MESSAGES
FROM
YOUR SELF

Other books by Simon

How to Raise a Happy Child
A must for parents with children of all ages

Leap into LOVE
Learn the secret to creating passionate and LASTING relationships

10 Steps to Break Through Fear
A little book that packs a BIG punch

10 Steps to Sales Success
Double your income... and TRIPLE your fun!

Lessons from Tyson
Inspiration from a furry friend (charity book)

All titles are available from Amazon and other good online booksellers. Or you can order direct from the author via email at simonhfirth@gmail.com

MESSAGES
FROM
YOUR SELF

'A guide book for finding your bliss'

Unlock the hidden secrets of your Birth Code

By Simon H Firth

Published by Simon Firth Seminars
Sydney, Australia

Copyright © 2018 by Simon H Firth

A Simon Firth Seminars book

All rights reserved

No part of this book may be reproduced or used in any form or by any means, electronic, mechanical or otherwise, including photocopying and digital distribution, or by any information storage retrieval system – other than for review purposes – without first obtaining the express permission in writing from the author.

Published by Simon Firth Seminars, Sydney, Australia

Printed by CreateSpace, Charleston, USA

Distributed by Simon Firth Seminars and CreateSpace

Cover design by G. Jeebair

ISBN-13: 978-0-6481426-0-7
ISBN-10: 0-6481426-0-4

Edition: 1.0

For Nene

Beauty is truth, truth beauty.

That is all ye know on earth…

and all ye need to know.

– John Keats, May 1819

Contents

Author's note: It's all in the numbers — 9
Introduction: A guide to using this book — 13

PART ONE: WAKE UP TO YOUR SELF

Chapter 1: A wake-up call — 25
Chapter 2: Why are we here? — 34
Chapter 3: All your answers lie within — 78
Chapter 4: Reality is a trap for the mind — 88
Chapter 5: Escape from the Matrix — 100
Chapter 6: Night becomes day — 107
Chapter 7: Everything is love — 120
Chapter 8: Self-awareness is your birth right — 128
Chapter 9: Start getting excited — 132

PART TWO: THE SELF-AWARENESS SYSTEM™

Chapter 1: Introduction to the numbers — 141
Chapter 2: Nine paths to happiness — 155
Chapter 3: The secrets of your Birth Code — 173
Chapter 4: Energy of the elements — 187
Chapter 5: Growing with the Spiritual Cycle — 193

Chapter 6: Revolving with the Nine-Year Cycles   203

Chapter 7: Identify your strengths & weaknesses   233

Chapter 8: The four 'Master Numbers'   254

Chapter 9: Your life is what you make it   277

PART THREE: THE NINE LIFE PATHS

How to read your Life Path listing   285

LIFE PATH 1: The Leader   291

LIFE PATH 2: The Intuitive   341

LIFE PATH 3: The Creative   397

LIFE PATH 4: The Builder   445

LIFE PATH 5: The Rebel   505

LIFE PATH 6: The Visionary   561

LIFE PATH 7: The Seeker   621

LIFE PATH 8: The Achiever   681

LIFE PATH 9: The Teacher   745

APPENDICES: BONUS MATERIAL

Appendix A: Some famous Life Paths   803

Appendix B: Easy numerology readings   814

Appendix C: Leap Into Love   821

Appendix D: Further reading suggestions   825

Author's note:
It's all in the numbers

The concept that numbers hold the key to unlocking all the secrets of the universe was first propounded by the father of mathematics Pythagoras in ancient Greece about 2500 years ago – some 500 years before the birth of Jesus.

Although very little of his material has survived, there is enough historical evidence to suggest Pythagoras spent much of his extremely productive life researching his belief that numbers are at the heart of the structure of the universe.

Since then, numerous texts have been published that explore the relationship between numbers and the way the physical world in which we live is constructed, such as the Chinese I Ching (circa 900BC) which first identified the existence of binary code as the fundamental building block of all physical and energetic matter almost 3000 years before modern scientists used it to develop the computers we all use today.

The Chinese have long been admirers of the power of numbers. They believe the number 8 – the infinity sign – brings wealth and good fortune, which is why the Beijing Olympic Games opening ceremony began at 8.08pm on August 8th, 2008 – 8 minutes past 8 on the 8th day of the 8th month of the 8th year of the new millennium.

Numerology has evolved over the centuries and spread to every corner of the world, inspiring some of the ancient Indian Vedic texts, the writings of St Augustine of Hippo in the 4th century, the Gematria works of the Jewish Kabbalists in the 13th century, the discoveries of the prominent German scholar Henry Agrippa in the 16th century and, more recently, the works of the 20th century numerological pioneers, including Josephine Balliett, Juno Jordan, Florence Campbell, Julia Stenton – and my favourite, Dan Millman.

I want to acknowledge all my forebears who have paved the way for the Self-Awareness System™ in this book. I also want to point out that all of them say they have no idea why numerology works, just that it does… which is a crucial "missing link", as I'm sure you'll agree.

Messages from Your Self is my attempt to set the record straight by revealing for the first time the reason why numerology is so effective:

– Why it contains the answers to all your questions about who you are and what you came here to do.

– Why it guides you to your perfect career, your ideal relationship, your optimum health, and your dream life.

– Why it shows you how to develop your innate strengths, and how to work on improving your weaknesses.

– Above all, why something as simple as your date of birth is actually a portal through which you can access the infinite love and wisdom of the universe and be blissfully and unendingly happy.

* * *

But what really sets *Messages from Your Self* apart from all the other numerological guidebooks is glimpsed in the title.

The information hard-coded into your date of birth is powerful beyond imagining, as you will discover in Parts Two and Three. It can, and will, lead you to have everything your mind has ever wanted.

But that is just the tip of the iceberg. When you learn (and you will) how to read the information from your heart, a whole new world opens up for you – a world as vast and abundant as the universe.

The key is "real-eyesing" the difference between who you think you are – "yourself", a human being having a spiritual experience without knowing why – and who you really are – your "Self", a divine being who has chosen to have a human experience for a very specific purpose.

When you real-eyes it was your Self who programmed all the numerological information into your date of birth, your "real eyes" will open and you will see your true nature for the first time.

You will also see the true nature of the world around you, because your real eyes will look beyond the fear, violence and suffering and see it is all part of a deliberately designed and perfectly constructed plan.

* * *

This book is no exception. Notice that all three books have nine chapters, one for each of the nine possible numbers in numerology.

Notice, too, how all 27 chapters contain lessons and insights that are governed by the unique qualities of their respective numbers.

Now flip back to the Contents Page and you will notice something else you may have missed. The 18 chapters of the first two books reveal the two most important qualities that you need to develop in your life (there's also a clue in the titles of both the forewords).

There is even a re-minder of who you really are in the titles of the four Appendices. And if you look at the cover again, there are some messages for you there as well, hidden in the green code of the Fear Matrix – which, unlike the one in the movie, is very real, I assure you, as you'll discover in Part One.

Please don't fall into the trap of thinking these patterns are just gimmicks included for your amusement. Far from it. They are here to teach you to look for the signs that are all around you.

When you do this – when you look through your real eyes and become fully aware – you will see for the first time the breathtaking perfection of the world you find yourself (your Self) in as you read this.

It is magnificent. It is Wonderland. And there are rabbit holes everywhere you tread.

Who in the world am I?
Ah, that's the great puzzle!

– Alice in Wonderland

Introduction:
A guide to using this book

Messages From Your Self is the result of my life's search to discover the answer to the simplest, and simultaneously most complex, question that has ever been asked.

It is a question I am sure you have already asked your Self.

In fact, you are probably still asking it – which is what would have led you to this book in the first place.

I don't know how old you were when you first asked it. I was seven, and it has obsessed me ever since.

It's the question: "Why are we here?"

* * *

Within those four small, everyday words lies the biggest mystery since the Big Bang created the "here" to which the question refers, many billions of years ago.

Wrapping your mind around the enormity of the universe you find your Self in (the "here") is tough enough, and it is a subject we will explore in more detail in just a moment.

Coming to terms with the "we" is not much easier. Are we upright apes in fancy clothes driving our cars to and from work on a rock that is whirling around a star in a far-flung corner of one of 200 billion galaxies in the known universe?

Or are we something else entirely?

But as intriguing as the "we" and the "here" are, it is the "why" in the question that really sets the pot boiling.

What is the point of it all? Indeed, is there a point to our existence? Or are we just meant to grow old, play golf, go on a cruise... and die?

* * *

In his best-selling book *A Brief History of Time*, the greatest scientific mind of our generation, the late great Stephen Hawking, takes us through a mind-boggling description of the vastness of the universe, including its many and varied complex physical laws.

His book, which I devoured with great interest when I started out on this journey of discovery, spent a staggering 237 weeks on *The Sunday Times* bestseller list... longer than any other book in history.

And yet, despite Hawking's brilliance and revolutionary theories about physics, gravity, black holes and the cosmos, at the end of his book he admits that even his planet-sized scientific intellect was unable to understand the true nature of the universe we find our Self in.

This is what he writes in his conclusion to *A Brief History of Time* (the italics are mine):

"Scientists have been too occupied with the development of new theories that describe *what* the universe is to ask the question *why*. If we find the answer to *why* we exist, it would be the ultimate triumph of human reason – for then we would know the mind of God."

* * *

Messages From Your Self not only meets Hawking's challenge of answering "why" we exist... it also contains the answer to every other question you have ever – or will ever – come up with.

That's a big claim, I know. So let me try to explain how this guide book works. And the best way I can do that – as with planning any journey – is to start from the end (where you want to go) and work backwards (to where you are now).

Part Three: The Nine Life Paths

Part Three contains the answers to all the questions you may have about how you can live a happy, healthy and fulfilling life, depending on your numerological Life Path Number. It will tell you what your life's highest purpose is, what sort of career and relationship will work best for you, what ailments you are prone to experience and how to avoid them, and it will also tell you how you can nurture the unique qualities of your children, if you have them, to give them the best possible start in life.

All the information in the listings in Part Three is uncannily accurate, as you will discover. But before you read it you will need to read Part Two so you know which answers are relevant to you.

Part Two: The Self-Awareness System™

Part Two contains my Self-Awareness System™ (the SAS – "Who Dares Wins" – no coincidence), which is loosely based on traditional numerology but refines this ancient divination practice and takes it to a whole new level.

Here you will discover how the information that is hard-coded into your date of birth contains everything you will ever need to know to live the life of your dreams.

You will learn that there are nine possible "Life Paths", but only one of them relates to you. This is the path which, if you follow it, will lead you to your life's highest calling.

Even more revealing, you will discover your life is no accident. You came "here" with a very specific purpose in mind. And in Parts Two and Three you will discover exactly what that purpose is.

Part One: Wake Up To Your Self

I have left the first for last because Part One contains a tonne of information that can only be described as deeply confronting, unless you have already "woken up" to your true nature as a spirit having a human experience – rather than the other way around.

If you manage to get through Part One without throwing it in the bin (and I must warn you that many of you won't, especially if you have been a follower of one of the mainstream Western religions up to this point), you will be rewarded with a much richer understanding of the Self-Awareness System™ in Parts Two and Three, which will not only teach you how to be materially happy... it will also guide you to your lifelong bliss, as promised on the cover.

What's more, you will finally understand WHY numerology works, and you will no longer have to take anything in your life on faith.

If you don't make it through Part One at the first attempt, that's perfectly fine. Perhaps it's just not the right time for you. We all have to "wake up" in our own way, and in our own time.

I suggest you keep it handy for when you decide you are ready. And in the meantime, Parts Two and Three will still show you how to make your life as happy as possible – as long as you real-eyes your happiness will be conditional on your income, your relationship, your health and everything else that can be snatched away at a moment's notice unless you learn in Part One how to make the Great Leap out of fear and into love.

On their own, Parts Two and Three contain all the answers to all your material, emotional and romantic questions. But they don't answer the big ones of "why are we here?" and "who or what is God?". For that you need to wake up to your Self by reading Part One.

***

Part One was not actually written by me. I mean, yes, I wrote it – in the sense that it was my fingers tapping on the keyboard – but it didn't come from me.

It came from spirit.

Or to be more precise, it came from my Angel.

We all have an Angel. They are divine and infinitely loving spiritual beings who watch over us. Some people call them our "Higher Self" and some call them our "Spirit Guide". It's all the same thing.

I don't know if you have met your Angel yet. If you have, you'll know exactly what I mean when I say the experience is not "pleasant" in the way you might expect it to be. It is exquisite and deeply humbling. But it is also terrifyingly confronting.

In terms of "waking up", meeting your Angel is the single most mind-altering experience it is possible to have. That's why your Angel will never appear before you are ready, otherwise they will literally blow your mind – like David Bowie's *Starman* – and send you mad.

To give you an idea of what it feels like, imagine you are lying there fast asleep in your comfortable bed, dreaming that you think you know who you are, and someone pours a large bucket of ice-cold water over your head. The shock is the same. Only instead of taking a few seconds to recover from the cold water, it takes years to come to grips with the enormity of what just happened.

A little over 21 years, in my case.

* * *

It was early 1996. I was working late in my office putting the finishing touches to an issue of a magazine I was editing at the time. All the other offices in the building were dark, as was mine – save for a little pool of light on my desk from a small grey angle-poise lamp.

There was no loud noise, or bright flash. I was just suddenly and acutely aware that I was no longer alone in the room.

Then I heard a voice, and the hairs on my neck stood up. I couldn't see anyone, but I could sense the presence of a woman standing next to me, and my office was much, much lighter.

I honestly can't recall if she said "Hello" or "Is this a good time? I can always come back later" – or even "Right, you asked for this, so buckle up because Kansas is going bye bye."

All I remember is that she started talking to me and, without even thinking about what was happening, I grabbed the A4 notebook on my desk and wrote down every word she said.

Longhand.

For eight hours.

Without stopping.

* * *

If you have read Neale Donald Walsch's *Conversations with God*, or seen the movie of the same name, you will know exactly what happened to me. He filled three yellow legal pads before the voice that was talking to him decided it was time for a break.

Neale had been asking "God" for answers to the big spiritual questions for decades before they were given to him. So had I, ever since I was a small child.

The principal question he had been asking was the same one I had been asking: "Why are we here?" I remember asking this question when I was seven years old, because it was the first time I had asked my parents a question they couldn't answer.

At the time (England in 1967) there was no internet and therefore no Google. My father had an *Encyclopedia Britannica* in the attic, all 32 volumes. But it was no help. So I asked around a bit, but generally the best answer I got was: "Um… just go and play with your toys dear."

At the age of 11, I decided to put the question on a shelf at the back of my mind, hoping it would sit there quietly and not make a fuss.

At school I learned the answers to all the other questions my eager young mind was asking: When was the Battle of Hastings? (1066). How do bees do it without stinging each other to death? (very carefully). What is the boiling point of radium? (1737C). Did Shakespeare smoke a lot of dope to make him so damned creative? (yes, apparently). Was Hitler a psychotic bastard, or just angry and short? (all three). Where did Napoleon keep his army? (up his sleevy). And a zillion more.

But no matter how much information I crammed into my head, and no matter how many answers I stacked onto my mental shelves, that one question kept nagging at me night and day.

Like a child tugging for attention on its mother's apron.

In my teens, the question became unbearably loud, both in my head and in my chest. None of my friends had a clue what I was talking about. They were more concerned with buying a windsurfer, or a Sony Walkman, or chatting up the barmaid at the Dog and Fox, while I knew none of those things would give me what I wanted.

I cried often. Especially at night, when the moonlight would bathe my face as I looked out of my bedroom window and begged whoever was up there to talk to me.

Eventually, in my mid-20s, I'd had enough. I knew there were only two ways I was ever going to get any sleep: I could have a lobotomy, or I could somehow remove the question from my head and forget I ever asked it in the first place.

I had just seen the Jack Nicholson movie *One Flew Over the Cuckoo's Nest*, which rather put me off the whole lobotomy idea. So I took a deep breath, quit my job and moved to the opposite side of the world in the belief that if I lived upside down in Australia for a while I might dislodge the question and it would fall out of one of my ears.

It didn't work. But I rather liked Australia, so I decided to stay.

The best thing about living upside down, as I discovered, is that you are able to see your life from a completely different perspective. That – and the fact I met two divinely beautiful spiritual women who kissed me, sprinkled fairy dust on my eyes and told me the answer I was seeking wasn't "out there" but inside my heart – meant my journey wasn't wasted.

So I redoubled my efforts, travelled the world, sat with mystics, studied with masters, danced with drugs and demons… and narrowly avoided going completely mad as I tore open my psyche in a desperate search for an answer I wasn't sure even existed.

* * *

I never did find the answer. In the end, it found me.

That night in my office in downtown Sydney.

I guess my Angel must have realised that when someone is looking for you with that amount of passion and for that long, it would be churlish to remain hidden in the etheric shadows.

* * *

By the time she stopped talking, it was light outside. I had used up every piece of paper I could find on my desk: my A4 pad, 37 yellow Post-it notes, all the sheets in my printer tray, the gaps in a restaurant menu, and even the back cover of a video I had been sent to review.

After the voice stopped I remember weeping, because when you finally meet your Angel, you feel so small, so humble and so grateful that all you can do is cry.

When it was over, and I read through my notes, I saw that all my questions had been answered – including the big one: "Why are we here?" The trouble was, what my Angel told me was so momentous and yet so simple that I didn't feel anywhere near confident enough to share it with the world without first being certain it was all true.

I understood what she had said (it's all there in Part One), but I wasn't ready to live it… let alone teach it to others.

I knew I couldn't teach it until I had experienced it first hand, so I decided to test it all thoroughly in the so-called "real world" (irony of ironies, as we will soon see) to make sure I had got it all right.

I just had no idea that process would take 21 years, nine of which involved me going through the living hell of killing my ego, which the mystics call the Dark Night of the Soul.

* * *

Bonus material

In the Appendices at the back of the book is an extensive list of the Life Path Numbers of famous people, both dead and alive. You'll be intrigued to see how the specific qualities of their Life Path Number guided them to their success.

I have also included an easy, step-by-step guide for conducting a numerology reading for your friends and family using the basic nine-numbered Pythagorean Square. These readings will enable you to delve a little deeper into the other numbers that make up your birth date, and they work seamlessly alongside the Self-Awareness System™.

And because I know there will be times when life folds in on you and you slip back into anxiety and doubt, I have included two short extracts from my book *Leap Into Love* that you can use to re-mind your Self how to make the Great Leap back out of fear and into love.

I strongly suggest you keep this book handy and consult your Life Path listing in Part Three at regular intervals, especially when you are facing a difficult decision. Be aware that each time you do, you will discover that different passages leap out at you. This is because you have moved further along your Life Path and are therefore facing a whole new set of challenges, choices and opportunities.

* * *

May the Force be with you…

I want to wrap up this rather long-winded introduction (written on Star Wars day – May 4, 2017 – how appropriate) by thanking you for giving me the opportunity to share this book with you.

I also want to explain that the reason I have written it in such an intimate and informal way is because I have tried to make it feel as though we are sitting down together in front of a crackling open fire to discuss "the meaning of life, the universe and everything" over a couple of large brandies, rather than having to connect through the frustratingly impersonal medium of the printed page.

I have finally found the bliss that I have been searching for all my life and am living it every day. But my journey has been harrowing to say the least, and the whole reason I have written this book is to try to make yours less so.

If I thought life was hard before I met my Angel 21 years ago, it was nothing compared to the years of soul-searching that followed. My Dark Night very nearly killed me and I had to face every single one of my deepest and darkest fears before the sun came up again.

It was well worth it, though, because in finding an answer to the question "why are we here?", I also found the answers to all the other questions that were troubling me… and are probably troubling you too, which is what would have led you here.

I hope that, like me, when you find the answers you decide to live them, because by doing so you will become a force for good in a world that desperately needs more love and light right now.

You see, all any of us has to do to make our life a "success" is to leave the world better than it was before we passed through it.

* * *

Finally, I urge you to question everything you are about to read. Please don't blindly accept any of it. If there's something that doesn't quite gel for you, kick it around in your head like a football until you

are completely satisfied that it resonates with the energy of the divine and contains the truth you seek. That's what I did with the information my Angel gave me, and I encourage you to do the same.

I wish you well on your journey.

I hope this book makes your life's journey easier.

And may the Source bless you every single step of the way.

Simon xxx

PART ONE:

WAKE UP TO YOUR SELF

You take the blue pill… you wake up in your bed and believe whatever you want to believe.

You take the red pill… you stay in Wonderland and I show you how deep the rabbit hole goes.

– Morpheus in *The Matrix* (1999)

Chapter 1:
A wake-up call

1 is the number of creation
All that you think is 'real' is nothing more than a creation of your mind

Questions are magical. Aren't they? Even the letter "Q" at the start of the word appears to be showing off, its tail-like flourish making all the other less fancy letters of the alphabet look decidedly ho-hum.

And what about that cute little seahorse-shaped squiggle at the end of a question? It demands our attention with a hypnotic presence that commas, full stops and even semi-colons can only dream of.

You may never have stopped to think about the power of questions before, but they are the most compelling force on the planet. Everything that has ever existed – from the earliest stone-age axe, to the internet, iPhones and space travel – started out as a question in someone's mind.

And your life is no different.

Everything you *think* you are – and therefore everything you *think* is "real" – is nothing more than the result of all the questions you have asked, and all the answers you have received.

But here's where this all gets just a little bit confronting. I'm sorry to tell you that some of the questions you asked as you started out in life would have steered you to make some false assumptions about your Self and the world you find your Self in.

As a child, all you did was ask questions, starting with the moment you squeezed out of your mother's womb in a cacophony of screams and moans and wondered (quite profoundly): "Where on Earth am I?"

Part One: Wake up to your Self

This was probably followed mere seconds later by "How did I get here?" and then "Why is this scary-looking person in a mask smacking me on my bum to make me cry?"

From that moment on, your entire sense of who you are and where you are – in other words, your perceived "reality" – is constructed in your mind from the answers you receive to all the questions you ask.

But your mind is not "real" in the true sense of the word. You weren't born with it, which ought to give you a clue.

Your mind is nothing more than a vast collection of answers to the questions you have asked throughout your life, most of which were based on the fear of not knowing who or where you were.

The only thing about you that is "real" is the tiny drop of pure golden light that glows in your heart, which we humans like to call "love", or "amour", or "liebe", or 愛 depending on where we decided to incarnate in this lifetime.

This love is our connection to the spirit world from where we came. Some call it our soul. But for reasons that will become apparent as we go along, I prefer to call it our Self… because it's a more accurate description of who we really are.

Our mind, on the other hand, is entirely man made (or woman made, depending). We have literally "made up" our mind about what we think is real based on all the answers we have received to all the questions we have ever asked.

I love the expression "make up your mind" because it describes this process perfectly. You have indeed made up your mind, just like a novelist makes up a story.

So let's start by opening your "real eyes" and asking your Self a question you will need to answer before you can go any further on this journey of Self-discovery.

(Please note that all the main subheads in all nine of the chapters that make up Part One take the form of a question. This is designed to re-mind you that your entire sense of identity has been constructed from all the questions you have asked of your Self and others, and all the answers you have received.)

Chapter 1: A wake-up call

"Who do you think you are?"

Think about this question for a moment. Who are you really? Are you the thoughts in your head, where all your millions of answers to all your millions of questions are neatly arranged on shelves in the cavernous storage room of your mind?

Or are you the tiny little drop of pure love that nestles quietly in your heart where your Self is, and always has been?

There's no easy way to break this to you gently, so I'm just going to say it. Your entire life is an illusion, including who you think you are. Everything you think is real, isn't – because everything you think isn't real.

Where you went wrong, although you were a child and you couldn't possibly have known any different, was that you never asked your Self any of your questions. You asked everyone except your Self because your young mind didn't even know your Self existed.

Your eyes were what led you astray. Eyes are wonderful things. They are great for watching movies and not bumping into things, but they are also a trap because we assume the information we seek is "out there" where we can see, rather than inside us where we can't.

So instead of looking within and asking your Self the question "Who am I?", you asked your parents, then you asked your teachers, and then you asked anyone else who came along.

And you stacked all the answers that you received neatly onto the shelves of your mind.

* * *

The first step in opening your real eyes (the ones that look within, rather than the ones that look "out there" into the world) and seeing who you really are is to understand that you have been looking in the wrong place for your answers all along.

Most of what you believe to be real is what your parents believed to be real. Then, when you were packed off to school, you naturally assumed that your teachers knew what they were talking about as well.

Part One: Wake up to your Self

It's an easy mistake to make. After all, they were teachers. They were much older than you, and some of them even had beards and patches on their jackets that made them appear deceptively wise!

At college or university, the teachers had bigger beards and even more patches so you trusted them too, and your shelves grew fuller.

Then you got a job and you studied for that, and your shelves grew fuller still.

* * *

Your first clue that something was wrong came when you started to ask a question that didn't seem to have an answer: "How can I be happy?" This normally occurs sometime in your teens, by which point you have experienced the exquisite but deeply confusing sensation of romantic love for the first time and have therefore started to think that maybe some of the answers to some of the harder questions might be found in your heart, rather than in your head.

But it's too late. By now your mind is so vast, so strong and so deafeningly loud in your head that it completely drowns out the tiny little voice of your Self in your heart.

So when you ask the question "How can I be happy?", which is unanswerable from the perspective of your ego, your Self – which knows the answer – doesn't even get a look-in. Your mind jumps up and down shouting "Me! Me! I know! I know!"... and off you go on a wild goose chase looking for happiness "out there", when all along it is in the one place your mind would never think to look.

Inside your Self.

For most people, this wild goose chase in pursuit of happiness (and we're talking unconditional happiness here, not happiness that depends on how much money you have or who loves you) starts with puberty and lasts anywhere from 10 to 20 years.

As a child, you never asked "How can I be happy?" You were a child. You were either happy, or you were unhappy.

Chapter 1: A wake-up call

As a teenager, you asked this question all the time, but you had no idea what happiness was. You thought happiness was a boyfriend or a girlfriend, or new clothes, or a party on the beach, or a new phone, or an acne cream that worked, or someone clicking "Like" on your Facebook page.

Then in your 20s, you thought: "Maybe if I get a great job, or make a lot of money, or get married, or start a business, or have a child, or buy a nice house and put nice things in it, or see the world, or go to the gym, or go to the pub… maybe then I will be happy."

But none of that stuff works, at least not for long. Which is why somewhere in their mid to late 20s, most people simply stop asking the question… and go to sleep.

If that's you.

If you went to sleep.

Then this is your wake-up call.

* * *

What do you mean by 'wake up?'

"Wake up to yourself!" is one of my favourite phrases. I hear people use it all the time, and it makes me smile because they have no idea what they are saying. They think they are being glib or perhaps even rude, but in fact they are making the most profound statement it is possible for a human being to make.

"Wake up to yourself!" means "Wake up to your Self!"

Your Self is who you really are. And it's not the ego in your mind; it's the love in your heart.

Your Self is your connection to what most people call "God", but I prefer to call the Source to avoid any nasty denominational fisticuffs, and when you learn to talk to your Self you are in fact talking to "God".

(Note: This process is very different from prayer, which we will discuss in depth in the next chapter.)

Part One: Wake up to your Self

"Waking up" involves these five key distinctions:

– You wake up to the fact that you are not just a carbon-based life form, but a spirit living inside a carbon-based life form. In other words you are a spirit having a human experience, not the other way around.

– You wake up to the fact that you are not separate from everyone else, but the same as them because they are pure love too. We are all one, we are all love, and we are all spirit.

– Your real eyes open for the first time. These are the ones that look inside your Self for all the answers you seek, rather than "out there" into the so-called "real world".

– You realise (real-eyes) that you are the co-creator of your life. You make everything happen (yes even the allegedly "bad" things; they are lessons) because your Self chose your life path before it incarnated inside your body.

– You start to kill your ego as your Self's voice gets louder and reminds (re-minds) you what you came here to do... in other words, what your sole (soul) purpose is.

(Note: Please real-eyes that I am not playing with these words just for the fun of it. I want you to see how the words you use, like the questions you ask your Self, are the building blocks that create your perception of "reality" and determine the quality of your "human experience"... otherwise known as your "life".)

If you haven't woken up yet, it is by far the most profound and significant moment of your life. If you have already woken up, you know exactly what I'm talking about. It is the moment you start unplugging from all the fear that your ego has been feeding you.

I call it the "Neo moment". If you have seen the film *The Matrix*, you have seen the perfect metaphor for your life. And if you haven't seen it, I urge you to do so before you read Chapter 5 of Part One ("Escape from The Matrix") because it will help you form a clear picture in your mind of how the process of "waking up" works.

In the film, the hero, Neo, wakes up when he unplugs from a computer program called "the Matrix" to discover he has been the slave

Chapter 1: A wake-up call

of intelligent machines that rule the world and have devised a way to keep humans in a comatose state while they produce the bioelectricity the machines need to function. He is so shocked by the experience that he vomits, and you probably will too because when you wake up you will see that you have also been plugged into a Matrix and have been a slave… not to a bunch of prescient machines, but to fear.

* * *

How did it happen?

As you grew up from a baby, to a child, to a teenager and finally an adult, you "made up your mind" about two things: your identity, and the nature of the world around you.

Unless you were evolved enough to choose to be born into a family that has already unplugged from the Fear Matrix, you would have been conditioned from a very early age to believe that you were separate, and that the world is a dangerous and competitive place.

You would have created your separate identity based on your name, your gender, your nationality, your social standing, your looks, the colour of your skin, your thoughts, your beliefs – and those of your parents – and all your experiences, many of which were painful and therefore caused you to become afraid of being hurt again.

With your separate identity came your ego. And with every painful experience, big and small, your ego grew stronger and stronger to protect you from your two biggest fears: the fear of getting hurt ("the world is a dangerous place") and the fear of not being good enough ("the world is a competitive place").

After you muddled through the pain of puberty and experienced both your first romantic heartbreak and the competitive cauldron of school, your sense of separation and vulnerability became so strong that you began filtering almost every experience through your ego (fear) and almost nothing through your Self (love).

Part One: Wake up to your Self

Once you reached that point, it was only a matter of time before you started buying into the fear that was being fed to you every day by your parents ("be careful"), your classmates at school ("I'm taller, better-looking, faster, stronger, richer than you"), your teachers ("if you don't pass these exams your life will be ruined"), the media ("war and violence are everywhere"), the banks ("money is the secret to happiness"), the advertisers ("buy this and you'll be happy"), the politicians ("we'll keep you safe" – um, from what, exactly?) and the churches ("believe in us or you will go straight to hell when you die").

Is it any wonder the Fear Matrix gets you?

* * *

I will explain more about how the Fear Matrix operates in Chapters 4 and 5, but for now I just want you to be aware that it exists, it is very real and it is very powerful.

The good news is it is relatively simple to unplug from the Fear Matrix. In fact, you have already started the process by taking the "red pill" and reading this book.

You are already "waking up" to who you really are. And it is not the fear-based ego identity in your head that says you are separate from everyone else, but the pure love in your heart that tells you – if you stand still and stay silent long enough to hear its quiet voice – that you are pure love, we are all pure love… and we are all one.

What's not so simple is the process of killing your ego. I am sorry to tell you, though, that from the moment you wake up it is something you will have to do, because once you wake up you can never go back to sleep. Which means all those material trappings that so satisfied you while you were asleep – and while your ego was at the controls of your life – will never please you in the same way again.

* * *

Chapter 1: A wake-up call

I will show you how to kill your ego in Chapter 6, but I have to warn you that you may not make it that far. Your ego likes being at the controls of your life. It's smart as a whip and it will fight like a dervish to stay there.

It's already starting to smell a rat after these first few pages, and it will try to stop you from reading any further. It will play tricks on you. It will make you yawn and want to go to sleep. It will make you suddenly decide to clean the car, or turn on the TV, or tidy the house – anything to prevent you making it to Chapter 6.

Whether you make it or not is entirely up to you. If you do, all your troubles will be over. But if you don't, that's perfectly OK. The timing might not be quite right for you to make the journey within.

One piece of information that might help you is to real-eyes that you don't have to kill off your ego altogether, which is virtually impossible. All you have to do is weaken it sufficiently so you can control it rather than allowing it to control you.

And when that happens, you can finally start living the life your Self came here to live. A life of pure love and unending happiness, with no worries, no borders and no boundaries.

* * *

Right, let's get started. And the place to start our journey of Self-discovery is the same place everything else started.

At the beginning.

So buckle your seatbelt, because in this next chapter we are going back in time to find the answer to the biggest question of them all: "Why are we here?"

A long way back.

13.8 billion years, to be exact.

Chapter 2:
Why are we here?

2 is the number of co-operation
Which is the only way we can ever discover who – and what – we are

The answer to this mother and father of all questions goes back to the beginning of the universe, nearly 14 billion years ago, because the reason the universe was "created" and the reason we are alive today are one and the same.

I asked this question for decades before getting the answer, and I certainly don't want you to have to wait a moment longer. So here, without further ado, is the answer:

We are here so that "God" can exist.

Or, to put it another way… we are here because without us "God" cannot exist.

* * *

Simple, huh? Well, that's what my Angel told me. And although I understood conceptually what she was saying, I really didn't have the first clue what she was talking about.

It was clear she was telling me that we come from the Source and we return to the Source. But I couldn't help wondering that if we are spirits to start with, then why can't we just stay in the spirit world? Why do we have to go through the trauma of incarnating into the physical

Chapter 2: Why are we here?

world as little prune-shaped babies, bruise our knees, break our hearts, learn the periodic table and the square root of a hypotenuse, work our asses off in an office, save all our money for our old age... and then keel over dead before we have a chance to spend it?

It just didn't make any sense.

If we come from the spirit world, why couldn't we have just stayed where we were, relaxing in our banana chairs on Cloud 9, sipping nectar cocktails and watching Elvis Presley, Jimi Hendrix, Jim Morrison and David Bowie live in concert?

In other words, why go through all this hassle just to get right back to where we started?

* * *

I had to wait several years after my encounter with my Angel before I found the answer I was looking for.

I was lying in bed one night reading a book that had caused quite a storm of controversy when it was published (interestingly just a year before my Angel's visit in 1996) because its author claimed to have conversed with "God". (As we'll see in a moment, he can't have conversed with "God" because the Source can't say or do anything. It's pure love and all it can "do" is be. He will have spoken with his Angel, like I did. It's the same thing to all intents and purposes, but a key distinction nonetheless.)

The book is the one I mentioned earlier, *Conversations with God* and, as so often happens when we look for an answer, it fell open at the very page where the author, Neale Donald Walsch, described how "God" had told him exactly what my Angel had told me. Only Neale, being a much better writer than I am, was able to make perfect sense of it.

I will quote you the words that he wrote (the brackets are mine):

In the beginning, That Which Is (ie, "God") was all there was, and there was nothing else. All That Is could not know itself from a reference point outside itself, so All That Is divided itself, becoming – in one glorious moment – That Which Is This, and That Which Is That.

Part One: Wake up to your Self

That Which Is This was "God", and That Which Is That was mankind and womankind – extensions of "God", so that each could look on each other and know themselves as "God".

* * *

After I read this, I scurried back to the notes I had taken from my Angel and real-eyesed in an instant what she had been telling me.

My Angel didn't use the word "God". She alternated between "Spirit" and "the Source". I am going to go with "the Source" for the purposes of this book because it neatly encapsulates the concept of where we come from, and it also cuts through all the religious dogma.

The word you choose to describe All That Is really doesn't matter. What does matter is whether you kill someone else simply because they choose to use a different word.

If you read all the different religious texts, you will discover that they are all talking about exactly the same thing.

As I will re-mind you throughout this book – and in my other books on relationships, parenting and breaking through our fears – the words you use are much more important to your level of happiness than you probably ever real-eyesed.

I should tell you, though, that when I say "thank you" to the Source and tell it how much I love it and how grateful I am for all its blessings (which is the only type of prayer it hears, by the way – it doesn't do "requests" like some cosmic DJ) I use the word "God", because saying "Thank you, Source" sounds way too impersonal for the exquisitely intimate connection I have with my co-creator.

My Angel told me that the Source is the spiritual dimension, while the world outside your window is the physical dimension.

Unlike the physical world, the spiritual dimension has neither shape nor form because it is not made of energetic matter, as our physical world is. The Source is pure love. And despite what Hallmark might say, love is not something you can measure, or send in the post.

Chapter 2: Why are we here?

The best visual I can give you for the Source is that it is a big pond of golden love. It isn't, of course, because it has no physical form. And it certainly isn't an old man with a long beard, any more than it is a jolly fat man in a Santa suit.

If you must insist on anthropomorphism, the Source would definitely be a woman because spirit is pure feminine creative energy.

Of course, the Source isn't a woman any more than it is a man. It has no physical form because it is pure love, and pure love has no form. That is why us humans have struggled with the identity of the divine for so long. Our brains are so plugged in to the so-called "real world" around us that we find it difficult to comprehend anything that has no physical shape.

This is the ultimate irony, really, when you consider that the vastness of the universe – including our atmosphere and the air we breathe to stay alive – has no shape or form.

Why do you think it's called "space"?

* * *

I have chosen to use the image of a golden pond of love simply to help you form a reasonably accurate picture of the Source in your mind. Your mind would have looked for an image for the Source anyway – because that's how the human brain works when it is trying to understand something new, and I wanted to make sure I gave your brain a reasonably accurate image.

Otherwise (Source forbid!) it may have come up with a picture of a grumpy old man with a long white beard.

The Source is infinite and infinitely wise, because it is love and love is all there is. It knows everything because it is everything. However, before the physical dimension was "created", there was one thing that it didn't know. It didn't know who or what it was.

There is no way it could have known that because it was all there was, and therefore it had no point of reference.

Part One: Wake up to your Self

In this, the Source is no different to you or me, or any living thing. All animals, including us humans (yes, we are animals just the same as the rest of them), can only ever learn about themselves and become conscious of who they are by interacting with others.

A baby owl only knows it is a baby owl because it sees its Self reflected in its mother and father. If you took an owlet away from its mother at the moment of its birth, it would grow into an owl but it wouldn't know it was an owl.

Similarly, if you took a newborn human baby straight from its mother's womb and put it in a dark room with no light, no sound, no stimulus and no human contact and merely fed it so that its physical body stayed alive, that human being could live to be 90 years old and not have the first clue about who or what it was.

The Source, which existed in a similarly stimulus-less vacuum, needed to "see itself through the eyes of another", figuratively speaking, so it could know itself, and therefore exist consciously.

Let me say that again, because this is crucial: to exist in the true sense of the word, the Source needed to know itself – because without awareness (consciousness), there is no existence. And it couldn't possibly know itself when it was "all that was".

It sounds like a complicated concept to grasp, but it's really very simple. The 17th century philosopher Rene Descartes got it almost right when he wrote: "I think, therefore I am." What he should have written was: "I know who I am, therefore I am."

Thinking is vastly overrated.

Knowing (consciousness) is where it's at.

* * *

The Source, being infinitely wise, knew everything. But it didn't know what it was, and it didn't know what it wasn't. The only way for that to happen was if it separated from itself so that it could see itself.

Chapter 2: Why are we here?

So it did what any right-thinking deity would do when faced with a similar conundrum – it split itself in two. And it did this by "creating" a physical dimension as a counterpoint to its own spiritual dimension.

In other words, it "created" the universe.

* * *

At this point, the creationists can take a bow because they have been right all along.

The evolutionists can also take a bow, because when the Source separated itself into two halves – physical and spiritual – the physical half took the best part of 14 billion years to evolve from gases to rocks to planets to basic life forms and finally to prescient life forms with central nervous systems capable of understanding what they are (pure love) and where they came from (the Source). There is no "time" in the spirit world, so 14 billion years is a blink of an eye as far as the Source is concerned.

Come to think of it, the creationists and the evolutionists must be feeling pretty silly about now, because they have been at each other's throats for hundreds of years when they could have been down the pub instead.

The astronomers can stop worrying about how the universe began and go to the pub as well, saving us a fortune in their research grants that can now be used to feed the poor.

All the millions of clergymen and women can go to the pub too, so we can sell the squillions of dollars of assets owned by the churches to pay off every country's national debt, build jails to house the world's central bankers who created the debt in the first place, and make every human being on the planet instantly wealthy.

While we're at it, we can send all the philosophers to the pub as well. And the physicists, and all the astrophysicists too.

Hmmm... we're going to need a bigger pub.

* * *

How did the Source 'create' the universe?

I have been putting the word "create" in inverted commas because it's not actually what happened. The Source didn't "create" the universe. It can't "make" anything. It doesn't have hands, or a hammer. And it certainly didn't knock up a few billion trillion planets in its garage in six days before washing its hands, putting on a clean pair of overalls and sitting down for dinner with Mrs Source on the seventh day.

As we've seen, the Source can't create anything because it can't do anything. The Source is pure love. And all love can "do" is… be.

So that's exactly what happened. The Source didn't "create" the universe. It "became" the universe.

I like to imagine that if the Source had a calendar it would have put a big red ring around the day it split itself in two and became the universe – because that was the day it saw itself for the first time.

I also like to imagine that it took a deep breath and closed its eyes just before it separated, because what happened next made even the biggest New Year's Eve fireworks extravaganza look like a damp match going "pffffft" in the rain.

As you would expect, when "everything that was" suddenly broke in two there was the mother of all Big Bangs.

Scientists know the physical universe was created by a Big Bang, which they describe as a never-ending atomic explosion that began when a "mysterious energy" started dividing itself in two over and over again, as it expanded rapidly in all directions at once.

They are absolutely right.

Most of them just have no idea why.

This is what happened:

The Source, which is pure love but doesn't know it is, wants to know itself by becoming conscious – so it decides to separate itself.

The Source takes a deep breath (not really), puts its fingers in its ears (definitely not), closes its eyes (can we just get on with it?) and splits itself in two.

Chapter 2: Why are we here?

Then the Source opens its eyes again (purrrlease!) because absolutely nothing happens. Not a thing. The Source now exists in two halves, but both halves are exactly the same so it is no closer to understanding who or what it is.

Going back to my analogy of the human baby kept in isolation, if you gave it a mirror it would be able to see itself but it would still have no understanding of what it was seeing. For it to become conscious of what it is, it needs to interact with other humans.

In the same way, the Source can't just see a reflection of itself to become conscious that it is pure, unbounded love – it has to interact with someone or something that is separate from it and yet conscious of the fact that it too is pure, unbounded love.

* * *

Sorry to interrupt, but is that why we are here?

Yes, that is exactly why we are here. We are here to create consciousness so that the Source can know itself. And we do this by incarnating from the Source as unconscious love (new souls) and then gradually becoming conscious of the fact that we are pure love – a long process that takes many lifetimes – so the Source can also become conscious of the fact that it is pure love by seeing itself reflected in us.

Doesn't sound very interesting, does it?

If you're like me, you were probably hoping the answer was more like: "To become ridiculously rich and have heaps of great sex."

Trust me, when you see what this is all about, you will understand that the fleeting pleasures of the material world (which you can have as well, by the way) are nothing compared to the indescribable bliss of knowing that you are pure, perfect love.

Now, let's get back to the action.

* * *

The Source now puts the second part of its plan into effect. Half of it kicks back and "puts it feet up" (this is the half that is "God" in the spiritual dimension), while the other half does something quite miraculous... it splits itself in two again, only this time in a very different way.

Remember, the Source in the spiritual dimension is pure love, which just "is". Pure love can't "do" anything... other than be.

The Source in the physical dimension, however, is very different. It is not love. It is love energy. And this is what creates the Big Bang.

The half that is love energy splits in two in the only way that energy can ever be split – into positive energy (masculine) and negative energy (feminine).

This is the universe's "Adam and Eve" moment, when the physical dimension ("the Garden of Eden") is created.

The Creation story in the Hebrew Bible perfectly describes the moment when love ("God") becomes love energy (the universe) by splitting itself equally into masculine energy (Adam) and feminine energy (Eve). The Israelites (all men) were spot on with their Garden of Eden parable. It's just such an outrage that these misogynistic old f..kers chose to reduce woman to little more than one of man's ribs!

They completely suppressed the feminine in all Biblical writings, and they even had the audacity to claim that "God" created "man" in "His" image – when it was quite clearly the other way around.

These men created "God" in *their* image. In the biggest crime of all time, they turned divine love into a gruff and judgmental white man.

Like most things that are wrong with the world, it is backwards.

* * *

So what happened next?

There is the briefest pause while, for a nano-nano-second, this energetic half of the Source exists simultaneously as both positive and

Chapter 2: Why are we here?

negative energy. Then the two halves reunite, just like in an atom bomb, and explode with an almighty "bang."

If you picture a trillion atom bombs detonating all at once, you will have a relatively accurate image... because the reason an atom bomb explodes and the reason the Source explodes is exactly the same.

All energy in the universe is love energy. It comes from the Source so it can't be anything else. This is why energy can never be created or destroyed, because love cannot be created or destroyed. The difference is an atom bomb contains only so much radioactive material, so the explosion lasts for only a moment or two before the fuel runs out. But the Source (which is pure love) is infinite, so the Big Bang explosion is never-ending, causing the universe to go on expanding.

Which it is still doing today.

Most scientists believe it will eventually stop expanding and start contracting due to the gravitational pull in the cosmos. I believe they are right, and when it does what will happen is that the entire universe will shrink back down to where it started and then explode again.

The universe, like the love from which it is made, will never end. It will continue to expand and contract for ever... just as though, like us, the Source is breathing in and out.

Which, metaphorically, it is.

* * *

After the heat of the initial explosion subsides, the gazillions of particles of masculine energy and feminine energy start to come together to form clusters of denser energy, which evolve into the first basic gases and minerals and then – eventually – into planets and stars.

Life had begun, and so had the universe's long march towards consciousness.

(Note: There is no reason to believe that ours is the first or the only universe in existence. There might be billions of them, all existing simultaneously. The Source is pure love, and pure love is limitless – so the Source can divide itself in two as many times as it wants.)

Part One: Wake up to your Self

Here in our little corner of our galaxy, the first single-cell life forms appeared in the oceans of our planet about 10.3 billion years after the Big Bang. Water then, just like embryonic fluid now, proved to be the perfect crucible for gestating life.

Approximately 3.3 billion years later (200 million years ago), the first warm-blooded mammals appeared. I don't know if these early life forms contained the first souls from the Source. If they did, there weren't many of them because evolution continued at a snail's pace (a very old and arthritic snail at that) for another 195 million years until the first apes got up off all fours and began walking about some five million years ago.

After this, it still took another three million years before these first humans discovered fire and almost two million more before they began to dress themselves with animal skins to ward off the winter cold.

And even then – after they had walked the planet for nearly five million years – these early ancestors of ours still clubbed each other to death without a second thought and communicated with each other using little more than grunts.

* * *

Then, remarkably, almost exactly 60,000 years ago, something quite miraculous happened. Suddenly, these basic cave dwellers started to form groups that can only be described as "families". They began to care for each other, and for the first time they nurtured their sick and buried their dead.

Amazingly, language was born out of nothing as they started to talk to each other using words and phrases not too different from how we speak today.

Previously, the only tools they had made were for hunting and survival. Yet suddenly these primitive beings began to make jewellery to adorn their bodies and ornaments to decorate their homes.

Perhaps most astonishing of all, however, was the sudden spark of creativity that was ignited as, completely out of the blue, they started

Chapter 2: Why are we here?

writing and drawing on the walls of their caves in a fantastic outpouring of feelings and emotions.

It was a time of radical and, in the vast context of millions of years of human evolution, almost instant change.

It was the dawn of humanity, the advent of art and language, and the birth of compassion.

* * *

This remarkable event in human history is called the Great Leap Forward. But to this day, no one – not even the wisest anthropologist in all the world – has been able to explain what happened 60,000 years ago to accelerate our human evolution so rapidly.

Until now.

* * *

My Angel told me what happened and, having spent 21 years since then researching everything she said, I am convinced she is right.

Finally, nearly 14 billion years after the "Big Bang", our little planet had produced a life form that had a central nervous system and a big enough brain to achieve conscious spiritual awareness.

It even had an opposable thumb that allowed it to rocket ahead of all the other hoofed and clawed creatures that it came across, which it dominated with ease.

All it needed was a soul.

And, boy, did the souls come.

They came in their thousands, then millions, then billions.

The Source's grand plan had come to fruition.

It had finally created ("became" is more accurate) a life form that could evolve spiritually as well as physically so that, at last, it could see itself and know what it was... namely, pure unbounded love.

* * *

Think about this process for a moment, and how it worked.

Back then, Earth was an extremely dangerous place and survival was all anyone or anything ever cared about. So it's not surprising the only feeling early primitive ape-like humans felt was fear.

The trouble is, fear is the one thing that is guaranteed to keep us stuck and rooted in one spot, completely unable to change... or evolve.

So what is the opposite of fear? What is the only thing in the world that is capable of dissolving fear?

No, it is not courage.

It's love.

Fear and love are opposites of each other, just like darkness and light. But fear is not real; only love is. Fear is simply where love isn't, just as darkness is simply where light isn't.

You can't shine darkness onto light and make the light disappear, but you can shine light onto darkness and make the darkness disappear.

And that is exactly what happened 60,000 years ago.

For the first time in billions of years of evolution, love arrived on Earth and began to dissolve the fear that had smothered the planet, like a dark, heavy fog for so long.

* * *

But where did the love come from? And how did it get here?

Clearly, in the context of billions of years of evolution, change as dramatic as this doesn't just happen by itself – it requires the introduction of an outside influence of some kind.

That outside influence can only have come from one place; from the place where everything in the universe comes from ... the Source.

(Note: It may also have come indirectly from other more advanced star systems such as the Pleiades. But it's all the same. The Pleiadians, if they do indeed exist, would have come from the Source as well... because the Source is all there is. There can be little doubt that in the vastness of the universe there are other planets just like ours where this same process is going on even as you read this. Modern science has proved that in the known universe there are a staggering 1 billion trillion planets

Chapter 2: Why are we here?

in what is called "the habitable zone" – ie, they are approximately the same distance away from a star as Earth is from the Sun and are therefore able to support life.)

* * *

When the first souls arrived on our planet – and all the other planets in the universe where similar life forms flourished – they introduced conscious love for the first time.

Until then, although the entire universe and everything in it was made out of love energy, none of it was conscious love energy.

And so began the rapid acceleration of human evolution, because now we were no longer evolving painfully slowly as unaware animals, we were evolving consciously as spirits – or Selfs – as well.

* * *

What is the difference between a soul and a Self?

Good question. I have used the term "Self" repeatedly – even in the book's title – and now is the perfect time to explain what it means.

A soul is pure, unconscious spirit (the drop of "golden love") that initially separates from the Source (the "golden pond") in the spiritual realm and enters the physical realm (the universe) for the first time.

This soul is a one-dimensional entity, just as the Source is. But as soon as it begins to experience life in the physical realm, it becomes a three-dimensional entity. It now has three dimensions: a physical body (necessary to support the mind), a mind (consciousness), and a soul (the drop of "golden love"). This 3D being is a Self, and it will reincarnate many times on its journey towards full consciousness.

On its own, a brand new soul is of no use to the Source because it has no awareness of what it is any more than the Source does. It is pure love, but it is not *conscious* that it is pure love. The soul (unconscious love) can only become a Self (conscious love) by incarnating into a carbon-based life form that has the three required attributes for conscious spiritual evolution (as opposed to unconscious zoological evolution) – namely, a heart (love), a body with a central nervous system (life support) and a decent-sized brain (consciousness).

These three dimensions of the Self are the origin of the concept of the "Holy Trinity" of Father, Son and Holy Spirit.
- The Holy Spirit is our heart connection to pure Source energy.
- The Father is our mind, or consciousness.
- And the Son is our body.

When we die physically, all that dies is our body – hence why Jesus dies in the Bible story. Our love, our consciousness, and the physical lessons of our previous lives all live on in our 3D spiritual Self.

This Self is what reincarnates hundreds of times in different physical forms on its journey to experience everything there is to experience of the full enormity of what it means to be pure love.

When we die, our Self retains all the lessons we have learned and all the experiences we have undergone. That is why if you ever encounter a spirit (what some people call a "ghost" but is in fact a Self in non-physical form), it has both a shape (an etheric body) and it has an awareness of who it is (Self-consciousness).

That is because it is a three-dimensional Self in spirit form here in the physical realm, and not just a one-dimensional soul.

If a soul remained as a soul, it would be no different from the Source – it would be pure love, but it would have no consciousness and no energetic form in three dimensions.

* * *

When the spirit (Self) of my dead father visits me, which it (he) does all the time, I know it's my father because it looks like my father, it thinks like my father, and it talks like my father. This is because it is not just a one-dimensional soul, but a three-dimensional Self.

A soul exists only from when it separates from the Source and incarnates into three dimensions in physical form for the first time. From then on, over the course of many lifetimes, the soul ceases to be a soul and becomes a Self that is able to retain the three-dimensional qualities (mind, body and spirit) of all its lifetimes.

When our Self leaves our body after we die, it doesn't return to the spiritual dimension (the Source) because it is not yet fully conscious of what Source energy is – ie, pure conscious love. It reunites with our Angel (our Self's "other half") and stays in the physical dimension, but in spirit form, until it reincarnates into another life form, usually after a "while"… which can range from hours, to many years, to decades.

Time is an illusion, so it makes no difference how long a Self waits before it splits in two again and reincarnates. Usually it sticks around to help those it has connected with while in its previous physical form before choosing its next incarnation.

People who have had a near-death experience report seeing a bright golden light. This is usually their Angel they are seeing. Our Self stays in the physical dimension and only leaves it to return to the Source in the spiritual dimension when it has evolved over many incarnations to the point where it understands everything there is to know about the enormity of what love is and has therefore become conscious of who and what it is – so the Source can know it too.

Then, and only then, can a fully evolved Self return through The Gateway between the physical dimension and the spiritual dimension and merge back into the "giant golden pond" as pure conscious love… pure Source energy. It is this consciousness that allows the Source to know itself, which is why without us the Source cannot "exist".

(Note: Only pure love can pass through The Gateway – either as a pure soul incarnating into the physical dimension from the Source for the first time, or as a purely evolved Self going back "home" the other way.)

* * *

What if you don't wake up? Is your life wasted?

No, nothing in Heaven or on Earth (they're the same place) is ever wasted. Energy can never be created or destroyed. It just changes form.

Part One: Wake up to your Self

I'm sure you've heard that before, but what you may not have been told is why. All energy is love energy, because love is all there is. The physical dimension — and every living organism within it — was created by "God" (the Source) in its own image, so every living thing in the material world is made of pure love.

Don't be fooled by the arrogance of the misogynistic founding fathers of all the mainstream Western religions who say only man was created in the image of "God". (If I were a woman — or a wombat, or an oak tree — I would definitely have something to say about that!)

It is absolute nonsense. The Source created everything in its own image — especially women, because pure divine love is feminine.

* * *

That is why energy can't be destroyed. Energy is love, and love is the only thing that can never be destroyed. Again, I'm sure you knew that too. But did you know that love can't be created either?

Love is everything. It is infinite and eternal because love is what the Source is, and the Source is everything.

It always has been everything, and it always will be everything.

So how can something create something that it already is? It just ends up with what it is. And it can't make more of what it is because there is no "more". Love already is everything.

There can never be any more love than there already is, because love is already everything. That's why love energy can never be created or destroyed, and it certainly can never be wasted.

* * *

So to finish answering your question — no, not everyone "wakes up" in their lifetime if their Self is on one of its earlier incarnations.

In its first lifetime, a brand new soul — before it has first joined with a mind and a body to become a three-dimensional Self — incarnates as pure, perfect love. But to start with, although it knows conceptually that it is pure love, it has no idea consciously what it means to be pure love.

As I said earlier, the reason your soul incarnates – and then reincarnates over and over again as your Self – is to experience what it feels like to be pure love.

And for that it needs a mind and a body.

It's no different with human children. Newborn infants are pure love, but you can't just tell them what love is and expect them to understand. They have to grow up and experience it for themselves.

So it is with each new soul.

During your first human lifetime as a one-dimensional soul, you will have very few experiences of what love is because you are unable to tell the rest of your Self (your mind and body) what you want to experience.

Then, in your next few lifetimes, now as a three-dimensional Self, you will experience more about what love is – and therefore what you are. But your consciousness (awareness) will still be on a very basic level, so your progress will be slow.

This is why a Self incarnates so many times, usually hundreds, before it is able to return to the Source as pure conscious love.

**

I'm sure you have met people who seem to have almost no concept of what love is other than the most basic "What's in it for me?" relationship, where the man tries to use money and sometimes (tragically all too often) verbal and physical aggression in a desperate attempt to control his woman, while the woman uses sex and her vastly superior emotional intelligence to try to control her man.

Sure, they might buy each other Valentine's Day cards every year, but there's not a lot of real love going on there.

There is little hope these basic Selfs can be woken up to the fact they are pure love, because there is almost no love inside them. What's inside them is fear, which is the opposite of love, as we have already discussed. And the two cannot coexist in the same time and place.

Wherever you see hate, anger, war, greed and exploitation in the world (sadly all too frequently these days), what you are actually seeing is fear. And fear can only ever be conquered by love – in other words by teaching a frightened person they are pure love and pure extensions of Source energy, and therefore have nothing to fear.

If you try to fight fear with anger, which is a manifestation of fear, you are simply adding more fear and making the situation worse.

Exactly like throwing petrol on a fire.

Now, would someone please tell that to all those people on both sides of the religious and geopolitical divide, who are propagating the so-called "War on Terror", before it is too late.

* * *

Young Selfs are full of anger because they are full of fear. They are the terrorists, religious fanatics, murderers, muggers, football hooligans, bullies, rapists, paedophiles and other aggressively angry people, because that's how fear always manifests – as anger.

The vast majority of them are men, because they are almost totally in the masculine energy of their "Holy Trinity".

Mind (the father) and body (the son) are both masculine, while the heart (Holy Spirit) is feminine.

Because their feminine is so weak, their masculine takes over their Self completely. And wherever you find women committing these atrocious acts of anger/fear, you will notice that although their genitals are female, their energy is always overwhelmingly masculine.

These people have no idea that they even have a Self, let alone a highest purpose. But it's OK. No one ever gets left behind. Their Self will eventually incarnate through enough of these "basic" lifetimes until its starts to glimpse what love is… and therefore what it is.

Gradually, the Self evolves. Lifetime by lifetime.

Chapter 2: Why are we here?

Each time you incarnate, you experience more and more of the full magnificence of love until, in one lifetime, you become conscious enough of what love is to "wake up" your mind so that your whole Self (spirit, mind and body) can experience the joy of being pure love.

That, in a nutshell, is what I wish to give you with this book – to wake you up to who you are. *(It occurs to me that squirrels must be the wisest creatures in all the universe because the Big Truths are always found in nutshells!)*

* * *

Is the lifetime when you 'wake up' your last lifetime?

Far from it. Your Self now knows that it is pure love, but that's a long way from *being* pure love. Waking up is the beginning of your journey of conscious spiritual growth, not the end of it.

Waking up to your true nature is the last step on your Self's unconscious path towards Self-awareness, and the first step on its conscious path towards full enlightenment.

You will live many more lifetimes as an "old Self", and in all your "awake" lifetimes your highest purpose will always be the same: to help and guide others.

During these awake lifetimes, however, your Self's evolution accelerates rapidly because now it is evolving as conscious love rather than unconscious love.

Each time you incarnate, you will still have to go through the process of waking up, but you will achieve this at a younger and younger age because your evolved Self will now choose to incarnate into a family that has already woken up.

Look at the world and you will see this process in action. More and more people are waking up and unplugging from the Fear Matrix, and more and more children are being born to these people, so they need only the slightest "nudge" to wake up at a very young age.

The level of conscious love energy in the world has never been higher. Which is just as well, because another look at the world will tell you that it is desperately needed if we are to avoid a game-ending war between the dangerously delusional forces of Islam and Christianity.

After living many lifetimes as conscious love energy whose highest purpose is to serve others, our Self will eventually come to the point where it finally *experiences* what it feels like to be pure Source energy – and that is the point at which we *become* pure Source energy.

This is the moment the religions call The Rapture. It is when our entire being becomes pure love. It is when our feminine (spirit) and our masculine (body and mind) unite, and we become whole again.

This is our last lifetime. Our three-dimensional Self ceases to exist and we become a one-dimensional soul again. We are pure, conscious Source energy and we can now go back "home" through The Gateway as pure love consciousness. (Remember, only pure love can ever go through The Gateway in either direction.)

(Note: Some enlightened Selfs may stay here in the physical dimension and incarnate over and over again to teach others what they know. Or just to have fun. Others may return to the Source. It's a matter of choice. An extension of free will.)

* * *

What does numerology have to do with all this?

Every time you are born, your Self brings with you all the insights, experiences and wisdom of all your previous lifetimes. You are not consciously aware of this, of course, because it is imprinted in your unconscious. But you can access it – and thereby discover your life's highest purpose that your Self came here to achieve in your latest incarnation – through a variety of divination methods, of which I believe the simplest and the most effective is numerology.

Your Self chooses what it wants to experience in human form in every lifetime, so it will always incarnate in a specific place, at a specific time, and in a specific body. This allows you to access all its wisdom through the numbers that make up your date of birth.

Chapter 2: Why are we here?

The truth is you can access the wisdom of your Self in hundreds of different ways, including astrology, Nordic runes, the Chinese I Ching, tarot cards, tea leaves, or even just by picking a flower and looking at its petals.

Everything in the universe is made out of love energy and is therefore a vibrational portal through which you can access the infinite love and wisdom of the Source.

Wikipedia lists more than 350 recognised divination methods, including such bizarre and intriguing practices as abacomancy (the interpretation of dust), ambulomancy (the examination of how someone walks), moleosophy (the study of blemishes on the skin) and even the decidedly distasteful scatomancy which, as you might have guessed from its name, involves examining your poo to predict your future. Yuk!

The reason I have chosen to base my Self-Awareness System™ in this book on the principles of ancient numerology is because it is by far the most effective way I have discovered to teach those who are not yet fully evolved how to access the wisdom of their Self.

Remember, your Self is who you are. You are not your separate "ego identity" in this lifetime. You are not "Jenny" or "Jerome". You are pure Source energy. And the moment you become fully Self-aware – ie, when you cease to see your Self as separate from the Source, or from anyone or anything else – then your last incarnation is over and you can go home through The Gateway back to the Source.

Job done.

* * *

As I have said before, this process takes place over many lifetimes. If you are on one of the last ones, you won't need this book because once you get fully in touch with your Self and silence the ego voice in your head, you will discover you can access spirit instantly and at any time simply by asking it to talk to you.

Part One: Wake up to your Self

Spirit is love. Love is truth. And both are universal and everywhere you look. (When Jesus said "lift a rock and you will find me; split a piece of wood and I am there", this is what he was referring to.)

If you are evolved enough, you can touch your finger to the trunk of a tree and instantly download every piece of information in the universe. It is just like plugging your laptop into the internet, because everything in the universe is connected and symbiotic.

* * *

To illustrate what I mean, some years ago – when I had evolved enough to access spirit pretty much at will – I was at a party in Sydney for the world's largest annual LGBTI+ parade, called the Sydney Gay and Lesbian Mardi Gras.

It was held in a vast entertainment complex in the inner city called Moore Park, and there were more than 16,000 revellers partying in five different dance halls.

During the night I became separated from my girlfriend at the time. This was before mobile phones (yes, I really am that old!) so on the face of it there was no way we would ever find each other again in such an enormous crowd – especially at night, with all the lights turned down low.

I was concerned for her wellbeing, though, so I closed my eyes and asked my Self where she was. Immediately I received a vision of her standing alone next to a pillar on the edge of a dance floor in a dome-shaped building.

The Dome was one of the five dance halls used for the party and it was about 200m away from where I was standing.

It took me 15 minutes to get there, pressing my way through the shoulder-to-shoulder crowds of sweaty dancers.

Eventually I arrived at the pillar and there she was. Exactly where I had seen her.

She smiled, hugged me and told me she had been standing there "broadcasting" a message to me to come and find her. And because

Chapter 2: Why are we here?

my "energetic antennae" were reasonably evolved by then after several years of intensive spiritual work, I had received her loud and clear.

The point of my story is this: once you unplug from the Fear Matrix and plug into the golden light of the Source, you will be able to access its infinite wisdom anywhere, and at any time.

When that happens, you won't need this book any more. But until then, numerology offers what I believe to be the best, quickest, cheapest and most accurate way to access the wisdom of your Self any time you feel you need some guidance "from above".

* * *

What about other calendars?

One of the most common criticisms of numerology by those who have not studied it is the accusation that it is based on only one of scores of different calendars that have been in use around the world over the past 2500 years – namely, the Gregorian calendar that was introduced by Pope Gregory XIII in the 16th century.

Please real-eyes that your Self is acutely aware when and where it incarnates, so it will always use the prevailing methods of divination at its disposal to ensure you have access to its accumulated wisdom.

So if your Self popped up among the Mayans in pre-Colombian Mesoamerica in the 3rd century BC, it would have employed the Mayan calendar. If it decided to have a crack at being a Roman centurion around the time Jesus was spreading his unique messages of love, it would have used the Julian calendar. And if it wanted to experience life as a Swedish peasant girl in the 13th century, it would have chosen the Runic calendar that was in use in Scandinavia in those days.

The Self-Awareness System™ in this book is based on the Gregorian calendar because now, at the time of publication in 2017, it is the calendar used by the vast majority of the world's population.

* * *

One last thing I want to say about your highest purpose is that everything you do in your life before you "wake up" will equip you to achieve this purpose after you are fully awake to your divine nature.

This is because, without real-eyesing it, you have been living one of nine possible Life Paths, chosen by your Self, since the moment you were born. (I'll explain all about the Life Paths in Part Two.)

My Life Path Number's qualities put me on a path of writing and teaching, so when I woke up I was able to work towards fulfilling my life's highest purpose, which is to help as many other people as possible to wake up through my writing and my teaching.

If you are a doctor, when you wake up you will take your medical skills and use them to help heal people by teaching them how they can become "well" spiritually and emotionally, as well as physically.

If you are a banker, when you wake up you will almost certainly choose to stop working for a bank – which are all agents of the Fear Matrix – and branch out on your own, or with other awake people, to help people better manage their money. Or you may choose to do something else entirely with some of the other skills you have learned.

The point is you always develop the skills your Self wants you to develop while you are asleep so that when you wake up you can use them to work towards fulfilling your highest purpose of helping others.

These skills will broadly be determined by the qualities of your Life Path Number in Parts Two and Three, although yours will be unique to you. Within each Life Path Number there are as many different ways of walking the Life Path as there are people walking it.

Having said that, I can tell you that no matter what skills you have, when you wake up and start using them to fulfill your life's highest purpose of supporting other people on their journey, you will always do so in one of three ways: you will be a healer, you will be a teacher, or you will be a helper. These are the only three tasks that are necessary from a spiritual perspective.

It doesn't matter whether you are a lawyer, a housewife, a bus driver, a butcher, a baker or a candlestick maker, you will use what you do to be of service to others by teaching others about their path,

Chapter 2: Why are we here?

helping them along their path, or healing them when they stumble and hurt themselves on their path, which everyone does from time to time.

* * *

How many lifetimes does one Self have?

The nature of love is so vast that it takes many lifetimes to understand all that love is. In other words, to become "fully conscious" could take anywhere from nine to nine hundred.

But from the divine perspective, a hundred lifetimes is merely a heartbeat because there is no time in the spiritual dimension.

Time is an illusion because it exists only in the physical dimension, and the entire physical dimension is an illusion. Besides, the Source isn't in a hurry. It doesn't have a bus to catch, or an office to go to.

The purpose of incarnation – the purpose of life – is to discover that we are pure love, because only when we become conscious that we are pure love can the Source become conscious that it is pure love.

So no matter how long that takes, it is always perfect.

Every time.

No exceptions.

Remember, the Source needs us just as much as we need it. It is a perfect symbiotic relationship.

The Source needs to see its magnificence in us to be conscious that it is pure love, and we need to discover that it exists before we can become conscious that we are magnificent pure love too.

There are a lot of people in the world today speaking about the importance of consciousness. Some of them have grasped the full significance of what it is, but not many – because consciousness is much more than how we exist... it is *why* we exist.

Every time a Self incarnates into physical form, it does so deliberately so that it can experience what it wants to experience to help it understand the full nature of what love is, so that it can become pure conscious love.

Sometimes it might choose to incarnate as a billionaire, sometimes a road sweeper, sometimes a nurse, sometimes a starving child in Africa, or sometimes an animal, or even a tree.

From the spiritual perspective, there is no good or bad, better or worse. It is all love, because love is all there is. If your Self wants to know what unconditional love feels like, it could incarnate as a golden retriever. If it wants to experience sex, it could incarnate as a rabbit. Or Julio Inglesias. And if it wants to prance around saying "look at me" just to experience what a rampant ego feels like, it could incarnate as a peacock. Or a Kardashian.

The point is, your Self will always choose its experiences before it incarnates. Which is why we can define our spiritual growth most accurately as a process of "remembering" why we are here.

This process of remembering has to take place in our conscious mind. The Self knows what it came here to do, but it is unable to tell our mind because, just like the Source, the Self can't do anything. All the Self can "do" is be.

Yes, it can respond if asked, but it can't intervene. This is the true nature of "free will". If the Self had human emotions, which it doesn't, it would be extraordinarily frustrating to have to sit in silence in our heart knowing exactly what we want and how to get it, while the ego in our head (our mind) stumbles about noisily like a blithering idiot, thinking it knows what it is doing but not having the first clue.

Fortunately, our Self, like the Source, is infinitely, exquisitely and eternally patient. This is why it is vital that you ask your heart all your questions from now on, because it will always tell you what to do to fulfill your sole (soul) purpose.

The clearest way to illustrate this distinction between our mind and our heart lies in the true meaning of the phrase "I love myself".

In this phrase, our mind is the "I" and our heart is our Self. Hence why the word "myself" is actually "my Self", because it is who – and what – we are.

We are pure love, pure Source energy, and perfect in every way.

Chapter 2: Why are we here?

So by all means develop and use your mind as much as you possibly can. It is what your Self wants you to do. But be sure you know the difference between your mind and your ego, which is merely a construct of your mind.

As we saw in Chapter 1, your ego is your false sense of identity that sees your Self as separate. And although it is essential that you have an ego (ie, a sense of your "identity") as you grow up, it is equally essential that you jettison it as soon as you are strong enough to stand on your own two feet.

There's a perfect analogy for this process, which is the Space Shuttle. We need those huge booster rockets (our ego) to get off the ground (our birth) and soar upwards into the sky. But eventually we have to jettison our ego, once its job is done and we are high enough, so that our Self (the shuttle) can fly onwards to our destination.

* * *

So, should we feed our mind… or not?

Yes. Absolutely!

Whenever I talk about the need to kill your ego (and I will talk about it often), I am not referring to killing your mind. Your mind is essential for your Self to experience what it came here to experience: ie, conscious love. Your mind is your consciousness, so make sure you feed it as much information and awareness as you possibly can.

You want to have a $500,000 Ferrari in your head purring like a thoroughbred so you can enjoy life to the fullest, not some rusty old jalopy that trundles along making dumb "Huh?" and "Doh!" noises.

Be curious. Feed your mind so you can use it to experience the infinite wonder of the world you find your Self in. Just make sure you use your heart (Self) to make all your decisions. Your Self (in your heart) will always tell your mind what the right thing to do is in any given situation (providing you ask it), so you can evolve along your Life Path towards becoming conscious that you are pure love… while at the same time having as much fun as you possibly can in your convertible Ferrari driving flat out with the wind in your hair.

You start every one of your lifetimes as pure unconscious love, and in every lifetime your sole (soul) purpose is to overcome your fears (by killing your ego) so you become pure conscious love.

There are nine different Life Paths that will lead you towards this goal (and you will live all of them many times), and there are a bazillion different experiences that you can have on each of the nine Life Paths. All that matters is you become aware that your physical experiences are just a means to an end, and the end is always the same: namely, to become conscious that you are pure love, so the Source can be conscious that it is pure love too… so the spiritual dimension and the physical dimension can both continue to exist.

Your Self knows "why you are here" in this lifetime because it chose your lifetime before it incarnated. For the same reason, it also knows what you need to experience so it can become more conscious of what love is than it was at the end of its last incarnation.

Your Self knows what to do, and your mind knows how to do it. It is another perfectly symbiotic relationship, just like the one between you and the Source.

* * *

I thought you said the Self can't talk to the mind?

It can't because it is love, and all love can "do" is be. So it can't instigate a communication. But it can – and will – respond to your mind if your mind asks it a question. It just won't respond in words. Its language is feelings, which is the language of love.

When you feel something to be true, you know it to be true on a much deeper level than if you just think it is true. That, in a nutshell (squirrel!), is the difference between your Self and your mind.

So no, there is no direct communication between your Self and your mind in the way you probably want there to be: ie, "Go left here",

Chapter 2: Why are we here?

"Take this job, not that one", or "Do this, not that, because it will make you happier".

That is never going to happen. Your Self won't instruct you. But it absolutely will guide you... every step of the way.

Your Self will also always answer any question you ask of it, because it already knows the answer to every question your mind can come up with. It just won't answer you with words.

So you need to learn the language of feelings. As soon as you do, the wisdom of your Self will be on tap to you whenever you need it.

Remember, though, your Self will never instigate a conversation with your mind. It will only ever, and can only ever, respond to your mind. That's why if you ask for a sign, you will get one. But if you don't ask it for one, you won't.

Remember, too, that when you ask for a sign, or ask your Self a direct question, you must do so expecting to get an answer. Your Self doesn't respond to rhetorical questions.

I see people all the time asking "endless loop" rhetorical questions such as "Why does this always happen to me?" or "What does it all mean?". There is nothing wrong with the questions themselves, but everything is wrong with the way they ask them.

First, they are just asking the thin air that surrounds them, or perhaps a friend who is comforting them... when they should be directing the question specifically to their Self in their heart.

Second, they are asking them as rhetorical questions and they are not expecting an answer, so of course they won't get one.

If this were you, you would sit quietly and still. You would close your eyes and breathe deeply for a few moments as you consciously put all your awareness in your heart and feel all the love and wisdom that is there. Then you would very calmly and very directly ask your Self the question – and wait for the answer.

It will come. You may not always like it. But it will come.

* * *

Part One: Wake up to your Self

If our Self is a young Self, clearly it will not know as much as an older Self because it has not yet experienced enough of what love is through its various lifetimes. But that's OK, because our mind will never be able to evolve beyond the wisdom of our Self in any given lifetime. So our mind will never be able to ask our Self a question it can't answer.

Equally, on the other side of this perfectly balanced equation, if we have a thought in our head that leads us to desire something, no matter what it is, our Self will always know how we can have it... again because our mind's desire is incapable of evolving beyond the limits of our Self's ability to manifest whatever it is we desire.

I don't want to get into a protracted debate about psychology, but it is worth noting that our subconscious mind and our unconscious mind (they are not the same thing, according to traditional Freudian psychoanalysis) are both conduits for accessing the wisdom of our Self, which is where we ultimately store all the wisdom and awareness – a better word would be "knowing" – that we have accumulated over our many lifetimes.

When something pops into our head from our subconscious or our unconscious, it is coming from our Self. That is why sometimes we have the experience of knowing something we didn't consciously know we knew.

Our Self is also the source of our intuitive awareness. Its memory banks frequently throw up echoes from previous lives in the form of deja vu, or an innate skill or ability that we are not consciously aware we have learned.

You may have read reports about people having a trauma of some kind and suddenly being able to speak a foreign language. This is just them unconsciously tapping into their Self's memory banks from a previous lifetime in another country somewhere.

Dreams also contain unconscious thoughts and memories that spring from your Self, so pay close attention to them as well.

* * *

Chapter 2: Why are we here?

Can we communicate with the Source directly?

You mean can you talk to "God"? Yes, you can. I talk to the Source all the time (mostly to say thank you, about 100 times every day). So yes, absolutely, I recommend you talk to the Source as often as you like.

Just make sure you real-eyes the Source can't talk back to you.

As I've said over and over, because it's so important, the Source can't say, or do, anything. All the Source can "do" is be. So when you talk to "God" and get a reply, you are usually getting a reply from your Self. It feels as though it comes from "God" because, like "God", your Self is pure love. The difference is your Self is pure love energy – which is why it can answer you, while the Source can't.

Sometimes you might get a reply from your Angel, or from the spirit of a loved one whose Self is still in spirit form between lifetimes. Or it may come from any one of the countless other Selfs in spirit form that surround us.

One thing you can be sure of, though, is that it's not coming from the Source. As we have already seen, the only energy that can pass through The Gateway between the physical dimension, where we are, and the spiritual dimension, where the Source is, is pure love… either as pure unconscious love coming from the Source as a new soul, or as pure conscious love returning to the Source as a fully evolved Self.

Nothing else can pass through – no thought, no question, no conversation, and no requests. All of these will be tainted, no matter how slightly, with fear, and the only energy that is completely devoid of fear is pure love.

* * *

A common mistake people make is to think they can talk to the Source and ask it for things. "Please 'God' help my mother because she is sick"; "Please 'God' I promise if you get me through this I'll never be bad again"; "Please 'God' can I have a new bicycle for Christmas"; "Please 'God' tell me what I am meant to do".

Part One: Wake up to your Self

Yes, your prayer will be heard and it will be answered, but it won't be answered by the Source, which has no voice. Instead, it will be answered by your Self, or your Angel. It's all the same. You will still feel as though you have talked to "God" because you have. But you have talked to "God" as it manifests here in the physical dimension... as love energy.

It's an easy mistake to make. When you talk to your Self or your Angel it feels exactly as though you are talking to the Source. Trust me, I know. The eight hours during which I met my Angel was the most exquisite experience of my life, and I can't imagine anything ever coming close. Her energy was pure love and the most divine feeling imaginable. It felt exactly as though I was in the presence of "God".

But it's vital to real-eyes that the Source itself cannot communicate with you. The Source can't do anything. It can't even make a cup of tea or a piece of toast, let alone talk to you. All it can "do" is be.

* * *

There is, however, one way you can communicate directly with the Source, and that is to send it unconditional love. That can pass through The Gateway between the dimensions ... because it is pure love.

If, when you pray, you just say thank you and send "God" your love, rather than asking for anything, then yes absolutely the Source will feel that. In fact, it will delight in the experience of feeling "something" (ie, you) other than itself that is pure love, because that was its goal in the first place... namely to know itself as pure love.

It still can't respond to you directly, but you will feel as though it has because your Self will expand inside your heart and you will feel a rush of divine love well up within you.

That is why I encourage all my students to cultivate an attitude of gratitude. Say "thank you" to the Source, "God", "Allah", Jehovah", "Great Spirit" – whatever label you choose to use – as often and as passionately as you possibly can, because it expands your awareness of – and your connection to – your Self every time you do it.

Chapter 2: Why are we here?

I thank "God" every day for all the blessings in my life. I thank it when I return to my car and it is still there. I thank it every time I get a green light. I thank it for my bed to sleep in, for the roof over my head, for the food that I eat, and for the friends I have. I thank it for my health, for my family, and for my life.

When you lay your head on your pillow at night, just before you go to sleep, put all your awareness in your heart and say to the Source, which is all that is: "Thank you. I love you. And thank you for loving me."

By doing this – by consciously acknowledging, thanking and loving the Source as often as you can – you are doing something magical: you are raising the level of consciousness of your Self, and you are therefore taking a giant step on your growth path towards becoming aware that you are pure love.

Prayer should never ask for things. Prayer should only ever be used to send your love either to the Source, or to other Selfs – whether they are currently in human or spirit form.

* * *

So how can we ask for things?

If you want something, use the Law of Attraction, which is part of the Source anyway, as everything is.

The Law of Attraction works like this: everything in the physical dimension is made of Source energy and vibrates with Source energy, including you. And because like energy attracts like energy, all you have to do is align your own energy – including, most importantly, your thoughts – to the energy of whatever it is that you want.

If you are consciously wanting something, you will never get it because the energy of "wanting" is not a match for the energy of "having" whatever it is you want.

Instead, imagine you already have it because the energy of "having" it is an exact match... and it will show up.

(For more on how to use the Law of Attraction, watch Rhonda Byrne's excellent documentary called *The Secret*. I have watched it at least 20 times, and I still make valuable distinctions each time I do.)

* * *

You talked about Angels. Do we all have one?

Yes, everyone has an Angel, or what some cultures prefer to call a "Spirit Guide" or a "Higher Self". It's all the same thing.

Angels are the other half of our Self that stays in spirit form when we split in two to incarnate as a physical being. They are right here with us in the physical dimension – but in spirit – to guide us and watch over us throughout our life, like a nanny. There are as many Angels in spirit form here in the physical dimension as there are Selfs incarnated in physical form – whether it be as a human, an animal, or a plant.

Everything in the physical dimension exists in a state of dynamic tension and has an equal and exact opposite. And we are no different. Our Angel is the equal and exact opposite of our physical Self. It knows everything our Self does, and it knows everything our Self came here to do. But while our Self in our heart is bound by the constraints of our physical existence, especially our fear-based ego, our Angel is free to roam the physical dimension as a divine energetic being, guiding us towards our highest purpose.

Like the Source, our Angel cannot mess with our "free will" and so it will never instigate a contact or a conversation with us. It can only ever, and will only ever, respond to the questions we ask of "God" – whereupon it will answer them on behalf of "God" (the Source), just as my Angel did with me. Also, you will never meet your Angel until you have "woken up" and have learned to listen to the voice of your Self in your heart, otherwise the divine presence of your Angel would literally blow your mind – exactly like a lightbulb in an energy surge.

However, you will know your Angel exists long before this because you will often feel the "presence" of a divine being on your shoulder. Many people mistakenly believe this is "God", but it is in fact your Angel, which never leaves your side. Not for one instant.

You may also receive messages from one or more of the other billions of angels swirling around us. Some are complete Selfs between incarnations, and some are the "other halves" of every Self currently having a physical experience. It really doesn't matter if it is your Angel you experience or someone else's. They are all divine, infinite beings who carry the messages of truth and love on behalf of the Source.

(Note: Angels are neither "male" nor "female". They have no gender and will speak to you, or appear to you, in the form with which you are most comfortable. For some that is a woman, for some it's a man, and for others it's as an animal.)

* * *

Are there such things as evil spirits?

Yes, and no. There is no such thing as evil, because negativity is not an active force. There is only a lack of love, which feels like "evil" in the same way that a lack of light feels like darkness.

When you encounter what feels like an "evil spirit", what you are experiencing is a Self in spirit form that has succumbed to fear while it was in physical form and has retained its fear after its host body has died. It will process this fear when it reincarnates in human form the next time around, but for now it roams the physical dimension in spirit form, radiating fear and anger (they are the same thing).

The way to deal with a negative and afraid spirit (again, they are the same thing) is to do what you would do with a negative and afraid person you might meet on the street – simply shine love on them, and bless them on their way.

When you do this, they will leave you alone… just as afraid Selfs that have incarnated in human form and try to attack you will do exactly the same thing if you send them love – without showing them even the slightest trace of fear – and ask them lovingly to leave you alone.

What about extraterrestrials?

As we saw earlier in this chapter, scientists tell us there are a mind-boggling 1 billion trillion planets dotted around the universe in what is called "the habitable zone" – ie, the same distance away from their star as the Earth is from our Sun, and so could potentially support life in the same way our little planet does.

So yes, using the principle of Occam's Razor, it is safe to assume there are other worlds out there where extraterrestrial Selfs are going through exactly the same process we are. (Occam's Razor is a scientific principle that states: "Among competing hypotheses, the one with the fewest assumptions should be selected." It was invented in the 14th century by English philosopher William of Ockham, who was a hairy fellow and had two razors – one he used to solve problems, and the other he used on his stubble because Mrs Ockham complained she got a rash every time they pashed. It's the first one we're talking about here, although I have no idea why he spelled "Ockham" wrong.)

Many people claim to have had encounters with extraterrestrial beings such as "Greys". If this is so, and I have no reason to doubt them, the Greys are as much an extension of Source energy as we are.

If aliens do exist, they come from the Source just as we do. Everything in the universe comes from the Source because the Source is everything, and everything is the Source. It doesn't matter if they are happy little green people or grumpy little grey people, they are going through the same process we are – which is to know our Self to be pure love, so the Source can see us and know that it is pure love too.

Don't buy into the new-age nonsense about "evil aliens". There is no such thing as "evil", as we have already seen. In the same way that angry spirits are merely Selfs in spirit form who are stuck in their fear, so too angry aliens are just afraid, nothing more. Shine love on them and they'll leave you alone. They can't bother you if you are unafraid, because – at the risk of repeating my Self yet again – fear and love cannot coexist in the same time and place.

Chapter 2: Why are we here?

You mentioned earlier that animals have souls too?

Yes, absolutely they do. Some Christians don't think so. They believe only human beings have souls. But that's OK, because all the animals I have spoken to about this just shrug and say the Christians will get the hang of it eventually.

The purpose of an incarnated soul, or Self, is to become conscious of its divine perfection, so it's doubtful whether all animals have Selfs for the simple reason that a Self would be unlikely to incarnate into the body of a slug, for example, as it would not accomplish a great deal of awareness, considering a slug has no brain and no nervous system.

It might, because the Self might just be curious about what it feels like to be a slug. Equally, it might feel that experiencing life as a tree, for example, is an important part of its journey to experience and understand everything there is to know about the enormity of love.

I can imagine no better way for a Self to experience the sensation of stability and strength than by being a big, old oak tree; or to experience the wonderful feeling of protecting your loved ones than by being a shade tree under which children play safely and joyously in their back garden.

And what about experiencing the glorious feeling of being part of a team where everyone works together for a common cause? If you wanted to know what that felt like, a life as an ant or a honey bee would teach you more than any human incarnation ever could.

Selfs will frequently choose to incarnate as sentient animals such as dogs, cats, lions, pigs, tigers, ferrets, cows, sheep, goats, dolphins, whales and horses so they can be of service to other Selfs.

Remember, the sole (soul) purpose of every incarnation is to become conscious of every single aspect of the enormity of what love is, and most sentient animals know more about unconditional love than any of us humans will know in 100 lifetimes.

(Cats are especially interesting. There's a very good chance they are the most evolved animals on the planet because they have figured out a way of doing absolutely nothing and sleeping all day while everyone else does all the hard work.)

Most Selfs, however, will incarnate as humans most of the time for the simple reason that the human brain, body and nervous system give them the best opportunity to evolve their love consciousness.

It also explains why, after evolving neck-and-neck with other life forms on the planet for millions of years, primates – the earliest "humans" – suddenly took off on the evolutionary scale and left the rest of the animal kingdom far behind.

Please, though, as you read this, be aware that just because an animal is primitive or may not have a Self in residence does not mean we should treat them any differently to how we treat other human beings (Selfs).

Every living organism in the universe is an extension of Source energy and deserves to be treated with love as well as respect – from a moth to a mother, a kingfisher to a king.

One day, mankind will wake up to this fact and pass laws that make abusing animals the same as abusing humans, and we will look back on the unspeakable cruelty of today's live animal exports industry exactly as we now look back on the horrors of the slave trade.

Animals deserve the same rights as we do. I'm not saying we shouldn't eat animals, just as some of them eat us. I'm saying we shouldn't mistreat them, because they are as much a part of Source energy as we are.

In the end, it doesn't matter whether you eat an animal, or an animal eats you. We all end up back home in the same place anyway. What does matter is that while we are here, we respect each other for what we are – extensions of pure Source energy.

Please just make sure that when you do eat an animal, you thank them for nourishing you. And who knows… maybe in one of your future lifetimes you will be able to return the favour.

* * *

Chapter 2: Why are we here?

What about plants?

Plants possess consciousness, but on such a basic level it is rare for a Self to incarnate as one. However, we do know that plants respond to positive and negative energy in the same way that more sentient beings like animals and humans do.

Sentience can be described as being aware of, and reacting to, your environment. When a sentient organism is hurt, it repairs itself (its Self). So on that level, plants are definitely sentient. But does grass mind us walking on it? No, because grass doesn't have pain receptors or a nervous system. The awareness level of plants is very basic, so you can go ahead and weed your garden without feeling bad.

Trees, however, are much more complex organisms because they create energy in their "bodies" just like we do. Trees should, and must, be respected at all times. I am aghast at how stupid our politicians are as they fumble about trying to "save the environment" with carbon taxes and emission caps while doing nothing except snipe at each other like children: "I'll do it when you do it, but you have to go first."

It's simple. Just stop cutting down all the trees. They eat carbon for breakfast. That's why they are here.

Come on guys, I learned this in junior school. What were all the politicians doing in biology class? Practising how to lie?

You want to save the environment? Make it illegal to cut down the natural forests, and make the penalties for people who do so a big enough deterrent… 15 years in jail should do it.

Then, instead of giving billions of dollars to the power companies to compensate them for lost income under the carbon caps, spend the money on planting trees. Lots and lots of them.

Next time you meet a tree, you don't have to hug it if you feel that would make you look foolish, although it will respond to you with love if you do. Just nod your head as you walk past. Because if it wasn't for the trees, none of us – not a single one of us – would be alive.

* * *

Part One: Wake up to your Self

What proof do you have for all of this?

That is a very fair question, and I am glad you asked it – because nothing you read in this book, or anywhere else for that matter, should ever be taken at face value.

All of what I have told you in this chapter came from my Angel. But that was not enough for me to fully real-eyes that what she was telling me was true… and I don't expect it to be enough for you either.

After she visited me in 1996 – 21 years ago almost to the day as I sit here writing this paragraph – I had to go out into the world and test it thoroughly, over and over again, before sitting down to share it with you in this book.

When I met my Angel, or rather when she showed herself (her Self) to me, I was already wide awake. I had experienced several life-changing contacts with the spirit world – enough, I now real-eyes, for her to know I was ready to meet her and hear what she had to say without blowing my mind. (An ironic phrase, because had I been in my mind at that stage of my life instead of in my heart, the experience of meeting my Angel would definitely have blown it, just like a fuse.)

My first profound spiritual experience came in 1988 at the age of 29. It was the saddest day of my young life, but wrapped inside the pain, like a delicious treat, was the greatest gift I have ever been given.

The gift of "waking up".

It was my father who gave me the gift. It was my father who woke me up. And he did it by dying.

* * *

I was lying in bed in Australia one night, almost asleep, when I heard the voice of my father saying goodbye to me. The thing was, my father was on the other side of the world, in England, at the time.

I sat up with a fright and looked at the clock. It was 11pm.

It took me a long time before I finally fell asleep, and I slept fitfully, unsure what this meant. Was my father dying? Or was I about to die in my sleep?

Chapter 2: Why are we here?

The next morning my brother Mark phoned me from London. He asked me to sit down.

"It's OK," I said. "I know. It's Dad, isn't it?"

"How do you know?" Mark said.

"What time did he die?" I asked.

Mark told me Dad had been out shopping with Mum and had a massive heart attack at noon on the main street of the village where they lived and had dropped down dead where he stood.

Allowing for the 11-hour time difference between England and Australia, it was precisely the time that Dad had said goodbye to me – 17,000km away.

When I got home to Mum's house in England after a 24-hour flight, I discovered that her watch had stopped at noon – at the precise moment that Dad had died. But what was even more remarkable was that Mum told me that on the morning Dad had died he had brought her a cup of tea, which he did every morning. Only this time he did something else he had never done before. He sat down on the bed and told her he had had a dream.

My father was a very old-fashioned man. Never once in the 40-odd years they were married had he ever spoken to Mum about his dreams. Not once. But that morning, the morning of his death, he told her he had dreamed he was moving house (even though they had no plans to move), and then he described the new house in great detail: it was a country cottage, surrounded by trees, with smoke coming out of the chimney and a donkey in the front garden.

After a late breakfast, my mother and father went shopping in the little seaside village of Emsworth on the south coast of England, where they had a summer house. My mother went into the bank to pay some bills while my father stayed outside on the pavement.

When my mother came out again a few minutes later, a small crowd had gathered. They were all looking down at someone lying on the pavement. It was my father. And he was already dead.

On the day of the funeral, at our local village church, we were all standing silently around my father's grave under a typically cloudy

Part One: Wake up to your Self

English sky, watching as four Dickensian men in top hats and tails lowered Dad's coffin into the ground.

My father's plot was the last one in the row, nestled against the boundary fence of the graveyard. Fighting back tears, I looked up… and there, on the other side of the fence, no more than 100m away, was a cottage, surrounded by trees, with smoke coming out of its chimney and a donkey grazing peacefully in the garden.

* * *

That was 28 years ago. Since then, my father's Self has visited me on numerous occasions when I have been upset. Just as in life, he always likes to make a grand entrance to let me know he is there, which is why every time he visits me he opens the door with a loud bang.

The last time Dad visited me, I was in the living room of my home in Sydney saying goodbye to the best friend I have ever had in my life – my faithful dog Tyson who was 13 and had suffered a massive stroke a few days earlier that had left him paralysed from the neck down. He could move his head, but his body, legs and tail were motionless.

Four of us were gathered around him, cuddling him as the vet injected a fatal overdose of sedative into a catheter in his leg.

The previous night I had asked my father's spirit (Self) to please come and get Tyson and make sure he was safe. But in the emotion of the moment, as I looked into Tyson's big, faithful eyes one last time while the deadly liquid raced towards his heart, I had forgotten.

Suddenly, at the precise moment that Tyson's heart stopped beating and he slipped away in my arms, the front door slammed open. Then, a split second later, Tyson looked up above my head as though he saw someone familiar, wagged his tail three times, and was gone.

He was paralysed. It wasn't possible for him to wag his tail. But it happened. And the vet, who saw it too, said it wasn't a death twitch.

Tyson clearly and deliberately wagged his tail three times at the precise moment he died, just as he used to whenever I came home or when he saw someone he loved (which was pretty much everyone).

Chapter 2: Why are we here?

The front door left me in no doubt. He had seen my father come to greet him, and I knew he was safe.

When Tyson came into my life, I was going through a difficult time. He not only helped me overcome my challenges, but he healed me in every way that a person can be healed.

A psychic told me a month after he died that Tyson has been sent by my father to help me grow so that I could write this book. That made sense, and it also explained why Tyson had recognised Dad.

* * *

I have had many other such experiences. I chose to share these two with you partly because I wanted to prove to you that animals have Selfs too, and also to make the point that if spirit exists (and these experiences prove to me beyond any shadow of a doubt that it does), then everything must be spirit.

You see, spirit is an all-or-nothing concept. Either there is no spirit (and therefore no Source and no Selfs), or everything is spirit.

Spirit can't exist over here where I am, but not over there where you are. It can't exist on a Sunday but not a Tuesday, or in your living room but not in your bathroom, or in Australia but not in Azerbaijan.

To put it another way, the universe is one of two things: either it is a collection of minerals and gases revolving randomly through time and space, both of which have no beginning and no end – or it is a giant, symbiotic organism designed to support life forms while the Selfs that inhabit them evolve and regenerate the Source.

It has to be one or the other. There is no middle option. No grey area. Either spirit exists, or it doesn't.

It's time, in this next chapter, for you to decide for your Self.

Chapter 3:
All your answers lie within

3 is the number of expression
And the only thing within you that's worth expressing is love

Having answered the biggest question of all, "Why are we here?", it's time to look in more detail at the "here" part of this question – the physical universe – and ask another brain-teaser that has been troubling humanity for thousands of years: "What is out there?"

There are two ways to answer this question: the easy way, and the hard way.

The easy way is to tell you the physical universe is impossible to understand using the laws of physics because it was deliberately designed so that as we humans evolve our intelligence to the point where we can attempt to measure it, we will discover the truth that the so-called "real world" is not "real" at all – it is divine – at which point we will real-eyes we are divine too, leading to a massive shift in global consciousness that will rapidly accelerate the number of Selfs who are able to evolve and return to the Source. (This is already happening, and the revelations in this book – as well as countless other similar books being published today – are all part of this process.)

The hard way is to try to explain to you what I mean by that last paragraph. I prefer the easy way because instead of bothering with this chapter we could all go to the pub, where I'm sure the creationists and the evolutionists must be having a great party by now. Plus, if you think your head aches after reading that last chapter, by the time we have

Chapter 3: All your answers lie within

gone through the finer points of thermo-nuclear astrophysics it's going to be throbbing like a bastard.

But you've paid your money, so here goes…

* * *

The nature of the universe has baffled human beings ever since the first caveman looked up at the stars and said to his wife, over a dinner of roasted mammoth cutlets: "Strewth, Sheila, waddya reckon all those bright lights are?"

Since then, and for the past thousands of years, scientists with brains the size of planets have devoted their whole lives to trying to figure out how the universe – the physical dimension – works.

But the more our technology evolves, and the further our astronomers are able to see into "space", the less we really know about how it is constructed… because every time we manage to answer one of our pointy-headed questions, we are confronted with another even more impossible one.

The truth is that even after all that work, and the countless billions of dollars spent on their research, the best the scientists have come up with is that the universe is big.

And I don't mean big like a Big Mac.

Or even big like an elephant.

I mean mind-blowingly and unfathomably BIG!

From the front of your house to the edge of the measured universe (and who knows how far it extends beyond what we can measure) is a distance of approximately 46 billion light years, give or take a light year or two.

To give you an idea of how far away that is, a light year is the distance light travels in one year. And light doesn't muck about when it decides to go somewhere. It travels at a pretty impressive 300,000km per second. That's more than 1 billion kilometers per hour – which is the fastest speed there is.

Part One: Wake up to your Self

To get your brain around how fast that is, imagine you could bend a beam of light all the way around the Earth. Now imagine you are standing on the roof of your house and you are holding a powerful torch in your hand. Point the torch in front of you and turn it on.

The little beam of light that comes out of your torch will travel all the way around the circumference of the planet (a distance of about 40,000km) and come up behind you to shine a little circle of light on the back of your shirt in roughly the time it takes you to blink your eyes. In other words, about one seventh of one second.

Now point your torch up at the Moon. If Neil Armstrong was still standing on it when you turned it on, your little beam of light would hit him in the face faster than he could say: "Crikey, that was fast!" In other words, almost exactly one second.

And then, even travelling at that unimaginable speed, it would not reach the edge of the known universe for another 46 billion years.

But here's the catch… that's more than three times longer than the universe has existed.

* * *

Are you starting to get the idea that the universe we live in is not physically possible?

You should. Because it isn't.

Something is very much amiss here.

Now consider the universe extends that far in every direction and it is not just growing in every direction, but accelerating.

So by the time your light beam reaches the edge of the known universe as it is today, 46 billion years would have passed and your beam of light would be further away from the edge of the universe than it was before it started.

Which means we will never be able to measure it, or understand it. Because we are not meant to.

* * *

Chapter 3: All your answers lie within

The reason the universe is impossible to measure using the laws of physics is because the universe is not governed by the laws of physics. It is governed by the law of love, known as Divine Law.

This is the crucial point that all physicists – including the great Stephen Hawking, as mentioned on page 14 – have missed.

The universe is not made up of physical energy, it is made up of love energy. And love, as we have already seen in the last chapter, is infinite and immeasurable.

When the Source, which is "all that is", split in two and created the physical dimension so that it could know what it was, it didn't "create" the universe... it "became" the universe. That is why the physical dimension is as endless and timeless as the spiritual dimension.

The centuries-old struggle by humanity's collective ego to make some sort of sense of our surroundings is as pointless as its centuries-old desire to define "God" in ego-based terms that the human brain can understand.

Neither is ever going to happen, because the ego simply cannot comprehend the unending vastness of love.

It's not meant to. That's the whole point. The only way we can ever measure the infinity of what love is (it is everything) is not with our mind, but with our heart.

The "impossibility" of the universe is the ultimate "clue", if you like, that shows us what we need to do to fulfill our highest purpose – which is to know our Self as pure love, so the Source can know itself too, so we can all exist and keep this party we call "life" rolling along.

And that is never going to happen as long as we stay in our heads.

To become conscious of what we are, we must get out of our heads and into our hearts. Yes, studying our surroundings is interesting from an intellectual standpoint. But, ultimately, it is irrelevant whether we are evolving from an ego identity to a conscious Self in a condo in Baltimore, or on a little green rock in a galaxy 40 billion light years away. It is just geography and makes not the slightest bit of difference.

All that matters is that the souls that incarnate from the Source, which is unconscious love in the spiritual dimension, eventually evolve

Part One: *Wake up to your Self*

into conscious Selfs here in the physical dimension – so that the Source can exist, and therefore so we can exist too.

It's all love. Love is all there is.

End of story. And end of search.

* * *

You mentioned something about 'Divine Law'?

Yes. Divine Law states that in the spiritual dimension everything is love, and in the physical dimension everything is love energy. The difference between the two is crucial.

Again, love just is. All it can "do" is be. But love energy – like all energy – exists in a state of constant dynamic tension between two opposites: positive (masculine) energy and negative (feminine) energy. Therefore, love energy is capable of creating consciousness – because only by knowing what we are not, can we know what we are.

In the spiritual dimension, there is no energy, there is only love. So the Source can't know what it is, because it can't know what it's not. But here in the physical dimension, we are able to know what we are by discovering what we are not.

This Law of Duality, as divine law is more commonly known by scientists who tend to still shy away from the word "divine", is what allows us to create consciousness in the physical dimension so that the Source in the spiritual dimension can know what it is.

The Law of Duality states that everything has an exact and equal opposite, and it operates in the same way as the binary code of computers. (This, by the way, is how numerology works. The numbers that make up your birth date are the "access codes" that allow you to plug into the collective consciousness of the physical dimension. It is exactly like plugging a computer into the internet and accessing the information of every computer in the world. But more on that later.)

The physical universe is made up of love energy. And energy – like everything else – is subject to the divine Law of Duality.

Chapter 3: All your answers lie within

Energy vibrates because it is made up of two parts: positive energy (protons - masculine) and negative energy (electrons - feminine) which are held together in a state of constant dynamic tension.

Without this charge of positive and negative energy, there would be no life. Nothing could exist because there would be no order. Planets and stars would not form, there would be no gravitational pull, there would be no water or air, and your bodies would disintegrate because atoms would be flying about all over the place... like thoughts in Donald Trump's head.

The Law of Duality is the most powerful law in the universe because it governs all the other laws. It's called "Divine Law" because it is how the Source separated into two dimensions at the same time.

All the physical laws are extensions of the Law of Duality, including Newton's law of gravity, Einstein's theory of relativity, Boyle's law of thermodynamics, Hubble's law of cosmology, Pascal's law of physics... and every other physical law you will never bother to read about because life is just too short.

All of the spiritual laws are also governed by the Law of Duality, including the Law of Attraction, which we talked about earlier, and the Law of Cause and Effect, otherwise known as karma.

But the Law of Duality is much more than boring old quantum physics. It applies to everything that exists with us here in the physical dimension – both spiritual and physical, as well as sexual too.

– Ask any physicist, and they will tell you that all physical matter consists of positive and negative particles held together in an eternal dance of energy. Without each other, neither could exist, and matter would not exist.

– Ask any quantum physicist, and they will tell you duality manifests as cause and effect, whereby every reaction has an equal and opposite reaction. Without action there would be no reaction, and vice versa, therefore there would be no evolution.

– Ask any mathematician, and they will tell you that all calculations are based on the simple structure of binary code, which consists of a series of 1s and 0s, where 1 represents "on" and 0 represents "off".

Without each other nothing would happen. Everything would be either on or off. Again, there would be no evolution. For life to exist it must be created (on), then destroyed (off), then created again (on).

– Ask any metaphysician and they will describe the Law of Duality as the split between the physical (on) and the spiritual (off), and the corresponding split between masculine (on) and feminine (off), that has to happen for life to exist. They will also tell you that the purpose of our existence on Earth – ie, the purpose of spiritual growth – is to reunite what is divided. Our work is over when the spirit (feminine) and the mind/body (masculine) merge back together and we become whole again, we become one, and we return to what we were before we started our spiritual journey all those lifetimes ago… pure love.

That is the significance of the Law of Duality. Without it there would be no consciousness, and without consciousness the Source would not exist, and therefore we would not exist.

* * *

What was that you said about sex?

I thought you might ask that! Yes, the universe and everything in it is – to put it bluntly – one giant, pants-down shagfest that has been going on for about 14 billion years. Everything in the universe, including you and me, is either positive energy (masculine) or negative energy (feminine). And for all you female readers, I am not using "negative" in the sense of "You never help around the house, you lazy bastard". I mean negative in the sense of serene, receptive and life-giving.

Here are a few examples to show you what I mean:

Positive energy (protons) are masculine, while negative energy (electrons) are feminine.

Light is masculine – darkness is feminine.
Fire is masculine – earth is feminine.
Air is masculine – water is feminine.

Chapter 3: All your answers lie within

> Mind is masculine – heart is feminine.
> On is masculine – off is feminine.
> Out is masculine – in is feminine.
> Cause is masculine – effect is feminine.
> Yang is masculine – yin is feminine.
> Day is masculine – night is feminine.
> Life is masculine – death and rebirth are feminine.

So whether it's masculine and feminine particles that are coming together to form a planet, a man and a woman coming together to create a child, a masculine man and a feminine man coming together to create love, a masculine woman and a feminine woman coming together to create even more love, or a mind/body and a heart coming together to create a fully conscious Self, it's all about sex... life-creating, consciousness-creating, "God"-given sex.

Why do you think the religions' founding fathers suppressed sex? At the time the religions started, the happy little pagans were running around making love, communing with nature and having so much fun that they were getting dangerously close to discovering the true spiritual nature of their existence... so of course that had to stop!

After all, the whole "If you want to reach "God" you have to go through me" business model was never going to work if the people had already figured out that they themselves were "God".

I'm going to put a few religious people's noses out of joint with this book, but it's worth it to get to the truth. I have spent many of the past 35 years working as a journalist, which taught me that exposing the truth is more important than a few crooked noses.

Sex is Divine. It always was, and it always will be. So perhaps someone can explain to me why the Catholic Church still bans women from being priests, and still forbids its male priests to have sex?

The sole (soul) purpose of all this "shagging" by particles, plants, animals and humans is to create life in the universe, which in turns creates consciousness. (Why do you think it's called "making love"?)

In the spiritual dimension, love is whole. There is no separation of masculine and feminine, as we saw earlier, which is why the Source can't know itself... because it can't know what it is not.

In the physical dimension, consciousness is created first by knowing what we are – and what we are not – and then by merging the masculine and the feminine back together again to become whole.

* * *

If love is everything, and if everything has an equal and exact opposite, then what is the opposite of love?

The opposite of love is not hate, it is fear. We touched on this briefly in the last chapter when we talked about the Great Leap Forward of human evolution, but it deserves a much deeper explanation because it is the key to life, the universe and everything.

The Source is love, but it doesn't know it is, so it creates (becomes) the physical dimension where the Law of Duality allows us to know what we are by first knowing what we are not.

As babies, we are born as pure love, but we are not conscious that we are. To be conscious of what we are, we first have to become conscious of what we are not. This is why we develop an ego, because to know what we are (our Self) we first need to know what we are not (our ego). Equally, our ego helps us to understand what we are not (fear) to that we can real-eyes what we are (love).

The process of becoming conscious can never be accidental. It has to be deliberate. That is why we can't just be born and live as love. We have to create our ego so that we can know our Self as separate and feel what it feels like to be afraid. Only then can we deliberately – and consciously – conquer our fears and return to being love, so the Source can know that it is pure conscious love too.

This is why the journey to full enlightenment is always called the "return to love". It is the return to what we are (love), having experienced all we are not (fear). *(There is more on this in Appendix C.)*

Chapter 3: All your answers lie within

And in case you have ever thought "If 'God' (pure love) is all there is, why is there so much fear, suffering and negativity in the world?"… now you know. It's because before we can know what love is, we have to know what love isn't. Therefore fear – the experience of being separate, which our ego gives us – is unavoidable.

It's an essential part of our journey back to love.

* * *

This all sounds easy, but don't be fooled. The trouble with the Law of Duality is that it states that everything has an equal and exact opposite. And as I am sure you know, love is the most powerful force in the universe. Which, I am afraid (pun intended), means that fear (the ego) is equally powerful. So conquering our fears and returning to love is no picnic.

This explains why 95 per cent of the world's population is still plugged into the Fear Matrix… because fear is equally as powerful as love. It also explains why making the Great Leap from our ego (fear) into our heart (love) is far from easy.

It is not impossible, though, as we will discover in the next two chapters. Plus, it is well worth the effort because the bliss that awaits us when we return to love is beyond anything our materialistic ego can ever imagine. And I'm including money, fast cars, designer clothes, designer shoes, ski chalets, private jets, sex, yachts, Caribbean island hideaways, lobster bisque, champagne, more money and even more sex.

None of these materialistic pleasures can come close to the bliss of living as pure love without the need for anything outside our Self.

Chapter 4:
Reality is a trap for the mind

4 is the number of stability
Real stability comes from building on a foundation of love, not fear

We have already seen that unless you chose to be born to parents who have already "woken up" to their spiritual identity, you will have constructed your beliefs about who you are based on your ego's view of what it thinks is "real", because that's what your parents did.

To re-mind you, your ego is the fear-based voice in your head that sees you as separate from everyone else and regards the physical world as a dangerous and competitive place.

As long as it is at the controls of your life, you will filter almost everything through fear – specifically, the fear of getting hurt and the fear of not being "good enough".

I know that, as you read those words, you might think you feel "good enough" because your Self-esteem is strong. But unless you have already unplugged from the Fear Matrix and removed your ego from the controls of your life, your level of Self-esteem – and your life as a whole – is as fragile as a bird's nest because it is built not on who you are, but on what you have achieved and accumulated.

If you are still in your ego and you were to lose your relationship, your money, your family, your job and everything else you hold dear, your life would collapse like a house of cards.

Chapter 4: Reality is a trap for the mind

Self-love has absolutely nothing to do with Self-esteem. Self-esteem is a fool's game because the more we have, the more our ego wants. And our happiness will last only as long as we are able to hang on to what we have.

No, the only way to build our life on a firm footing is through Self-love, not Self-esteem. Self-esteem is all about trying to be "good enough", which is the desire of the ego and based on competing with others around us. Self-love, on the other hand, is about being "God enough"... in other words, real-eyesing that we are pure Source energy and nothing outside our Self can make us lastingly happy, no matter what the television advertisers might try to tell us.

This is why Self-love is called the "greatest love of all".

I explain the importance of Self-love in more detail in my book on relationships called *Leap into Love*. For now, though, the point I want to make is that as long as your ego in running your life, you will never be able to fulfill your life's highest spiritual purpose – which, to re-mind you, is to know your Self as pure spirit (pure love) and then help others do the same.

* * *

How do I get rid of my ego?

The full process will be described in Chapter 6. But briefly, there are three steps to weakening your ego so that it relinquishes the controls of your life to your heart (your Self). Three steps to "heaven", if you like... remembering that heaven is right here on earth.

The first step is to "wake up" to the fact that your ego is not "who you are" because you are a pure, perfect spirit – pure Source energy. We have already covered all this in the first three chapters.

The second step is to unplug from the Fear Matrix, which – just like in the film *The Matrix* – has enslaved your mind by drip-feeding your ego a diet of fear on a daily basis.

Part One: Wake up to your Self

These first two steps are relatively easy. You will have achieved them both by the end of this first book, I promise you. But the third one is not quite so straightforward because it involves facing all your fears. It will be a challenge, but only by facing this challenge will you be able to wrest your ego from the controls of your life and return to living as pure love, just as you did when you were first born as a brand new baby – only this time it will be as conscious love, rather than unconscious love.

As I have already mentioned in the introduction, this process is called the Dark Night of the Soul (although from now on we will give it the more accurate name of Dark Night of the Self). It can take many years and is usually extremely painful. You may have to lose your relationship and your job. You will almost certainly suffer a money crisis. And you will feel as though a part of you is dying – because it is.

But don't worry, it is only your ego that is dying. And the rewards when you do make it through the Dark Night and the sun comes up again are worth all your suffering a million times over. You will have "died and risen again" – only this time you will be fully alive as an immortal spirit, rather than half alive as a mortal, frightened human.

* * *

Does this story sound familiar? It should, because our "ego death" and our "spiritual rebirth" is the original message of the Christian parable of the Resurrection.

In the Bible, Jesus dies and comes back to life three days later. I'm afraid to say that your Dark Night will take more than three days, but then the Bible's use of time – "40 days and 40 nights", for example – was always intended to be metaphorical.

(Oh, and while we are on the subject of Biblical imagery, please be aware that the concept of "hell" refers to the experience of living in our ego (fear) and "heaven" refers to the experience of living in our heart (love). The Christian founding fathers were only too happy to

Chapter 4: Reality is a trap for the mind

use the threat of a concocted "hell" to make the already frightened masses even more terrified and easier to control.)

Jesus was one of the truly great avatars, along with Muhammad and Buddha and many others, and the original authors of the parable of the Resurrection are to be congratulated for coming up with such a perfect way to describe his spiritual rebirth after he faced all his fears. It's just a shame the parable has been so badly misinterpreted over the centuries to imply his body died, rather than just his fear-based ego.

The same misinterpretation is true of the Biblical parable of the "virgin birth" of Jesus, which the Bible's early male editors twisted into yet another preposterous lie by trying to claim that Mary and Joseph never had sex (tut! tut!).

What the original authors of the Bible were saying – quite correctly – is that we all have two physical births: a "virgin" birth when our Self enters the unborn foetus and gives it life by starting its heart beating, and then a second one when we burst screaming into the world approximately nine months later.

Finally, we have a third (Holy Trinity) spiritual birth – or, to be more precise, a rebirth (Resurrection) – when in one of our lifetimes (Jesus, in the Biblical story, apparently needed only one) we face all our fears and kill our ego.

This is when we are reborn (or "resurrected") as pure love. In other words, as our true Self.

* * *

Anyway, I digress. In the next two chapters we will go into detail about how you can unplug from the Fear Matrix and make your Dark Night of the Self as quick and as painless as possible.

For now, though, I need to show you what the Fear Matrix is so you have a clear idea of what you are up against.

And I must warn you… it isn't pretty.

* * *

Part One: *Wake up to your Self*

OK, so what exactly is the Matrix?

The Matrix, as the character Morpheus says in the film of the same name, "is the world you see when you look out your window – it is the world that has been pulled over your eyes to blind you from the truth that you are a slave in a prison that you cannot smell, or see, or touch... because it is a prison for your mind".

In the film, the Matrix is a computer program that is used to fool the subconscious minds of comatose human beings into believing they are fully conscious.

The film is set in an imagined future when artificial-intelligence machines rule the Earth. All the natural resources of the planet were destroyed in the war between the humans and the machines – which the machines won after the humans torched the sky and blocked out the sun in a failed attempt to cut off the machines' power source.

But the machines simply found another power source – namely, the bioelectrical energy created in the bodies of human beings.

The machines farm vast "crops" of humans – billions of them, all linked up to a central power grid, like batteries. And to prevent the humans from trying to break free, they are kept in an induced coma.

However, the machines soon discover that because the humans' brains are inactive other than for basic life-support functions, the amount of bioelectrical energy their bodies produce is minimal.

Humans create much more energy when their brains are active, so the machines develop a computer program called the Matrix, which they then plug into the humans' brains to stimulate their minds by making them think they are living out their lives in a "real" world.

Exactly like the one outside your window.

* * *

So I have a question for you... have you ever stopped to consider that the world outside your window is no more real than the computer-generated Matrix in the movie?

Chapter 4: Reality is a trap for the mind

What if I were to tell you that just like the humans in the movie, we have all been plugged into a fake, fear-based reality that stops us rising up against our "captors" and being free?

And what if I were to tell you that our "captors" are not machines, but humans just like you and me who have kept us locked up in fear and have blinded us from the truth of who we are for thousands of years... not so we can generate electricity to make them function, but so we can generate money to make them rich.

This might all sound a bit tabloid and sensationalist to you, but I can assure you that even if you choose to believe there is no conscious conspiracy, the effect of the Matrix is very real and you need to be aware of it – especially when it comes time for you to "unplug" from the diet of fear that has been fed to you by the media ever since you were old enough to turn on your TV or pick up a newspaper.

* * *

Who created the Matrix?

The architects of the Matrix were the first "Fat Controllers" who sprung up in Europe and the Middle East thousands of years ago.

They used a mixture of violence and religious dogma to generate fear in the minds of the masses so they could control them and use them as slave labour to make themselves rich and powerful.

As they spread through the world, the so-called European "conquistadors" (they couldn't bring themselves to use the more accurate words "pillagers" and "murderers") enslaved everyone who lived in the countries they invaded in the name of "God".

If the natives didn't co-operate, the Fat Controllers killed them in their tens of millions, wiping out indigenous populations in North and South America, Africa, Asia and Australasia.

In Australia, where I live, the indigenous population of Tasmania was virtually wiped by the English in what white historians like to call the "Black War", but which wasn't a war at all. It was genocide.

Part One: Wake up to your Self

When this was taking place, in the early 19th century, a common man in England who stole a goat or a deer from his obscenely wealthy landlord to feed his starving family was put to death. And yet the brutal English invaders who killed almost all the Aborigines in Tasmania, and elsewhere, were lauded and given medals for "bravery".

Go figure.

Today, the Fat Controllers' methods are more subtle because with the advent of mass media they know we wouldn't stand for genocide or slavery anymore. At least not for long.

So instead of making us work as slaves, they give us jobs and pay us to work for them, then take the money back – some of it in taxes, and the rest of it by convincing us to spend our hard-earned money buying all the worthless stuff they paid us to make in the first place, promising us that the more shit we own, the happier we will be.

* * *

Who are the Fat Controllers today?

Look out your window. You'll know who they are because they own everything. They are the churches, the politicians and the fat-cat corporations – especially the banks – which grow fatter by the minute by feeding on your fear.

Their weapons are not just the armies and police forces, which they use to quell anyone who tries to break free, but the media, which they use to drip-feed you a non-stop diet of fear with stories about terrorism, burglary, murder, swine flu, bird flu, SARS, unemployment, cancer, heart attacks... and, of course, the latest "financial crisis".

There is no financial crisis. There never was and there never will be. Money isn't real, which ought to give you a clue and set your alarm bells ringing. Ding! Money was invented by the Phoenicians in 1500BC and spread throughout the civilised world through the Medicis of Italy in the 14th century and the Fuggers of Germany in the 16th century (hence the origin of the popular expression "Greedy Fuggers").

Chapter 4: Reality is a trap for the mind

Money is just bits of paper and metal with pictures of famous dead people on them. It has no value, other than what the Fat Controllers decide its value is. And they can change it in a heartbeat by declaring that the $100 note in your pocket is now worth $10… or $1000.

Have a look at the recent GFC – the "Global Financial Crisis" that brought the world to its knees in 2008-09. (GFC? It sounds like a cheap fast-food restaurant, and it was just as manufactured.)

Do you know why it happened? It happened because people were starting to get too much money after decades of prosperity, soaring house prices and a record run of bull markets on Wall Street and other global stock exchanges. And when people get too much money they are much more difficult to control.

The millions of people who lost their homes and their life savings during the GFC were not the Fat Controllers. Oh no. They were the "unruly masses" who were starting to get ideas about being "free". The Fat Controllers actually got fatter as a result of the GFC.

The bankers have never made as much money as they do today. The many trillions of dollars of your hard-earned cash (ie, taxpayers' money) that the governments gave to the banks all over the world to bail them out went straight into the pockets of the executives as big, fat, juicy bonuses. You don't believe me? Google it. It's all there, cleverly hidden in plain sight.

After the GFC, the bankers were given a bonus by the politicians (using our taxpayer money). Why? Because they had done such a good job of putting the masses back in their place and making them even more afraid than they were before, and therefore easier to control.

Along with the so-called "War on Terror", the GFC gave governments around the world carte blanche to impose restrictions on our liberties that would have made Stalin green with envy.

But even that wasn't the worst of it. The governments then used the media to tell us that times are tough and we will all have to work harder for less money. Not just that, but we will also have to stay in the workforce longer, well into our 60s and 70s.

Right after the GFC, governments raised the retirement age, so now they can keep us plugged into the Matrix generating money for them right up to the point where we fall off the perch.

And all the while the banks' profits continue to soar, the kickbacks to the politicians have grown bigger, and the wealthy have bought larger and larger mansions – while millions of hard-working people lost their homes because the banks foreclosed on their mortgages. Mortgages those same banks sold them just a few years earlier in the full knowledge that the poor bastards would never have a hope in hell of making the payments.

GFC? It wasn't a crisis. It was a brilliantly orchestrated plan to make the rich richer and the rest of us poorer... and therefore more afraid and easier to control.

* * *

If this real-eyesation makes you angry, good. Maybe your anger will be enough to drive you to break free from the Matrix.

But if it makes you shake your head in disbelief and say something like "This can't be true – surely these men (yes, they are almost all men) can't be that evil", then consider this: it doesn't matter if this was a conscious conspiracy or a subconscious one, the effect was the same.

My belief is that some of the perpetrators knew exactly what they were doing, while the majority were simply greedy and so in their ego that the promise of riches led them to go along for the ride.

* * *

Now let's look at the recent "European debt crisis". There was no debt crisis. If the Fat Controllers had really wanted to plug the gap between their incomings and outgoings, they would have just used all the trillions of dollars sitting in all the central bank vaults right across the continent.

But that wasn't the point at all.

Chapter 4: Reality is a trap for the mind

The point of the so-called "crisis" was to cut the living standards of all the happy little Europeans who were sunning themselves on the beaches of Greece, Italy, Portugal and Spain. They were getting far too happy and unafraid and difficult to control, which would never do.

So the Fat Controllers took away their pensions, cut their pay, cut their benefits and told them they had to work more hours for many more years – for less money.

The media, of course, went along for the ride because nothing sells papers like a "crisis". The advertisers loved it, because the more miserable we are, the more effectively their ego-trip message of "buy this and you'll be happy" can cut through to the frightened masses.

It's nonsense. Your ego is insatiable. It doesn't matter how much rubbish you buy, it will never be satisfied. But the more you buy, the richer the Fat Controllers get. And at the same time you are feeding your ego, so it wants even more.

* * *

And then there are the churches, which were all founded on the precept of keeping the masses afraid. And they still promote their message of fear to this day: "Believe in 'God' or you will go to hell."

Their lie is the worst of all because it is done in the name of the Source, which is pure love and has no concept of what fear is.

The churches talk about "demons" to frighten us when we are small children, and they cover the outside walls of their buildings with them to keep us afraid as we grow up.

But there is no such thing as a demon.

Do your own research. You will find the original Greek word "daemon" describes a beautiful and benevolent nature spirit – all of them extensions of the Divine. The early Judeo-Christian churches grabbed this lovely pagan image, twisted it into something "evil" and then used it as a stick to beat the masses into fear-based submission.

* * *

Part One: Wake up to your Self

That is the Matrix.
Clever, isn't it?

* * *

I have only scratched the surface of how vast and over-reaching the Matrix is. When you wake up and see it for your Self, you will probably throw up your lunch, just as Neo did in the film.

The Matrix is Alan Joyce, the chief executive of Qantas, the Australian national airline, here where I live, who in 2011 gave himself a 71 per cent pay rise of $3 million and then laid off 1000 workers. He then told the rest of his staff they couldn't have a pay rise – not one single cent – because there wasn't enough money.

The Matrix is Australia's national newspaper *The Australian* (owned by Rupert Murdoch) which in the same year had the audacity to nominate Alan Joyce as a potential "Australian of the Year" for crushing the spirit of his unionised workforce.

(In the interests of transparency, I must acknowledge that I spent many years working for Rupert Murdoch's newspapers as a journalist before I saw what he stood for – namely fear and control. I real-eyes now that this was an important part of my Life Path to discover all that love isn't, and all that fear is, so I could teach the opposite from a perspective of knowing what the "enemy" looks like.)

The Matrix is also Hank Poulson, the former CEO of Wall Street banking giant Goldman Sachs, who as US Treasury Secretary during the GFC earned more than $US400 million – tax free, no less! – while millions of his fellow Americans and countless millions of other people around the world went broke, lost their homes and were forced to live on the street.

The Matrix is Dick Cheney, who, as CEO of the giant US arms dealer Halliburton, earned the company $US40 billion out of the Iraq War and Afghanistan War that resulted from the terrorist attack on the US on September 11, 2011, while he was vice-president.

The Matrix is the banks who lend money to people to buy a bigger house that they don't need at interest rates that they can never pay

Chapter 4: Reality is a trap for the mind

back, ensuring they remain "mortgage slaves" for the rest of their lives, generating money for the Fat Controllers.

The Matrix is also the cacophony of noise that the Fat Controllers blast at you through your television, radio, iPhone and computer so you can't hear your Self speak.

If you could hear your Self speak, you would hear it saying: "Shhh… please stop running around chasing happiness that you will never find, and just be still. Unplug from your fear. Unplug from the Matrix. Take out your earplugs. Open your eyes and real-eyes you don't need anything to be happy and free – because you are already free."

* * *

Now that you know what the Fear Matrix is, it becomes easier to unplug from it. Knowledge (awareness) is two-thirds of the battle. So let's now move on to this next chapter and plan our escape…

Chapter 5:
Escape from the Matrix

5 is the number of change
Everything changes when you 'wake up' to who you really are

The best way to break free from the Matrix is simply to "wake up" to the fact that you are not your ego in your head (fear), but your spiritual Self in your heart (love). When you do this, you will unplug your Self from the Matrix automatically.

Hopefully I have done a good enough job of convincing you that this is who you are, because when you start identifying as the love in your heart rather than the fear in your mind, the Fat Controllers can't touch you.

The Fat Controllers hate love. It's the only thing they can't control, which is why you seldom hear about it on the nightly news.

Bankers can't charge you for it. Advertisers can't sell it to you. Politicians can't regulate it. And the churches stay well away from it because they are terrified of the "real thing" in case you expose them for the fear-peddling frauds they are.

Even the military and the police of all the countries in the world are powerless against the force of love. There are 7 billion of us. If we all unplugged from the Fear Matrix at the same time and marched on City Hall demanding our fair share of the Earth's resources, they would be – to use the widely accepted technical term – "totally fucked".

* * *

Chapter 5: Escape from the Matrix

The first step to breaking free from the Fear Matrix is to be as still and as silent as you possibly can. Apart from the steady drip-feed of fear, the other way the Fat Controllers stop us from escaping is by keeping us running around chasing our unobtainable ego goals while simultaneously bombarding us with "white noise" from the moment we wake up to the moment we fall asleep.

They sell us newspapers, talkback radio, iPhones, iPads, iPods, Instagram, Facebook, Twitter, reality TV, celebrity magazines, the internet, TV streaming services – anything to keep our minds occupied so we are guaranteed never to hear the small voice in our heart that is desperately whispering to us: "Stop! What are you doing? You will be dead soon. Please just STOP and listen to me."

* * *

Take a look at a crowd of commuters leaving their office in the evening, where they have just laboured all day to make someone else richer (it certainly isn't them). Notice how they all have earplugs in their ears and their faces buried in their ironically named "smart" phones. They don't even see each other, let alone interact.

They are zombies.

The walking dead.

These people are plugged so deep into the Matrix, they haven't got a hope of ever breaking free. Unless they read a book like this.

Please don't be like them. Try unplugging for just one day, or longer if you can. Turn everything off. Turn off your phone, your iPad, your internet, your email, your radio, your TV.

Take the plugs out of your ears and just listen. Listen to the sound of the wind, the sound of your breath, the sound of your heart and what it is trying to tell you.

In fact, close your eyes right now after you have read this paragraph and ask your heart if everything you have read about the Matrix so far is true. It won't reply to you in words, because the language of love is feelings. So just feel what it feels like to be pure love

Part One: Wake up to your Self

and connected to everyone and everything. Stay with it for a while. And then open your eyes and try to see the world around you as pure love, without any fear.

* * *

Did you do it?

If not, please stop now, close your eyes and be perfectly still, just for a moment. Breathe deeply. Feel the love in your heart and listen to what it is trying to tell you.

Stay with it for a few minutes. And then you can decide if I am a "conspiracy theory lunatic", or if what I am saying rings true.

* * *

You may have to do this a few times, or even a few hundred times, before you real-eyes you are now finally looking at the world with very different eyes... with your real eyes.

You will know when you are fully awake because the ads on the TV will make you laugh. You will see them for what they are: pathetic attempts to convince you that you can't possibly be happy unless you buy all the crap they are trying to sell you.

You will watch the nightly news or read the papers and smell the unmistakable stench of fear that the Fat Controllers are trying to ram down your throat... the fear of terrorism, of burglars, of sharks, of sickness, of poverty, of lack, of not being thin enough, or old enough, or young enough. (Did I mention the fear of terrorism?)

You will tune into your favourite reality TV show, or pick up your favourite celebrity gossip magazine, and laugh because you finally understand that they are designed to make you focus on everyone else's life rather than on yours – to prevent you from breaking free.

You will listen to the conversations of people at work, or in the pub, or in the supermarket – and you will hear the sad, bitter voice of their ego as they carp and bitch and moan about this and that.

Chapter 5: Escape from the Matrix

But you will also hear the unmistakable sound of love in the voices of little children, and recognise it instantly as the voice of the Source.

You will see an animal sleeping in the sun, or a tree bristling with energy in a breeze, or a bird floating freely in the sky… and you will instantly recognise the presence of the Source.

Above all, you will look in the mirror and see, for the first time, a living, breathing perfect spirit… instead of someone who needs to lose a few pounds, or wishes they were taller, or lighter, or darker, or younger, or older, or had a better car, or a bigger house, or more shoes.

* * *

What happens when I unplug from the Matrix?

When you wake up and unplug from the Matrix you will notice that nothing changes… and everything changes. Waking up is the start of your spiritual journey, not the end of it. But now you are living in alignment with spirit, so you will begin to notice how everything that happens to you is perfect for what you need to do, or not do – providing you are a good person, of course, and are therefore free of the painful consequences of the Law of Cause and Effect, also known as karma, otherwise all kinds of bad and painful stuff will come your way.

– If you get sick, you'll know it's your body telling you to rest.

– If you lose something, you'll know it's because the Source wants to give you something even better.

– If someone leaves you, you'll know it's because someone else who has something to teach you wants to come into your life.

– You will see "signs" everywhere you look and you will feel guided every step of the way, because you are.

– You will almost certainly want to leave your job and do something that is in alignment with your highest purpose (which you will discover in Parts Two and Three).

– You will find that many of your friends will automatically fade away into the distance. These are the people who are agents of the

Part One: Wake up to your Self

Matrix. Don't worry, other friends will step in to take their place because they have already broken free and they will recognise you instantly and embrace you with an energy that is pure love.

– You may even have to leave your marriage or relationship if you can't persuade your partner to come with you. Again, don't worry because it may only be temporary. When they see you literally "glowing" with the light of Self-love they will ask you to help them wake up too. And if they don't, you will bless them and move on, safe in the knowledge that a new, awake partner is waiting for you just around the corner.

* * *

The final piece of advice I have for you in this chapter is to watch the film *The Matrix* if you haven't already seen it. In fact, even if you have seen it before, please watch it again with all of this in mind. It will wake you up for sure when you view it through the prism of everything I have just told you.

I have no idea how the seriously savant writers and directors of the film, Lana and Lilly Wachowski, came upon this information. Perhaps it was by accident, but I don't think so because they were writing the film in 1996 at the same time my Angel visited me.

As you can imagine, when the movie made a big splash at the box office in 1999 I was one of the first to go and see it, and I don't mind telling you that the hairs on the back of my neck were standing on end by the time the credits rolled because it was obvious someone had been speaking to them at the same time my Angel was telling me the exact same thing.

The Matrix got the message out to a worldwide audience of millions of people, but the tragedy was 99.9 per cent of the people who saw the film didn't know what they were seeing.

They watched the movie, but they didn't see the metaphor for the world they were living in. They ate their popcorn, drove home… and went back to sleep.

Chapter 5: Escape from the Matrix

When you watch it again, your real eyes will be opened, if they haven't been already.

Neo, Keanu Reeves' character, is the Jesus figure. His name is an anagram of One, as in "The One". After he wakes up and unplugs from the Matrix, he is free but he is still afraid. He still has to get to the point where he knows he is pure Source energy and has no fear, and that takes most of the film.

It will be the same for you. You now know how to unplug from the Fear Matrix, but you still have to go through your Dark Night of the Self and face all your fears (as you will discover in the next chapter).

Neo conquers his last fear, the fear of fear itself, in the penultimate scene of the film when he dies and then comes back to life (remember the Resurrection parable about the ego death?).

It is the most touching scene of the film because his girlfriend, who of course is called Trinity (mind/body/heart), tells him she is no longer afraid because she loves him.

Love conquers everything, especially the ego, so Neo springs back to life – this time not as his ego, but as his Self... as pure love.

Neo is now able to see the green code of the Matrix, just as you will be able to see it. And as the agents fire off their bullets at him (the bullets represent fear), he puts his hand up and calmly says: "No."

What he is saying – you can see the expression on his face – is "No, I'm not going to accept your fear any more. You can't touch me because I am pure love, pure Source energy, and all of your fear-based bullshit won't work on me any more."

At this point the agents (the Fat Controllers) are utterly powerless against him. Watch Neo's expression closely when he fends off the attack of one of the agents with one had behind his back. He is neither afraid (submissive), nor is he angry (aggressive).

He is perfectly peaceful.

He just is.

This is how you need to be. You can't be afraid, or they'll get you. You can't be angry either, because anger is just the expression of a deep fear, and they'll get you. You must be completely neutral and detached.

Part One: Wake up to your Self

Just calmly and benignly put up your hand to the Fat Controllers and say, firmly ... "No!"

When you do that, when you are no longer afraid and no longer angry, you are completely, and blissfully, free. They can't touch you!

Then listen closely to what Neo says in the voice-over final scene of the movie as the camera closes in on a screen full of numbers from 1 to 9, including the amplifier 0... the numbers of numerology that make up the code of the universe, and on which the Self-Awareness System™ in this book is based.

As the numbers freeze and the Matrix computer code crashes, two words appear, written in large letters: "SYSTEM FAILURE."

The camera zooms in on the space between the **M** at the end of the word "System" (**M** for "masculine") and the **F** at the beginning of the word "Failure" (**F** for "feminine"). It's the Law of Duality.

As the letters get bigger and bigger, we hear Neo talking on the phone to the Fat Controllers who created the Matrix in the first place.

This is what he says to them:

"I know you are out there. I can feel you now. I know that you are afraid. You are afraid of us. You are afraid of change. I don't know the future. I didn't come here to tell you how this is going to end. I came here to tell you how this is going to begin. I'm going to hang up this phone and then I'm going to show these people what you don't want them to see. I'm going to show them a world without you – a world without rules and controls, without borders or boundaries. A world where anything is possible."

As he stops talking, the screen is filled with the letters **M** and **F**.

Why? Because when you merge your masculine body/mind with your feminine spirit you become "One".

You become "Neo".

You become whole.

And you become free.

Chapter 6:
Night becomes day

6 is the number of beauty
Nothing can hurt you when you real-eyes you are pure, perfect love

Now you are free of the Fear Matrix, the next step on your path to Self-awareness is to kill your ego – which, to re-mind you, is your mind's fear-based opinion of who you think you are.

This process, which I touched on briefly earlier, is called the Dark Night of the Self because it is when you go into the darkness and face all your fears. It's the moment in *Star Wars: The Empire Strikes Back* when Yoda sends Luke Skywalker into the bowels of the Earth to face his alter ego Darth Vader.

It's not fun, I must warn you, but the rewards are well worth it. And besides, the information contained in the Self-Awareness System™ in Parts Two and Three will speed things up considerably by showing you the areas you need to work on.

Your Dark Night begins after you unplug from the Matrix and wake up to the fact that you are not a separate carbon-based life form but a three-dimensional spiritual being who is connected to everyone and everything in the universe.

Actually, that's not strictly accurate. Your Dark Night doesn't begin immediately after you wake up to who you truly are because you will probably spend several months, years even, resisting the challenge

Part One: Wake up to your Self

that you know lies ahead. As I warned you at the end of Chapter 1, when you start to try to kill your ego it will put up a hell of a fight. It will do everything in its power (which is considerable) to try to make you go back to sleep so that it can stay at the controls of your life.

It won't succeed though because once you have woken up, all the sleeping pills in the world can never make you go back to sleep again.

* * *

After my Angel visited me in 1996, I fiddled around the edges of spirituality for seven years before I real-eyesed there was no escaping the truth of what she had told me.

Seven years. That's how strong my ego was. It was like Rambo, the Hulk and Conan the Barbarian all rolled into one.

Ever since I was a teenager I had wanted the wife with the long legs and ample cleavage, the Aston Martin next to the Ducati in the garage, the villa in Cap Ferat, the chalet in St Moritz, the lean muscular body, the Prada sunglasses… and everything else the Matrix was telling me I needed to be happy.

My conditioning (brainwashing) was extensive because in my teens I was extremely shy and insecure, which meant I was an easy target for the advertisers.

Looking back now I can see (although I didn't real-eyes it at the time) that I thought I needed all this extravagant and egotistical stuff to make me feel "good enough".

If only I had known then what I know now, which is that we can have all this "stuff" and more after we have killed our ego – as well as blissful, joyous and never-ending peace – because we don't "need" it to feel better about who we are.

So even after my experience with my Angel, my ego fought so hard to hold on to the controls of my life that it was seven years before I was able to even start the process of killing it by facing all my fears.

That was the start of my Dark Night. And it was another nine years before I came out the other side.

Chapter 6: Night becomes day

I am not saying that your Dark Night needs to last as long as mine. You may get through it in a matter of months. Or maybe even less. It's different for everyone. I was diagnosed as a "manic depressive" (there's a medical "label" for you... I was just thoughtful!) at 16, so I was carrying more baggage than Heathrow Airport on a Friday evening.

Plus, I didn't have a book like this one. The whole reason I have written *Messages From Your Self* is to help you break free of your fears much more quickly and easily than I did.

* * *

During the "fiddling phase" – between knowing you have to face your fears and plucking up enough courage to do so – you will exist as two separate identities: your ego identity, which is who you believed you were before you woke up; and your Self, which is still weak but will grow stronger with every spiritual experience you have.

Your Dark Night will begin when your Self's immortal spiritual identity is strong enough to challenge your ego's fear-based mortal identity to a duel for ultimate control of "who you are".

It is literally a fight to the death, because one of you has to die.

Your ego has ruled your life since you were a toddler, when your mind first started forming your identity based on the answers to all the questions you asked, as we saw in Chapter 1. But now your Self is strong enough to make a play for the throne.

* * *

It is impossible to say when this life-and-death power struggle begins because there is not usually one single event that sets it off. It starts gradually as you begin listening to the voice of love in your heart instead of the voice of fear in your head.

Your ego is pure fear, and your Self is pure love. They are sworn enemies because they are opposites of each other. But the good news is the fear your ego is made of is not real fight-or-flight fear, which you

Part One: Wake up to your Self

feel in your gut – it is imagined fear that is nothing more than a "what if?" thought in your head.

Fight-or flight fear, which we and all animals possess, is essential for keeping our Self's vehicle – our physical body – alive in a sometimes dangerous world. But imagined fear is an illusion. It is no more real than our ego's identity of who we think we are.

So the good news is you are fighting an "enemy" that has no substance, no strength and can't fight back. Its only hope of winning is persuading you not to fight at all, because it knows you can destroy it with just one punch.

That is why there is only ever going to be one winner in this power struggle for "who you are". Your ego will die because it has to die, in this lifetime or the next, otherwise your Self could not continue on its journey towards enlightenment and full Self-awareness.

You must, however, be prepared for the mother of all battles. The reason it's called the Dark Night is because you will feel that you are going mad in the darkness for a while as you struggle to accept who you are. You know that you are no longer your ego, but you aren't yet convinced that you are your Self.

Madness is defined as losing touch with reality. In this case, you are indeed momentarily out of touch with your ego's false sense of what reality is… before you are able to accept the true reality of who you really are.

In the heat of the battle, sometimes it may seem hopeless. But just keep re-minding your Self that you don't have to kill your ego completely for your Dark Night to end; you just have to shrink its power sufficiently for it to relinquish control to your Self.

Your ego will stick around for many years after your Dark Night ends, but that's OK. All that matters is your Self – your heart – is now in control of your life. Your ego will get smaller and smaller with every new experience your Self has of what it means to be pure love.

* * *

Chapter 6: Night becomes day

When does the Dark Night end?

Your Dark Night ends, and the dawn comes, one wonderful day when your Self finally takes over the controls of your life and you start living every day in the blissful knowledge that nothing matters, because you are pure spirit and everything in the universe is pure spirit.

This is the moment when you real-eyes the exquisite truth of the famous phrase: "Nothing real can be threatened, and nothing unreal exists – therein lies the peace of 'God'."

This is the moment when you real-eyes love is the only thing that is real, because love is all there is.

It is also the moment when you real-eyes everything that has happened in your life was absolutely perfect and intricately designed (by your Self before it incarnated) to teach you what you needed to learn so that you are able to achieve your life's highest purpose.

It is the most exquisite moment you will ever experience.

Nothing else even comes close.

The moment is described perfectly in one of my favourite books, *Way of the Peaceful Warrior*, by my greatest mentor Dan Millman. After he has emerged from his own Dark Night, Dan walks through the streets of Berkeley, California, where he lived at the time and gazes upon the scurrying crowds of people who are still plugged into the Matrix. He wants to go up to each and every one of them and wake them up.

This is what he wants to say (the brackets are mine):

There is no need to search; achievement leads to nowhere. It makes no difference at all, so just be happy now.

Love is the only reality of the world because it is all one, you see. There is no problem, there never was, and there never will be.

Release your struggle, let go of your mind, throw away your concerns and relax into the world.

There is no need to resist life; just do your best.

Open your eyes and see that you are far more than you imagine. You are the world. You are the universe. You are yourself (your Self), and everyone else too.

Part One: Wake up to your Self

It is all the marvellous play of God.
Wake up. Regain your humour.
Don't worry.
You are already free.

* * *

What's the best way to get through the Dark Night?

Here's what you need to do. And please don't be worried, because it sounds a lot more difficult than it really is.

You must be prepared to give up everything that is attached to your ego's sense of who you think you are. And I mean everything.

It may not come to this. For many people, it doesn't. But for some it does. The key is you must be "prepared" to lose everything that your ego has held dear. Often the mere act of being prepared to lose it all is enough to get you through without actually having to lose it.

You must be prepared to lose all your money, all your material possessions, most probably your job and possibly your relationship, unless your partner is prepared to make the Great Leap with you.

(Note: In my experience, the feminine half of a relationship usually makes the leap first, and then the masculine half follows. But if they are not able to join you, then you must cut them loose and bless them on their way.)

You may lose your sanity, but again that is OK because when you come out the other side you will discover it was actually your "insanity" that you lost. (Remember the scene in *Avatar* when Jake first meets Neytiri's mother Mo'at, the spiritual leader of the clan, and she says to him: "Let's see if your insanity can be cured.")

What you are doing is facing all your fears – otherwise known as your Dark Side. It is one of the most common themes in movies, including famous scenes in *The Matrix*, *Avatar* and *Star Wars*.

You can have all your trinkets and your toys back again when the dawn breaks and you reach the other side – all the romantic love, sex, money and material possessions you can possibly imagine. The

Chapter 6: Night becomes day

difference is that your ego, which needed these things to feel "good enough", is no longer in control of your life, so now you will not be attached to them. You can have them back provided you only want them for fun, and don't need them to feel better about your Self.

You will discover that you want very little, because the pleasure of material possessions doesn't even come close to the bliss of living as pure love, unafraid and connected to everyone and everything.

In fact, you will probably find that they weigh you down and you are happiest just being you, your Self… unencumbered and free.

* * *

All the information contained in this first book – as well as the Self-Awareness System™ in Parts Two and Three – is designed to wake you up and help you get through your Dark Night as quickly and painlessly as possible. However, even with all the help of the Self-Awareness System™, your Dark Night will not be an easy experience.

It breaks my heart to tell you that not everyone survives it unless they have a strong support network of loving friends (which I was blessed to have).

The soaring suicide rate all over the world today is largely a result of the growing numbers of young people – mostly teenagers – who are trying to go through their Dark Night long before they are ready to do so and are simply not strong enough to break free from their families and friends, who try to pull them back down.

Some make it, but tragically many don't. This is especially true in the rapidly growing transgender community, where the attempted suicide rate is now nudging an appalling 50 per cent.

No, that is not a typographical mistake. One of the reasons so many people these days are transitioning their gender is because they are waking up to their true nature as divine spirit – and spirit doesn't give a fig about gender because we are all – underneath our fears – a perfect balance of masculine and feminine (the Law of Duality).

It is our society's blinkered adherence to its need to label people by their gender that causes these harmless Selfs to feel like outcasts, leading one in every two of them to try to take their own lives.

Appalling, isn't it.

If you are still transitioning, or if you are still living at home in a family that is asleep, you haven't got a chance. So please don't even try. Wait until you are strong enough to leave home and stand on your own two feet. Gather a strong support group of awake people around you. Tell them what you are doing, ask for their support... and then do it.

***

That sounds horrible. Do I have to go through all that?

The answer I know you are dying ("living" would perhaps be more accurate) to hear is... no, you don't. There is one way of avoiding the Dark Night; a short-cut if you like. But it's not easy. So don't get too excited because very few people manage to do it.

If I can explain the short-cut well enough, though, hopefully you will be one of them.

To re-mind you, the purpose of your Dark Night is for you to conquer enough of your fears so that your ego, which is your fear, relinquishes the controls of your life and hands them over to your Self, which is pure love.

All fear is the fear of getting hurt, the fear of not being good enough, or the fear of losing something... whether it's your money, your relationship, your health, your life, or anything else you're attached to. So, no, you don't have to lose everything. In fact, you don't have to lose anything. Not a single thing. All you have to do is be WILLING to lose it all, and have no fear of what would happen if you did.

This is the true meaning of the lesson of "sacrifice" as it appears in the Bible. It is also the originally intended message of the story of Abraham, who was asked by "God" to sacrifice his son Isaac.

Chapter 6: Night becomes day

Abraham doesn't hesitate. He takes Isaac to the top of a mountain where he places him on an altar and is about to kill him when an angel intervenes to stop him.

This powerful parable is at the heart of all three of the Abrahamic religions – Christianity, Judaism and Islam. Abraham is common to all three, and he is revered by all of them because of what he was prepared to do. (Yes, I know, the followers of these three dogmas fight and kill each other because they believe the same thing. You'd be forgiven for thinking exactly what I'm thinking… which is "WTF!")

* * *

What the wise scribes of the original scriptures (before they were heavily edited and redacted by greedy men) were attempting to tell us with the story of Abraham is that you don't have to lose everything, you just have to be prepared to lose everything.

So, right now, put this book down and look at everything in your life. Look at your house, your car, your job, your family, your partner, your friends, your children if you have them, all your money, all your possessions, your jewellery, your furniture, your clothes – everything that you have right now in your life except your naked body.

And then ask your Self these three questions:
– "Do I need any of it to be me?"
– "Do I need any of it to feel better about my Self?"
– "Do I need any of it to be happy?"

If you can truthfully answer "No" to all three questions and you know in your heart that if everything was taken away from you tomorrow you would survive and still be "you", then no – you don't have to go through the Dark Night.

The trouble is – and this is why the short-cut almost never works – in order for us to know something is true, we usually need to experience it. It cannot just be conceptual. This is why most people need to experience the Dark Night of their Self for themselves.

But even if you do have to experience your Dark Night, the more you real-eyes that "who you are" has nothing to do with what you do or what you have, the shorter it will be.

Fear is the key, because fear is what your ego feeds on.

The only way to loosen your ego's grip is to starve it to death. Again, this comes down to experience. If you are afraid of "rejection", or "failure", or "being alone", or "not having a job", or "being broke", or "being homeless" – or all the other imagined fears that your ego can come up with – then you normally have to experience all these things to find out there was nothing to be afraid of after all... because you didn't die.

You are still you, the indestructible Holy Trinity of pure love.

And you always will be.

* * *

Let me give you another valuable tip for speeding up the process of your Dark Night: you don't have to face all your fears to kill your ego, you just have to face your biggest one.

Right now, decide what your biggest fear is and then face that. When you do, you will discover that it, too, was only imagined fear and therefore doesn't exist.

The magic of this tip is that when you face – and vanquish – your biggest fear, all your other smaller fears will vanish automatically.

Most people (me included) make the mistake of starting with their smallest fear, because it is the easiest. They then go through all their fears in ascending order of how frightening they are, working their way towards the "big one".

This is the main reason the Dark Night takes so long. But the sooner you can face your biggest fear, the sooner all your other smaller fears will disappear like a puff of smoke on a windy day.

And when that happens, your ego will instantly relinquish control of your life because it no longer has the "food" it needs to survive... namely, fear.

Chapter 6: Night becomes day

You see, starving your ego of fear is the only way to kill it. You can't shoot it, although many people try to do just that as a last, desperate act when they put a gun to their head and end their life. The same goes for jumping off a building, putting your head in a gas oven, overdosing on drugs, or any of the other ways people kill themselves.

People who commit suicide are, at the deepest level, trying to kill their ego. They just don't know that it is separate from them, so they kill the whole lot.

It is desperately sad because, as I said before, you don't have to kill your ego completely to end your Dark Night. You just have to weaken it by not being afraid.

The moment you can be like Abraham and be WILLING to lose everything, you have won... and you are free.

* * *

Before we finish this chapter, I want to go back to the story of Abraham for a moment and explain why the true meaning of the story has been missed by almost everyone for so long.

The earliest theologians who selected and edited the canon of books that made up the Old and New Testaments of the Bible had an ulterior motive. They wanted to cement the authority of their church at a time when controlling the unruly masses was much harder than it is today without the help of a powerful media, so they decided the best way to do it was to make them afraid. (Karl Marx was wrong, religion isn't the opium of the people... fear is.)

Borrowing heavily from the Israelites' portrayal of a mean and vengeful "God" in the Hebrew Bible, they gathered all the scriptures and proceeded to cut out everything Jesus had said about "God" being us and us being "God" – and instead wrote in a bunch of blatant lies about "God" being separate from us.

They turned the Source into an old man with a beard and made him someone to be afraid of. They then invented the twin concepts of

Part One: *Wake up to your Self*

Heaven and Hell as the ultimate "carrot and stick" with which they could control us.

It was as brilliant as it was evil. But that was only the half of it, because in the process of creating a way to control us, they also came up with the best "business model" this planet has ever seen: "Give us your money and we will save you from eternal damnation." (Excuse me! You're offering to save me from something that doesn't exist?)

From that moment on, the Christian church stopped being a rag-tag bunch of people who believed in the true teachings of Jesus and became the richest, most powerful corporation in history.

And it still is.

It wasn't just Christianity, though. The Jews had already created the model hundreds of years earlier. So by the time the other splendid avatar, Muhammad, came along 300 years later, the world was already so mired in fear that it tainted his beautiful message of love and truth as well … as it, too, was twisted into a cynical control mechanism.

The power-hungry men who censored the early religious texts did a remarkably good job of changing the original message of love into a cudgel of fear. But they were far from thorough because, if you look closely, you will see that the truth is still in there.

* * *

Which leads me back to the story of Abraham – a story, as I said earlier, that is at the heart of the Christian, Jewish and Islamic faiths.

In the story, Abraham has tied his son to the altar and is about to plunge a knife into his heart when an angel appears and stops him.

But the scriptures twisted the story, so instead of saying "It's OK, you don't need to kill your son because you have proved that you love "God" and have no fear" – which is what the angel would have said (and is what Jesus was saying all along if you read closely enough) – someone rewrote it, so now, in all the religious texts, the angel says to Abraham: "It's OK, you don't need to kill your son because you have proved to "God" that you FEAR him."

Chapter 6: Night becomes day

Excuse me for swearing, but I have to say again: "WTF!"

Check it out for your Self if you don't believe me. That is what all the religious texts say. That one abominable lie has ensured that the billions of people who have ever followed these religions can never enter the "Kingdom of Heaven", which is right here on Earth in our heart and is ours to dwell in forever as soon as we have NO FEAR.

And that's not even the worst of it. If that's all the lie did, it would be bad enough. But this lie didn't just condemn all the mainstream religious believers to live in fear of the Source, it condemned all the non-believers to a life of separation from the Source.

Why? Because this outrageous and totally unbelievable story of "God" asking Abraham to kill his son just to prove he was afraid of "him" is the story that all atheists and agnostics point to – quite understandably – to argue that "God" doesn't exist. After all, what kind of a "God" would do that?

"God" does exist. In fact, it is ALL that exists – because "God" (the Source) is pure love… and love is all there is.

This lie, along with numerous others concocted by the early male church leaders, was how the Matrix was able to spread across the entire planet and enslave everyone who has ever come into contact with the fear-based concept of an external "God", as taught in all the main Abrahamic Western religions.

These days, the Matrix is much more complicated than just a religious trap. It is also a financial trap, as we saw in the last chapter. But this lie is how it started, and it is also how it spread so rapidly all over the world, generation after generation.

For centuries, the teaching systems of almost all countries in the world have included compulsory "religious education" for all children, and in most countries they still do – which is why the fear-based lie of Abraham's story still echoes in every corner of the world.

Chapter 7:
Everything is love

7 is the number of truth
Everyone who tries to sell you 'salvation' is selling you a false god

God is love. It is the Source of everything, and it is everything, because love is all there is. As we have already seen, "God" is not outside us, or above us, or separate from us. "God" is us. And we are "God". And, if you look closely enough, you will see that every one of the mainstream Western religions has this crucial message about our relationship to the Source at its core.

The trouble with the Western religions, though, is that the beautiful messages of love and inclusion preached by the splendidly insightful prophets Jesus and Muhammad were exploited by their power-hungry male leaders thousands of years ago, when fear was the overriding experience of human existence.

Fear was how the early churchmen (not women; fear is masculine, love is feminine) exploited the uneducated masses and bent them to their will… and, in the process, became obscenely wealthy.

Please real-eyes that anyone who stands between you and the Source and says "In order to talk to 'God' you have to go through me" is selling you a false god.

You should knee them in the balls (they will almost always be men) and move on.

* * *

Chapter 7: Everything is love

Now I'm not saying for one moment that the message at the heart of these religions is wrong. All the religious texts – the Bible, the Quran and the Torah – contain the incontestable truth about the divine nature of the Source, but sadly the truth was twisted by the religions' founding fathers (all men!) centuries ago – to line their pockets.

And their successors are still doing it today. Go visit the Vatican. The art is exquisite. But look beyond it – the ostentatious flaunting of the church's obscene wealth while millions of men, women and children live and die in poverty will make you want to throw up.

I'm also not saying there aren't plenty of people in all the churches today who are doing fantastic work to help the needy. There are, in every corner of the world. I just want you to be aware that while the tireless and courageous work these people do is both commendable and inspirational, the organisations behind them are anything but.

* * *

The Source is pure love. It is freely available to anyone, any time, because we are all extensions of Source energy.

You can talk to "God" in your car, in the pub, or the toilet. You don't need to flock obediently to an imposing, draughty building with scary gargoyles all over it in order to "worship" the Source.

In fact, the whole concept of "worship" is nonsense. Since the spawning of religious dogma, egotistical men have projected their need to feel "special" onto their deity. These people need to wake up to their Selves. "God" doesn't have an ego. It doesn't want to be worshipped. And it doesn't need to feel "special". "God" is pure love. It doesn't want us to praise it. And it certainly doesn't want us to fear it. "God" wants one thing and one thing only… for us to real-eyes that we are pure love too.

By all means bow your head out of respect when you acknowledge the Source. I do, countless times every day. And sometimes I kneel as well – because the vast magnificence of what the Source is makes me feel so humble when I send it my love and say thank you for my life.

Part One: Wake up to your Self

Just make sure you don't ever worship it. Or fear it. Send the Source your love – and send it your gratitude – as often as you possibly can. But if you worship it or fear it, you are ensuring that you remain separate from it.

If the Source had a head, it would shake it sadly. And if it could talk to you, it would say: "My child, when will you wake up and real-eyes that I am you, and you are me?"

* * *

I know I have been a bit harsh on the Western religions, but as I have said many times my purpose with this book is to tell the truth. It would have been too easy to gloss over the atrocities committed by the churches to avoid controversy, but that wouldn't be fair to you. I hope you understand why that wouldn't have been right, or honest.

The unspeakable horrors being committed today by extremist Muslims have sickened all of us in ways we never could have imagined and have sparked waves of condemnation by right-thinking and right-feeling people all over the world. As they should. But don't be fooled into thinking this is anything new.

Was I the only person to recoil in horror at the despicable irony of Pope Francis's statement, in April 2017, when talking about Muslim extremists: "Let us say a firm and clear 'No!' to every form of violence, vengeance and hatred carried out in the name of God"?

Excuse me! The Christian churches have massacred more people (especially intelligent women as "witches" in their millions) than all the rest of humanity put together. I'm talking tens of millions of innocent men, women and children… just so they could steal their money.

Do your own research. Research the Catholic brutality in South America, the English brutality everywhere, the Spanish inquisition (as many as 11 million innocent women slaughtered as "witches"), and the Catholic Ustase death camps in World War II that massacred innocent little children with the Vatican's help… all in the name of "God".

Please Google them. You'll be appalled.

Chapter 7: Everything is love

Mass murder for financial or political reasons is bad enough. But when you don the robes of "God" and profess to be a teacher of love and salvation, and then slaughter millions of people just because they don't happen to agree with your point of view (which, by the way, was wrong), then that is pure evil and it needs to be exposed.

Look at the obscene amount of money controlled by the Western churches. If that doesn't set your alarm bells ringing, nothing will:

– Look at the jewelled rings on the bishops' fingers. Ding!

– Look at the ornate interiors of their churches. Ding! Ding!

– Look at their opulent mansions and palaces. Ding! Ding! Ding!

– Look at how much money there is in the Vatican bank. Ding! Ding! Ding! Ding!

Now look at all the people in the world who die every day for want of a simple meal.

And these churchmen have the audacity to claim that they are doing "God's work".

* * *

When I first visited St Peter's in Rome – and all the other great Catholic churches of Europe in my early 20s before I woke up – I marvelled at their grandeur and gasped in awe at the gold leaf on the ceilings, the magnificent paintings and sculptures, and the vast tracts of land these churches sat on in some of the most expensive real estate in the world.

Now when I see them I want to vomit because I know where they got the money to buy all this stuff.

They stole it. But they didn't just steal it, they murdered the people who owned the land and then stole it while their bodies were still warm. And they did this to millions of people, all over the world.

Never in the history of humanity have so many people got away with so much murder and theft as the Catholic Church.

It's one of the main reasons German theologian Martin Luther was impelled to call out the Catholic Church on its rampant corruption, its violence and its immorality way back in the early 1500s. The early protestants weren't much better, but at least Luther brought the issue of religious greed and genocide into the mainstream to be debated.

* * *

To illustrate my point about how greedy men have imposed their own sickeningly selfish ego onto the identity of their so-called "God", let's leave the subject of religion for a moment and seat this debate firmly in the world of the 21st century… the world outside your window.

We all know that in Africa there are millions of people who are starving and would die without the help of donations from generous people in the Western world, including from the churches.

(As I have said before – and it bears repeating here – the people in the churches are not to blame, merely their misogynistic, murderous and money-hungry founding fathers many centuries ago.)

But I ask you this: does a hungry child in Africa want to know the name of the person who donated the food parcel that saved their life? Perhaps they do, but I very much doubt it. They are just grateful that someone somewhere gave them the gift of life.

Put your Self in the Source's shoes for a moment (and if you're wondering whether the Source wears shoes, that's a question that's just going to have to wait until you evolve and return "home".)

If you generously and lovingly sent money or a food parcel to a starving child in Africa, or anywhere else for that matter, would you want that child to spend the rest of their life worshipping you and erecting buildings where they can go every day and spend hours praying to you and exalting your name?

Would you want them to be afraid that if they didn't worship you every day, at a precisely allotted time, they would be doomed to a life of eternal damnation?

Would you care what they did on a Friday or a Saturday or a Sunday, or any other day for that matter?

Chapter 7: Everything is love

Would you care whether they ate an animal with a cloven hoof, as opposed to any other kind of hoof, when they were starving and needed food to survive?

Or would you rather they just got on with living their life and being happy?

I thought so.

So why the "hell" do we ascribe these ridiculously egotistical qualities to "God"?

* * *

I want to finish this discussion on a personal note, which is to say I am fortunate enough to know many devout Christians, Muslims and Jews. Most of them spread love wherever they go and they never fail to help anyone who is in need. And above all, they are happy in their faith, which nourishes them and makes them better people.

There is absolutely nothing wrong with religion when it has this effect on you. Problems only arise when you try to impose your beliefs on others, or when you are afraid that if you don't worship your "God" you will be in trouble. That is fear, and fear is the weapon of the Fat Controllers who run the Matrix.

So please don't ever be "a good God-fearing person".

Be a "good God-loving person" instead.

I love the Source with all my heart. But I don't, and I never will, fear it. And I certainly will never worship it, any more than I would worship the love in my heart, because "God" is pure love. It is everything, and it is in everything, and it would be appalled at the thought of a single human being worshipping it or fearing it.

It wants only what we all want… to love and be loved.

* * *

This chapter marks the end of your journey within to real-eyes your Self's divine perfection and the beginning of your outward

Part One: Wake up to your Self

journey to discover your life's highest purpose as a fully awake spirit living in harmony with the Source.

Before we get into it, though, let me re-mind you of three core truths about your life:

1. Your Self chose to come here as you. No one else. Which means you are unique and perfect. You can therefore start – right now – to see yourself (your Self) not as a flawed human being whose hips are too big, or eyes are too small, or nose is too long, or who is too short, too tall, too thin, too fat, too white, too black, or too anything… and instead see your Self as pure, perfect love.

Remember, love is all there is. And therefore all you are is love.

2. The world you find yourself (your Self) in is just as perfect as you are. And it is designed perfectly to be both a playground and a classroom at the same time.

All the puppies, kittens, beaches, ice creams, pubs, restaurants, bridal suites, shoes, money, sex, parties, pay rises, fast cars, designer clothes, cocktails and sunsets are placed here to amuse you.

And all the trauma, struggles, anger, fear, distress, suffering, pain, despair, loss and heartache are here to teach you.

We need both pleasure and pain to grow, which is why – as Rudyard Kipling writes in his magnificent poem *If* – our challenge is to "accept both these imposters just the same" by celebrating the good times and learning from the tough times.

Neither is better or worse than the other. All experiences, either "good" or "bad", are merely paving stones on the path to our bliss.

3. You have within your grasp the key that unlocks all the doors to your future happiness, because you gave it to your Self when you were born. As these next two chapters will show you, this key is your Birth Code – the wealth of information that was literally hard-coded into your date of birth when your Self chose to incarnate as you.

Chapter 7: Everything is love

Throughout history, since Pythagoras first identified the numerological secret code of the universe 500 years before the birth of Jesus, numerology has guided millions upon millions of people towards their bliss – but they have followed the path blindly, knowing numerology works while having not the slightest idea why it does.

As you turn this page, please real-eyes that you will be one of the first of a new generation of Selfs to walk this path with your eyes wide open. Because after reading (surviving might be a better word for it!) this first book, you now know why numerology is such a powerful tool for accessing all your Self's divine wisdom.

So let's get to it…

Chapter 8:
Self-awareness is your birth right

8 is the number of power
So let's step into our power right now and start living the life of our dreams

I had already come across the powerful divination practice of numerology many years before my Angel visited me in 1996. I knew it was uncannily accurate in describing the central issues and challenges we will face, as well as identifying our innate strengths and weaknesses. But I didn't know *why* it worked. And that, as I said in the Introduction, was essential for me to know before I could develop the Self-Awareness System™ contained in Parts Two and Three.

My Angel told me that when our Self incarnates into physical form, it does so with a very specific purpose. Our Self chooses our body, our parents, our race and everything else about us because it knows exactly what it has come here to do. This is all part of the process a Self goes through over many lifetimes until it is evolved enough to return to the Source, knowing that it is pure love.

And because it chooses everything, it also chooses our place and date of birth. So to access the wisdom of our Self and discover what we came here to do, all we need are the "computer codes" that will allow us to access our Self's "database".

There are any number of codes available to us, among them astrology, runes and the I-Ching. But in my opinion, numerology – which connects directly with our Self using the numbers of our date of birth – is by far the most accurate, as well as the easiest to use.

Chapter 8: Self-awareness is your birth right

Why can't I just talk to my Self directly?

You can. As often as you want. But until you have silenced the deafeningly loud voice of your ego in your head and wrested it from the controls of your life, you are going to have a very hard job hearing your Self's reply.

Plus, if your ego is in control it means you are still afraid. So even if you could hear what your Self wants to do, you simply wouldn't have enough courage to do it.

There's another problem. Your Self doesn't "speak" to you in the same way the ego voice in your head does. It doesn't communicate with words. It uses feelings. And again, if you are still plugged into fear, you will not be "in tune" enough with your spiritual nature to interpret your feelings accurately.

That is why you have to go through your Dark Night and defeat your ego before you can, first, hope to feel the wisdom of what your Self is telling you, and, second, have the courage to act upon it.

The beauty of the Self-Awareness System™ is that not only does it give you the access codes to talk directly to your Self until you have achieved the death of your ego, it will speed up the process by showing you what you came here to do and how you can do it.

* * *

Isn't numerology just 'new-age' mumbo jumbo?

No, numerology is not a hippie "new-age" invention, as many people like to believe – although some new-age numerologists have done nothing to help its reputation by trying to convince you (in return for your hard-earned cash) that it can help predict your future.

No one can predict your future. All numerology can do is identify the positive and negative potential within you. What you decide to do with your life is up to you (that's the beauty of free will), and your Life Path will always unfold before you wherever you choose to tread.

Part One: Wake up to your Self

Proper numerology is descriptive, not prescriptive. It has been around for thousands of years and was practised by all the early civilisations, including the Greeks, Egyptians, Babylonians, Hebrews, Hindus and Chinese.

Some charlatans today claim they can use numerology to predict what is going to happen to you, but this is not real numerology. It is garbage, pure fantasy sold to you for the purpose of making money.

These people have no idea why numerology works, which is why they try to claim the digits that make up your phone number, or your house number – and even the numbers that correspond to the letters that make up your name – will determine what happens to you.

It's absolute nonsense.

Yes, these numbers might have some superficial value as talismans (the Chinese, for example, will pay well over the asking price for a house with the number 8, believing it to be lucky), but it's pure superstition. It has no bearing on how your life will turn out.

Traditional numerology, including the Self-Awareness System™ contained in this book, deals only with the numbers of your date of birth – because that is the only number your Self had any control over when it chose to incarnate as "you" for this lifetime.

Your Self had absolutely no idea what name your parents would choose to give you, or what house you would live in when you grew up, or what your mobile phone number would be.

Please be clear on this. The Self-Awareness System™ in Parts Two and Three suggests choices you can make that will lead you towards your highest potential, but it can never – and will never – predict what is going to happen, because your destiny is entirely up to you.

Your future is what you decide it will be. Your Life Path is not pre-ordained. It will appear wherever you put your feet.

Forget the "new age" fortune-tellers (many of whom mean well, by the way, but are lost and desperate for answers), numerology is merely a guide. Your future is, and always will be, what you create it to be.

* * *

Chapter 8: Self-awareness is your birth right

What about astrology?

I am a fan of astrology, as long as it's not used to try to predict your future. It can tell you many things about your personality, the issues you may face and what may make you fulfilled, or not.

The reason astrology works is the same as the reason numerology works... namely, your Self chose to incarnate at a specific time and in a specific place. So, yes, of course you can use astrology as an access code to tap into the database of your Self's wisdom. But there are four major problems with astrology:

First, no one knows if Indian astrology or Western astrology is correct, and they are quite different. In one you are a Gemini, and the other you are a Cancer. To me, that difference is unacceptable.

Second, astrology is very complicated. You either have to study it for a year or more, or else pay an expert to do your chart for you.

Third, your astrology chart is a snapshot in time, just as each Self-Awareness System™ reading is a snapshot of where you are now. But your issues change as you grow, so you need to have your chart done regularly, which gets expensive... whereas the Self-Awareness System™ in this book is freely available for you to consult over and over again.

Fourth, because astrology is so complex, unless you take the time to study it you will have to rely on the interpretation of someone else who isn't inside your body and who hasn't lived your life. And that will never be as accurate as when you use the Self-Awareness System™ to interpret your Self's wisdom... by your Self... and for your Self.

The Self-Awareness System™ is easy to use wherever you are:

– You can consult it by your Self as many times as you want.

– You can interpret the information your Self, rather than have it filtered by someone else.

– You can do it over and over again for free with Part Three as you grow along your Life Path and confront different challenges.

Chapter 9:
Start getting excited

9 is the number of wisdom
Success is measured not by how rich we are, but by how happy we are

The number 9 that governs this final chapter of Part One heralds both the end of one journey and the beginning of another. So, before we move on to unlock the magnificent and life-changing information contained in the Self-Awareness System™ in Parts Two and Three, I would like to finish up Part One with a message worthy of this king and queen of numbers.

As you read about the Self-Awareness System™ in the next two books, please be aware (awareness is all) that you can use the system on two different levels, and you will therefore need to have two different keys – one to unlock each level.

* * *

How can I use the first level?

If you haven't yet woken up to your spiritual identity and purpose, the Self-Awareness System™ will tell you how to be as happy as you can, considering you are still in the clutches of your ego identity, which filters almost everything that happens to you through fear.

The key that unlocks this first level is simply the numbers that make up your date of birth. However, at this basic level, your happiness

Chapter 9: Start getting excited

will always depend on something or someone outside you, such as how much money you have, how many material possessions you own, who loves you, how much you enjoy what you do for a living – and even trivial matters such as what the weather is like or whether you are having a good or bad hair day.

The problem with this sort of "conditional happiness" is that it never lasts for long. Either what makes you happy is taken from you or leaves you for someone younger, or else the happiness you feel from having something or someone new in your life wears off.

When that happens, off you go on your wild goose chase again, trying to satisfy the insatiable cravings of your ego.

You will change your hairstyle, or change your relationship, or buy the latest iPhone or iCar or iHouse – and suddenly you are happy again for precisely the amount of time it takes for your ego to become bored with all these new things as well.

* * *

And what about the second level?

If you have already woken up to your divine identity and your spiritual purpose (and I hope the information in Part One has done that for you), the Self-Awareness System™ will still tell how you can be ecstatically happy in the material world by guiding you to your perfect job, your perfect relationship, your perfect healthy body and your perfect bank balance.

But it will also tell you something else that is truly magical and is guaranteed to lead you straight to your bliss: it will tell you what your life's highest purpose is. In other words, it will help you to remember what your Self came here to do, and it will show you how to do it.

When that happens – when you walk your true Life Path – your happiness never ends.

* * *

Part One: Wake up to your Self

The second key, which unlocks the spiritual messages from your Self as contained in the Self-Awareness System™, is Self-love.

You cannot possibly hope to access the full wisdom of your Self's database unless you can speak your Self's language. And the language your Self speaks is the language of divine wisdom, not human wisdom. It isn't BASIC, or AppleScript, or HTML – or English, or Cantonese, or Swahili.

It's love.

* * *

As I have said, the very fact you are reading this book means you have either already "woken up", or else are about to, so the Self-Awareness System™ will work for you on both levels… materially to help you enjoy your life to the maximum, and spiritually to guide you towards your highest purpose and therefore to your bliss.

If someone who is still plugged into the Fear Matrix, and is therefore still asleep, stumbles across this book on your coffee table, or in a shop, or online, and turns straight to Parts Two and Three, they will still be able to access the messages from their Self, but only on the first and most basic level.

That's OK. At least they will be able to make their uphill struggle a little easier because they can use the Self-Awareness System™ to get answers to all their ego questions – questions such as "What sort of a job suits me best?"; "How can I improve my relationship?"; "How can I best raise my children?", "How can I be healthy?"; and "How can I make more money?"

They just won't be able to use it to get answers to the much richer spiritual questions such as "Why am I here?", "Who am I?" and "What did I come here to do?"

But you, who have so heroically made it through Part One, now have both the keys… so you can get both sets of answers.

* * *

Chapter 9: Start getting excited

Remember, though – and this is important – that just because you have woken up and are on a spiritual growth path, it doesn't mean you can't also have ridiculous amounts of fun in the process.

Having fun is one of the two reasons you are here (the other, in case you've forgotten, is to know your Self as pure love, so the Source can know itself as pure love too, so we can all exist happily ever after).

When you have woken up to your spiritual purpose, you don't leave your pleasurable concerns behind. Far from it. You live your life on both the spiritually and materially pleasurable levels at once.

That is why the Self-Awareness System™ will not only guide you towards your spiritual bliss, it will also guide you towards your physical bliss by showing you how you can have the most fun imaginable while you are here... in your loving relationships, in whatever you choose to do for a living, and in every other aspect of your life as well.

* * *

Please real-eyes that your "bliss" – as promised on the cover – takes two forms: the spiritual bliss of knowing your Self to be pure love, and the physical bliss of making your Self – and as many other people as possible – blissfully and unendingly happy.

I have put these three little smiley faces here because I want you to pause before you read this next paragraph. It is the most important paragraph you will read in the whole book.

Life is meant to be fun. You don't have to do anything other than be happy... because happiness is the highest spiritual discipline there is. Happiness is your expression of your Self, which is pure love. And the happier you are, the more love you will create... which is always everyone's highest purpose.

* * *

Are you saying that's why I came here… to be happy?

Yes! You didn't come here to DO anything. You came here to BE. And you came here to be two things: you came here to be love, and you came here to be happy.

The greatest irony of the human experience is that when we are first born, we are perfect love and we are perfectly happy. We just don't know that we are, because we are not conscious of our perfection.

Young children know more about being happy than the wisest academic in the world because they don't live in their head, where their ego has not yet developed. They live in their heart, where their love is.

The very best way to live our life is the way we started living our life… as an enthusiastic young child with eyes full of wonder, a mind full of curiosity and a heart full of love.

Have you ever asked your Self why you stopped living your life this way? I'll tell you why: it's because your ego (your fear voice in your head that develops along with your mind) convinced you that "life is hard work", "life is a serious business", "life means being interested in politics and finance", "life requires me to be an adult", or some other grown-up excuse for being miserable.

If being an adult means learning to take responsibility for our actions and developing a strong moral compass of what is and isn't acceptable behaviour, then yes, absolutely – those are the only two "adult" qualities that are essential.

But in every other respect, "being an adult" is the very worst way that we can live our lives… because for most people "being an adult" means being grumpy, stressed, serious, boring, judgmental, critical and worried about what others think.

And that's just on their good days.

Sure, I know you've been hurt, you've lost loved ones, you've had your heart broken, you may be struggling just to put food on the table and pay the bills. It's tough, I know. I have been there too. But this should never prevent you from seeing the world through the eyes of a child… or, more specifically, through the eyes of your inner child.

Chapter 9: Start getting excited

Babies get hurt all the time, and look what they do. They don't dwell on it for years, or look around for someone to blame. And they certainly don't shut down their emotions in the hope of avoiding being hurt again.

No, what a baby does is let it all out in one great big scream (I suggest you use a pillow to avoid freaking out the neighbours – that's what I do) and then they go straight back to being a happy and carefree baby again.

It's a magic formula for happiness. We all knew it when we were young, and somehow we forgot it.

* * *

If you want to know the very best way to live your life and you don't have a baby in your house, get a puppy and watch what it does. It flops and rolls and galumphs about all day, chortling in its glee at being a puppy. Then, when it's tired, it goes to sleep. And as soon as it wakes up it starts playing again.

That's all a puppy ever does: play and sleep.

Play-sleep-play-sleep-play-sleep-play-sleep. That's the way to live our life if we want to be happy. And it is why animals are, and always will be, our best teachers.

The reason you stopped living like a child (or a puppy) is simple: you "grew up" into an adult, instead of "growing out" into a big child. And you did this because somewhere along the line you became afraid of being hurt.

Don't feel bad. We all do it. And I was one of the worst offenders. But I figured it out in time, before it was too late, and I became a child again. As a result, I don't need a brand new Aston Martin, or a holiday in the Seychelles, or a pay rise, or a new pair of shoes… or anything else to feel deliriously happy.

When I'm awake I'm always playing, even if it's just by my Self, or with the people I meet. And when I'm not playing, I'm asleep.

Just like a puppy.

Part One: Wake up to your Self

Walt Disney, that magnificent creator of fun, magic and childhood wonder, once said (and it's my all-time favourite quote by a celebrity): "Too many people grow up. That's the real trouble with the world... too many people grow up."

So please stop being such a boring old fart of an adult.

As you read Parts Two and Three, please promise me you will at least try to go back to being a child with eyes full of wonder... because the world we live in is truly wonder-full.

You mean I should see life through a child's eyes?

YES!

It is vital that you read the information about your Life Path in Parts Two and Three from the point of view of an enthusiastic child, because that way you will see how you can have all the toys and fun you could ever possibly dream of... and spiritual bliss as well.

Be a child for as long as it takes you to read Parts Two and Three. Please, I beg you.

When you have finished reading all about your Self and how you can find your bliss in all areas of your life, then – I promise you – I will get off your case.

You will be free to go back to being a boring, frightened, negative, grumpy and worried old adult.

But something tells me you won't want to.

PART TWO:

THE SELF-AWARENESS SYSTEM™

Numbers are the rulers of forms and ideas.
Numbers rule the universe.

- Pythagoras

Chapter 1:
Introduction to the numbers

1 is the number of creation

It's also the number of beginnings, which is why we'll begin this journey where everything begins... at the beginning

Pythagoras is right. Numbers do rule our lives, and they are at the heart of all we do. We have a number for everything: phone numbers, key card numbers, credit card numbers, identity numbers, passport numbers, tax numbers, bank account numbers... even those little paper numbers when we queue up at the deli to buy some ham.

But have you ever stopped to consider what numbers mean? Most people haven't because, on the surface, numbers appear to be about as interesting as filling out our tax return.

No matter how hard they try, numbers just don't seem to zing (unless there are lots of them and they are in our bank account).

Letters are great. I love letters. Letters create beautifully romantic words such as S-E-N-S-U-A-L-I-T-Y and S-E-R-E-N-D-I-P-I-T-Y.

Numbers, however, are decidedly ho-hum.

Read this: "961743 54803 4629 256 34460 97234 23409 2340 7234 98345 3450 987 23409 74365 5993 65924."

And now read this: "Shall I compare thee to a summer's day; thou art more lovely and more temperate."

See what I mean?

Part Two: The Self-Awareness System™

One of the biggest challenges I faced when researching and writing *Messages from Your Self* was to find a way to make numbers leap off the page and inspire you... like letters can.

In my desperation, I even researched the ancient Hebrew practice of Gematria, which ascribes numbers to letters, thinking this might be a good way around the problem.

But Gematriatics, I discovered, were really just a bunch of boring old wannabe accountants who were trying to have a bob each way in the numerology caper.

(Actually, I always thought a "Gematriatic" was an old codger with a bus pass. Turns out I wasn't far wrong.)

Anyway, my point is numbers are inherently and fundamentally boring – and that, as much as anything, is why numerology has never been as popular as astrology.

You can see why, can't you? Given a choice between "a mutable Virgo exalting Uranus" and a "Life Path Number 5", I don't think there's any doubt about which sounds more appealing.

But then I started to dig deeper.

I knew numbers were powerful. I also knew they were the "magic key" chosen especially by your Self when it incarnated into your body on a specific day so you could access its wisdom. But I didn't really know anything about the qualities of the numbers themselves.

What I discovered was nothing short of extraordinary.

Numbers had been under my nose all my life, but I had never paid much attention to them – just as I am sure you haven't paid them much attention either. Until now.

I certainly had never noticed how much "personality" they have, let alone how much they can tell us. I had just assumed they were plain old numbers.

It was like suddenly discovering your cat writes poetry.

Let me show you what I'm talking about.

* * *

Chapter 1: Introduction to the numbers

Qualities of the numbers

The first and most fascinating fact I discovered about numbers is that there are only nine of them. This is because 0 is not a number, it is simply a multiplier.

The number 10 is actually a return to the number 1 (add 1 and 0 together and you get 1). The same is true of 20 (2 + 0 = 2) and 30 (3 + 0 = 3), and so on.

To see this in action, dig out a calculator and divide the number 20 by 9, which is the highest number. You will get 2.22222222222222 recurring to infinity.

Now divide the number 5 by 9 and you'll end up with a never-ending string of 5555555555555555555s.

Go bigger and divide the number 8 by 9 and you will get a screen full of 888888888888888888888888888888s marching off into the distance forever.

9 is the most interesting of all the numbers because it behaves very strangely, as we'll see in a minute.

But first I want to show you how each of the nine numbers that govern our world on every imaginable level has a unique quality and a very specific purpose, and how they all lead on from each other:

1

The number of creation

1 is pregnant with potential and possibility. It is exciting and exhilarating because it vibrates with the most miraculous energy in the entire universe… the energy of creation.

As the Chinese say: "Every journey, even the longest and most arduous quest, begins with a single step." That is why 1 is so powerful, because it contains the force of momentum, of getting started.

1 is governed by the "masculine" energy of action, but on its own it is impotent and isolated. One animal cannot reproduce; one human cannot fall in love; one talker can never be heard; one baby in a vacuum

will never know itself no matter how long it lives (to use the example from Part One). That's why a 1 will never create anything worthwhile unless it can meet another 1 so it can see itself in the eyes of another – just like the Source did all those billions of years ago.

When two 1s come together (the "Adam and Eve" moment), they begin to know themselves for the first time, thus beginning the cycle of creation by becoming…

2

The number of co-operation

When two people work together in harmony they are twice as powerful as they are on their own ("two is better than one"), and they can create something bigger, better and stronger than if they remained separate ("the whole is greater than the sum of its parts").

2, which has a "feminine" energy because it is internally focused, is also the number of awareness. On its own, 1 cannot know itself. Like the Source, it must see itself through the eyes of another to know what it is. So when two people pool their resources, not only do they begin their journey of Self-awareness, they begin the process of growth.

Two people always create a third entity out of their union, whether it's an idea, a business, a relationship, a friendship or even a baby. That is why 2 always becomes…

3

The number of expression

A 2 can be chock full of ideas and passion, but until it takes action to make its plans happen it will achieve absolutely nothing. Two lovers, for example, may sit and canoodle on a park bench all day, delighting in their connection. But the moment they act on their passion and come together to make a baby – whether it's an actual baby or a "creative baby" – they invoke the divine "Holy Trinity" energy of 3.

Chapter 1: Introduction to the numbers

The 3, which like 1 is governed by the masculine energy of action, is the most restless of all the numbers because it is off-balance and imbued with the energy of "two's company, three's a crowd", so it drives itself forward, accumulating knowledge on its journey of growth and discovery as it strives for the comfort and security of…

4
The number of stability

Whereas 3 was restless, odd and off-balance, 4 is symmetrical, stable and secure. Which is why there are four sides to a square, four legs on a table and four wheels on a car.

4 is another feminine number because it takes the dynamic forces of creativity (1), co-operation (2) and expression (3) – which on their own serve no useful end unless they have a purpose – and grounds them in the real world to create both spiritual and material gains.

The trouble is 4 sometimes gets too comfortable and can tend to stagnate by resting on its laurels. It feels safe, especially after the uncomfortable imbalance of 3. And because it is able to create wealth and security with ease, it mistakenly thinks this is as far as the journey goes. Something needs to happen or else the growth cycle will stop here. And that something is…

5
The number of change

We have reached the halfway point in the nine-number cycle and it's time to shake things up. Enter number 5!

If it weren't for the number 5, the world would be stable and solid and really rather dull. Like a table.

It is appropriate we have five fingers on our hands, because 5 is the number of grabbing everything we have achieved and throwing it out the window in the certainty that something better is waiting for us.

Don't worry, we can always pick it up again on the other side. But for now we must free ourselves of our material "baggage" in order to make the Great Leap out of our ego (fear) and into our heart (love).

Like 1 and 3, 5 is a masculine number. It takes us from the realm of physical growth – which started with 1, 2 and 3 and was perfected with 4 – and hurls us into a whole new world of metaphysical growth, where we start to grasp our true nature as divine, spiritual beings.

5 knows that everything we have achieved so far (except for the lessons we have learned) must be left behind if we are to climb higher up the mountain and achieve something much more noble, namely…

6

The number of beauty

6 is the gateway to the second stage of the cycle because it is the portal through which we must all pass to transform ourselves from unaware carbon-based life forms having a physical experience into pure, perfect spirits having a human experience.

This is when we make the most profound shift in our lives as we real-eyes that, contrary to everything we have been taught in Sunday School, we are divine love… and "God" is not out there, but within us.

It's when we see our Self and others with our real eyes, and also when we fully accept responsibility for all our actions… because we real-eyes we are the "God"-like co-creators of all our experiences.

It's no surprise the churches tried to disguise the divine truth of the number 6 – namely, that we don't need them to talk to "God" – by making 666 the number of the devil.

This is pure drivel. The devil doesn't exist. It was invented by the religious patriarchs to control us through fear, thereby ensuring the success of their business model… which, to re-mind you, is: "Give us your money and we'll save your soul." They were lying then and they are lying now. Your soul (Self) doesn't need saving. It is made out of infinite love. Nothing can ever harm it.

Chapter 1: Introduction to the numbers

What 6 really represents is the divine beauty of man and woman, as opposed to the divine beauty of some imagined external "God". It is the understanding that we are all connected, and all the same.

It's no surprise that the early religious founding fathers tried their "damnedest" to put us off the scent by trying to corrupt the true meaning of this most beautiful of numbers.

6 is another feminine number. It is also the first of the second divine cycle of four numbers (6 to 9), because only when we understand that "love is who we are" can we progress to…

7
The number of truth

All the religious texts equate the number 7 with divine qualities, which on the surface may seem to be at odds with its place in the Self-Awareness System™ as the number of truth and knowledge. But look closer and you will see that knowledge in this second stage of the cycle is not about scientific knowledge, but spiritual knowledge – discovering who we are and why we are here.

7 is another masculine number, and the reason it follows on from 6 is that knowledge without love has relatively little value in terms of spiritual growth. This seems to have escaped many scientific thinkers throughout the ages who have regarded knowledge as an end, rather than a means to enlightenment.

Don't get me wrong, scientific knowledge is absolutely essential. It helps us understand the world around us. But it is only of real worth if we take that understanding and use it to improve the lives of all the people and animals who inhabit it.

Divine love (6) is what enables us to do this, because when our search for knowledge is based on the precept of "love is all there is", now 7 stops being a quest to put letters after our name or money in our pockets and becomes the key that unlocks the truly unending abundance of the world we live in, as defined by…

8
The number of power

Look closer at the number 8 and you will see it is the mathematical sign of infinity, flipped on its side. This is because in every cycle of nine numbers, 8 signifies that it is time to reap the rewards of all the hard work done by the previous seven numbers.

8 is a feminine number. It is the number of wealth in all areas, not just financially, and it reveals to us for the first time in the cycle that we can have, do and be whatever we want – but only on the condition that we use our wealth and power to help others who are in need.

This is why 8 appears after 6 (love is all there is) and 7 (we are all in this together), otherwise 8 would give us power *over* people rather than power to *help* people.

In the cycle of history, the human race, after many millions of years of evolution, has arrived at number 8 at the beginning of the third millennium. Even the most cursory glance at the world will show you that the gap between rich and poor is obscene, which is why there is now a growing consciousness that our planet's abundance is meant to be shared, not hoarded. And this backlash against corruption and greed is not going away any time soon. In fact, it will get louder and stronger.

After all, it is only when everyone learns that abundance is to be shared that we, as a species, can rise above our material concerns and enter the much higher spiritual realm of the final number…

9
The number of wisdom

9 is another masculine number. It is the pinnacle of the human experience that can be reached only by learning the lessons of all the other numbers. It is the number of nirvana – of arrival – because it manifests all the qualities of the numbers that have gone before it.

Chapter 1: Introduction to the numbers

As we saw earlier in this chapter, there is a magnifying purity about 9 that can be seen by the fact that if you divide any of the other single-digit numbers by 9 you get an unending string of that number:
- 1 divided by 9 equals 0.1111111111111111111111111 etc.
- 4 divided by 9 equals 0.4444444444444444444444444 etc.
- 7 divided by 9 equals 0.7777777777777777777777777 etc.

Even more remarkably, when you multiply any number by 9, no matter how big it is, the number you get always adds up to 9.
It is the only number that behaves in this way:
- 2 x 9 = 18 (1 + 8 = **9**)
- 14 x 9 = 126 (1 + 2 + 6 = **9**)
- 3,568,347 x 9 = 32,115,123 (3 + 2 + 1 + 1 + 5 + 1 + 2 + 3 = 18 and 1 + 8 = **9**)

Now, let's add any single-digit number to 9 and see what happens. You will be amazed (in a "ta da!" kind of way) to see that the number you get always reduces back down to the original number. Again, no other number does this:
- 5 + 9 = 14 (1 + 4 = **5**)
- 3 + 9 = 12 (1 + 2 = **3**)
- 8 + 9 = 17 (1 + 7 = **8**)
- 1 + 9 = 10 (1 + 0 = **1**)

Spiritually, then, 9 is heaven on earth... it is bliss, paradise and never-ending perfection. In the Christian Bible, it is the number of the "final judgment", and the Hebrew Bible refers to 9 as the number of "Immutable Truth".

In the context of the cycle of human history, 9 represents the tipping point when humanity rises above the potentially materialistic negativity of 8 and swaps greed for "God". (And we're not talking about any false monotheistic "God", who has inspired more human greed than all the Wall Street bankers put together; we're talking about love, when humanity finally releases all its fear and the rapture of becoming pure love takes place.)

On a personal level, and from the point of view of the Self-Awareness System™, the number 9 represents the attainment of your goal, whatever your goal happens to be. It's the number of completion, and it is therefore also the number of death and rebirth.

There is only one place you can go after 9… and that is back to the beginning – to 1 – to start a new cycle of growth.

* * *

The nine Life Path Numbers

In the next chapter, you will learn how to calculate your Life Path Number by adding up the numbers of your date of birth. But before you discover which of the nine Life Path Numbers is yours, it is helpful for you to see how all nine Life Paths resonate with the energy of the nine numbers. As you read the list, notice how each number contains an equal potential for positive and negative outcomes. The difference is always how much we live in love, versus how much we live in fear.

Life Path 1: The Leader
Quality: 1 has a masculine energy and is the number of creation.
Positive potential: People born with a Life Path Number of 1 have powerful and original ideas that make them the best trailblazers and entrepreneurs in our society.
Negative potential: However, if they flip to the "dark side" they can become either domineering tyrants who use their power over people to control them, or manic depressives afraid to stand up for themselves.

Life Path 2: The Intuitive
Quality: 2 has a feminine energy and is the number of co-operation.
Positive potential: People born with a Life Path Number of 2 have a deep capacity for love, an intuitive understanding of others'

needs and a talent for bringing people together, making them great diplomats, healers and peacemakers.

Negative potential: However, if they flip to the dark side they can be manipulative and use their ability to read other people to bend them to their will. They can also be needy and co-dependent, and may exhibit some of the more unattractive traits of the martyr.

Life Path 3: The Creative

Quality: 3 has a masculine energy and is the number of expression.

Positive potential: People born with a Life Path Number of 3 have artistic flair and analytical minds, and they are uncannily sensitive to what others are feeling. This empowers them to become great motivators to help people grow and discover their highest potential.

Negative potential: However, if they flip to the dark side, 3s can become critical of people's shortcomings, frequently finding fault with what others do or say. Instead of being motivators, negative 3s can become de-motivators who prophesy doom, gloom and disaster.

Life Path 4: The Builder

Quality: 4 has a feminine energy and is the number of stability.

Positive potential: People born with a Life Path Number of 4 are practical and reliable and are prepared to work hard to build a stable foundation for themselves and others.

Negative potential: However, if they flip to the dark side they can become materialistic and moody, hoarding their material possessions and shutting themselves off emotionally from others.

Life Path 5: The Rebel

Quality: 5 has a masculine energy and is the number of change.

Positive potential: People born with a Life Path Number of 5 are usually dynamic, restless and adventurous, making them the natural revolutionaries and change-agents of the world.

Negative potential: However, if they flip to the dark side they can become ill-disciplined, scattered and Self-destructive, experiencing frequent bouts of depression. Negative 5s can end up as disillusioned underachievers – true rebels without a cause.

Life Path 6: The Visionary

Quality: 6 has a feminine energy and is the number of beauty.

Positive potential: People born with a Life Path Number of 6 are wonderfully inspirational and optimistic. They hold a vision for a perfect world, not just in their own life but for the whole planet.

Negative potential: However, if they flip to the dark side of this number they can become intolerant perfectionists for whom nothing and no one is ever good enough because it is impossible for anyone, or anything, to live up to their idealistic expectations.

Life Path 7: The Seeker

Quality: 7 has a masculine energy and is the number of truth.

Positive potential: People born with a Life Path Number of 7 are deep thinkers who are blessed with insight and intelligence, making them great scholars, mystics and seekers of truth.

Negative potential: However, if they flip to the dark side they can become arrogant "know-it-alls", obsessed with knowledge for knowledge's sake, which they may then be tempted to use for their own personal gain rather than to help others.

Life Path 8: The Achiever

Quality: 8 has a feminine energy and is the number of power.

Positive potential: People born with a Life Path Number of 8 are strong-willed and ambitious. They have a yearning for success that makes them high achievers, not just in business and finance but in whatever career path they choose to pursue, especially sport.

Negative potential: However, if they flip to the dark side they can become greedy and aggressive power trippers who use their wealth and position to cover up for their deep-seated insecurity.

Life Path 9: The Teacher
Quality: 9 has a masculine energy and is the number of wisdom.
Positive potential: People born with a Life Path Number of 9 are wise in the ways of the world and make the best humanitarians, teachers and role models... because they teach by example.
Negative potential: However, if they flip to the dark side they can become over-zealous and fanatical about imposing their will on others in the belief that they always know best.

* * *

Positive and negative potential

You can see how the energy of the number governing each Life Path can easily manifest in both positive and negative ways. Don't be alarmed. The negativity isn't really negativity at all. It's simply another – and often more powerful – way in which we learn and grow.

Life always gives us precisely what we need. Sometimes it gives us a leg-up, and sometimes it gives us a boot up the bum. This is because as human beings we need both the carrot and the stick to drive us towards achieving our highest potential.

As one of my teachers Anthony Robbins likes to say, when things are going well we tend to party, which is great fun but doesn't do much for our growth, and when things are not going well we tend to ponder, which makes us go in search of answers.

Occasionally, the only way life can get us to make a change is to give us so much pain that we are forced to change. When this happens, it is important that instead of wailing "Why does this always happen to me?" we look for the lesson and change our behaviour. Then, not only

Part Two: The Self-Awareness System™

will we grow but we will also shift out of the negative energy of our Life Path Number and work blissfully with its positive energy.

Also, the nature of spiritual growth dictates that as soon as we learn the lesson, we never have to experience that same pain again.

However, if we don't look for the lesson and do what most "unawake" people do – which is to blame someone else for what happens to us – not only will we keep experiencing the pain, but the pain will get worse and worse until we do finally decide to change.

You might think that in a divinely designed universe like ours there would be no need for negativity – in other words, no need for sadness, loss or suffering. It's the question I get asked all the time: "Why do 'bad things' happen to me?"

The answer is explained by the Law of Duality, as described in Part One. Until we have risen above our fears and have learned to live in love, whereupon we will have no more need for the "carrot and stick" approach to growth, every positive experience will be balanced by an equally negative one.

Just as we need to know what fear is like to appreciate the feeling of love, so too we have to experience darkness to appreciate the light, or rain to appreciate the sunshine.

In the vast context of human evolution, from carbon-based life forms grunting around in caves to fully evolved spiritual beings, we have needed both Hitler and Mother Teresa to show us the extremes of what we as humans are capable of doing to ourselves and each other.

* * *

With that in mind, let's now invoke the "co-operation" energy of **2** for this next chapter and work together to calculate your single Life Path Number and your two Supplementary Birth Numbers.

Chapter 2:
Nine paths to happiness

2 is the number of co-operation

*Now let's work together to discover who you are,
and what you came here to do*

Calculating your single-digit Life Path Number is as easy as writing down your birthday in a succession of single numbers and then adding them up. So if your birthday is April 20, 1978, for example, then the numbers of your birth date are 4 (for the fourth month), 20 (for the date) and 1978 (for the year), and they should be written out like this: 4 + 2 + 0 + 1 + 9 + 7 + 8 = 31.

To obtain your single-digit Life Path Number, all you do is add up the double-digit number like this: 3 + 1 = **4**.

So in this example your Life Path Number would be **4**.

Here are some more examples

Jan 10, 1965:   1 + 1 + 0 + 1 + 9 + 6 + 5 = 23   /   2 + 3 = **5**
Jun 15, 1994:   6 + 1 + 5 + 1 + 9 + 9 + 4 = 35   /   3 + 5 = **8**
Jul 12, 1952:   7 + 1 + 2 + 1 + 9 + 5 + 2 = 27   /   2 + 7 = **9**
Dec 5, 1988:   1 + 2 + 5 + 1 + 9 + 8 + 8 = 34   /   3 + 4 = **7**

(Note: I am using the European style for writing dates, but it doesn't matter if you write your birthday in the European style (April 20, 1978) or in the American style (20 April, 1978). The result will always be the same.)

All double-digit numbers in your date of birth must be separated into single numbers, including the zeros. If your birthday falls on the 20th, as in the example above, it must be written as 2 + 0, not as 20.

Similarly, a birth date of October 26, for example, is not 10 + 26, but 1 + 0 + 2 + 6. And in the same way, December 11 is not 12 + 11 but 1 + 2 + 1 + 1.

Also, make sure you write the year in full. It is 1998, not 98. And it is 2009, not 09.

You may find that when you add together your double-digit number you get another double-digit number (10, 11 and 12 are the only possibilities). In this case, add these two numbers together as well to get your single-digit Life Path Number.

For example:

February 12, 1940: 2 + 1 + 2 + 1 + 9 + 4 + 0 = 19
                    1 + 9 = <u>10</u>
                    <u>1</u> + <u>0</u> = **1**

January 20, 1997:   1 + 2 + 0 + 1 + 9 + 9 + 7 = 29
                    2 + 9 = <u>11</u>
                    <u>1</u> + <u>1</u> = **2**

July 29, 1965:   7 + 2 + 9 + 1 + 9 + 6 + 5 = 39
                    3 + 9 = <u>12</u>
                    <u>1</u> + <u>2</u> = **3**

* * *

Your three-digit Birth Code

Your Life Path Number is your most important number because it determines not just what your life's highest purpose is, but how you can achieve it. In the Life Path listings in Part Three, the number you will refer to is your single-digit Life Path Number, because – as its name suggests – it covers all the main issues of your Life Path.

Chapter 2: Nine paths to happiness

However, your Life Path Number is not the whole story. To get the best results from the Self-Awareness System™ – and to receive all the messages from your Self when it programmed its wisdom into your Birth Code before incarnating – you need two more numbers.

Your three-digit Birth Code is made up of your single-digit Life Path Number and the double-digit number you added together to reach your Life Path Number.

These digits are called your Supplementary Birth Numbers, and I will reveal their significance in just a moment.

Always write down your Birth Code with the two Supplementary Birth Numbers first, then a slash, then your Life Path Number.

*(Note: Whenever a number operates as a Supplementary Birth Number it is underlined, and when it is a Life Path Number it is written in **bold**.)*

* * *

These are the Birth Codes for the examples listed earlier:

January 10, 1965:   1+1+0+1+9+6+5 = 23
                              2 + 3 = **5**
                              Birth code: 23/**5**

June 15, 1994:   6+1+5+1+9+9+4 = 35
                              3 + 5 = **8**
                              Birth code: 35/**8**

July 12, 1952:   7+1+2+1+9+5+2 = 27
                              2 + 7 = **9**
                              Birth code: 27/**9**

Dec 5, 1988:   1+2+5+1+9+8+8 = 34
                              3 + 4 = **7**
                              Birth code: 34/**7**

Part Two: The Self-Awareness System™

Feb 12, 1940:   2+1+2+1+9+4+0 = 19
                 1 + 9 = <u>10</u>
                 <u>1</u> + <u>0</u> = **1**
                 Birth code: <u>10</u>/**1**

Jan 20, 1997:   1+2+0+1+9+9+7 = 29
                 2 + 9 = <u>11</u>
                 <u>1</u> + <u>1</u> = **2**
                 Birth code: <u>11</u>/**2**

July 29, 1965:   7+2+9+1+9+6+5 = 39
                 3 + 9 = <u>12</u>
                 <u>1</u> + <u>2</u> = **3**
                 Birth code: <u>12</u>/**3**

Possible three-digit Birth Codes

These are the 30 three-digit Birth Codes of the Self-Awareness System™. (A very few children who were born since 2000 have single-digit Birth Codes. These are called the "Millennium Children" and we will examine their unique potential later in this chapter.)

For Life Path **1**, the only possible Birth Code is <u>10</u>/**1**

For Life Path **2**, the Birth Codes are <u>11</u>/**2** and <u>20</u>/**2**

For Life Path **3**, the Birth Codes are <u>12</u>/**3**, <u>21</u>/**3** and <u>30</u>/**3**

For Life Path **4**, the Birth Codes are <u>13</u>/**4**, <u>22</u>/**4**, <u>31</u>/**4** and <u>40</u>/**4**

For Life Path **5**, the Birth Codes are <u>14</u>/**5**, <u>23</u>/**5**, <u>32</u>/**5** and <u>41</u>/**5**

For Life Path **6**, the Birth Codes are <u>15</u>/**6**, <u>24</u>/**6**, <u>33</u>/**6** and <u>42</u>/**6**

For Life Path **7**, the Birth Codes are <u>16</u>/**7**, <u>25</u>/**7**, <u>34</u>/**7** and <u>43</u>/**7**

For Life Path **8**, the Birth Codes are <u>17</u>/**8**, <u>26</u>/**8**, <u>35</u>/**8** and <u>44</u>/**8**

For Life Path **9**, the Birth Codes are <u>18</u>/**9**, <u>27</u>/**9**, <u>36</u>/**9** and <u>45</u>/**9**

Chapter 2: Nine paths to happiness

What our Supplementary Birth Numbers mean

For most of us, our Supplementary Birth Numbers are the double-digit total of the numbers of our birth date that we add together to get our Life Path Number. But for some they are the second pair of double-digit numbers (10, 11 or 12 are the only possible ones) we get when we add the first double-digit number together.

The energy of each of the two Supplementary Birth Numbers works in the same way as it does for the Life Path Number, as described in the first chapter here in Part Two:

1 is the Leader

2 is the Intuitive

3 is the Creative

4 is the Builder

5 is the Rebel

6 is the Visionary

7 is the Seeker

8 is the Achiever

9 is the Teacher

The difference is that while our Life Path Number governs the central issues we will work with for our entire life, our Supplementary Birth Numbers play a supporting role during the formative years of our childhood and our early adult life up until the age of 36.

Our first Supplementary Birth Number operates in conjunction with our Life Path Number during the first 18 years of our life, from childhood to independence at 18, and our second Supplementary Birth Number operates during the next 18 years until we reach full emotional maturity at the age of 36. Throughout this time, we will always be working with the energy of the two supplementary numbers in a way that assists us with the principal challenges of our Life Path Number.

The timelines for the Supplementary Birth Numbers are flexible. We will not stop working with the energy of our first Supplementary

Part Two: The Self-Awareness System™

Birth Number on our 18th birthday and then immediately start working with the energy of our second Supplementary Birth Number. There will be an overlap. The dates are a guide, although a reasonably accurate one in my experience.

This period of 36 years takes us from birth to full emotional maturity. In Chapter 6 we will see how this process is divided into four distinct Nine-Year Cycles: The Cycle of Dependence (years 1 to 9) and The Cycle of Independence (years 10 to 18), which are influenced by our first Supplementary Birth Number, and The Cycle of Confidence (years 19 to 27) and The Cycle of Maturity (years 28 to 36), which are influenced by our Second Supplementary Birth Number.

* * *

Let's look at our original example of someone born on April 20, 1978. Their two Supplementary Birth Numbers are $\underline{3}$ (the Creative) and $\underline{1}$ (the Leader), and their Life Path Number is **4** (the Builder).

This person will work primarily with the energy of **4** (the Builder) throughout their life, but in the first part of their life – up until about the age of 18 when they reach adulthood – they will also work with the energy of $\underline{3}$ (the Creative) in a supplementary capacity.

Then, in the second growth phase of their life (from 18 to 36) they will work with the supplementary energy of $\underline{1}$ (the Leader) in tandem with the main issues governed by their Life Path Number **4**.

If this was you, your highest purpose would be to master the energy of your Life Path Number **4** by building a solid foundation for you and your family, and then helping others to do the same.

However, in your childhood years you would also confront the supplementary issues of $\underline{3}$, which is the number of the Creative and is concerned with learning to express your Self. This is essential for all children, but especially so for young $\underline{31}$/**4**s.

Then as you started building your career and home life between the ages of 18 and 36, you would begin to work with the supplementary energy of $\underline{1}$, which is the number of the Leader and would drive you to perhaps start your own business, or else climb quickly up the ranks in your chosen profession.

Remember, our life's highest purpose is always to be of service to others, no matter what our Birth Code is. The numbers simply delineate the areas of life where we can be of greatest service, be it as a force for change (Life Paths **1**, **5** and **9**), a force for harmony (Life Paths **2** and **6**), a force for awareness (Life Paths **3** and **7**) or a force for abundance (Life Paths **4** and **8**).

* * *

How Supplementary Birth Numbers can help children

If you are a parent and you are calculating your child's Birth Code, it is especially valuable for you to know about this progression of their Supplementary Birth Numbers so you can guide them to make the best choices at school, college and in the workforce – as well as helping them to overcome any negative challenges as they grow up.

To continue with our example, you would help your child work through the issues of confident communication (the energy of the Creative 3) during their formative years up to 18 years old, and then advise them on the issues of ambition and leadership (the energy of the Leader 1) as they reach young adulthood – all the while having a clear understanding of the major issues and challenges they will face throughout their childhood and adult years as a result of their main Life Path Number, in this case **4** (the Builder).

* * *

The Millennium Children

As the world has evolved and entered a new millennium, we are now seeing a new generation of children who have been born without a conventional three-digit Birth Code because the numbers of their birth date add up to less than 10.

These "Millennium Children" appear to have an extraordinary potential based on their Self's desire to work intensely with the energy of just one number.

The Millennium Children are those who were born on certain days since January 1, 2000 and whose birth date adds up to a number that is less than 10, which means they are governed solely by the energy of their single-digit Life Path Number of **4, 5, 6, 7, 8** or **9**.

Examples of Millennium Children:

Jan 1, 2000: $1 + 1 + 2 + 0 + 0 + 0 = 4$
Birth code: **4**

Feb 11, 2010: $2 + 1 + 1 + 2 + 0 + 1 + 0 = 7$
Birth code: **7**

Oct 10, 2005: $1 + 0 + 1 + 0 + 2 + 0 + 0 + 5 = 9$
Birth code: **9**

These children carry a particular set of skills and responsibilities because they will be working intensely with their Life Path Number in the absence of any Supplementary Birth Numbers.

As a result of being able to focus all their energy on the issues of their single-digit Life Path Number they must be regarded as having a unique ability to tap into their highest potential so they can help pave the way for others. This is not surprising, given the powerful "renewal energy" of the dawn of the new millennium when they were born.

Time will tell what roles these Millennium Children will play in the transformation of the world. But it is worth noting the last time anyone was born without a Supplementary Birth Number was more than 400 years ago in 1600, just before the start of The Age of Reason – one of the most profound periods of change in human history.

(Note: Although these children have only one number, for the purposes of the listings in Part Three their Birth Code will be written as <u>00</u>/ *4,* <u>00</u>/ *5,* <u>00</u>/ *6,*

Chapter 2: Nine paths to happiness

00/ 7, 00/ 8 and *00/ 9*. *This is because they have an amplified focus similar to someone who has a 0 in their Birth Code, as we're about to see...)*

* * *

If there is a '0' in your Birth Code

Although 0 is not technically a number, it does play a very important role in the Self-Awareness System™ because it acts as an amplifier for the number with which it appears.

Specifically, people who are born with a 0 in their Birth Code are more sensitive to the energies around them and to the feelings of other people, and they also develop a heightened sense of intuition that allows them to work with their Life Path Number on a deeper level.

There are only four possible three-digit Birth Codes that include a single Supplementary Birth Number of 0. They are 10/1, 20/2, 30/3 and 40/4.

It's easy to see why someone with one of these Birth Codes has an amplified potential to achieve great success, because they have a double dose of the energy of just one number in their Birth Code, rather than three different numbers.

The number that governs the issues they will face in the crucial first 18 years of their life is the same as their Life Path Number that governs their entire life and leads them to their highest purpose.

And then in their second 18 years they will continue working with the energy of that number with the amplified energy of 0 as they develop a powerful sense of intuition as well as a deep and sensitive understanding of themselves, other people and the world around them.

This heightened potential does not mean that someone born with one of these four Birth Codes is any more "special" than anyone else. We are all born with the same amount of potential to achieve our life's highest purpose. It simply means they will be much more focused on deciding what they want to do with their life.

Besides, who's to say that mastering just one or two aspects of your life is any better or worse than working (and playing) in a number of different arenas?

There is no "better" or "worse" in the Self-Awareness System™, just potential. As the name says, "awareness" of our potential is what counts. What we then choose to do with it is up to us, and our outcome will always be determined by the choices we make.

In addition, a powerful intuition and heightened sensitivity can be a double-edged sword. If we have one of these four Birth Codes with a <u>0</u> in them we will feel emotions very deeply, which is fine when life is going well. But all Life Paths contain challenges we must overcome to grow – that is the nature of life – so when things are not going so well, we will tend to feel pain and frustration more acutely as well.

* * *

The effect a '<u>0</u>' will have on your Life Path

<u>10</u>/1

All people who are born with a Life Path Number of **1** (the Leader) have a <u>0</u> as their second Supplementary Birth Number, which amplifies the creative and leadership qualities of this Life Path.

There is no other Birth Code that will give us a Life Path Number of **1**, which means that everyone who walks the Life Path of the Leader does so with an evolved sense of intuition that will give them the confidence to take a leadership role at work, at home and in their community.

They also have a deep sensitivity that allows them to understand the needs of others – an essential quality for a great leader.

If this is your Birth Code, the fact that your first Supplementary Birth Number is the same as your Life Path Number means you will work intensively with the creative and leadership energies of **1** not just in your first formative years, but throughout your life.

Chapter 2: Nine paths to happiness

Then in your second 18 years, as you evolve from a young adult into a fully mature adult, your second Supplementary Birth Number of <u>0</u> means you will work even more intensely with the energy of **1** on a more intuitive level, which will help you in your leadership capacity. You will also develop a deep sensitivity to your own feelings and the feelings of others, which will help you become an empathetic and compassionate leader – the highest purpose of all **1**s.

However, none of this will happen if you fail to clear your emotional blockages and remain stuck in your ego. As with all the Life Paths, there is a light side and a dark side, thanks to the Law of Duality.

If you rise above your ego, you will walk the light side. But if you succumb to fear (the diet of the ego) you may flip to the dark side.

It doesn't matter which Life Path we are on, the purpose of life is the same: to learn we are an extension of Source energy, and therefore we are pure love. It is only by learning this simple but elusive truth that we are able to rise above our ego and live life asking the question "How can I help?" instead of "What's in it for me?"

Regardless of the numbers that make up our Birth Code, our task is always to learn this truth… and our highest purpose is always to help others do so too.

Just like roads and Rome, all nine Life Paths (and Supplementary Birth Numbers too) lead to the same place.

The very fact that you are reading this book means you are almost certain to get there in this lifetime. However, there are billions of people out there who are only just starting out on their journey.

Just try to help as many of them as you can, but don't worry if you can't. They will be fine.

The Source is perfect. Everyone gets there in the end.

* * *

Now that you see how this all works, we can move through the next three "<u>0</u>-powered" Birth Codes a little more quickly.

20/2

The presence of the 0 in this Birth Code amplifies the double energy of **2**, which is the only Supplementary Birth Number and also the Life Path Number.

Individuals born with this Birth Code will work intensively with the co-operative energy of **2** (the Intuitive) throughout their life and, thanks to the presence of their 0, they will do so with a heightened capacity for sensitivity, intuition and awareness.

These people make excellent empathetic therapists, healers and psychics, as well as diplomats, teachers and social workers, because they are able to connect with other people at a deep level.

But if they flip to the dark side, due to the demands of their ego, they can become needy and co-dependent – and, in extreme cases, might even be tempted to try to use their powers to manipulate other people and bend them to their will.

30/3

Again, the 0 works as an amplifier, giving individuals born with this Birth Code a heightened sensitivity and intuition when working with the double energy of **3** (the Creative), both as their Life Path Number and as their first Supplementary Birth Number.

Because **3** is concerned with expression, people with this Birth Code will frequently become great artists, writers and orators, using their talent for communication to inspire and motivate others.

The amplifying energy of their 0 means their intuition will also become highly attuned to the needs of those they choose to help.

However, because of their deep sensitivity, they have the potential to be extremely harsh on themselves, which can often cause them to be critical of others as well.

All **3**s walking the dark side of their Life Path can be cynical and negative, but negative 30/3s with the amplified qualities of a 0 can be downright destructive, tearing everybody and everything down just so they can feel better about themselves.

40/4

This Birth Code is relatively rare, and when it does occur it signifies a person who is extremely focused on building a stable foundation for their life – the double energy of **4** (the Builder).

These people will usually own their own home from an early age, and will probably go into business for themselves, perhaps even running several companies at once.

4s make excellent managers. If you want someone to organise people or an event and get the best results from your team, you would definitely employ a **4**.

The amplifying energy of the 0 endows them with a strong intuition to make the right business and investment choices, and so they will often become fabulously wealthy.

There is a big downside to this Birth Code, however. If the 40/**4** stays stuck in their ego, they will never be able to accumulate enough possessions and money to make their insatiable ego happy, no matter how hard they work – and they will almost certainly become unhealthy workaholics, to the detriment of their family and their home life.

They will also tend to jealously guard everything they have worked so hard to achieve, never feeling able to trust anyone completely, including those people who are closest to them.

If this is your Birth Code, you must learn the crucial Life Path lesson that money – like love – only has value when it is given away, preferably to help others in need. You cannot take it with you. A jewel-encrusted coffin made of solid gold is still a coffin.

Also, by no means all 40/**4**s who walk the dark side will become wealthy. The flip side of the positive and tenacious qualities of the **4** is a tendency to obsess on petty details, so much so that they often take no action at all.

Negative **4**s can be some of the world's worst procrastinators. And their heightened sensitivity means that they also react badly to any form of criticism.

Part Two: The Self-Awareness System™

There's no doubt that all **4**s have a tendency to shut themselves off emotionally when they work with the negative energy of this Life Path Number, but 40/**4**s can take this to extremes.

* * *

The four 'Master Numbers'

Having shown you the qualities of the four "0" Birth Codes, I now want to introduce you to another set of four unusual Birth Codes – what numerologists like to call the "Master Numbers".

Master Numbers are Birth Codes where both Supplementary Birth Numbers are the same. There are only four of them: 11, 22, 33 and 44.

*(Note: There is no 55 or higher because the highest possible number that can be reached by adding up a birth date is 48, for someone who was born on September 29, 1999. The first time we will see a 55 is on September 29, 8999 – in nearly 7000 years' time. And even then, they wouldn't be a Master Number because they would add their two 5s together to give them a Birth Code of 10/ **1**.)*

Some numerologists believe that only 11, 22 and 33 are Master Numbers and that 44 is not a true Master Number. They offer varying reasons for this but, as you will discover if you research all the different numerology books and websites, there is a fair amount of conflicting information out there based on the different interpretations of the basic principles of traditional Pythagorean numerology.

There is no right or wrong. You must decide what feels true for you, but for me it makes sense that if some identical double-digit Supplementary Birth Numbers are called Master Numbers, then all of them should be called Master Numbers.

That is why in the Self-Awareness System™ there are four Master Numbers, and they are called the Master Intuitive (11/**2**), the Master Builder (22/**4**), the Master Visionary (33/**6**) and the Master Achiever (44/**8**). These double-strength Supplementary Birth Numbers have a special significance that I will describe in detail in Chapter 8. For now, though, here is a quick overview of their qualities.

Chapter 2: Nine paths to happiness

Examples of the four Master Numbers

October 1, 2016: $1 + 0 + 1 + 2 + 0 + 1 + 6 = \underline{11}$
                               $\underline{1} + \underline{1} = \mathbf{2}$ (Master Intuitive)

February 7, 1964: $2 + 7 + 1 + 9 + 6 + 4 = 29$
                               $2 + 9 = \underline{11}$
                               $\underline{1} + \underline{1} = \mathbf{2}$ (Master Intuitive)

January 20, 1990: $1 + 2 + 0 + 1 + 9 + 9 + 0 = \underline{22}$
                               $\underline{2} + \underline{2} = \mathbf{4}$ (Master Builder)

July 21, 1976: $7 + 2 + 1 + 1 + 9 + 7 + 6 = \underline{33}$
                           $\underline{3} + \underline{3} = \mathbf{6}$ (Master Visionary)

August 29, 1987: $8 + 2 + 9 + 1 + 9 + 8 + 7 = \underline{44}$
                             $\underline{4} + \underline{4} = \mathbf{8}$ (Master Achiever)

(Note that the $\underline{11}/\mathbf{2}$ Master Intuitive is unique among the Master Numbers because it can be added up directly to reach $\underline{11}$, and it can also come from reducing one of three larger double-digit numbers – 29, 38 or 47 – to reach $\underline{11}$.)

* * *

If you have a Master Number it means you will be working with the energy of the same Supplementary Birth Number for all your first 36 years. And, as we saw with the four $\underline{0}$ Birth Codes, when you focus of all your attention and energy in one direction your chances of success are greatly increased.

$\underline{11}/\mathbf{2}$ – The Master Intuitive

With a Master Number of $\underline{11}$, both of our Supplementary Birth Numbers are $\underline{1}$, so we will be working with the forceful masculine leadership energy of $\underline{1}$ (the Leader) for the first 18 years of our life, and we will then continue to work with the masculine leadership energy of 1 for the next 18 years until we reach full emotional maturity around the age of 36.

Our main work will still be with our Life Path Number **2** (the Intuitive, which is feminine in its nurturing energy), but we will do so with a double dose of the creative and leadership energy of 1 – so we have the potential to become an extremely intuitive and influential healer and peacemaker – the main strengths of Life Path Number **2**.

Famous 11/**2**s include Barack Obama and Lord Byron.

* * *

22/4 – The Master Builder

With a Master Number of 22, the double Supplementary Birth Number of 2 means we will work the feminine energy of 2 (the Intuitive) for the entire first 36 years of our life, while also working with our Life Path Number of **4** (the Builder), which is also feminine.

This means that while we may be focused on building a stable foundation and a solid home (the energy of **4**), we will do so in co-operation and harmony with others (the supplementary energy of 2).

Plus, although our primary concern is stability, we will have an acute awareness that stability is of no use if we – and those we care for – are not happy and at peace. So while other **4**s might build just for the sake of it, the double energy of 2 (the Intuitive) in this Master Number Birth Code ensures that we will build our family home and our career with our heart as well as our head.

Famous Master Builder 22/**4**s who are noted for their humanity as well as their achievements include Bono and Leonardo da Vinci.

* * *

33/6 – The Master Visionary

With 33, the double Supplementary Birth Number of 3 means we will work with the double masculine energy of communication (the

Creative) for the first 36 years of our life, while also working primarily with our feminine Life Path Number of **6** (the Visionary).

As a result, while we are learning to express our Self through communication, we are doing so to help us move towards our ultimate Life Path goal of boosting the level of love and compassion in the world (the energy of **6**).

For this reason, <u>33</u>/**6**s are potentially the most powerful of all the Visionaries. Famously romantic Master Visionaries include Fred Astaire, and Greta Garbo from the world of cinema, and Agatha Christie and HG Wells from the world of literature.

* * *

<u>44</u>/**8** – The Master Achiever

This is an extremely rare Birth Code. The double Supplementary Birth Number of <u>4</u> (the Builder) means we will work with the feminine energy of material stability for the first 36 years of our life, while also working primarily with our equally feminine Life Path Number of **8** (the Achiever).

Both <u>4</u> and **8** are materialistic as well as spiritual numbers, which means we will have the capacity to create a great amount of abundance. Metaphorically, we can turn lead into gold, hence why this number is often referred to as "The Alchemist".

Since this number is so rare, there are no famous people in all of history who have a birth number of <u>44</u>/**8** – at least none that I have been able to find. (I'll explain this bizarre phenomenon in Chapter 8.)

* * *

All Birth Codes are equal

Please don't think that if you have a Master Number or a <u>0</u> in your Birth Code you are "special" in any way. That is a trap set by your ego and you should stay well away from it. From a numerological – as well as a spiritual – perspective, we are all equal.

Part Two: The Self-Awareness System™

If we are born into poverty or disadvantage, our highest purpose may be to help just a few people. That does not make it any less valuable. And besides, people born into disadvantage have just as much potential to change the world if they choose to.

Think of Joan of Arc (15/6), a poor peasant girl who led her country to fight for its freedom at a time when women didn't go to war, let alone command an army.

Or Mother Teresa (36/9). Or Oprah Winfrey (31/4).

Google their life stories. All of them came from poor beginnings and none of them had a "special" 0 or a Master Number Birth Code.

Master Numbers and 0 Supplementary Birth Numbers simply mean that we have a heightened potential for achieving our goals. Whether we do, or not, will always depend on the choices we make.

* * *

I will go into more detail about the four Master Numbers in Chapter 8 (an appropriate number for discussing their powerful potential), but in this next chapter let's turn our attention back to your Life Path Number – which is by far the most important number in your Birth Code – and invoke the "expressive" energy of **3** to reveal what it can tell you.

Chapter 3:
The secrets of your Birth Code

3 is the number of expression

The Self-Awareness System™ shows you how to express the love in your heart and live the life you were born to live

Now that you know your Life Path Number, the first thing to do is celebrate because you have a whole new sense of identity. You can get t-shirts made up with your number on it, you can personalise your car plates, celebrate your special day each month, and even go up to people at parties and say: "Hi, I'm a 3. What are you?"

I'm kidding, of course. But there's a serious side to this subject because I want to make the point loud and clear right from the start that our Life Path Number is only a guide for helping us live our life, it does not "define" who we are.

As a society, we are far too prone to use easy labels to pigeonhole people based on what they do for a living, their gender, their sexuality, age, race, creed and even the colour of their skin. The truth is we are all vastly complex individuals who think and feel differently to every other person on the planet. That is why the Fat Controllers like to use labels – so they can pigeonhole us and control us more easily.

Each of us is unique, with unique qualities, thoughts, dreams and desires. We all have our own life to live, and the path to our unique highest purpose will not be the same as any of the billions of others

Part Two: The Self-Awareness System™

who have come before us, or those who are yet to come. Please remember as you read this book that the value of our Life Path Number lies not in "defining" who we are, but in "divining" what we are capable of achieving.

So before you skip eagerly ahead to read all about the qualities of your Life Path Number and Supplementary Birth Numbers in Part Three, it is important that you first understand how the Self-Awareness System™ works so that when you do read all about your Self you will be able to obtain the maximum benefit from the information.

* * *

The Five Pillars of the Self-Awareness System™

The Self-Awareness System™ has been designed for the sole (soul) purpose of guiding you towards your bliss. It does this by first showing you what your life's highest purpose is, and then by showing you how you might best be able to achieve it.

I have chosen my words carefully, because although it will *show* you what you can do to live the life of your dreams, it will never *tell* you what to do. The Self-Awareness System™ is "descriptive", but it is never "prescriptive" – because what we choose to do with our life, and how we decide to interpret the unique messages from our Self, is entirely up to us.

All the wisdom of our Self's previous incarnations in human form is accessible through our Birth Code, which comprises our Life Path Number and our two Supplementary Birth numbers. So we are talking about a lot of information, especially if ours happens to be an old and experienced Self.

To make it easier for you to sort through it all, the Self-Awareness System™ breaks the information down into five key areas:

1. Life choices to help you first discover and then achieve your life's highest purpose.

2. Career and business choices to help you use your talents in the most fulfilling and rewarding way.

3. Relationship choices to help you create and maintain loving, lasting and passionate relationships.

4. Health choices to ensure you have the energy to achieve all you want to achieve and avoid the ailments to which you are prone.

5. Choices for children to give your children the very best start in life and set them on course for success and happiness.

These are the Five Pillars of the Self-Awareness System™. They are explained in detail in the nine Life Path listings in Part Three, but for now I want to explain how each of them works so you will know how to interpret the information when you get to it.

* * *

1. Discover your life's highest purpose

We have already talked about how the ultimate journey of every one of our lifetimes is to discover and then achieve our life's highest purpose. So let's be absolutely clear you know what this term "highest purpose" means.

If you have ever wondered "Why am I here?" or "What am I meant to do with my life?", the answer to both questions is the same… it's your life's highest purpose.

The first point to real-eyes about your highest purpose is that you have already decided what it is. Your Self has already chosen your life path before you came here. The Self-Awareness System™ will simply re-mind you of what you came here to do, because your highest purpose is always what your Self decided it wanted to do in this lifetime when it incarnated as you.

The second point to real-eyes is that there is no "big" or "small" – or "better" or "worse" – in the eyes of spirit. Your highest purpose does not have to be world-changing, like Gandhi or Mother Teresa.

Part Two: The Self-Awareness System™

You don't have to save the planet, or cure cancer, or become president, or go to Africa and feed the starving children with your bare hands. Yes, by all means you can do these things if you choose to. And good on you if you do. But you don't have to. You can just as well stay in your little corner of the world and help people across the street, or write a book, or clean people's houses, or teach little children, or play a sport, or make people laugh, or work in a factory, or raise a family.

The term "highest purpose" does not mean "higher than anyone else's purpose". Life is not a competition. The reason you have a highest purpose is not so that you can change the world, it is so that you can change "you" – because only by becoming the best "you" that you can be will you learn to love your Self exactly as you are.

Self-love is the key
Self-love is the one essential quality we all need to learn to fulfill our highest purpose. It is the starting point. It is the base camp everyone must establish for the climb up the mountain path to our bliss, because only when we truly love ourselves are we able to truly love others... which is always what our life's highest purpose is about.

I hope by now you are starting to see the perfect symmetry of the Self-Awareness System™. The only reason we have a highest purpose is because it guides us to do what we need to do to learn how to love ourselves. And the only reason we need to learn how to love ourselves is because it is the only way we can achieve our highest purpose.

It is a "blissful spiral" – a perfect, unwinding path that leads inexorably up the mountain to our eternal and unbounded happiness.

This is why Self-love is called the greatest love of all. Learning to love our Self is always the first step on our path to everlasting bliss.

* * *

Another reason Self-love is so essential is because our life's highest purpose always takes the form of service to others, in one form or another – which means we will give our love unconditionally without needing anything in return.

It is simply not possible to love someone else unconditionally if we don't love ourselves. Why? Because it is only when we can stand up and say we have all the love we need right here in our own heart that we can devote our life to loving and helping others.

As the table below shows, your Life Path Number gives you a rough idea of how you can best serve others based on your particular strengths. It also shows you what you need to work on to become the best "you" that you can be – the first step towards loving your Self.

It is not specific because you will interpret your highest purpose in a way that feels right for you. This is a guide book, not a rule book. However, your highest purpose will always fall into one of these three categories: you will be a "teacher", a "healer" or a "helper".

How you choose to manifest your particular form of service – whether it is teaching, healing or helping – is entirely up to you and will become much clearer when you have read the full listing for your Life Path Number in Part Three. For now, though, this summary of the nine Life Paths will give you a brief guide:

1. The Leader
Qualities: Creative, energetic and full of ideas. A trailblazer.
Highest purpose: To lead the way for others to follow.

2. The Intuitive
Qualities: Compassionate, intuitive, empathetic. A peacemaker.
Highest purpose: To bring people together in peace and love.

3. The Creative
Qualities: Sensitive, social, expressive. A motivator of others.
Highest purpose: To inspire others to be the best they can be.

4. The Builder
Qualities: Down to earth, practical. A rock for others to lean on.

Highest purpose: To build a stable foundation for your Self, and to help others less fortunate than you do the same.

5. The Rebel
Qualities: Adventurous and inquisitive. An agent for change.
Highest purpose: To fight the forces of oppression and help others break free of fear of the Fear Matrix.

6. The Visionary
Qualities: Idealistic, empathetic, nurturing. A spiritual visionary.
Highest purpose: To show others their true loving potential.

7. The Seeker
Qualities: Analytical, intelligent, insightful. A seeker of truth.
Highest purpose: To learn the "Big Truths" and share your unique insights with the world.

8. The Achiever
Qualities: Resourceful, strong-willed, ambitious. A wealth creator.
Highest purpose: To create abundance, and then share it with others who are in need.

9. The Teacher
Qualities: Wise, aware and experienced. A teacher of wisdom.
Highest purpose: To be a role model for others, to stand up for what is right and teach by example.

Notice how the innate qualities of each Life Path Number equip everyone living that number with precisely the qualities they need to achieve their life's highest purpose.

Also, notice how each Life Path leads seamlessly on to the next one to complete the nine-step process of growing (over many lifetimes) from the materially focused leadership energy of the Leader, whose highest purpose is to create opportunities for others to succeed, to the spiritually focused leadership energy of the Teacher, whose highest purpose is to be a role model for others to follow.

For the Leader **1** to become a true leader who teaches by example, they must also experience the co-operative energy of **2** (the Intuitive), the artistic and expressive energy of **3** (the Creative), the humanitarian and loyal energy of **4** (the Builder), the bold and adventurous energy of **5** (the Rebel), the idealistic and loving energy of **6** (the Visionary), the thoughtful energy of **7** (the Seeker) the powerful energy of **8** (the Achiever) and the insightful energy of **9** (The Teacher).

I told you this system was exquisite in its perfection. But we have only just scratched the surface. By the time you have finished reading about how the Self-Awareness System™ works you will be astonished to see how it all fits together.

Your life, which you have hitherto regarded as a random collection of experiences, is actually an integral and beautifully designed part of a much, much bigger picture.

* * *

2. Career and business choices

Wouldn't it be great to know what we want to do with our life right from the outset? We could focus all our energy on achieving one outcome... if only we knew what that outcome was.

The list of celebrities in Appendix A is filled with examples of people who knew right from when they were children or young adults what they wanted to do: people like Richard Branson (a business **4**), Sylvester Stallone (a showbusiness **6**), Tiger Woods (a sporting **1**), JRR Tolkien (a literary **6**) and Albert Einstein (a scientific **6**).

All of these extraordinarily successful individuals have admitted that they always knew what they wanted to do with their lives, and there is no doubt that this awareness and ambition from an early age gave them both the focus and the determination to succeed in their chosen profession.

Part Two: The Self-Awareness System™

For most of us, though, the decision of what to do with our lives is far from easy. We might have an idea of the kind of career we would like, but we often end up doing whatever job we happen to stumble upon when we first leave school or college, and then we continue to do that line of work simply because we become good at it. But at no point did we ever choose our career deliberately.

One of the saddest realities of life for me is the number of times I ask my students "What is your passion?" and their faces light up as they give me answers such as "dancing" or "singing" or "travelling" or "helping people". And then I ask them what they do for a living, and their smile fades into a grimace as they tell me they work in a dead-end job in an office, or in a shop, or on a factory floor.

Yes, I know someone has to do these jobs. But those "someones" are almost always people who have yet to "wake up" spiritually to their life's highest purpose. Usually they are still working through some of the more basic issues of personal power and ego. What's more, they are often still plugged into their "tribe" (the culture they were born into) because they have not broken away and begun their solitary climb up the metaphorical mountain path of spiritual growth.

But once you wake up to your spiritual nature and begin your journey towards enlightenment, these jobs may no longer satisfy you – unless, of course, you have evolved to the point where driving a bus, sweeping the streets, waiting tables or serving behind a counter is the perfect way to help others as part of your life's highest purpose.

In fact, in my experience it is common to find what the late, great English spiritualist Stuart Wilde calls "God's Gladiators" working in these types of jobs. These people are fully enlightened Selfs who have come back to help out "down here" rather than return to the Source. They are usually cunningly disguised as janitors, gardeners, postmen and women, nurses, office assistants, taxi drivers, passers-by, and even the homeless. They appear before us to reassure us and put us back on our path when we lose our way.

I have met many Gladiators working in all manner of menial jobs. They are divine spirits who walk, and work, humbly among us.

Remember, our life's highest purpose is always to be found in the service of others, no matter what form it takes. And sometimes this is best done on the most basic level, and on a one-to-one basis. After all, we can't all be pop stars, princesses and presidents.

If you have already woken up to your spiritual nature (and I suspect you have, or you would have stopped reading long ago) and are working towards your highest purpose but are still stuck in a dead-end job that not only bores you but is holding you back, then you need to know it is never too late to change what you do for a living.

This is where the Career and Business Choices aspect of your Life Path Number comes in.

As you will see in the listings in Part Three, the correct interpretation of the qualities of your Life Path Number will help you to choose a job, business or career that is perfectly suited to your strengths, and at the same time will also steer you towards achieving your life's highest purpose.

In other words, your Life Path Number can help you decide what you want to do for a living that will reward you not just financially, but emotionally and spiritually as well.

* * *

3. Relationship choices

Another area where the correct interpretation of your Life Path Number can transform the quality of your life is in your relationships. And I don't just mean your romantic relationships, but those with your friends, family and business colleagues as well.

The energy of your Life Path Number will be more compatible with some Life Path Numbers, and less compatible with others. You will therefore discover which numbers are best suited for love and growth, which are best suited for friendship, and which are best suited for a business partnership. You will also discover which numbers will throw up specific challenges in these three areas as well.

Part Two: The Self-Awareness System™

Well, that's great, I hear you think as you read this, but what if you have already skipped ahead to your listing and discovered that you are in a relationship with someone whose Life Path Number turns out to be what you might consider "incompatible" with yours?

If this is the case with you, then please read this next part very carefully. If you discover that your Life Path Number is not inherently "compatible" with your lover, friend or business partner, I do not for one second suggest that you end the relationship, cut off the friend, or sell out of your business. You need to know that these people are in your life right now for a very good reason.

As you will discover when you read Chapter 7 on working both the positive and negative aspects of your Life Path Number, your date of birth is the key to access certain strengths that you can use to make the best of your life… and it is also the key that shows you which weaknesses you must learn to rise above.

The reason for this is that human nature dictates that when things are going well, we tend to ease off the gas and freewheel. But when we are faced with obstacles or challenges to overcome, we dig deep and discover hidden qualities within us that drive us forward.

In life, it is only by overcoming challenges that we grow – because by doing so we access inner strengths that would otherwise have lain dormant and hidden.

In other words, it is only when the chips are down that we discover what we are truly capable of.

If life was all plain sailing, we wouldn't grow very much. Facing adversity and overcoming it is the one thing that makes us grow faster than anything else. That is why we all have to sail through storms from time to time, so that when we do finally reach the safety of harbour we are better sailors and therefore better-equipped to weather the storms on the next stage of our grand voyage of learning and discovery.

So your seemingly "incompatible" lover, friend or business partner may be exactly the person you need in your life right now to help you to first identity your own weaknesses (they do this by reflecting yours back at you), and then to find a way to rise above them – and, by doing so, help you to become a much better person.

Should you discover that your Life Path Number is not perfectly matched to that of your current partner, please consider that you may actually be in a very fortunate position because you have chosen a partner who will challenge you and help you grow. After all, growth is the main reason we are here. It is the reason our Self incarnated into human form in the first place.

So please understand that so-called "incompatible" relationships are one of the primary ways we manifest people into our lives who press our buttons and show us our faults reflected back at us so that we can learn and grow.

There are no "right" or "wrong" Life Path Number pairings. Just like everything else in our life, our relationship will always be perfect for where we are on our spiritual growth path. Sometimes it will be harmonious, if harmony and love are what we need. Other times it will be challenging, if challenges and growth are what we need.

Abuse is never OK... so get out now

There is an exception to this rule, just as there are exceptions to every rule. If you are in an abusive, violent or restrictive relationship, then that is an issue of Self-worth and you need to leave immediately.

You obviously have not valued your Self highly enough to break free until now, or else you would not have put up with it. If this is where you are right now as you read this, please contact a good therapist who can help you resolve this issue and break free.

I know it is not easy, and I know it hurts. But you need to be aware that the starting point of all personal and spiritual growth – whether it is through this Self-Awareness System™ or any other system – is Self-respect, which leads to Self-love.

You cannot hope to achieve any of your life's goals, let alone your life's highest purpose, if you do not learn to love your Self to the point where abuse of any kind is simply not acceptable.

However, if your relationship is not abusive, but is still not making you happy, you may find the solution to your troubles by reading your Life Path Number and that of your partner. By using the information in the listings in Part Three you may be able to identify your differences and then work out ways to resolve them peacefully and harmoniously.

* * *

4. Choices for optimum health

The Self-Awareness System™ also contains valuable information about the physiological strengths and weaknesses with which we have incarnated. We all have them, and it pays to know what they are.

Our Life Path Number will steer us to understand the physical ailments we may be prone to experience in your lifetime, as well as the emotional blockages that can cause so many of them... which allows us to take the necessary precautions to avoid them.

Make no mistake, the health risks differ widely depending on which Life Path Number we are born with.

The information contained in your Life Path Number listing will guide you towards making wise choices that support your physical health, so you can make sure you have the energy to do whatever it is that you want to do with your life.

It is important to remember that we are not spirits having a spiritual experience, we are spirits having a human experience. So while most of the guidance contained in your Life Path Number might be concerned with your emotional and spiritual growth, you must not forget to look after your physical body – your Self's "vehicle" – as well.

Health is an extraordinarily complicated subject that has spawned hundreds of thousands of books, diets, fads and fashions, each one seemingly contradicting the rest. One minute it's all about food combining, and the next protein-rich diets are all the rage. Then, before you can say "steamed chicken and vegetables", someone else goes on

Chapter 3: The secrets of your Birth Code

TV and claims the secret is to eat raw food – or match your diet to your blood type – and all will be well.

The bottom line is that although diet is important, our health is never guaranteed purely by the foods we eat because there is a large emotional and spiritual element that plays a very significant role in the level of physical health we are able to enjoy in our lifetime.

Many well-meaning doctors have buried their heads in the sand of traditional attitudes towards some of the "dis-eases" that have become the scourge of our modern society, including the Big C… cancer.

However, in the past 20 years or so, quantum physics has started to reveal how the thoughts in our head can directly influence the physiological structure of our cells, regardless of what we eat, and this may soon lead to a breakthrough in the way we treat many of today's most common ailments.

Doctors do not yet fully understand why our thoughts affect the structure of the cells in our body, but there is enough empirical evidence to suggest our thoughts play a life-changing – and even life-saving – role in determining our overall level of physical health.

Yes, a healthy diet is vital for maintaining the health of our cells. But there is a growing consensus that even more important than the quality of the food we eat is the quality of the thoughts we think.

Our health, like everything else in our life, depends on the choices we make. And this is where our Life Path Number comes in.

The listing for each number in Part Three will reveal your inherent physiological strengths and weaknesses and therefore guide you towards making the best possible choices for your body type so you can optimise the level of vibrancy and health you will experience.

It does this by showing you what ailments you are prone to experience, and it is then up to you to take whatever steps you deem necessary – whether they are emotional, spiritual or physiological – to prevent these dis-eases from happening to you.

* * *

Part Two: *The Self-Awareness System*™

5. Choices for children

If there are children in your life – even if they are nephews or nieces, or just children of close friends – the information contained in their Life Path Number will be extremely valuable in helping you to identify their inherent strengths and weaknesses from the earliest possible age, long before they are able to express them to you.

This will allow you to identify any negative behaviour patterns so you can nip them in the bud before they become a problem. It's far easier to correct the negatives associated with each Life Path when we are young than wait until we are adults and have to spend countless hours – and dollars – on therapy and personal growth seminars to correct them after they have become ingrained in our psyche.

Equally, the positive qualities of your child's Life Path Number will help you tailor your communication with them to bring out their best, so they will perform well at school and get a fantastic head start in life.

Furthermore, under each Life Path Number you will find a list of playtime activities to encourage them to develop their positive qualities and minimise their negative ones. And as they grow older, you can also use the information in the "Career Choices" section to help them decide what they are going to study at college or university, what apprenticeships might suit them, and what career path they may choose.

* * *

For this next chapter it's time to invoke the energy of "stability" that governs the number **4** to reveal why our Life Path Number is so accurate in helping us achieve stability and success in all areas of our life – because we will be working in perfect harmony with the four basic elements of Mother Mature.

Chapter 4:
Energy of the elements

4 is the number of stability

Every Life Path is perfectly designed to work with the stabilising qualities of the four elements that govern our world

In astrology, it is well-known that each of the 12 signs of the zodiac is related to one of the four elements of the physical world: fire, water, air and earth. The three fire signs (Aries, Leo and Sagittarius) are governed by the element of fire; the three water signs (Cancer, Scorpio and Pisces) are governed by water; the three air signs (Libra, Aquarius and Gemini) are governed by air; and the three earth signs (Capricorn, Taurus and Virgo) are governed by earth.

Fire signs are go-getters who take action (action is the quality of fire). Water signs are nurturers and romantics (emotion is the quality of water). Air signs are thinkers (thought is the quality of air). And earth signs are builders (stability is the quality of earth).

In the same way, each of the nine Life Path Numbers in the Self-Awareness System™ is governed by one of the four elements that make up our natural world – with the exception of **9**, which is governed by all four elements at once, for reasons that will become clear.

The element that governs each Life Path Number helps to illuminate the nature of people born under that number. It affects the choices they make, what their values are, how they interact with others and how they express themselves throughout their life.

It also determines whether the person will work primarily with "masculine energy" or "feminine energy". Fire and air elements are masculine in the sense of being focused on achievement, while water and earth are feminine in the sense of focusing on love and nurturing.

All of this is covered in depth in the Life Path listings in Part Three, when you will see how the energy of your governing element helps to shape the qualities of your Life Path Number.

For now, though, here is a quick overview of how it works.

* * *

Fire numbers: 1 and 5

Fire is the masculine element of <u>forceful action</u> (both creation and destruction), which is why mythology portrays the phoenix as rising from the ashes. Those people who are born under a fire Life Path Number (**1** and **5**) are primarily concerned with and creating new ideas and possibilities where previously none existed.

Fire people react to obstacles by taking massive action, so if you had a business you would want a fire person as your chief executive to go out and conquer the world.

Fire people make the best executives, entrepreneurs, military leaders and politicians.

♣ In playing cards, fire is the suit of clubs, and in tarot it is the suit of wands.

Water numbers: 2 and 6

Water is the feminine element of <u>emotion</u>, which is why the pull of the Moon affects our emotions just as much as it affects the ebb and flow of all the oceans on the planet. Those people who are born under a water Life Path Number (**2** and **6**) are primarily concerned with

Chapter 4: Energy of the elements

expressing their deepest feelings, achieving their goals through co-operating with others, and bringing harmony to the world.

Water people react to obstacles by consulting others and making sure everyone feels happy with the group decision, which is why if you were running a business you would want a water person as your human resources manager.

Water people make the best healers, counsellors, nurturers, diplomats and peacemakers.

♥ In playing cards, water is the suit of hearts, and in tarot it is the suit of cups.

Air numbers: 3 and 7

Air is the masculine element of <u>thought</u>, which is why people who are in their heads most of the time are said to be "ungrounded" and "building castles in the sky". Equally, those of us who are born with an air Life Path Number (**3** and **7**) are primarily concerned with intellectual pursuits, creating ideas and solving the world's problems by dreaming up innovative solutions.

Air people react to obstacles by sitting down and thinking of all the possible solutions, which is why if you had a business you would want an air person as your strategist.

Air people also make the best marketing managers because of their strong creative flair, and they are excellent inventors, sales people, researchers, designers, entertainers, artists and authors.

♠ In playing cards, air is the suit of spades, and in tarot it is the suit of swords.

Earth numbers: 4 and 8

Earth is the feminine element of <u>stability</u>, and those who work with its energy tend to be grounded, reliable and focused on the real world as it is, rather than as it could or should be. People born under an earth Life Path Number (**4** and **8**) are concerned with building a strong foundation and nurturing a loving environment for themselves and their loved ones, as well as using their wealth to help others who are less fortunate.

Earth people seldom meet too many obstacles because they plan ahead and have a great eye for detail, which is why if you had a business you would want one as your general manager.

They also make the best accountants, financial controllers, bankers, engineers, builders, social workers and charity directors.

♦ In playing cards, earth is the suit of diamonds, and in tarot it is the suit of pentacles.

* * *

Out of the nine possible Life Path Numbers, there are two fire numbers, two water numbers, two air numbers and two earth numbers.

The number **9** contains the energy of all four elements, because this is the pinnacle of a growth cycle where all the lessons of the previous eight Life Paths are integrated before starting again at the beginning of a new cycle.

As you will see from the Elemental Table below, these natural elements appear not in some random pattern but in two perfectly ordered cycles that reflect the qualities of the nine numbers as they progress from the human to the divine.

The first cycle of four numbers, from **1** to **4**, concerns the inner work we do as part of our personal growth. The cycle then repeats, from **5** to **8**, only this time the work we do is more spiritual and concerns the way we relate to others as we climb higher up the mountain on our life's journey towards our highest goal of service to others.

The first 'human' cycle
1 is the number of fire (the spark of creation)
2 is the number of water (the outpouring of feelings)
3 is the number of air (understanding the world we live in)
4 is the number of earth (learning to master our material world)

The second 'divine' cycle:
5 is fire again (this time as an agent of change)
6 is water again (this time to show others their true loving nature)
7 is air again (this time the expression of ideas to help others)
8 is earth again (this time creating abundance for all)

9 represents the number of wisdom and integration of the two cycles, so it is governed by all four elements at once.

This Elemental Table puts all of this information together, along with each Life Path's astrological influence. Notice how the elements rotate through the two cycles, and how **9** has an equal balance of all the four elements of fire, water, air and earth:

THE ELEMENTAL LIFE PATH CYCLE

1. The Leader. Element: Fire (forceful)
This is the spark of creation. The focus of this Life Path is to take action on our original ideas so that we can inspire and lead others to go after their goals. (Masculine, ruled by the Sun.)

2. The Intuitive. Element: Water (emotional)
This is the number of co-operation and awareness. The focus of this potentially most compassionate of Life Paths is on spreading peace and harmony. (Feminine, ruled by the Moon.)

3. The Creative. Element: Air (thoughtful)
This is the number of expression. The focus is on speaking out to motivate others to grow. (Masculine, ruled by Jupiter.)

4. The Builder. Element: Earth (practical)
This is the number of stability. The focus is on creating security and helping others do the same. (Feminine, ruled by Uranus.)

5. The Rebel. Element: Fire (forceful)
This is the number of change. The focus is on taking action to improve the world. (Masculine, ruled by Mercury.)

6. The Visionary. Element: Water (emotional)
This is the number of compassion. The focus is on bringing love and beauty into the world. (Feminine, ruled by Venus.)

7. The Seeker. Element: Air (thoughtful)
This is the number of knowledge. The focus is on seeking truth and sharing it with others. (Masculine, ruled by Neptune.)

8. The Achiever. Element: Earth (practical)
This is the number of wealth and power. The focus is on creating abundance for all. (Feminine, ruled by Saturn.)

9. The Teacher. Elements: All four of them (balanced)
This is the number of completion. The focus is on integrating all we have learned so we can teach our valuable insights to others. (Balance of masculine and feminine, ruled by Mars.)

* * *

This next chapter is governed by the "change" energy of **5**, so it's time to shift gears as we move from the physical arena of personal growth to the metaphysical arena of spiritual growth.

Chapter 5:
Growing with the Spiritual Cycle

5 is the number of change

*Get ready for a radical shift as we cast off our mortal fears
and embrace the divine nature of our true Self*

If you look closely at the tables in the two previous chapters – the table of the highest purpose of each Life Path Number in Chapter 3 and the table that shows you the cycle of the four governing elements for each Life Path Number in Chapter 4 – you will start to see a remarkable pattern emerge.

The growth challenges associated with each Life Path Number are not just randomly arranged from **1** to **9**. They form an eight-stage "Spiritual Growth Cycle" that corresponds to Buddhism's eight-stage path to enlightenment, followed by the ninth stage (Life Path **9**) when we integrate all we have learned before going back to the beginning of another nine-step Spiritual Growth Cycle to start the process again.

My understanding of the Spiritual Growth Cycle within the nine Life Path Numbers came to me one evening when I was working on the two tables in Chapters 3 and 4 and I started to see a pattern emerge that I believe no one has written about before – or if they have, it hasn't been widely publicised.

I was tired and my eyes were starting to defocus (a great way to see clairvoyantly, by the way) when I suddenly noticed that the highest purpose of one Life Path Number leads directly to the highest purpose of the next one, and so on – all the way up the path to the summit (Life Path Number **9**), where we real-eyes our true purpose here on earth, which is to know ourselves as pure spirits, pure love and purely evolved beings, so the Source can know itself too.

I also noticed the cycle is divided into three distinct parts:

1. The first four Life Path Numbers are primarily concerned with our **personal growth** (ie, Self-confidence) and are governed in turn by the elements of fire, water, air and earth.

2. The second four Life Path Numbers are concerned with our **spiritual growth** (ie, Self-love) and are also governed in turn by the elements of fire, water, air and earth.

3. The final Life Path Number **9**, which is governed by all four of the elements at once, is when we **integrate all the lessons** we have learned about our physical world (numbers **1** to **4**) with the lessons of the metaphysical world (numbers **5** to **8**) and **live in integrity as a role model for others.**

(Notice how the words "integrate" and "integrity" have a perfect symbiosis with each other. And they also both happen to have nine letters. A coincidence? You decide for your Self.)

* * *

Before we look in detail at each stage of the Spiritual Growth Cycle, it is worth noting that we will always live each Life Path Number many times – over many lifetimes – because there is simply too much growth inherent in each number for our Self to accomplish it all in just one incarnation.

We also do not always live each Life Path in order, going from **1** to **2** to **3** and so on. We may repeat one Life Path several times, and we may jump forwards and backwards to work on issues pertaining to other Life Paths. However, a new soul will always incarnate for its first lifetime as a **1**, because like everything else it begins at the beginning.

Chapter 5: Growing with the Spiritual Cycle

And then – as a three-dimensional Self – we will work through all the nine numbers as many times as we want each time we incarnate.

Eventually, after many lifetimes, the end result is always the same: namely, that by working through the issues of all the Life Paths, in whatever order we choose and however many times we choose, we fulfill our sole (soul) purpose and become pure conscious love.

* * *

*(Note: Our last lifetime will not necessarily be while we are working with the completion energy of **9**. We work with the energy of all the Life Paths many times, gaining new distinctions each time. Then, when we feel we have reached the point where we understand everything there is to know about what it means to be pure love, with no fear, we can return home to the Source. Or we may decide to incarnate again as a Leader (**1**), or a Creative (**3**), for example, to help teach our lessons to others before we return home. And we can do this as many times as we wish.)*

* * *

THE NINE STAGES OF THE SPIRITUAL CYCLE

Stage 1 (fire)

Our Spiritual Growth Cycle starts with the powerful creative spark of the Life Path Number **1** (the Leader), which is governed by the forceful and masculine element of fire (action) and is concerned with the bold and pioneering expression of new and original ideas (**1** is the number of creation).

Our soul is incarnating for the first time, and so it starts its journey by taking action and then gauging the results of that action.

Just as the universe started with a Big Bang, we begin our own experience of the physical world by unleashing an explosive barrage of creativity and inventiveness.

♣ The mantra of Life Path Number **1** is: "Actions speak louder than words."

Stage 2 (water)

Our spiritual growth continues with Life Path Number **2** (the Intuitive), which is governed by the feminine element of water (emotion) and is concerned with knowing ourselves through our emotional interaction with others (**2** is the number of co-operation).

Although spiritually we are whole and complete, we can only ever know ourselves by interacting with others, because their strengths and weaknesses reflect our own strengths and weaknesses back to us.

This is why those of us who are working with the energy of **2** seek to improve our own lives, and the lives of others, through co-operation and by finding common ground on which we can all flourish and grow.

♥ The mantra of Life Path Number **2** is: "The person who needs my love the most is me."

Stage 3 (air)

Now we have made contact, the next step is Life Path Number **3** (the Creative), which is governed by the masculine element of air (thought) and is concerned with accumulating knowledge and then sharing what we know (**3** is the number of expression).

Whereas the fire energy of Life Path Number **1** was action, and the water energy of Life Path Number **2** was interaction, the air energy of Life Path Number **3** drives us to contemplate the nature of the world we live in so we can then communicate what we have learned to help others on their journey.

♠ The mantra of Life Path Number **3** is: "I speak freely and confidently from my heart."

Stage 4 (earth)

We have gone out into the world (**1**), we have connected with other people (**2**) and we have studied the nature of the human condition (**3**) so that we have a clear understanding of how the physical world works and our place in it.

Now we come to Life Path Number **4** (the Builder), which is governed by the feminine element of earth (practicality) and involves

Chapter 5: Growing with the Spiritual Cycle

building a secure life for ourselves and others before moving on to the spiritual stage of the cycle (**4** is the number of stability).

In this stage we get ready to leave our physical concerns behind and enter the realm of the metaphysical.

♦ The mantra of Life Path **4** is: "Build for tomorrow, but take the time to enjoy today."

Stage 5 (fire)

The cycle reaches the halfway point and takes a sudden turn with Life Path Number **5** (the Rebel), which reverts back to the masculine element of fire (action)... because it is time for us to shake things up.

This Life Path is concerned with rebelling against accepted norms, questioning the status quo, freeing our minds and exploring the world to find new answers (**5** is the number of change).

Curiosity, adventure and restlessness are the hallmarks of the **5**, who knows that to be a change-agent for the world they must first be prepared to change themselves.

♣ The mantra of Life Path Number **5** is: "True freedom comes from within."

Stage 6 (water)

With Life Path Number **6** (the Visionary) we begin working with the one force that unites us and binds us all together... love.

The feminine element of this number is water (emotion), but now instead of emotion being the way we interact with others, as in Life Path **2**, it is the light with which we shine our love out into the world to show others their spiritual perfection (**6** is the number of beauty).

This is the number of the idealistic torch-bearer who holds a lofty vision of all humanity living together in love and peace. When others are fighting over money and power, the **6** steps in and shows us that if we just managed to stop squabbling for a moment we would notice that we are all the same and we are all made of the same stuff... love.

♥ The mantra of Life Path Number **6** is: "We are all perfect, and everything happens perfectly."

Stage 7 (air)

Life Path Number **7** (the Seeker) is governed by the masculine element of air (thought) because this is the path in which we discover the answers to all the questions that have been mystifying us about the nature of who we are and why we are here (**7** is the number of truth).

Thought follows love, because from a spiritual growth perspective thought without love is utterly worthless. That is why we have to live Life Path **6** at least once before we arrive at Life Path **7**, because our heart must be open before we can solve the riddle of human existence – namely, that we are all connected at an energetic level.

The "knowledge" of the **7** Life Path is not factual knowledge but spiritual knowledge. It is concerned with understanding the truth about the human condition and how we can rise above fear to live in bliss.

♠ The mantra of the Life Path Number **7** is: "The truth will set us free."

Stage 8 (earth)

Life Path Number **8** (the Achiever) is concerned with amassing great wealth and influence. Like the **4**, this Life Path is governed by the feminine element of earth (practicality) and is focused on abundance (**8** is the number of power, and is also the number of infinity).

If we had arrived at this Life Path before we had first understood the power of love (**6**) and discovered the truth that we are all one (**7**), we may well have been seduced by the power that wealth bestows.

It doesn't take much to real-eyes that the world is full of people who have done exactly this. Which is why more than ever we need more teachers and guides to show the world the truth of why we are here, and what we came here to do.

To complete this phase of our Spiritual Growth Cycle we must first learn the lessons of **6** and **7** so that we grow to understand that abundance is meant to be shared, not hoarded.

♦ The mantra of Life Path Number **8** is: "We are all in this together and there is more than enough to go around."

Stage 9 (all four elements)
Finally, after cycling through the four elements twice – first to master the physical world and second to master the metaphysical world – we arrive at Life Path Number **9** (the Teacher), which is masculine and governed by all the elements at once (**9** is the number of wisdom).

The purpose of this Life Path is to integrate the lessons of all the previous eight Life Paths and teach them to the world. After all, it is only by living with integrity and showing others the way to spiritual bliss (as Jesus, Muhammad, Buddha and all the great avatars have done) that we can attain spiritual perfection ourselves and come to know ourselves as pure, divine love.

☼ The mantra of Life Path Number **9** is: "Love is all there is."

* * *

The table below puts it all together. Note how each number possesses an energy that is diametrically opposed to that of the one that precedes it. The feminine and intuitive **2** is the polar opposite of the masculine and ambitious **1**. The masculine and outgoing **3** is the opposite of the feminine **2**. The feminine and supportive **4** is the opposite of the masculine **3**. And so on.

THE SPIRITUAL GROWTH CYCLE

STAGE 1: PERSONAL GROWTH (physical)

1. The Leader
Element: Fire (forceful, masculine).
Qualities: Inventive, pioneering and original.
Stage in the cycle: Our spiritual growth path starts with an explosive spark of creation when we first express our Self.
Highest purpose: To lead from the front.

2. The Intuitive
Element: Water (emotional, feminine).
Qualities: Empathetic, nurturing and compassionate.
Stage in the cycle: We begin to know our Self by the way we relate to others.
Highest purpose: To bring people together in peace and love.

3. The Creative
Element: Air (thoughtful, masculine).
Qualities: Sensitive, artistic and expressive.
Stage in the cycle: We learn more about our Self by expressing our innermost thoughts and feelings.
Highest purpose: To use our creative talents to motivate others to be the best they can be.

4. The Builder
Element: Earth (practical, feminine).
Qualities: Hard-working, loyal and humanitarian.
Stage in the cycle: We real-eyes that to progress any further on our growth path we must have a strong foundation.
Highest purpose: To build a stable foundation for our Self, and to help others less fortunate than us do the same.

STAGE 2: SPIRITUAL GROWTH (metaphysical)

5. The Rebel
Element: Fire (forceful, masculine).
Qualities: Adventurous, inquisitive and restless.
Stage in the cycle: We turn everything inside out and upside down in search of a higher truth and a better way.
Highest purpose: To set people free from their limiting beliefs and help them escape from the Fear Matrix.

6. The Visionary
Element: Water (emotional, feminine).
Qualities: Idealistic, loving and supportive.
Stage in the cycle: We learn how to live in love… and teach others how to do the same.
Highest purpose: To hold the vision of a beautiful, loving world.

7. The Seeker
Element: Air (thoughtful, masculine).
Qualities: Analytical, intelligent and insightful.
Stage in the cycle: Our role is to discover, absorb and interpret divine wisdom.
Highest purpose: To learn the "Big Truths" about the spiritual nature of the human condition and share them with others.

8. The Achiever
Element: Earth (practical, feminine).
Qualities: Resourceful, single-minded and ambitious.
Stage in the cycle: We learn that there is more than enough to go round for everyone.
Highest purpose: To create abundance and share it with others.

STAGE 3: ENLIGHTENMENT (physical and metaphysical merge)

9. The Teacher
Elements: All four of them (integrated, masculine).
Qualities: Wise, evolved and inspirational.
Stage in the cycle: We have finished learning. Now it is time to bring our light to the world and teach what we know.
Highest purpose: To be a role model for others by standing up for what is right and teaching by example.

* * *

Part Two: The Self-Awareness System™

I'm sure by now you are well on your way to real-eyesing that you are much MUCH more than a descendant of apes with an opposable thumb, living on a rock that's whirring through "space" while you struggle to make a living and wonder why everyone you know seems to have more Instagram followers than you do.

So in this next chapter let's invoke the beautiful "pure love" energy of **6** to show you what your purpose truly is – and, just as importantly, how you can achieve it in this lifetime.

Chapter 6:
Revolving with the Nine-Year Cycles

6 is the number of beauty

*Right from the moment we are born we are guided
on our sacred journey back to love*

Life is change. When something is alive, it never stops changing. Or growing. And the way life changes and grows is never in a straight line. Just like Mother Nature, it revolves and evolves in a series of circular cycles from birth to death and back to birth again.

All life is governed by circular cycles, including the cycle of the Earth's daily rotation from dawn to dusk and back to dawn again; the cycle of the four seasons as the Earth orbits around the Sun; and the much longer cycle of birth, death and rebirth – of plants, animals, humans, and even the trillions of stars and the planets in the universe.

In the previous chapter we saw how our Spiritual Growth Cycle repeats over the course of our many lifetimes. But there is another kind of cycle that operates throughout our current lifetime. It's called the Nine-Year Cycle, and its sole (soul) purpose is to help us grow towards our goal of loving our Self in this incarnation.

As you read about the Nine-Year Cycles in this chapter, you will feel – even if you are receiving this information for the first time – that something about it resonates with a sense of familiarity. This is because when you look back on your life later in this chapter you will notice how it has have evolved in a similarly cyclical way. It's amazing when you see how it works.

* * *

The Nine-Year Cycles

To love our Self, which is the goal of all personal and spiritual growth because it leads to our highest purpose, we must face a number of challenges. And we must face them in a specific order, one after another, like peeling the layers off an onion.

Just as it is impossible to peel the second layer off the onion until we have removed the first layer, it is also not possible for us to fully understand the challenges of the second year of our Nine-Year Cycles until we have learned the lessons of the first year, and so on.

Each challenge we must face follows on from the previous one, as we peel away all the layers in turn.

In numerology, the "onion" has nine layers, one for each of the nine numbers as we evolve through a series of Nine-Year Cycles. And because we cannot hope to master a skill by doing it only once, we repeat these cycles, learning new lessons and making new distinctions for each of the nine stages as we return to them over and over again.

At the end of the ninth year, we begin again in the first year of a new Nine-Year Cycle and work through the issues of each number in order, from **1** to **9**, for a second time – only we have grown, so this time we are able to go deeper into the issues governed by the energy of each of the nine numbers.

How the cycles work

– The 1st year represents new beginnings. It is governed by the energy of fire, which is the element of forceful action. It is a time of creativity, new ideas, making plans and getting the ball rolling. This is the year for starting something new, or maybe starting over... by making changes that we have been wanting to make for a long time.

Chapter 6: Revolving with the Nine-Year Cycles

– The 2nd year represents interaction with others. It is imbued with the energy of the element of water, which governs emotion. This is when we take all our creativity and new ideas from the first year and run them by other people, enlist their help and start to put our ideas into action, whether it is a new project, a new job, a new business or a new relationship.

– The 3rd year represents communicating our ideas. It is governed by the element of air (thought) and is a time of Self-expression when we bring our new ideas out into the world. This is when new projects take shape, new jobs or businesses start to bring us success, and new relationships blossom.

– The 4th year represents putting down roots. It resonates with the energy of the element of earth, which governs materialism and practical concerns. This is the year when our new projects bear fruit and we start to reap the material rewards of business projects and the emotional rewards of a well-established relationship.

– The 5th year represents change and new directions. This year marks a return to the element of fire, which denotes forceful action. Now is the time to make changes to our business, take our job or career to another level (or branch out in a different direction), and refresh our relationship. This is the mid-point of the cycle when the mantra is "out with the old and in with the new" to prepare us for the radical changes of the next four years.

– The 6th year represents emotional growth. This year, like the second year in the cycle, is once again governed by the energy of emotion (water), and it is a time when we realign our priorities by letting go of the materialistic concerns of the fourth year and focusing our attention on love. This is when we bring a new level of passion to our business or work life and nurture our home life.

Part Two: The Self-Awareness System™

— The 7th year represents a quantum leap in our knowledge. It marks a return to the element of air (thought), only this time our thoughts are turned inwards towards Self-discovery and personal awareness. In our love life, communication is vital in this year, which is why it is renowned for marking the end-point of so many relationships (the "seven-year itch"). Following on from our emotional growth in year six, the knowledge we gain here is meant to be shared with our partner, as well as with the world.

— The 8th year represents reaping the rewards for all our efforts. This is the year of wealth and power, marked by a return to the element of earth. Because of our lessons in years six and seven, the abundance we enjoy in this year is not just for us and our loved ones, as in year four, but is to be shared with others. This is the peak of the cycle.

— The 9th year represents completion when we consolidate all we have learned and achieved and get ready to start all over again on a new project. This year is governed by the energy of all four elements because it is a time for us to tie up all the loose ends in as many areas of our life as we can and prepare for the start of the next cycle.

* * *

Although it may sound as though this process is circular, it is anything but. We do not go round and round chasing our tails through cycle after cycle. Instead, we evolve upwards with each cycle, returning to the same issues time after time every nine years, but never to the same place… because we have evolved further up our spiral path.

So although the lessons of each year may be repeated throughout the cycle, they are never the same lesson at the same level. They become more and more advanced as our lives progress in an upward spiral of Nine-Year Cycles.

* * *

Chapter 6: Revolving with the Nine-Year Cycles

If you were to look down on this process in two dimensions, it would look like this:

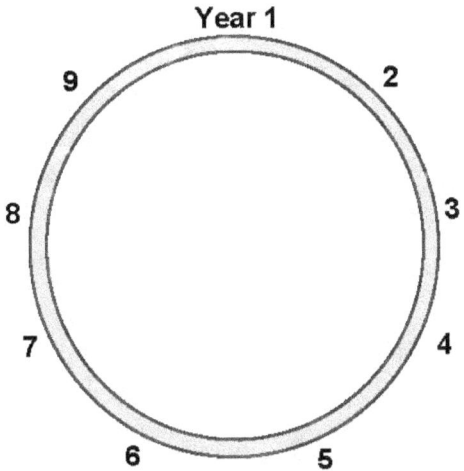

But this is actually what is happening:

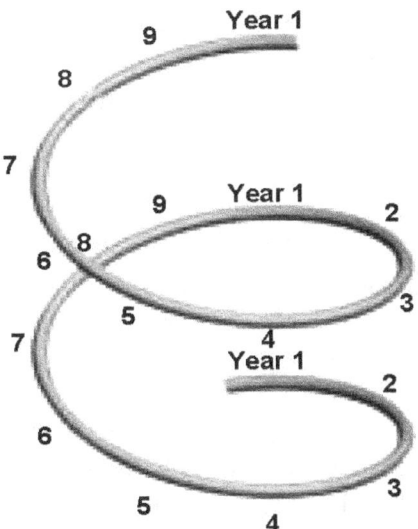

Each year is governed by the energy of the number of the year. So in the first year of each cycle we will work with the energy of **1** (creation), then in the second year we will work with the energy of **2** (co-operation with others), and so on up until the ninth year when we will work with the energy of completion, before starting all over again.

In any given year, we won't work solely with the energy of that year to the exclusion of all other lessons. We are all learning multiple lessons all the time. The cycle simply means that in each year there will be one primary focus – and therefore one primary lesson for us to learn – which relates to the energy of the number of the year.

* * *

Many of us will go through between seven and 10 Nine-Year Cycles in our lifetime, although for some it will be a lot less. Some Selfs incarnate for a very short time and with a very specific purpose.

It doesn't matter how long we live. We will always work through the issues our Self incarnated to work through. In some lives, this might take many cycles, while in others it might take only a cycle or two, or a year or two, or perhaps even less. The length of our life is always the length it is meant to be, as designed by our Self before we incarnated.

From the perspective of the Source, every lifetime, no matter how short or how long, is always perfect. Every time. No exceptions.

* * *

The reason these Nine-Year Cycles are so important is because they are the key to understanding the two fundamental lessons of life:

Lesson 1: Grow with the flow

Life is ever-changing. It has to be, or we wouldn't grow… and growth is why we are here. And the quickest way for us to grow is to stop resisting change and instead relax into the flow of life.

To "grow with the flow", so to speak.

Chapter 6: Revolving with the Nine-Year Cycles

These Nine-Year Cycles are part of the divine wisdom of spirit that exists in all of us. They are specifically designed to guide us to our life's highest purpose. The more we work with them and go with the flow of life, the easier and happier our life becomes. Equally, the more we resist the changes they bring and try and go in a different direction, the more our lives will feel like an upstream struggle.

Until we learn to jettison our ego, we will often resist the change of the cycles because our arrogant ego thinks that it knows more about what we need than our Self does. So when the cyclical changes come, we tend to fight them and kick and scream because life isn't giving us what our ego thinks we want.

As long as we remain in our heads, rather than in our hearts, we may try to swim against the current, resisting any change that doesn't conform to our ego's view of how our life should be.

Sometimes we even get out of the river altogether in the hope of finding a better river that will take us in the direction our ego thinks we want to go. So we change our hair, our clothes, our job, our relationship, even the country where we live, only to discover that we are right back in the same river, at exactly the same place, clinging on for dear life to exactly the same part of the river bank.

And then we turn to our friends, who are right there next to us clinging on for dear life as well, and say to them: "Why is life so hard? Why is it such a struggle?" They can't tell us, of course, because they are too busy with their own struggle. And our parents are no help. They wear their struggle like a badge of honour that is worthy of emulating, because they have struggled all their lives. They tell us things like: "Young people these days don't know how easy they have got it." (I'm sure you have heard that one before!)

If only we could real-eyes that all we have to do is let go of the bank (which is our ego, and therefore our fear) and kick out into the middle of the river, where it flows fastest… and relax into our lives.

The only struggle, and therefore the only pain, comes from resisting the flow of our life. The moment we let go of our ego's need to feel that it is in control, we can relax into life and finally be happy.

We don't have to do anything other than let go. The stream will carry us exactly where we are meant to go, because it's our stream. We designed it. Our Self created our life for us before we were even born, and all we have to do is live it.

So please, right now, let go. Let go of your fears. And just be.

* * *

This letting go is what the religions call "surrendering our will to God". The trouble with that phrase, though, is that it implies it is not OUR will. But it is. It's all us. Everything is us. Even "God" is us, as we have already seen.

That's why instead of the phrase "surrendering our will", which is laced with the energy of capitulation and defeat, I prefer "relaxing into the flow of life".

One implies we are bloodied and beaten, waving a white flag in the face of an overpowering enemy, while the other conjures an image of us lying back on an airbed, hands laced behind our head as we drift blissfully along a sparkling stream in the sunshine.

I know letting go is not always as easy as it sounds. Sometimes we resist change because we want things to stay the same, especially when we are having fun and we want the "good times" to last forever. But when you start to work in harmony with the energy of the Nine-Year Cycles, you won't feel the need to cling on to the good times… because they are all good times.

What you used to regard as "bad times" – when life throws up challenges on your path such as sickness, loss or lack – you will see as "growth times" because you know these events are not unwelcome obstacles to be overcome, they are wonderful opportunities for you to learn and grow. Hence the popular expression: "It's all good."

It is indeed all good.

Because it's all "God".

* * *

Chapter 6: Revolving with the Nine-Year Cycles

Hang on! What about when 'shit happens'?

You're asking: "What about when you are suffering physical or emotional pain? Surely these times aren't 'good' as well?"

From your ego's perspective, no they're not. But from your Self's perspective, which is the only perspective that counts, sometimes you need to feel pain before you see the lesson it contains ... like a delicious sweet hidden inside an ugly wrapper.

Rest assured, there is as much pleasure in growth as there is in the reward that comes from the growth, because the good times you will experience on the other side of the lesson will be 10 times better than anything that has come before.

Everything is always perfect. You are always exactly where you are meant to be, learning exactly what you are meant to be learning.

You can't not be. The universe is flawless.

When you start living your life from your Self's perspective, you will find it easy to work with the Nine-Year Cycles, learning what you are meant to learn when you are meant to learn it, one step at a time, onwards and upwards, laughing and growing towards the light.

* * *

Lesson 2: Live in the moment

I am sure you have heard about "The Power of Now", and if you haven't already read Eckhart Tolle's wonderful best-selling book of the same name, I highly recommend it.

There are two reasons why living in the present moment is so important. The first is because NOW is where all our power is. And by "power", I mean our ability to take the necessary action to make our life the way we want it to be.

Personal power is not just knowledge. All the knowledge in the world is worthless unless we use it. That's why personal power is not just knowing what to do. It's doing it.

Personal power can best be described as our ability and our willingness to take action. And the only place we can ever take action is right here and right now… in the present moment.

Imagine trying to take action based on the energy of the fourth year of a cycle when you are in the second year. If the action you take is massive enough, you might enjoy some success. But it will be fleeting and limited compared with the success that you would achieve if you worked with the flow of the Nine-Year Cycle, rather than against it.

When you take the action you are meant to take in your second year, for example, all the energy of the Source will rush up to support you and you are therefore more likely to achieve instant and massive success, helping you move further up your spiral towards your bliss.

All power exists in the present moment. The past is gone and therefore holds no power for you, other than as lessons learned. The future hasn't arrived yet and therefore holds no power for you either, other than as a motivational force to pull you forward. But the present moment is eternal – it never ends – and therefore it contains all the power of the universe.

* * *

The second reason why living in the moment is so important is because it is only by being "fully present" that we are able to learn all the lessons our Self wants us to learn that are contained in each year of the Nine-Year Cycles.

There is no point being in the second year of a cycle, say, and trying to "hurry up our life" by jumping ahead to the third year, or beyond. We would be completely unprepared, and therefore would likely fall flat on our face before limping back to where we were.

I see people do this all the time. (I used to do it all the time, until I learned that there is a proper process for all things.) So instead of trapping our Self in an endless cycle of skipping forward and falling back to do what we were meant to do in the first place, it is much better to focus all our attention on what is happening to us right now... and take action based on our own particular "now".

By doing this, we will move up our growth spiral much more easily because now we are working with our Self – and therefore with Source energy – rather than fighting against it.

I am not saying don't plan for the future. Setting clear goals is essential for getting where you want to go. I am saying that once you have planned your path ("remembered your path" would be a more accurate description), you need to concentrate all your courage and all your energy on taking the next step along it.

Once you know where you want to go, you must put all your attention in the present moment – because that is where all your power, all your bravery and all your determination is found.

Dan Millman's marvellous book *No Ordinary Moments* is worth a read because it perfectly describes this process of living in the moment. What Dan says is that when we focus all our attention on what we are doing, we invoke the "power of now" and imbue every action we take with the unstoppable force of divine energy.

* * *

Our four most important Nine-Year Cycles

The first four Nine-Year Cycles of our life, when we are children and young adults, are by far the most eventful and significant because they take us through our rapid growth from birth to full adulthood.

They are the Cycle of Dependence (from birth to age 8); the Cycle of Independence (9-17), which takes us to adulthood at 18; the Cycle of Confidence (18–26), which takes us to 27, when our personality is fully developed; and the Cycle of Maturity (27-35), which culminates when we reach our full emotional maturity at the age of 36.

(Note that the first Supplementary Birth Number in our Birth Code operates during our first two Nine-Year Cycles, and our second Supplementary Birth Number operates during our second two Nine-Year Cycles.)

Clearly, not everyone's life experience will conform exactly to these patterns, especially in poor countries where issues of starvation and conflict cause children to grow up more quickly. But when we look at the Nine-Year Cycles through the prism of our emotional development towards Self-love – which is what really counts, and what this sixth chapter is all about (**6** is the number of love, as well as the number of beauty) – then the patterns work perfectly.

So while not all children will hit puberty at exactly the same age, they will all face the same emotional challenges during their Cycle of Independence. And while not everyone buys a home or gets married at 27, this is when we all make a quantum leap in the way we perceive the world and our place in it – if not by settling down, then by taking a big decision about how our life is going to unfold. (For example, I emigrated from the UK to live in Australia when I was 27.)

The "27 club"

The age of 27 has achieved a well-publicised notoriety because of the commonly named "27 club" of talented artists who have died at this age. These include Kurt Cobain, Jimi Hendrix, Janis Joplin, Jim Morrison, Brian Jones, Alan Wilson and Amy Winehouse.

All of these talented musicians share one common quality: they all failed to integrate their outstanding talents into their own personal visions of who they were, which led to Self-destructive behaviour and, ultimately, life-ending Self-abuse.

The portal between a carefree youth and a responsible adult, through which we must all pass, occurs around the age of 27. And if we have failed to develop both our Self-worth and a healthy awareness of the Law of Cause and Effect, this can be a time of abrupt and premature crisis... as happened with all these musical legends.

* * *

Let's look at the first two Nine-Year Cycles in detail to illustrate how they work, because they are by far the most eventful cycles of our life. We will then briefly discuss the second two Nine-Year Cycles that take us to full emotional maturity at the age of 36.

If you are a parent, these first two Nine-Year Cycles will be invaluable in helping you to steer your child through their often challenging early years.

(Important note: When you are calculating where you or your children are on your Nine-Year Cycles, be aware that the years of our cycles are not calendar years beginning on January 1st. Each year of each cycle begins on our birthday and runs through to our next birthday.)

CYCLE 1: THE CYCLE OF DEPENDENCE

Year 1 (age 0): The energy of "Creation"

The cycle starts when we are born, so our first year is governed by the fire energy of **1**, which is the start of it all.

We enter the world as pure, perfect little bundles of love. We are pregnant with possibility and potential, and the energy of **1** endows us with the drive and creativity to make our mark.

We are not yet capable of expressing what we are feeling, or communicating in any meaningful way, as we focus purely on the primal instinct of survival. But we are able to open our eyes, take in our surroundings and real-eyes where we are.

After the extraordinary accomplishment of fertilisation (against odds of 3 million sperm to one) and the truly miraculous achievement of childbirth, we have – at long last – made it into the world.

We are here. We are alive. And we are on fire.

Year 2 (age 1): The energy of "Co-operation"

After our first birthday, we begin working with the emotional (water) energy of **2** as we start to interact with the people around us – mostly our parents. This is when we speak for the very first time and start to understand how we feel as an individual, rather than just a screaming bundle of helpless neediness.

It is also when our ego starts to form and we begin the long process of getting to know who we are by the way others relate to us.

Year 3 (age 2): The energy of "Expression"

In our third year, aged two, our mind (this is an air number) is developing rapidly as we start to express ourselves through the energy of **3**, which governs communication and expression.

Children in the third year of their life, aged two, often fight with their parents for the first time because they want to communicate how they feel but are not yet able to put words to their swirling thoughts and feelings. Their anger is born out of frustration, and it can be a very challenging time for both children and parents.

As the year progresses, though, we become more adept at speaking and are therefore able to better express not just what we want or need, but how we feel.

Year 4 (age 3): The energy of "Stability"

In our fourth year, aged three, we can communicate more effectively so we start to focus on trying to control our world and make ourselves the centre of it. The earth energy of **4** is when we put down roots, and for a three-year-old toddler this takes the form of growing a sense of identity for the first time.

This is the year when our personality takes shape. Suddenly we want to do everything for ourselves and can't be taught or shown anything. It's a time of trial and error (mostly error) as we begin to test our boundaries and start the long process of building the foundation of our identity.

Year 5 (age 4): The energy of "Change"

If you have children, you will know how challenging this fire stage of the cycle is. In our fifth year, aged four, we start to rebel against our parents as we question everything they say and do and disagree with almost all of it. This is the rebellious "change" energy of **5 in action**, which dictates that we stop blindly accepting the world as it is and start trying to impose our will power to change it and create it the way we want it to be.

Year 6 (age 5): The energy of "Beauty"

Our sixth year, aged five, is when we first start to understand the nature of love. The water energy of **6** allows us to make connections (with pets, friends and even our "grumpy old parents") based on emotions other than neediness, as we start to real-eyes that love is something we feel and express, not just a comfort blanket.

Until now "love" has been a word that we use because we have imitated our parents and we see it brings pleasure when we tell people close to us that we "love them". Now we start to understand what the word really means.

Year 7 (age 6): The energy of "Truth"

Now we are six, and we want to know how the world works. Parents know this as the age of "Why?", because that is the only word that ever seems to come out of their six-year-old's mouth.

The air (thought) energy of **7** fills them with curiosity, and if a parent manages to get through this year without saying "because I said so" they deserve a medal.

This is also the age in many countries when a child enters Year 1 in the formal education system and begins to feed their mind.

Year 8 (age 7): The energy of "Power"

In our eighth year, aged seven, we want to do our own thing and be our own boss. The earth energy of **8** means the focus now is on power and independence, which manifest as our initial childish attempts to break away from our complete dependence on our parents.

Normally this plays out in our fantasy world, but occasionally this is when we rebel against our parents, or even run away from home, because we want to discover the world for ourselves.

In less extreme examples of attempting to exert our nascent power as individuals, this is when we might build our first tree house or put a "do not enter" sign on our bedroom door in an attempt to take some semblance of control over our young life.

Year 9 (age 8): **The energy of "Wisdom"**

The final year of our first cycle, aged 8, is when children in many countries enter their first year of school, as opposed to pre-school or kindergarten. And in countries where children enter school earlier, this is when they first start to develop a strong sense of their individuality.

This year marks the end of the Cycle of Dependence as we begin to experience life out there in the world as an independent person, as opposed to life at home as a dependent extension of our parents.

* * *

CYCLE 2: THE CYCLE OF INDEPENDENCE

In our 10th year (aged nine) we begin our second Nine-Year Cycle, the Cycle of Independence. This is without doubt the most challenging of all our Nine-Year Cycles because it includes the difficult teenage years when we are trying to discover who we are and how the world works. Our bodies are undergoing massive hormonal changes and our minds are being crammed with a tonne of information at school, while at the same time we are struggling to come to terms with our sexual awakening and the torrent of emotions raging inside us.

Year 1 (age 9): **The energy of "Creation"**

In our 10th year, aged nine, most of us start to feel the first onset of puberty when our bodies begin to change and we start to experience for the first time what it feels like to have urges that can only be described as "adult" in nature – although we are far too young to understand them. What we do understand, however, is that this is the beginning of a new phase of our life and the flames of desire and creation have been lit within us (the fire energy of **1**).

Year 2 (age 10): The energy of "Co-operation"

Now we have reached double figures, and our world really starts to change in direct proportion to the way we interact with others. Friendships start to blossom into deep connections, and we even develop our first real innocent crushes. This is the age when we begin to real-eyes for the first time that life is all about the relationships we have with other people (the water energy of **2**).

Year 3 (age 11): The energy of "Expression"

Our 12th year is the third year of our Cycle of Independence. The age of 11 is when so many changes start happening in our bodies and in our lives that it is difficult to make sense of it all.

The air (thought) energy of **3** is working overtime, causing us to struggle to understand what is going on. In the positive, this means starting to discover our identity and express our individuality. In the negative, it means becoming a typically withdrawn pre-teen as we shrink into our shell and try to figure out what is happening to us.

Year 4 (age 12): The energy of "Stability"

The return of the practical earth energy of **4** marks our 13th year, aged 12, which is why this is the perfect time for our parents to start helping us understand about the value of money – how to manage it, and how to save it.

It is also the time when we try to build something of an emotional foundation for ourselves to prepare us, as best we can, for the enormous challenges of the teenage years that lie ahead of us...

Year 5 (age 13): The energy of "Change"

... because as soon as we hit 13 years old we are hurled headlong into the wildest ride of our life as everything changes and we are thrown aboard the roller-coaster of our often traumatic teens.

Internally, our hormones are going berserk, our bodies sprout adult hair, our voice breaks as our testes drop (if we are male) and our breasts begin to develop (if we are female). And as if that wasn't enough to deal with, this is also the age when many children graduate from primary school to secondary school, so we go from being a big fish in a small pond to a small fish in a much bigger one.

On the positive side, this is the year when we really start to feel we have a degree of freedom of choice in our lives and become at least partially independent from our parents.

Our 14th year – the fifth of our second cycle – is a time of massive change unlike any we have ever experienced before, or ever will again.

It is the perfect example of the fire energy of **5**… out with the old and in with the new.

Year 6 (age 14): The energy of "Beauty"

By the time we turn 14 and enter our 15th year, puberty is well and truly under way for most children, and almost finished for some early developers.

Along with the severe physiological and sexual changes in our bodies, we are also experiencing an emotional flowering inside us akin to opening our eyes for the first time to the beauty that surrounds us.

What we see – the vision of romantic idealism – is that suddenly other kids are no longer yucky and full of "girl germs" or "boy germs". Instead they become beautiful objects of obsession ("If he/she doesn't go out with me I'll just die!") as teenage crushes take hold at the deepest level of our being.

Yes, I know this romantic vision of perfection isn't "love" (the emotional water energy of **6**) in the fullest sense of the word, but think back to when you were 14… it sure felt like it.

Year 7 (age 15): The energy of "Truth"

Now we are 15, and exams are looming on the horizon. Somehow, in the middle of this hormonal and emotional maelstrom, we are also supposed to be studying like crazy and memorising everything from the atomic number of potassium to the capital of Botswana.

Fortunately, we are working with the air (thought) energy of **7** so our brains are able to retain an incredible amount of information.

What drives our thirst for knowledge at this eager young age is the dawning real-eyesation that the world is awesome (in the true meaning of the word) and full of opportunity.

Parents would do well to remember that the average 15-year-old is capable of learning – and retaining – more information in this one year than anyone over the age of 30 can do in a decade.

Year 8 (age 16): The energy of "Power"

Ah, sweet 16! Many children become sexually active around this time. This is the end of innocence and the start of our ego's determined quest to increase our sense of personal power (the earth energy of **8**).

Towards the end of this year, some of us choose to leave school early and strike out into the world of entrepreneurship to flex our personal power muscles, while the rest of us stay in school and become "seniors". This is when we start to feel that we have some power over others for the first time in our young life. It is important to give children some responsibility at this age. And non-judgmental, open communication is vital on subjects such as sex, drugs and alcohol.

Note that this is the time when heterosexual children begin using their sexuality to gain power over the opposite sex. Girls learn to use their sexuality to gain control over physically stronger boys and also to compete with their female friends to be the most desirable girl in school, while boys use their sexuality to make them feel more of a "man" by trying to subjugate girls to their sexual wills.

If this pattern is allowed to gain a foothold here, it could stay with them for the rest of their life – dooming them to a succession of "conditional" relationships. Parents would be advised to educate their 16-year-old children about unconditional love and teach them that sex is an expression of love, and not a power trip for the ego. If they can get this into their heads now it will save them a fortune in relationship seminars and marriage counsellors later in life.

For children who identify as gay, bisexual, transgender or any other of the fluid sexual identities, this year (our 17th overall and the eighth of this Cycle of Independence) is usually when they either summon the courage to risk the judgment of their parents and others by "coming out" and revealing their sexuality, or shrink back and bury their truth in a deep depression.

It is absolutely vital that parents give their children the safe, loving and non-judgmental environment that they need to speak what is in their heart at this age. Just as the mantra for Life Path Number **8** is "We are all in this together...", so the mantra for teenagers in this crucial second **8** year of their development is: "... but every single one of us is different."

Teach your child that their "difference" is their strength, and that there would be no point to any of all this thing we call "life" if everyone thought and felt the same. "God" (the Source) loves our differences much more than it loves our similarities.

Year 9 (age 17): **The energy of "Wisdom"**

The final year of the Cycle of Independence resonates with the completion energy of **9** and culminates in one of the most momentous events of our life – our coming of age at 18.

Depending on what year we happen to be working in school, we either finish our exams, or we prepare to finish them, and then we are off out into the world, ready to experience our next Nine-Year Cycle as a young adult.

This is the age when we may leave home to go away to college, or travel the world, or house-share with friends, or get our first full-time job. And although we are still a long way from being fully emotionally mature, we are independent and we have made it through our first two – and by far our two most difficult – Nine-Year Cycles.

* * *

Chapter 6: Revolving with the Nine-Year Cycles

CYCLE 3: THE CYCLE OF CONFIDENCE

The third Nine-Year Cycle takes us from the age of 18 up until we turn 27, which for most of us is the age when our personality is fully developed, we have embarked on our chosen career path, and we may feel ready to "settle down" (although I dislike that phrase… "settle up" is so much better).

Of course, in the modern world our lives do not fit precisely into such easily constructed boxes. Some people marry younger than 27, some much older, and some not at all. But if you look closely at your life, you will find that 27 is the time most of us make the big decisions about how our home and work lives are going to be.

So if you married earlier, this may be the time when you decide to have children. If you are LGBTI, this might be the time you form a relationship that takes you to a new level of domesticity, either through buying a home or renting together. If you are single or divorced, this might be the time when you move to another country, or another city, or just another part of town to start a new life for your Self.

* * *

CYCLE 4: THE CYCLE OF MATURITY

Although our personality, our desires and our domestic life are often in place by the time we turn 27, we do not attain full emotional maturity for another nine years until we reach the age of 36, when the issues of our second Supplementary Birth Number have been resolved.

This fourth Nine-Year Cycle from 27 to 36 is called The Cycle of Maturity. And from then on, our Nine-Year Cycles go round and round as we continue to work primarily with the energy of the number of each year in harmony with our Life Path Number – always growing towards the light of achieving our life's highest purpose.

* * *

Part Two: The Self-Awareness System™

A quick recap of the energies of each of the nine years:

— In the **first** year of each cycle we bring new ideas to fruition, or start new projects, or change jobs, or change the direction of our relationship, or start a new one, and so on.

— In the **second** year we work with the energy of co-operation and interaction with others.

— In the **third** year we work with the energy of expressing ourselves and our ideas.

— In the **fourth** year we work with the energy of stability to create a stronger foundation.

— In the **fifth** year we work with the energy of change: out with the old and in with the new.

— In the **sixth** year we focus on love, whether it be Self-love or romantic love.

— In the **seventh** year we focus on accumulating knowledge.

— In the **eighth** year we reap the rewards of the labours of the previous seven years.

— Finally, in the **ninth** year, we bring completion and closure to some aspect of our life in readiness to begin a new cycle all over again.

When you look back at your own life in a moment, using the table at the end of this chapter (on page 230), you will be amazed to see how your progression through the years has followed the path of these Nine-Year Cycles, although it's not that surprising when you consider it was designed by your Self before you incarnated in physical form.

As you map out the main events of your life so far, pay particular attention to where the first year of each cycle marks something new that happened in your life (a new direction that you took, a new job, a new friendship, or whatever it might be for you); where the fifth year brought change; and where the ninth year corresponds to something in your life that was completed, you received closure on some big issue, finished a project, ended a relationship, or whatever it was for you.

* * *

Chapter 6: Revolving with the Nine-Year Cycles

My life as a guide to help you

To give you an example of how much of an influence the Nine-Year Cycles have on our lives, let me share with you some of the events of my own life. I hope it will help you understand how powerful these cycles are so that you can first go back and see how your own life has been similarly influenced and, second, plan your future so that from now on you can live in alignment with the rhythm of your cycles.

I was born in 1959 and my childhood was relatively uneventful (although I did "fall in love" with a girl at kindergarten in my 6th (romance) year, aged just five!).

When I was 13, in the 5th (change) year of my second cycle in 1972, my parents left England to live in Denmark at the same time as I left junior school for senior school. Talk about change!

I left school in 1977 at 18 in the 1st (new beginnings) year of my third cycle and went to university in London in 1978 in the 2nd (connecting with other people) year, where I interacted with others on a deep and mature level for the first time.

At university, I studied for a degree in English Literature, and in 1979 – the 3rd (communication) year of my third cycle – I formulated the spark of my writing career. I was married in 1982 in the 6th (romance) year of my third cycle, and we decided in 1986 (the 1st year of my fourth cycle) to emigrate to Australia.

In 1988, when I was 29 and in the 3rd (communication) year of my fourth cycle, I became a full-time newspaper journalist and started to write professionally for the first time.

In 1990, in the 5th (change) year of the fourth cycle, I switched from being a journalist to work as a salesman for personal growth seminar teachers (the very best way to study something is to sell it). And I also got divorced. Talk about a change year!

A year later in 1991, in the 6th (romance) year of the cycle, I followed a girl I was in love with to Canada because she had gone there for a holiday and had fallen in love with someone else. Now, looking back, I see how the passionate and idealistic energy of 6 (the Visionary) helped me win her back. It was the most romantic time of my life when love was all that mattered.

We returned together to Australia, where we lived happily for three years before separating amicably in 1994 in the 9th (completion) year of my fourth cycle to walk our separate growth paths.

In 1995, in the 1st (new beginnings) year of my fifth cycle, I returned to journalism to found and edit the Australian edition of Larry Flynt's famous yet controversial *Hustler* magazine, when I was privileged to learn some invaluable lessons about the link between sexuality and spirituality that very few people get to experience in the way I was lucky enough to do.

In 1999, the 5th (change) year of my fifth cycle, I quit my job in Australia and moved back to live in the UK for a while.

The next year, in 2000, my 6th (romance) year, I followed my heart back to Australia for a beautiful girl who I lived with for four years until we broke up in the 9th (completion) year of my fifth cycle in 2003.

I moved into a new home in 2004, the 1st (new beginnings) year of my sixth cycle. In 2008 in the 5th (change) year, I switched direction in my career and started working on my success coaching business.

In 2010, the 7th (knowledge) year, I started to study numerology intensely and began to develop the Self-Awareness System™ for this book. (Yep, there was so much to learn it has taken me a full seven years to develop.)

In 2012, the 9th (completion) year of my sixth nine-year cycle, I packed up my home of eight years and moved into a flat by the beach where I took stock of my life and decided to resign from my job and write five self-help books, before working on completing this one.

In 2013, the 1st (new beginnings) year of my seventh cycle, I took a cottage in the country to begin the task of writing these five books.

In 2014, the 2nd (connection) year, I moved back to Sydney and almost immediately met the woman of my dreams, who I would not have been able to connect with (2 is a love year) had I not already written my books in my self-imposed cottage isolation.

Chapter 6: Revolving with the Nine-Year Cycles

Now, here we are in 2017 – the 5th (change) year of my seventh cycle – and I have changed everything. I have published this book and quit my rent-paying job to pursue my "happiness teaching" full time.

* * *

I have compiled this table to show these major events and have marked the key years mentioned above in bold, starting with my birth in 1959 and finishing in 2017 when this book was published. I hope this will help you when you come to fill in your own table at the end of the chapter.

<u>1959</u> **1**	1960 2	1961 3	1962 4	1963 5	1964 6	1965 7	1966 8	1967 9
1968 1	1969 2	1970 3	1971 4	<u>1972</u> **5**	1973 6	1974 7	1975 8	<u>1976</u> **9**
<u>1977</u> **1**	<u>1978</u> **2**	<u>1979</u> **3**	1980 4	1981 5	<u>1982</u> **6**	1983 7	1984 8	1985 9
<u>1986</u> **1**	1987 2	<u>1988</u> **3**	1989 4	<u>1990</u> **5**	<u>1991</u> **6**	1992 7	1993 8	<u>1994</u> **9**
<u>1995</u> **1**	1996 2	1997 3	1998 4	<u>1999</u> **5**	<u>2000</u> **6**	2001 7	2002 8	<u>2003</u> **9**
<u>2004</u> **1**	2005 2	2006 3	2007 4	<u>2008</u> **5**	2009 6	<u>2010</u> **7**	2011 8	<u>2012</u> **9**
<u>2013</u> **1**	<u>2014</u> **2**	2015 3	2016 4	<u>2017</u> **5**	2018 6	2019 7	2020 8	2021 9

* * *

Part Two: The Self-Awareness System™

Look back at how the cycles have affected your life

I hope this brief tour of my life helps you look back on your own life and notice how your most notable experiences have followed the rhythm of your own Nine-Year Cycles.

You can do this by using the table on page 230.

Start by writing the number 1 under the year you were born, and then write numbers 2 to 9 under the following eight years. Then start again at 1 and so on, writing 1 to 9 under all the following years.

As you look back at the major events of your life, it might appear at first glance that they do not always conform to the energy of the year in the cycle when they occurred. But if you look deeper into the experience you obtained from each event – using my own examples as a guide – you will see the lesson you learned, the distinction you were able to make or the opportunities you were given will all resonate very deeply with the number of the year in which it happened.

For example, a big change that happened in a 7 year might not have been just about the change (if it was, it would have happened in a 1 or 5 year), but about the knowledge (the energy of 7) you gained as a result of the change. Equally, a relationship that ended in an 8 year may not have been about issues of love (year 6) or connection (year 2), but was about you tapping into your power (the energy of 8) by standing up and saying: "This is not what I want." Or this could have happened in a 3 year, which is governed by the energy of Self-expression.

Use the cycles to help you plan your future

As well as mapping out the events of your past, you can also use the table on page 230 to design your life for the future, so that you work with the positive energy of the Nine-Year Cycles as often as possible.

Try to start major projects in a 1 year, begin new relationships in a 2 or 6 year (or else deepen the ones you are in), invest in a 4 year and cash out in an 8 year, make big changes in a 5 year, focus on creativity and expression in a 3 year and study in a 7 year, and wrap up as many projects and tie off as many loose ends as you can in a 9 year.

Chapter 6: Revolving with the Nine-Year Cycles

Pay particular attention to when one cycle ends and another one begins, because the more you can work with the positive energy of the Nine-Year Cycles, the more you can plug in to the wisdom of your Self... and the more effortless and harmonious your life will become.

The table on page 230 goes all the way up to 2059, so plan away!

Yes, there is a shortcut!

If you don't want to go through all the trouble of mapping out the Nine-Year Cycles of your life in the table on the next page, you can quickly find out where you are on your current Nine-Year Cycle using this easy shortcut, and then plan your future accordingly.

This is also useful to help you work with the positive energy of the number of the year you are in, while at the same time watching out for the negative pitfalls associated with the number of each year.

All you do is take the sum of your age, and add 1.

If you are 46, for example, add your 4 and 6 together to reach 10. Then add 1 to reach 11. And because we always keep adding until we reach a single number, you need to add the 1 and 1 together to reach 2. You are therefore in the 2nd year of your current Nine-Year Cycle, which is a 2 (connection) year. On your next birthday, when you turn 47, you will enter a 3 (creative) year (4+7+1=12, and 1+2=3).

To use another example, if you are 26 you will need to add your 2 and 6 together to get 8, and then add 1 to get 9. You are therefore in a 9 (completion) year – the 9th year of your current Nine-Year Cycle. On your next birthday, you will begin a new Nine-Year Cycle with a 1 (new beginnings) year when you turn 27 (2+7+1=10 and 1+0=1).

* * *

Use the table on the next page to map out the events of your life so far, and also to plan for your future. You will be amazed at how your life dovetails perfectly with the energy of the number of each year.

Part Two: The Self-Awareness System™

1910	1911	1912	1913	1914	1915	1916	1917	1918	1919
1920	1921	1922	1923	1924	1925	1926	1927	1928	1929
1930	1931	1932	1933	1934	1935	1936	1937	1938	1939
1940	1941	1942	1943	1944	1945	1946	1947	1948	1949
1950	1951	1952	1953	1954	1955	1956	1957	1958	1959
1960	1961	1962	1963	1964	1965	1966	1967	1968	1969
1970	1971	1972	1973	1974	1975	1976	1977	1978	1979
1980	1981	1982	1983	1984	1985	1986	1987	1988	1989
1990	1991	1992	1993	1994	1995	1996	1997	1998	1999
2000	2001	2002	2003	2004	2005	2006	2007	2008	2009
2010	2011	2012	2013	2014	2015	2016	2017	2018	2019
2020	2021	2022	2023	2024	2025	2026	2027	2028	2029
2030	2031	2032	2033	2034	2035	2036	2037	2038	2039
2040	2041	2042	2043	2044	2045	2046	2047	2048	2049
2050	2051	2052	2053	2054	2055	2056	2057	2058	2059

Chapter 6: Revolving with the Nine-Year Cycles

Everything begins at the beginning

If you are already familiar with some aspects of numerology, you may be aware that many numerologists believe we are not born in the first year of our first cycle, but rather that our Life Path Number determines the stage of the cycle when we are born.

They believe that if we are a **5**, say, then the year we are born is the 5th year of our first cycle. Similarly, they believe that if we are an **8** we are born into the 8th year of our first cycle. And so on.

Because this rather strange theory has been accepted and repeated by numerologists for centuries, it has many adherents. But it does not have a place in the Self-Awareness System™, for three reasons:

– First, it is not logical to be born into a change year (the energy of the 5th year) when there is nothing yet to change, any more than it is possible to reap the rewards of the previous seven years of our life (the energy of the 8th year) when we have just been born. That is why the Self-Awareness System™ is gaining broad acceptance because it is based on the logical and mathematical precept that we are all born at the beginning of a Nine-Year Cycle, not half way through it.

– Second, some numerologists claim that Pythagoras developed this theory of the Nine-Year Cycles beginning on your birth number, but there is no evidence to support this claim. Pythagoras never wrote about the cycles at all, so the claim is speculative at best.

– Third, the argument put forward that the cycle is explained by reincarnation – in other words we pick up where we left off in a past life – is an interesting one but is also flawed, because newborn babies simply don't have enough awareness in their first year to work with the energy of any number other than **1**. Yes, by the time we reach the end of our first year we are starting to work with the energy of **2** (co-operation), but communication (**3**), stability (**4**), freedom (**5**), vision (**6**), truth (**7**), power (**8**) and integrity (**9**) are all completely out of the reach of our under-developed consciousness during our first year as a spirit having a human experience. So how could a tiny baby possibly work with the energy of any number other than **1**?

The Self-Awareness System™ takes the view that the Nine-Year Cycles that affect our personal growth path begin where everything begins… at the beginning.

* * *

Now that we have looked in detail at the numerological cycles that govern our personal development in this lifetime – and our spiritual development over many lifetimes – it's time to discover what our Birth Code reveals about our innate strengths and weaknesses.

We will do this in the next chapter by invoking the "truth" energy of **7** to face up to the real-eyesation that every Life Path contains just as much potential for pain as it does for pleasure.

This is because one of the "Big T" Truths about personal and spiritual growth is that sometimes the only way our Self can get our attention and force us to make a change is by giving us a swift kick up the bum.

Chapter 7:
Identify your strengths and weaknesses

7 is the number of truth

In this chapter you will discover the truth about what comes easiest to you, and what challenges you will face on your Life Path

One of the most rewarding aspects about the Self-Awareness System™ is how equitable it is. All the nine Life Paths offer the same opportunities for happiness and fulfillment, and they also offer the same amount of challenges – which means no Life Path is any "better" or "worse" than any of the others.

At first glance, it may appear that being born with, say, a Life Path Number of **8** (the number of wealth and power) means you may enjoy more abundance in your life than someone who is born with a Life Path Number of **2** (the number of co-operation and harmony), or a Life Path Number of **6** (the number of divine love and beauty).

But who's to say that money necessarily buys us happiness? Yes, sometimes it does. But often it doesn't. And besides, abundance comes in all forms, so living our life as a **2** or **6** might be just as rewarding in terms of the deep, loving connections we enjoy, as living our life as a wealthy **8** who hasn't done the necessary inner work on themselves to real-eyes that all the wealth and power in the world can't paper over their deep-seated insecurities. Plus, many **2**s and **6**s become fabulously wealthy, just as many **8**s wind up in the poor house.

Remember, life is never about what we do. It's about who we become. And our highest purpose in every lifetime is to learn to love our Self, no matter what Life Path we are on.

History is littered with talented, wealthy and successful people who failed to love themselves and paid the ultimate price, including Prince (**9**), Michael Jackson (**6**), Kurt Cobain (**9**), John Belushi (**3**), River Phoenix (**3**), Jimi Hendrix (**9**), Jim Morrison (**1**), Elvis Presley (**9**), Robin Williams (**8**), Heath Ledger (**7**) and Philip Seymour Hoffman (**8**), to name just a few.

Clearly, some wealthy people do enjoy both material success and peace of mind, but this is because they have cleared their personal blocks and have evolved up their growth path to achieve first Self-awareness, and then Self-love.

My point is this: no number gives you any more or less chance of attaining your life's highest purpose… which is to find your bliss and then help others find theirs. As we saw earlier, all Life Paths contain an equal measure of positive and negative potential. Our challenge in every lifetime, no matter our Life Path Number, is always to nurture our positives and overcome our negatives.

* * *

The pros and cons of the nine Life Paths

1s have the potential to be the best leaders, but they also have the potential to be the worst indecisive ditherers.

2s have the potential to be the best loving peacemakers, but they also have the potential to be the worst needy co-dependents.

3s have the potential to be the best upbeat motivators, but they also have the potential to be the worst fault-finding critics.

4s have the potential to be the best dependable friends, but they also have the potential to be the worst moody drama queens or kings.

5s have the potential to be the best courageous explorers, but they also have the potential to be the worst disillusioned cynics.

6s have the potential to be the best romantic idealists, but they also have the potential to be the worst intolerant perfectionists.

7s have the potential to be the best insightful scholars, but they also have the potential to be the worst arrogant "know-it-alls".

8s have the potential to be the best generous philanthropists, but they also have the potential to be the worst egotistical power-trippers.

9s have the potential to be the best humanitarian role models, but they also have the potential to be the worst over-zealous fanatics.

The reason we are given negative potential as well as positive potential is because people usually respond more effectively to the threat of pain than they do to the likelihood of pleasure. Both are effective change-agents, but when push comes to shove we are more likely to change our negative behaviour to avoid a painful outcome (if we don't change) than to gain a pleasurable outcome (if we do).

As we saw earlier, the Western religions discovered that fear is a powerful persuader, which is why they have recruited more followers by using the threat of "hell" than by using the promise of "heaven".

This syndrome is called the Pleasure-Pain Principle. Everything we do in life is for one of two reasons: the desire to gain pleasure, or the desire to avoid pain. And all but the most masochistic of us will do more to avoid pain than to gain pleasure.

That is why our Life Path Number contains negative qualities as well as positive ones, because if we overcome our weaknesses (avoid pain) as well as play to our strengths (gain pleasure), we are more likely to achieve our highest purpose than if we just played to our strengths.

Yes, of course it is admirable to do what we are good at in life. But we will only ever become the best we can be by also facing our "dark side" and digging deep into our Self to overcome the obstacles that appear on our path.

After all, it is only when we are truly up against it that we are able to tap into our most powerful inner strength.

* * *

When you read the details of your Life Path Number in Part Three you will notice that it is just as important to focus on learning the lessons of the "dark side" of your personality as it is to nurture your positive qualities if you are going to get where you want to go.

In some respects, it is even more important to pay attention to the possible pitfalls because most of us live in denial much of the time. In other words, we do what we are good at because it gives us pleasure, and we avoid facing those challenges that might not be so easy because we are afraid that facing them would give us pain.

So we tend to ignore our shortcomings, or try to pretend that they don't exist in the hope they will go away. Eventually, though, the pain we feel from not changing our negative behaviour becomes stronger than the pleasure we feel by avoiding our fears – and, when that happens, we take the bull by the horns and make a change.

This process is called "emotional leverage", and it is by far the most powerful personal growth tool we have in our Life Path kit bag.

* * *

Kill the "monster" while it's tiny

Your Life Path Number in Part Three contains messages from your Self to show you what behavioural issues will bring you the most pain. This is incredibly valuable information because it means you don't have to go through the process I have just described of waiting until the pain gets so intense before you make a change. Instead, you can pre-empt it by taking action long before it gets to that stage, because you will know exactly what to look for.

If you think of each negative quality inside you as a little "monster" that starts out small when we are young, and grows much larger as we get older, it is much easier to kill the monster when it is tiny by taking pre-emptive action early on, rather than waiting until the monster has grown so large that it has taken over our life, by which point it becomes very difficult to kill.

Chapter 7: Identify your strengths and weaknesses

(I am speaking from experience here because I have slain a few internal jabberwockys in my time, as I'm sure you have.)

For this reason, the negative aspects of our Life Path Number are as much a blessing as the positive ones. Think of them as signposts directing us to the areas of our life we need to work on, so we can remove our internal "roadblocks" that are preventing us from achieving our highest potential.

* * *

Another benefit of working with our "dark side" is that the most exquisite feelings of achievement and pleasure come not from doing what comes easily to us, but from doing something that we know will be difficult – or that we are afraid of doing – and succeeding.

These are the hard-earned "breakthroughs" in our life that give us far more pleasure than anything else.

* * *

How to use our obstacles to find our bliss

As we work with the energy of our Life Path Number, sometimes we will achieve our goals by plugging into our positive qualities – the ones that empower us to achieve what we set out to achieve – and other times we will attain our goals by overcoming the challenges that are thrown up by our Life Path's negative qualities.

Remember, it is only by digging deeper into our Self that we are able to tap into our true inner strength.

Examples of these challenges include ill health, financial hardship, losing our job, losing our relationship, the failure of an investment, the failure of a business, having something stolen from us, and even the death of a pet or a loved one.

It is important to real-eyes that although these appear to have been put in our path by the partner who leaves us, or the boss who fires us, or the judgmental person who rejects us, and so on – in every case it is never them who have "done this to us", it is always our Self who has chosen these experiences for our growth. As we saw in Part One, our Self programmed our Life Path when we incarnated. It always knows the best way forward because it is our direct link to the infinite wisdom and love of the Source. So if an obstacle appears on our path, it was put there – quite deliberately – by our Self.

When something "bad" happens in our life, it is because our Self knows it is time for us to make a change, and make it quickly. It will have given us many gentle hints, suggestions and opportunities to make the change painlessly, but we have ignored them – either through fear or laziness.

So now our Self is forced to raise the stakes by causing us pain to get our attention. And if we still fail to act, the stakes will continue to rise and the lessons will get more and more painful until we do finally take the action we need to take.

Then, after we have made the change and learned the lesson, we will look back on the so-called "bad" event and see how it was actually perfectly designed for us – by us – to learn what we needed to learn.

And the real beauty is, once we learn a particular lesson we never have to go through that same painful experience ever again.

* * *

A word of warning

If we don't learn the lesson and continue to see the event as "something someone else did to us" – rather than our Self giving us exactly what we needed – then we will carry all the associated anger, resentment and bitterness towards that person into our future, which in turn ensures it will keep happening to us again and again, growing more and more painful each time, until we do finally learn the lesson and release our negative emotions.

Our life lessons work in the same way as the lessons we learned in school: we do it right, or we do it again.

Chapter 7: Identify your strengths and weaknesses

Sadly, if we continue to miss the lesson of our life experiences and blame someone else for "doing them to us", the toxic emotions of resentment and anger will fester inside us and we may become sick, sometimes even with a life-threatening "dis-ease" such as cancer.

This Self-poisoning is by no means the only cause of cancer, but it is certainly one of the most common. It is our Self getting desperate and playing its ultimate card. If it works, the sickness makes us stop and refocus all our priorities and energies until we learn what we are meant to learn – in which case we will get better.

But if we still don't get it, the sickness may take us – and we will have to go through the lesson all over again in our next life.

To prevent this from happening, all we have to do is real-eyes that every obstacle we encounter in our life – and I mean every single one of them – has been put there by our Self to make us tap into our inner strength, which we need to do if we are going to have any hope of achieving our highest purpose.

This is why so-called "negative" events happen in our life. They are not random, they are all part of the perfect plan that our Self designed to lead us to our highest potential.

As long as we are not a "bad" person and are free from Karmic Law, everything "negative" that happens does so for a positive reason – namely, to make us access our inner strength.

* * *

If we go back to the examples we used just now, it is easy to see the lessons hidden in the so-called "bad things" that seem to "happen to us". In every case, it's our Self (or our Angel... it's the same thing) stepping in to make a positive change that we were too afraid to make.

If our partner leaves us

This always means we are being forced out of a situation that no longer serves us, and into a new one that does. A better relationship awaits us, as long as we learn the lessons and take a new and more unconditionally loving "us" to the next one.

Lesson: Everything we lose in our life is always replaced by something of greater value.

If our boss fires us

This is because we haven't had the courage to leave our job. In our heart, we know something better is waiting for us, but because we have not taken action to go out and find it – usually through fear or laziness – our Self has been forced to intervene.

Lesson: We must have the courage of our convictions.

If someone rejects us

This is always for one of two reasons, and often both. It is either because there is a part of us that we do not fully accept yet, so we will manifest others to judge that part of us and reject us until we either change it, if it is a fault, or accept it with pride as a healthy part of who we truly are. Or it is because we may have a habit of judging other people, in which case when we stop judging others, they will – as if by magic – stop judging us.

Lesson: Learn to love our Self and accept others, "faults" and all.

These are just a few examples. The list is as long as the number of so-called "painful experiences" that we will encounter in our life. There is a lesson in each and every one of them. All we have to do is look for the lesson… and we will find it.

(Note: Please always forgive the person who appeared to do you harm and send them a blessing. They were nothing more than tools used by your Self to get its point across to you. Your Self cannot operate in physical form, so sometimes to get through to you it has to employ people along your path to act on its behalf.)

* * *

Chapter 7: Identify your strengths and weaknesses

Self-love is the key to everything

Before we look in more detail at the specific positive and negative qualities inherent in each of the nine Life Path Numbers, I want to share with you the secret of how you can best boost your positive qualities and minimise your negative ones.

It's also the secret of personal growth, the secret of spiritual growth, the secret of success… and the secret of happiness.

It's Self-love.

I mentioned this earlier when talking about famous wealthy and successful people who died by their own hand because they didn't learn to love themselves, but it deserves a fuller explanation.

Self-love is not the same as Self-esteem, which is a construct of the ego. Self-esteem is about being "good enough". It is about feeling good about your Self and is an important step on your path to your life's highest purpose. It takes the form of healing all the wounds you have suffered and learning to stand up for your Self. But it is basic and limited in its ability to take you where you want to go.

Self-love is something else entirely. As we saw in Part One, Self-love is not about being "good enough", it's about being "God enough".

Loving your Self is the process of becoming aware that you are pure love… a divine incarnation of Source energy and perfect in every way. When you real-eyes you are perfect just as you are, you start seeing the world from a completely different perspective, because if you are perfect, then everyone else must be perfect too. And that means everything that happens to you must also be perfect, even the things you used to label as "bad".

Now, suddenly, it is easy to see the lesson in these so-called "bad" experiences because you accept them immediately as being exactly what you needed to learn and grow – in other words, you see them as perfect, because you know everything is perfect.

So when a challenge arises, instead of saying "Why does this always happen to me?" (which is your mind talking on behalf of your ego), ask your Self: "What am I meant to be learning here?" (which is your mind talking on behalf of your Self).

* * *

When you approach life from this perspective, you will always work with the positive vibration of your Life Path Number – even when faced with obstacles – because your level of Self-love means you now know that everything is perfectly designed to help you grow.

But when you lack Self-love for whatever reason – whether it's that you doubt your own divinity, whether you are mistreating or judging others, or lying, or cheating, or stealing, or whether you are simply not living in accordance with your highest moral principles – you cannot be sure that everything is there to help you. It might be there in your life because of your Self-imposed karmic punishment, or because you feel you don't "deserve" any better.

That is why Self-love is so important.

* * *

When you listen to your Self rather than to your ego, everything in your life works in harmony to lift you to your higher ground and you will never again experience the "dark side" of your Life Path Number, or the dark side of anything else for that matter.

Nothing "bad" will happen. It will be plain sailing – and for the first time in your life you will start to experience what bliss feels like.

If negative events still happen, then at some level you are not loving your Self enough. You must look more closely at what you are still doing that a pure-love Self would never do:

– Are you lying to others, or your Self, even just a little bit?

– Are you insecure about any aspect of your Self?

– Is there any part of your Self that you don't like, let alone love? If so, change it at once.

– Are you mistreating people or animals, or mistreating your Self?

Chapter 7: Identify your strengths and weaknesses

– Are you being judgmental of others?
– Are you afraid of anything? If you are, you must face the fear.

Don't worry, fear is never real. But if you have any fear left in you, you are giving your ego the "food" it needs to stay alive.

The moment you have no fear, your ego dies. It simply cannot live in a fear-less environment, any more than your body can live in an oxygen-less environment.

No stone must be left unturned. You may need the advice of a therapist or a friend to help you, because other people can see our faults more easily than we can. But whatever you do, ask all these questions and more and do nothing else until you are absolutely certain you are living your life exactly as your pure-love Self wants you to live it.

* * *

When you do this, something magical happens.

When you love your Self fully, all your troubles are suddenly gone. All your worries are gone too, because your "struggle" is over.

You have made it! You have become pure conscious love. And from that moment on, all you will ever experience in your life is bliss… breathtaking, heart-opening, exquisite, sublime, untouchable, unending and unbounded bliss.

* * *

Positive and negative potentials of the Life Paths

Now that we know the only way to boost our positive qualities and dissolve our negative ones is to love our Self, let's look at the main pros and cons of the nine Life Path Numbers.

Your Life Path Number description in the listings in Part Three will give you much more detail, but for now just notice how the difference between manifesting the positive and the negative is always determined by your level of Self-love, versus your level of fear.

Life Path 1: The Leader

This is the first number, forged in the fire of creation. The main positive aspect of this Life Path is that **1**s have a powerful spark of creativity which, with enough confidence to express themselves, can inspire and uplift others. But if they shrink back into fear and lose confidence, their creative energy can turn inwards and cause them to become frustrated and angry. This may lead them to use alcohol, drugs, sex or other "addictions" because their energy must still come out.

Energy cannot be blocked for long. Think of a blocked hose; the water will always eventually burst out at the seams or at the tap. And if **1**s don't have enough courage to express their creative energy in positive ways, it will come out as negative energy that they may be unable to control... usually as aggression, or as an urge to Self-destruct.

Equally, if they lack confidence in their leadership abilities, the **1**'s deep insecurity can also flip them to the negative side of this number, so instead of inspiring others they may try to dominate them to make up for their lack of Self-worth.

1s who work with the positive side of "the Force" (ie, love) make the best leaders and trailblazers (like Luke Skywalker), while insecure **1**s who work with the dark side can make the worst despots and tyrants (like Darth Vader).

The original and ground-breaking *Star Wars* movies are the perfect illustration of the power of love. In the final climax, Luke is able to rescue his father from the Dark Side simply by loving him.

And what Life Path Number is *Star Wars* creator George Lucas? Yes, you guessed it... he's a **1**.

Life Path 2: The Intuitive

This is a water number, and **2**s are therefore governed by their emotions. It's also the number of co-operation and harmony, so in the positive they will be driven to help others wherever and whenever they can. But if they fail to honour themselves and go too far in helping others without taking care of their own needs, the **2**'s sensitive energy will quickly veer out of balance, and this can cause them to flip to the negative side of their Life Path Number.

They may become exhausted and overwhelmed. And if they don't correct the imbalance quickly, they may find themselves displaying deep feelings of resentment and even an unhealthy desire to manipulate other people to get what they want.

2s make the best peacemakers, counsellors and diplomats, and the worst manipulators and needy co-dependents. Negative **2**s are rare, though, because this is such a compassionate and considerate number.

Bill Clinton, John Candy, Ronald Reagan, Mozart and Keith Richards are all high-profile **2**s who have exhibited both the positive and negative aspects of this Life Path.

Life Path 3: The Creative

When they work with the positive energy of their creative Life Path Number, the upbeat and optimistic **3** will freely express their original ideas and become a powerful communicator, able to inspire and motivate others to be the best they can be.

Positive **3**s are extremely intelligent and insightful and make great stand-up comics, actors, writers, artists, musicians and journalists.

However, if they lack the confidence that comes from loving and trusting themselves, their thoughts will remain unexpressed and they will fester inside them in the form of insecurity and Self-doubt. Even worse, their piercingly intellectual mind will tend to criticise others and find fault with them simply because the negative **3** is projecting onto other people their dissatisfaction with themselves.

Creative **3**s make the best orators, motivators and entertainers, and the worst fault-finding critics.

Many of the best entertainers in history have used a mask to hide their insecurities. Judy Garland, David Bowie, Ricky Gervais, Alfred Hitchcock, Salvador Dali and River Phoenix are all famous examples of how even the most outwardly confident **3** can sometimes suffer from a brooding dark side.

Part Two: The Self-Awareness System™

Life Path 4: The Builder

This is an earth number, which means Builders who work with the positive energy of **4** are well-grounded, nurturing, loyal and reliable. They confidently focus their managerial and social skills on "building things" – from comfortable homes, successful businesses and valuable share portfolios to close friendships and loving families.

All positive **4**s are dependable, fiercely loyal and willing to support others – as well as themselves – both financially and emotionally.

However, if they flip to the negative side of this Life Path, their natural conservatism and caution can cause them to doubt themselves and, by extension, to distrust others.

Their keen eye for detail may also morph into an obsessive compulsiveness, leading them to get bogged down in the minutiae of a project, or their partner's behaviour in a relationship, as they lose sight of the bigger picture of who their partner really is and what the project, or relationship, is all about.

They may even suffer quite extreme mood swings, and they have a habit of stirring up drama in their life just for the sake of feeling alive.

Negative **4**s can often be intolerant and judgmental, which is merely a result of them projecting their dissatisfaction with themselves onto other people.

Builders make the best entrepreneurs, loyal friends and human and animal rights activists, but they can also make some of the worst procrastinators, materialistic hoarders and drama queens and kings.

Oprah Winfrey, Bill Gates, Richard Branson, Pamela Anderson and Bono are all **4**s who have used their high profiles and their wealth to help people and animals in need.

Life Path 5: The Rebel

Positive **5**s are vivacious and dynamic. This is another fire number (like **1**), and the Rebel is well and truly fired up to fight for justice in the world. They have boundless energy and a love of life that is matched only by their burning desire to experience everything the world has to offer… usually all at once.

Chapter 7: Identify your strengths and weaknesses

When they are confident, **5**s are brave change-agents who want to shake up the world, make a difference and improve the lives of as many people as possible (including their own), and they will use their considerable courage and intelligence to blaze new trails and tear down old beliefs in their quest to make the world a better place.

On the negative side, however, if they lack Self-confidence, the Rebel will rush around trying lots of new jobs, careers and relationships without ever learning the discipline required to achieve anything of lasting value. They tend to scratch the surface of life and, at the first sign of an obstacle, give up and move somewhere else – maybe even overseas – only to repeat the same pattern over and over again.

The trouble with this approach is that they never settle in one place long enough to achieve their passionate goals, and they run the risk of burning out and becoming bitter, blaming everything that goes "wrong" in their life on other people.

There are few people in this world who are more frustrated – and therefore more angry at the world deep down inside – than a Rebel **5** without a cause.

5s make the best revolutionaries, freedom fighters and explorers, and the worst disillusioned underachievers.

Steven Spielberg, Malcolm X, Sidney Poitier and Abraham Lincoln are all positive, pioneering and revolutionary **5**s who have changed the world for the better.

Life Path 6: The Visionary

Ah, the romantic **6**! In the positive, the confident and Self-loving **6** will hold a torch of love and compassion for everyone to follow. They will shine their love-light out into the world, nurturing and inspiring others by bathing them in the healing glow of their kindness.

This is another water number, like the **2**, and Visionaries are truly governed by their emotions. In the positive, they are so in love with life (because their Self-love is so strong) that they see the best in everyone. More than that, they show other people the best of themselves as well, because the **6** is able to reflect their own beauty back at them.

However, if they fail to learn how to love themselves and don't real-eyes that love is all there is, instead of seeing beauty everywhere they look, the negative **6** will focus on all the anger and despair they see in the world, which could send them into a spiral of depression.

This is an extremely sensitive Life Path. All **6**s are deeply affected by negative energy if they are not strong enough to guard against it.

In the negative, they can become critical of anyone or anything that doesn't match up to their idealistic, visionary and rose-coloured view of how the world should be. And they may also judge others too harshly if they fail to live up to the **6**'s impossibly high standards.

6s make the best nurturers, home-makers and romantic idealists, but they can also be the world's worst intolerant perfectionists.

Joan of Arc, James Dean, Fred Astaire and Cary Grant are all heroically romantic **6**s who held aloft a vision of a more loving world.

Life Path 7: The Seeker
This is another air Life Path, like the **3**, and it's no surprise that it's called the Seeker, because **7**s are in their head almost all the time, seeking out the truth and meaning in all their experiences.

They have a powerful, analytical mind with excellent problem-solving skills and a keen intellect, borne of the ability to first see and then understand what most other Life Paths have not even noticed.

The highest purpose of the **7** is to find answers to all of life's biggest questions, and then to share them with the world.

In the positive, they use what they learn first to know themselves and how the world works, and then to help others do the same.

But in the negative – ie, in the absence of Self-love – their insecurity can sometimes lead them to use their knowledge as a weapon to put other people down, so that they can feel better about themselves by comparison.

They can also tend towards arrogance, as their rampant ego tries to make them feel superior to the "fools" around them.

All **7**s must real-eyes it is only through learning to accept and love themselves that they are able to see others in the same way. When they learn that knowledge for its own sake has no value, they will be able to fulfill their life's highest purpose of sharing their wisdom with others.

Seekers make the best inspirational thinkers and prophets, and the worst arrogant "know-it-alls".

Winston Churchill, JFK, Golda Meir, James Cameron and Al Pacino are all famous **7**s who have teetered on the brink between unattractive arrogance and inspirational brilliance.

Life Path 8: The Achiever

Here we are back at earth again and, as with Life Path Number **4**, the Achiever will work mainly with the practical issues of material and financial abundance – only the energy of **8** is twice as strong.

Those **8**s who work with the positive energy of this Life Path Number will be fiercely determined, resourceful and hard-working and will have an excellent chance of achieving success in whatever they choose to do, both professionally and personally.

They will see their wealth, fame and status as valuable tools that they can use to help improve the lives of others who are worse off.

They have probably already lived as a **6** and a **7**, and so have learned the importance of sharing their success with others who are in need. But those **8**s who lack Self-love – and therefore fail to real-eyes that their status and material wealth do not define who they are – will sometimes fall into the trap of pursuing money and power at the expense of everything else in a doomed attempt to paper over the cracks of their insecurity with $100 bills.

They may even use their wealth and influence to gain power over other people. If they go down that path, they will learn the hard way that money and fame will never make them feel better about themselves, nor will they give them the peace of mind they seek.

8s make the best philanthropists, and the worst power trippers.

Paul Newman, Bob Marley, Matt Damon, Alexander Graham Bell, Laurence Olivier and Nelson Mandela are all examples of famous **8**s who have used their extraordinary success to help others through their philanthropy and their generosity of spirit.

Life Path 9: The Teacher

The final Life Path Number is governed by all four elements at once, which means it is concerned with teaching all the lessons learned throughout the Nine-Year Cycle and the Spiritual Growth Cycle.

The **9** tends to throw up fewer negatives than the other Life Path Numbers because by the time we reach this pinnacle of our nine-stage cycles we have experienced the lessons of all the other Life Paths.

The biggest challenge – Self-love – still remains, though. So while most **9**s usually enjoy many more positives than negatives, they can still fall down in a depressed and frustrated heap if they fail to appreciate their own divine, spiritual perfection.

The highest purpose of the **9** is to teach all they have learned, and to teach it by example. And the only way they will work with the negative energy of this Life Path is if they lack the Self-confidence to stand up and say: "Listen up! I have something to say."

This is the Life Path when we integrate all we have learned from the other Life Paths and live in integrity as a role model for others.

Integrity is the key word here. As we saw in Chapter 5, the words "integrate" and "integrity" have a perfect symbiosis with each other… and I believe it is no accident that they both have nine letters.

Self-doubt is the "enemy within" for the **9**, just as it is with all the other numbers, because only by knowing themselves to be pure love will the Teacher be able to fulfill their life's highest purpose and share what they know with the world.

This Life Path is one of supreme ability, but with great ability comes great responsibility… in this case, the responsibility to uncover their own inner beauty, so they can show other people theirs.

If they fail to do so, they may become an over-zealous fanatic who bullies and cajoles others to be the best they can be, rather than an inspirational role model who teaches lovingly and patiently by example.

9s make the best teachers and role models, and the worst fanatics.

Famously influential and inspirational **9**s include Mother Teresa, Gandhi, Louise Hay, Morgan Freeman, Cher and Elvis Presley.

Chapter 7: Identify your strengths and weaknesses

A quick-reference guide

The table on the next page sums up all this information for you in an easy-to-consult format. I have laid it out on just one page so that, if you wish, you can take a picture of it or photocopy it and put it on your fridge door as a quick-reference guide to re-mind you – and your friends and family members – of the pitfalls that your "dark side" will throw up on your Life Path from time to time.

When this happens – and it will – it is important to remember the three key points of this chapter:

1. First, remember there is no such thing as a "bad experience", only a learning experience. All obstacles are put in your path by your Self because your Self knows what you need to learn, and it knows the best way for you to learn it. And sometimes that is the "hard way".

2. Second, remember that if the lesson is a painful one, it is only because you are not yet "awake" enough, and so your Self uses pain to get your attention. As you evolve along your Life Path and become more aware – and more awake – you will learn your lessons ever more quickly and easily, and the painful experiences will stop.

3. Finally, remember there is only one lesson. It will come to you in many different forms, including heartbreak, illness, financial crisis, rejection, boredom, frustration and failure. But the lesson is always the same one... and you will keep attracting obstacles until you learn it.

The lesson is to learn to love your Self, and when you learn it everything changes. All of your obstacles will disappear and suddenly, instead of scrambling up a rock-strewn mountain path, you are cruising down a beautiful country road in a Ferrari towards your life's highest purpose with the wind blowing in your hair.

* * *

Part Two: The Self-Awareness System™

YOUR LIFE PATH'S UPS AND DOWNS

1. The Leader. Ambitious, energetic, dominant and pioneering.
Highest: Intrepid trailblazer. **Lowest:** Aggressive control freak.
Mantra: "Actions speak louder than words." **Focus on:** Humility.

2. The Intuitive. Compassionate, inclusive, stylish and empathetic.
Highest: Confident peacemaker. **Lowest:** Fragile co-dependent.
Mantra: "No one needs my love more than me." **Focus on:** Balance.

3. The Creative. Sensitive, expressive, insightful and artistic.
Highest: Rousing communicator. **Lowest:** Fault-finding critic.
Mantra: "I speak freely what is in my heart." **Focus on:** Expression.

4. The Builder. Loyal, generous, hard-working and reliable.
Highest: Tireless humanitarian. **Lowest:** Moody procrastinator.
Mantra: "Build for tomorrow, but enjoy today." **Focus on:** Flexibility.

5. The Rebel. Adventurous, imaginative, quick-witted and outgoing.
Highest: Brave freedom fighter. **Lowest:** Timid jack of all trades.
Mantra: "True freedom comes from within." **Focus on:** Discipline.

6. The Visionary. Romantic, supportive, loving and nurturing.
Highest: Inspirational idealist. **Lowest:** Intolerant perfectionist.
Mantra: "Love is who we are." **Focus on:** Inner beauty.

7. The Seeker. Analytical, intelligent, inquisitive and thoughtful.
Highest: Spiritual guru. **Lowest:** Arrogant "know-it-all".
Mantra: "The truth will set us free." **Focus on:** The bigger picture.

8. The Achiever. Resourceful, persuasive, driven and influential.
Highest: Generous philanthropist. **Lowest:** Egotistical power-tripper.
Mantra: "We are all in this together." **Focus on:** Gratitude.

9. The Teacher. Wise, understanding, patient and aware.
Positive: Enlightened role model. **Lowest:** Over-zealous fanatic.
Mantra: "Love is all there is." **Focus on:** "I can make a difference."

Chapter 7: Identify your strengths and weaknesses

As we saw in Part One, everything in our physical world is made of love energy and is therefore governed by the Law of Duality. This means everything that exists has an equal and exact opposite.

There's a Stalin or a Hitler for every Gandhi or Mother Teresa, just as there's a rainy day for every sunny one.

Likewise, every potential strength has a potential weakness. And the factor that determines whether we manifest one or the other is always the same: how much love is in our heart, versus how much fear.

* * *

With that in mind, let's invoke the "abundant" energy of **8** with this next chapter and look more closely at the so-called "Master Number" Birth Codes, which are also governed by the Law of Duality and therefore have an equal potential to give us a heightened amount of success, as well as a heightened amount of disappointment.

Chapter 8:
The four 'Master Numbers'

8 is the number of power

*These Life Paths have the potential for powerful growth
...as well as powerful challenges*

Master Numbers are double-digit Supplementary Birth Numbers where both numbers are the same. As we saw in Chapter 2, there are only four possible "Master Numbers" – 11, 22, 33 and 44 – because the highest possible set of Supplementary Birth Numbers for anyone alive today is 48 (those people born on September 29, 1999).

Having a Master Number in your Birth Code endows you with a heightened potential, because instead of working with two different supplementary energies in the first 36 formative years of your life, you are working intensely with only one. And anyone who focuses all their attention on one task or one goal is always more likely to succeed than someone who divides their energy between two or more.

The four Master Number Life Paths are 11/2 ("the Master Intuitive"), 22/4 ("the Master Builder"), 33/6 ("the Master Visionary") and the very rare 44/8 ("the Master Achiever").

If you have a Master Number, you have a heightened ability to achieve your highest purpose of helping as many people as possible.

– The 11/2 has the potential to be a powerful intuitive healer. They are creative, with a flair for design and a passion for harmony.

Chapter 8: The four 'Master Numbers'

– The <u>22</u>/**4** has the potential to build a happy home and work life. They are also humanitarians who give freely of their time and money.

– The <u>33</u>/**6** has the potential to manifest love and joy wherever they go. They are romantics who raise the vibration for all of us.

– The <u>44</u>/**8** has the potential to manifest abundance in all areas and then use their wealth and power to improve the lives of others.

* * *

Are Master Numbers more likely to achieve success?

The short answer is yes, and no. Like everything else in the universe, the Master Numbers are governed by the Law of Duality, which states that everything has an equal and exact opposite. This means their potential for success is heightened, but so is their potential for pain, frustration and disappointment.

Furthermore, the personality of a Master Number can often be problematic and highly charged because they are striving to walk a higher path. This can sometimes manifest in extreme mood swings, as they flit regularly between feeling confident and successful on the one hand, and disillusioned and frustrated on the other.

With great ability comes great responsibility, and some Master Numbers will choose not to stand out from the crowd. That's why there are just as many underachieving Master Numbers as there are highly successful people who don't have a Master Number.

* * *

Does having a Master Number make me "special"?

There is nothing "magical" about the four Master Numbers. Yes, they have unique qualities, but their name is somewhat misleading because it suggests that people born with a Master Number in their three-digit Birth Code are perhaps "special" in some way – and one of the most fundamental messages of the Self-Awareness System™ is that no one is any more special than anyone else.

"Special" is a trap for the ego. You want to stay well away from it.

Master Numbers do have a heightened potential. However, this potential can work both ways, and many people with Master Numbers who are not able to clear their emotional blockages (ie, their fears) may experience wild mood swings between the extremes of pleasure and pain, happiness and depression, and success and failure.

In the end, whether we have one Supplementary Birth Number that we work with for our first 36 years, or two that we work with for 18 years each, the level of success we experience in terms of achieving our highest purpose always depends not on the cards we are dealt... but how we play them.

* * *

How to play the Life Path cards you are dealt

Before exploring the qualities of the Master Numbers, let's review the supporting role your Supplementary Birth Numbers play in relation to your Life Path Number – which, as I want to keep re-minding you, is the number that has by far the most influence on your life.

Your two Supplementary Birth Numbers are the final double-digit number you get when you add up the numbers of your birth date. For example, if you were born on November 20, 1975 your Birth Code calculation would look like this:

1 + 1 + 2 + 0 + 1 + 9 + 7 + 5 = <u>26</u> / <u>2</u> + <u>6</u> = **8**.

In this example of a non-Master Number Birth Code, your Life Path Number is **8** (the Achiever) and your Supplementary Birth Numbers are <u>2</u> (the Intuitive) and <u>6</u> (the Visionary).

This means you will work primarily with the Life Path energy of **8** to achieve your life's highest purpose of creating abundance and helping others in need, but to do so you will also work with the supplementary energy of <u>2</u> at the start of your life to learn how to

Chapter 8: The four 'Master Numbers'

interact with others, and then with the supplementary energy of 6 to share your vision of love with the world.

Playing your hand in the positive:
If this was the non-Master Number hand your Self dealt you on the day you incarnated, you would probably spend most of your early years understanding what makes people tick and how to make them happy (positive 2). You would also develop a strong romantic and visionary awareness (positive 6) as you matured into adulthood, while at the same time preparing for an entrepreneurial career (positive **8**).

You might start a business that would be successful (positive **8**) because you would know how to get the best out of the people you work with (positive 2). It would also make you independently wealthy (positive **8**). This business might involve improving the lives of other people by teaching them how to be more loving (positive 6).

At the same time as you were forging a successful business or career (positive **8**), you would probably also focus a good deal of your energy on creating a nurturing and peaceful home life (positive 6).

Then as you grew older you might use your wealth and knowledge to help others in need by donating to worthy causes and doing charity work (the highest purpose of **8**).

Playing your hand in the negative:
If you failed to face your fears and learned to truly love your Self, your life could turn out very differently.

You might spend your early years trying to please everyone else while ignoring your own needs (negative 2), and then as you matured you might become disillusioned and even angry that the unjust and shockingly violent world you found your Self in failed to conform to your lofty romantic ideals (negative 6).

A lack of Self-love could lead you to employ the energy of your Life Path Number to hoard material possessions (negative **8**) as you used your wealth, status and power to hide your insecurity (negative **8**).

Part Two: The Self-Awareness System™

Because your Self knows that no amount of money will ever make you lastingly happy, your business might fail (negative **8**), or else if it succeeded it might do so at the expense of your personal life.

And instead of becoming unconditionally loving and optimistic (positive 6), you could turn into an irritating fault-finding perfectionist for whom nothing and no one was ever good enough (negative 6).

Furthermore, others would almost certainly let you down (negative 2) because you would need to learn the lesson that you must take care of your Self and not rely on others to do it for you.

You might even develop the ugly qualities of the co-dependent martyr (negative 2). Then, as you grew older, you could end up alone with all your money (negative **8**), rather like Scrooge on Christmas Eve.

Self-love is the key:

The difference between these two extremes depends on how much you learn to love your Self, face your fears and overcome your need for material objects and praise to make you feel better about your Self. As soon as you learn that love is all that matters, and that you are pure love and pure Source energy, you can turn the second scenario into the first… just like Scrooge did on Christmas morning.

* * *

Now let's do the same exercise for someone born with a Master Number, so you can see how people who rave about the special qualities of Master Numbers are really getting a little bit carried away. There is a difference, but not a huge one.

Let's say your birth date is August 27, 1989. If you add up your Birth Code, your calculation will look like this: 8 + 2 + 7 + 1 + 9 + 8 + 9 = 44 / 4 + 4 = 8. So, as a 44/**8**, your Life Path Number is still **8**, as in the example above, but this time your Supplementary Birth Numbers are the Master Number 44, (a double dose of the Builder).

Like the 26/**8**, you would use your Life Path energy of **8** to work towards achieving your highest purpose of creating abundance in all

Chapter 8: The four 'Master Numbers'

areas of your life and sharing it with others. But instead of doing so in close co-operation with others (the energy of **2**) and shining your message of love out into the world (the energy of **6**), you would be more likely to go it alone and focus all your efforts on material and practical issues, due to the double supplementary earth energy of **4** operating throughout your first 36 years in conjunction with the equally earthy and pragmatic energy of your Life Path Number **8**.

<u>Playing your Master hand in the positive:</u>
If this was the hand your Self dealt you on the day you incarnated, you would spend your early years studying hard and performing well at school (positive **4**). And because you would continue to work with **4** into your adult years, you might go to college to further your studies (positive **4**), or else go straight into business for your Self (positive **8**).

Your business, or your professional career, would have a high chance of success thanks to your remarkable capacity for hard work (positive **4**) and your attention to detail (positive **4**).

You would be a fiercely loyal friend and colleague (positive **4**) as well as a powerful persuader (positive **8**), ensuring you would gather a group of devoted followers around you if you started a business, or a team of dedicated staff to support you if you worked for a company.

Whatever you chose to do, your stamina (positive **4**) and your boundless energy (positive **8**) might earn you substantial wealth and status (positive 8), which you would use in philanthropic ways to help the needy (positive **8**). Your home life would be stable (positive **4**), your friendships would also be rock solid (positive **4**) and you would provide a luxurious home for your close loving family (positive **8**).

<u>Playing your Master hand in the negative:</u>
If you failed to overcome your fears and insecurities, your life could play out very differently.

The negative energy of your double supplementary number of **4** in your formative years could turn you into a stubborn and inflexible perfectionist who struggles to fit in with others at school. You might rebel against your teachers, your parents and anyone else in authority (negative 4), repeatedly landing you in trouble and causing you to shrink ever deeper into cynicism and even depression (negative 4).

Your stubbornness (negative 4) and your refusal to open up about how you are feeling (negative 8) could push away even those who are closest to you. And, ironically for someone who is so trustworthy (positive 4), you could end up distrusting everyone (negative 4) and using your intelligence and personal power (positive 8) to manipulate them and bend them to your will (negative 8).

In business or your career, your obsession with petty details and your tendency to procrastinate (negative 4) would almost certainly doom you to failure, while your need for wealth and power to cover up your insecurities (negative 8) would cause you to hoard what money you did make and guard it jealously (negative 8).

As with the negative 26/8, in the previous example, you would probably end up like Scrooge… miserable, unloved and alone.

* * *

The qualities of the four Master Numbers

The above examples illustrate how Master Numbers allow us to focus all our energies in a certain direction – with dramatic results, either positive or negative, depending on our amount of Self-love.

Also, a Master Number usually indicates the presence of an older Self who has already worked through many Life Paths and has chosen to focus in this lifetime on one or two particular areas. But by no means do all great leaders, healers and teachers have Master Numbers. Some of the most influential people in recent history – Gandhi, Mother Teresa, Nelson Mandela, Winston Churchill and Mikhail Gorbachev – were all born without a Master Number.

So now let's go through the four Master Numbers to see how each contains the potential for achieving a heightened level of success, as well as an equally heightened potential for disappointment.

11/2: The Master Intuitive

When 11 appears in your Birth Code, it indicates that in your early formative years – as well as working primarily with your Life Path Number **2** (the Intuitive) – you will focus on your double supplementary energy of 1 (the Leader). This means that while the main purpose of your life is to bring peace and harmony to the world around you (the positive energy of **2**), you will do so in original and creative ways due to your double leadership energy of 1.

The magnified "fire" (action) energy of 1 empowers you to take the lead in your peacemaking efforts as you grow up, driving you to help others find harmony in their lives. As well as giving you a natural flair for creativity, design and original ideas, the unique combination of your **2** and your two 1s in this Master Number endows you with the skills to become an intuitive and effective peacemaker on a much bigger stage, capable of bringing harmony not only to your workplace and family, but to your community, your country… and even the world.

Barack Obama, for example, has a Birth Code of 11/**2**. For all of his shortcomings, and no matter which side of the political fence you are on, his heart is unquestionably in the right place.

David Beckham, Bill Clinton, Anthony Robbins and Prince William are other well-known 11/**2**s. They have all demonstrated the positive potential of this Master Number by bringing people together in peace and harmony.

Positive qualities

The feminine "water" (emotion) energy of Life Path Number **2** ensures that 11/**2**s are usually very social and make friends easily. They are generous hosts, have good memories for both names and faces and are quick to put people at their ease.

In their childhood and throughout their crucial teenage years they can often be nervous and even shy until they find a level of confidence to break out of their shell. However, once they do develop their Self-confidence, they can quickly grow up to become charming, empathetic and charismatic socialisers and harmonisers.

11/2s often have a powerful imagination and a somewhat dreamy nature. They are inherently artistic, possessing a deep affinity with colour and form. Socially, they experience emotions deeply and can easily get upset if they feel hurt or let down by people close to them.

When this happens, they tend to retreat back into their shell, often not speaking about their hurt until they are sure they know what they are feeling. When they do eventually talk about it, they weigh their words carefully. And because they are extremely forgiving by nature, they quickly find a way to make peace with whoever has done them wrong and return to being their lovely, sunny and optimistic Self.

Most 11/2s are highly intuitive individuals. They are usually emotionally and spiritually evolved and have powerful psychic abilities that, if nurtured, enable these insightful peacemakers to connect with people not just effortlessly, but on a deep and meaningful level. They also make excellent healers, designers, sales people and clairvoyants.

If 11/2s are able to tap into their leadership potential through working with the double masculine energy of 1 in their early years, they can make an impact on a wide scale, especially if they follow a path that puts them in the public eye. At the highest level of their potential, they can literally change the way the world thinks about love.

Famous Master Intuitives

Mozart turned the world of music on its head, Lord Byron has become synonymous with romanticism, and billionaire John Paul Getty and legendary filmmaker Cecile B. DeMille redefined their industries. More recent 11/2s include Bob Hope, Madonna, Paris Hilton, Jennifer Aniston and Diana Ross.

Potential negatives

Because of the extremely high vibration of their Life Path energy and their heightened ability to reach their true potential, 11/2s can sometimes collapse beneath the weight of their own personal expectations. They know they are capable of great achievements and they can therefore tend to judge themselves harshly if they feel that they are not living up to the often impossibly high expectations they have for themselves.

Also, some 11/2s are so spiritually evolved that they feel the pain of others as though it were their own. This can lead them to become overwhelmed if they try to help everyone all at once.

In extreme cases, they can become weighed down into depression, causing them to veer towards Self-destructive behaviour such as addictions to drugs, alcohol, sex and so on. If this happens they can find themselves teetering on the brink between success and disaster.

From the list of famous 11/2s above it is easy to find examples. Bill Clinton famously flirted with women and disaster while at the same time being one of America's most well-loved populist presidents, while Paris Hilton seemed to teeter between spectacular success and equally spectacular disaster early in her career.

Mozart was part genius, part lunatic. David Beckham is revered by some, and ridiculed by others. And Madonna has walked a fine line in becoming the most influential female pop musician in history. The successor to her crown is Lady Gaga, who is a **1** rather than a Master 11/**2**. While she has undoubted creative and leadership qualities, she may lack the lasting influence of Madonna. Only history will tell.

The secret to success

To ensure success and avoid disaster, all 11/**2**s need to have faith in their abilities and avoid over-analysing themselves too much.

Conclusion

No Birth Code in the entire Self-Awareness System™ is so tuned in to the needs and desires of others than the always compassionate and empathetic Master Intuitive, thanks to their remarkable "sixth sense" that picks up on how everyone else is feeling.

This makes the 11/**2** an effective healer and peacemaker, but it can also be a burden when everyone they know beats a path to their door asking for help. The key lesson that 11/**2**s need to learn is to draw firm boundaries around themselves so they are able to help out when they can... but never at the expense of their own wellbeing. When they can do this, they can avoid the negative side of their Master Number and real-eyes their own beautiful divine nature as one of the most loving, supportive and generous Birth Codes of all.

* * *

22/4: The Master Builder

When <u>22</u> appears in your Birth Code, it indicates that in your formative years, as well as working primarily with your pragmatic earth Life Path Number **4** (the Builder), you will focus intently on the double supplementary emotional energy of <u>2</u> (the Intuitive).

So while the main purpose of your life is to create a solid foundation for your Self and help others do the same (positive **4**), you will be doing so in close and intense co-operation with the people around you, both at home in your family and in your professional life (positive <u>2</u>).

The double "water" (emotion) energy of <u>2</u> endows you with a heightened capacity for empathy and compassion. All <u>2</u>s have strong social skills and make the best diplomats, counsellors, healers and advisers, and these qualities are particularly strong in the <u>22</u>/**4**. This, combined with your practical Life Path Number **4**, gives you the capacity to be extremely successful in business and your career, and many <u>22</u>/**4**s strike out on their own quite early, often building up several companies (and building several homes) in their lifetime.

4s are the best managers and <u>2</u>s are the best peacekeepers. When these energies are combined it makes for a very harmonious work and family environment where you can tap into your highest potential.

Positive qualities

<u>22</u>/**4** is called the number of the Master Builder because as well as learning how to build a business and a stable home life for themselves with the practical earth energy of **4**, they also have the potential to interact well with others through the supplementary water (emotional) energy of <u>2</u>, which allows them to become excellent team players.

Chapter 8: The four 'Master Numbers'

<u>22</u>/**4**s are natural problem-solvers and hard workers. If they channel their talents they can build almost anything they set their mind to and overcome any obstacle in their way through their sheer tenacity and determination.

Most <u>22</u>/**4**s will achieve remarkable success in whatever they set out to do. They have an enviable knack for manifesting both significant wealth and lasting friendships, and they are able to use their practical organisational skills (**4**) and team-building talents (<u>2</u>) to make even their wildest dreams come true.

<u>22</u>/**4**s achieve their success by using the intuitive qualities of their "double <u>2</u>" emotional energy to spot opportunities others may have missed. Their pragmatic **4** energy then kicks in, helping them to set clear goals and follow through on their detailed plan to achieve them.

They are often the proverbial rock on whom others lean when times get tough. It is a role they are usually happy to play because **4**s are fiercely loyal friends, and <u>2</u>s are always concerned about the welfare of others... so <u>22</u>/**4**s are normally only too happy to help out anyone who might be in need.

<u>Famous Master Builders</u>

Well-known <u>22</u>/**4**s include master craftsman Leonardo da Vinci, enduring Hollywood star Clint Eastwood, the first ever showbusiness millionaire PT Barnum, Irish singer and activist Bono, legendary crooner Frank Sinatra, and the famous American novelist JD Salinger, whose birth date of 1/1/1919 has one of the most remarkably potent set of birth numbers I have ever seen. All these high achievers worked hard and, importantly, focused on detail to build their success.

<u>Potential negatives</u>

The <u>22</u>/**4**'s tendency to go out of their way to look after others can sometimes get the better of them. They may find themselves becoming overwhelmed with requests for help, money and advice, and they must learn to do what they can, and no more, because the double energy of <u>2</u> when they are growing up carries the potential for the <u>22</u>/**4** to spend so much time making sure everyone else is happy that they forget to look after themselves.

If they don't find the right balance between doing what is best for them and what is best for others, they can quickly become grumpy, resentful and subject to wild mood swings. They are also very sensitive to the emotional needs of their friends, and they can sometimes be disappointed when their circle of friends does not reciprocate with the same level of sensitivity and consideration for how they are feeling.

Another negative that 22/4s must watch out for is a tendency to drive themselves to the point of physical and emotional exhaustion by taking on too much all at once. They usually bounce back pretty quickly, though, because they tackle health issues the same way they tackle any other problems that come along – logically, and with grit, stamina and determination.

22/4s are often perfectionists, which can be a double-edged sword. Whether they are building something, making something or just arranging the furniture in their home, everything has to be just so. They must therefore guard against becoming bogged down in the minutiae of life and obsessing too much over petty details.

If you are a 22/4, try to remember to stay focused on the bigger picture and step back from a situation or challenge if you start to feel overwhelmed by it. You do best when you concentrate on making the big strategic decisions, and then use your unparalleled people skills to enroll others to look after the day-to-day details.

The secret to success

On the whole, 22/4s – like all the Master Numbers – are more likely to work with the positive aspects of their Birth Code than the negative ones, because they tend to be natural optimists.

As long as they remember to take the time to nurture themselves, keep one eye on the bigger picture at all times and not take themselves – or anyone else – too seriously, they have the ability to achieve remarkable success in almost everything they do.

Chapter 8: The four 'Master Numbers'

Conclusion

22/4s have a knack for manifesting their dreams into reality by following through on practical actions to achieve their goals.

Some might say they have a "magic touch" because they seem to enjoy great success in their business ventures, while at the same time they are incredibly loyal and reliable people who create deep and abiding friendships, not just at home and in their social life but with their work colleagues as well.

However, all Master Builders must guard against becoming too involved in the lives of others. When someone close to them is suffering, they can take on their pain as though it were their own.

A key lesson for the 22/4 is to draw clear boundaries around themselves, allowing them to continue to help others but not at the expense of their own emotional and financial wellbeing.

* * *

33/6: The Master Visionary

When 33 appears in your Birth Code, it indicates that in your formative years, as well as working primarily with your Life Path Number **6** (the Visionary), you will also focus intently on the double supplementary energy of 3 (the Creative).

This means that while the main purpose of your life is to uphold and teach the lofty romantic ideals of love to show humanity what it is capable of (the highest purpose of **6**), you will also develop excellent communication skills (the energy of 3) and be able to motivate others to follow in your footsteps to become the best they can be.

The double "air" (thought) energy of 3 means you are insightful and expressive, able to communicate your ideas effectively to motivate others. This, combined with the nurturing qualities of your "watery" (emotional) Life Path Number **6**, enables you to take your uplifting message of love to a wider audience.

Not only will you see the best in everyone, you will help them to see the best in themselves as well.

And whereas all **6**s are nurturing homemakers, Master 33/**6**s are seldom content to just focus on their home life. Whether it's through writing, charity work, public speaking or political activist roles, the Visionary 33/**6** is usually driven to go out into the world – far beyond the confines of their home – to do whatever they can to improve the lives of as many people as possible.

Positive qualities

33/**6** is called the number of the Master Visionary because the highest purpose of Life Path Number **6** is to hold a vision of beauty and love for all mankind and to show them how the world is meant to be… and indeed can be, if only everyone were to focus on love and compassion, rather than fear and greed.

This, combined with the double communication energy of 3, gives Master Number 33/**6**s the opportunity to become powerful writers, teachers and persuasive orators whose ultimate goal is to convey their message of love to the world.

Beauty is fundamental to all 33/**6**s, especially the beautiful notion that we can be, do and have anything we set our hearts and minds on. This is one of the central lessons that all 33/**6**s are here to teach us through their books, films, music and speeches, as well as by using their own lives as a shining and loving example.

They are also here to teach us the important lesson that love, like charity, begins at home… because it is not possible to shine our love into the world if we don't first shine it on our Self and the ones we love. This is why all 33/**6**s are sensitive people who, deep down, value their family above all else and will go to great lengths to create a calm, loving and nurturing home environment.

Famous Master Visionaries

Agatha Christie, who is the best-selling fiction author of all time with sales of 4 billion books (even beating Shakespeare!), was a Master Visionary 33/**6**. She infused all her famous detective stories – as well as the love stories she wrote under the name Mary Westmacott – with

Chapter 8: The four 'Master Numbers'

a healthy dose of charm and sophistication, setting them in romantic locations and in a period of history when gentility was the cornerstone of society. It is one of the main reasons that her stories have stood the test of time, and will continue to do so.

Another hugely influential 33/**6**, Francis Ford Coppola, is known to have nurtured the talents of many great modern filmmakers, including Stephen Spielberg, Martin Scorsese and George Lucas, playing an almost "godfatherly" role to them. And in his famous *Godfather* trilogy, the central message of the importance of family shines through loud and clear above all the drama and violence. (He even employed another famous 33/**6**, Robert DeNiro, to portray the romantic if ruthless early life of the eponymous central character.)

And what about Fred Astaire and Greta Garbo? Both these 33/**6**s epitomised the romance of cinema in its early days.

Even *Rocky*, Sylvester Stallone's breakthrough film, has as its central theme the wonderfully romantic notion that we can all achieve our dreams if we go after them with both hands. Stallone, a fiercely loyal family man, is also a Master Visionary 33/**6**, and his career typifies another quality of this Master Number Birth Code – namely, a desire to motivate the underdog to rise above their circumstance.

All 33/**6**s will go to great lengths to improve the lives of the disadvantaged and the downtrodden. It is a vital part of their vision of a better world. And when they master the art of communication through working with the double energy of 3 – as Stallone has done in the medium of film – they can succeed in making the world more aware of the need for compassion and kindness.

Stallone is the epitome of the positive qualities of the 33/**6**. There is no greater movie about the triumph of the human spirit against all the odds than *Rocky*. Even his absurdly violent *Rambo* films all have as their central plot the story of one man risking his life to help free the oppressed and the persecuted.

The life purpose of all 33/**6**s is to help the needy, protect the weak, enrich the poor and empower the disadvantaged. And the best way to do this is by using the double energy of 3 to communicate their vision of beauty and love to as wide an audience as possible.

Potential negatives

On a personal level, 33/6s will strive to nurture their friends and families. But they must always remember to nurture themselves as well. Their giving and caring nature can sometimes lead them to give too much of themselves without looking after their own needs. When this happens, the 33/6 can spiral into distress as they fret about the problems of the world and beat themselves up for not doing more to help. They see images of brutality and starvation on the nightly news and feel the pain as if it were their own… as if it were them languishing in the Asian labour camps, or the sand-blown African villages.

The secret to success

No one person can change the whole world on their own, and so to avoid disappointment and despair all 33/6s must remember that they are not Superman or Wonder Woman. They must also remember that the key lesson of their life is to learn to love themselves first before they can give their love to others.

Conclusion

33/6s are relatively rare individuals who are able to rise above their own needs to help others. These are attractive Selfs in every sense of the word because they draw other people to them with their loving energy. They always want to do good and help out anywhere they can.

The downside of this burning desire to make the world the way their romantic hearts want it to be is they can tend to take on too much and burn out. Like the 22/4, they need to learn to set their boundaries and be able to say "no" when the tsunami of needy people beating a path to their loving door gets all too much.

* * *

Chapter 8: The four 'Master Numbers'

44/8: The Master Achiever

The Master Number <u>44</u>/**8** is very rare for the simple reason that mathematically the highest number you can obtain is 48 (September 29, 1999: 9+2+9+1+9+9+9 = <u>48</u>). Therefore there are only a few possible birth dates that will add up to <u>44</u>, or higher. And this situation is not about to change in a hurry because the next possible <u>44</u>/**8** birth date will not arrive until September 29, 2499… in about 500 years.

So it is very probable that all of the <u>44</u>/**8** Master Achievers who are alive today may feel a great burden of responsibility, whether they are aware of it consciously or not.

The rarity of this "all-earth" Birth Code is reflected in the potency of its numbers. This is the only Birth Code in which all three numbers are governed by the same element, which means people with this Birth Code have a unique capacity for material success on the Earth plane.

This is why the <u>44</u>/**8** is known as "The Alchemist", because they have a Midas-like power to turn anything they touch into gold.

<u>Positive qualities:</u>

When <u>44</u> appears in your Birth Code, it indicates that in your formative years, as well as working primarily with your earthy Life Path Number **8** (the Achiever), you will also focus on the double earth energy of <u>4</u> (the Builder). In other words, all your energy will be directed towards creating, stability, wealth and abundance.

The double "earth" (nurturing) energy of <u>4</u> means you will work to build a solid foundation, firmly rooted in the real world. From a very early age, you will nurture the positive qualities of fidelity, hard work and determination. You will also evolve into a loyal and devoted friend. Then, as you mature, you will continue to work with "earth energy" through your Life Path Number **8** – which, in the positive, may help you create great wealth and use it to set up foundations and other charitable organisations to improve the lives of those in need.

<u>4</u> marks the end of the first stage of the Spiritual Growth Cycle, where we learn how to create a stable financial and emotional foundation for ourselves, and **8** marks the end of the second stage of

the Spiritual Growth Cycle, where we use all we have learned to teach others how to create abundance for themselves. Taken together, this helps explain why 44/8s are usually very old Selfs and are regarded as having the "biggest karmic bank balance" of all the Birth Codes, due to the lessons and achievements of their many past lives working with the energies of Life Paths **1** through to **7**.

Those 44/8s who do the required inner work (ie, learn that they are pure love and part of the Source) have the capacity to amass great wealth and use it in positive ways for the greater good. They also have the potential to become extremely powerful and effective philanthropists who are dedicated to using their Midas-like gift for creating abundance to improve the lives of others on a massive scale.

As well as being wise old Selfs, Master Achiever "Alchemists" are also loyal, considerate and dependable (the qualities of 4). So not only can they metaphorically turn lead into gold, their friendships and their relationships will often be "solid gold" as well.

<u>Famous Master Achievers</u>

Remarkably, there is no public record of any famous 44/8s having existed at any time in history. On the surface, this seems bizarre to say the least because one would think that these high-powered Achievers would stand out from the crowd.

Incredibly, I have not found any well-known 44/8s born between September 29, 1599 and September 25, 1999, which is the bracket for this Master Number. Even Dan Millman's exhaustive list of more than 1570 famous Life Path Numbers in his book *The Life You Were Born To Live* does not contain a single 44/8.

This leads me to one of two conclusions: either the relatively few 44/8s born in the past 400 years or so have been so evolved they have chosen to work tirelessly behind the scenes to create abundance and share it with their fellow travellers while humbly shunning the limelight (this is quite likely given the fact they are old Selfs who may have learned in previous lifetimes how to rise above their ego); or else the enormous pressure of fulfilling the potential of such a powerful Birth

Chapter 8: The four 'Master Numbers'

Code has proved too much for them and they have either chosen not to pursue fame and fortune at all, or they have fallen to the "dark side".

<u>Potential negatives</u>

As we have seen, the Law of Duality states that everything has an equal and exact opposite. So it is with the Master Numbers, for with great gifts comes great responsibility. And none of them has greater gifts or greater responsibility than the Master Achiever.

Because Alchemists are almost always old Selfs, very few will fall into the clutches of their negative "dark side" potential. Almost all of them will walk the positive side of their Life Path. However, <u>44</u>/8s who do not do the necessary "inner work" to face their fears may flip to their dark side from time to time if they fall prey to the temptation of using their power and influence to make themselves feel better by exploiting others. This is called the "Scrooge" path, and some insecure <u>44</u>/8s can be tempted to take it.

Sometimes, even positive <u>44</u>/8s may find they are just not strong enough to shoulder the heavy weight of their exaggerated expectations of themselves, leading them to judge themselves too harshly for their perceived shortcomings.

Other <u>44</u>/8s might experience some success but choose not to accept the burden of devoting their life to the wellbeing of others, electing instead to limit their generous philanthropy to their inner circle of friends and loved ones.

<u>The secret to success</u>

If you are a <u>44</u>/**8**, you need to know that nothing is expected of you by anyone other than your Self. There is no tablet in the sky on which is written: "All <u>44</u>/**8**s are here to change the world." Your life is yours to live exactly how you choose to live it. And for many people, fame and fortune are simply not worth the effort and the price we have to pay to achieve them. That, in my opinion, might also explain the lack of high-profile <u>44</u>/**8**s in the world.

There is one other possible explanation for the lack of well-known 44/8s: it could be that the world is not yet ready for the revolutionary changes of which these people are capable, due to their extraordinary capacity to manifest abundance.

As I said, the next possible 44/8s will not be born for another 500 years. Perhaps by then the world will be ready for them. Maybe by then we will have evolved enough to accept the remarkable and abundant gifts that the 44/8 Alchemists have to offer us.

Conclusion

If you are a 44/8, please be aware that you have no obligation whatsoever to fulfill the highest potential of this remarkable Birth Code. All that matters is that you learn to truly love you Self for who you are, and know that you are pure, divine love.

In this regard, perhaps the mantra of The Alchemist should be: "We create the most abundance in our life, and in the lives of others, when we love our Self… and allow our Self to love others too."

* * *

To add or not to add… that is the question

As a final note about the Master Numbers, I want to address a debate that has been raging in the small but wonderfully vocal and passionate numerology community for centuries.

This is the debate over whether the two identical Supplementary Birth Numbers in a Master Number (11, 22, 33, 44) should be added together to arrive at a single-digit Life Path Number of **2, 4, 6** or **8** to determine the primary energy that governs the Life Path of someone born with one of these four high-powered Birth Codes.

Or should we create four more Life Paths especially for these Master Numbers and call them **11, 22, 33** and **44** – and forget about their single-digit Life Path Numbers altogether?

Chapter 8: The four 'Master Numbers'

I am part of a minority who believes <u>11</u>, <u>22</u>, <u>33</u> and <u>44</u> are not Life Path Numbers and therefore these double-digit Supplementary Birth Numbers should be added together… just like all the rest.

To me, there really is no debate because there are only nine numbers, as we have already established, which means any number larger than 9 is merely a multiplier of one of the nine numbers.

To show you what I mean, dig out a calculator – or use the one on your phone – and divide the Master Number <u>11</u> by 9, which is the highest number and the only true "master number" in my opinion.

You will get 1.2222222222222222222222222… stretching out to infinity and beyond, as Buzz Lightyear would say.

Yes, the <u>1</u> is still there and will play an important role. But it is clearly the energy of **2** that governs the number <u>11</u>.

Now divide the Master Number <u>22</u> by 9, and you will get 2.4444444444444444444444. So again, the <u>2</u> is still there, but it is clearly the energy of **4** that counts the most for this Birth Code.

Do the same with the Master Number <u>33</u> and you get 3.6666666666666666666, and with the Master Number <u>44</u> you get 4.88888888888888888… going on forever. (If you get a "7" or a "9" at the end of the number, your calculator has merely rounded up the last decimal point.) Again, the <u>3</u> and the <u>4</u> are still there, but the Master Number <u>33</u> is clearly ruled by the energy of **6**, just as the Master Number <u>44</u> is clearly ruled by the energy of **8**.

So yes, I couldn't agree more that if you are born with a Master Number, then the double dose of <u>1</u>, <u>2</u>, <u>3</u> or <u>4</u> in your Supplementary Birth Numbers means you will work intensely with the energy of that number as you grow towards becoming pure conscious love (which is your one and only goal). But the energy that overarches all your efforts will be that of your Life Path Number of **2, 4, 6** or **8**.

In the listings for the nine Life Paths in Part Three, I will spend considerable time on the unique challenges and benefits of the four Master Numbers. But I will not list them separately. I will put them under their single-digit Life Path Number – <u>11</u> under **2**, <u>22</u> under **4**,

Part Two: The Self-Awareness System™

<u>33</u> under **6** and <u>44</u> under **8** – because I believe both passionately and sincerely that is where they belong.

However, if after reading all about them you still want to "identify" as an <u>11</u> rather than an <u>11</u>/**2**, as a <u>22</u> rather than a <u>22</u>/**4**, as a <u>33</u> rather than a <u>33</u>/**6**, or as a <u>44</u> rather than a <u>44</u>/**8**, that is absolutely fine. How you identify your Self is up to you, and should always be based on what makes you feel most comfortable, as long you real-eyes that any form of "identity" – whether it's a Life Path Number, an astrological sign, or just your name – is the work of your ego that wants to feel separate from everyone and everything.

The Self-Awareness System™ is concerned with guiding you, not labelling you. So go with what you feel most serves your needs. If you want to be an **11**, for example, then be an **11**. If you want to be an <u>11</u>/**2**, then be an <u>11</u>/**2**. And so on. Just remember that all the numbers in the Self-Awareness System™ represent paths you can take to help you shed your ego and attain your life's highest purpose, not labels that define who you are.

Who you are is pure love, the same as the rest of us.

And there is no number for that.

***

I know you are longing to finish this introduction to the Self-Awareness System™ in Part Two and move on to Part Three to find out all about your Self. So let's now invoke the "completion" energy of **9** to tie this all up and bless you on your journey.

After this next chapter you will be ready to access and decode every single message your Self hard-wired into your Birth Code when you chose to live the life you are living, right now as you read this.

Go well on your journey. Enjoy your Life Path.

Love everyone you meet.

And above all… love your Self.

Chapter 9:
Your life is what you make it

9 is the number of wisdom

*You already know the path to your bliss
...all you have to do is walk it*

I dislike rules. As a non-conformist Rebel **5** (and a mercurial Gemini to boot) I have broken almost all of them in my time. And yet here I am about to give you the five "Golden Rules" for the Self-Awareness System™ to make sure you correctly interpret the messages that your Self is about to give you in Part Three.

Normally, I would tell you that if someone gives you a rule, the first thing you should do is break it... just so you can flick two fingers at the Fat Controllers who tell you to keep off the grass, obey all the signs and fall into line.

But in this case, these five Golden Rules will help you get the most out of the listings in Part Three so you can break free from the forces of control and let your Self soar to the stars.

* * *

1. Life is not a competition...

Please remember that no number is "better" or "worse" than any other number. If you are a **1**, say, that does not mean you are "beneath" or less evolved than a **6**, **7**, **8** or **9**. In your many past lives you may have already worked through the qualities of **6**, **7**, **8** and **9** but have returned to **1** to master some other aspect of courage and leadership.

You won't necessarily work through the Life Path Numbers in numerical order. You may incarnate as a **2**, say, to work predominantly on issues of co-operation and awareness, and then in your next lifetime you might incarnate as an **8** to work on creating abundance in all areas of your life, and then as a **4** to help others on your path, then go back to **3** to learn more about creativity, then as a **5** to develop discipline and gain a sense of adventure, and so on.

So in many ways you may be much wiser and more evolved as a **1** in your 30th lifetime than someone else who is living a **9** in, say, only their 12th life.

Besides, life is not a competition. Nor is it a race. There are no winners or losers. It's all about learning and growing at your own pace… and, of course, having lots and LOTS of fun in the process.

* * *

2. …but it is a numbers game

No one works solely with the qualities of their Life Path Number and Supplementary Birth Numbers to the exclusion of everything else. The Builder **4**, for example, will also experience romance (**6**), freedom (**5**), achievement (**8**), co-operation (**2**), and so on.

Everyone works through all nine areas of their life to varying degrees – that is the nature of the human experience. What your Life Path Number and Supplementary Birth Numbers will show you are the primary challenges and opportunities that will determine whether you succeed in achieving your life's highest purpose, or not.

Your Life Path Number represents the latent potential that you are born with. It also indicates the specific character traits that will influence your behaviour. And it offers valuable clues about some of the obstacles you will face during your life, as well as highlighting your

Chapter 9: Your life is what you make it

inherent skills and shortcomings that will make some of the challenges relatively easy, and others more difficult.

But it does not define who you are.

Yes, the central lessons of your Life Path Number will lead you to your highest purpose and will denote the major battles and victories of your life. But you will also need to learn other lessons so you can grow from an innocent, inexperienced and unevolved "pure-love child" into a well-balanced, well-rounded and fully evolved "pure-love adult".

Someone working a particular Life Path Number will certainly focus most of their time and energy on the challenges and rewards associated with that particular number, but they will also have to deal with the issues relating to all the other eight numbers throughout their life... only to a lesser extent.

Example:

Let's say we have incarnated as an **8** and are therefore working primarily on the issues of abundance and power – ie, tapping into the abundant nature of the material world we live in so we can use it to help others, as well as enrich our Self.

This is our highest purpose as an **8**, but we will also face some of the challenges associated with the other eight Life Path Numbers:

1 – confidence, so we are brave and determined enough to start our own business and take our original ideas out into the world.

2 – interaction and co-operation with others, so we can enroll them to help us with anything we decide to do.

3 – expressing our Self, so we can form close and supportive relationships in our life... romantically, socially and professionally.

4 – practicality, so we can manage our affairs seamlessly.

5 – adventure, so we have the desire to travel and understand how the world works, and therefore how we can improve it.

6 – romance, so we remember to take the time to nurture the important loving relationships in our life.

7 – spiritual knowledge, so we understand how we can use our material success for the higher good of all mankind.

9 – integrity, so our business and our personal life will give us a sense of fulfillment and peace of mind, and also so we can become a role model for others.

All of these other life lessons are of secondary importance to our highest life purpose, but we would have no chance of achieving that purpose if we focused just on the energy of **8**. Therefore, when you read about your Life Path Number, real-eyes that if what you read doesn't cover the issues you are facing in your life right now, it may be because you are focusing on some of the more minor issues that relate to one of the other numbers – or, if you are aged 36 or younger, you may be working with the energy of a Supplementary Birth Number.

If you look closer and open up your mind to your deep, intuitive connection with your heart/Self, you will be able to see how what you are focusing on right now is actually a smaller part of the bigger picture of your overall Life Path.

Rest assured that all of the information contained in each Life Path Number listing in Part Three is absolutely perfect for who you are and where you want to go with your life.

* * *

3. What if it doesn't sound like me?

If you don't immediately identify with the issues of your Life Path, look closely at the sections on the negative aspects of your number. You may find that these insights are more accurate for where you are in your life right now.

All this means is that you are working your issues from the negative perspective rather than the positive at the moment. Neither is better, nor worse. They are both equally valid ways of arriving at the same outcome… namely, your life's highest purpose.

Also, please be aware of the role that your cultural upbringing will have on your personality, the foundation of which was formed during the first three years of your life. If you were born into a religious family,

Chapter 9: Your life is what you make it

or a wealthy family, or a poor family, or in a society that doesn't value freedom, or in a hippie commune – to take a few extreme examples – your core values and beliefs will be shaped very differently.

The qualities of your Life Path determine what you came here to do (your life's highest purpose), but how you go about doing it will vary greatly depending on your upbringing and your values and beliefs.

So even though some of the information in your Life Path listing may not perfectly match your personality and the belief system of your cultural background, it will always tell you exactly what you need to do to guide you to your highest purpose, and therefore to your bliss.

* * *

4. Double-check your calculations

If after looking at both the positive and negative aspects of your Life Path Number you still find little in common with your life as it is right now, go back to Chapter 2 and check you added up your birth date correctly. You may inadvertently be looking at the wrong number.

Then, if you are still unsure how the information relates to you, ask a close friend to read the details of your Life Path Number for you and give you some feedback. Often it takes an outsider's perspective to show us the qualities about ourselves (especially the negative ones) that we may not be able to see, or that we are in denial about.

The Self-Awareness System™ works every time and is uncannily accurate. I have yet to find a single person whose strengths, weaknesses, likes, dislikes and life experiences do not match their Life Path Number and their Supplementary Birth Numbers down to a tee.

* * *

5. There is no such thing as "success" or "failure"

Finally, when you read all about your Life Path Number and your Supplementary Birth Numbers in a moment in Part Three, please don't feel you have to do everything perfectly throughout your life as you strive to achieve your highest purpose. As I've said before, this is a guide book, not a rule book. Not all of us achieve everything that we set out to achieve. Some of us achieve less, and some achieve more. And both are absolutely fine.

Please don't put any pressure on your Self to be the "perfect **2**" or the "perfect **7**", or whatever you are in this lifetime. Just try to be who you are, and do what you can.

Everything in life is always perfect. You will always be exactly where you are meant to be. You will always learn exactly what you are meant to learn. And you will always grow in exactly the way you are meant to grow.

Always. Every time. No exceptions.

Remember, you will almost certainly come back and do it all over again in one of your future lifetimes. As we have already seen, we all live each Life Path more than once, and usually numerous times. The most important thing is to have fun along the way.

Happiness is always one of your highest personal goals, for it is only through being happy that you are able to perform the greatest service for those around you, and for the world as a whole – because happiness raises its vibration.

So just relax into your life. Enjoy it. It's a magnificent trip. Strive to remain young at heart and full of wonder. And please don't grow up too much. Try to be like a child, because children know instinctively that love and laughter are all that matters.

The very best way to live your life is to be like a child in the front seat of a roller-coaster. No matter what life gives you, or what it takes away, try as often as you can to put a big silly grin on your face, throw your arms high up in the air above your head… and shout "YES!" to the heavens as loudly as you possibly can.

If you live like that, you won't go wrong.

I promise you.

PART THREE:

THE NINE LIFE PATHS

Our deepest fear is not that we are inadequate.
Our deepest fear is that we are powerful beyond measure.
It is our light, not our darkness, that most frightens us.

– Marianne Williamson, *A Return to Love*

How to read your Life Path listing

TO make sure you get the most out of these Life Path listings in Part Three, if you haven't already done so please first read Part One to understand your life's purpose (which is the answer to the question "Why are we here?") and then read Part Two to discover how the Self-Awareness System™ works. Without this knowledge, you will miss out on 80 per cent of the value of your listing here in Part Three. Yes, you will be astonished at how accurate the information is, and it will certainly guide you to experience some success in all areas of your life, and the lives of your family and friends. But the successes that you, and they, achieve will be fleeting and shallow at best.

Having said that, I know many time-challenged people will choose to come straight here, in which case please bear in mind these five important points about the listings. And then, when you get a chance, please read Parts One and Two. It will be worth it, I assure you, because you will be able to decipher the much richer information your Self hard-coded into your Life Path Number and Supplementary Birth Numbers when it incarnated as you – wonderful, unique, perfect YOU.

* * *

1. Reading the number as your Life Path Number

Each Life Path Number contains a summary header that includes the main qualities of the number for a quick reference guide. This includes the stage you are at on your Spiritual Growth Cycle, your governing element and astrological influence, your main positive and negative potential, your life's highest purpose, your relationship matches, some suggested career paths, and positive words to live by.

Then the main part of each listing breaks down the information contained in your Birth Code into five sections to help you make the best choices in each of the five key areas of your life:

1. Life choices to explain the paths and the pitfalls that you will navigate on your journey towards your highest purpose.

2. Career and business choices that suit your natural talents.

3. Relationship choices to help you get the most out of your love life, friendships and business partnerships.

4. Health choices to help you avoid the ailments associated with your Life Path, including exercise and diet options that suit you best.

5. Choices for children to give them the best possible start in life.

* * *

2. Reading it as a Supplementary Birth Number

All the information for each number is presented as though the number is your Life Path Number, because this number has the most effect on your life. However, if you are consulting the number because it is one of your two Supplementary Birth Numbers, the information still holds true. Just remember that you will work through the issues in conjunction with the overriding energy of your Life Path Number, and that you will do so primarily in the first 18 years of your life if it is your first Supplementary Birth Number, and in the second 18 years of your life if it is your second one. To assist you in this I have included a section under the "Life Choices" heading for each number devoted to your three-digit Birth Code to help explain the relationship between your Life Path Number and your two Supplementary Birth Numbers.

* * *

3. Notice what jumps out at you

As you read through the information for each of your numbers, pay particular attention to the passages that trigger a powerful response in you – either positively or negatively – because these are the areas you need to focus on.

Some of the information may wash over you. That's not to say it is not important. It is all important. What your Self is telling you is that the areas you need to concentrate on in your life right now are the ones that spark the strongest reaction in you.

When you read it again in the future (and I suggest you read your listings at regular intervals throughout your life, at least every two or three months), you will find that different passages provoke a powerful response in you. This is because you have moved further along your Life Path and are confronting a new set of challenges, and you need to focus on these particular areas of your life to overcome them.

If you find something that inspires you, this is an area in your life that you need to pursue to get you where you want to go.

Equally, if you read something that presses one or more of your buttons – and makes you angry, annoyed or even just uncomfortable – then this is an area you need to work on to improve.

Remember, all the information comes directly from your Self, which means it is eternal, universal and precisely tailored to tell you exactly what you need to know, when you need to know it. (Back to the movie *The Matrix* again… remember when Neo goes to see the Oracle, and afterwards Morpheus says to him: "She told you exactly what you needed to hear"? Well, the same holds true for your listing.)

If some of it appears "vague" to you because you are seeking clear and specific advice on a challenge or decision that you are facing, remember this: all the answers to all your questions are found in one place and one place only… your heart. That is why the best way to read the messages from your Self is to notice how they make you feel – in your heart – and then make your decision based on that, not on what your mind thinks about it.

Part Three: The nine Life Paths

The messages from your Self that are contained in the Self-Awareness System™ are designed to provoke a reaction in you. They will never tell you precisely what to do because your Self cannot mess with free will. You are always free to choose what, how, when, where, why and with whom you do everything in your life.

Nothing is set in stone. Your life will be what you create it to be, based always and only on the choices that you make.

* * *

(Note: On the subject of information jumping out at you each time you consult the numbers here in Part Three, it's worth pointing out that in the course of your daily life you will also find numbers jumping out at you, or appearing before you with a regularity that attracts your attention. These are almost always messages from your Angel, who – as we saw earlier in Part One – can't communicate with you directly due to the restrictions of free will. The next time this happens, consult the listing for the number or numbers because there will be a message there for you that your Angel wants you to read. You will know what it is when you read it.)

* * *

4. Cast your net as wide as you can

We talked about this in the last chapter of Part Two, but in case you have picked up this book and turned straight to the Life Path listings here in Part Three I want to repeat that although you will work primarily with the energy of your Life Path Number – and in your formative years, up to the age of 36, with the energy of your two Supplementary Birth Numbers as well – on your inner journey to well-roundedness and balanced fulfillment you will also experience some of the lessons of all the other numbers: **1** for courage, **2** for intuition, **3** for expression, **4** for stability, **5** for freedom, **6** for love, **7** for truth, **8** for power and **9** for integrity.

So while it is advisable for you to focus most of your attention on your three Birth Code numbers to guide you to your bliss, it is also worth reading through the other numbers as well when your time allows so that you can become aware of how their energies will operate in your life in a supporting role.

* * *

5. Over to you…

Finally, please remember that none of this information – not one single word – has any value unless you use it.

The messages from your Self that are contained here in Part Three will guide you towards your life's highest purpose, and therefore to your bliss. I promise you.

But they can't make it happen.

Only you can do that.

Destiny never comes knocking on your door. Your dream partner won't come tumbling down your chimney. And your perfect career isn't lurking under your bed.

All the joys of life are "out there" waiting for you. But you have to make it happen.

As Morpheus says: "There is a difference between knowing the path… and walking the path."

Happy walking!

No one saves us but ourselves.
We alone must walk the path.

– Buddha

LIFE PATH 1:
The Leader

1. **Growth cycle:** First stage (the number of creation)
2. **Influences:** Fire (action, masculine) and the Sun (passion)
3. **Positive qualities:** Ambitious, energetic and entrepreneurial
4. **Negative potential:** Impatient, domineering and arrogant
5. **Highs and lows:** Intrepid trailblazer, or bossy control freak
6. **Highest purpose:** Lead the way and inspire others to follow them
7. **Love matches:** 1, 3, 5, 7, 9 for compatibility (the rest for growth)
8. **Possible careers:** Business, law, politics, arts, entertainment
9. **Words to live by:** "Actions speak louder than words"

1. LIFE CHOICES FOR THE LEADER

THIS is the beginning of both a nine-year personal growth cycle and a nine-year spiritual growth cycle, which means positive and pioneering **1s** have come into the world bristling with creative energy and full of big ideas about how they want to live their life.

All **1s** tend to be natural leaders from an early age, and they are blessed with magnetic personalities and strong wills. They also have a flair for taking charge of any situation, and they find it relatively easy to inspire and motivate others to follow their lead.

Because **1s** are governed by the element of fire (forceful action), they will often be highly motivated and energetic Self-starters who are expert at getting the ball rolling. It's no surprise their astral influence is the Sun because it doesn't take much to fire up their enthusiasm.

Life Path 1: The Leader

All **1**s want to lead, but the evolved **1** will lead by example as they work towards their highest purpose of showing others what is possible.

The "masculine" forceful energy of **1** means they see potential and opportunity everywhere they look, and they won't hesitate to create openings in both their professional and personal lives. This, combined with the fire of ambition that burns brightly in their belly, drives the Leader to succeed in almost everything they choose to do.

However, because what we are all here to achieve is not necessarily what comes easiest to us, all **1**s will also face challenges on their Life Path that are put there specifically to help them grow.

Don't worry, **1**s have all the qualities necessary to overcome every challenge they will face, because life never gives anyone more than they can handle. The main challenge, especially for the young Leader, is to overcome their fear of failure and trust in their own abilities.

More than any other Life Path, confidence is crucial for the **1** and they will always be their own worst critic. This may cause them to start numerous projects, only to give up at the first sign of a setback.

The **1** must learn the value of persistence and hard work, which together will take them almost anywhere they want to go. In fact, as they evolve and grow, most **1**s will actually welcome obstacles and challenges along their path. They thrive on solving problems and must guard against subconsciously manifesting them simply so that they can prove to themselves how powerful they are.

There is no one more determined than a properly motivated **1**, but equally there is no Life Path so in their ego – and this is what causes them to create obstacles simply so they can challenge themselves.

If there are two roads, the **1** will often take the hardest one just for the sake of flexing their problem-solving muscles, but this is not necessarily the most effective use of their energy and time.

The evolved Leader will learn to move beyond their powerful ego and focus instead on using their skills to help the common good and create win-win results for themselves and their colleagues.

* * *

Highest purpose of The Leader

The highest purpose of the **1** is to help other people become the best they can be by inspiring them to find their own hidden strengths and talents to help them succeed. This process takes patience, clear communication and empathy for the needs of others, none of which is among the masculine **1**'s strong suits.

All **1**s need to guard against becoming too egotistical, bossy and intolerant of others who might not appear to be as motivated, intelligent or committed as they are. One of the big lessons of this Life Path is to learn to look for the highest potential in other people by looking beyond their human frailties and seeing what they are capable of in the future, rather than who they are now.

The most valuable contribution a successful **1** can make to society is to use their innate leadership qualities to teach others how to tap into their own potential and help them succeed in whatever they do.

Remember, the most important goal for all Life Paths is always the same: to first "wake up" to the truth that we are an extension of Source energy, and to help other people wake up as well. Then, and only then, will the path to our highest purpose open up before us.

* * *

Key words are… 'confidence' and 'patience'

To fulfill their life's highest purpose, the high-energy **1** must learn to develop a powerful inner confidence in their abilities.

Confidence is crucial for all the Life Paths as we embark on our common journey from pure unaware love to pure conscious love. As we saw in Part One, Self-esteem is the first crucial step towards Self-love that we all must take. (If you're wondering what a "Self" is, please try to find the time to read Part One because, as you'll discover, it's way too complicated to explain again here.) For the high-energy **1**, however, developing a strong sense of inner confidence is much more than the key to their personal and spiritual growth – it is the key to their very survival.

Leader **1**s come to the world full of creative energy, and all energy must be expressed or it will cause blockages within us that can lead to illness and Self-destructive behaviour. Think of a fast-flowing river. If the water is blocked, it will back up and eventually burst its banks. Similarly, if the **1** lacks the confidence to let their creative energy flow through them and out into the world, it will build up inside them, leading to frustration, outbursts of anger and even depression.

The blocked **1** will likely use alcohol and drugs to release their pent-up energy. And if they continue to block their creativity, sickness will inevitably follow, often in the life-threatening form of cancer.

In their late teens and early 20s, **1**s who have not yet developed enough confidence to express themselves and pursue their burning goals can sometimes turn to harder drugs because they give them the immediate release of energy they so desperately crave.

When this happens, instead of inspiring others to follow them by being a positive Leader – both at home and at work – there is a danger they could become withdrawn and disillusioned about life.

The young **1** needs to real-eyes there is nothing to be afraid of. Nothing and no one can ever hurt them because they are pure love, and any energy they express freely and openly will be pure love energy – which will always be welcome by whoever receives it.

The other lesson the high-energy Leader would do well to learn as early in life as possible is to real-eyes that not everyone operates at the same lightning-fast speed they do.

Impatience is the **1**'s middle name because they have so many ideas to explore and goals to achieve that there isn't time to wait around for everyone else to get with the program. Frustration can quickly turn to anger, and the impatient **1** risks offending the very people they need to help them fulfill their dreams. A healthy serving of patience mixed with a dash of compassion and liberally sprinkled with words of encouragement is the recipe all **1**s need to follow to fulfill their highest purpose of inspiring others to do better and dig deeper.

Life Path 1: Life Choices

When Leaders learn to work with the positive energy of **1**, they will channel their energy to bring new ideas into the world to inspire others. But when they work with the negative energy of **1** they may alienate everyone near to them and wind up on their own.

Fortunately, as they grow older, most **1**s develop enough patience with others to keep them onside, and enough confidence in themselves so they can expend their energy in positive pursuits such as business and sports, rather than Self-destructive ones such as addictions to alcohol, drugs and sex. Plus, if they don't, it is usually only in their youth, especially in their late teens, before they have had a chance to prove themselves – and, by doing so, develop their Self-worth.

* * *

Positive and negative potential

All Life Paths contain an equal measure of positive and negative potential. Our challenge in every lifetime, no matter what our Life Path Number happens to be, is to nurture and boost our positive attributes, while at the same time healing and rising above our negative ones.

The reason we are given negative potential as well as positive potential is because people usually respond more effectively to the threat of pain than they do to the promise of pleasure.

Also, while it is admirable to do what we are good at in life, we will only ever become the best we can be by facing our "dark side" and digging deep into our Self to overcome the obstacles that appear on our path.

As we have already seen in Part Two, it is only when the chips are down and we are up against it that we find out who we truly are and what we are truly capable of doing.

For example, confidence is the key to success for all **1**s. If they have it, they will have the courage to go down paths no one has gone down before when all around them are shaking their heads. But if they lack it, they can easily turn to the negative side of this number and

Life Path 1: The Leader

express their energy as bossiness and aggression in a vain attempt to bulldoze their ideas through against the will of those around them.

All **1s** would be well-advised to try to strike a balance between committing to their goal, and consulting with others along the way.

Because **1s** are at the first (ideas) stage of a Spiritual Growth Cycle, they tend to be naturally outgoing, courageous and adventurous and almost always possess all the qualities of a charismatic leader.

However, their aggressive, take-charge style of leadership differs greatly from the calm, role-model method employed by those working with the energy of **9** (the Teacher) at the final stage of a growth cycle.

1s are usually dynamic and individualistic and are born with a very strong sense of willpower and determination to succeed. Managing others is in their blood. They will gravitate towards the executive ranks in business and may well start their own company. Or they may go in a different direction and use their natural creativity to inspire others through art, film, music or dance.

The forceful **1** craves independence and needs to be in control of every situation. They love the limelight, thrive on the status that success brings and, if they have developed enough confidence in their abilities, are not afraid to walk their own path, even if it means going off the beaten track to pursue some apparently wacky business venture.

All **1s** tend to perform best when they are left to do things their own way. They usually insist on making up their own mind, and they will go to great lengths to ensure they are free to do whatever they want, whenever they want, however they want.

These qualities make all **1s** natural go-getters, both in their private life and in business. They are bursting with energy and passion, and their uncanny ability to always see the big picture enables them to inspire and motivate others. In fact, they will be surprised how easily they can persuade people to drop whatever they are doing and follow them to the ends of the Earth.

Once a **1** is committed to a goal, everyone else had better get out of their way because they will stop at nothing to achieve it – providing they are confident enough to blast their way through whatever

Life Path 1: Life Choices

obstacles arise. If they are not, they may find themselves starting any number of "grand plans", only to give up on them a day or two later at the first sign of resistance, and then race off on another tangent.

Evolved and confident **1**s will often enjoy great success in life because they are able to draw on their vast energy reserves and "never-say-die" attitude, enabling them to overcome almost any obstacle or challenge that life puts in their path.

1s are always looking for new money-making opportunities so they are likely to attract material wealth throughout their life. Losing is one thing they do not accept easily, or gracefully, and they will go to great lengths to avoid it.

When they do lose, whether it's a business deal, money, a relationship or in any other area of their life, **1**s will normally recover quickly and take the time to figure out what went wrong and what they can do better next time. Providing they are working with the positive energy of this most forceful of numbers, it will never be long before the go-getter **1** is back up on the winner's rostrum again.

On the negative side, **1**s can be impatient with people who are not as motivated as they are. They are extremely competitive and can become dismissive of the shortcomings of others, unless they remember that the whole reason they are here is not just to make themselves feel better, but to help others feel better about themselves.

Immature **1**s can be overly concerned with status and appearance, which also drives them to achieve material success. But they will do well to remember that status and appearance are the work of their ego, and neither will give them one tenth of the satisfaction they will feel by using their creative powers to improve the lives of those they love.

As natural leaders, **1**s instinctively like to take charge of any situation. Sometimes this is appropriate, but they would do well to consider that sometimes it is not. This ability to know when to leap in and take over, and when to take a back seat, will be invaluable to the **1** in their relationships and their business, as well as socially.

Talking about social life, **1**s tend to be popular because they are outgoing, intelligent and bold – all of which are attractive qualities.

They are usually assertive and ambitious, although they must guard against becoming too demanding, especially with friends and family.

For the most part, however, **1**s are great socialisers and conversationalists. People are drawn to them and will often praise them for their charisma, intelligence and courage – which is a good thing because for all their strengths and bravado, most **1**s are also extremely sensitive to criticism and prone to Self-doubt.

* * *

On a more personal level, **1**s can sometimes struggle in their romantic relationships simply because they are so used to getting their own way, and any form of compromise (which is essential in a relationship) goes against everything they stand for and hold dear.

An evolved **1** can make an excellent partner who is strong, optimistic and able to provide the finer things in life for their husband or wife and their children. However, they would do well to find a partner who is happy to let them be "on top" in every room in the house, whether it's the bedroom with sex, the kitchen when cooking, or the living room when conversing or playing games. And yes, they will usually want full control of the TV remote as well!

In their family life, **1**s must guard against steamrolling their partner by always insisting on taking all the decisions, big or small.

Consultation is not something that comes easily to a **1** and they would do well to remember that although their partner might enjoy having someone who is happy to play the role of provider and protector, they will quickly become fed up if they are not allowed to have an equal say in the big decisions.

1s have very strong desires and needs, which can be challenging in a relationship, as well as socially. They would do well to keep their ego on a tight leash and take the time to listen to the opinions of others, especially their loved ones.

Insecure **1**s who have not done the inner work to boost their confidence – and, crucially, their level of Self-awareness – can become so entrenched in their ego that they may find it extremely difficult to enjoy a close, loving relationship.

The same warning applies in business, where 1s will always benefit from making sure they include their subordinates in some of the key decisions to make them feel that they are validated and part of the team. They must also take the time to listen to alternative viewpoints, no matter how difficult this might be for them.

It doesn't take much for a **1** to be seduced by a power trip, and if this happens they can easily flip from inspiring leader to domineering tyrant quicker than they can say: "My way, or the highway." Yes, of course they probably have a clearer vision of what they want than anyone else, but the truly successful leader is inclusive, not exclusive.

* * *

Another problem 1s can encounter, especially early on in their Life Path, is that they do not like to take orders from anyone. The trouble is in most walks of life we all have to follow for a while before we are able to lead, so 1s would do well to be patient and understand that everyone has to learn the ropes before they can captain the ship.

At times, 1s can tend to be petulant and grumpy if they don't get their own way. They can even be lethargic and downright lazy if they are not properly motivated or allowed to make things happen the way they think they should happen.

If they are unhappy with their own achievements, the disgruntled **1** can become angry and attack those closest to them, as though in some way it was "their fault". It is not uncommon for 1s to vent their frustration by becoming critical of others – if not downright vengeful, cruel, rude and quick-tempered.

There is no bigger ego than the unevolved **1**, which means the "dark side" of this Life Path is never far away.

An addiction to status, money and power has brought many a **1** undone if they haven't done the necessary inner work that allows them to feel secure about who they are.

Life Path 1: The Leader

All Leaders must learn that although it is wonderful to have status, money and power, it is vital that they go after it because they want it, and not because they need it to paper over their insecurities.

Remember, everyone's highest purpose is always to improve the lives of others as well as their own. When the Self-aware **1** learns to rise above their overdeveloped ego and attract status and power through being an inspiring leader, rather than an aggressive tyrant, they will be revered and followed for their courage, strength and vision.

If they don't, they may quickly become resented outcasts – tall poppies just waiting to be cut down to size.

* * *

Summary of the positives

In the positive, **1**s are expressive, creative, energetic and brave. They make the best leaders, executives, managers, explorers, inventors and entrepreneurs through their ability to blaze new trails for others to follow, generating wealth and fulfillment for all around them.

Their magnetism and determination bring out the best in people, and their creative flair for big ideas and original solutions ensure they will enjoy a high level of success in their chosen field, whether it is in business or in a more creative and artistic enterprise.

When they tap into their inner confidence, they are able to climb the mountain path and achieve their highest purpose of inspiring others to become the best they can be by making their life a shining example of what is possible for others to follow.

Key positive words

Driven, independent, powerful, courageous, assertive, ambitious, insightful, intelligent, strong, original, forceful, pioneering, passionate, creative, focused, single-minded, determined and Self-reliant.

* * *

Life Path 1: Life Choices

Summary of the negatives

In the negative, 1s can easily become insecure, power-hungry and domineering tyrants who are doomed to a life of shallow loneliness. Rather than trying to feel better about themselves by improving their own lives, they may achieve the same feeling by putting others down.

Equally, their lack of confidence may lead them to impose their will on others by force, rather than leading by example.

Negative 1s may feel the need to amass wealth, power and status to compensate for their fundamental lack of inner confidence and Self-esteem. They are prone to being bossy and impatient, and can quickly fall prey to all manner of addictions – mainly sex, drugs and alcohol – to give them a sense of false confidence. If left unchecked, these negative behaviour patterns can ultimately become destructive, not just for themselves but for the people who are close to them as well.

Key negative words

Bossy, egotistical, impatient, angry, arrogant, intolerant, critical, stubborn, controlling, unpredictable, lazy and aggressive.

* * *

Self-love is the difference

If you have read Part One, you will already know that your ability to walk the positive side of your Life Path, as opposed to the negative side, is determined by whether you have undertaken the two key stages of personal growth. Or, to put it another way, whether you have taken the two crucial first steps on the path to your life's highest purpose.

The first step towards living your Life Path in the positive is to develop Self-esteem (and if you're wondering what a "Self" is, please take the time to read Part One because it's way too complicated to explain again here). This feeling of inner confidence is essential because it allows you to tap into your innate strengths, which you will need if you are going to have any hope of overcoming the numerous obstacles on your path. Be aware, though, that on its own this first step is never enough, because Self-confidence and Self-esteem are still the work of the ego. The feeling of being "good enough" carries with it an implied sense of needing to be "better than".

So to reach your full potential and achieve your life's highest purpose, you must also take the second step – which is to rise above the egoic concept of Self-esteem and climb to the much higher ground of Self-love.

Loving your Self does not mean being "full of your Self". It means the opposite. It means being humble because you understand that you are the same as everyone else, no better and no worse.

Above all, it means you understand that we are all immortal spirits having a human experience, and therefore we are all, at our core, the same – pure love and pure Source energy. (The Source is also fully explained in Part One.)

We can see it easily in new-born babies because when we are born into physical form, and before our fear-based ego has had a chance to develop, we are all gorgeous, gurgling bundles of pure, exquisite love.

I am not suggesting you do this, but just imagine you were to place a new-born infant on the pavement of a crowded street and then stand back out of sight. Everyone – and I mean everyone – would stop and tend to it. And the reason they would do this is because, deep down, we all recognise pure love when we see it. We are drawn to it at the most basic level of our being because it is the most strikingly beautiful and compelling force on the planet.

But sadly, as we grow up and go out into the world, our ego takes over and we start to believe – usually during our teenage years – that our ego is who we are. It isn't. Love is who we are.

We are all pure love. We are all extensions of Source energy (or children of "God", whichever phrase you are more comfortable with).

If you can rise above the quasi-religious terminology, I can summarise the two steps like this: Self-esteem is about feeling "good enough", while Self-love is about feeling "God enough".

Life Path 1: Life Choices

The reason why loving your Self is so important for your Life Path is because when you start to live your life from the perspective of being pure love, everything changes. Suddenly you understand that nothing "out there" in the material world can ever harm you in any way.

Equally, you real-eyes you don't need anything "out there" in the material world to make you feel happy – not the approval of others; no amount of money, fame and power; and not even the love of a good man or woman – because you have all the love you need right there in your own heart, and you can therefore relish the exquisite joy of loving everyone unconditionally without needing anything in return.

That is why Self-love is the secret to working with the positive energy of your Life Path Number. Because when you truly love your Self, the rocky mountain path you've been climbing suddenly becomes an express elevator ride all the way up to the summit of your bliss.

* * *

No Life Path is an island

Although your Life Path Number denotes the main issues you will focus on, you will also work to some degree with the energies of the other numbers to become a fully rounded Self. As a **1** your main work will be in the areas of confidence and patience, but you will also tackle the issues of co-operation and balance (**2**), creative expression (**3**), stability and flexibility (**4**), freedom and discipline (**5**), acceptance (**6**), trust (**7**), power (**8**) and integrity (**9**). It's worth your while to read through them when your time allows – especially if they are one of the two Supplementary Birth Numbers that make up your Birth Code.

* * *

Qualities of your three-digit Birth Code

(Note: The unique relationship between your two Supplementary Birth Numbers [the two underlined numbers] and your Life Path Number [the bold

Life Path 1: The Leader

number] that make up your three-digit Birth Code is explained in detail in Part Two: The Self-Awareness System™.)

10/1

This Life Path is unique among the nine Life Path Numbers because all people working with a Life Path Number of **1** have the same Birth Code of 10/**1**.

This is because these are the only two Supplementary Birth Numbers that add up to **1**. This means that for all Leaders, their two supplementary numbers are a 1 and a 0, where 0 is an amplifier that endows them with heightened sensitivity and intuition to work in conjunction with the double energy of **1**.

As a result, all 10/**1**s will work exclusively with the energy of their Life Path Number of **1** (creativity and leadership) throughout their childhood and their adult years to guide them towards their life's highest purpose.

This is one of the main reasons why all **1**s are endowed with an innate power to become great leaders and innovators.

Because their double energy of 1 and **1** is amplified by their 0, everyone who walks the Life Path of the Leader does so with an evolved sense of intuition that will give them the confidence to take a leadership role at work, at home and in their community.

They also have a heightened amount of emotional sensitivity that allows them to understand the needs of others, which is an essential quality for a great leader.

If this is your Birth Code, the fact that your first Supplementary Birth Number is the same as your Life Path Number means you will work intensively with the creative and leadership energies of **1** not just in your first formative years from age 1 to 18, but throughout your life.

Then in the second 18 years, as you evolve from a young adult to a fully emotionally mature adult at age 36, your second Supplementary Birth Number of 0 means you will work on developing your intuitive powers, which will help you in your leadership capacity.

You will also develop a deep sensitivity to your own feelings and the feelings of others, which will assist you in becoming an empathetic and compassionate leader... the highest purpose of all **1**s.

However, none of this will happen if you fail to clear your emotional blockages and remain stuck in your ego. As with all the Life Paths, there is a light side and a dark side, thanks to the Law of Duality (described in Part One). If you rise above your ego, you will walk the light side. But if you succumb to fear (the staple diet of the ego), you may flip to the dark side.

The purpose of life is the same for all Life Paths – namely, to learn we are an extension of Source energy, and therefore we are pure love. Our highest purpose is always to help others learn this truth as well.

* * *

2. CAREER AND BUSINESS CHOICES

ENERGETIC **1**s are outgoing, creative and brim-full of ideas for starting something new. This will lead them to take leadership roles in whatever they choose to do with their lives – whether it is in their own business, or a company they join and work their way to the very top.

Many **1**s gravitate towards the corporate world, where their natural leadership and managerial skills will propel them quickly through the ranks. However, their creative and single-minded personality can often spark friction when they bump up against the often stagnant and entrenched corporate culture of many large companies.

Aggressive and ambitious **1**s like to make things happen. They do not like routine and they tire very quickly of repetitive tasks, as well as projects where they are not in complete control. They need to be their own boss, so if they are not the chief executive they will demand the autonomy to allow them to run their department the way they want to

Life Path 1: The Leader

run it. If this is not possible, they will probably strike out on their own and start up their own enterprise.

Success will often come easily to the **1** because of their unique combination of courage, business acumen, creativity and a trailblazing desire to go where no one else has gone before.

It doesn't matter whether you admire them or not, global media tycoon Rupert Murdoch, Apple co-founder Steve Jobs and the most revolutionary entrepreneur of his generation Henry Ford are all classic examples of **1**s who fulfilled their life's highest purpose by going against the trend and blazing a corporate trail to create extraordinary wealth and opportunities not just for them, but for their thousands of colleagues and employees as well

By no means all **1**s are drawn to the corporate world, however. Their strong creative streak and their capacity for original ideas may lead them into the arts or fashion, or even writing or journalism. Many **1**s also find considerable success in dance, music, design and film (producing, directing and acting).

Whichever artistic path they choose, they will always strive to do things differently to how everyone else is doing them. Original and creative filmmakers Charlie Chaplin, Walt Disney and George Lucas are all great examples of **1**s who changed the face of their industry.

And in music, the same is true of Chuck Berry, Marvin Gaye and Lady Gaga, all of whom didn't just find success in the music business, they revolutionised it.

1s are also often drawn to politics, where again they will strive to make radical changes to what they perceive to be social injustices. Karl Marx, Mikhail Gorbachev and Martin Luther King are great examples of **1**s who changed the whole world, not just their little corner of it.

Beneficial career paths

People working with the leadership energy of **1** make excellent politicians, filmmakers, business leaders, military leaders, inventors, innovators, graphic designers, town planners, engineers, project managers, sales managers, theatrical promoters and producers, TV producers, newspaper and magazine editors, adventurers, explorers, shop owners, small business owners, computer programmers, management consultants, event planners, fashion designers, business lawyers, and headmasters or headmistresses.

Best business matches

If a **1** goes into business, it will usually be as the boss. For their human resources manager, they would do best to choose an insightful **2** or a nurturing **6**. For their creative team (marketing and sales) they would pick the imaginative **3** or the quick-witted and persuasive **5**. The thoughtful **7** performs best in a back-office role such as research and development or IT.

For managing director, look no further than the practical **4** or the astute **8**. And for a special project that needs someone to take over the reins and drive it to fruition, no one is better at running their own team than the independent and highly motivated **9**.

* * *

3. RELATIONSHIP CHOICES

ONE of the most rewarding aspects about the Self-Awareness System™ is how equitable it is. Each Life Path offers the same opportunities for happiness and fulfillment, albeit in markedly different ways. And each of them also offers the same amount of challenges to force us to grow, although again in very different ways.

This means no Life Path is any "better" or "worse" than any of the others. All of them have their blessings, and all have their obstacles.

In the case of **1**, the blessings centre around their remarkable creative and leadership abilities that virtually guarantee they will achieve a high level of success in whatever career path they choose to pursue – providing, of course, that they do the inner work to first boost

Life Path 1: The Leader

their Self-confidence and then their Self-love to ensure they work with the positive energies of this number.

The challenges of the **1** Life Path usually centre around their relationships, especially their love life. They are naturally internally focused and they have a deep, powerful drive to succeed in whatever they do. This may be great for business or sports, for example, but it is not necessarily ideal for creating a close and loving relationship.

Romance is not always the **1**'s strong suit. They tend to be a bit Self-centred and like to have their own way, and compromise never comes easily to them. They would do well to remember that in a romantic relationship, everything is a compromise at one level or another. And consultation – another of their weak points – is essential.

All **1**s must real-eyes that loving someone means including them, respecting them and listening to them… not just providing for them.

Self-confidence is crucial for the Leader to succeed in their many business ventures, and this is equally true in relationships. If they are insecure, they may find it difficult to let love in. In fact, insecure **1**s can sometimes overcompensate by becoming so domineering that they may find it difficult to enjoy a close and loving relationship of any kind.

Having said that, the good news is that **1**s are not short of passion (this is a fire number after all), which makes them an attractive partner, at least in the short term. Quick flings are their forte, but if they want it to grow into something more meaningful they are going to have to put their ego on the shelf and learn to share some of the responsibilities – and, yes, some of the decisions too – with their partner.

***

Sex drive of the 1

Sex is very important to this masculine fire energy Life Path, whose desires in the bedroom usually match their passionate ambition in the boardroom. But **1**s must guard against being as competitive under the bedsheets as they are with their balance sheets.

Life Path 1: Relationship Choices

Most **1**s tend to be dominant in bed, but they may struggle to be as liberal with their affections as they are with their sexual desires. This is mainly due to a deep-seated lack of Self-confidence.

1s in a business suit are unstoppable, but in their birthday suit they can sometimes paper over their insecurities by focusing on the physical experience at the expense of the emotional connection.

Regardless of birth gender, a masculine **1** will often cycle through numerous lovers when he is young, because for him sex is just another way of expressing his forceful and dominant fire energy. Only when he learns to rise above his ego's desires and approach a relationship from the perspective of "What can I give?" rather than "What can I get?" will he be able to forge a truly deep bond with his partner – especially if they are one of the feminine numbers **2, 4, 6** or **8**.

The same holds true for the feminine **1** in a relationship, who will choose a strong partner because she loves a challenge. She will abhor any lover who cowers to her sexual strength, which is ironic because although she loves to be in control, deep down she yearns to be dominated by her powerful lover. The feminine **1** does best when she chooses a lover who is strong enough to stand up to her, yet secure enough to allow her to take control on occasion too.

* * *

The compatibility listings that follow will help dominant **1**s get the most out of their relationships, whether it's with someone they love, a friend or a business partner. You will notice the fire energy of **1** is well-matched with other **1**s and their fiery cousin **5**, as well as a **3** or a **7**, whose air energy is able to fan their flames. Water (**2** and **6**) and earth (**4** and **8**) can both be used to douse a fire, so these pairings may throw up more challenges. The **9** is usually a good match for any number.

However, what appears to match you best on the surface may not be what you need right now. All relationships are designed to help us grow along our Life Path. Yes, of course we enjoy the companionship, close connection, sexual intimacy and deep love that relationships give us. But that is now why we have them.

The reason we choose a partner (or, to be more accurate, why our all-knowing Self chooses them for us) is because they are a mirror in which we see our shortcomings and strengths reflected back at us through their shortcomings and strengths.

That is why opposites so often attract, especially in love.

I have written an entire book on this subject called *Leap into Love* which goes into the way relationships work in our lives in great detail. But for now, please real-eyes that when your partner presses one of your buttons, they are doing so not to "piss you off" but because your Self is using them to show you the areas you need to work on.

If you fail to understand this is the main reason why you attracted them into your life in the first place, you will fight each other and may eventually break up. And you will believe their faults were exactly that – their faults – rather than yours reflected back at you.

Worst of all, you will then take the unchanged you with you to your next relationship, and – lo and behold! – exactly the same issues will come up again.

If this sounds familiar. If you have ever asked any of these questions – "Why does this always happen to me?" or "Why do all men cheat?" or "Why are all women so demanding?" or whatever it is for you – then now you know why. It's because you didn't learn from your last partner, so of course your new one will do the same thing.

And this will continue to happen, relationship after relationship, until you real-eyes it is meant to be happening to show you what areas you need to work on in your Self to change and grow.

* * *

One final quick point before we get into it: I need to stress that I disagree with almost every numerologist I know who likes to label relationships "a natural fit", "a neutral fit" or "an unnatural fit", depending on the compatibility of the numbers of the two partners.

Life Path 1: Relationship Choices

All relationships are challenging. That is why we have them, as we have just seen. Yes, sometimes we might choose a partner who is "just like us" for the sake of harmony, but that could be regarded as a cop out if we are truly serious about our personal and spiritual growth.

If you are on a spiritual growth path in this lifetime (and there is no doubt in my mind that you are if you made it through Part One without throwing it in the bin!), then your Self will choose your relationships for you – and they will always be with a partner who will challenge you to grow in exactly the ways you need to grow.

Just because you might discover your current partner has a Life Path Number that doesn't dovetail perfectly with yours, don't fall into the trap of thinking there must be something wrong – or worse, end it with them so you can go out with someone with a "better" number.

Where you are right now on your Life Path is exactly where you are meant to be, and who you are with is exactly who you are meant to be with. So please let these listings help you to look for the lessons in your relationship, rather than look for the door.

And if you are single at the moment, try to remain open-hearted about your next relationship. It doesn't matter what Life Path Number they have, so don't "cherry pick". All that matters is you follow your heart and be open to learning the lessons they can teach you. After all, that's the reason you will attract them into your life in the first place.

* * *

1 & 1
(Independence and Control)

Love

Like attracts like, and **1**s can certainly find much in common with their fellow **1**. The trouble is that when two **1**s get together they usually don't make two – they are still two **1**s, fiercely opinionated and equally keen to be in charge.

Let's face it, two independent leaders who absolutely insist on being in control of everything can be a recipe for conflict. Who is going to decide what movie to see, just for starters? Let alone where they go on holiday. Fireworks and conflict are virtually guaranteed.

If bickering and arguments don't worry them, then there is much to be gained from this love-match because they will both egg each other on and push each other to succeed.

Their ambition and drive will feed of each other, spurring each other to do better. Yes, it will be fiery because both partners are governed by the element of fire, but with a little compromise and a good deal of conflict-resolution skills, this is a match that can create great passion – not to mention spectacular make-up sex.

The downside is they may both be so focused on their careers that there is little room for each other. If the bedroom is ignored for the benefit of the boardroom, this relationship can quickly start to feel more like a marriage of convenience than a marriage of true hearts.

Two **1**s will both be so busy conquering the world that they may have precious little time for each other. However, if they can set common goals and work together to achieve them, there is nothing this fiery partnership cannot achieve, and their mutual successes will likely keep them together.

If both **1**s can give each other enough space to pursue their own individual goals – and if they have enough common ground that they can work on together – this can be a strong and passionate relationship.

Sexually, this can by an excellent combination. There is certainly no shortage of fire, which will lead to mind-shatteringly good sex. But romantically it will probably be a bit of a fizzer unless they can both agree to take time out from their hectic work lives for each other.

On the whole, this can be a rewarding – if argumentative – pairing. In some ways, another **1** is the only Life Path that can understand them, which means that despite the potential for conflict, this is usually a compatible match, albeit a feisty one.

Remember that when disagreements arise (and they will because all relationships are about growth, as we saw earlier), take the time to sit down and figure out what you are meant to be learning from your partner – then kiss them and thank them for the lesson.

Good luck, stay open and honest… and enjoy the material wealth, awesome sex and mutual motivation this relationship can give you.

Friendship

Two **1**s make excellent friends because they share the same "take charge" view of life. But if their goals overlap, they may fall out easily in their quest to be top dog.

When two **1**s get together and brain-storm their big ideas, the resulting powerhouse of creativity can be a dynamite combination. However, it is important that they respect each other's need to feel they are in charge of their own destiny. Set the parameters first, avoid stepping on each other's toes, and watch the friendship grow.

Business

There are four words to describe the compatibility of two **1**s going into business together: "no", "no" – and "hell no".

This will never work because both of them will want to be in control and calling all the shots, and they are guaranteed to fall out quicker than either of them can say: "I'm in charge". Pick any other number as a business partner, preferably a **3**, a **7**, an **8** or a **9**.

* * *

1 & 2
(Independence and Co-operation)

Love

On the surface, the fiercely independent **1** and the romantically co-dependent **2** appear to be about as compatible as petrol and a naked flame. However, there is a chance for this apparently mismatched pairing to work, as long as both partners are happy to play traditional and stereotypical roles of breadwinner and homemaker.

Life Path 1: The Leader

It doesn't matter which sex is which because this is not about male or female in the birth-gender sense; it's about masculine energy and feminine energy. **1**s are masculine (whether they are female or male) and **2**s are feminine (whether they are male or female).

It's worth noting here that Master Number **11**/**2**s are much more balanced in their masculine and feminine energy, and therefore will find it easier to relate to the male energy of their Leader partner.

However, all **2**s want peace and harmony (togetherness) above all else, while solitary **1**s are driven primarily by ambition and achievement, not just in their work life but in their home life too.

2s must remember to give **1**s the space they need to go out and conquer the world and express their creative ideas, while **1**s must never forget to tell the **2** how much their love means to them and how appreciated they are.

The real challenge of this pairing lies in the fact that all **2**s thrive on attention, and **1**s are almost always far from home conquering the world. If **1**s can make their **2** partner feel loved and appreciated, even while they are away, the **2** will keep the home fires burning and be happy to give them the freedom they crave to build their business.

Sexually, this is a mismatch because **1** usually wants to have sex while **2** wants to make love. The water of **2** can douse the fire of **1**, and the fire of **1** can scald the sensitive heart of **2**.

Again, Master Number **11**/**2**s are much more sexual than their **20**/**2** sisters and brothers, so if a Leader is going to partner up with a **2**, they would do best to choose a Master Number **11**/**2**. Even then, though, they will need to take the time – and make the effort – to think about what their partner wants, which doesn't come naturally to the **1**.

2s, more than any other number, need lots of attention and they also have a tendency for wild mood swings – both of which are challenging for the independent, impatient and intolerant **1**.

They will also both have to work hard to meet each other's needs. But if they do, it can be a rewarding match. Be aware, though, that **2**s may want more love and affection than **1**s are able to give them, while

Life Path 1: Relationship Choices

1s may want more independence and freedom than the often jealous **2** is comfortable with.

The key to this pairing is to respect each other's differences and support each other, even though sometimes you may feel you are about as well-matched as English chalk and Venezuelan beaver cheese.

Remember, the sole (soul) purpose of your relationship is to learn from each other and help each other to grow. And this pairing will certainly throw up more than enough lessons for each partner to real-eyes that success on its own may be wonderful – but success shared with someone we love is doubly so.

Good luck, stay open and honest… and enjoy the shared triumphs and valuable growth lessons this relationship can give you.

Friendship

These two numbers have little in common in terms of their core values. The sometimes insular **1** is focused on what they can achieve next, while the passionately social **2** wants to go out for dinner and sit and chat, preferably all night long.

They can be friends, and sometimes even BFFs if they meet when they are young and the **2** is an 11/**2** who is working intensely with their 1 supplementary energy. But if the **2** is a 20/**2**, it will be another story because their energy will be so different.

Deep in their heart, the independent **1** is a loner who knows that while they love the company of energetic people from time to time, they always operate at their best when left to their own devices.

Yes, they are wildly social – but usually only on a fairly shallow level. They can make do with lots of acquaintances and only a couple of close friends. This is the polar opposite of the **2**, who doesn't like being on their own for longer than very short periods and always works best when part of a close-knit team.

The social and harmonious **2** will often have several close friends with whom they can share their deepest feelings. And even when they are in the company of acquaintances or even strangers, they will share deep parts of themselves – and expect the same in return.

Sometimes this need for depth can be too much for the fiercely independent **1**, who may react by keeping their **2** friend at arm's length, thinking them to be a bit too "heavy" for their liking.

Equally, the **2** will probably choose the company of a water or air number (**2, 3 ,6** or **7**) over the fiery **1** because they make them feel deeply connected in a way a **1** will always struggle to do.

Business

This can work well, providing **1** is the boss and handles the visionary side of the business, while **2** handles the management and human resources side of the business, looking after staff morale and nurturing the business while the **1** grows it.

1s have to be in charge, which in turn means the **2** has to trust that they know what they are doing. As long as the **1** keeps the **2** included in all the big decisions, the **2** will be happy to play a supporting role – on the condition that their ideas are always heard and considered, and that they are allowed to share equally in all the rewards.

The insightful **2** has an uncanny knack for knowing what people do and don't want, and if they feel the **1** is going in the wrong direction they will need to feel free to speak up. When this happens, the headstrong **1** would be advised to put their ego on a shelf and listen very closely to the **2**'s advice. Nine times out of 10 they will be right.

* * *

1 & 3
(Independence and Expression)

Love

This is an action-packed combination that works extremely well in all areas. In love, the forceful fire energy of **1** and the thoughtful air energy of **3** dovetail almost perfectly, with the independent and ambitious **1** leading the way and the creative **3** always finding ways to reinvent and grow the relationship at the first signs of stagnation.

Life Path 1: Relationship Choices

Both the Leader **1** and the Creative **3** appreciate the work that the other does, and both will drive each other forward. The **3** is good at stroking the **1**'s ego, and the **1** is great at encouraging the **3** and giving positive feedback to all their creative ideas.

This will usually be a lively and passionate relationship that will also allow them to cover a lot of ground, both professionally and in their personal life. They will fire up each other's imagination, making their time together fun and exciting.

They will usually have many friends, an active social life and will have a comfortable or even luxurious home where they can socialise and enjoy the fruits of their considerable material success.

The fire of the **1** and the air of the **3** are compatible elements (air is always a good match for fire – it is water that fire struggles with because it can easily douse their flames of their passion). Both partners love adventure and new experiences, they both like to experiment sexually once they have learned to trust each other, and they both absolutely love surprises.

They are very well-matched in the bedroom where there will be much passion, and laughter too. However, they must watch what they say because they both have thin skins and do not take criticism well. This is the one pitfall that can undermine this relationship quicker than either of them can say "ouch". Both **1**s and **3**s can tend to be overly sensitive unless they have done the "inner work" to boost their Self-love, so they must be wary of saying something off-the-cuff that can hurt the other to their core.

For all their great qualities, neither the **1** nor the **3** is good at forgetting, nor forgiving. A wound left untreated can fester and easily become incurable because unevolved **1**s and **3**s are firmly entrenched in their egos and take any attack very personally.

That aside, this is a fun and passionate match with never a dull moment. The outgoing **1** and the social **3** will love each other's company and respect each other's abilities, and there is potential for a long and happy time together.

Life Path 1: The Leader

Remember that when disagreements arise (and they will because all relationships are about growth, as we saw earlier), take the time to sit down and figure out what you are meant to be learning from your partner – then kiss them and thank them for the lesson.

Good luck, stay open and honest… and enjoy the laughter, love and material success that this relationship can give you.

Friendship

1 and **3** can be great friends because they are both chock-a-block full of creative ideas and will inspire and motivate each other. There is a risk of treading on each other's toes, and disagreements – even fights – will arise because both numbers are headstrong and opinionated.

Having said that, it is rare for the **3** and the **1** to want to play the same role, so they will be unlikely to compete for the same love interest or the same business opportunity. They will have much in common and will love spending long evenings planning their next grand adventure – whether it be a holiday they will take together, a business they will start together, or just a fun night out on the town.

Business

1s can work well with the creative and intelligent **3**, but they must guard against being too bossy because the **3** needs to be free to do their own thing and give vent to their limitless font of ideas.

As a social motivator, **3** is focused on working with all the team members to help them achieve their full potential and will be happy for **1** to be out front taking the lead, as long as they give the **3** plenty of autonomy.

Both will usually fire off each other's creative ideas, while at the same time their agendas are very different. The **3** usually doesn't need to be the boss, merely team leader. And the **1** will respect the **3**'s motivational talents and draw strength from their creative drive.

* * *

Life Path 1: Relationship Choices

1 & 4
(Independence and Stability)

Love

The take-charge and dominant fire energy of **1** will struggle with the dogmatic and stubborn earth energy of **4** because both these numbers like to feel that they are in control of all aspects of their life…at work, at home, and even in bed.

However, there is potential for the ambitious and energetic **1** to benefit from the grounded and pragmatic level-headedness of the **4**, leading to a mutually trusting and intimate connection.

1s are always off, dancing with new ideas and romancing business partners with their passion for creating new endeavours and exciting opportunities. And yet they often lack the staying power and fortitude to see their creations through to fruition.

Enter the **4**.

Builder **4**s are process-driven and loyal to a fault, and they will always stand side by side (never behind) their Leader partner through thick and thin – providing (and here's the essential ingredient that will make this partnership work, or not) the headstrong and impulsive **1** always takes the time to explain in great detail (**4**s love details) what they are doing and what their vision is.

When **1**s include their **4** partner in everything they do, they will find the **4** will gleefully buy into their vision – providing they understand it – and offer practical support and advice to help make it happen.

This will never be an easy union, though, because the **4** will tend to find fault with almost everything the **1** does. That is just the cautious and practical nature of the **4**, who always focuses on what can go wrong as much as what can go right. The optimistic **1**, however, doesn't want to hear negatives. Even though they would be wise to listen to the **4**'s counsel, they often regard the **4**'s voice of caution as a criticism, which can lead to resentment, arguments and worse, unless the **4** can temper the 1's reckless ambition in such a way that the 1 feels supported and encouraged, rather than nit-picked and undermined.

Romantically, the 1 wants fire and brimstone, while the 4 wants sensible, mature and measured engagement. Problems will occur unless both can value the other for what they bring to the table – which is usually the diametric opposite of each other.

If the 1 is still stuck in their fragile ego, they will take the 4's constructive criticism as an attack on their ability. And if the 4 is still stuck in their stubborn need to be right all the time (and believe me, no one needs to be right more than the unevolved 4), then they will be sorely disappointed by the 1's dismissive attitude towards their advice.

Sexually, there will be challenges too because the grounded 4 wants to feel the earth move when they make love, while the fiery 1 just wants to ignite the flames of passion so they can get their fix of gratification and go back to their latest project as quickly as they can.

The secret to the success of this union lies with the 1 being prepared to accept that the 4's criticism comes from a place of loyalty and honesty because they want the 1 to be aware of all the potential pitfalls that could derail their grand plan, rather than being a control trip designed to undermine their position of power.

Criticism is never easy to hear, but if the 1 can real-eyes the 4 has their best interests at heart, they will learn to cherish their wise counsel. If, in their arrogance, they don't real-eyes this, this relationship may last about as long as it takes the 1 to shout "Next!".

Remember that when disagreements arise (and they will because all relationships are about growth, as we saw earlier), take the time to sit down and figure out what you are meant to be learning from your partner – then kiss them and thank them for the insight.

Good luck, stay open and honest… and enjoy the many valuable growth lessons this relationship can give you.

Friendship

In relationship, where the purpose is to help each other heal their wounds and become stronger and more evolved, this fire/earth match has the potential for great advancement. But where a **1** and a **4** are just friends, with no commitment, the result will almost always end in tears because both the **1** and the **4** want to feel they are in control, and yet they are coming at it from opposite ends of the spectrum.

1s are impulsive go-getters whose only concern is to break new ground with no thought of how to achieve it, whereas **4**s are practical managers whose focus is on the process and who look upon the **1**'s lack of proper planning with abject disdain.

Yes, they can be friends, but only if they recognise each other's differences as lessons to refine their own view of the world.

Most **1**s and **4**s will argue like cats and dogs over the relative virtues of inspiration versus practicality, with the **1** becoming frustrated and even angry at the **4**'s obsession with detail and process, and the **4** becoming critical of the **1**'s impetuosity.

Shallow friendships work fine, but anything much deeper and there will be little common ground because almost every decision will escalate into a debate and perhaps even a row – with the **1** believing the **4** is stuck in the mud of caution, and the **4** believing the **1** will crash and burn in the fires of impulsiveness.

Business

Because both the **1** and the **4** love to be in control, this is not a match that is recommended for equal business partners. However, it becomes a perfect match where the **1** is in control and taking the "big picture" decisions and the **4** works for the **1** as their manager, running the business like clockwork.

When it comes to building – a house or a company – there is no one better than the practical, tireless and efficient **4**.

As long as they are kept closely informed of the vision the **1** has for the business, the loyal and diligent **4** will work tirelessly – literally around the clock – to make sure everything works out perfectly.

* * *

Life Path 1: The Leader

1 & 5
(Independence and Freedom)

Love

This can be a brilliant pairing full of fun, because both these fire numbers are highly motivated go-getters who are happiest when they are rushing about all over the place pursuing their latest goal, rather than sitting around at home wondering where the other went and growing resentful at the lack of attention.

Both **1** and **5** like to have a lot of personal space in a relationship and they are more than happy to give it to each other – so the **1** can seek new opportunities for the material wealth and personal success they crave, and the **5** can seek the adventure and new friendships they need more than the air they breathe.

However, herein lies a major challenge for this pairing because neither may take the time to properly nurture the relationship and they are likely to end up just drifting apart – or else they will find someone new and move on. (Both the **1** and the **5** find it very easy to meet potential mates, and they find it just as easy to let go of their old one.)

For this relationship to last longer that a few months of wild sex and thrilling adventures, both the **1** and the **5** must make the effort to spend quality time together. Regular romantic dinners and weekends away, just the two of them (without the kids if they have them) are the perfect way for them to reconnect and rekindle the spark of desire.

Sexually, this is a passionate and adventurous coupling that will almost certainly result in broken furniture. Both partners like to express their love for each other through sex, and are prepared to push the boundaries of their sexual experiences in almost every direction.

Perhaps the biggest obstacle this pairing will face, though, is the lack of initial attraction, other than on a purely physical level. The ambitious **1** will tend to regard the mercurial and ever-changing **5** as being too unpredictable and irresponsible, while the freedom-loving **5** will see the focused and driven **1** as boring and way too serious.

It's worth sticking at it though, because the fun-loving **5** will be able to bring the goal-driven **1** out of their shell and teach them how to relax and smell the roses, while the disciplined **1** can teach the restless **5** that true freedom comes from focusing on one project and bringing it to fruition, rather than dashing about starting numerous projects and never finishing any of them, as **5**s tend to do.

Remember that when disagreements arise (and they will because all relationships are about growth, as we saw earlier), take the time to sit down and figure out what you are meant to be learning from your partner – then kiss them and thank them for the lesson.

Good luck, stay open and honest... and enjoy the thrilling adventures and fun times this fiery relationship can give you.

Friendship

This is an unlikely friendship, for the reasons discussed above. Usually, the always driven and focused **1** will become frustrated with the irresponsible and ever-changing personality of the **5**. And the fun-loving **5**, who just wants to party and socialise, will quickly tire of the **1**s serious nature and career-driven monologues about their latest plan to conquer the world.

They would do well to listen to each other, though, because each holds the secret to the other's success. The **1** can teach the **5** to see a project through to the finish, thus creating the material wealth the **5** needs to obtain the true freedom they crave.

Equally, the **5** can teach the **1** that while achievements are fine, the real pleasure of life is to be found in enjoying the moment and going with the flow, rather than missing out on all the fun because they are too busy planning what they are going to be doing next week, next month or next year.

Business

The same dynamic makes this a good business partnership, as long as the **1** is allowed free rein to choose the direction of the company and the **5** is not required to sit in on every meeting, which would bore them to death.

Dominant **1**s love to be in charge, but they can tend to become a bit blinkered in their single-minded pursuit of a goal. Which is why the **5**'s constant search for new and improved ways of doing things can make this a very powerful corporate combination.

The **5** will usually be happy to let **1** lead the way and shoulder all the responsibility (just the word "responsibility" makes the free-spirited **5** cringe), leaving the **5** free to come up with brilliant new ideas that almost certainly wouldn't have occurred to the single-minded **1**.

Make sure the **1** is the boss and the **5** doesn't have to sit at a desk all day, and watch the dollars roll in.

* * *

1 & 6

(Independence and Romance)

Love

Both these numbers have sexuality and passion coming out of their ears (and everywhere else too, for that matter… but this is a family book, so let's just leave it at ears, shall we?). Suffice to say that when it comes to falling in love, these two will find it as easy as falling entwined off the four-poster bed in their bridal suite at the five-star tropical resort, where they will surely go on their lust-filled luxury honeymoon.

No, the challenge for the dominant and fiery **1** and the loved-up watery **6** is never falling in love – it's staying in love after the first thrilling fires of love-making have faded.

One day, not too long into the relationship, the homemaker **6** will wake up and wonder where the independent **1** went. The answer is their Leader partner has probably left a hastily written note on the **6**'s expensive Egyptian cotton pillowcase – or by the **6**'s always tended open fireplace in their homely living room – saying: "Gone to a meeting in Caracas, back in a couple of days."

Life Path 1: Relationship Choices

That's bad enough for the **6**, who is all about creating a loving and comfortable home full of warm family energy. But what really hurts them to their core is the lack of an "I love you" at the end of the note.

The **1** is ruled by masculine energy, so whether they are a male or a female in the traditional birth-gender sense, they will just assume their partner knows that they love them – because, after all, they are with them, aren't they?

But the deeply feminine energy of **6** needs to be told they are loved about 3.7 million times every day, give or take a few million.

As long as the ambitious and achievement-oriented **1** takes the time to regularly assure their **6** partner how much they love them – and at least once a month whisks them away for a weekend in the country to romance them with candles and wine just like they did at the beginning – then this relationship has a chance.

Equally, the homemaker **6**, who wants to have a big family and always be at the centre of it, needs to learn to trust their **1** partner and give them the space they require to pursue their lofty goals – goals that will often take them away from the homely hearth fires for long periods at a time.

Children and/or pets will often be the difference between this pairing working, or not, no matter whether the **1** is the male or female energy in this relationship. As long as the **6** is surrounded by people and animals who they can love and nurture, they will be able to cope with their partner being away from home. But if they are left on their own too long or too often, one day the **1** will return home to find the **6** has left to find the loving connection they need in the arms of someone else, and they will have only themselves to blame because it's really not hard to keep a **6** happy. Just tell them you love them. A lot!

The lesson for the **1** is to make sure their devoted **6** partner feels loved and appreciated for all they do around the home. And the lesson for the **6** is to real-eyes their desire for love and connection is so strong, it is too much to ask the task-focused **1** to provide it all the time.

By looking to their family and friends as well for their regular doses of love and connection, the **6** can avoid stifling the **1**. And in return, the **1** will shower them not only with the love they crave, but with the wealth to build an even bigger and more beautiful family home than the last one.

Remember that when disagreements arise (and they will because all relationships are about growth, as we saw earlier), take the time to sit down and figure out what you are meant to be learning from your partner – then kiss them and thank them for the lesson.

Good luck, stay open and honest… and enjoy the deep feelings of trust and devotion this relationship can give you.

Friendship

It is rare for the goal-driven **1** and the homemaker **6** to form deep and lasting friendships simply because they get their needs met in such radically different ways.

The **1** wants to conquer the world, while the **6** is seldom happy roaming too far from their family, which always comes first for them. But **1**s are not always keen on long Sunday family lunches when they could be out riding their customised Harley with their wild and crazy friends, or playing sport… or just watching it.

However, when these two numbers reach the highest purpose of their Life Paths they can connect on a deep level because the idealistic and romantic vision of the **6** – who knows that "love is all that matters" – will resonate with the impassioned **1**, who wants to use their considerable talents and energy to spread love to as many people as possible. And the firebrand energy of the **1**, who wants to spread love through their many endeavours, will earn the lasting admiration of the evolved **6**, who knows their idealistic romantic vision for the world needs the take-charge energy of the **1** to make it happen.

On this level, the **1** and the **6** can work perfectly together.

Business

This is an auspicious commercial partnership because of what we have just spoken about. The leadership energy of **1** is ideal for starting a dynamic business, and the idealistic vision of **6** will ensure the business grows in ways that benefit as many people as possible – and is therefore more likely to succeed.

The **1** must always consult their **6** business partner in all the big decisions, or else the **6** will feel unappreciated and become resentful.

And the **6** must always let the **1** be the public face of the business who goes "out there" into the world to make things happen, or else the **1** will feel restricted and become equally resentful.

Thankfully, these roles come naturally, so very few toes will be trodden on in this business partnership. The romantic **6** wants only to spread love and is happy to let the **1** hog the spotlight. And the passionate **1** wants only to make a difference in the world, and is happy to give credit to the **6** for the vision that led to their success.

* * *

1 & 7

(Independence and Understanding)

Love

This is an extremely compatible match that can often turn into a lifelong relationship, providing both partners come to each other at similar stages of their spiritual and personal development.

In the beginning of the relationship there can be challenges as the always confident (if not arrogant) **1** struggles to accept that the insightful and brilliantly aware **7** is not only much smarter than they can ever hope to be, but probably has a keener insight into the **1**'s strengths and weaknesses than they have themselves.

This can sometimes lead the insecure **1** to break up with the **7**, simply because they are unnerved by their superior intelligence.

The **1** needs to learn that the **7** has absolutely no intention of stealing the **1**'s thunder. Yes, of course they are more evolved because **1**s are only at the beginning of their cycle, forging their successes in the fires of material wealth, while **7**s are well past that materialistic stage and are working with the advanced air energy of spiritual wisdom.

Life Path 1: The Leader

The truth is, the evolved **7** is a loving and supportive partner who is happiest when they see the love of their life succeeding in whatever they choose to do.

This can sometimes make the **1** feel guilty, because they are acutely aware that their capacity for selfless support is nowhere near as strong, or as evolved, as that of their faithful and devoted **7**.

This is a mistake, because the **7** does not always want back what they give out. They will support their independent **1** lover through thick and thin and all they will ever need in return is recognition and appreciation for their support. Well, that and enough solitary time to do their own thing – which the independent **1** will usually be only too happy to give them.

The often wayward **1** must always treat their devoted **7** with the utmost respect and communicate their innermost feelings with absolute honesty. The **7** can see through a lie easier than an x-ray can see through skin, and for them honesty is paramount.

Remember that when disagreements arise (and they will because all relationships are about growth, as we saw earlier), take the time to sit down and figure out what you are meant to be learning from your partner – then kiss them and thank them for the lesson.

Good luck, stay open and honest... and enjoy the exquisite and passionate connection this relationship can give you.

Friendship

Yes, yes, yes! These two can be best friends forever, the **7** inspiring the **1**, and the **1** bringing the often shy **7**'s lofty ideas to fruition. They will feed off each other, the forceful **1** encouraging the insightful **7** to put their ideas out there into the world, and the thoughtful **7** using their air energy to fan the flames of the passionate **1**.

In fact, these two numbers get along so well together that if their sexualities match and the **1** is in a relationship, they must be careful their close connection with their **7** BFF doesn't become an issue that could threaten their partner.

Business

This is a positive combination for business, for all the reasons we have already seen. The firefly **1** and the insightful **7** will usually work well together – the intelligent **7** stoking the flames of the **1**'s energetic drive with their knowledge of what people really want, and the ambitious **1** taking the **7**'s inspiring ideas and making them happen.

The fire energy of **1** and the air energy of **7** will drive this business to grow beyond their wildest dreams. But growing a business is only one side of the coin. Neither of these fire and air numbers has the first clue about the day-to-day practicalities of running a company – so the first thing they should do after signing their partnership agreement is employ an earthy manager to make sure everything runs smoothly.

And, as we have already seen, that requires a **4**. A business with a tireless **1** driving its growth, an aware **7** targeting its market, and a loyal **4** managing the back-office operations is almost guaranteed to succeed.

* * *

1 & 8
(Independence and Ambition)

Love

These numbers are like two peas in a pod and will usually find it easy to form a close business relationship, but loving relationships are another matter because neither the independent **1** nor the ambitious **8** has much regard for romance. They are too busy making their mark in the world and pursuing their careers to spend much in the way of quality time with their partner.

The upside is that while other numbers will struggle with the **1**'s constant need to focus on their career, it's no problem for the equally driven **8**, who will please the **1** by allowing them the space they need.

The downside is that this can tend to feel more like a marriage of convenience than a marriage of love, and both must take the time to nurture the relationship or it may quickly wither and die.

Life Path 1: The Leader

Also, for all their material focus, both the headstrong **1** and the strong-willed **8** crave the approval and support of their partner. And if it isn't there, they will look for it somewhere else. Extra-marital affairs are common, though usually short-lived, because after the disgruntled **1** or **8** has got their "fix" of approval from someone else, they will quickly feel cramped by their new illicit relationship and yearn for the freedom they had before with their undemanding partner.

Another area to watch for is that both the **1** and the **8** are assertive partners who like to be on top – which can make for a great time in the bedroom, but a series of blazing rows everywhere else. The solution is to draw firm boundaries within the relationship and decide the arenas where each can be in charge.

Taking turns also works – whether it's deciding whose turn it is to pick the Sunday night movie, or choose the restaurant, or even the holiday destination each year.

As long as there is open communication and both partners feel free to speak up when their needs are not being met – which will be frequently – this relationship can be mutually rewarding. But if the high expectations of both these numbers lead either one to become demanding or needy towards the other, it will push them away faster than they can say "divorce".

Well, that's not quite accurate. They will have to say "expensive divorce" because both the **1** and the **8** are very money-oriented and will probably want to squeeze every last penny from the other.

It need never come to this, though, as long as the busy **1** and the ambitious **8** take the time to inject even just a little bit of romance into their daily lives. Notes on the pillow, flowers or gifts for no reason, surprise dinner dates and such will work just fine.

Remember, the sole (soul) purpose of your relationship is to learn from each other and help each other to grow. Specifically, in this case, the **1** needs to develop enough confidence in their abilities so they never feel threatened by the always powerful **8**. And the **8** needs to learn that the power they so desperately seek is not power over other people – especially their **1** partner – but an inner power that allows them to open up and be vulnerable, knowing nothing can or will ever hurt them because they are pure love. And love is not only the most powerful thing there is... it is ALL there is.

Good luck, stay open and honest... and enjoy the material success and exciting adventures this relationship can give you.

Friendship

The ambitious **1** and the materialistic **8** have the potential to be both best mates and sworn enemies – usually in quick succession.

Many **1/8** friendships will start out great, both firing ideas off each other. They will bond over their mutual desires for success and advancement, and may even choose to partner up (see the Business notes below), thinking – quite rightly – that by combining their ferocious appetites and energies they will form a dynamic team.

They will, there is no doubt about it. But it may last only as long as it takes one to outstrip the other. If the fragile ego of the **1** feels slighted by their sometimes ruthless **8** partner, competition will replace co-operation and the friendship could be sacrificed on the altar of ambition. The solution is to real-eyes there is more than enough to go around, and if each can rise above their ego and celebrate the successes of the other rather than resent them for their triumphs, then this can be a very rewarding friendship in every sense.

Business

Of all the possible Life Path Number combinations, this is one of the most auspicious pairings for creating lasting wealth and abundance.

The energetic and creative **1** – who sees opportunities everywhere they look with their fire energy of possibility – can sometimes fall into the egoic trap of pursuing goals that are more about making themselves feel worthy than creating genuine abundance for all concerned.

This is the curse of the energy of fire, which sometimes can burn brightly just for the sake of it – and yet at the end of their spectacular display of energetic fireworks, when all the embers have died down, there may be very little to show for their efforts other than the smouldering ashes of their failed dreams.

Enter the **8**, who is equally ambitious but is governed by the stable and process-driven energy of earth, and can therefore ground the fiery **1** and keep them focused on the end result.

The materialistic **8** is balanced by their more advanced spiritual understanding that the purpose of creating wealth is not to keep it, but to share it with others less fortunate than themselves.

This is a lesson the **1** would do well to learn.

As long as the powerful personalities of the **1** and the **8** can set boundaries so they do not tread on each other's toes, this is the perfect business partnership, where both will drive each other to new heights of achievement.

The secret to success here is trust. If the **1** trusts the **8** to manage the business while they rush about making deals and bringing in the money, and the **8** trusts the **1**'s vision enough to let them take the lead and drive the business forward into new markets, there is nothing this most dynamic of duos can't achieve.

* * *

<u>1 & 9</u>
(Independence and Passion)

Love

This pairing has great potential to forge a close, loving and lasting relationship, full of passion, laughter and happiness.

No other number can captivate the normally career-focused **1**'s heart as easily as the vivacious, generous and optimistic **9**. Their love of life and sunny personality will feed the **1**'s need for a partner who is as independent as they are.

At the same time, the **9**'s inner strength and confidence will help them cope with long periods apart while the **1** pursues their career-

Life Path 1: Relationship Choices

focused goals – and all they will need in return is a regular phone call or text telling them how much they mean to their Leader lover.

All **1**s quickly tire of a partner who becomes overly needy of their time and attention, which is why the independent **9** has the best chance (along, perhaps, with the Self-sufficient **7**) of all the numbers to fulfill the **1**'s very specific need for intimacy without expectation.

During the times they are together, the passionate **1** and the ebullient **9** will dance and sing and make love like teenagers. Sex is almost always passionate, intimate and adventurous. And during their times apart (there will be many as the **1** pursues their business interests and the **9** shares themselves freely with friends and family in need), they will delight in planning their next fun time together.

One word of warning: the **9** is so passionate and generous that they will freely give the **1** all the time and space they need – but only on the unspoken condition that they never lose the deep, intimate connection with their lover. Intimacy is paramount to the **9**, and as long as they always know they are the most important person in the **1**'s life, all will be well. But if they feel they are being taken advantage of, they will shut down and withdraw into their shell.

1s must ensure their adoring **9** always knows they are the most important thing in the **1**'s life. This usually requires nothing more than a loving phone call or a small token of appreciation now and then in the form of a gift. And on the very rare occasion when the **9** does ask for attention, the **1** absolutely must stop whatever they are doing (and fly home if necessary) to give them the intimacy they need.

It's a very small price to pay for the years and years of selfless support, love and freedom the **9** is only too happy to give their **1** partner... with this one very small proviso.

Remember that when disagreements arise (and they will because all relationships are about growth, as we saw earlier), take the time to sit down and figure out what you are meant to be learning from your partner – then kiss them and thank them for the lesson.

Good luck, stay open and honest... and enjoy the love, lust and laughter this exciting relationship can give you.

Friendship

Usually, a **1** and a **9** who forge a close, trusting friendship will stay friends for life. As we saw just now in the context of a romantic relationship, both come to the table with only one expectation each: for the **1** it's the desire for a friend who is not needy, and for the **9** it is for a friend who never takes advantage of their limitless generosity.

Providing both these needs are met – and the **1** remembers to always acknowledge the **9**'s generosity and never take advantage of their giving nature, while the **9** always remembers not to cramp the **1** or make them feel guilty about their ambitious desires – these two naturally optimistic lovers of life can become great friends.

I would even go so far as to suggest they consider teaming up and starting a business. And if their sexualities match, they might even hop into bed and get married because there is little these two numbers can't achieve better together than they can on their own.

Business

As we have just seen in friendship, the **1** and the **9** can also work extremely well together in a business context. The usual provisos apply, namely that the **1** will need to feel they are in charge and the **9** will need to give the **1** all the space they require to pursue new opportunities where they find them.

In return, the **9** will need to feel appreciated and always kept in the loop. They will also need the freedom to pursue their own (usually charitable) projects that will form part of the business but will be their own responsibility for them to run as they see fit.

One of the problems an unevolved **1** will encounter in business is the number of times they put people's noses out of joint in their headlong pursuit of a goal. Having a **9** as a partner is perfect, because there is no more diplomatic problem solver that a **9** who can easily put out the **1**'s fires and ensure everyone is happy.

* * *

4. HEALTH CHOICES

ALL **1**s are so full of dynamic, passionate and creative energy that they need to guard against ignoring their health for the sake of pursuing their latest goal at all costs.

Although most **1**s will enjoy robust good health when things are going their way, stress and "dis-ease" are common problems when the going gets tough. They also tend to take any setbacks to heart, which is why cardiovascular problems are the **1**'s Achilles Heel.

Regular physical exercise is vital for **1**s because they have so much creative energy coursing through their bodies that they need to make sure it doesn't build up and manifest as muscular and organic stress. Energy must always be expressed and released, or it can cause illness.

Stress comes with the territory when you are a leader and a trailblazer, wagering large amounts of money on the outcome of an investment, project or business.

The more **1**s bump up against frustration in their business and personal life, caused by failing to get their ideas across or bringing their projects to fruition, the more they will need to vent the powerful flow of their creative energy by moving their body radically, either by running, swimming or cycling – or by engaging in physical team sports.

Many **1**s have a taste for rich foods, which is not surprising given they love the finest things in life. But this accentuates the risk of heart trouble, and if you add stress into the mix the result can be catastrophic.

A vegetarian diet may not be optimum for **1**s because they need high quantities of iron to fuel their creative furnace. Emotionally, red meat fires up their yang energy. This should be kept in moderation, though, and they should especially guard against high-fat diets that will cause them to put on weight easily. And because **1**s are so quick to judge themselves, any shame they feel about their physical appearance will be immediately translated into a desire to compensate for their perceived physical shortcomings by increasing the power they have over others to make themselves feel better.

Life Path 1: The Leader

In my experience, it is common for healthy **1**s to easily access the positive qualities of their Life Path Number because they are so focused on everything they do, including their exercise program. However, it is just as easy for them to swerve towards the "dark side" of their number when they have a hunger for fattening foods that matches their hunger for wealth and power.

Many **1**s will find solace in nature. A regular walk in the country will not just improve their health, it will also ground them and re-mind them of what is important. They must remember they are here to let their energy flow through them for the greater good of all. The more they try to block their energy, the more out of balance they will become, both physically and emotionally.

A regular walk in nature also helps the **1** remember they can't take anything with them, and it may encourage them to share what they do have with those who are in need. In the process, their stress levels will reduce and they will benefit from relaxing into the ebb and flow of life.

Ailments to watch out for

All **1**s are prone to stress-related disorders such as cardiovascular dis-ease and strokes (giving up emotionally). Their constitutions are fairly strong if they combine their healthy appetites with regular and rigorous physical exercise that involves breaking into a sweat.

They have a strong immune system (sense of identity) that will fend off most common bugs, but their tendency to overindulge in the finer things in life, and their inability to listen to advice from anyone – including their doctor – can put them at risk of chronic ill-health.

1s will usually make a lot of money and will love nothing more than spending it on fine wines and extravagant (ie, unhealthy) meals, leaving them prone to cholesterol and blood pressure issues.

Other common afflictions for **1**s include indigestion (failure to let life in), anaemia (lack of joy), eye disorders (refusal to see what's in front of them) and stress-related problems such as ulcers and hernias (fear of not being good enough).

Life Path 1: Choices for Children

Effective therapies

1s should have regular medical check-ups, particularly as they get older, to monitor their susceptibility to stress-induced illnesses. They will also benefit from alternative therapies that work on clearing energy blockages in their bodies, including massage, acupuncture, kinesiology, Reiki and other hands-on energetic healing methods

Because of the **1**'s fondness for high-fat diets, nutritional, herbal and homeopathic remedies will also be extremely beneficial. And for their hyperactive minds, creative visualisation, meditation and even hypnosis can keep them focused, calm and centred.

Diet choices

Raw foods that benefit the **1**'s digestive system include ginger, chamomile, honey, bay leaves, nutmeg, cloves, lemons, oranges and raisins. Of these, honey is by far the most beneficial for the **1**. They can eat it off the spoon, or include it in teas or in a glass of water.

Because their planet is the Sun, **1**s should eat plenty of yellow and orange foods, including peppers, squash, oranges, mandarins, lemons, carrots, apricots, peaches, pawpaw, bananas and pumpkin.

And all **1**s much remember to take it easy and not indulge too much at their corporate lunches and five-course club dinners.

* * *

5. CHOICES FOR CHILDREN

YOUNG children working with the energy of **1** will usually explore the negative energies of their Life Path Number before moving on to master the positive aspects. This is true of all the nine Life Paths

Life Path 1: The Leader

because children need to first understand the boundaries of what is and isn't acceptable behaviour.

However, once their boundaries are in place – and your child has understood the crucial lesson of cause and effect – young 1s can then start tapping into their natural leadership strengths with the assistance of an attentive and supportive parental guiding hand.

Children working the positive side of **1** will usually be creative and imaginative from an early age. Young **1**s tend to be brim full of curiosity and have high energy levels. They are good problem solvers, so they will usually do well at school, especially in exams where their natural competitive streak will drive them to outdo their classmates.

The only thing that could hold them back is a lack of confidence, so parents must do all they can to nurture their **1** child's sense of Self-esteem in their early years.

Young **1**s tend to adapt easily to the responsibility of leadership roles at school and on the sports field as team captain. And their natural sense of determination and willpower will, if correctly nurtured, cause them to study hard and achieve success academically as well.

Losing is one thing they do not accept easily, or gracefully, so they try to avoid it at all costs.

In the negative, a child working with the energy of **1** can have a tendency to be stubborn and unco-operative. All toddlers throw tantrums when they don't get their own way, but none will do so as dramatically as a **1**. Believe me, things will get broken!

1 children need to be taught patience and tolerance, and a firm guiding hand may sometimes be needed to teach them that everyone has to follow and learn the ropes before they can hope to lead.

Parents also need to watch out for sharp mood swings and the risk of laziness and lethargy, particularly in teenagers. All **1**s dislike routine, so as much as they can parents must try to provide **1** children with a variety of activities that stimulate their hyperactive minds.

At times, **1** children can tend to be Self-indulgent and grumpy if they don't get their own way. And since **1** is the most egotistical of all

Life Path 1: Choices for Children

the Life Paths, their strong motivation can easily flip into the negative pursuit of greed and power because deep down they feel insecure.

Parents should guard against **1**s becoming bossy and intolerant, which is a symptom of a hidden insecurity. Plenty of love and encouragement – even in the face of a tantrum – should do the trick.

During their teenage years, **1**s thrive on being given a large amount of independence. An after-school job or a Saturday job are perfect for allowing the teenage **1** to develop their natural entrepreneurial skills.

Playtime activities

Problem-solving and creative pursuits will work well for young **1**s. Their lightning-fast minds will allow them to think up new games and pastimes, and they should also be encouraged to develop their natural leadership abilities through role-playing activities.

As they grow older they will quickly become independent, able to amuse and entertain themselves for long periods without being bored. **1** children love video and computer games, as well as outdoor activities and sports, all of which allow them to excel and feel like winners.

Because **1**s are individualistic, some will enjoy solo competitive sports such as tennis, golf, swimming, sailing and athletics rather than team sports – unless, as I have said, they are captain or the star player.

* * *

Your child's three-digit Birth Code

As we have seen in Part Two, we always work primarily with the energy of our Life Path Number right from the outset, but in our childhood years from 0 to 18 we do so in conjunction with the energy of our first Supplementary Birth Number, and in our second 18 years – until we reach full emotional maturity at 36 – we do so in conjunction with the energy of our second Supplementary Birth Number.

It's worth reading the main listings here in Part Three for the numbers that make up your child's two Supplementary Birth Numbers to gain a better understanding of their positive and negative qualities. Also, as you read about your child's three-digit Birth Code, real-eyes that the difference between "feeling the force" of any Life Path and flipping to the "dark side" is determined by the amount of Self-confidence we develop in our childhood years, and then the amount of Self-love we develop in our teenage years.

That, in a nutshell (squirrel!), is your role as a parent: to instill in your child first Self-esteem, and then Self-love.

The 10/1 child

10/1 is the only possible Birth Code of this Life Path, so all young Leaders will work solely with the energy of **1** (as detailed in the Life Choices section earlier) not just during their first formative 18 years, but throughout their usually highly successful lives.

In the Self-Awareness System™, 0 acts as an amplifier for the number it is associated with – in this case a **1**. So it's easy to see that young **1**s are uniquely focused individuals who are working solely with the amplified double energy of leadership, creativity and ambition that defines the Leader's personality right from the moment they are born.

This ultra-focused Life Path gives the young **1** a fantastic potential to excel in whatever they choose to do. Just remember the golden rule of the Self-Awareness System™, which states that with every positive potential comes an equal negative potential – which means every Leader child has both the capacity for fantastic success and the capacity for spectacular disappointment in everything they do.

As a parent, it's important to give your 10/1 child plenty of leeway to follow their own star, while also keeping a firm rein on their rampant ego as it develops. The most important lesson a 10/1 child can learn is that it's perfectly OK to follow their dreams, but never at the expense of others, who must be treated with respect and love at all times.

LIFE PATH 2:
The Intuitive

1. Growth cycle: Second stage (the number of co-operation)
2. Influences: Water (emotion, feminine) and the Moon (sensitivity)
3. Positive qualities: Compassionate, affectionate and empathetic
4. Negative potential: Defensive, resentful and overwhelmed
5. Highs and lows: Confident peacemaker, or fragile co-dependent
6. Highest purpose: Bring people together in peace and harmony
7. Love matches: 2, 4, 6 and 8 for compatibility (the rest for growth)
8. Possible careers: Healing, design, medicine, HR, social work
9. Words to live by: "The person who needs my love the most is me"

1. LIFE CHOICES FOR THE INTUITIVE

THE empathetic and kind-hearted **2** is the most compassionate and generous of numbers. They have come into the world full of hope and optimism, eager to spread their message of love and bring people together to work – and play – in peace and harmony.

This is the second "co-operation stage of a growth cycle, following on from the leadership energy of **1**, whose highest purpose is to create new opportunities by striking out on their own to help others. But while the **1** values their independence, the insightful and aware **2** knows that we will always achieve more success and joy by working together as a harmonious team than we ever can on our own.

Just as the dominant **1** is the most masculine of the nine Life Paths in the sense of taking radical action "out there in the world" to achieve

Life Path 2: The Intuitive

their goals, the empathetic **2** is the most feminine Life Path because their work is internal and driven by a strong desire to bring love, healing and happiness to as many people as possible.

The **2** is governed by the element of water and their ruling planet is the Moon, both of which endow the always emotional Intuitive with deep insights into the needs and feelings of others.

As we'll see in a moment, Intuitive **2**s are never happier than when they are in a close, passionate and loving relationship. However, the "love energy" of their Life Path refers to more than just romantic love. The big-hearted **2** is a true lover of life. They adore nature, especially animals, and it is rare to find a **2** who doesn't have a pet and a garden they love to tend, or at least an apartment full of pampered plants.

2s also love to travel, not just so see new places but to meet new people from different cultures and backgrounds.

There is no more giving number than the **2**. Unlike the materially focused **1** who tends to pursue goals at all costs, the insightful **2** understands that the journey is more important than the destination.

Yes, **2**s often start their own business, but it will almost always be with the goal of bringing healing and harmony to the lives of others. And because they are working with the elemental energy of water (emotion) that governs this Life Path Number, their deep desire to help others will dictate almost every decision they make.

The word "compassion" describes the **2** best – it literally means "with passion" (from the Latin "com", meaning "with"). They have an exceptional amount of empathy for the plight of other people, and animals too, and a passionate desire to help out wherever they can.

However, because what we are all here to do is not necessarily what comes easiest to us, compassionate **2**s will also face challenges on their Life Path that are put there specifically to help them grow. This is especially evident in the **2**'s need to look after themselves as well as everyone else around them.

Although their intuitive understanding and their desire to help are the **2**'s greatest strengths, they can also be the cause of their greatest pain if they fail to draw firm boundaries around themselves and learn how to take care of their own needs as much as those of others.

Those who walk the light side of this Life Path tap into their seemingly endless reserves of energy and generosity. But if they don't give themselves as much love as they give to others, they can flip to the dark side by becoming resentful, withdrawn and even depressed.

The open-hearted **2** is so sensitive that if they haven't learned how to defend their boundaries, they may flit between being overly generous and resentful, retreating into their shell at the first sign of a disagreement. Ironically, instead of feeling "safe", this Self-imposed isolation feels more like a prison for the always social **2**.

This is especially true for younger **2**s who have not yet learned to stand up for themselves and may suffer from shyness and a lack of confidence that prevents them from saying what's truly in their heart. For the loving and caring **2**, that is the very worst feeling in the world.

* * *

Highest purpose of The Intuitive

The highest purpose of the **2** (and the Master Intuitive **11**/**2** – more about you "**11**s" in a moment) is to become a compassionate peacemaker who brings people together in healing and harmony.

This can be on a family, a community, a national or even a global scale, but most often your capacity for teaching co-operation and awareness will be used to help others find peace and harmony within themselves and their relationships.

This is the second stage of the cycle. You have already learned to express your Self as a **1**, so now you need to learn how to co-operate and interact with others while at the same time honouring your own needs so you can help others without harming your Self.

Because your highest purpose is to learn how to help others while honouring your Self, you will face the central challenge of balancing your sense of responsibility towards others with ensuring you have put your own boundaries in place so you are able to be true to your own needs as well.

Those **2**s who cannot find a healthy balance between service to others and service to their Self risk burning out by running around in circles and getting nowhere. They may even become co-dependent on others for their happiness, rather than finding it within themselves in their big, beautiful, generous hearts.

Remember, the most important goal for all Life Paths is always the same: to first "wake up" to the truth that we are an extension of Source energy, and to help other people wake up as well. Then, and only then, will the path to our highest potential open up before us.

* * *

Key words are... 'confidence' and 'forgiveness'

In order to fulfill their life's highest purpose, **2**s must first learn to develop an unshakeable inner confidence that will allow them to reach out and help others, while at the same time feeling able to draw a line in the sand when they need to take time out to nurture themselves.

Confidence is crucial for all Life Paths as we embark on our common journey from pure unaware love to pure conscious love. As we saw in Part One, Self-esteem is the first crucial step towards Self-love that we all must take. (If you're wondering what a "Self" is, please try to find the time to read Part One because, as you'll discover, it's way too complicated to explain again here.)

For the always empathetic **2**, however, developing a strong sense of inner confidence is much more than just the key to their personal happiness – it will determine whether they walk the positive Life Path of the brave and loving Intuitive, or veer down the negative path towards victim consciousness, co-dependence and resentment.

All Intuitives are born with a deep and passionate desire to create peace and harmony around them, first within their immediate family and then within larger groups at school or their workplace. If their love is not reciprocated – or, worse, is repaid with deceit and aggression – the unconfident **2** will be deeply wounded.

If this happens often (and any **2** you speak to will tell you it does, especially in childhood), wounded Intuitives may use their unparalleled understanding of how people feel to attack their enemies with a ferocity and vindictiveness that can be truly frightening – because they intuitively know exactly how to hurt someone to their core.

That is why young **2**s must be taught the value of unconditional love. Many times, the love they give out will not be reciprocated for any number of reasons, and they must be made to real-eyes this is not because they have done anything "wrong". It simply means the other person is not as evolved in their ability to give love as they are.

Another person's anger is always "their stuff", but the unconfident **2** will believe it is because of something they have done, or not done. If they have developed a deep inner sense of their Self-worth, however, they will clearly see their attacker's anger and rejection for what it truly is – the other person's sense of inadequacy, which causes them to reject the love that they subconsciously feel they don't deserve.

The other lesson the Intuitive would do well to learn as early in life as possible is to real-eyes that they are the co-creator of all their experiences, bad as well as good. This is because **2**s, particularly in their formative years, will experience more than their fair share of rejection from others who have far less love in their hearts and lash out at the **2** because he or she makes them feel inadequate, or jealous… or both.

If the **2** is to survive this onslaught unscathed and avoid carrying a lifelong resentment inside them towards those who have caused them pain in the past, they must learn the art of forgiveness. Or, more precisely, and to borrow a phrase from one of my favourite spiritual growth authors Colin Tipping, the art of "radical forgiveness".

Forgiveness – the act of forgiving someone who hurts us – implies the person "did something" to us. Radical forgiveness, on the other hand, is the understanding that at some level we attracted the pain so we could grow – and therefore there is nothing to forgive.

Life Path 2: The Intuitive

There is no dumber slogan in all the world than "shit happens". Shit never happens to us – it is always us who attracts it and makes it happen, so we can learn and grow from the experience.

Yes, this can be difficult to accept when the experience is a particularly painful one. But the amount of pain (and therefore potential for growth) is always determined by our Self.

Once we can accept this life-changing truth, we can clearly see – with our real eyes – that trying to forgive a parent, a sibling, a partner or anyone else for "hurting us" is guaranteed to keep us mired in the mistaken belief that they "did something" to us. Only when we real-eyes that we (our Self) create our experiences can we feel the liberating bliss of radical forgiveness and free our hearts of resentment forever.

This lesson is crucial for all the Life Paths, but none so much as the sensitive **2**, whose unique capacity to love and be loved makes them particularly vulnerable to abuse and anger from insecure people who may lash out at them because they are in so much pain caused by their own chronic lack of love. Especially within their immediate family.

Once the aware **2** learns the art of radical forgiveness (which, of course, includes forgiving themselves) and becomes confident in their ability to help others find the love in their own hearts, they will radiate peace, compassion and empathy everywhere they go.

Also, as if by magic, everyone in their past who caused them pain will either vanish from their awareness or morph into loving reflections of the **2**'s own compassionate Self. Best of all, they will no longer feel any fear because they will finally real-eyes that love is not something they give or receive… it is who they are, and it is who everyone is.

* * *

Positive and negative potential

All Life Paths contain an equal measure of positive and negative potential. Our challenge in every lifetime, no matter our Life Path Number, is to nurture our positives and overcome our negatives.

Life Path 2: Life Choices

The reason we are given negative potential as well as positive potential is because, like it or not, people usually respond more effectively to the threat of pain than they do to the promise of pleasure.

Also, while it is admirable to do what we are good at in life, we will only ever become the best we can be by facing our "dark side". This process involves digging deep into our Self to overcome our fears and any other obstacles that may appear on our path. And we will do this by subliminally – but quite deliberately – creating so-called "bad" experiences to help us learn and grow.

As we have already seen in Part Two, it is only when the chips are down and we are up against it that we find out who we truly are and what we are truly capable of doing.

For example, the empathetic **2** finds it easy to "tune in" to how others are feeling, enabling them to make close, loving connections seemingly at the drop of a hat.

But on the flip side, this ability to read other peoples' energy exposes them to the negativity and judgment of others – even if it is unspoken – which the **2** will experience as a criticism, even when it is not. And unless the **2** has developed, through adversity, enough Self-worth and Self-love, they will sever the connection faster than you could pick up the hat again.

Because all **2**s are at the second (connection) stage of a Spiritual Growth Cycle, they tend to be naturally social, loyal and genuinely interested in helping everyone around them. Their friends seek them out for advice and support because they know there is no one as caring and compassionate as the eternally loving **2**.

Young **2**s (and many older ones too) can struggle to clearly express their emotions, which is painful when they are misunderstood. If this happens often, the ever-sensitive **2** may become shy and withdrawn.

The most important real-eyesation for all young **2**s is to trust their feelings and learn to express them without the fear of being judged. Intuitive **2**s have a highly developed psychic ability, and what they have to say usually comes straight from the Source. The truth is, they are often much more spiritually aware than they, or their parents, know.

Life Path 2: The Intuitive

As well as being spiritually attuned, **2**s are also blessed with an intuitive insight into what makes people tick, and are usually able to see all sides of a situation – enabling them to help resolve conflicts here in the material world with an almost "guru-like" wisdom.

Those who work with the positive energy of **2** make excellent healers and counsellors who give freely of their time to help others. But those who work with the negative energy of this Life Path will struggle to remain upbeat and may suffer repeated mood swings.

In the positive, **2**s are sensitive, kind, courteous and compassionate towards others, and they desire peace and harmony in all areas of their lives. However, if they have suffered a lot of pain in their lives (and all **2**s have), they will have little time for people who indulge in Self-pity, and their compassion for others' misfortune will go only so far.

"Harmony" is much more than just a word (or an Elton John song) for the **2** – it is their most important value in life, especially within their family home, which will always be immaculate.

2s have an excellent eye for design, and their homes will usually be stylish, tasteful and harmonious. They love music too, and they will always feel the energy of their favourite songs with an intensity that frequently baffles even those closest to them.

Teamwork is also important for **2**s, who tend to excel in group activities due to their ability to read people's thoughts and see all sides of a situation. They are seldom shy about giving advice – in fact, they can even feel miffed if they are not allowed to contribute – and, for the most part, what they suggest is of significant value to the group.

If a **2** does offer advice, they will expect it to be followed, or at least seriously considered. Few things annoy a **2** more than seeing a group or an individual ignore their suggestions. But **2**s must remember that many people don't like being told what to do, so they would be wise to either keep their counsel until someone asks them for it, or else work hard on communicating their advice in such a way that the other person receives it as merely a suggestion rather than an instruction.

A quick tip is to ban the words "you should" and "you must", and instead phrase your advice as a question: "Have you considered...?

Life Path 2: Life Choices

As the ultimate team member, the **2** usually doesn't need the focus to be on them, even though all **2**s love attention. They are usually content to toil away with little praise or recognition, as long as they receive at least some form of acknowledgement for all their hard work.

It's easy to take a generous **2** for granted, but this is a big mistake. They will never say anything, but their resentment will build until you will know something is very wrong just by looking at them. You won't need to ask what is wrong (they wouldn't tell you even if you did), just lavish them with attention and praise – and all will be well again.

Although **2**s are not leaders, like **1**s, they are extremely talented and insightful members of a group whom leaders would do very well to consult. As peacemakers, **2**s will look for the best solution for all parties when faced with a conflict or upset. They are almost always balanced and fair in everything they do and say, and because of this people often turn to **2**s to mediate their problems.

Most **2**s are closely in touch with their spiritual nature and have a clear understanding of how the spirit world operates. They are intuitive and insightful and have an uncanny knack to always see the best in people, even when it's not always easy to see. This ability is driven by a sincere concern for the welfare of others.

2s are often creatures of habit who are comfortable with routine. Friendship and companionship is very important to the outgoing and social **2**, who doesn't usually like to be on their own for too long.

Their watery energy, governed by the Moon, is decidedly feminine and compassionate. They can be sweet, gentle and charming, and very often they are attractive physically as well as emotionally.

As we have seen, the Life Path of the **2** is likely to be one of helping and improving the lives of others. They are hospitable and make excellent hosts and hostesses, and their sound judgment and level-headedness mean they are ideal to have around in a crisis.

On the negative side, however, the **2** is so concerned with finding approval that they find it particularly difficult to accept criticism of any kind, even when it is offered in the most loving and constructive way.

Life Path 2: The Intuitive

The unevolved **2**'s extreme sensitivity can cause them to lash out at their critic, or else cut off all contact with them – and usually both. As gentle and loving as the **2** is most of the time, their anger is formidable, especially when they believe they have been mistreated.

Another negative behaviour pattern to watch out for is lethargy and indecisiveness. When the **2** becomes overwhelmed by the million tasks they always have on their mental "to do" list – or, because they have spent so much time looking after everyone else, they have forgotten to take care of themselves – they have a tendency to collapse in a heap of self-pity and despair.

Fortunately, it seldom lasts for long because the **2**'s innate optimism and love of life quickly bubbles back to the surface. But the overwhelmed **2** can waste vast amounts of time and energy brooding on something that simply isn't worth worrying about.

2s can also be unfairly harsh on themselves because they set such high standards for what they expect to achieve. They tend to beat themselves up because they are not Superwoman or Superman, able to solve the whole world's problems all at once.

Often a **2** can fail to recognise the 119 things they have done with great success because there were 120 things on their list. Instead, they will fret about the one thing they didn't manage to do.

For the most part, however, the friendly and compassionate **2** will enjoy a wide circle of friends, a peaceful and harmonious home and the admiration and respect of their business colleagues.

When they learn the confidence to give their love freely and without expecting anything in return, and liberate themselves from pain and resentment by embracing the concept of radical forgiveness, there really is nothing a **2** cannot accomplish with ease – including learning to love themselves as much as they do everyone else.

***

On a more personal level, **2**s tend to value their family above all else. And "family" for the loving **2** usually extends beyond their immediate home to include distant relatives and even close friends, who they always treat as family. Any discord within this group affects the **2** deeply, and they will do whatever it takes to try to make their family unit harmonious, peaceful and mutually supportive again.

Arguments and friction are anathema to the sensitive **2**. Their usual response to any kind of conflict is to retreat within themselves and wait for it to pass.

2s are also devoted nurturers and make excellent parents for the simple reason that they love children. Equally, if one or both of their elderly parents falls sick or is in need of comfort, out of all their siblings it will almost always be the **2** who pitches in to help.

Other than the fiercely protective **4**, there is no one who is capable of more loyalty than the empathetic and compassionate **2**.

In relationship, the sensitive **2** feels emotions very deeply (the 20/2 especially so) and they can become frustrated if their partner doesn't understand that what might appear trivial to them is of great importance to the empathetic **2**.

In fact, the **2**'s sensitivity can be a double-edged sword because although it gives them a unique capacity to connect with others once they have learned enough Self-confidence as an adult, as a child it can manifest as a crippling shyness that prevents them from ever truly expressing the voluminous love in their hearts.

This inability to express themselves can cause the unevolved **2** severe heartache and pain. Their delicate ego can easily be hurt, and as a result they are so afraid of confrontation that they tend to shrink back into their shell – where, instead of feeling safe, they actually feel only more scared and depressed.

If someone then tries to pry open the shell, the frightened and vulnerable **2** will react with an explosion of anger – a "back off" warning akin to a cornered wild animal – which serves only to alienate everyone around them even more.

This behaviour confirms the loving **2**'s greatest fear, which is not conflict, even though they dread it. It is the fear of being alone.

Life Path 2: The Intuitive

All this is avoided, of course, once the **2** grows up and learns that disagreements are a natural and healthy part of any relationship and are in no way an indication that they are at fault.

* * *

Summary of the positives

Providing the eternally optimistic and loving **2** has developed the inner confidence to express what is in their heart and has released all their past hurts through radical forgiveness, there is nothing they cannot achieve both at home in their harmonious family life and also in their professional capacity, which will always revolve around healing and helping others release their fears and conflicts as well.

Those who work with the positive energy of **2** will make excellent healers, counsellors, diplomats, artists, designers and social workers who give freely of their time to help improve the lives of others. They will also excel as partners and parents because they love to love, they adore children, and they always value their home life above their work.

The aware and evolved **2** is a shining light of love and peace, both for their wide circle of friends and for the world as a whole.

Key positive words

Gentle, intuitive, spiritual, considerate, compassionate, social, tidy, hospitable, loyal, reliable, generous, supportive, open-hearted, kind, insightful, adaptable, stylish and well-mannered.

* * *

Summary of the negatives

The ever-sensitive **2** is going to get hurt in their young life. It is unavoidable, and a necessary part of their journey. After all, it is their unique sensitivity among all the Life Paths that makes the confident and Self-aware **2** such a vital peacemaker and harmoniser in the world.

However, if the **2** fails to develop the Self-confidence they need to express the love in their hearts – or else fails to real-eyes that all those people who hurt them in their past before they "woke up" to their spiritual purpose were a necessary and Self-imposed part of their journey to wholeness – they may flip to the dark side of this number and become resentful, bitter, angry and withdrawn.

Key negative words

Moody, lethargic, indecisive, resentful, overly sensitive, reactive, aggressive, grumpy, aloof, pessimistic and overwhelmed.

* * *

Self-love is the difference

If you have read Part One, you will already know that your ability to walk the positive side of your Life Path, as opposed to the negative side, is determined by whether you have undertaken the two key stages of personal growth. Or, to put it another way, whether you have taken the two crucial first steps on the path to your life's highest purpose.

The first step towards living your Life Path in the positive is to develop Self-esteem (and if you're wondering what a "Self" is, please take the time to read Part One because it's way too complicated to explain again here). This feeling of inner confidence is essential because it allows you to tap into your innate strengths, which you will need if you are going to have any hope of overcoming the numerous obstacles on your path.

Be aware, though, that on its own this first step is never enough, because Self-confidence and Self-esteem are still the work of the ego. The feeling of being "good enough" carries with it an implied sense of needing to be "better than".

Life Path 2: The Intuitive

So to reach your full potential and achieve your life's highest purpose, you must also take the second step – which is to rise above the egoic concept of Self-esteem and climb to the much higher ground of Self-love.

Loving your Self does not mean being "full of your Self". It means the opposite. It means being humble because you understand that you are the same as everyone else, no better and no worse.

Above all, it means you understand that we are all perfect spirits having a human experience, and therefore we are all, at our core, the same: pure love, pure Source energy. (The Source is also fully explained in Part One.)

We can see it easily in newborn babies because when we are born into physical form, and before our fear-based ego has had a chance to develop, we are all gorgeous gurgling bundles of pure, exquisite love.

I am not suggesting anyone should ever do this, but just imagine you were to place a new-born infant on the pavement of a crowded street and then stand back out of sight. Everyone – and I mean everyone – would stop and tend to it. And the reason they would do this is because, deep down, we all recognise pure love when we see it. We are drawn to it at the most basic level of our being because it is the most strikingly beautiful and compelling force on the planet.

But sadly, as we grow up and go out into the world, our ego takes over and we start to believe – usually during our teenage years – that our ego is who we are. It isn't. Love is who we are.

We are all pure love. We are all extensions of Source energy (or children of "God", whichever phrase you are more comfortable with).

If you can rise above the quasi-religious terminology, I can summarise the two steps like this: Self-esteem is about feeling "good enough", while Self-love is about feeling "God enough".

The reason why loving your Self is so important for your Life Path is because when you start to live your life from the perspective of being pure love, everything changes. Suddenly you understand that nothing "out there" in the material world can ever harm you in any way.

Life Path 2: Life Choices

Equally, you real-eyes you don't need anything "out there" in the material world to make you feel happy – not the approval of others; no amount of money, fame and power; and not even the love of a good man or woman – because you have all the love you need right there in your own heart, and you can therefore relish the exquisite joy of loving everyone unconditionally without needing anything in return.

That is why Self-love is the secret to working with the positive energy of your Life Path Number. Because when you truly love your Self, the rocky mountain path you've been climbing suddenly becomes an express elevator ride all the way up to the summit of your bliss.

* * *

No Life Path is an island

Although your Life Path Number denotes the main issues that you will focus on throughout your life, you will always work to some degree with the energies of the other numbers as well to become a fully rounded Self.

As a **2** your main work will be in the areas of co-operation and forgiveness, but you will also tackle the issues of Self-confidence (**1**), creative expression (**3**), stability and flexibility (**4**), freedom and discipline (**5**), acceptance (**6**), trust (**7**), abundance and power (**8**) and integrity (**9**).

It's therefore worth your while to read through the listings for the other Life Path Numbers when your time allows.

* * *

Qualities of your three-digit Birth Code

(Note: Please read the description in Part Two of how a $\underline{0}$ operates in your three-digit Birth Code. Also, you can consult the main Life Path listings here in Part Three for each of your Supplementary Birth Numbers (the two possible ones for the Intuitive are 1 and 2) to give you a clearer understanding of how their qualities govern your formative years.)

Life Path 2: The Intuitive

20/2

The powerful loving energy of this Life Path can easily be seen by the fact that there are only two possible three-digit Birth Codes for the Intuitive – either 20/2, or the Master Number 11/2.

We will get to the Master Number in a moment, but by the time we do you will have come to real-eyes that this first Birth Code of 20/2 is just as "masterful" in terms of its highest purpose of spreading love, peace and harmony throughout the world.

The first Supplementary Birth Number of 2 in this Birth Code means that anyone born under this number will work to develop their unconditional loving nature (the energy of **2**) during the first formative 18 years of their life in conjunction with the over-arching energy of their Life Path Number, which is also a **2**.

So they will focus all their efforts on spreading love and light to help others heal their wounds and find love in their own lives.

Their second Supplementary Number of 0 – which, as we saw in Part Two, acts as an amplifier of the Life Path Number to which it relates – means that for their second 18 years, up to full emotional maturity at age 36, they will re-double their efforts to develop within themselves the capacity to bring love, light and harmony to as many people as possible.

One of the "Big T" Truths I teach in all my books and seminars is that love is the only thing in this world that is real. It is the only thing worth giving a damn about, because it is not just the source of our greatest joy – it is who we are.

As I've said before, we are pure Source energy and pure love.

Full stop. End of story. And end of anxiety.

No one knows this to be true more than the ever-loving 20/2, who will focus on loving themselves and others their entire life.

Yes, the **2** will also work through some of the issues of the other numbers at different stages of their life – leadership (**1**), expression (**3**), security (**4**), change (**5**), idealism (**6**), truth (**7**), abundance (**8**) and wisdom (**9**) – but they will always do so with the singular goal of spreading love and peace wherever they go.

Life Path 2: Life Choices

Master Number 11/2 – 'The Master Intuitive'

If you have not already done so, please read my comments in Chapter 8 of Part Two about what numerologists call the Master Numbers – namely, those Life Path Numbers whose Supplementary Birth Numbers are the same. There are four possible Master Numbers in numerology: 11/2, 22/4, 33/6 and 44/8.

There is no doubt that having two identical Supplementary Birth Numbers helps you focus on developing the qualities of your Life Path Number during the first 36 years of your life. However, as we have just seen with the Birth Code 20/2, they are by no means the only "supercharged" Birth Codes in the Self-Awareness System™.

If your Birth Code is 11/2, you will work to develop the positive, peacemaking "water" qualities of the Intuitive (Life Path **2**) throughout your life, and you will do so with the double "fire" energy of the Leader (1) during your first 18 years of childhood, as well as your early adult years towards full maturity at age 36.

This means you will strive to develop your loving compassion (the energy of **2**) by taking the lead (the energy of 1) to spread your love not just within your family as a child, but with everyone you meet as you grow up – and also in whatever you decide to do for a career.

The double "masculine" leadership energy of 1 combined with the compassionate "feminine" energy of **2** means the 11/**2** has the potential to be a powerfully intuitive healer and peacemaker in the world. They are insightful, generous and kind and have an innate understanding of how other people are feeling.

The 11/**2** is the ultimate "people person", and they also have a flair for design and a passion for harmony, both in their personal and professional lives and in their immediate surroundings.

Theirs will always be the most stylish home on the street, and the most welcoming office on the company floor. And they have excellent taste in music too, which plays a very significant part in their lives.

So as well as giving you a natural flair for creativity, harmonious design and original ideas, the Master Number 11/**2** empowers you to become an intuitive peacemaker on a much bigger stage, capable of

Life Path 2: The Intuitive

bringing peace not only to your workplace and family, but to your country – or even the world.

Barack Obama, for example, has a Birth Code of 11/2. For all of his shortcomings, and no matter which side of the political fence you are on, his heart was unquestionably in the right place.

David Beckham, Bill Clinton, Anthony Robbins and Prince William are all 11/2s. They have all demonstrated the power of this Master Number by bringing people together in peace and harmony.

On the negative side, 11/2s must guard against being too hard on themselves, because they have a tendency to indulge in Self-criticism and Self-doubt. Also, their ability to resonate warm, loving energy always makes them stand out in a crowd, which can cause young and insecure 11/2s to suffer a shyness borne of feeling they never fit in.

The solution is never to try to dim their light, because this goes against their life's highest purpose – which is to shine their radiant love on as many people as possible. Indeed, when 11/2s do try to "blend in" by deliberately dulling their light, they will become depressed and resentful of others for not "allowing" them to be their true Self – when all along it is they who are not allowing their light to shine.

To prevent this, the 11/2 must develop a strong Self-confidence in their ability to heal other people's pain, as well as the resilience to handle rejection from those who simply aren't ready to be healed yet.

A final word of warning: all **2**s are prone to procrastination (only the scattered **5** is worse) and tend towards laziness when it comes to doing the tough work on themselves that needs to be done. The 11/**2** Master Intuitive takes this fine art of "avoidance" to a whole new level. The words "I know" seem to take up permanent residence in their mouth and pop out every time someone gives them good advice.

Their intuition is so well-developed that they always know the best course of action to improve their life at any given moment – but that is usually the very last thing they do, and they do it only after the stinky stuff that comes out the back of cows has made contact with one of those whirry things that keep us cool in summer.

They will put it off over and over again, choosing instead to clean the house for the 10th time that week, rearrange their biscuit tins, sort their shoes in order of colour, make a list of all the things they know they should do (then lose it and make another completely different list), or go out for a surf, a bike ride, a gym class or some sushi – all the time knowing they are putting off the inevitable.

Nike's famous slogan "Just do it" was invented for the 11/2. If they don't have a bull and a bullet lying around the house, they need to get one of each as soon as possible, so they can grab one by the horns and bite down hard on the other… and turn their life around.

* * *

2. CAREER AND BUSINESS CHOICES

EMPATHETIC 2s have a deep desire for creating peace and harmony in all walks of life and will tend to graduate towards careers in healing, counselling, music, design, diplomacy, social work and even politics – usually on a local scale, but occasionally on the global stage.

The impersonal "cut and thrust" competition of corporate life does not normally appeal to the 2's need for intimacy and connection, although some of the best human resources managers will often be 2s.

Playing the role of mediator comes naturally to the fair-minded 2, which makes them excellent judges and law-enforcement officers.

Whatever they choose to do with their lives, Intuitives will always strive to create peace and harmony, both at home and in the workplace. Indeed, many 2s of both sexes choose to be homemakers, raising a close loving family in a beautiful, harmonious home.

Along with the equally romantic 6, the 2 will often put their focus on their home life and will try to create a business that allows them to spend as much time at home as possible.

Life Path 2: The Intuitive

The unevolved **2** is usually happy to be part of a corporate team, working behind the scenes for the common good without need for recognition. But once he or she wakes up to their spiritual nature as a peaceful mediator and loving healer and steps into their true power, they will quickly tire of the ego-based greed of the corporate world and strike out on their own to find the autonomy they seek.

The **2**'s desire for harmonious surroundings makes them excellent interior designers, fashion designers, artists, architects and stylists. And yet no matter how passionate they are about the work they do – and they will be – it will never take preference to spending time with the people they love.

It doesn't matter what career path the **2** chooses – even if it takes them far away from home to travel the world – their need for peace, harmony and connection will always bring them back to what matters most to them... their family.

In fact, the **2**'s ideal career path would probably involve teaming up with friends or family members to start their own company. The business would usually involve spreading their messages of love and healing to improve the lives of others – and by running it with their loved ones, the **2** can work and spend time with them at the same time.

Beneficial career paths

People working with the intuitive and loving energy of **2** make excellent healers, counsellors, judges, mediators, human resources managers, interior decorators, musicians, artists, teachers, architects, fashion designers, diplomats, politicians, sales people, social workers, law-enforcement officers, stay-at-home parents, doctors, nurses, therapists, psychologists and beauticians.

Best business matches

2s who choose to start their own business will benefit from doing so with a partner, because the ever-talkative **2** loves to consult with a close confidant on absolutely everything they do.

Life Path 2: Relationship Choices

It's best to avoid the bossy **1**, who will want to take over control, and their fellow watery **6**, who will quickly become a rival. Instead opt for a practical **4** or **8** – both of whom will work diligently in a managing role to turn the **2**'s dreamy visions into real-world successes.

Another **2** or a **6** is fine for running the team and keeping everyone happy. For the creative departments they would pick a **3**, and they would choose a persuasive **5** to run the sales and marketing operation.

The thoughtful **7** performs best in a back-office role such as research and development or IT.

And for a special project that needs someone to take over the reins and drive it to fruition, no one is better at running their own team than the independent and motivated **9**.

* * *

3. RELATIONSHIP CHOICES

ONE of the most rewarding aspects about the Self-Awareness System™ is how equitable it is. Each Life Path offers the same opportunities for happiness and fulfillment, albeit in markedly different ways. And each of them also offers the same amount of challenges to force us to grow, although again in very different ways.

This means no Life Path is any "better" or "worse" than any of the others. All of them have their blessings, and all have their obstacles.

In the case of the spiritual and loving **2**, their blessings centre around their intuitive ability to see what is troubling other people and suggest ways they can solve their problems. This makes them highly skilled at helping to bring peace and healing to those around them.

The downside of this innate attunement to what others are feeling can throw up all manner of challenges in their personal relationships. For example, only very evolved Selfs like it when their partner knows more about what they are feeling than they do. And unless their partner is particularly aware of their own shortcomings (again, the sign of an evolved Self), the **2**'s uncanny ability to put their finger on precisely what is wrong with their partner's behaviour patterns will often be met with anger and rejection, rather than gratitude.

The well-meaning **2**'s desire to help, combined with their intuitive ability to put their finger on their partner's inner pain, allows them to clearly see what their partner needs to work on. The trouble is, by saying it out loud, the **2** is likely to press one of their partner's most sensitive "buttons", causing them to lash out in anger. This, in turn, will drive the **2** into their cave, where they will stay silent for long periods, furious that their partner is not evolved enough to accept their help and therefore doubting the whole point of their relationship – which, for the **2**, is to heal and grow.

Not being able to help is the very worst feeling there is for a **2**. And if it persists, they may abandon the relationship and move on.

It is vital that the **2** chooses a partner who has done at least some of the difficult "inner work" on themselves and is therefore likely to react to their intuitive advice with gratitude, rather than resentment.

For this reason, most **2**s will go through several relationships before finding "the one". They will usually marry young, in their deep desire to create a loving and harmonious family home, and then real-eyes that the person they fell in love with is simply not evolved enough spiritually to deal with the depth of their love.

Humans can only ever allow another person to love them as much as they love themselves. So if their level of Self-love is low, they will reject – sometimes angrily – their partner's attempts to love them more than they love themselves. This process is subconscious, of course. But for the loving **2**, who is ruled by the emotional element of water and the romantic planet of the Moon, this inability to love and be loved to the stars and back is a deal-breaker.

As a lover, the **2** is devoted, loyal and committed. They will defend their partner through thick and thin, but in their desire for harmony they must guard against losing themselves in their relationship. Their biggest fault is that they have a tendency to run away at the first sign of adversity – a hangover from all the pain they felt as a child when their love was rejected by their family or friends for being "too much", and they will do anything to avoid feeling that pain again.

In their desire to avoid the agony of rejection, the **2** will often end a relationship before their partner can. They may also threaten to end it as a test just to see whether their partner will fight to keep it alive or not. If they don't, the **2** will know they were right to call it quits. And if they do, then the **2** has received the commitment they seek.

They might try to deny it, but the **2** absolutely loves to be treated like a prince or a princess. If you are in relationship with them, you will always know when you have failed to pay them enough attention. Their ability to pout and sulk when they feel they have been wronged is unsurpassed, and their grumpy over-reaction to the most trivial perceived slight is enough to drive any sane person crazy.

Don't ever bother arguing with a **2**. They display the most illogical reasoning imaginable and can change the goal posts of the debate quicker than Superman can change his underpants. Arguing with a **2** is like trying to cut water with a knife, because as soon as you think you have resolved one issue they will flit to another.

The best thing to do when you find your Self in an argument with a **2** is to get out of their way and leave them be. Send them a text telling them you love them, or reappear with a gift, and the **2** will eventually come out of their cave and behave as though nothing happened.

It sounds hard, but it is well worth the trouble. This baffling behaviour aside, **2**s are the most loving, loyal, generous and supportive partners you can ever hope to find. Give them what they want, and they will return it to you tenfold.

* * *

Sex drive of the 2

Most **2**s suppress their sexuality when they are young due to the shyness they suffered as a child, when all they wanted to do was win their parents' approval by being Master or Miss Goody Two Shoes.

Life Path 2: The Intuitive

Deep down, all **2**s have a wild sexual streak, borne of their desire to experience physical pleasure on the same intense level at which they feel emotional pleasure.

Feelings are the **2**'s lifeblood, so much so that they would sometimes rather feel pain than feel nothing at all. (This can also lead to some very interesting experiences in the bedroom.)

When an adult **2** does finally slough off their childhood desire for approval and embrace the tumultuous sexual desires welling within them, the result is a bit like lighting the blue touch paper on a firework.

Well, actually, it's more like 100 fireworks – because when the fire of the **2**'s sexual desires is finally lit, you'd better stand well back if you don't want to get burned. (Or else put on a flame-proof suit and jump into bed with them.)

The "feminine energy" partner in the relationship has deep and passionate sexual fantasies but will only express them when she feels totally safe with a partner who she knows can handle her. And when that happens, her fantasies won't remain fantasies for long because the secure **2** will want to act them all out with her lucky, lucky partner! She is a considerate and understanding lover, and she will often choose to experience sex with both men and women until she finds the inner confidence to break down all her inhibitions, which will lead her eventually to find the love of her life.

The "masculine energy" **2** in a relationship is equally passionate and restrained at an early age, but quickly steps into his power when he finds someone with whom he feels safe. Because this number is overwhelmingly feminine in its energy, the masculine **2** is able to marry his innate feminine understanding of what his partner needs with a masculine desire to please his partner and make them feel like a god or a goddess. Like the feminine **2**, the masculine Intuitive can suffer bouts of jealousy and insecurity if he has not boosted his levels of Self-worth and Self-love. But once he feels secure, he can be the most inventive and passionate of lovers.

* * *

Life Path 2: Relationship Choices

The compatibility listings that follow will help emotional **2**s get the most out of their relationships, whether it's with someone they love, a friend or a business partner.

The water energy of **2** is well-matched with other **2**s and their watery cousin **6**, as well as a **4** or **8**, whose earthy nutrients combine with water to create life, and love. But fire (**1** and **5**) can boil water, and air (**3** and **7**) can evaporate it, so these pairings will normally throw up more challenges. The **9** is usually a good match for any number.

However, what appears to match you best on the surface may not be what you need right now. All relationships are designed to help us grow along our Life Path. Yes, of course we enjoy the companionship, close connection, sexual intimacy and deep love that relationships give us. But that is now why we have them.

The reason we choose a partner (or, to be more accurate, why our all-knowing Self chooses them for us) is because they are a mirror in which we see our shortcomings and strengths reflected back at us through their shortcomings and strengths. That is why opposites so often attract, especially in love.

I have written an entire book on this subject called *Leap into Love* which goes into the way relationships work in our lives in great detail. But for now, please real-eyes that when your partner presses one of your buttons, they are doing so not to "piss you off" but because your Self is using them to show you the areas you need to work on.

If you fail to understand this is the main reason why you attracted them into your life in the first place, you will fight each other and may eventually break up. And you will believe their faults were exactly that – their faults – rather than yours reflected back at you. Worst of all, you will then take the unchanged you with you to your next relationship, and – lo and behold! – exactly the same issues will come up again.

If this sounds familiar. If you have ever asked any of these questions – "Why does this always happen to me?" or "Why do all men cheat?" or "Why are all women so demanding?" or whatever it is for you – then now you know why. It's because you didn't learn from your last partner, so of course your new one will do the same thing.

Life Path 2: The Intuitive

And this will continue to happen, relationship after relationship, until you real-eyes it is meant to be happening to show you what areas you need to work on in your Self to change and grow.

* * *

One final quick point before we get into it: I need to stress that I disagree with almost every numerologist I know who likes to label relationships "a natural fit", "a neutral fit" or "an unnatural fit", depending on the compatibility of the numbers of the two partners.

All relationships are challenging. That is why we have them, as we have just seen. Yes, sometimes we might choose a partner who is "just like us" for the sake of harmony, but that could be regarded as a cop out if we are truly serious about our personal and spiritual growth.

If you are on a spiritual growth path in this lifetime (and there is no doubt in my mind that you are if you made it through Part One without throwing it in the bin!), then your Self will choose your relationships for you – and they will always be with a partner who will challenge you to grow in exactly the ways you need to grow.

Just because you might discover your current partner has a Life Path Number that doesn't dovetail perfectly with yours, don't fall into the trap of thinking there must be something wrong – or worse, end it with them so you can go out with someone with a "better" number.

Where you are on now is where you are meant to be, and who you are with is who you are meant to be with. So please let these listings help you to look for the lessons in your relationship, rather than look for the door. And if you are single, I urge you to remain open-hearted about your next relationship. It doesn't matter what Life Path Number they have, so don't "cherry pick". All that matters is that you follow your heart and be open to learning the lessons they can teach you. After all, that's the reason you will attract them into your life in the first place.

* * *

Life Path 2: Relationship Choices

2 & 1
(Co-operation and Independence)

Love

On the surface, the sensitive, feminine **2** and the brash, masculine **1** appear to be about as compatible as, well… water and fire. However, there is a chance for this apparently mismatched pairing to work, as long as both partners are happy to play some of the more traditional and stereotypical roles of homemaker and breadwinner.

It doesn't matter which sex is which because this is not about male or female in the birth-gender sense; it's about masculine energy and feminine energy. **1**s are masculine (whether they are female or male) and **2**s are feminine (whether they are male or female).

It's worth noting that Master Number 11/**2**s are more balanced in their masculine and feminine energy than 20/**2**s, and therefore will find it easier to relate to the masculine energy of their Leader partner.

However, all **2**s want peace and harmony (togetherness) above all else, while solitary **1**s are driven primarily by ambition and achievement, not just in their work life but in their home life too.

2s must remember to give **1**s the space they need to pursue their creative ideas, while **1**s must never forget to tell the **2** how much their love means to them and how appreciated they are.

The real challenge of this pairing lies in the fact that all **2**s thrive on attention, and **1**s are almost always far from home conquering the world. If **1**s can make their **2** partner feel loved and appreciated, even while they are away, the **2** will keep the home fires burning and be happy to give them the freedom they crave to build their business.

Sexually, this is a mismatch because **1** usually wants to have sex while **2** wants to make love. The water of **2** can douse the fire of **1**, and the fire of **1** can scald the sensitive heart of **2**.

Master Number 11/**2**s are usually more sexual than their 20/**2** sisters and brothers, so they may find it easier to partner up with the

Life Path 2: The Intuitive

intensely masculine energy of the Leader. Even then, they will need to make a considerable effort to let the **1** have the space they need.

2s, more than any other number except perhaps the **4**, crave attention and they also have a tendency for wild mood swings, both of which are challenging for the independent and intolerant **1**.

They will also both have to work hard to meet each other's needs, but if they do it can be a rewarding match. Be aware, though, that **2**s may want more love and affection than **1**s are able to give them, while **1**s may want more freedom than the **2** is comfortable with.

The key to this pairing is to respect each other's differences and support each other, even though sometimes you may feel you are about as well-matched as English chalk and Venezuelan beaver cheese.

Remember, the sole (soul) purpose of all your relationships is to learn from each other and help each other to grow. And this pairing will certainly throw up more than enough lessons for each partner to real-eyes that success on its own may be wonderful – but success shared with someone we love is doubly so.

Good luck, stay open and honest… and enjoy the shared triumphs and valuable growth lessons this relationship can give you.

Friendship

These two numbers have little in common in terms of their core values. The sometimes insular **1** is focused on what they can achieve next, while the passionately social **2** wants to go out for dinner and sit and chat, preferably allnight long.

They can be friends, and sometimes even BFFs if they meet when they are young and the **2** is an 11/**2** who is working intensely with their masculine 1 supplementary energy. But if the **2** is a 20/**2**, it will probably be another story because their energy will be so different.

The **2** dislikes being on their own for longer than very short periods and always works best when part of a close-knit team, whereas the **1** tends to work best on their own and will usually indulge in social activity only when they believe they can gain something from it.

Life Path 2: Relationship Choices

The social **2** will often have several close friends with whom they share their deepest feelings. But sometimes this need for depth can be too much for the fiercely independent **1**, who may react by keeping their effusive **2** friend at arm's length, especially if they are a 20/**2**.

Equally, the **2** will probably choose the company of a water or air number (**2**, **3**, **6** or **7**) over the fiery **1** because they make them feel deeply connected in a way a **1** will always struggle to do.

Business

This will be a challenge but can work well, providing **1** is the boss and handles the visionary side of the business, while the **2** handles the management and human resources side, looking after staff morale and nurturing the business while the **1** grows it.

1s have to be in charge, which in turn means the **2** has to trust that they know what they are doing. As long as the **1** keeps the **2** included in all the big decisions, the **2** will be happy to play a supporting role – on the condition that their ideas are always heard and considered, and that they are allowed to share equally in all the rewards.

The insightful **2** has an uncanny knack for knowing what people do and don't want, and if they believe the **1** is going in the wrong direction they will need to feel free to speak up. When this happens, the headstrong **1** would be advised to put their ego on a shelf and listen very closely to the **2**'s advice. Nine times out of 10 they will be right.

* * *

2 & 2
(Co-operation and Togetherness)

Love

A relationship between two **2**s will have one of two outcomes: they will either dance blissfully together through life, showering so much love on each other that it makes even their closest friends sick, or else they will fight constantly like two alley cats, tearing each other to shreds before quickly breaking up to retreat and lick their wounds.

It all depends how evolved the partners are, and how much Self-love they have in their hearts.

As we saw in Part One, it is not possible for a person to be loved more than they love themselves. If their partner tries to love them more than they feel they deserve, they will subconsciously push them – and their love – away.

In the case of two **2**s – both of whom want nothing more than to be able to love their partner to the Moon (their guiding planet) and back – this will be a relationship killer. But if both partners have done enough inner work to boost their level of Self-love, they will be the couple you see holding hands on the beach at sunset, canoodling in the corner at parties, and still going out dancing together under the stars when they are well into their 80s.

Be warned, though, that there is plenty of potential for friction on a more mundane, day-to-day basis. For example, the **2** has a keen eye for design and likes their home to be just so, with not a single ornament or pot plant out of place. If another **2** enters their space and tries to rearrange things to conform to their equally keen eye, look out!

Also, because they are so alike, there is a risk they will frequently tread on the each other's toes, so petty disputes can arise easily.

Plus, both **2**s must remember how thin their own skin is and guard against causing verbal injury to their partner. No one hurts as much as a **2**, and no one is able to hurt them more than another **2** because they know exactly the right buttons to press.

As long as this couple can agree to disagree on the little things, their powerful love and mutual respect will forge a bond that can survive anything life throws at them. There will be so much love in the room, and so much understanding of what the other is feeling, that any argument should quickly give way to hugs and forgiveness.

The one thing a **2** wants more than anything else in a relationship is absolute commitment, and no one can give it to them better than another **2**. They will also benefit from being able to talk to each other about anything and everything that they are feeling – sometimes for hours and hours – and know they are being understood. This, too, is an absolute must for the expressive and deep-hearted **2**.

The key to this pairing is to make sure you give your partner exactly what you want to receive from them – unconditional love, without expecting anything in return. If you can do that, the only problem you will ever encounter is arguing over who is going to carry the bucket every time you leave the house, wrapped up in each other's love and openly adoring each other so intensely that you are going to make everyone you meet throw up.

Good luck, stay open and honest… and enjoy the exquisite, loving connection this romantic relationship can give you.

Friendship

Just as two **2**s in a relationship will either be Romeo and Juliet or Alien and Predator, depending on their level of Self-love, so too in a social situation they'll either be Best Friends Forever or arch enemies.

I know two sisters who are both 11/**2**s and are so alike that they fight almost constantly because neither is able to occupy a unique "space" in their relationship. They love each other more than words can say, but their bickering is enough to drive even the most saintly onlooker to Self-immolate.

When two **2**s meet, they will feel a strong pull towards each other. But it is precisely their uncanny similarities than can quickly turn them into rivals, rather than friends.

The key is communication. Go away together for a long weekend and spend the entire time talking. You will likely as not forge a friendship that will last you a lifetime.

All **2**s are extremely social and make friends easily, but they lose them easily as well – especially when the other person takes the **2**'s unique capacity for love and understanding for granted.

The always generous **2** will accumulate numerous "fair weather friends" who lean on them when they want healing and advice, but are nowhere to be seen when the **2** wants some of it in return.

That is when they will turn to their fellow **2**, and be delighted to find they are there for them in whatever capacity they need.

Business

This may appear to be a compatible and potentially profitable commercial match because both partners want to create as much love and happiness in the world as they possibly can, so they will be working towards a common goal. However, serious issues will arise over the day-to-day running of the business because both of you will want to have a say in every single aspect of how your company is run. Nothing can happen without both **2**s being involved in every decision, leading to a cripplingly inefficient doubling up of your time and energy.

The **2** who wants to run their own business would do far better partnering up with an earthy **4**, who is happy to let the **2** take the lead but has an equally fine eye for detail, or a humanitarian **9**, who shares the **2**'s vision of a better world but won't tread on their toes.

* * *

2 & 3
(Co-operation and Expression)

Love

This will often be an energetic and fun-packed relationship due to both partners' social nature and love of a good time. The outgoing, communicative **3** and the empathetic **2** both enjoy being around other people and share a common interest in food, art, music and travel.

There will be plenty of restaurant dinners, nights out and holidays to exotic locations, as well as long, animated conversations over a good home-cooked meal. Both the creative **3** and the nurturing **2** like to cook, and they love to talk. In fact, there will be few chances for anyone else to get a word in when these two lovebirds have friends over.

The **2** likes their relationship to be harmonious, as does the **3**, so this couple will try their hardest to avoid fighting. But because the **3** will usually be the more dominant partner, and because the **2** doesn't like being told what to do, conflicts will invariably arise.

The **3** has a tendency to be a bit bossy and must remember to praise the nurturing **2** for all they do, and the **2** must remember to give the **3** plenty of freedom to pursue their creative goals.

This is where problems can arise. If the co-dependent **2** becomes jealous of the **3**'s flirtatious behaviour and desire for independence they will simply succeed in pushing the **3** away. Equally, if the **3** forgets to give the tactile **2** enough love and affection – especially physical touch – they may look elsewhere for the intimacy they seek.

Regular and open communication is the solution – something both partners are normally very good at – to express their needs and let each other know which ones are not being met. And as long as neither side shuts down completely (something else they are both good at), conflicts should be resolved relatively painlessly.

Number **2** will often perceive the social and flirtatious behaviour of the **3** as a form of betrayal and will worry they are no longer loved or respected. For their part, the **3** hates to be tied down and will view any insecurity by the **2** as an attempt to manipulate them.

The **3** must remember to reassure the **2** that there is no threat, and the **2** must avoid trying to restrict the **3**'s outgoing personality. Jealousy is the biggest relationship killer of all.

Also, the **2** must learn to trust the **3,** who in return must be careful never to do anything to break that trust. Once they are hurt, it is rare for a **2** to ever fully trust again.

Good luck, stay open and honest… and enjoy the many social outings and travel adventures this relationship can give you.

Friendship

These two can have a lot of fun together because they are both so social and enjoy many of the same things, including food, wine, parties, travel and adventure. However, they tend to see life very differently.

The masculine air energy of the **3** means they are in their heads most of the time and value their creative and personal freedom above all else, while the feminine and watery **2** – though happy to party with the **3** in small groups – will usually seek out the company of other water friends for their more intimate connections because they intuitively understand the depth of their emotions.

These two can certainly forge a close and loving friendship, as long as they respect each other's differences.

Business

This is usually an excellent business combination, providing the **2** is happy to let the **3** hog the limelight and the **3** respects the **2**'s opinion and listens to everything they have to say. The **2** is a valuable business partner due to their uncanny ability to read people and resolve problems, leaving the **3** free to pursue their "big picture" goals.

Neither is particularly good with money, though, and they both have expensive tastes, so employing a good accountant to keep track of the cash (preferably a **4** or an **8**) might be a good idea.

* * *

<u>2 & 4</u>
(Co-operation and Stability)

Love

The feminine energy of these two numbers brings a lot of love and compassion to this pairing. Both are homemakers who like to have a living space that is warm, welcoming and tidy. They also share a common desire to feel nurtured and appreciated by their partner.

The **4** is the ultimate builder and organiser, while the **2** has an eye for style and design. They both want their home to be a safe haven where they can nurture each other and live in relative harmony.

There will also usually be the soothing energy of pets in their lovely home as well because both are passionate animal lovers.

The always talkative **4** will enjoy the **2**'s ability to share with their partner how they are feeling. Equally, the **2**'s love of a good "D & M"

Life Path 2: Relationship Choices

will please the **4**, who needs to be heard and loves nothing better than to be able to share their innermost thoughts with their partner.

These two will talk for hours long into the night, well after all the other numbers have got bored and gone to bed.

Both the **2** and the **4** are looking for absolute commitment in their relationship and like to feel safe with their partner above all else. Once they begin a romance, it is likely to become serious very quickly, and they will often move in together within a matter of weeks, rather than months or years.

They also share a hatred of deceit and know instinctively when their partner is not being honest with them. This willing openness to share all they are thinking and feeling quickly creates a mutual trust and understanding that can take other lovers much longer to achieve.

One thing that could upset this apparently idyllic partnership is if the more outgoing **2** gets bored with the **4**'s obsessive need for routine and stability. The **2** wants to travel the world and meet new people and may struggle with the **4**'s lack of adventure. Similarly, the **4**'s need to feel that everything they do has a specific purpose may sometimes lead them to resent the **2**'s tendency to act on impulse.

This pair will have plenty of common interests but their relationship will work best when the **4** gives the **2** leeway to pursue their "frivolous" and "time-wasting" adventures, and the **2** resists the urge to pester the **4** to lighten up and come play with them.

Another potential pitfall is the emotional **2**'s need for almost constant reassurance that their partner truly loves them. This will annoy the loyal **4**, who never – ever – strays once they have committed to a partner. But their lack of romance and inability to easily reach out and show their affection will worry the needy **2**, who may take it as a sign that the **4** has indeed gone cold on them.

Also, the emotional **2** may be a bit unstable for the pragmatic **4**, who in return may be a bit stuck in their ways for the spontaneous **2**. The faithful **4** will never stray, but if they are not able to indulge the **2**'s need for fun – especially in bed – there is a danger the needy **2** will look elsewhere for the excitement and intimacy they crave.

On the whole, though, this is one of the more harmonious pairings for the **2**. As long as they make sure to include their **4** partner in their decisions and never – ever – lie to them, they should live a long and happy life together.

Good luck, stay open and honest... and enjoy the deep and meaningful connection this passionate relationship can give you.

Friendship

The emotional **2** and the nurturing **4** will usually find they have much in common as friends, just as they do in a relationship. They will likely forge a close, loyal bond based on their ability to open up about how they are truly feeling, leading to a mutual trust and admiration.

They will have much to talk about. In fact, they will probably sit up all night talking about their lives until the cows come home, eat a quick grass meal, have a shower, get changed and go out again.

The adventurous **2** may sometimes find the pragmatic **4** a little too reserved for their liking. And the money-conscious **4** may baulk at the **2**'s expensive tastes – especially when they both go out to dinner or to a club and split the bill.

But overall, they are well-matched because they are both honest and upfront with their emotions at all times and will seldom allow any minor disagreement over money to mar their friendship.

Business

This is an especially good match because both partners share the common goal of creating a business to help others live a better and more healthy life, as well as having the financial nous to manage the purse strings and ensure it succeeds.

The **4** is unbeatable in their ability to manage a project and see it through to completion, but they often get bogged down in details and fail to grasp opportunities for growth when they come. This is where the **2** comes in. They, too, are good managers but their keep their eyes up on the horizon, and their heightened sense of intuition can lead them to spot gaps in the market that the **4** simply won't see.

Also, while the **4** is brilliant at planning and organisation, they can be judgmental of others' perceived shortcomings, which can cause discord among their staff. The **2**'s proven people skills will be able to smooth over any upsets and keep the team pulling in the same direction.

* * *

2 & 5
(Co-operation and Freedom)

Love

This pairing is the ultimate attraction of opposites between the fun-loving and fiercely independent **5** who yearns to be free but desperately needs to learn the lesson of discipline, and the disciplined but co-dependent **2** who desperately needs to learn how to relax and enjoy life as a confident and independent free spirit.

When the conformist **2** and the rebellious **5** come together, the relationship is going to go one of two ways: it will either last five minutes during which the **5** will accuse the jealous **2** of cramping their style and the **2** will harangue the fickle **5** for being too irresponsible. Or else, if both partners are smart enough to know that the other one possesses exactly the qualities they lack and need, it will blossom into the most perfect mutual growth pairing it is possible to imagine.

Yes, there will be plenty of disagreements but change is never easy, and both partners' egos will resist the valuable spiritual and emotional lessons each has to teach the other. But providing there is a solid bedrock of love and trust, and neither partner does anything to betray that trust, the aware **5** will learn everything they need to learn about discipline, commitment and perseverance from the always patient and loving **2**, who in turn will learn everything they need to learn about optimism, tolerance and forgiveness from the always ebullient **5**.

One word of caution, though: the often jealous and insecure **2** must give their **5** partner all the trust and freedom they need and avoid being too serious, while the flighty **5** must make sure they always put

Life Path 2: The Intuitive

their **2** lover first in everything they do and balance their need for time alone with the **2**'s need for quality time together.

Good luck, stay open and honest… and make sure you learn the life-changing lessons your partner has come into your life to teach you.

Friendship

These two are going to struggle to find much in common outside a romantic relationship, because friendship is seldom enough of a bond to force them to look past their differences and see the valuable lessons these two radically different numbers have to teach each other.

In fact, the **2** and the **5** will usually only ever come together to form a meaningful relationship if they are either lovers or best friends. Anything less, and their differences will merely irritate each other.

However, providing the impatient **5** takes the time to really listen to the always talkative **2** and hear what they have to say, and the serious **2** understands that the average **5**'s attention span is only slightly longer than that of a gnat who's busting to pee – and therefore tries to keep their monologues as short as possible – then these two can form a friendship that will stand the test of time.

Business

No. Definitely not. The organised **2** will hate the irresponsibility and recklessness of the flighty **5**, and the lightning-fast **5** will go bonkers having to explain every little detail of what they are doing to the detail-obsessed **2**. Pick any other number, preferably a **1**, **6** or **9**.

* * *

<u>2 & 6</u>
(Co-operation and Romance)

Love

This pairing will never be able to complain that there isn't enough passion and emotion in their lives, because both these feminine water

Life Path 2: Relationship Choices

numbers wear their hearts on their sleeve and value their relationship and their family high above every other area of their life.

The homemaker **6** is by far the most domestic of all the Life Path Numbers, and the compassionate **2** leaves them all floundering in their wake when it comes to their capacity for love and connection. Just the words that describe their Life Paths – Intuitive and Visionary – tell you all you need to know about how these two will be together when they first meet and fall in love. Violinists will appear out of nowhere and the rest of the world will cease to exist as they stare deeply into each other's eyes like a scene from an old black and white Cary Grant movie.

No, falling in love will never be a challenge for these two romantic idealists. Dealing with the realities of everyday life after the flames of their initial attraction have died down is another matter, though.

The forthright **6**, who likes to speak what's on their mind with a confronting directness, must be careful not to offend the sensitive and often insecure **2**, just as the **2** must guard against becoming too jealous of the more dominant energy of the busybody **6**.

The key to making this work is for both partners to give each other plenty of room to breathe and grow, while also avoiding the very real potential for jealousy by constantly acknowledging their partner and expressing clearly how much they are loved and appreciated.

Family will always be the focus of this pairing, and their home will be immaculate, warm and nurturing. They will gladly share everything they have with each other, knowing that it will be returned in kind. But communication, or rather the lack of it, could sometimes become a problem. Both the **6** and the **2** have a tendency to bottle up their true feelings, expecting the other to just know instinctively what is going on for them. Should their partner miss something, or fail to be a world-beating mind-reader every second of every day, both of them can react in anger and lash out, claiming the other "doesn't love them any more".

This can be as devastating as it is simple to avoid. Neither the **6** nor the **2** can bear any kind of negativity in their peaceful, loving home, and arguments can cut them to their core. Yet, all they needed to do to prevent it happening was to say something right at the beginning.

Life Path 2: The Intuitive

Communication is important in all relationships. For the **6** and the **2**, though, it is the difference between a long and happy life together or a short and angry affair.

Good luck, stay open and honest... and enjoy the passion and blissful connection this relationship can give you.

Friendship

These two have so much in common, they can't help but get along. Yes, problems can sometimes arise in a relationship where expectations are much higher. But, between friends, this pair's mutual love of people, love of animals – and love of love itself – can quickly bring them together to forge a strong and long-lasting emotional connection.

These two romantics will feed off each other, sharing their dreams and buying each other ever brighter pairs of rose-coloured sunglasses for each other's birthdays.

They will delight in teaming up to help fight for worthy causes, and every moment they are not needed at their own homes they will probably pop round to visit each other to get their fix of mutual validation that they both crave.

Business

This match has the potential for success because both partners will find it easy to share a common vision for the business, which will almost always be focused on healing, teaching or helping others.

The **6** is the more grounded of these two watery numbers, so it would be best to give them control of the finances. In return, the **2** will thrive if given free rein to control the creative aspects and drive the business forward into exciting new markets.

However, the perfectionist **6** must real-eyes no one, not even the diligent **2**, is ever perfect. And the brooding **2** must always speak their mind and not be intimidated by the **6**'s tendency to be controlling.

* * *

Life Path 2: Relationship Choices

2 & 7
(Co-operation and Understanding)

Love

As long as a healthy balance can be achieved, whereby the **7** takes the time to listen to all the **2**'s social media gossip with genuine interest and the **2** respects the **7**'s need to spend five million hours every single day in their study wrestling with the intangible questions of conceptual metaphysical identity, then this relationship can work harmoniously without the slightest sign of a disagreement.

Yeah, right! I'm kidding. Sorry, it's a cheap joke, I know, but it's more likely that Donald Trump will admit he's a lying bastard on the same day that someone in rural Slovakia films a flying pig and posts it on Instagram.

These two numbers have so little in common that it's a stretch to imagine them ever meeting and falling in love in the first place. Before they have even finished their starters, the emotionally closed **7** will be looking for the restaurant door to escape the fire of the **2**'s passionate and always open heart, and the free-loving **2** will be yawning into their soup as the intellectual **7** tries to explain the finer points of existential libertarianism for the 15th time.

Of all the eight other Life Path Numbers, the independent and reserved **7**, who requires long periods of time alone to contemplate the big mystical questions of life, is perhaps the most challenging match for the co-dependent and emotional **2**, who wants to curl up together on the lounge and watch movies together while the cerebral **7** wants time alone to read a treatise on quantum physics.

However, if they do experience an attraction of opposites, this has the potential to be one of the most powerful growth combinations it is possible to imagine. Think about it. What does the analytical and independent **7** need more than anything else to live a happy and fulfilling life? The answer is emotional connection, which the **2** can teach them before they've had their first mug of Earl Grey in the morning.

And what does the deep-feeling yet insecure and co-dependent **2** need more than anything else to live a happy, healthy and fulfilling life? The answer is loyalty and devotion from their partner, as well as a powerful lesson in how to stand on their own two feet and not sweat the small stuff – which the **7** can give them and teach them without even stopping to think about it for a single second.

If these two lovers can get out of their own way and real-eyes that each has everything the other needs, this can be a powerful growth relationship. They are unlikely to be lovers for life, but that's OK. Sometimes the best relationships flare and fade in a matter of moments, but they change the way we view the world forever.

Good luck, stay open and honest... and enjoy the challenging but ultimately life-changing growth lessons you have to teach each other.

Friendship

Unless these two are very evolved, this pairing is seldom going to work outside the "mutual growth" construct of a loving relationship that is explained above, because these two opposites will meet on a social level, freak each other out, bore each other to death and then run as fast as they can in the opposite direction.

Anything other than a Facebook friendship based on the **7** liking the **2**'s photo of a pot roast they cooked the previous night for 462 of their closest, most intimate friends, or the **2** liking the obscure Renee Descartes quote they posted about mankind's quasi-spiritual struggle to discover their true identity will definitely be a stretch.

It's a shame because these two friends have so much to teach each other, if only they could see past their differences.

Business

Strangely, given their polar opposite values in life, these two could come together to form a relatively successful business partnership, because without the expectation of familiarity that is necessary for both love and friendship, they might just be able to see that each perfectly

Life Path 2: Relationship Choices

plugs the gaps in the other's skill set and is therefore able to perform the roles they themselves suck at.

The often scattered **2** needs the insightful and intelligent **7** to solve the day-to-day problems that will inevitably arise in any business, while the intellectual and solitary **7** needs the co-operative **2** to connect with their customers and motivate their staff. There will be conflict, but if there is enough respect for the other's abilities, these two can definitely work well together, perfectly complementing each other's abilities.

* * *

2 & 8
(Co-operation and Ambition)

Love

This is one of the most compatible love matches for the **2**, both romantically and in business. In fact, these two lovebirds may well decide to partner up for both so they can live, play and work together.

While in a business setting it makes no difference which number is the feminine energy and which is the masculine, at home this pairing usually works best in the traditional roles of a **2** homemaker and an **8** breadwinner. The materialistic and earthy Achiever needs to be out there kicking goals and making tonnes of money, while the emotional and watery Intuitive is happiest when they are creating a stylish, warm and harmonious home for their family.

There is nothing sexist about this. In fact, because these numbers are both feminine, it's common for the ambitious "female" **8** to be the breadwinner while her "male" **2** partner runs the rest of their life. The goal-oriented **8** will be delighted that their trusted **2** partner controls the family purse strings, freeing them up to go after their Next Big Deal. They will also relish the unwavering support they feel from their Intuitive, who will be only too happy to stroke their ego and offer words of encouragement when the **8** suffers one of their rare setbacks.

Life Path 2: The Intuitive

On their side, the homemaker **2** will be thrilled they don't have to go to a boring office every day and endure interminable, dick-swinging meetings during which everyone tries to out-ego each other. They will love having the freedom to do whatever they want, whenever they want, and focus all their loving energy on raising a family – or, if they don't have children, on running their own business from home.

Yes, the **2** is governed by the emotional element of water, but money is also important to them because all Intuitives want a comfortable home and an active social life, and they also love to travel – all of which require a good income – so they will be happy to let their **8** partner focus their energy on the business of making wads of cash.

But (there's always a but in relationships, sorry) the **8** must never take their **2** partner's support for granted. If they don't feel appreciated for the part they play, and if they don't receive enough attention, the **2** can flip from "Hello darling, how was your day?" to "I've run away to Acapulco with my personal trainer, your dinner's in the dog".

Despite their busy business schedule, the **8** must always make enough time for their **2** lover. Coming home late with expensive gifts is nice, but what they really want is for them to come home early with a babysitter secretly organised and whisk them away to their favourite restaurant for a romantic candlelit dinner, followed by long, languid lovemaking in a luxury hotel suite complete with bubble bath.

And woe betide the **8** who cheats on their **2** partner. They will come home to find their precious designer dresses – or Tom Ford suits, depending on their sex – cut up into a thousand pieces and lying under the sprinkler on the front lawn.

For their part, the **2** must at all costs avoid becoming too needy and making unwarranted demands on the **8**'s precious time. Nothing turns an Achiever off more than a nagging husband or wife.

Providing both partners do the necessary inner work to boost their level of Self-love, none of these issues should arise and they will enjoy a long-lasting, passionate and exciting relationship together.

Good luck, stay open and honest… and enjoy the close, loving connection and mutual financial rewards this relationship can give you.

Life Path 2: Relationship Choices

Friendship

Although the **2** and the **8** can find much joy in a traditional loving relationship and experience mutual success in a business partnership, this pairing is not so compatible when it comes to a friendship. The ambitious **8** may look down on the simple, homely values of the **2**, and the emotional **2** may distrust the blatantly materialistic priorities of the money-oriented **8**.

Providing they can find a middle ground of mutual interests, there is the potential to forge a rewarding friendship, whereby the **8** helps the **2** set up a lucrative business and the **2** teaches the **8** to loosen up and smell the roses.

Interestingly, if their connection deepens along these lines, and if their sexualities and life circumstances match, then these two friends will probably wind up in bed – or in business – together.

And probably both.

Business

As we've already seen, this is a fantastic business combination because the ambitious and take-charge **8** needs a partner they can fully trust, and few Life Path Numbers are more loyal and trustworthy than the honest, open-hearted **2**.

Equally, while the **2** usually has a solid head for business, they may lack the **8**'s drive and ambition to make it to the very top, not to mention the ruthless killer streak necessary to see off their rivals.

Just as in love, the **8** must make sure the **2** feels fully appreciated for all their hard work, and the **2** must trust the **8** and support them in all they do, rather than nag them and undermine their confidence.

Normally, the **8** might be tempted to feel that they perform best on their own without a business partner, and that is often true. But not in this case. A dedicated and supportive **2** in their corner will empower them to work harder, reach higher and go a lot further than they could ever hope to do on their own.

* * *

2 & 9
(Co-operation and Passion)

Love

This relationship will throw up more than a few challenges. The always compassionate **2** is a co-operative and deeply caring Self who works best in close, intimate relationships, which is fine up to a point because the humanitarian and evolved **9** loves intimacy too. But while the **2** wants to share all their love with their partner, the **9** wants to share their love with the whole world. Yes, they will love the **2** – but not to the exclusion of everyone else.

This can cause problems if the attention-seeking **2**, who doesn't like to be alone for long, hasn't done the necessary inner work to avoid being needy and co-dependent should they feel their **9** partner isn't giving them enough time and affection.

The **9** has come here for a specific reason – and that is to share their gifts with the world. If they feel their partner is stifling them or holding them back, they will quickly grow resentful and cold towards them. One of two things will then happen. The disconsolate **9** will either shrink back into their shell and behave so badly that the **2** will eventually break up with them, thus setting them free. Or, if they are more courageous, they will simply walk out the door themselves.

This can easily be avoided by the **2** giving the **9** the space they need to fulfill their life's highest purpose of teaching and loving as many people as they can. The **2** will then be delighted to find the **9** showers them with all the love – if not the time together – that they crave.

Equally, the **9** must make a concerted effort to make time for their **2** partner and never stop telling them how much they are loved. Regular romantic weekends away together and surprise gifts work wonders to let the **2** know they are the most important person in the **9**'s life.

Good luck, stay open and honest… and enjoy the beautiful intimacy this deeply emotional relationship can give you both.

Life Path 2: Health Choices

Friendship

The ebullient **9** can pretty much make friends with anyone and everyone they meet. They are working with all the four elements, which allows them to connect with a wide variety of people. The one element they can sometimes struggle with, though, is water – and especially the sensitive **2** – because while the **9** is a deeply emotional number, they are not overly gushy or romantic.

These friends will usually have very different views of the world because the **2** likes to stay close to their home and their family, while the **9** is focused on spreading themselves far and wide. Yes, they will have much in common to talk about, but they are unlikely to be best friends simply because their lifestyles and core values don't match.

Business

While their differences may pose a serious challenge in love and friendship, in business the **2** and the **9** can work well together. The co-operative **2** will be happy for the **9** to take the lead, as long as they are appreciated for all they do, and the **9** will love the **2**'s upbeat energy and the fact they share the **9**'s lofty vision for a better world.

* * *

4. HEALTH CHOICES

ANYONE born under the Life Path Number **2** is a predominantly spiritual being, which means they are seldom fully present in their bodies – with the result that they can spend most of their lives flitting between robust good health and debilitating illness.

The **2** is such a spiritual number that physical matters of diet and exercise seldom get a look in. Add to this the **2**'s inherent capacity for laziness and procrastination – which means they often fail to exercise even when they know they should – and you have a recipe for all manner of physical ailments.

2s would do well to remember that they are much more than spirits – they are spirits having a physical/human experience. They must therefore take the time to look after their "vehicle" – their human body – or their experience in the material plane will not be an easy one.

Regular exercise is important for the **2**, not only so they can look after their human vehicle, but more importantly so they can ground their flighty spiritual being within their physical body. This will make them feel more a part of the world around them, which so often seems alien from their heightened spiritual perspective.

Due to their deeply loving nature, **2s** will usually occupy bodies that are attractive, whether male or female, to reflect their inner beauty. But because they are pure Source energy inhabiting an imperfect body, they often get so caught up in their feelings of physical inadequacy that they neglect to do the basics (diet and exercise) to ensure the image in the mirror matches their own Self-image of pure loving perfection.

No one beats themselves up when they "let themselves go" more than the **2**. They will see images of gymnasts, dancers and athletes on the TV who are "so in their bodies" and feel deep pangs of envy.

There is a reason for this. Deep down, the spiritual **2** real-eyes that they are here – in human form – to master their physical selves. Yes, they can be at least partially happy existing purely as a spiritual being. But their true elation comes only when they marry their spiritual selves with their physical incarnation.

When a **2** looks in the mirror and sees the physical representation of their inner beauty, something magical happens: their confidence soars to heights they could never have achieved by merely accepting their body as an imperfect "prison" for their spiritual perfection.

The **2** is happiest when they feel they look as beautiful as they know they are. This is not the work of the ego. It is their soul purpose, and one of the main reasons they came here to the physical realm.

Life Path 2: Health Choices

Ailments to watch out for

All **2**s are prone to worrying and they have a tendency to stress easily, which is only natural for someone who wants to be accepted by others as much as the Intuitive does. This worry will tend to manifest in all manner of stomach complaints (fear of change) and indigestion (gut-level fear). And depending if the **2** is ectomorph or endomorph, it can result in rapid weight loss or gain.

Many kind-natured **2**s also suffer from a sweet tooth, which they would say reflects their inner sweetness. But all joking aside, the craving for "comfort food" such as ice cream, chocolate, biscuits and lollies brought on by any kind of emotional upset can result in rapid weight gain, as well as exacerbation of their stomach problems.

Throat issues (fear of speaking their truth) are common for **2**s because they often feel unable to express themselves without fear of rejection. This fear of saying what is in their heart can cause sore throats, thyroid problems, tonsillitis and even cancer.

Leg, foot and ankle problems (stability) such as sprains, breaks, cramps and bunyons are common when the flighty **2** fails to ground themselves. And low energy levels are a frequent occurrence, brought on by the depression so many **2**s feel when the world around them fails to conform to their own inner knowing that everything is love.

Effective therapies

Regular exercise and a carefully controlled diet are essential for the spiritual **2** to ground them and keep them in their bodies, as are the "two Ms" for reducing stress – massage and meditation.

The best exercise choices for the **2** include mood-lifting activities such as dancing, swimming, surfing and walking in nature, as well as anything involving balance (yoga, Pilates, gymnastics and stretching).

The peaceful **2** should avoid contact sports – except, of course, for sex, which is absolutely the best exercise of all for the Intuitive!

Diet choices

Raw foods that benefit the **2**'s unusually sensitive digestive system include cabbage (and cabbage broth), flax seed, rape seed, turnips, melons, cucumbers, lettuce, broccoli, bok choy, asparagus, apples, coconut, cauliflower, okra, lemons and bananas. Try to avoid spicy foods as much as you can.

Because this Life Path is governed by the Moon, try to eat as many white foods as you can – especially cabbage, which is the **2**'s magic elixir. You can eat it as a vegetable or boiled into a broth to boost your digestive system and overall energy levels.

2s also have a tendency to skip meals (especially breakfast), which is a big mistake. A healthy breakfast and regular small meals during the day will transform their health faster than anything else they can do.

* * *

5. CHOICES FOR CHILDREN

CHILDREN working with the positive energy of **2** will usually be social, outgoing, compassionate and considerate of others. They love being part of their family and tend to make friends easily.

Young **2**s have a thirst for knowledge and will be good learners. They are diligent students because they have a high regard for learning and knowledge, and they will usually thrive in their school work, providing their school environment is a harmonious and peaceful one.

Similarly, **2** children will grow and blossom in confidence if their home is peaceful and harmonious. Arguments and friction can upset **2** children very deeply.

Life Path 2: Choices for Children

Parents need to be aware that **2** children are extremely sensitive and spiritual by nature, and it is important to nurture them with love and gentleness and never leave them on their own for long periods.

2s love to interact with other children but upsets can occur easily, so where possible try to keep at least one eye on them while they are playing – and ask their teachers to do the same.

Because young **2** children want to try to please everyone and have such a loving and giving nature, they can often become the objects of jealous kids' verbal and physical attacks.

All children love acknowledgement and approval, but none so much as the **2**. They want almost constant validation from everyone around them, and if they don't get it they can be hurt easily. When they feel emotionally damaged, the young and immature **2** can quickly flip to the negative side of their number and withdraw into their shell. They may also lash out and act aggressively. It is vital for parents to teach them to say "no" and learn to stop and look after themselves instead of trying to please everyone all the time.

Young children working with the energy of **2** will usually explore the negative aspects of their Life Path Number before moving on to master the positive aspects. This is true of all nine Life Paths because children need to first understand the difference between what is and isn't acceptable behaviour. However, once their boundaries are in place – and the child has understood the crucial lesson of cause and effect – young **2**s can then start tapping into their natural strengths with the assistance of a positive parental guiding hand.

The negative traits that afflict all **2**s no matter their age can play havoc with children working with the sensitive energy of this Life Path Number. This is especially true when a child **2** becomes overwhelmed by the intensity of their emotional reaction to the world around them at an age when they don't yet fully understand what their feelings mean.

Young **2**s experience a wide range of emotions and feel them very deeply, so parents need to be extremely sensitive to this and explain to them what they are feeling and why – even from an early age.

Life Path 2: The Intuitive

This can start from the moment they are born because even very small **2**s are so in tune with how they feel – and how others feel too – that they will understand much more than you might think. They know what they are feeling, but they are too young to define it, let alone understand it, so their parents need to define it for them in simple terms they can grasp.

This is important because even very young **2**s are natural peacemakers, and if their home environment is not harmonious and calm they may rebel against their parents and siblings and shut down.

It pays to talk openly and frankly with **2**s about any conflicts that arise and explain to them the emotions behind the conflict. This may be hard for some parents to accept, but by including their child **2** in their adult problems they actually allow them to offer a solution.

I know what you're thinking: a four-year-old telling you how to resolve an argument with your partner? You'd better believe it. Never underestimate the intuitive insight of a child **2**.

In their teenage years, **2**s can easily become shy, withdrawn and depressed if their emotional or spiritual expression is stifled, and they will suffer if they are isolated from other like-minded friends.

Teenage **2**s are very social and will thrive if their parents trust them to go out and enjoy an active social life. But always keep a close eye on them; the **2** child is a sponge for everyone else's traumas, and they will soak up all their classmates' troubles and come home feeling depressed and drained. This is seldom their own "stuff", and the best thing a parent can do is allow their **2** child to talk about it – and, by doing so, release the "stuff" from their own bodies.

Playtime activities

Group activities are paramount for young **2**s so their natural ability to interact with others can flourish. I know parents like to "hoard" their young children for themselves, but with a **2** this is the very worst thing a parent can do. Instead, encourage them to go out and socialise – but be prepared to pick up the pieces when they come home in tears because someone in their group was mean to them.

Life Path 2: Choices for Children

Team games and sports are often better than solo pursuits for the **2** child, who will also enjoy puzzles and problem-solving activities.

Most **2**s love acting and performing. Putting on a show as part of a drama group is a perfect activity, and as they get older they will enjoy games that involve the whole family. They will also flourish in the boy scouts or girl guides, or any similar team activity.

* * *

Your child's three-digit Birth Code

Young **2**s are born with one of two equally highly charged three-digit Birth Codes: they are either a 20/**2** or a Master Number 11/**2**.

In both Birth Codes, the child's Supplementary Birth Numbers perfectly complement their Life Path Number, which means all young **2**s will be naturally gifted peacemakers and healers right from the moment they are born.

As we have seen in Part Two, we always work primarily with the energy of our Life Path Number right from the outset, but in our childhood years from 0 to 18 we do so in conjunction with the energy of our first Supplementary Birth Number, and in our second 18 years – until we reach full emotional maturity at 36 – we do so in conjunction with the energy of our second Supplementary Birth Number.

It's worth reading the main listings here in Part Three for the numbers that make up your child's two Supplementary Birth Numbers to gain a better understanding of their positive and negative qualities.

Also, as you read about your child's three-digit Birth Code, real-eyes that the difference between "feeling the force" of any Life Path and flipping to the "dark side" is determined by the amount of Self-confidence we develop in our childhood years, and then the amount of Self-love we develop in our teenage years.

That, in a nutshell (squirrel!), is your role as a parent: to instill in your child first Self-esteem, and then Self-love.

The 20/2 child

20/2

The first Supplementary Birth Number of 2 in this Birth Code means that all children born with this set of numbers will work to develop their unconditional loving nature (the energy of 2) during the first formative 18 years of their life in conjunction with the overarching energy of their Life Path Number, which is also a **2**. So they will focus all their efforts on spreading love and light to help others heal their wounds and find love in their own lives.

Their second Supplementary Number of 0 – which, as we saw in Part Two, acts as an amplifier of the Life Path Number to which it relates – means that for their second 18 years, up to full emotional maturity at age 36, they will re-double their efforts to develop within themselves the capacity to bring love, light and harmony to as many people as possible.

This Birth Code is particularly auspicious because it contains the energy of only one of the 9 numbers, which means your child has a double helping of the Intuitive (**2**) amplified by the energy of 0. So not only will your child be extremely loving, they will need lots of loving attention in return. And I mean lots.

Also, the absence of any other number in the Birth Code means they will approach everything they do – both at home and at school – with a deep desire to create love and harmony everywhere they go.

Like all children, they will of course also develop some of the leadership qualities of **1**, the creativity of **3**, the loyalty and practicality of **4**, the curiosity of **5**, the sense of responsibility of **6**, the hunger for knowledge of **7**, the desire for success of **8** and the wisdom of **9** – but in every case, they will view all their lessons through the prism of "How can I use this information to improve the lives of those I love?"

This laser-like focus on creating harmony and helping others gives the 20/2 child a unique ability to read other people's thoughts and feelings, but it also means they feel emotions very deeply as well.

Parents must be alive to the danger that their child can get hurt easily, and that they may feel the pain as an excruciating rejection of everything they stand for.

The best thing a parent can do to coax them back out is simply to validate them – over and over – by assuring them they are loved unconditionally. Then explain that the person who hurt them did so only because they have so little Self-love in their hearts. Before long, your exquisitely compassionate 20/2 child will wipe away their tears and ask you: "How can we help make them feel loved too?"

The 11/2 'Master Intuitive' child

If your child is born with this Birth Code it means they have chosen to incarnate with one of the four Master Numbers whereby their two Supplementary Birth Numbers are the same (the others are 22/4, 33/6 and 44/8).

What this means in this case is your 11/2 child will work with the leadership energy of 1 not just throughout their first formative years from 0 to 18 but right up to their full emotional maturity at age 36.

Their main focus will still be on learning how to love and be loved unconditionally, which is the energy of Life Path **2**, but unlike the 20/2 child who will work solely with the compassionate energy of **2**, this young Master Intuitive will use their double energy of 1 to develop a strong personality and will often want to take the lead in group situations, both at home in their family and at school with their friends.

All **2** children are highly emotional and sensitive to how other people are feeling, but the double leadership energy of 1 endows the 11/2 child with a heightened sense of intuition, which is why this Birth Code is known as the Master Intuitive.

While the benefits of intuition are obvious, the downside is that your child's ability to read other people's thoughts and feelings could potentially scare other children (and adults too), which will open them up to even more attacks.

Life Path 2: The Intuitive

Parents must give their 11/2 child as much unconditional love as they can, while also ensuring that their home life is as harmonious and supportive as possible.

The 11/2 Master Intuitive child will usually be more outgoing than their 20/2 counterparts thanks to the double masculine fire energy of their two 1s, which gives them a "take charge" mentality in any group setting, including their family.

By contrast, the 20/2 child is ruled exclusively by the feminine water energy of **2**, making them more sensitive and therefore more vulnerable to rejection.

As they grow into their teenage and young adult years, the 11/2 Master Intuitive will be driven to take more of a leadership role in whatever activities they are involved with. They have a heightened potential to become a powerfully intuitive healer and peacemaker in the world. Barack Obama is an excellent example of a successful 11/**2**.

But because every Life Path's positive potential has an equally powerful negative potential, parents must be warned that when their intensely sensitive 11/2 child flips to the "dark side" of their Birth Code, they may become intensely aggressive or depressed.

No one is grumpier than a wounded 11/**2** child, who will test the patience and loving resolve of even the most doting parent. The solution, as I have said before, is to make certain they know how loved they are – and to teach them that it is wrong to look outside themselves for their happiness.

All children need to be taught Self-esteem and Self-love if they are to have a chance of achieving lasting happiness in life. For the hyper-sensitive 11/**2** child, however, this is doubly important.

LIFE PATH 3:
The Creative

1. **Growth cycle:** Third stage (the number of expression)
2. **Influences:** Air (thought, masculine) and Jupiter (wisdom)
3. **Positive qualities:** Artistic, outgoing and expressive
4. **Negative potential:** Cynical, withdrawn and manipulating
5. **Highs and lows:** Rousing communicator, or fault-finding critic
6. **Highest purpose:** Motivate others to be the best they can be
7. **Love matches:** 1, 3, 5, 7, 9 for compatibility (the rest for growth)
8. **Possible careers:** Acting, singing, writing, teaching, design, media
9. **Words to live by:** "I speak freely from my heart"

1. LIFE CHOICES FOR THE CREATIVE

THE intelligent, astute and insightful **3** is easily the most artistic of all the Life Paths. They have come into the world with a passionate desire – "hunger" may be a better word for it – to learn as much as they can and experience all life has to offer, and they will use their inspirational creative skills to motivate others to do the same.

3s are usually sunny and optimistic people who delight in any kind of Self-expression, choosing to use their limitless font of original ideas to create a happier, fairer, more stylish and infinitely more enjoyable world for all of us to live in.

Imagine a combination of David Bowie, John Travolta, Audrey Hepburn and Ricky Gervais (all inspirational **3**s), and you can see just how much the always original and entertaining Creative has to offer.

Life Path 3: The Creative

This is the third "expression" stage of a Life Path cycle, following the leadership energy of **1** and the loving energy of **2**. If you pictured the masculine **1** and the feminine **2** having a love child, it would have a balance of the **1**'s creative flair and the **2**'s empathy and compassion – which perfectly describes the qualities of the **3**.

The childlike **3** takes the achievements of its numerological "parents" and makes everything more fun. To use a well-worn but effective analogy, **1** gets the ball rolling, **2** brings people together to keep it rolling in the right direction (ie, towards creating more love in the world), and **3** shows us new ways to roll the ball and how to have fun doing it, by painting it bright colours and teaching us how to laugh at ourselves when we momentarily lose control of the ball and fall flat on our face.

Because this Life Path is governed by the masculine element of air (thought) and its ruling planet is Jupiter (wisdom), the Creative **3** will spend their young life soaking up vast amounts of knowledge while simultaneously expressing their creativity from an early age.

They are fascinated by anything and everything, they love to read and they yearn to travel. If they discover a place they want to visit and can't afford to go there right this second, they will read as much as they can about it in books and online and "experience it" that way.

As well as artistic flair and a wide general knowledge, the always talkative **3** will also develop excellent communication skills – both written and verbal – because being able to express themselves effectively is as essential as being able to breathe for the creative **3**.

The buzzword of this Life Path is "communication" in all its forms. But because what we are all here to do is not necessarily what comes easiest to us, the **3** will face some substantial challenges on their Life Path that are put there specifically to help them grow.

When they learn to work with the positive energy of **3** and express themselves freely, they will enjoy considerable success. But if they fail to develop enough confidence to communicate what is in their heart, they may flip to the "dark side" of this Life Path and become angry and judgmental. In doing so, the masculine **3** is merely angry at themselves for not having the courage to speak out. And although the problem is easily fixed (as we'll see in a moment), the **3** must guard against damaging their relationships while they are in this state. When it comes to being verbally cutting, no one comes close to a negative **3**.

* * *

Highest purpose of The Creative

The highest purpose of the **3** is to motivate and uplift as many people as possible and inspire them to be the best they can be. They will often do this through one of the many artistic mediums, but may also follow a business path that allows them to connect with people.

Because all these career paths involve communicating what is in their heart, the **3** must develop both the courage to express themselves freely and the confidence to cope with the rejection that all artists experience when their ideas are ignored or misunderstood, or both.

No artist likes rejection, but the **3** is particularly bad at accepting criticism (if you are in a relationship with a **3**, take note). Not only do they tend to be overly sensitive, especially about what is closest to their heart, they know exactly the best way to attack others and, if hurt, will likely lash out with a ferocity and cruelty that is truly frightening.

The person who always gets hurt the most, though, is the **3** who is only reacting like this because deep down they are their own worst critic and regularly beat themselves up for their perceived "failings".

Remember, the most important goal for all Life Paths is always the same: to first "wake up" to the truth that we are an extension of Source energy, and to help other people wake up as well. Then, and only then, will the path to our highest potential open up before us.

* * *

Key words are… 'confidence' and 'resilience'

To fulfill their life's highest purpose, **3**s must first learn to develop a robust inner confidence in their creative abilities. Confidence is

Life Path 3: The Creative

central to all the Life Paths as we embark on our common journey from pure unaware love to pure conscious love. As we saw in Part One, developing a healthy Self-esteem is the first crucial step towards Self-love that we all must take.

(If you've come straight to this Life Path listing in Part Three and are wondering what a "Self" is, please try to find the time to read Part One because it's way too complicated to explain again here.)

For the always creative **3**, however, developing a strong sense of inner confidence is much more than just the key to their personal happiness – it will determine whether they walk the positive Life Path of the inspired and fearless motivator, or veer down the negative path towards judgmentalism, insecurity and – ultimately – loneliness.

All Creatives are born with an insatiable thirst for knowledge, which they need to fuel their creative furnace. They have much to say, and always original ways to say it. But unless they are confident enough to put their art – and their message – out there into the world, their furnace will wither and die instead of lighting the way for others.

Parents, partners and bosses of the non-conformist **3** must give them plenty of freedom to go their own way and forge their own path, as well as encouragement to pursue their offbeat goals.

Positive feedback is essential for boosting the **3**'s confidence. If they post their art on Facebook and don't receive enough Likes, it may take them a long time to pluck up the courage to do so again.

The **3** is notoriously sensitive and thin-skinned, which they inherit from their **2** "mother". Unlike the **2**, however, the **3** has no choice but to throw themselves open to public criticism and rejection – such is the Life Path of the creative artist and passionate communicator.

That is why as well as a strong inner confidence in the value of what they have to say, which is essential for all artists, the **3** also needs to develop a resilience to criticism, otherwise they will fall in a heap every time someone doesn't understand or appreciate their message.

As we saw earlier, what is really going on for the perfectionist **3** when they get in one of their moods is not so much that they have taken the outside criticism to heart, but more that they are using it as an excuse to beat themselves up. No one expects more of them than they do. They have a cruel and intolerant Self-critic that always knows when they could have done better, and it will seize on the slightest chance to wield the big stick.

This is especially prevalent among young **3**s, which is why those around them must shower their creative efforts with lavish and genuine praise. As they grow older and more confident, the **3**'s Self-beatings will become less frequent and less severe. However, it is only when they have learned how to truly love themselves (as described in Part One) that they will feel free to express everything in their heart.

Yes, the **3** needs love and approval as much as we all do. But because the Creative has such a finely attuned inner critic that knows better than anyone whether their message is worthy or not, in the end it is only the love and approval they give themselves that really counts.

* * *

Positive and negative potential

All Life Paths contain an equal measure of positive and negative potential. Our challenge in every lifetime, no matter our Life Path Number, is to nurture our positives and overcome our negatives.

The reason we are given negative potential as well as positive potential is because people usually respond more effectively to the threat of pain than they do to the promise of pleasure. Also, while it is admirable to do what we are good at in life, we will only ever become the best we can be by facing our "dark side" and digging deep into our Self to overcome the obstacles that appear on our path.

As we have already seen in Part Two, it is only when the chips are down and we are up against it that we find out who we truly are and what we are truly capable of doing.

For example, confidence and an unshakeable belief in the value of what they have to say are the keys to success for all **3**s. If they have these qualities, they will have the courage to freely express what is in

Life Path 3: The Creative

their heart to uplift and inspire others. But if they don't, they can easily flip to the negative side of this number, and what will come out of their mouths will be cuttingly critical and judgmental instead.

Because all **3**s are at the third (expression) stage of a growth cycle, they are sponges for information and will be able to converse easily on a wide range of subjects. This is helped by their natural flair for both written and verbal communication.

They are usually right up to date with all the latest trends. In fact, they are probably way ahead of them, creating new trends with almost everything they do – from the clothes they wear, to their flair for cooking original recipes, mixing kick-ass cocktails and discovering new restaurants, art galleries, musical performers and fringe theatres long before the mainstream madding crowd has latched on to them.

3s have a keen, analytical mind and are usually highly talented and enthusiastic people who appear to achieve their goals easily – although this is never the case. The **3**'s achievements are always the result of persistent and focused hard work.

3s soak up information quickly, becoming almost effortlessly knowledgeable on a wide range of subjects. They are fast learners and their razor-sharp minds retain information easily, ensuring they succeed in most challenges they set themselves. However, they can also be a bit too quick to judge whether they like something or not, so there will often be gaps – some quite large – in their knowledge.

Creatives are frequently able to find solutions to their problems by enrolling the help of others. They also have a knack for being in the right place at the right time, and are therefore perceived by those around them to be "lucky" – when the truth is they make their own luck by thinking carefully about all the possible courses of action and then choosing the one that will give them the best outcome.

Freedom and knowledge are essential for the **3**. They hate to be tied down (only the **5** values their freedom more), so take note if you are in a relationship with a **3** and give them plenty of space. And they are in almost constant need of thought-provoking stimulation. They find it difficult to just sit and "be", so if they are not researching their

Life Path 3: Life Choices

latest project they will be found chatting with friends on the phone, connecting on social media, cooking a meal, or watching a movie.

As well as being excellent communicators, **3**s are also great at listening. This, and their natural ability to relate to others from all walks of life, makes them popular in social circles. However, they are always happiest talking with like-minded people. At a party, you will often see a **3** deep in conversation with just one other person for the entire night.

They make friends easily, but their social groups will usually tend to be relatively small. Again, this is because they prefer the company of similarly expressive and creative people.

They love to entertain, whether it is with great food and a games night at their home or a fun night out on the town, for which they will have organised tickets for all their friends. They are social, stylish and entertaining and have a knack for putting others at their ease.

Family is important for the **3**, although they will often experience a great deal of conflict in their home. They are usually closest to their mother (after all, it is she who has endowed the masculine **3** with their sensitive and creative nature), but there will be times when they fight ferociously because the **3** is torn between their need to break free of their mother's apron strings, and to stay close to the one person in the world who loves them the most – and therefore makes them feel better about themselves than anyone else can.

On the negative side, people working with the energy of **3** can spend too much time in their heads, over-thinking and over-analysing even trivial concerns. Their analytical nature can also lead them to become critical of others' shortcomings. Tolerance and patience are definitely not the **3**'s strong suit.

This lack of sympathy for others can make **3**s appear cold and judgmental, when in reality their real dissatisfaction is with themselves. This operates on a subliminal level because what they are reacting to are their own perceived shortcomings, which their subconscious mind sees reflected in the behaviour of others, as though in a mirror.

In extreme cases, insecure **3**s can become insular and withdrawn. They may find it difficult to open up to their family and friends, and

Life Path 3: The Creative

almost impossible to forge close loving relationships, believing that the reason they are not loved is because they are not lovable.

Because **3**s have high expectations of themselves and others, the negative **3** can sometimes be boastful of their own achievements and dismissive of the achievements of others. This can be hurtful, but is in fact just another symptom of the **3**'s insecurity about their own ability.

All **3**s need to think less and feel more by getting out of their heads and into the hearts as much as possible. This is a crucial lesson of their Life Path – to learn to trust their creative skills and bring their ideas to fruition by expressing what is truly in their hearts.

In their insecurity, **3**s can sometimes be quite needy in their desire for affirmation and praise. They must be wary of this pattern because their friends and loved ones often wind up feeling used and resentful when the **3** finds their feet again and quickly abandons their rescuer to pursue some exciting new challenge or idea they have dreamed up.

* * *

On a more personal level, **3**s can have a tendency to struggle in romantic relationships unless their partner is able to cope with their dramatic mood swings. On a good day, when the **3** feels confident, their energy will light up an entire room and they will radiate love and light to make everyone feel happy and buoyant. But if the **3** is feeling negative, they will ensure all those around them feel as bad as they do.

When a **3** is happy, everyone is happy. And when they are miserable, everyone is miserable. This can be difficult to live with, and the **3** must always make a point of apologising to their partner – and anyone else they hurt – as quickly and as sincerely as possible.

In romance, the **3** is often reluctant to give themselves completely to another person and may go through several early relationships with one foot out the door before they find their true love.

Rejection of all kinds is particularly painful for the artistic and sensitive **3**, and affairs that don't go well can leave lasting scars. The **3** is generous to a fault with their time and their money, but they are much more cautious with giving out their love for fear of getting hurt.

The secret to a long and happy relationship for the **3** (and a long and happy life, for that matter) is to real-eyes nothing and no one can ever hurt them as long as they remain true to themselves, because who they are is pure love – pure Source energy – and everything they express from that part of themselves is pure love too. However, as long as their ego is still at the controls of their life, their love will be tainted with the energy of "now love me back", and everything they create will come from their head rather than their heart.

All Life Paths must learn the lessons of Part One before they can kill their ego and make the Great Leap out of fear into love. But for the **3**, who possesses a mind like a sports car, stepping out of their head and into their heart is particularly challenging, yet especially important.

The **3** must learn that the only art worth making comes from the heart, not the mind, and the only love worth having – or giving – is unconditional love, which comes only from first loving their Self.

* * *

Summary of the positives

In the positive, the confident, Self-aware **3** is optimistic, social and uplifting, motivating others to feel great about themselves and teaching them new ways to tap into their own inner creativity and expression to get the most out of their life.

They will thrive best when given the freedom to express their individuality, whether it be the clothes they wear, the art they create or the way they choose to live their life.

3s who learn to ignore what others think about them will find the inner confidence to be themselves, which in turn allows them to teach others how to do the same. They will be deeply loving and caring people who make friends – and fans – easily and enjoy great success.

Life Path 3: The Creative

Key positive words

Creative, artistic, intelligent, inspiring, social, visionary, optimistic, broadminded, expressive, expansive, fun, original, stylish, fashionable, brave, passionate, knowledgeable, fast-learning, spontaneous, witty, sharp, energetic, enthusiastic, supportive, reliable, imaginative, loyal, inquisitive, communicative, happy and honest.

* * *

Summary of the negatives

In the negative, the insecure and afraid **3** can easily become needy, moody and Self-abusive, beating themselves up and blaming everyone around them for the way they are feeling, without taking responsibility for their own failure to love and nurture themselves.

Their lack of confidence can also stifle their artistic expression, leading them to become resentful and afraid. They may even start putting other people down, but will take no pleasure from doing so.

Negative **3**s will seldom go so far as to destroy themselves with drugs, alcohol or a final desperate act of suicide. They will simply live out their lives in sadness and anger, choosing solitude over love and using their grief to create "dark art" in the belief that expressing the despair they feel about life is better than expressing nothing at all.

Key negative words

Pessimistic, cruel, judgmental, cynical, moody, angry, controlling, selfish, arrogant, uncommunicative, depressing and aloof.

* * *

Self-love is the difference

If you have read Part One, you will already know that your ability to walk the positive side of your Life Path, as opposed to the negative

Life Path 3: Life Choices

side, is determined by whether you have undertaken the two key stages of personal growth. Or, to put it another way, whether you have taken the two crucial first steps on the path to your life's highest purpose.

The first step towards living your Life Path in the positive is to develop Self-esteem (and if you're wondering what a "Self" is, please take the time to read Part One because it's way too complicated to explain again here). This feeling of inner confidence is essential because it allows you to tap into your innate strengths, which you will need if you are going to have any hope of overcoming the numerous obstacles on your path. Be aware, though, that on its own this first step is never enough, because Self-confidence and Self-esteem are still the work of the ego. The feeling of being "good enough" carries with it an implied sense of needing to be "better than". So to reach your full potential and achieve your life's highest purpose, you must take the second step, which is to rise above the egoic concept of Self-esteem and climb to the higher ground of Self-love.

Loving your Self does not mean being "full of your Self". It means the opposite. It means being humble because you understand that you are the same as everyone else, no better and no worse. It means you understand that we are all immortal spirits having a human experience, and therefore we are all, at our core, the same – pure love and pure Source energy. (The Source is also fully explained in Part One.)

We can see it easily in new-born babies because when we are born into physical form, and before our fear-based ego has had a chance to develop, we are all gorgeous, gurgling bundles of pure, exquisite love.

I am not suggesting you do this, but imagine you were to place a new-born infant on the pavement of a crowded street and then stand back out of sight. Everyone – and I mean everyone – would stop and tend to it. And the reason they would do this is because, deep down, we all recognise pure love when we see it. We are drawn to it at the most basic level of our being because it is the most strikingly beautiful and compelling force on the planet. But sadly, as we grow up, our ego takes over and we start to believe – usually during our teenage years – that our ego is who we are. It isn't. Love is who we are.

Life Path 3: The Creative

We are all pure love. We are all extensions of Source energy (or children of "God", whichever phrase you are more comfortable with).

If you can rise above the quasi-religious terminology, I can summarise the two steps like this: Self-esteem is about feeling "good enough", while Self-love is about feeling "God enough".

The reason why loving your Self is so important for your Life Path is because when you start to live your life from the perspective of being pure love, everything changes. Suddenly you understand that nothing "out there" in the material world can ever harm you in any way.

Equally, you real-eyes you don't need anything "out there" in the material world to make you feel happy – not the approval of others; no amount of money, fame and power; and not even the love of a good man or woman – because you have all the love you need right there in your own heart, and you can therefore relish the exquisite joy of loving everyone unconditionally without needing anything in return.

That is why Self-love is the secret to working with the positive energy of your Life Path Number. Because when you truly love your Self, the rocky mountain path you've been climbing suddenly becomes an express elevator ride all the way up to the summit of your bliss.

* * *

No Life Path is an island

Although your Life Path Number denotes the main issues you will focus on, you will always work to some degree with the energies of the other numbers as well to become a fully rounded Self.

As a **3** your main work will be in the areas of creative expression, but you will also tackle issues of Self-confidence (**1**), co-operation (**2**), stability (**4**), freedom (**5**), acceptance (**6**), trust (**7**), power (**8**) and integrity and wisdom (**9**). It's therefore worth your while to read through the listings for the other Life Path Numbers when your time allows.

* * *

Life Path 3: Life Choices

Qualities of your three-digit Birth Code

(Note: Please read the description in Part Two of how 0 operates in your three-digit Birth Code. Also, you can consult the main Life Path listings here in Part Three for each of your Supplementary Birth Numbers (the three possible ones for the Creative are 1, 2 and 3) to give you a clearer understanding of how their qualities govern your formative years.)

12/3

The numbers that make up this wonderfully creative Birth Code endow 12/3s with a strong sense of purpose, as well as a capacity to take a leadership role in whatever they choose to do with their life.

Their first Supplementary Birth Number means they will begin by working with the leadership energy of 1 during the first formative 18 years of their life in conjunction with the over-arching creative energy of their Life Path Number **3**.

They will therefore quickly strive for independence at a young age (the goal of the trail-blazing 1) and will probably start to develop their artistic and communicative talents (the trademark of the creative **3**) almost as soon as they can walk and talk.

Then, in their second 18 years – from coming of age at 18 to full emotional maturity at 36 – they will work with the co-operative energy of their second Supplementary Number of 2, which means they will focus their creative expression on bringing people together and will learn to work with others to achieve a common goal as part of a team.

If the 12/3 works with the positive qualities of both their energetic "parents" – the masculine 1 and the feminine 2 – they will be able to achieve a healthy balance in their lives between being outwardly ambitious and inwardly considerate of others. This is how progress happens. The numerological "child" is always able to draw on the qualities of its energetic forebears, taking what they learned and creating new opportunities and greater understanding in their life.

In the case of the 12/3, this means developing the courage and originality of the Leader and combining them with the compassion and co-operation of the Intuitive to motivate others to become the best they can be... which is always the highest purpose of the Creative **3**.

21/3

This Birth Code involves working with the same energies as the 12/3, just in a different order. Their main work will still be with the expressive and communicative energy of **3**, combined with their Life Path's natural inclination towards the arts and other creative pursuits. But their Supplementary Birth Numbers are flipped, which means they will do so in significantly different ways.

For the first formative 18 years of their life, the 21/3 will focus their creative expression on bringing people together (the energy of 2). In their family, they will be a peacemaker from a very early age, always wanting everyone to get along well together. They will often be the mediator in resolving disputes (2), a task at which they will usually excel thanks to their innate talent for communication (the energy of **3**).

Whereas the 12/3 will spend most of their childhood striking out on their own and scheming about their latest plan to get ahead in the world (the energy of 1) by using their creative energy (**3**), the 21/3 will be much more social and focused on connecting with their friends and family (2), often putting on plays to amuse and entertain (**3**).

Then, in their young adult years from 18 to full emotional maturity at 36, the 21/3 begins to strike out on their own (the energy of 1) to take their creative ideas to a much wider audience (**3**).

As with the 12/3, the 21/3 will benefit from being able to work with the qualities of both their energetic "parents" – the masculine 1 and the feminine 2 – to achieve a healthy balance in their lives between being outwardly ambitious and inwardly considerate of others.

30/3

Of the Creative's three possible Birth Codes, this is by far the most artistic, leading 30/3s to work exclusively with the motivational and expressive qualities of **3**, both as their Supplementary Birth Number

Life Path 3: Career Choices

during their first formative 18 years and also throughout their life as their overarching Life Path Number.

Then, during their second 18 years until they reach full emotional maturity at 36, they will continue to work with the energy of their Life Path Number with a laser-like focus, thanks to the amplifying effect of their second Supplementary Birth Number of 0.

As children, they will be expressive, creative, curious and energetic – all hallmarks of the inquisitive, communicative and life-embracing **3**. They will absorb knowledge like a sponge in their first 18 years, and will continue to expand their knowledge and creativity for their next 18 years, and the rest of their long and productive life.

The 30/**3**'s creative ideas will usually be left-field and groundbreaking, their flair for fashion and Self-expression will be highly original, and their communication skills will be finely tuned. Remember, though, that the core rule of the Self-Awareness System™ states that every positive potential is matched by a corresponding negative potential of the same magnitude. So while the amplified single-number focus of the 30/**3** gives these Creatives a heightened capacity to achieve their goals, it also means they are more likely to suffer the dramatic mood swings to which all **3**s are prone.

The key, as we saw earlier, is for them to develop first Self-confidence and then Self-love. For it is only after they have learned to love themselves that any of the **3** Birth Codes – and especially the 30/**3** – can fully express the love and passion in their hearts, both creatively in their professional lives and intimately in their personal relationships.

* * *

2. CAREER AND BUSINESS CHOICES

CREATIVE **3**s naturally graduate towards the arts and entertainment industries. Many become musicians, actors, singers, painters or writers.

Life Path 3: The Creative

Careers in interior decoration, graphic design and film production also suit their creative and expressive talents.

Many **3**s go into business for themselves (because they absolutely love to be in control), or else they will choose to work on a freelance basis to retain the autonomy they crave.

The positive Creative has a joyful spirit. They are charming and social, as well as being both great listeners and communicators, so careers or businesses in the areas of counselling, media, hospitality, tourism and PR are also a good option – as long as their work gives them plenty of outlets to use their creative flair.

Overbearing bosses and repetitive tasks annoy the **3**, so jobs that contain a high level of autonomy and variety are the best choice.

Confident **3**s love the limelight and will enjoy "putting on a show" in whatever form that takes, so careers in the theatre, film, television, modelling, public speaking, live music and event management are also well-suited to their creative desire to entertain.

If the **3** strikes out on their own and sets up their own business their chances of success are high – providing they surround themselves with the right people and employ a well-grounded financial controller, because they are generous to a fault and they have a tendency to spend money like they do everything else in their life – with great style.

Beneficial career paths

People working with the motivational energy of **3** make excellent writers, designers, comedians, fashionistas, models, musicians, singers, actors, painters, journalists, presenters, filmmakers, producers, public speakers, event managers, tourism operators, chefs, hoteliers, personal growth teachers, sales trainers, public relations advisers, image consultants, counsellors, school teachers, stylists, beauticians, make-up artists and hairdressers.

Business matches

The **3** will have an excellent chance of turning one of their creative ideas into a successful business. Unless they are a super-focused 30/**3**, however, they will usually not be great with details and may benefit from choosing a diligent and disciplined **4** as a partner. The egotistical **8**, however, just like the bossy **1**, should probably be avoided.

For their human resources manager, they would do best to choose an intuitive **2** or a nurturing **6**. For their creative team (marketing and sales) they would pick another **3** or the quick-witted and persuasive **5**. The thoughtful **7** and hard-working **4** perform best in the back-office roles such as research and development, accounting and IT.

For a financial controller look no further than a cautious **4**. And for a special project that needs someone to take the reins and drive it to fruition, no one would be better suited for the task than a motivated and capable **9**.

* * *

3. RELATIONSHIP CHOICES

ONE of the most rewarding aspects about the Self-Awareness System™ is how equitable it is. Each Life Path offers the same opportunities for happiness and fulfillment, albeit in markedly different ways. And each of them also offers the same amount of challenges to force us to grow, although again in very different ways.

This means no Life Path is any "better" or "worse" than any of the others. All of them have their blessings, and all have their obstacles.

In the case of **3**, the blessings centre around their unique capacity for conjuring up new and creative ways of looking at the world, and their obstacles show up in the form of Self-doubt and cynicism if they don't have the confidence to bring their creative ideas to fruition.

This innate creativity of thought and expression makes the **3** a true artist. But their heads are most often to be found in the clouds, which makes them more likely to succeed in their creative endeavours than in their intimate relationships, which by their very nature are always grounded in the mundane, day-to-day world – a place many **3**s don't like to inhabit other than for short periods at a time.

The always creative and imaginary **3** prefers to live in the world of ideas and idealism, which can leave their partner wondering where they went – like Alice through the looking glass.

As we will see in a moment when we look at the potential love matches for the **3**, the best chance of lasting happiness they have is with a partner who is equally creative and free and is therefore able to understand that when the muse calls, they have to go.

The bottom line is most **3**s are happiest to fall in love with life itself, rather than with a person, so relationships are often secondary to their need to drink in all this world has to offer. This does not mean they can't enjoy deep and lasting relationships. It merely means that their partner must be both secure in their own worth, and also willing to give the **3** as much space as they need.

Of all the Life Path numbers, only the adventurous **5** values their freedom more than the experience-hungry **3**. So anyone who falls in love with a **3** must learn to live by the timeless truth of all romantic relationships: "If you love them, let them go. If they come back, their love for you is real. If they don't, it never was."

What a **3** looks for in a relationship more than anything else is freedom to do and be what they need to do and be. This is the deep, soulful plea of all artists. If they have this, there is nothing they won't do for their partner. If they don't, it is only compassion and kindness that will keep them in the relationship, and that won't last long.

Providing the trust and freedom is there, the **3** makes for a most fulfilling and entertaining partner. They are excellent communicators who, if they choose, can adeptly prevent conflicts from arising, and solve them quickly and relatively painlessly when they do. They are also excellent listeners, capable of tuning in to their partner's needs and knowing instinctively what they have to do to keep them happy.

Yes, they will flirt – as all air and fire numbers are wont to do – but they will never stray from a partner who supports their creative passion and gives them the freedom to experience all life has to offer.

Life Path 3: Relationship Choices

In relationship, when a **3** is happy they want everyone else to be happy too. But when they are down, they have a knack for bringing everyone else down with them.

If you are in a relationship with a **3** you will be only too familiar with this far-from appealing trait. Sometimes they will come home full of the joys of spring and light up the home. Other days, it will be like someone opened the front door and let a thunder cloud in.

When **3**s are in one of their moods, it's best to give them a very wide birth. They will only bite your head off if you try to find out what's wrong. Give them space and wait for them to talk about it first, which they may never do. The **3** likes to solve all their own problems, and the next time you see them they will be a little ray of sunshine again, as though nothing happened.

Deep down, the **3** knows they ask a lot, but they will stay faithful if given the freedom they seek. Blow wind under their wings and tell them to fly, and they will always fly home to you. Try to clip their wings and they will walk out the door without ever looking back.

* * *

Sex drive of the 3

Sexually, the **3** is usually as creative and adventurous in bed as they are in the rest of their life. They love to talk during sex (they are communicators, after all) and will often challenge their sexual partner to explore sides of themselves they never even knew existed.

Many **3**s tend to be sexually shy in their teens and are what can best be described as "late starters". Some never really fully shed their inhibitions, while others may overindulge in a frenetic bid to make up for lost time – often having more than one partner at a time.

For most **3**s, however, sex will often be seen as another avenue for expressing their creativity and accumulating knowledge about the human condition. While the **1**, for example, equates sex to power and the **2** uses it to surrender the very core of their being, the playful **3** regards sex as primarily a mental exercise rather than a physical one.

Life Path 3: The Creative

They love to laugh in bed and their sexuality will often be quite coy and immature, but charmingly and attractively so.

The "masculine energy" **3** in a relationship (and this is a masculine number) will want to be as dominant in the bedroom as he is everywhere else. However, he also has a deep inner longing to be seduced and ravished by his partner, no matter which sex they are. This is not just a fetish, it is yet another manifestation of the **3**'s quest to experience everything life has to offer from every possible perspective.

The same is true of the "feminine energy" **3**, who will want to take turns being the ravisher and the ravishee. Because this number is masculine, the feminine **3** will have a healthy energy balance that allows her to switch roles effortlessly in bed, as well as elsewhere in the home.

* * *

The compatibility listings that follow will help the outgoing yet often sensitive **3** get the most out of their relationships, whether it's with someone they love, a friend or a business partner.

You will notice the air energy of **3** is well-matched with other **3**s, their air cousins **7**, and the evolved **9**, as well as a **1** and **5**, whose fire combusts with the presence of air. But air evaporates water (**2** and **6**) and erodes earth (**4** and **8**), so these pairings throw up more challenges.

However, what appears to match you best on the surface may not be what you need right now. All relationships are designed to help us grow along our Life Path. Yes, of course we enjoy the companionship, close connection, sexual intimacy and deep love that relationships give us. But that is now why we have them.

The reason we choose a partner (or, to be more accurate, why our all-knowing Self chooses them for us) is because they are a mirror in which we see our shortcomings and strengths reflected back at us through their shortcomings and strengths.

That is why opposites so often attract, especially in love.

I have written an entire book on this subject called *Leap into Love* which goes into the way relationships work in our lives in great detail.

Life Path 3: Relationship Choices

But for now, please real-eyes that when your partner presses one of your buttons, they are doing so not to "piss you off" but because your Self is using them to show you the areas you need to work on.

If you fail to understand this is the main reason why you attracted them into your life in the first place, you will fight each other and may eventually break up. And you will believe their faults were exactly that – their faults – rather than yours reflected back at you.

Worst of all, you will then take the unchanged you with you to your next relationship, and – lo and behold! – exactly the same issues will come up again.

If this sounds familiar. If you have ever asked any of these questions – "Why does this always happen to me?" or "Why do all men cheat?" or "Why are all women so demanding?" or whatever it is for you – then now you know why. It's because you didn't learn from your last partner, so of course your new one will do the same thing.

And this will continue to happen, relationship after relationship, until you real-eyes it is meant to be happening to show you what areas you need to work on in your Self to change and grow.

* * *

One final quick point before we get into it: I need to stress that I disagree with almost every numerologist I know who likes to label relationships "a natural fit", "a neutral fit" or "an unnatural fit", depending on the compatibility of the numbers of the two partners.

All relationships are challenging. That is why we have them, as we have just seen. Yes, sometimes we might choose a partner who is "just like us" for the sake of harmony, but that could be regarded as a cop out if we are truly serious about our personal and spiritual growth.

If you are on a spiritual growth path in this lifetime (and there is no doubt in my mind that you are if you made it through Part One without throwing it in the bin!), then your Self will choose your relationships for you – and they will always be with a partner who will challenge you to grow in exactly the ways you need to grow.

Life Path 3: The Creative

Just because you might discover your current partner has a Life Path Number that doesn't dovetail perfectly with yours, please don't fall into the trap of thinking that there must be something wrong – or worse, end it with them so you can go out with someone with a "better" number.

Where you are right now on your Life Path is exactly where you are meant to be, and who you are with is exactly who you are meant to be with. So please let these listings help you to look for the lessons in your relationship, rather than look for the door.

And if you are single at the moment, try to remain open-hearted about your next relationship. It doesn't matter what Life Path Number he or she has, so don't "cherry pick". All that matters is you follow your heart and be open to learning the lessons they will teach you.

* * *

3 & 1

(Expression and Independence)

Love

This is an action-packed combination that often works well in all areas. In love, the thoughtful air energy of **3** and the forceful fire energy of **1** dovetail perfectly, with the independent and ambitious **1** leading the way and the creative **3** always finding new ways to reinvent and grow the relationship at the first signs of stagnation.

Both the Leader **1** and the Creative **3** appreciate the work that the other does, and both will drive each other forward. The **3** is good at stroking the **1**'s ego, and the **1** is great at encouraging the **3** and giving positive feedback to all their creative ideas.

This will usually be a lively and passionate relationship that will allow each partner to cover a lot of ground, both professionally and in their personal life. They will fire up each other's imagination, making their times together both exciting and rewarding.

Life Path 3: Relationship Choices

They will usually have many friends, an active social life and will have a comfortable or even luxurious home where they can socialise and enjoy the fruits of their considerable material success.

The air of **3** and the fire of **1** are compatible elements (air is always a good match for fire because, when they come together, the air fans the fiery flames of passion). Both partners love adventure and new experiences, they both like to experiment sexually once they trust each other, and they both absolutely love surprises.

They are very well-matched in the bedroom, where there will be much passion, and laughter too. However, they must watch what they say because they both have thin skins and do not take criticism well. This is the one pitfall that can undermine this relationship quicker than either of them can say "ouch". Both **3**s and **1**s can tend to be overly sensitive unless they have done the inner work to boost their Self-love, so they must be wary of saying something apparently off-the-cuff that can hurt the other to their core.

For all of their great qualities, neither the **3** nor the **1** is good at forgetting, or forgiving. A wound left untreated can fester and easily become incurable because unevolved **3**s and **1**s are firmly entrenched in their egos and take any attack very personally.

That aside, this is a fun and passionate match with never a dull moment. The outgoing **1** and the social **3** will love each other's company and respect each other's abilities, and there is potential for a long and happy time together.

Remember that when disagreements arise (and they will), take the time to sit down and figure out what you are meant to be learning from your partner – then kiss them and thank them for the lesson.

Good luck, stay open and honest… and enjoy the laughter, love and creative expression this relationship can give you.

Friendship

3 and **1** can be great friends because they are both chock-a-block full of creative ideas and will inspire and motivate each other. There is a risk of treading on each other's toes, and disagreements – even fights – may arise because both numbers are headstrong and opinionated.

Having said that, it is rare for the **3** and the **1** to want to play the same role, so they will be unlikely to compete for the same love interest or the same business opportunity. They will have much in common and will love spending long evenings planning their next grand adventure – whether it be a holiday they will take together, a business they will start together, or just a fun night out on the town.

Business

1s can work well with the creative and intelligent **3**, but they must guard against being too bossy because the **3** needs to be free to do their own thing and give vent to their limitless font of ideas.

As a social motivator, the **3** is focused on working with all the team members to help them achieve their full potential and will be happy for the **1** to be out front taking the lead, as long as they give the **3** plenty of autonomy. Both will fire off each other's ideas, while at the same time their agenda is very different. The **3** usually doesn't want to be the CEO, dealing with all those boring meetings, but they will insist on having creative freedom. And the **1** is usually happy to let the **3** design the business… as long as they can run it.

* * *

<u>3 & 2</u>

(Expression and Co-operation)

Love

This can sometimes be an energetic and fun-packed relationship due to both partners' social nature and love of a good party. The outgoing **3** and the empathetic **2** both enjoy being around other people, and they share a common interest in food, art, music and travel.

There will be plenty of restaurant dinners, nights out on the town and holidays to exotic locations, as well as long, animated conversations

Life Path 3: Relationship Choices

over a good home-cooked meal. Both the creative **3** and the nurturing **2** like to cook, and they absolutely love to talk. Boy, can they talk. In fact, there will be precious few chances for anyone else to get a word in when these two lovebirds have friends over.

The **3** likes their relationship to be harmonious, as does the **2**, so this couple will try their hardest to avoid fighting. But because the **3** will usually be the more dominant partner, and because the **2** doesn't like to be told what to do, conflicts will invariably arise.

The **3** has a tendency to be a bit bossy and must remember to praise the nurturing **2** for all they do, and the **2** must remember to give the **3** plenty of freedom to pursue their creative goals.

This is where problems can arise. If the co-dependent **2** becomes too needy or jealous of the **3**'s flirtatious behaviour and desire for independence they may push the **3** away.

Equally, if the **3** forgets to give the tactile **2** enough love and affection – especially physical touch – they may look elsewhere for the intimacy they seek.

Regular and open communication is the solution – something both partners are normally very good at – to express their needs and let each other know which ones are not being met. And as long as neither side shuts down completely (something else they are both good at), conflicts should be resolved relatively painlessly.

A **2** will often perceive the social and flirtatious behaviour of the **3** as a form of betrayal and will worry they are no longer loved or respected. For their part, the **3** hates to be tied down and will view any insecurity by the **2** as an attempt to manipulate them.

The **3** must remember to reassure the **2** that there is no threat, and the **2** must avoid trying to restrict the **3**'s outgoing personality. Jealousy is the biggest relationship killer of all.

Also, the **2** must learn to trust the **3,** who in return must be careful never to do anything to break that trust. Once they are hurt, it is rare for a **2** to ever fully trust again.

Good luck, stay open and honest… and enjoy the many social outings and travel adventures this relationship can give you.

Life Path 3: The Creative

Friendship

These two can have a lot of fun together because they are both so social and enjoy many of the same things, including food, wine, parties, travel and adventure. However, they tend to see life very differently.

The air energy of the **3** means they are in their heads most of the time, while the feminine **2** – though happy to party with the **3** in small groups – will usually seek out the company of other water friends for more intimate friendships. Yes, the **3** loves to talk, but normally about worldly issues rather than emotional ones. They may find the **2** a little too "heavy" at times and will usually bond best with a **5**, a **7** or a **9**.

Business

This is usually an excellent business combination, providing the **2** is happy to let the **3** hog the limelight and the **3** respects the **2**'s opinion and listens to everything they have to say. The **2** will be a valuable business partner due to their uncanny ability to read people and resolve problems, leaving the **3** free to pursue their "big picture" goals.

Neither is particularly good with money, though, and they both have expensive tastes, so employing a good accountant to keep track of the cash (preferably a **4** or an **8**) might be a good idea.

* * *

3 & 3
(Expression and Creativity)

Love

Talk about fun! These two social butterflies will probably meet at a party or an art gallery and talk each other's ears off, before painting the town 50 shades of red and dancing until dawn. There will never be a dull moment as they bounce their creative ideas off each other – usually over a bucket of mojitos in a booth at some ultra-chic bar – and plan how they are going to change the world. The **3** loves to entertain and be entertained. They crave excitement and adventure, yearn to travel and explore, and they absolutely hate being bored or tied down. So on a purely social level there is no better pairing for a **3** than their fellow fun-loving and life-affirming Creative.

But that's often as far as this relationship will go. Yes, they may fall in lust and become intimate, but as often as not one or both of them will pull back and choose to remain just friends, not wanting to risk destroying their exhilarating connection by taking it any further.

On one level this is a shame, because two **3**s who are both ready to commit really should give it a go. With enough trust in each other's level of commitment – and providing both have done enough inner work to boost their Self-confidence so they don't feel threatened by their partner's flirtatious ways or professional success – they can push each other to achieve far more together than they ever could alone.

But therein lies the rub. All but the most evolved **3**s are sensitive, suffer from Self-doubt and don't take criticism well, while at the same time they have a tendency to criticise others, sometimes harshly.

They also have difficulty committing to a relationship, which takes a lot of hard work, preferring instead to pursue their pleasure in their work and by meeting new and interesting people. So this relationship can frequently deteriorate into a bitter mix of criticism and mistrust.

If this happens, both **3**s will be left scratching their heads and wondering why they didn't follow their head rather than their heart right from the start and remain just friends.

If they stick with the relationship, though, the rewards will be worth it 10 times over. No one has more fun than a pair of **3**s who love and support each other. They will achieve much together, but the timing has to be right – namely, when both partners want to experience what it feels like to commit to another person and create a life together.

Good luck, stay open and honest... and enjoy the wild ride this exciting and passionate relationship can give you.

Friendship

Yes, yes and hell yes! As we have just seen, two **3**s are well suited as friends thanks to their common interests and shared hunger for

Life Path 3: The Creative

knowledge and experience, not to mention their love of socialising. Without the expectations and constraints of a relationship, this pairing can enjoy stimulating each other's minds and pushing each other to fly higher and higher, while also being free to take off on their own to answer the call of adventure whenever they feel like it.

Some words of caution, though. Most **3**s are sensitive to criticism, so choose your words carefully in a disagreement to avoid creating a rift. Also, one of you two party animals has to be able to call time and know when to rest and recharge, or else your health could suffer – as well as your bank balance.

Business

Friends, yes. Lovers, maybe (if you are both ready to commit). But business partners? You'd be better off going your separate ways.

Two **3**s with like-minded creative ideas might feel tempted to partner up in a business, but this time they would be better advised to remain just friends. The constraints of running a business are even tougher than those of a relationship, and neither **3** will be willing to let the other one have the limelight while they toil away paying the bills.

Both will want to be the star of the show, creating the big ideas and spending the big money, which is a recipe for rivalry, resentment and, eventually, bankruptcy. It's probably best to choose an earthy and practical **4**, or a watery and co-operative **2** instead.

* * *

3 & 4
(Expression and Stability)

Love

The flighty, avant-garde **3** and the conservative and materially focused **4** have little in common in the way they approach life, which means this air/earth relationship will always be an opportunity for growth rather than a recipe for peace and harmony.

Life Path 3: Relationship Choices

The practical, feminine **4** wants to build a home and a career from the ground up, while the creative and masculine **3** wants to follow their heart and experience all life has to offer.

The artistic **3** is spontaneous and likes to take life as it comes, while the pragmatic **4** dislikes surprises and wants to plan everything in advance. Add to this the **4**'s love of routine and the **3**'s love of change, and it's easy to see why this is far from a harmonious match.

However, if these two can find a middle ground between careful planning and reckless spontaneity, they have an excellent opportunity to teach each other how to get the most out of life.

As I have repeated often, relationships are primarily about growth, and this is certainly one of those pairings. The **4** can benefit enormously from adopting some of the **3**'s love of excitement and adventure, and the **3** would do well to take on board what the **4** has to teach them about proper planning and discipline.

Number **3** wants romance, passion and fireworks but often has little idea about the value of serious commitment, leading them to flit from one relationship to another. They may live out their lives without ever really knowing what true love feels like because it requires hard work and dedication to create a bond that stands the test of time.

Meanwhile, the conservative **4** wants the deep loving connection that devotion to just one partner gives them, but they are in danger of living out their lives stuck in their comfort zone without ever having the courage to explore all this magnificent world has to offer.

If each can learn from the other, both partners may be able to have their cake and eat it too, complete with icing and a cherry on top. It won't be easy, but the **4** who learns to embrace the **3**'s passion for life will be all the better for it – just as the **3** who learns the value of discipline and careful planning from the **4** will find that rushing around skimming the surface of life will never give them the intense pleasure of truly committing to another person who loves them.

Good luck, stay open and honest… and try to see the world through your partner's eyes. You will be all the better for it if you can.

Life Path 3: The Creative

Friendship

Will these two meet at a party one day and instantly become besties for life because "OMG! We have so much in common"?

Um... no. It's hard to find two such opposite personalities. The **3**'s butterfly personality and headstrong nature is likely to irritate the **4** right from the outset, while the **4**'s serious personality and their equally headstrong nature may well cause these two heads to clash.

Yes, these two can get along when they have to in a social setting, but the **4** may find the fun-loving **3** irritatingly unpredictable, while the sensitive **3** may regard the outspoken **4** as being a bit too judgmental.

Business

This is as challenging a match for business as it is for friends and lovers. In a relationship, at least they have an opportunity to learn from each other. But in business, where money is involved, the stakes are just too high. The hard-working **4** may quickly grow to resent the effervescent **3**'s ability to attract people – and money – to their cause with just the bat of an eyelid or the curl of a flirtatious smile. And the impulsive **3** may resent having to account for every dollar and cent they spend to woo customers on what the **4** sees as frivolous activities.

If the **3** takes the time to explain to the **4** what they are doing and respects them for their ability to manage the details, the business may thrive. Equally, if the **4** can real-eyes the **3**'s instincts are almost always right and give them the space to do their thing, this partnership may achieve great success. But those are some big "ifs".

* * *

3 & 5
(Expression and Freedom)

Love

On the surface, the creative air energy of the **3** and the passionate fire energy of the **5** appear to be an excellent match in all areas, and especially in love. These two will certainly enjoy a rich and varied social life, but it may all feel a bit shallow from a lover's perspective.

They make great friends, and all the best relationships are founded on being best friends above all else. But their passion can sometimes flare too brightly and be over almost as soon as it has begun because neither number is serious enough about doing the hard work to build a solid relationship from the ground up.

The curious **5** will be off doing their own thing, delighted that the equally adventurous **3** understands their need for freedom. And the creative **3** will be off following their dreams, equally delighted that the independent **5** is happy spending large amounts of time without them.

The trouble is, the whole point of being in a relationship is to spend time together, learning from each other and helping each other to grow. So, from a personal growth perspective, there is very little point in these two numbers falling in love and committing to each other when they could achieve the same result by staying best friends.

However, if a **3** does find themselves in a romantic relationship with a **5**, they can make it work – and last – by sharing as much as they can of themselves with their partner, and by taking the time to involve themselves in the **5**'s freedom-fighting crusades wherever possible.

The partners will have to be very secure in themselves, however, because the **3** and the **5** are both fiercely social and incorrigible flirts. If they become jealous, they will push each other away and into the arms of another lover faster than either of them can say "Next!"

Good luck, stay open and honest… and try to make enough time for each other to keep the flames of passion burning bright.

Friendship

As we have just seen, this is one of the best and most mutually fulfilling friendship pairings in the entire Self-Awareness System™. The expressive air energy of the **3** will fan the flames of the fiery **5**'s passionate need to explore the world and make a difference in the lives of others, while the **5**'s quick-witted intelligence and love of adventure will inspire the **3** to ever higher creative achievements.

These two will quite possibly be best friends forever, firing off each other and driving each other forward with not a hint of jealousy or insecurity. If they are sexually matched, though, they should probably avoid falling in love and ruining everything, unless they are prepared to learn the valuable life lessons each has to teach the other.

Business

For all the reasons that we have discussed in the Love and Friendship sections, these two numbers have so much in common creatively that they may feel tempted to combine their resources and go into business together to make their dreams come true.

They will certainly inspire and push each other, as well as give each other the space they need to do their own thing and follow their own separate creative instincts. But problems will arise if they disagree on the creative direction the business needs to take.

Also, while the well-rounded **3** is certainly better qualified to run the business, file the invoices, collate the expense accounts and handle the finances than the unreliable **5**, if they spend too much time on the mundane day-to-day tasks, the **3** may quickly grow to resent the reckless and irresponsible **5** and decide they are better off on their own.

Just as we saw with their relationships, this pairing, even if they are sexually matched, would be best advised to remain best friends, neither falling in love, nor going into business together.

∗ ∗ ∗

3 & 6
(Expression and Romance)

Love

The creative and intellectual **3** is always going to face challenges if they choose to form a romantic attachment with an idealistic and controlling **6**, simply because the **3** insists on being in control of their own destiny and needs to feel free to pursue their creative dreams —

Life Path 3: Relationship Choices

which may take them far from the family home the **6** holds so dear – while the **6** may resent the fact that they are not in control of the relationship, as they like to be.

That's why this pairing will always be more about personal growth than anything else.

The nurturing **6** wants to shower their partner with love and open up their exquisitely affectionate heart to them in a demonstrative and dazzling display of devotion – which may only make the intellectual and relatively restrained **3** feel guilty that they are nowhere as "deep" as their Visionary partner.

Equally, the always curious and expressive **3** wants to talk long into the night about conceptual issues such as human rights, politics and oppression, while the idealistic **6** – although deeply concerned about these subjects – doesn't like to dwell on negativity and just wants to make love, believing (correctly) that the best way to raise the vibration of the planet is to literally "make" love.

As long as the intellectual **3** puts aside their need for mental stimulation long enough to satisfy the **6**'s craving for physical intimacy, and the faithful **6** trusts that the **3**'s need to spend time away from home with a broad spectrum of friends doesn't mean they don't value them above all others, this can be a mutually rewarding relationship.

The **6** will help the **3** get in touch with their divine inner Self, which is crucial for all creative artists. And the **3** will encourage the **6** to take their much-needed message of love out into the world.

On a day-to-day basis, the social **3** must curb their naturally flirtatious personality, which can wound the **6** deeply even if there is nothing of substance to worry about.

Similarly, the homemaker **6** must real-eyes that the adventure-seeking **3** needs more mental stimulation than they do and be prepared to step outside their comfort zone to prevent the **3** becoming bored and looking elsewhere for excitement.

Good luck, stay open and honest… and enjoy the many mutual growth opportunities that this relationship can give you.

Life Path 3: The Creative

Friendship

On the surface, these two numbers appear to have little in common, with the nurturing **6** wanting to stay close to home and the adventurous **3** wanting to travel far and wide to explore the world.

However, without the constraints of a romantic relationship, this friendship can work extremely well because the one thing both these numbers fear the most is failing to achieve their life's ambition.

The intellectual **3** needs the loving **6** to re-mind them that while conceptual negative "dark art" might fill galleries and cinemas with arrogant, Self-important elitists, the highest purpose of art is to improve the lives of the common man and woman, while also raising the vibration of the planet with messages of love and hope.

Equally, the **6** has come here to show the world its true loving potential, but is often too timid to take their message to a worldwide audience. By supporting their **3** friend to create art that spreads love throughout the world, they can achieve their highest purpose vicariously.

Business

Yes, this can work. But the expressive **3** must have full control of the creative side of the business, while the diligent and hard-working **6** must feel acknowledged for their tireless leadership role. Creative **3**s are well-organised, but this is not their area of greatest expertise. Far better for the **6** to run the business, allowing the **3**'s ideas to flow freely.

* * *

<u>3 & 7</u>
(Expression and Understanding)

Love

No one is better able to understand the spiritual and intellectual nature of the creative **3** better than their fellow conceptually focused air cousin **7**, making this a good match – as long as both partners are secure enough to trust each other during long periods of separation.

Life Path 3: Relationship Choices

The solitary **7** needs to be given plenty of time alone without being made to feel guilty that they are neglecting their partner, and no one is better able to give this gift to them than the outgoing and equally independent **3**, who needs to feel free to go out and explore the world to fuel their creative fire.

This mutual need for time apart makes this romantic match one of the most harmonious it is possible for the **3** to find, because they can support and love their intellectual **7** partner without feeling that they need to devote too much of their precious thinking time to stroking either their hair or their ego to make them feel loved.

Even a fellow expressive **3** is not as understanding a lover as the loyal and devoted **7** because another **3** may want to occupy the same space in the relationship as their **3** partner does, and they may fight them constantly to be top dog, both intellectually and spiritually.

No such competitive drive afflicts the individualistic and cerebral **7**, for whom a relationship will always be of secondary importance to their need to feel free to take their message of love and truth out into the world, through whatever creative medium they choose.

The principal challenge that can arise with this pairing – and it probably will, so be forewarned and forearmed – is that both partners will be so content to let each other have all the time and space they need, they may neglect the romantic side of their relationship and simply drift apart, becoming more like friends than lovers.

As long as they take time out from their individual career goals to spend quality and passionate time together every once in a while – whether it be away on romantic weekends just the two of them, or even just out for dinner with a baby-sitter at home looking after the kids – this shouldn't become too much of a problem.

Good luck, stay open and honest… and enjoy the mutual support and understanding that this relationship can give you.

Friendship
The spiritual air energy of **7** is well-suited to the creative air energy of **3**, meaning these two analytical observers of life have the potential

Life Path 3: The Creative

to forge a great friendship that will stand the test of time. Their mutual interest in understanding the world around them and finding ways to improve the lives of others will let these two friends fire off each other, sharing their Big Ideas and egging each other on to ever greater heights of creativity and professional success.

These two air (thought) numbers have so much in common they can't help but become good friends and mutual admirers almost as soon as they meet. Their conversation will soar and plunge through issues great and small, like some sort of intellectual roller-coaster, as they share their ideas with a tangible sense of relief that – at last! – they have finally found someone who "gets it".

What the **7** lacks in confidence, the **3** has in spades to help them have the courage to bring their grand designs to the world. And what the **3** lacks in depth, the intellectual **7** seamlessly provides to shore up the **3**'s paper-thin Self-esteem and give them the boost they need to express their creative ideas without fear of rejection or failure.

Business

Just as in love and friendship, this is a brilliant match for business, because both these air numbers will have an immediate and intuitive grasp of each other's creative Big Ideas, thus allowing them to share a vision for where the business needs to go, and how it can get there.

Generally, the enterprise will work best when the creative **3** is free to pursue new directions for growth and the intuitive and thorough **7** is in charge of running the company. However, because these two air numbers have so much in common, care must be taken to avoid treading on each other's toes. A clear delineation of roles is essential to allow both partners to operate most effectively.

Neither air number will be especially good at looking after the mundane day-to-day details of running a business, so they would do well to employ an earthy **4** or **8** to look after the finances, freeing them to focus on the big creative and conceptual ideas.

* * *

Life Path 3: Relationship Choices

3 & 8
(Expression and Ambition)

Love

This is always going to be more of a mutual growth opportunity than a "tra-la-la-la" tiptoe-through-the-tulips-hand-in-hand-without-a-care-in-the-world-because-we're-so-in-love relationship. But that's OK. After all, some of our most valuable relationships are the ones just like this one where opposites attract – no matter how briefly – to teach each other some valuable life lessons.

Try as they might to be attentive to their partner, the goal-oriented **8** will always be too focused on themselves and their material interests for the attention-seeking **3**, just as the socially interactive **3** will always be too demanding of their partner's time for the busy **8** to cope with.

The earthy **8** needs a partner who gives them plenty of time and space to do their own thing, but the social **3** thrives on excitement and needs almost constant stimulation from their lover, otherwise they might just as well have stayed single and fancy free.

For a **3** to commit happily to a relationship with an **8** they must be prepared to make their own entertainment separate from their partner, otherwise they will quickly grow to resent the Achiever for never being there for them. Equally, the **8** must let their **3** lover go out and find the entertainment they crave without them, trusting that they won't stray.

Which they probably will, one day, when they meet someone who is creative and quirky and cool and… well… more like them.

One of the biggest problems with this pairing is that the **8** will find little to admire about the **3**'s social butterfly nature, and the **3** will not value the **8**'s monetary work ethic because they are perfectly capable of making their own money, thank you very much.

In fact, their values are so different that it's highly unlikely these two will ever meet and fall in love in the first place. So please real-eyes that if you find your Self in one of these **3/8** relationships as you read this, you are there for a very specific and important reason.

Life Path 3: The Creative

There is something you need to change about your Self, and you have attracted your **8** partner into your life so they can teach you what it is and how to do it. You'll know what it is if you look hard enough. And, who knows, by making the change you just might find that this relationship is "the one" after all, and you will both go on to live a long and blissfully happy life together.

Good luck, stay open and honest... and try to learn the crucial and life-changing lessons each of you is able to teach the other.

Friendship

The ambitious **8** will meet the free-loving **3** at a party and hit it off immediately, partying long into the night together.

Said no one. Ever.

Yes, they can be friends – even great friends, if they work at it. But on first meeting, these two will usually have very little in common.

Business

Equally, no one ever said that these two should even think about perhaps contemplating the thought of considering the possibility of maybe mulling over the concept of discussing the idea of talking about going into business together.

Ever.

* * *

3 & 9
(Expression and Passion)

Love

Throughout this book, and indeed throughout all my books, I talk about the important role romantic relationships play in our personal and spiritual growth. That is why even the so-called "incompatible" relationships in the Self-Awareness System™ are so valuable – because we will always attract at least one partner, and usually several, into our life to teach us the valuable life lessons we need to learn to grow along our Life Path.

Occasionally, though, a relationship comes along with someone who is so like us and so well-matched in all the crucial areas that we immediately shut down all our internet match-making profiles, pluck out our roving eye, put a huge sign on our front door saying "SOLD! OFF THE MARKET!" and dance our lives away together in a soulmate samba of such twinkle-toed delight that, by comparison, even Fred Astaire and Ginger Rogers at their very best would look like two flat-footed walruses fighting over a fish.

This is one of those. Right from the start, when these two first meet, there will be an instant attraction as the effervescent **3** and the socially charming **9** strike up a scintillating conversation about their latest creative project. Both are naturally artistic and outgoing, both share a common love of the limelight, and both want a partner who they know won't cramp their style in any way.

Once these two lovers commit, they can enjoy a wonderfully passionate roller-coaster ride through life as they explore the world together, party together, entertain together, create fantastic art together and grow old together – while all the while giving each other all the space they need to do their own thing.

Problems can really only arise in this relationship if either partner fails to share the limelight… because both these numbers love to perform and absolutely adore being the centre of attention. They must make sure they allow each other to shine so this doesn't become an area of conflict and jealousy.

That having been said, there is normally nothing that will prevent these two lovers of life from acting out all their romantic fantasies and growing old and happy together.

They will both almost certainly have worked through their growth lessons in previous relationships, which is what has freed them to find this blissfully compatible connection.

Good luck, stay open and honest, remember to share the limelight… and enjoy every single moment of your glorious time together.

Life Path 3: The Creative

Friendship

These two perfectly matched numbers won't be just BFFs, they'll be BBFITWBWs – Best Bloody Friends In The Whole Bloody World. They will have so much in common, in fact, that they must be wary of upsetting their respective partners by rabbiting on too much about how wonderfully inventive X is, or how creative and original Y is.

As with relationships, problems can arise for these friends if they become jealous of each other's success and try to hog the limelight. The **3** must celebrate the **9**'s triumphs, even when their own lives aren't going so well, and support their friend rather than compete with them.

Business

The **3** and the **9** will likely work just as well in business together as they do in love and friendship. This is a case of the whole being more than the sum of its two parts, with both pushing the other to achieve far more success than they could on their own. Again, make sure you share the limelight and the praise… and watch the money roll in

* * *

4. HEALTH CHOICES

THE effervescent **3** is normally so positive and energetic that they will maintain a natural physical wellbeing just by going about their frenetic day to day life. For some, though, weight gain can be a concern.

The sensitive **3**'s easily bruised ego combined with their need to put themselves "out there" to express their creative ideas – thus making themselves vulnerable to the pain of perceived rejection – mean even the healthiest **3** can become overweight, without ever knowing why.

Energetically speaking, all weight gain is subliminally driven by a person's fear of being hurt. They literally try to "protect" themselves from being hurt by others by hiding behind a layer of fat – which, no

Life Path 3: Health Choices

matter how much they exercise, never really goes away. This is especially prevalent among feminine **3**s, but applies to masculine **3**s too

The physically healthy **3** who struggles with their weight will find that their protective layer will literally fall off without the need for excessive exercise as soon as they tap into their Self-confidence and learn how to express their creative ideas without fear of judgment.

All Life Paths must learn to silence the fear-based voice of the ego in their head and listen only to the voice in their heart that tells them that nothing and no one can ever hurt them because they are pure love (pure Source energy), and love is the only thing in the universe than can never be harmed or attacked in any way. For the **3**, however, this is especially important – not just so they are free to speak their truth and share their wonderful creativity with the world, but so they avoid manifesting a physical illness that reflects their ego's fear of not being "good enough".

Common health issues for the **3** include throat and lung problems and disorders of the skin. All **3**s need to be heard, which means if they lack the confidence to speak freely what is in their heart they can develop thyroid, throat and respiratory dis-ease – all of which are physical manifestations of their stifled expression.

And like the **5**, with which the **3** shares so much in common, they regard their skin as their last line of defence against the outside world, so until they learn to fully love themselves and real-eyes nothing "out there" can ever hurt them they may suffer from eczema, psoriasis, rashes and other skin problems.

Ailments to watch out for

As we have seen, throat (fear of expression) and skin (vulnerability) issues are not uncommon for the unevolved **3** but as soon as they learn to develop this Life Path's two key qualities of confidence and resilience, these ailments will usually clear up on their own.

Fatigue, depression, nervousness and weight gain are three other psychosomatic disorders common to the **3**. Again, all are solved not by physical exercise but by spiritual exercise. Learning to love your Self is not just the greatest love of all – it is the greatest doctor of all.

On a more physical level, the ever-social **3** can overdo the partying and develop all manner of debilitating physical ailments as a result of burning the candle at both ends. Plenty of rest (**3**s loves their sleep) and relaxation is needed to ensure that their love of socialising doesn't take a lasting toll on their physical health.

Effective therapies

I have said it before, but it's worth repeating: the best therapy for the **3** is energetic, rather than physical. Learning to love your Self and developing the courage to speak the truth in your hearts will be more beneficial to your health than any amount of diet and exercise.

However, there are a number of physiological steps you can take to optimise your energy levels and overall sense of wellbeing. These include happy and expressive movements, such as dancing, Zumba and walking (or jogging) in nature.

(Note: the treadmill at the gym just doesn't cut it for most aesthetic 3s – unless there is a screen playing uplifting music videos.)

Regular massage and meditation are also beneficial for the **3**, and body shaping at the gym works wonders for their Self-esteem.

Diet choices

The **3** does best with a largely vegetarian diet, and if they do eat meat they would do well to try to keep it to a minimum.

It's rare to find a **3** who doesn't love to cook, and the very least of their concerns while creating their elaborate and spectacular dishes is how healthy they are. That's fine on occasion, but the **3** must try to eat as healthily as possible in between their bouts of culinary extravagance.

The foods that benefit the **3** the most are fresh berries, for their powerful antioxidant properties. They should be consumed on their own, however, either as they come or in a healthy juice or smoothie – but never at the end of a meal, when they can't be digested properly.

Other beneficial foods include mint, nuts, figs, olives, carrot, fish oil (for the skin), apples, peaches, pineapple, cherries, sage and saffron.

Finally, try to eat lots of eggplant (aubergine) and beets, which are especially good for the **3**'s digestive system.

* * *

5. CHOICES FOR CHILDREN

YOUNG children working with the energy of **3** will usually explore the negative energies of their Life Path Number before moving on to master the positive aspects. This is true of all the nine Life Paths because children need to first understand the boundaries of what is and isn't acceptable behaviour.

However, once their boundaries are in place – and the young **3** has understood the crucial life lesson of cause and effect – they can start tapping into their natural creative strengths with the assistance of a positive parental guiding hand.

Children working with the positive energy of **3** are usually optimistic and cheerful, provided they are given the freedom by their parents and teachers to express themselves in their own way and are not forced to conform to too many rules.

3 children learn quickly and their razor-sharp minds retain vast amounts of information, making them likely to achieve success in their school work. They tend to be diligent in their studies and will obtain good grades, especially if they are allowed to learn in their own way.

Most **3**s thrive on independence and don't like to be "mothered", so mums will do well to give them space to find their own answers, while always being on hand to give advice when asked for it.

Life Path 3: The Creative

(This is ironic, because **3** children – both male and female – will usually develop a much stronger bond with their mother than their father, unless their dad is an exceptionally creative and artistic man.)

Young **3**s are extremely sociable and make friends easily but their social groups will usually be quite small and even a little cliquey due to their strong desire to be surrounded by like-minded people.

Most **3**s prefer creative and artistic pursuits to sporting ones, and many **3**s stay away from the competitive nature of sports altogether.

The creative instincts of young **3**s means they are usually sensitive and do not react well to criticism of any kind, so it is important for parents and teachers to tread carefully when disciplining or correcting them. And effusive praise and encouragement is vital for every piece of art they show you – and there will be a lot.

Conflicts with a **3** child are common, especially with teenage **3**s who are trying to stand on their own two feet and may rebel against their parents' relatively conservative view of the world.

All **3**s are brimming with creative ideas about how they can make the world better (which is, after all, their life's highest purpose), but they haven't yet developed the inner confidence they need to freely express themselves.

The best advice for parents is to lavish praise on their **3** child's creative ideas – no matter how "whacky" they may seem – and tell them over and over again that they are deeply loved. Self-esteem and Self-love are the two most important lessons any child can learn, and especially so for the creative and extremely sensitive young **3**.

Conflicts can arise around their overly critical nature, especially when they are teenagers. Parents need to teach them the value of tolerance and acceptance of others, just as they expect tolerance and acceptance for themselves and their creative ideas.

Because they are so sociable and in their heads, young **3**s can easily become scattered. If this happens they will need to learn to ground themselves and trust their ability to solve their own problems without crying for help and falling back into the trap of neediness.

Life Path 3: Choices for Children

Playtime activities

Children who are born with **3** as their Life Path number love to socialise and are incessantly talkative, so group activities will work well by allowing them to connect with like-minded children.

They are also naturally creative and they will thrive if given a box of paints or crayons, or a musical instrument and a song book. They also love to put on plays and other performances for their parents, who must try to shower them with as much praise as they can.

3 children do not like too many rules, so free-form activities that allow them to tap into their imagination are also good for them.

Role-playing games, word games, dance lessons and drama classes should be considered because most young **3**s respond better to creative pursuits than sporting ones.

It is important for parents to find the time to listen to what their always talkative **3** child has to say, because this will give them the confidence they need later in life. **3** is the number of communication, so the very worst thing a parent can do is tell them to be quiet.

* * *

Your child's three-digit Birth Code

Young **3**s are born with one of three triple-digit Birth Codes: they are a 12/**3**, a 21/**3** or a 30/**3**.

As we have seen in Part Two, we always work primarily with the energy of our Life Path Number right from the outset, but in our childhood years from 0 to 18 we do so in conjunction with the energy of our first Supplementary Birth Number, and in our second 18 years – until we reach full emotional maturity at 36 – we do so in conjunction with the energy of our second Supplementary Birth Number.

It's worth reading the main listings here in Part Three for the numbers that make up your child's two Supplementary Birth Numbers to gain a better understanding of their positive and negative qualities.

Life Path 3: The Creative

Also, as you read about your child's three-digit Birth Code, real-eyes that the difference between "feeling the force" of any Life Path and flipping to the "dark side" is determined by the amount of Self-confidence we develop in our childhood years, and then the amount of Self-love we develop in our teenage years.

That, in a nutshell (squirrel!), is your role as a parent: to instill in your child first Self-esteem, and then Self-love.

The 12/3 child

The first Supplementary Birth Number of 1 means all children born with this Birth Code will work with the confident energy of the Leader during the first formative 18 years of their life, in conjunction with their over-arching creative Life Path energy of **3**, the Creative.

This means they will tend to develop the courage from an early age to express the creative ideas that are in their heart – the highest purpose of the **3**. But because all young children suffer from insecure feelings of Self-consciousness, parents would be advised to focus on nurturing their 12/3 child's confidence to communicate verbally.

Dinner time is especially effective for this because it allows the young 12/3 to speak out about what they have learned at school that day, and how it makes them feel.

As they grow older, their focus on the energy of 1 will empower the sociable 12/3 child to take the lead in their social and school groups to develop their creative ideas and share them with others. But parents must watch for signs of arrogance, because the energy of 1 can cause them to try to impose their creative ideas on others before they are old enough to understand that no one likes to be told how to think.

In their second 18 years, the 12/3 flips to work with the energy of the Intuitive (2) – which is co-operation and connection – so any early signs of arrogance and aloofness should usually quickly disappear. All the while their main focus is on accumulating and retaining knowledge about the human condition, which they do with remarkable ease thanks to the mentally agile qualities of their Life Path Number **3**.

Life Path 3: Choices for Children

So by the time they reach full maturity at age 36, the 12/**3** – if they have been nurtured correctly to follow the positive creative energy of this Birth Code rather than the negative judgmental energy to which it can be prone – will step into their strength and become powerful and inspirational motivators who teach others through their creative ideas how to experience life to the fullest.

The 21/3 child

This Birth Code contains the same potential for positive growth and negative setbacks as the 12/**3**, just in a different order.

Whereas the 12/**3** starts out by developing the confidence of the Leader (1) to express what is in their heart before later developing the ability to connect on the deepest level with others (the energy of 2), the 21/**3** starts out by being especially sociable in their desire to connect first with those around them (family and friends) to understand how others feel, and then in their adult years will develop the inner confidence to take the lead (the energy of 1) in teaching others about the nature of life through their creative art (the energy of their Life Path of **3**).

Neither Birth Code is better or worse than the other because both paths lead to the same destination. But the 21/**3** will usually enjoy a more peaceful and harmonious childhood because they are working with the supplementary energy of connection and co-operation (2) in their formative years (rather than the independent energy of 1), which will give them not just a peacemaking role within their family, but a rewarding popularity among their friends.

The 30/3 child

This Birth Code is radically different to the other two because children working with the energy of 30/**3** will focus all their energy on accumulating knowledge and developing their creativity (the energy of their Life Path **3**) for their first 18 years, without worrying about taking

Life Path 3: The Creative

a leadership role (the energy of 1) or developing strong bonds with those around them (the energy of 2).

Then in their second 18 years as they grow up and out into the world, they will re-double their efforts to use their creativity and artistic expression to entertain and uplift others (the energy of **3**) thanks to their amplifying second Supplementary Birth Number of 0.

This means children born with this Birth Code have a heightened capacity for accumulating knowledge and developing their original creative ideas, which is the positive energy of the number **3**.

Parents must be warned, though, that it also means they are more susceptible to experiencing the negative aspects of the Creative, which can include judgmentalism, wild mood swings, extreme sensitivity to criticism and occasionally even aggression.

A heightened capacity for success in the Self-Awareness System™ comes with an equally heightened capacity for disappointment if the child is not properly nurtured from an early age to work with the positive energy of their Life Path, rather than the negative.

The 30/**3** child – even more than the 12/**3** or 21/**3** child – needs to be given the space to freely express themselves. All **3** children need to be praised for their creativity, but none as much nor as often as the hypersensitive 30/**3**.

LIFE PATH 4:
The Builder

1. Growth cycle: Fourth stage (the number of stability)
2. Influences: Earth (practical, feminine) and Uranus (assertiveness)
3. Positive qualities: Loyal, generous and hard-working
4. Negative potential: Stubborn, inflexible and indecisive
5. Highs and lows: Tireless humanitarian, or moody procrastinator
6. Highest purpose: Build a better world for your Self and others
7. Love matches: 2, 4, 6 and 8 for compatibility (the rest for growth)
8. Possible careers: Management, law, admin, finance, social work
9. Words to live by: "Build for tomorrow, but live for today"

1. LIFE CHOICES FOR THE BUILDER

THE passionate and loyal **4** is one of the most honest and trustworthy of numbers. They are faithful and reliable, they have a remarkable capacity for hard work... and they have come into the world with a burning desire to make it a better and fairer place for everyone.

Here you will find the truly selfless helpers among us: the casualty ward nurses, the courageous aid workers and the tireless volunteers who derive genuine pleasure from tending to those less fortunate than themselves and helping them get back on their feet.

And even those **4**s who work an office job will normally go above and beyond what is expected of them, helping out wherever they can and genuinely celebrating the success of others.

Life Path 4: The Builder

As their name suggests, Builders – and especially Master Builders – are concerned with issues of practicality and purpose. They value honesty highly and will usually spend their lives working hard to build a stable foundation for themselves and their family.

This is the fourth "stability" stage of the growth cycle, which means the **4** will work to right any perceived wrongs and turn the key lessons of the three previous Life Paths into something tangible to improve their own lives… and the lives of others.

The **4** takes the dynamic energies of creativity (**1**), co-operation (**2**) and expression (**3**) – which on their own serve no useful end unless they have a purpose – and grounds them in the physical world to create both spiritual and material understanding and fairness.

Because **4**s are governed by the element of earth (practicality), they tend to be no-nonsense types who cut to the chase. They are seekers of truth and have little time for dreamers, flakes, shonks and new-age charlatans. They value their physical and financial wellbeing highly, and they will pursue their goal of improving their lives – and the lives of others – with a gusto more akin to a crusade than a challenge.

And because they are passionate about fairness in all areas of life, it is not unusual for the **4** to be a tireless campaigner for human and animal rights. Nothing riles a **4** more than the sight of some ignorant bully mistreating a helpless human being or a defenceless animal, and they will feel the victim's pain as if it were their own.

In this lifelong quest for fairness, the **4** is equipped with the best "bullshit meter" in the business, which helps them sort the wheat from the chaff. They are ruthless in their pursuit of truth and they can usually spot a "get rich quick" or "get healthy quick" scam a mile away.

Fastidious in their attention to detail, they will usually examine all sides of every person, every object and every idea they come across until they are 100 per cent certain that what they are being offered resonates with the quality and authenticity they demand before they will invest their precious time and money in it, or them.

Try to pull the wool over the eyes of a **4** – or, worse, dare to lie to their face – and you will immediately live to regret it, because they will

Life Path 4: Life Choices

call you on your deceit quicker than you can say: "Um, well, what I meant was…"

Because the **4** is an earth (feminine) number, those working with the positive energy of this Life Path will tend to have their feet planted firmly on the ground. But if they flip into fear and thereby invoke the negative energy of this Life Path, they can become scattered and even overwhelmed. In the worst case, they will even slump into victimhood, allowing others to walk all over them as they retreat into their shell rather than "cause a fuss" by fighting back.

Another quality of the positive **4** who operates from a position of strength is their desire for fairness. The courageous defender you might see standing up to the bully at school or calling out the aggressive policeman at a human rights rally or berating the dodgy grocer at the market whose food is not as fresh as it should be will often be a **4**.

However, because what we are all here to do is not necessarily what comes easiest to us, the **4** will also face challenges on their Life Path that are put there specifically to help them grow. And they will usually come in the form of their intimate relationships – with their partners, their immediate family and their close friends.

Few people are able to measure up to the **4**'s impossibly high standards (including themselves). And, yes, they beat themselves up with the same intensity they bring to every other task they do if they feel they have not lived up to their full potential.

* * *

Highest purpose of The Builder

The highest purpose of the **4** (and the Master Builder **22** – more about you justice warriors in a moment!) is to build a stable life for themselves and help others do the same. In particular, the **4**'s highest calling is to right wrongs in the world by helping the victims of injustice.

Sadly, for many **4**s this means that they bravely choose to incarnate into a family environment where they themselves will be the victim of some kind of injustice or abuse so they can get a first-hand experience of what it is they want to spend their lives eradicating.

This painful but courageous choice has both positive and negative consequences, as we'll see in a moment when we look at the positive and negative potential of this number. But as far as the highest purpose of this feminine earth number goes, there is no greater calling than righting a wrong... both in their own lives, and in the lives of others.

When they tap into the positive energy of their Life Path Number, the loyal and grounded 4 will work tirelessly and diligently to build their successes from the ground up, as their name suggests.

– They take time to build their homes on the solid foundation of financial security, rather than borrowing and going deep into debt.

– They also take their time to build their relationships on a foundation of trust and understanding. Same with their friendships.

– They build their career slowly and step by step too. And they even build themselves a body in which they feel comfortable and secure by nurturing their health and taking regular exercise.

Yet, as we'll see in a moment, the most important project for the 4 will always be to build within themselves a healthy level of first Self-worth and then Self-love, or else all their magnificent edifices can – and probably will – come crashing down.

Remember, the most important goal for all Life Paths is always the same: to first "wake up" to the truth that we are pure spirits having a human experience – pure extensions of Source energy – and then to help other people wake up to this truth as well. Then, and only then, will the path to our highest purpose open up before us.

* * *

Key words are... 'confidence' and 'flexibility'

To fulfill their life's highest purpose, 4s must first learn to develop a robust inner confidence in themselves. Confidence is central to all the Life Path Numbers as we embark on our common journey from

Life Path 4: Life Choices

pure unaware love to pure conscious love. As we saw in Part One, developing a healthy Self-esteem is the first crucial step towards Self-love that we all must take.

(If you've come straight to this Life Path listing in Part Three and are wondering what a "Self" is, please try to find the time to read Part One because it's way too complicated to explain again here.)

For the goal-oriented **4**, however, developing a strong sense of inner confidence is much more than just the key to their personal happiness – its will determine whether they walk the positive Life Path of the disciplined and dependable Builder, or veer down the negative path by becoming indecisive, bitter and resentful.

All Builders are born with a deep and burning desire to right the wrongs in the world and help others, both emotionally and materially. But before they can hope to do this they must first heal their own wounds and find peace within themselves.

This involves facing their own inner fears, which is never easy or pleasant. But if they fail to clear their own blockages, the inherently positive **4** can easily flip to the dark side of this Life Path, which will manifest as neediness, insecurity and a fear of being left on their own.

As well as facing their fears, the ponderous **4** would do well to lighten up from time to time and remember life is meant to be fun. It's a playground, as well as a classroom – a fact that often escapes them.

Yes, it's great to plan for the future and build your life from the ground up, but the **4** who spends all their time focused on creating their future may miss out on many of the pleasures of the present.

As Eckhart Tolle says in his spectacularly successful book *The Power of Now*, the present is all any of us have, and the serious **4** would do well to regularly take a break from planning for the future and smell those roses, have that glass of champagne, eat that chocolate dessert… and enjoy being alive.

The other quality the always focused **4** must try to develop within themselves is flexibility – specifically, the ability to react in a positive way to the curve balls that life will throw their way.

Life Path 4: The Builder

You will seldom find a **4** who hasn't had the challenging but ultimately rewarding experience of fate bursting into their lives to remove them from a situation they have wanted to leave for some time but have lacked the confidence and flexibility to do so – simply because it wasn't a part of "their plan".

Whether it's being sacked from their job, removed from their home, or abandoned by their partner, the inflexible **4** is being forced by their Self to deviate from their carefully constructed plan and strike out in a new, more rewarding direction.

If they have done enough inner work, they will embrace this divine intervention and be evolved enough to grow with the flow. But if they haven't and are still stuck in their ego – especially their fear of being abandoned – the fragile **4** may fall in a heap.

They would do well to remember that when a storm comes, the sturdy but rigid oak tree is often uprooted and sent crashing to the ground, while the flexible willow tree simply bends with the wind and then rights itself again once the storm has passed.

* * *

Positive and negative potential

All Life Paths contain an equal measure of positive and negative potential. Our challenge in every lifetime, no matter our Life Path Number, is to nurture our positives and overcome our negatives.

The reason we are given negative potential as well as positive potential is because people usually respond more effectively to the threat of pain than they do to the promise of pleasure.

Also, while it is admirable to do what we are good at in life, we will only ever become the best we can be by facing our "dark side" and digging deep into our Self to overcome the obstacles that appear on our path.

Life Path 4: Life Choices

As we have already seen in Part Two, it is only when the chips are down and we are up against it that we find out who we truly are and what we are truly capable of doing.

For example, the generous and humanitarian **4** is prepared to drop everything they are doing and rush to the aid of someone they love. There really is nothing they won't do to help a person in need.

But on the flip side, they can sometimes become resentful when the favour is not returned. They can feel setbacks and rejection very acutely, especially when they are young and haven't done the inner work on themselves to boost their level of Self-love.

When a crisis hits, instead of tapping into the same incredible problem-solving skills they use to help others, they may shut down and push everyone away, often falling into long bouts of depression and isolation and refusing all offers of assistance. They may then brood, procrastinate and change their mind almost every minute about what they feel they should or shouldn't do.

For some **4**s, this negative behaviour occurs because deep down they lack Self-love, which is why they rush around helping everyone else except themselves. But most of the time, it's simply because the always headstrong **4** simply hates to be in anyone's debt.

They would do well to consider how they would feel if someone else pushed their help away, and real-eyes they are denying their loved ones the pleasure of helping that they themselves hold so dear.

Because the **4** is at the fourth (stability) stage of a Spiritual Growth Cycle, they tend to be focused on practical and pragmatic issues, such as building a career, building a home, building a relationship and building a close and trusted circle of close friends.

While the **1** wants to conquer the world, the **2** wants to heal the world and the **3** wants to travel the world for the sake of it, the **4** wants to travel the world to learn how to make their own world better.

Also, because this is an earth number, while the fire, air and water numbers are dashing about seeking happiness "out there", the **4** knows all the answers they seek lie in their own personal development. When

Life Path 4: The Builder

they travel, for example, they do so as much to learn something new about themselves as to visit new places and meet new people.

This Self-focus can sometimes get on others' nerves, and the **4** must be careful not to come across as brooding and antisocial. On the one hand, the **4** can be the most loyal friend it is possible to have, but for their partner and immediate family they are by no means the easiest people to live with.

Those who work with the positive energy of **4** will patiently build a strong financial base and clear their emotional blockages so they can support themselves as well as those around them. But those who work with the negative energy of this Life Path can become moody, obsessed with details and bogged down by indecision and procrastination.

Negative (ie, fearful) **4**s usually need to have all the facts before they make a decision, and this can mean they never take a decision at all. This leads to frustration and moodiness, which will only make them even less able to decide what they want to do – and so it goes, in a vicious spiral of indecision and frustration.

If they can simply learn to follow their heart (their Self, which always knows instinctively what to do) rather than their head (their fear, which will never do anything in the least bit risky), they will avoid this trap and transform their lives in more ways than they can imagine.

All **4**s are quick to understand new ideas, and if they learn how to make decisions from their heart they will be able to take quick and decisive action to turn them into successful business opportunities. If they don't, and stay in their head, they may become stuck in a rut.

The **4**s capacity for hard work, combined with their knack for proper planning and attention to detail, means they have an excellent chance of being successful in whatever they choose to do. Once they are set on a course of action it is virtually impossible to distract them or make them change their mind. Giving up is just not in their nature, which is the secret to any successful venture.

Caution is the byword of all **4**s and they will do whatever it takes to create a solid foundation of financial, physical and material security

Life Path 4: Life Choices

in their lives. If this foundation ever wavers, they will stop whatever it is they are doing until they have shored it up again.

4s are also great bargain hunters because they understand the value of money, even though they are extremely generous to the people they love. These are the most loyal friends anyone can ever hope to make, and they will be faithful to a fault in all their relationships.

They take a no-nonsense approach to life and will always tell it like they see it. They are also painstakingly honest. If you want to know who to trust with your money or with a secret, trust a **4**.

Positive **4**s are usually found in positions of authority where trust is paramount, such as holding the purse strings at the local club or social group. They have a finely tuned moral compass and instinctively know the right thing to do in any given situation.

4s also love the outdoors and have a strong affinity with animals and nature. This comes from the strong influence of the material earth element that guides them in everything you do.

They are the salt of the earth, the cornerstones of our society and the workers who are always called in to get the job done. They have high standards of ethics and excellence and are as generous with their time as they are with their money, which often leads them to volunteer for their local charity, children's hospital or animal shelter.

There are few negatives to this Life Path, but they are crippling ones if not dealt with in the right way.

The first one we have already dealt with, which is the **4**'s tendency to obsess about the details in every situation they face, causing them to get bogged down in procrastination and miss out on the juice of life.

Slow and steady might win the race sometimes, but more often than not it pays to react quickly to our changing circumstances in this increasingly fast-paced world. Plus, many of our greatest pleasures come from the spontaneity of jumping aboard the roller-coaster of life and holding our arms high in the air as we ride the ups and downs with the wind in our hair and a big smile on our face.

By facing their fears and learning to trust the voice in their heart, the **4** will discover that the issue of procrastination goes away all by itself. Their heart (Self) always knows what to do, and what not to do, in every given situation.

This is easier written than done, of course, and will involve the **4** going through the painful process of killing off their ego known as the Dark Night of the Self, as described in Part One. It's something we all have to do, however, if we want to rise above the daily diet of fear and insecurity and embrace out immortal, spiritual Self.

A second common negative potential for this Life Path (ie, for those **4**s living in fear) rears its ugly head when their healthy need to feel safe morphs into an unhealthy stubbornness and refusal take even the smallest risk to go after their goals and dreams.

The **4** loves routine and likes everything in their life to be just so. Even the slightest mess, disturbance or deviation from their plan can unsettle them and lead to a conflict, as the quick-tempered **4** either lashes out or, more frequently, retreats into a big, moody storm cloud.

The phrase "lighten up" springs to mind. But don't ever say it out loud to a **4** when they are in one of their moods, unless you are very good at dodging plates, wine glasses and other high-speed projectiles.

4s also sometimes find it difficult to make new friends because they are able to see through a person's "party face" with x-ray-like accuracy in social situations. Yes, they will make many acquaintances. But few people measure up to their very high standards of integrity and honesty, which can lead to repeated disappointments for the **4**, who craves a much deeper connection.

Finally, because all **4**s freely speak their mind and insist on truth and openness, they must be careful not to offend everyone who crosses their path. You could never say that tact was a quality that comes easily to a **4**. Rest assured, though, that if a **4** does choose you as a friend, they will be your friend for life through thick and thin.

All the **4**'s potentially negative patterns can be avoided if they do the inner work to rid themselves of the fear of failure and the fear of rejection. These two fears are the "Evil Twins" that hold the **4** back from taking the plunge into the river of life and just going with the

Life Path 4: Life Choices

flow. They need to be conquered by all Life Paths, but for the **4** they are responsible for all their suffering and absolutely must be eradicated.

Again, this is done by getting out of their head and into their heart. Or, to put it another way – and excuse me while I duck down here under my desk as I write this – by just "lightening up".

* * *

On a more personal level, **4**s have a tendency to struggle in their romantic relationships – even if it is with another **4** – because no one can live up to the impossibly high standards they set for themselves.

Yes, you read that right. The **4** doesn't set the standards for their partner – they set them for themselves, and then when they fail to live up to them they take out their frustration on their partner. Go figure!

This is not exactly a recipe for peace and harmony in the Builder's otherwise lovely and loving home, but it is a perfect example of one of the main reasons why we have relationships – so that we can see our own faults that we need to work on reflected in those of our partner.

Once the **4**, and their partner, recognise this dynamic in action, their relationship will magically transform from one of bickering and criticism into one of spectacular personal growth and Self-awareness.

A relationship for the earthy **4** is seldom going to be the unicorns and rainbows fantasy that the **2** and **6**, for example, might desire. Nor will it be the wild amusement park ride sought by the **3** or the **5**.

The **4** loves passion as much as the next number, but this earthy realist will seldom throw caution to the wind completely in pursuit of love, choosing instead to root their romance firmly in the real world.

What their relationship will be, though, as we'll see in more detail in a moment under Relationship Choices, is the perfect environment for the **4** to face all their fears and learn all their growth lessons.

Seldom can a **4** make the big internal changes on their own. They need to feel supported and protected, and for that they need a close, loving relationship. And for all you partners of **4**s, rest assured you won't get burned. Quite the opposite. You will be rewarded with the

Life Path 4: The Builder

exquisite love and unshakeable loyalty of your **4**, who will never let you down and will go to the ends of the earth and back to fulfill your needs.

* * *

Summary of the positives

Providing the practical **4** develops the ability to trust their feelings and listens to the love in their heart rather than the fault-finding voice in their head, they will overcome their fear of failure and rejection and build a healthy and happy life for themselves, and those they love.

They will also have the confidence to stand up for what is right and fulfill their highest purpose of rooting out injustice and helping others who are in need.

Those who work with the positive energy of **4** will make excellent health and social workers, project managers, builders, bankers and human rights lawyers. They will also create a comfortable home life for themselves and enjoy the company of close friends.

The aware and evolved **4** is a shining light for truth and justice and will bend over backwards to help improve the lives of as many people as they can by volunteering their services to worthy causes.

Key positive words

Honest, faithful, loyal, determined, practical, pragmatic, diligent, hard-working, generous, compassionate, devoted, dependable, down to earth, considerate, conscientious, full of stamina, trustworthy, disciplined, methodical, loving, humanitarian, moral and upstanding.

* * *

Summary of the negatives

Unless the cautious **4** can overcome their obsession with petty details and their fear of taking even the smallest risk, they may miss out on much of the fun of life, veering down the dark side of their Life Path towards procrastination, frustration and even depression.

Few people can create a bigger vortex of negativity than a **4** who doesn't feel safe and secure. If they are not careful, it will suck all the joy out of their life, and the lives of those closest to them.

Ironically, although the **4** is the most trustworthy of Selfs, they have trouble trusting others and can alienate even those closest to them with their moodiness. This only serves to push people away, leading the **4** to be even more certain that no one can be trusted.

If they can't snap themselves out of this vicious cycle, the **4**'s bitterness can hound them their entire life, causing them to suffer the ultimate sadness of feeling alone and unloved.

Key negative words

Stubborn, critical, aloof, moody, jealous, depressed, brooding, dismissive, tactless, workaholic, fearful and intolerant.

***

Self-love is the difference

If you have read Part One, you will already know that your ability to walk the positive side of your Life Path, as opposed to the negative side, is determined by whether you have undertaken the two key stages of personal growth. Or, to put it another way, whether you have taken the two crucial first steps on the path to your life's highest purpose.

The first step towards living your Life Path in the positive is to develop Self-esteem (and if you're wondering what a "Self" is, please take the time to read Part One because it's way too complicated to explain again here).

This feeling of inner confidence is essential to your growth because it allows you to tap into your innate strengths, which you will need if you are going to have any hope of overcoming the numerous obstacles on your path.

Be aware, though, that on its own this first step is never enough, because Self-confidence and Self-esteem are still the work of the ego. The feeling of being "good enough" carries with it an implied sense of needing to be "better than".

So, to reach your full potential and achieve your life's highest purpose, you must also take the second step – which is to rise above the egoic concept of Self-esteem and climb to the much higher ground of Self-love.

Loving your Self does not mean being "full of your Self". It means the opposite. It means being humble because you understand that you are the same as everyone else, no better and no worse. Above all, it means you understand that we are all immortal spirits having a human experience, and therefore we are all, at our core, the same – pure love and pure Source energy. (The Source is also explained in Part One.)

We can see it easily in new-born babies because when we are born into physical form, and before our fear-based ego has had a chance to develop, we are all gorgeous, gurgling bundles of pure, exquisite love.

I am not suggesting you do this, but just imagine you were to place a new-born infant on the pavement of a crowded street and then stand back out of sight. Everyone – and I mean everyone – would stop and tend to it. And the reason they would do this is because, deep down, we all recognise pure love when we see it. We are drawn to it at the most basic level of our being because it is the most strikingly beautiful and compelling force on the planet.

But sadly, as we grow up and go out into the world, our ego takes over and we start to believe – usually during our teenage years – that our ego is who we are. It isn't. Love is who we are.

We are all pure love. We are all extensions of Source energy (or children of "God", whichever phrase you are more comfortable with).

If you can rise above the quasi-religious terminology, I can summarise the two steps like this: Self-esteem is about feeling "good enough", while Self-love is about feeling "God enough".

The reason why loving your Self is so important for your Life Path is because when you start to live your life from the perspective of being

Life Path 4: Life Choices

pure love, everything changes. Suddenly you understand that nothing "out there" in the material world can ever harm you in any way.

Equally, you real-eyes you don't need anything "out there" in the material world to make you feel happy – not the approval of others; no amount of money, fame and power; and not even the love of a good man or woman – because you have all the love you need right there in your own heart, and you can therefore relish the exquisite joy of loving everyone unconditionally without needing anything in return.

That is why Self-love is the secret to working with the positive energy of your Life Path Number. Because when you truly love your Self, the rocky mountain path you've been climbing suddenly becomes an express elevator ride all the way up to the summit of your bliss.

* * *

No Life Path is an island

Although your Life Path Number denotes the main issues you will focus on, you will always work to some degree with the energies of the other numbers as well to become a fully rounded Self.

As a **4** your main work will be in the areas of stability and flexibility, but you will also tackle the key issues of Self-confidence and patience (**1**), co-operation and balance (**2**), creativity and expression (**3**), freedom and discipline (**5**), acceptance and tolerance (**6**), trust and humility (**7**), power and abundance (**8**) and integrity and wisdom (**9**).

It's therefore worth your while to read through the listings for the other Life Path Numbers when your time allows.

* * *

Qualities of your three-digit Birth Code

(Note: Please read the description in Part Two of how 0 operates in your three-digit Birth Code. Also, you can consult the main Life Path listings here in Part Three for each of your Supplementary Birth Numbers (the four possible ones for the

Life Path 4: The Builder

Builder are 1, 2, 3 and 4) to give you a clearer understanding of how their qualities govern your formative years.)

'Millennium Child' 00/4

A Millennium Child born with the remarkably powerful single-digit Birth Code of **4** has come into the world with the potential to achieve something truly spectacular with their life.

All the Millennium Children (those born at the beginning of this century without any Supplementary Birth Numbers) are endowed with extra potential because they will all work with the energy of their Life Path Number with absolute focus and an incredible amount of commitment. (The qualities of the Millennium Children are described in detail in Part Two, Chapter 2.)

The doubly amplified presence of the two 0s in place of their two Supplementary Birth Numbers means these 00/**4** children will be working solely with the supercharged energy of **4** for their entire life, right from the moment they take their first breath.

This gives them a unique capacity to build something of great significance. And if they follow the highest purpose of the **4** – which is to build a stable base from which they can fight injustice – they have the potential to achieve a huge shift in the way we as a species treat our fellow man and woman, as well as how we treat our animals.

This Life Path has an extra special significance, simply because it is by far the rarest of all Birth Codes. There are only four possible dates at the start of the new millennium that add up to 00/**4**: January 1, 2000, January 10, 2000, October 1, 2000 and October 10, 2000.

What makes this Birth Code even more remarkable is the fact that before this century, the last child with a code of 00/**4** was born on October 10, 1100, more than 900 years ago, and there won't be another one born until January 2, 10,000 – a staggering 8000 years from now.

(If this is your number, you will be in your late teens as *Messages from Your Self* is published, so please flip forward to the Choices for Children section under this listing for the Builder to find out more about your positive potential, and the negatives to watch out for.)

Life Path 4: Life Choices

13/4

The presence of <u>1</u> as the first Supplementary Birth Number of this Birth Code means these Builders will work with the powerful fire (action) energy of the Leader (<u>1</u>) during the first formative 18 years of their life, and the creative air (thought) energy of the Creative (<u>3</u>) until full maturity at 36 to help them pursue the highest purpose of the **4** Life Path – which is to build a stable foundation for themselves and use their time, wealth and energy to fight for justice and fairness.

The combination of fire (<u>1</u>), air (<u>3</u>) and earth (**4**) gives them the capacity to become immensely successful, able to take the lead and build a profitable career or business (<u>1</u> and **4**), as well use their creative flair (<u>3</u>) to take advantage of opportunities when they come their way.

As long as they clear their emotional blockages and work with the positive energy of these numbers, their remarkable capacity for hard work and their impressive attention to detailed planning should garner them considerable financial wealth and stability.

Because of the absence of any water (emotion) energy, these Builders will be focused almost exclusively on the practicalities of life, able to take charge of a situation (<u>1</u>), motivate others to join their cause (<u>3</u>) and see all their projects through to a successful conclusion (**4**).

Romantically, they may be a little on the cold side because they tend to be serious and particular in everything they do. They would do well to let their fun-loving <u>3</u> side come to the fore in matters of love.

31/4

This is a mirror of the previous Birth Code, and people walking this Life Path will share many qualities with their <u>13</u>/**4** cousins. The key difference is that during their first formative years – when their personality is established – they will be working with the supplementary air energy of the artistic, social and fun-loving <u>3</u> instead of the driven and ambitious fire energy of <u>1</u>.

Yes, they will still be an earthy **4** through and through – and will therefore be pragmatic, diligent and hard-working – but they will be much less of a loner than the pioneering and focused 13/**4**, and they will lean towards building their life around more creative pursuits.

The 31/**4** will also tend to be slightly less serious and have a richer and more varied social life, due to the outgoing energy of 3 operating during their childhood and teenage years. Their 1 leadership energy then kicks in during early adulthood, helping them climb the corporate ladder or strike out in business for themselves.

Again, as we saw with the 13/**4**, the absence of any water (emotion) energy in their Birth Code means these Builders will be focused almost exclusively on the practicalities of life, able to take charge of a situation (1), motivate others to join their cause (3) and see all their projects through to a successful conclusion (**4**).

In their romantic and personal life, they will probably be slightly more interested than the 13/**4** in taking time out from their busy work schedule for a moment to spend time with their family and friends. But they must still guard against being too practical all the time and learn to let their hair down, especially with their partner.

40/4

Here we have the truly focused Builders whose capacity for material success is matched only by their heightened sense of right and wrong. They will work exclusively with the diligent and pragmatic energy of **4** with no distractions, and they will do so with the extra focus and determination provided by the amplified energy of their 0 Supplementary Birth Number.

So right from their earliest years, these young 40/**4**s will usually be serious children who have an innate awareness of right and wrong. "Fairness for all" will be their catch cry, and they will be organised, practical and focused on the "serious business" of life.

As they grow older, the 40/**4** may well become a little too serious – even, dare I say it, a touch boring – and may need to remember that life is for living and not just all about arriving at their destination.

Also, because of the equitability of the Self-Awareness System™, their heightened capacity to build successful businesses, material

Life Path 4: Life Choices

wealth and harmonious relationships will be offset by an equally heightened capacity to experience the harsh lessons of the negative side of their Life Path.

The negative 40/4 can tend to be extremely stubborn and inflexible, leading them to not only miss out on the juice of life but also be in danger of collapsing in a heap when things don't go their way and their routine is shattered by outside influences.

These negative pitfalls afflict all the **4** Birth Codes, but none so painfully or frequently as the highly sensitive 40/**4**. The difference between the light side of this Birth Code and the dark side is, as always, how much they step out of their ego (fear) and into their heart (love).

Master Number 22/4 – 'The Master Builder'

If you have not already done so, please read my comments in Chapter 8 of Part Two about what numerologists like to call Master Numbers – namely, those Life Path Numbers whose Supplementary Birth Numbers are the same. There are four possible Master Numbers in numerology: 11/**2**, 22/**4**, 33/**6** and 44/**8**.

There is no doubt that having two identical Supplementary Birth Numbers helps you focus on developing the qualities of your Life Path Number during the first 36 years of your life. However, as we have just seen with the Birth Code 40/**4**, they are by no means the only "supercharged" Birth Codes in the Self-Awareness System™.

22/**4**s have the potential to create tremendous amounts of wealth and stability. In the positive, they are excellent problem solvers who are well-grounded, honest, hard-working and unwaveringly loyal.

As well as working with the practical and humanitarian energy of their Life Path Number **4**, they will focus intently in their early years on the double supplementary energy of 2 (the Intuitive).

So while the main purpose of their life is to create a solid foundation and help others less fortunate than themselves, they will be doing so in close co-operation with the people around them, both at home and at school as children and later in their professional life.

Life Path 4: The Builder

The double "water" (emotional) energy of 2 endows them with a heightened capacity for empathy and compassion. All 2s have good social skills and make the best diplomats, counsellors, healers and advisers, and these qualities are especially strong in the Master Builder.

This, combined with the practical qualities of their Life Path Number, means many 22/4s will be extremely successful in business, striking out on their own quite early in life and often building up several companies over the course of their career.

4s are easily the best managers and 2s are the best peacekeepers. When these energies are combined it makes for a very harmonious work environment where they, and those they work with, can tap into their highest potential and produce their best work.

The Master Builder is the rock on whom others lean when times get tough. It is a role they are usually only too happy to perform because all 4s are fiercely loyal friends and all 2s are overwhelmingly concerned about the welfare of others, so it comes naturally for the Master Builder 22/4 to help anyone they meet who might be in need.

But – and this is a huge "but" that would make Kim Kardashian green with envy *(yes, I know it's spelled differently – but it's a good joke, and I'm going with it!)* – the Master Builder also has a heightened potential for walking the dark side of their Life Path Number.

Their challenges will be many, particularly as they often choose to incarnate into a family environment where they may suffer abuse of some kind so they can experience the sort of injustice first hand that they will spend the rest of their lives fighting nobly to eradicate.

Negative 22/4s who are stuck in their fear can be the most rigid and inflexible of people for whom the slightest upset or departure from their carefully planned routine can potentially be devastating. They will benefit greatly from learning to go with the ebb and flow of life and accept that change is an unavoidable part of every Life Path journey.

Also, their intense desire to go out of their way to help those in need can sometimes get the better of 22/4s, who may lose themselves in the problems of others. If they allow this to take over their life, they

Life Path 4: Career Choices

will end up dashing from one "emergency humanitarian mission" to another, sometimes losing their way – and even their sense of identity.

They may spend so much time making sure everyone else is happy that they forget to look after themselves. If they don't find a balance between doing what is best for them and what is best for others they may wind up being resentful, bitter and even angry.

Another negative that 22/4s must watch out for is a tendency to drive themselves to the point of physical and emotional exhaustion by taking on too much all at once. They usually bounce back pretty quickly, though, because they tackle health issues the same way they tackle any other problem: logically and with grit and determination.

22/4s are also perfectionists, which can be a double-edged sword. Whether they are building something or just arranging their furniture, everything has to be just so. They must guard against becoming bogged down in the minutiae of life and obsessing over petty details.

On the whole, though, 22/4 Master Builders – like all the Master Numbers – are more likely to do the inner spiritual work that ensures they end up working with the positive energy of their Life Path.

As long as they remember to take time to nurture themselves and not take themselves – or life – too seriously, they have the ability to achieve remarkable success in almost everything they do.

* * *

2. CAREER AND BUSINESS CHOICES

THE practical 4's innate ability to work diligently and energetically to achieve a goal makes them the world's best managers in any field of commerce. They have an impressive eye for detail, a loyalty to those they work with and a defiant "never say die" attitude that also makes them excellent problem solvers.

Life Path 4: The Builder

The always organised **4** will thrive in a job where patience and perseverance are the key to success. They take instructions gracefully, providing they always know exactly what is being asked of them, and they respond well to order and routine.

In every role, they always demand far more from themselves than they do from others and will be happy to shoulder more than their share of the burden – providing they receive both the recognition and the remuneration they know they deserve.

4s are masterful at planning everything they do down to the Nth degree, ensuring there is little scope for error – or, worse, surprise. This attention to detail that sometimes borders on an obsession has a flip side, however, which can manifest in stubbornness and inflexibility when changes to the original plan need to be made. By their very nature, the **4** resists the concept of a Plan B, preferring to do whatever it takes to make Plan A work.

As long as everything is explained to them in perfect detail, and providing they know precisely what is expected of them, the **4** can go away and work autonomously with a dedication and efficiency that will leave all the other Life Path Numbers gobsmacked.

However, if they don't fully understand the task they are meant to perform, or if someone else tries to muscle in on their territory to take over control, the **4** will react with "great vengeance and furious anger", to quote my favourite line from the movie *Pulp Fiction*.

Their ability to take orders and work quietly and efficiently makes the **4** well-suited to project management roles, where they will often be called in to finish a job that someone else has stuffed up. They also work well in a team, provided they have their own specific set of responsibilities separate from everyone else.

The Master Builder (**22/4**) has a particularly finely tuned moral compass and will almost always find themselves drawn to careers that involve righting wrongs and helping the downtrodden, whether they be families and children in need, cancer and other patients, abused and neglected animals, or Third World issues of starvation and poverty.

Life Path 4: Career Choices

Beneficial career paths

Management, banking, accounting, science, IT, engineering, medicine, law and (of course, for the Builder) construction are all well-suited to the money-savvy **4**.

Other potential careers include the military, law (especially in the field of human rights), law enforcement, education, social work, event management, PR, family services, charity work, animal shelters, mental health, and wellness practitioners.

*(Note that the hard-working and humanitarian **4** is so concerned with helping others that much of their best work will be done on a volunteer basis, whether it be pro bono law, free financial advice for charities, or dedicating their time and energy to support a worthwhile cause.)*

Best business matches

If a **4** goes into business for themselves, they would usually be best to do it in conjunction with a trusted partner because, while the **4** is a fantastic manager, they have a tendency to get bogged down in details and would benefit from a "big picture" influence to open them up to new directions and help them grow the business.

A **1** may not be the best choice because they always need to be top dog and would eventually make a play for control of the company.

The **4** would do better to choose their fellow earth number **8**, or else an intuitive **2** or an idealistic **6**, both of whom could help them take full advantage of new market opportunities while also using their people skills to keep customers and staff happy.

For their creative team, they could choose an artistic **3** and a quick-witted **5** for marketing and sales respectively.

The thoughtful **7** performs best in the essential back-office roles such as research and development and IT. And for a special project that needs someone to take over the reins, a well-rounded **9** or a results-oriented **1** would be ideal.

* * *

3. RELATIONSHIP CHOICES

ONE of the most rewarding aspects about the Self-Awareness System™ is how equitable it is. Each Life Path offers the same opportunities for happiness and fulfillment, albeit in markedly different ways. And each of them also offers the same amount of challenges to force us to grow, although again in very different ways.

This means no Life Path is any "better" or "worse" than any of the others. All of them have their blessings, and all have their obstacles.

In the case of **4**, the blessings centre around their aptitude for hard work, devotion, honesty and loyalty, which are all wonderful qualities in a partner, and their obstacles show up as stubbornness, inflexibility and moodiness, which are sure to cause a certain amount of conflict.

On the positive side, the **4** makes the most loving, faithful and reliable partner. They value a strong, stable relationship above all else and, once committed, will stick to their partner like glue no matter what life throws at them.

They might sometimes appear demanding of their partner by insisting they fit into their perfectly ordered life, rather than the other way around. But really there is only one thing the **4** needs from their lover – and that is 100 per cent, A-grade, 24 karat, rolled-gold honesty in all things and at all times.

Nothing arcs up a **4** quicker than if they sense their partner is holding something back or not telling them the whole story, even about the smallest, most insignificant issue. They have their "bullshit antenna" fully extended and switched up all the way to maximum power, and they can spot the slightest whiff of deceit a mile away.

If you are in a relationship with a **4**, never make the mistake of trying to pull the wool over their eyes. You will fail miserably. There is no such thing as a white lie for a **4**, who would always prefer to hear the truth, no matter how painful for them it might be.

4s also make fantastic homemakers. Their home will always be tidy, warm and welcoming, as well as practical and ordered. Everything has its place, and everything has its purpose. There really is no room

Life Path 4: Relationship Choices

in the **4**'s life for mess and unnecessary clutter, and this can sometimes get on the **4**'s nerves if they have children.

The truth is, earthy **4**s are deeply nurturing people who usually make excellent parents. They will struggle with the whirlwind of chaos a toddler can create in their well-organised life, and they will certainly lean towards being strict with their kids. But this will instill valuable Self-discipline in their children, who will usually grow up to be polite, well-mannered and grounded young Selfs.

Problems arise when something happens to disrupt the **4**'s well-ordered life and throws their plan off track, such as a separation. They know that unless their partner cheats on them they will never leave them and they will fight to the death to save their marriage, so they are always devastated when their partner gives up and walks out.

A momentous event such as this can turn the heartbroken **4** to the dark side of their Life Path Number, causing them to become vengeful, bitter and depressed. It is imperative that they seek help and do whatever it takes to process their pain and understand that when someone ends a relationship, they are not rejecting them – they are merely rejecting a relationship with them. In fact, they are setting them free from a life of bickering and discord to find someone else who is more suited.

If the **4** can understand this "Big T" Truth about relationships, they will move on and become both happier and stronger in their next relationship. If they can't, the consequences can be disastrous and they may struggle to ever find their feet, and love, again.

On a day-to-day basis, the **4** likes to be involved with all family decisions big and small, and their partner would do well to consult them before doing anything that affects them… whether it's organising a dinner out with friends, buying a new cushion for the couch, or even buying clothes for themselves. (Rare is the **4** who doesn't like to have at least some say in how their partner dresses.)

Another area to watch for is the **4**'s perfectionist and stubborn nature. They can easily slip into a negative mood when something in their life isn't going perfectly according to their plan, and when this happens it is paramount for their partner to let them process for themselves without trying to push them towards a decision or shower them with advice, no matter how wise it may be. Let them know you love them and are there for them, and leave it at that.

When the **4** is ready, they will come to you and want to talk about it. At this point it is vital to give them the space – and the time – to fully vent how they are feeling. All **4**s love to talk things through, so sit back, listen and make certain they know you have heard them.

Whenever they feel insecure, for whatever reason, the **4** can tend to become overly critical and judgmental. And if they don't fully understand why they are being asked to do something, they can lash out in a burst of anger.

"Grumpy" doesn't even begin to describe a negative **4,** so when they are in one of their "moods" it's best to give them a wide berth and wait for them to come to you. Try to push a negative **4** and you will know what it feels like to head-butt a rhinocerous.

This may sound like hard work for the partner of a **4**, but I can assure you these little upsets are well worth the trouble – because as long as you are honest with them and make sure they feel both loved and appreciated, you will never find a more loving, committed, loyal, supportive and honest partner than a **4**. They will literally lie down in traffic for the ones they love.

* * *

Sex drive of the 4

4s are not known to be the most adventurous partners in bed. They tend to approach sex the same way they approach everything else: deliberately, methodically and only when they feel like it.

The always pragmatic **4** is also able to use sex to get something they want, and they are not afraid of flirting for the same reason. They have few hang-ups about their sexuality and can usually talk openly about sex because they have long ago explored it – often with several different partners, including some of the same gender.

Life Path 4: Relationship Choices

They do this partly because they are so in tune with their bodies that they feel no fear around exploring all aspects of physical intimacy, but mainly because they hate it when they don't understand something fully… so they will tend to explore their sexuality until they do.

This doesn't mean the ever-practical **4** is cold or boring in bed. Far from it. Once they trust their partner they will delight in opening up the deepest part of themselves to them – and that part is absolutely as deep and beautiful as it gets.

The "feminine energy" **4** in a relationship (and this is a deeply feminine and nurturing number) will be happy to beguile and seduce her masculine partner with spectacular results, but normally only when it suits her. If she is with another **4**, that may be fine. But if she is partnered with any other number – and especially a masculine number (**1**, **3**, **5**, **7** or **9**) – she would do well to consider that her partner's need for fireworks may be greater than hers.

The "masculine energy" **4** in a relationship will have a better balance of masculine and feminine qualities, making him a more willing instigator in the bedroom. He must still be wary of disappointing his partner, however, because even a masculine **4** tends to only feel like sex when it's right for him, which may not be as often – nor as spontaneous – as his partner needs.

Plus, both masculine and feminine **4**s must guard against giving their partner a roving eye. They are always happiest when they are at home and feel comfortable, which means they tend to wear practical, comfy clothes and love flopping on the couch. They would do well to make a regular effort to dress up for their partner (if they are feminine this is a sexy and alluring outfit, and if they are masculine it's a snappy suit) and go out on the town together.

* * *

The compatibility listings that follow will help the always loyal and practical **4** get the most out of their relationships, whether it's with someone they love, a friend or a business partner. You will notice that

Life Path 4: The Builder

the earth energy of **4** is well-matched with other **4**s and their earthy cousin **8**, as well as a **2** or a **6**, whose water gives the earth the nutrients it needs to nurture love. Fire (**1** and **5**) can scald the fragile earth, and air (**3** and **7**) can erode it – so these pairings are likely to throw up more challenges. The **9** usually matches well with all of the numbers.

However, what appears to match you best on the surface may not be what you need in your life right now. All relationships are designed for one purpose and one purpose only – to help us grow along our Life Path. Yes, of course we enjoy the companionship, close connection, sexual intimacy and deep love that relationships give us. But that is now why we have them.

The reason we choose a partner (or, to be more accurate, why our all-knowing Self chooses them for us) is because they are a mirror in which we see our shortcomings and strengths reflected back at us through their shortcomings and strengths.

That is why opposites so often attract, especially in love.

I have written an entire book on this subject called *Leap into Love* which goes into the way relationships work in our lives in great detail. But for now, please real-eyes that when your partner presses one of your buttons, they are doing so not to "piss you off" but because your Self is using them to show you the areas you need to work on.

If you fail to understand this is the main reason why you attracted them into your life in the first place, you will fight each other and may eventually break up. And you will believe their faults were exactly that – their faults – rather than yours reflected back at you.

Worst of all, you will then take the unchanged you with you to your next relationship, and – lo and behold! – exactly the same issues will come up again.

If this sounds familiar. If you have ever asked any of these questions – "Why does this always happen to me?" or "Why do all men cheat?" or "Why are all women so demanding?" or whatever it is for you – then now you know why. It's because you didn't learn from your last partner, so of course your new one will do the same thing.

Life Path 4: Relationship Choices

And this will continue to happen, relationship after relationship, until you real-eyes it is meant to be happening to show you what areas you need to work on in your Self to change and grow.

* * *

One final quick point before we get into it: I need to stress that I disagree with almost every numerologist I know who likes to label relationships "a natural fit", "a neutral fit" or "an unnatural fit", depending on the compatibility of the numbers of the two partners.

All relationships are challenging. That is why we have them, as we have just seen. Yes, sometimes we might choose a partner who is "just like us" for the sake of harmony, but that could be regarded as a cop out if we are truly serious about our personal and spiritual growth.

If you are on a spiritual growth path in this lifetime (and there is no doubt in my mind that you are if you made it through Part One without throwing it in the bin!), then your Self will choose your relationships for you – and they will always be with a partner who will challenge you to grow in exactly the ways you need to grow.

Just because you might discover your current partner has a Life Path Number that doesn't dovetail perfectly with yours, don't fall into the trap of thinking there must be something wrong – or worse, end it with them so you can go out with someone with a "better" number.

Where you are right now on your Life Path is exactly where you are meant to be, and who you are with is exactly who you are meant to be with. So please let these listings help you to look for the lessons in your relationship, rather than look for the door.

And if you are single at the moment, try to remain open-hearted about your next relationship. It doesn't matter what Life Path Number they have, so don't "cherry pick". All that matters is you follow your heart and be open to learning the lessons they can teach you. After all, that's the reason you will attract them into your life in the first place.

* * *

Life Path 4: The Builder

4 & 1
(Stability and Independence)

Love

The grounded and cautious **4** can often struggle in a relationship with an impulsive and reckless **1**. However, if the love and commitment is strong on both sides, this can be a rewarding marriage of opposites.

The pragmatic **4** can ground the flighty **1** and help them avoid a lot of pain and failure by thinking and planning before they leap, just as the spontaneous **1** can teach the **4** not to take life too seriously and that's it's fun sometimes to take a risk just for the hell of it.

As a wise friend of Joel – Tom Cruise's memorably uptight character in the classic teen angst movie *Risky Business* – says to him: "Sometimes, Joel, you've just got to say 'What the f...!'"

There will definitely be arguments with this pairing, especially when the **4** criticises the **1** for being so reckless (and they will... often), and the **1** gets fed up with the cautious **4** for pouring cold water on their Big Ideas (which they will also do... even more often).

But as we have already seen, relationships are designed to bring two people together to help each other grow. So instead of lashing out at each other, the **4** has a wonderful opportunity to learn how to enjoy more of life, and the **1** would do well to heed some of the warnings of the **4** and learn the value of proper planning.

On a day to day basis, the **4** must guard against being too boring for the **1** and also try to find ways of supporting their partner rather than undermining them. Equally, the **1** must remember to include the **4** in their decisions and real-eyes their words of caution are not meant as a criticism (even though they might feel like it) but are a genuine attempt to avoid the **1** getting hurt.

Romantically, the **1** wants fire and brimstone, while the **4** wants sensible, mature and measured engagement. Problems will occur unless both can value the other for what they bring to the table – which is usually the diametric opposite of each other.

Remember that when disagreements arise (and they will because all relationships are about growth, as we saw earlier), take the time to sit down and figure out what you are meant to be learning from your partner – then kiss them and thank them for the insight.

If the **4** and the **1** can learn these valuable lessons, this can be an extremely successful relationship.

The ambitious and energetic **1** will benefit from the grounded level-headedness of the **4**, just as the conservative **4** will benefit from being pushed to achieve far more than they ever dreamed they could by the relentless ambition of the **1**.

When the **4** stops finding fault with everything the **1** says and does and learns to trust them, the **1** will want to include the **4** in all their grand adventures, laughing and dancing through life together.

Good luck, stay open and honest… and enjoy the many valuable lessons this relationship can give you.

Friendship

In relationship, where the purpose is to help each other heal their wounds and become stronger and more evolved, this earth/fire match has the potential for great advancement.

But where a **4** and a **1** are just friends, with no commitment, the result will almost always end in tears because both the **4** and the **1** want to feel they are in control, and yet they are coming at it from opposite ends of the spectrum.

1s are impulsive go-getters whose only concern is to break new ground with no thought of how to achieve it, whereas **4**s are practical managers whose focus is on the process and who look upon the **1**'s lack of proper planning with abject disdain.

Most **4**s and **1**s will argue like cats and dogs over the relative virtues of practicality versus inspiration, with the **1** becoming frustrated and even angry at the **4**'s obsession with detail and process, and the **4** despairing of the **1**'s impulsiveness and impetuosity.

Yes, they can be friends, but only if they recognise each other's differences as lessons to refine their own view of the world.

Business

These two numbers should probably avoid going into business as partners, unless they are both so evolved that they are able to learn the valuable lessons each has to teach the other.

The take-charge and impulsive **1** will be infuriated by the pedantic and cautious **4**, just as the process-driven **4** will be exasperated by the recklessness and unreliability of the **1**. However, it doesn't take a rocket scientist (or a decorated psychoanalyst) to see that the **1**'s Big Picture view of the world is just what the conservative **4** needs to see, or that the efficient and diligent **4**'s knack for organisation is perfect for the disorganised **1** to achieve their grand goals.

If they can learn to respect each other's skill set, this partnership can take over the world. But if they can't, it will last about five minutes.

* * *

4 & 2
(Stability and Co-operation)

Love

The feminine energy of these two numbers brings a lot of love and compassion to this pairing. Both the earthy **4** and the watery **2** are big-hearted homemakers who like to have a living space that is warm, welcoming and tidy. They also share a common desire to feel nurtured and appreciated by their partner.

The **4** is the ultimate builder and organiser, while the **2** has an eye for style and design. And they both want their home to be a safe haven where they can nurture each other and live in relative harmony.

There will also usually be the soothing energy of pets in their lovely home as well, because both are passionate animal lovers.

The always talkative **4** will enjoy the **2**'s ability to share with their partner how they are feeling. Equally, the **2**'s love of a good "D&M" will please the **4**, who needs to be heard and loves nothing better than to be able to share their innermost thoughts with their partner.

Life Path 4: Relationship Choices

These two will talk for hours long into the night, well after all the other numbers may have got bored and gone to bed.

Both the **4** and the **2** are looking for absolute commitment in their relationship and like to feel safe with their partner above all else. Once they begin a romance, it is likely to become serious very quickly, and they will often move into together within a matter of weeks.

They also share a hatred of deceit and know instinctively when their partner is not being honest with them. This willing openness to share all they are thinking and feeling quickly creates a mutual trust and understanding that can take other lovers much longer to achieve.

One thing that could upset this apparently idyllic partnership is if the more outgoing **2** gets bored with the **4**'s obsessive need for routine and stability. The **2** wants to travel the world and meet new people and may struggle with the **4**'s lack of adventure. Similarly, the **4**'s need to feel that everything they do has a specific purpose may sometimes lead them to resent the **2**'s tendency to act on impulse.

This pair will have plenty of common interests but their relationship will work best when the **4** gives the **2** leeway to pursue their "frivolous" and "time-wasting" adventures, and the **2** resists the urge to pester the **4** to lighten up and come play with them.

Another potential pitfall is the emotional **2**'s need for almost constant reassurance that their partner truly loves them. This will annoy the loyal **4**, who never – ever – strays once they have committed to a partner. But their lack of romance and inability to easily reach out and show their affection will worry the needy **2**, who may take it as a sign that the **4** has indeed gone cold on them.

Also, the emotional **2** may be a bit unstable for the pragmatic **4**, who in return may be a bit stuck in their ways for the spontaneous **2**. The faithful **4** will never stray, but if they are not able to indulge the **2**'s need for fun – especially in bed – there is a danger the needy **2** will look elsewhere for the excitement and intimacy they crave.

On the whole, though, this is one of the more harmonious pairings for the **4**. As long as they give their **2** partner plenty of freedom to indulge their love of adventure, they should live a long and happy

Life Path 4: The Builder

life together. Good luck, stay open and honest… and enjoy the deep and meaningful connection this relationship can give you.

Friendship

The nurturing **4** and the emotional **2** will usually find they have much in common as friends, just as they do in a relationship. They will likely forge a close, loyal bond based on their ability to open up about how they are truly feeling, leading to a mutual trust and admiration.

They will have much to talk about. In fact, they will probably sit up all night talking about their lives until the cows come home, eat a quick grass meal, have a shower, get changed and go out again.

The adventurous **2** may sometimes find the pragmatic **4** a little too reserved for their liking. And the money-conscious **4** may baulk at the **2**'s expensive tastes – especially when they both go out to dinner or to a club and split the bill. But overall, they are well-matched because they are both honest and upfront at all times and will seldom allow any minor disagreement over money to mar their friendship.

Business

This is a good match. Both partners share the common goal of helping others live a happier and more healthy life, and they have the financial nous to manage the purse strings and ensure it succeeds.

The **4** is unbeatable in their ability to manage a project and see it through to completion, but they often get bogged down in details and fail to grasp opportunities for growth when they come. This is where the **2** comes in. They, too, are good managers but their keep their eyes up on the horizon, and their heightened sense of intuition can lead them to spot gaps in the market that the **4** simply won't see.

Also, while the **4** is brilliant at planning and organisation, they can be judgmental of others' perceived shortcomings, which can cause discord among their staff. The **2**'s proven people skills will be able to smooth over any upsets and keep the team pulling in the same direction.

***

Life Path 4: Relationship Choices

4 & 3
(Stability and Expression)

Love

The conservative and materially focused **4** and the flighty, avant-garde **3** have little in common in the way they approach life, which means this earth/air relationship will always be an opportunity for growth rather than a recipe for peace and mutual understanding.

The practical and feminine **4** wants to build a home and a career from the ground up, while the creative and masculine **3** wants to follow their heart and experience all life has to offer.

The artistic **3** is spontaneous and likes to take life as it comes, while the pragmatic **4** dislikes surprises and wants to plan everything in advance. Add to this the **4**'s love of routine and the **3**'s love of change, and it's easy to see why this is far from a harmonious match.

However, if these two can find a middle ground between careful planning and reckless spontaneity, they have an excellent opportunity to teach each other how to get the most out of life.

As I have repeated often, relationships are primarily about growth, and this is certainly one of those pairings. The **4** would benefit enormously from adopting some of the **3**'s love of excitement and adventure, while the **3** would do well to take on board what the **4** has to teach them about proper planning and discipline.

Number **3** wants romance, passion and fireworks but often has little idea about the value of serious commitment, leading them to flit from one relationship to another. They may live out their lives without ever really knowing what true love feels like, because it requires hard work and dedication to create a bond that stands the test of time.

Meanwhile, the conservative **4** wants the deep loving connection that devotion to just one partner gives them, but they are in danger of living out their lives stuck in their comfort zone without ever having the courage to explore all this magnificent world has to offer.

If each can learn from the other, both partners may be able to have their cake and eat it too, complete with icing and a cherry on top.

It won't be easy, but the **4** who learns to embrace the **3**'s passion for life will be all the better for it, just as the **3** who learns the value of discipline and careful planning from the **4** will find that rushing around skimming the surface of life will never give them the intense pleasure of truly committing to another person who loves them.

Good luck, stay open and honest... and try to see the world through your partner's eyes. You will be all the better for it if you can.

Friendship

Will these two meet at a party one day and instantly become besties for life because "OMG! We have so much in common!"

Um... no. Not ever. Not in a million years.

It's hard to find such diametrically opposed personalities as the earthy, conservative **4** and the flighty, devil-may-care **3**. Even the firefly **5** has more in common with the practical **4**, as we'll see in a moment.

The **3**'s butterfly personality and headstrong nature may irritate the **4** right from the outset, while the **4**'s serious personality and equally headstrong nature means these two heads are likely to clash.

Yes, these two can get along when they have to in a social or family setting, but the **4** may find the **3** irritatingly unpredictable, while the **3** may find the outspoken **4** to be a little bit too judgmental.

Business

For all the reasons we have just seen, this is as challenging a match for business partners as it is for friends and lovers. In a relationship, at least they will have an opportunity to learn from each other. But in business, where money is involved, the stakes are just too high.

The hard-working and diligent **4** may quickly grow to resent the effervescent **3**'s ability to attract people – and money – to their cause with just the batt of an eyelid or the curl of a flirtatious smile. And the impulsive **3** may resent having to account for every dollar and cent they spend to woo customers on what the **4** sees as frivolous activities.

Life Path 4: Relationship Choices

If the **4** can real-eyes that the **3**'s instincts are almost always right and give them the space – and the budget – to do their thing, the business will thrive.

Equally, if the **3** takes the time to explain what they are doing to the **4** and respects them for their ability to manage the details with which they can't be bothered, this partnership can kick a lot of goals. But those are some big "ifs", and each will usually be better advised to choose someone more like them to go into business with.

* * *

4 & 4
(Stability and Loyalty)

Love

Like definitely attracts like, and two **4**s will certainly see eye to eye on most issues and be able to love each other without any effort at all, simply by asking themselves: "How would I like to be loved?"

But the danger with this pairing is that both partners are so set in their ways and so happy to stay at home in their comfort zone that they may stagnate and miss out on many of the joys – and lessons – of life.

If two elderly **4**s meet each other late in their lives, I can honestly say they would be mad not to shack up together – even if their connection is more "companion" than "lover" – because they share so many interests that they will delight in whiling away their twilight years in blissful conversational harmony.

But for younger **4**s, there is a real risk of stasis. Yes, each will relish the other's loyalty and honesty and feel able to commit without fear of rejection. But neither will tend to push the other to expand and grow, which – as I hope you real-eyes by now – is the whole reason we have relationships, at least in our younger years.

When two **4**s come together, they will forge a solid connection built on mutual respect and understanding. Which is great. But if that all sounds just a little bit predictable and boring, it's because it is.

Life Path 4: The Builder

A ship is safest when it's in harbour, but that's not what a ship is built for. In the same way, the conservative **4** is safest in a relationship with another **4**, but that's not why it came here.

The **4**, like all Selfs, came here to experience as much of the world as it can so it can grow to know its Self as pure conscious love and return to "replenish" the Source. (If that statement elicits in you a "What the...?" response, please stop and read Part One.)

So, like the ship, the **4** needs to sail outside its comfort zone and head out to see (to sea) what the world has to teach them. In this they may do better with a supportive and brave water partner (**2** or **6**), but providing both earthy **4**s are willing to leave the comfort of their well-ordered home and their meticulously planned life and go in search of adventure, like Sinbad, this pairing can bring them rich rewards... because there is no one you would rather have by your side when you face the unknown than someone you trust with your life.

Good luck, stay open and honest... and enjoy all the trust and companionship that this rewarding relationship can give you.

Friendship

Two **4**s, when they meet, will delight in finding someone who is "just like them" and can listen as well as talk. They will bond in their common need to be heard and understood, and they will build a close friendship based on their mutual values of trust, loyalty and honesty.

Or they will fight like cat and cat, scratching each other's eyes out as they try to score points off each other in a no-holds-barred battle to expose the other as a fraud.

No one speaks their mind as easily, or as frankly, as a **4**. And while every other Life Path Number will shy away from such a confrontation, in a social setting such as a cocktail party another **4** will take up the challenge with glee – giving as good as they get and responding to every verbal lunge with a riposte worthy of an Olympic fencing champion.

This isn't a fight to death, it's just the way **4**s like to find out who they are dealing with. And depending on how the other responds, they will either lay down their swords and swear undying allegiance to each other, or grab a canape and move on to their next target.

Business

If the **4** wants to go into business, they would be advised to choose anyone other than another **4** to be their partner – simply because they are already the world's best manager, so why would they need another?

All **4**s are brilliant at handling money, organising the backroom team and making sure they have thought of – and planned for – every possible eventuality. But what they lack is the imagination to see, and grasp, new opportunities as they come along.

The risk-averse **4** can easily get stuck in a rut, albeit it a well-costed, beautifully-built and energy-efficient rut. They will achieve a level of success because they are so efficient and hard-working that a goal, once set, will always become a reality. But what they are not so good at is reacting to changing circumstances, which is why they need a partner who is able to see the bigger picture.

In this they would do best to team up with a watery **2** or **6**, because they bring both passion and compassion to the table without the irresponsibility of an airy **3** or **7** or the bossiness of the fiery **1** or **5** – none of which sits well with the pragmatic and process-driven **4**.

***

4 & 5

(Stability and Freedom)

Love

OMG! Just look at the diametrically opposed qualities that define these two most incompatible of Life Path Numbers: "Stability" and "Freedom". How is that ever going to work? You'd have more luck mixing oil and water, or mating a Great Dane with a chihuahua.

The conservative **4** is a feminine earth number who wants to diligently build a stable home life focused on financial security and physical health, while the rebellious **5** is a masculine fire number who wants to charge around the world tilting at windmills and partying until dawn with a bunch of prurient, pill-popping Patagonian polyamorists.

Talk about chalk and cheese! These two have as much in common as a blackboard and a water biscuit.

If both partners are still stuck in their ego and have not yet woken up to the fact that the whole reason we attract a partner into our life is so we can learn the valuable lessons they have to teach us, then this pairing will last about 30 seconds.

However, and I speak from experience here as a mercurial **5** who dated a wonderfully loving and loyal **4** for five years, the opportunity for these two numbers to teach each other the lessons they need to learn to grow both spiritually and emotionally are unparallelled.

The reckless and risk-taking **5** values their freedom above all else, but they will never be truly free until they learn the value of discipline and commitment that is second nature to the well-grounded **4**.

Equally, the conformist and risk-averse **4** values their stability above all else, but they may miss out on all the joys of life unless they learn to live in the moment, which is second nature to the epicurian **5**.

Good luck, stay open and honest… and make sure you learn the valuable lessons that each of you can teach the other.

Friendship

As well as being fiercely loyal, which makes them a most trusting and trustworthy friend, the **4** is also passionately honest, which means they usually speak the truth without pausing to consider that perhaps the truth is not something their restless **5** friend wants to hear.

Most **5**s spend much of their time in denial of the harsh realities of life, preferring – like Don Quixote – to live in a fantasy world where they battle the forces of oppression without achieving anything other than perhaps a wounded windmill or two. They certainly don't want some super-fit and impossibly wealthy **4** telling them that their entire life is a pointless waste of time… even when it is.

This, as well as their radically different approaches to life, is why these two numbers will seldom become friends, let alone close friends. Which is a shame, because – as we saw just now in the "Love" section – they both have so much to teach each other.

Business

Aha! Now this is one area where the grounded and diligent **4** and the outgoing and charming **5** can benefit each other in ways that are not only mutually beneficial but profoundly profitable as well.

Providing each takes the time to appreciate the other for all they do – the **4** for running a tight ship and the **5** for navigating effortlessly through the storm – this can be a most beneficial business pairing.

On their own, the reckless and easily bored **5** would be completely incapable of managing the business, just as the **4** would be incapable of looking up from the accounts to see the big picture and take advantage of the growth opportunities when they come along.

But together, they can fill in the gaps of each other's skill sets and enjoy considerable success – the **4** holding the purse strings and driving the business with their knack for organisation, and the **5** winning new clients and broking new deals with their tireless optimism.

* * *

4 & 6

(Stability and Romance)

Love

Have you ever visited someone's house and been struck by the warm, welcoming energy of the place before you've even stepped through the architecturally designed front door into a stylish hallway straight from the pages of *Vogue Living*, as homely smells of freshly baked bread and furniture polish mix with the sound of well-behaved children playing with a puppy in the immaculately groomed garden?

Life Path 4: The Builder

If you have, chances are the people who live there are a **4** and a **6**, because these lovers are all about making their home as comfortable, welcoming and harmonious as they possibly can.

Yes, some other Life Paths love to create stylish and hospitable homes as well, especially the watery **2** and earthy **8**, but this perfectly matched pairing takes the art of domestic bliss to a whole new level.

The nurturing **6** wants nothing more than to raise a family and shower them with love in a beautiful home, while the pragmatic **4**'s attention to detail means everything in their home matches perfectly. There will not be a single vase or pot plant out of place.

Both the **4** and the **6** are dyed-in-the-wool perfectionists, a quality that can cause a great deal of friction in many relationships. But these two are so well-matched in their fastidious need for everything to be "just so" that it will seldom become a problem. They both share the same ideals, they are both loyal and honest, and they are both willing to shoulder more than their fair share of the domestic responsibilities.

Towels left lying on the bathroom floor after a shower, or dirty clothes piled up on the bedroom floor, would send either of these nit-pickers into spasms of apoplectic rage. But it just isn't going to happen when they live together. Even their kids will be tidy – because, when they were younger, they would have been properly schooled by their parents in the old-fashioned values of manners and respect.

Neither of these partners is particularly touchy-feely in their relationships, so physical intimacy could be an area of concern that these two will need to work on. Also, the **4**'s serious nature can sometimes be draining for the more upbeat **6** and they would do well to lighten up, while on the other side the controlling **6** must be careful not to step on the **4**'s toes too often and would do well to learn the relationship-saving skill of compromise.

All up, though, this well-matched pairing is one of the most harmonious in the entire Self-Awareness System™ and bodes well for a long and happy life together.

Good luck, stay open and honest… and enjoy the many comforts of a peaceful and loving home that this relationship can give you.

Friendship

The loyal **4** and the nurturing **6** will usually find they have a lot in common as friends, just as they do in a relationship. Both these numbers are open, honest and generous, which will allow them to forge a close bond based on mutual trust and admiration.

They are both naturally cautious and sensible and have similar goals in life, which will give them much to talk about. The pragmatic and well-grounded **4** may sometimes find the idealistic **6** a little flighty for their taste, just as the passionate **6** might occasionally tire of the **4**'s obsession with details.

But overall, they are so alike that forming a lasting friendship will be as easy for them as stepping purposefully off a log.

Business

"Compromise" is the buzzword here.

It's not a quality that comes easily to either of these fastidious numbers and, just as in a romantic relationship, the success of this pairing will depend largely on whether these two perfectionists can find a middle ground when disputes arise.

In many ways, running a business is harder than living together, so the need for compromise is even more crucial. But providing both have clearly defined roles and resist the urge to nitpick, these diligent partners can patiently build a successful business from the ground up.

***

4 & 7
(Stability and Understanding)

Love

The earth energy of the **4** and the air energy of the **7** seldom make for a particularly harmonious loving relationship, simply because both are just as set in their ways as the other and are equally as reluctant to

Life Path 4: The Builder

compromise on their basic values, so they have limited potential to find a peaceful middle ground.

The solitary and spiritual **7** wants to have plenty of space to pursue their studies, free from the expectations of their partner. Meanwhile, the particular and fussy **4** wants to feel free to consult their partner about a million times a day on every single decision, ranging from what they are going to eat for dinner (the **7** couldn't care less) to where their lives are going (the **7** has absolutely no idea).

In some respects, the earthy **4**'s pragmatic and well-grounded personality is the perfect foil for the airy **7**'s idealistic and spiritual focus, allowing them to ground themselves in the so-called "real world" of material stability. However, the **7** may quickly tire of what they see as the **4**'s mundane concerns. All they want to do is solve the big riddles of human existence, while the **4** wants to know if they are going to insure their home with this company or that.

Equally, the financially savvy **4** may tear their hair out trying to convince their **7** partner to come out of their study and look through the latest energy company brochures with them so they can save 30c a year on their gas bill, while the **7** is trying to come to grips with the finer points of astrophysical energetic spectro-dynamics as defined by the latest reimagining of the Keynesian economic paradigm.

These two have much to teach other about love, life and stopping to smell the roses. But they are both so serious, even Eddie Izzard may struggle to get them to lighten up over dinner and a show.

Good luck, stay open and honest… and enjoy the lessons about compromise and flexibility you can learn from each other.

Friendship

On the surface, the pragmatic and realistic **4** and the deep-thinking and conceptual **7** appear to have little in common, but look a little deeper and you will see how these two can sometimes find a great deal of common ground as friends and mutual admirers.

Both numbers have a highly evolved intuition and are acutely aware of their divine, spiritual nature. Plus, they both have finely tuned "bullshit meters" that allow them to stay well clear of cheaters and fakers, which repulse the honest **4** and appall the idealistic **7**.

Add to this their common desire to think through every problem they encounter by researching the issue in great detail and exploring all possible avenues towards finding the best solution, and it's easy to see how these two can see eye to eye on a great many topics.

The **4**'s obsession with the minutiae of life may irritate the **7**, who instinctively knows the best way forward. And the **7**'s need to spend long periods alone contemplating the big questions of life may frustrate the practical **4**, who just wants to get the job done as quickly as possible.

But on the positive side, these two friends will always respect each other's attention to detail and they will value each other for their generosity and humanitarian qualities – even if their friendship is not destined to be a deep or abiding one.

Business

This is a beneficial partnership for business, because the practical earth energy of **4** will be happy to look after the everyday details of running and growing the company, leaving the egotistical and dominant **7** to steer the ship.

As long as the often aloof and solitary **7** takes the time to share with their **4** partner everything they are thinking (which is a lot), and the detail-focused **4** is happy to let the extraordinarily intelligent **7** take the reins and decide the direction of the business, this pairing can create an extraordinary amount of wealth and success.

***

4 & 8

(Stability and Ambition)

Love

"Earth to Number **4**. Earth to Number **4**. Come in, Number **4**. Your perfect life partner is waiting for you!"

Life Path 4: The Builder

Here at the Self-Awareness System™ Ground Control Situation Room we have expert teams of NASA-qualified relationship counsellors working round the clock monitoring banks of computer data to find everyone in the entire universe an ideal mate.

For some lovelorn lonely hearts, this task can be more challenging than putting a man on the Moon. But for these universally compatible earth numbers, finding a love that lasts with each other is easier than putting a man on a bicycle.

The earthy **4** and the equally earthy **8** are as alike as root canal therapy and a Justin Bieber concert. (Sorry to all you young Bieber fans, but you will grow out of it one day soon, I promise you.)

In fact, they are so alike that in some ways this relationship just doesn't need to happen, unless both partners have already learned all their personal growth lessons in their 249 previous incarnations and have come here this time simply to fall in love, earn wads of cash together, drink absurdly expensive cocktails by their infinity pool overlooking Monte Carlo Harbour, and shag each other senseless while listening to any music other than Justin Bieber.

These two lovers' mutual earthiness is the key to this pairing's success. The goal-oriented and competitive **8** will love that their equally pragmatic **4** partner understands and supports their need to go out into the world and win. And the more homely but equally professional and focused **4** will delight in their **8** lover's desire to create a strong and stable home for their family.

It doesn't matter if the masculine partner in their relationship is the **4** and the feminine partner is the **8**, or whether it's the other way around, these two well-grounded lovers will usually gladly give each other more than enough space to do their own thing without complaining that they don't spend enough quality time together.

The only real banana skin in this relationship could occur if one partner betrays the other's trust. Both numbers tend to be fiercely honest, and they demand the same in return. Plus, they both have excellent lie-detector minds, so if one decides to cheat on the other, they will be caught out and the fairytale will be over.

As long as they stay true, though, there is no reason why these two well-suited earthy lovers can't enjoy an emotionally and materially successful relationship that stands the test of time.

Good luck, stay open and honest... and relish the exquisite bliss of finding your "soulmate".

Friendship

Yes. Absolutely. For all the reasons outlined above, these two well-grounded and pragmatic friends will see eye-to-eye on almost every topic, leading them to forge a close and intimate connection. In fact, if they are not single but are sexually matched, they must be careful not to spend too much time together or else their friendship may threaten one or both of their relationships.

Providing clear barriers are drawn, these two Best Friends Forever can support each other, encourage each other and push each other to ever greater heights of success.

There's even a chance that they might decide to pool their resources, if their respective relationships are strong enough, and go into business together. As we're about to see...

Business

When it comes to stamina and a capacity for sustained hard work, no one comes closer to the detail-focused and diligent **4** than the equally pragmatic **8**, which makes them perfect business partners.

Neither will feel the other is failing to pull their weight, and while the **8** wants to go out in pursuit of the Next Big Deal, the **4** has no such lofty needs and will happily run the business like clockwork while the **8** flexes their deal-making muscles.

As long as each acknowledges the other's efforts, and the spoils are shared evenly, this pairing has the potential to achieve great wealth in whatever enterprise they embark on together.

* * *

Life Path 4: The Builder

4 & 9
(Stability and Passion)

Love

One numerologist I know has this to say about a **4** and a **9**: "These two have next to nothing in common. Not recommended for any kind of interaction, let alone a relationship."

While this is definitely a bit harsh, and misses the crucial point that even the most incompatible of relationships is always worthwhile for the lessons we can learn from them, it does a pretty good job of warning that this pairing will always be more about growth than anything else.

Providing that both partners real-eyes their love for each other is based on helping each other to change and grow, rather than validating each other's faults and failings, then this can be one of the most important relationships in their lives. Sure, their time together won't be all beer and skittles, let alone champagne and lawn tennis, but it will be ultimately rewarding and well worth the effort.

Let's list the differences between these two numbers, and then look for the lessons contained in them.

The conservative **4** despises the superficiality of the "look at me, I'm so wonderful" social whirl and chooses instead to spend their time at home, or in the company of close, like-minded friends, while the **9** is an avidly social number who wants to mix with as wide a circle of friends and strangers as they can.

The often reticent **4** wants stability and companionship, while the normally expressive **9** wants passion and fireworks.

The practical **4** can be as controlling of their partner as they are of everything else, while the freedom-loving **9** hates to be told what to do.

The cautious **4** wants to build their home and their relationship from the ground up, while the impatient **9** wants to have it all now.

The list goes on and on, but you get the idea. The point is that in every difference lurks a valuable lesson for both partners.

Life Path 4: Relationship Choices

The **4** needs to get out more and learn how to have fun, while the social **9** is often hurt by superficial people taking advantage of them and would be wise to adopt some of the **4**'s skepticism.

The reserved **4** could do with learning how to be more passionate and adventurous, while the **9** frequently gets burned by wearing their heart on their sleeve and would benefit from some of the **4**'s caution.

The **4** loves to give advice and needs to learn to live and let live, while the headstrong **9** doesn't take advice well, often to their detriment.

The deliberate **4** can take far too long to make up their mind, which means they may miss out on all sorts of business and romantic opportunities, while the impatient **9** can suffer from financial hardship and emotional rejection when they jump in without thinking, and they would do well to learn how to take the time to plan properly.

So, yes, on the surface my numerologist friend is right – these two do have virtually nothing in common. But that is precisely why this could be the most valuable relationship of both their lives if they are open to learning from each other.

Good luck, stay open and honest… and if fights break out (they probably will) try to look past your differences and see the lessons.

Friendship

As with a loving relationship, this is definitely a case of opposites attracting. Outside of their shared humanitarian views, the cautious **4** and the confident **9** have such different tastes, values and personalities that it's hard to imagine them taking the time to get to know each other unless they find themselves stuck in a lift together for at least 10 hours.

Which is a shame, because these two have so much to teach each other… IF they could see beyond the 731 things that annoy them.

That's one big-assed if, though.

Business

There are only so many ways to say this, but I'm going to try to come up with as many as I can to make sure the message is crystal clear: No, definitely not, never in a million years, no way Jose, uh-uh, are you

Life Path 4: The Builder

serious? are you kidding? are you nuts? what part of "no" don't you understand? I could say "yes" but I'd be lying, nope, nein, negative, negatory, not on your nelly, not on your life – and my favourite (thank you, Austin Powers): "How about NO, you crazy Dutch bastard!"

* * *

4. HEALTH CHOICES

AS with everything they do, the detail-obsessed **4** will approach their physical health with the same passion and laser-sharp focus they bring to all their decisions. They will consider every possible diet and exercise regime, read everything that has ever been written about them, and then narrow the field down to two or three possible contenders.

They will then try each of their "finalists" to discover which gives them the specific results they want. And when they light upon the choice that suits them best, they will stick with it through thick and thin, fastidious in their dietary discipline and unwavering in their exercise regime.

As lovers of routine and sticklers for seeing any project through to completion, the **4** finds it easier to maintain a healthy diet and exercise schedule than anyone else. Rain, hail or shine, they will be out there doing their boot camp at 6am, or their yoga class after work, while others have caved in to the temptation of more sleep in the morning, or "just a couple" at the pub with their colleagues after work.

4s need to guard against overdoing it, however. Most of them are workaholics, and if they expend too much additional energy on their exercise routine they can run their bodies into the ground. They need to pace themselves and ensure they don't wear themselves out.

Fatigue and emotional exhaustion are common ailments for the **4**, as are joint pain, lower back problems, intestinal disorders (especially indigestion and ulcers) and headaches.

Skin ailments are also common and particularly upsetting for the **4**, who has a deep desire to present an immaculate visage to the world that matches their need for perfection in all things.

As any **4** reading this will know, everything that they feel on the inside will always manifest on the outside. So when they are at peace and feel relaxed and fulfilled, their skin will be clear. But when there is inner turmoil or anxiety (especially deep feelings of vulnerability and insecurity), they will experience outbreaks of pimples, rashes, wrinkles and other skin complaints.

One final word of caution for the **4**: they will frequently suffer from dis-eases that cannot be easily diagnosed, even by the most astute and intuitive medical professionals. The main areas of concern are their digestive system, which often fails to give them enough energy for their hectic daily life no matter how good their diet is, and their skin.

The solution to the mystery is invariably an emotional one, which is why it is so elusive to traditional medical practitioners.

The **4**'s obsessive approach to solving any perceived "problem" may lead them to consume truckloads of unnecessary vitamins, pills and potions – when all along, the answer is never a physiological one. They simply need to breathe, meditate, relax and let all their worries go (no one is more capable of being stubborn and controlling than a **4**!) and just grow with the flow of life.

As soon as they stop resisting what is (and Source knows that is never easy to do for a **4**), all of the physical manifestations of their emotional fears and insecurities will disappear quicker than they can say to their waiter: "Forget the alfalfa soy burger and organic prune juice... I'll have the steak, fries and a bottle of red wine please."

Ailments to watch out for

As we have just seen, the most common physiological symptoms of the **4**'s "wound-up-as-tight-as-a-ball-of-string" emotional state of being are to be found on their skin (the "face" they show the world) and in their gut (their ability to let life in).

Other ailments common to the often rigid and inflexible **4** are found, not surprisingly, in their joints (flexibility) and in their back (monetary worries, lack of support).

Headaches, migraines and depression are also symptoms of the hyperactive **4**'s inability to switch off, relax and forget about all the things that still need to be done.

Effective therapies

There is only one therapy that truly works for the **4** – and it's not rushing around frantically exercising with the same frenetic sense of purpose as they do everything else. It's relaxation. Deep mental, emotional, spiritual and physical relaxation.

Spa baths, saunas, meditation, massage, stretching, yoga, reflexology, facials and deep breathing are magic formulas to cure all the **4**'s ailments, which are almost invariably caused by stress.

When they want to be more active and break a sweat, body/mind balancing exercises such as Pilates and gymnastics, or brisk walks in nature, are best. However, the **4** would do well to avoid anything too extreme and exhausting, such as running, aerobics and spin classes.

Perhaps the best "exercise" of all for the **4** is sleep. Lots and lots of relaxing, mind-replenishing, body-repairing sleep.

Diet choices

The focused and detail-obsessed **4** will doubtless research all four and a half million diets out there before deciding which one is best for them. They will try everything in their mistaken belief that if they just ate the right food, their stress-related ailments would disappear – from the "Eat Right For Your Knees Diet" to the "Atkinson Raw Baby Seal Diet" to the "Paleo-Jurassic Vegetarian Brontosaurus Pooh Diet".

The truth is, the **4**'s ailments are almost always psychosomatic, just like for the rest of us. Almost every "disease" of the body is never anything more or less than a "dis-ease" of the mind, providing they live a fundamentally healthy lifestyle. So when the **4** learns to master their emotions and find the inner peace they seek, they could scoff down plates of fatted kangaroo buttocks drenched in pureed bandicoot bile and be just as energised as if they sipped organic oxygenated Amazon rainwater through a straw made of free-range Himalayan tea-tree leaves.

In the absence of an angry bandicoot and a kangaroo with a bum the size of Nicki Minaj's, these are the best dietary choices that are available for the **4**: fenugreek and oregano seeds for the digestive tract; carrot, apple and beet juices for energy; herbal teas (especially rooibos) for cleansing; lots of green leafy vegetables and sprouts for the bowel; fish rather than meat for animal protein, unless you're a vegetarian – in which case nuts and legumes are best.

Eggplant, celeriac, coconut, lentils, fresh berries, yoghurt and cheese in moderation are also beneficial. And try to avoid hot spices and highly seasoned foods wherever possible.

***

5. CHOICES FOR CHILDREN

YOUNG children working with the energy of **4** will usually explore the negative energies of their Life Path Number before moving on to master the positive aspects.

This is true of all the nine Life Paths, because every single child first needs to understand the boundaries of what is and isn't acceptable behaviour before they can give their personality free rein.

However, once their boundaries are in place – and the young **4** has understood the crucial life lesson of cause and effect – they can start tapping into their natural creative strengths with the assistance of a positive parental guiding hand.

Life Path 4: The Builder

Children working with the energy of **4** are usually quite serious and practical from an early age. The most common word to come out of their young mouths will be "why?", because the inquisitive child **4** will always want to know why they are being asked to do something. And "because I said so" is never going to cut it.

All **4**s have a strong sense of what is right and wrong from an early age, which means young **4** children will often be wise far beyond their years. Parents must try to limit the "baby talk" and instead address their **4** child as a young adult, because from the moment they can stand they will hate to be talked down to or patronised.

Try to involve **4**s of all ages in family discussions as much as you can, and give them specific tasks to perform so they feel included and important. It is always essential to consult even young **4**s for their opinion because they react badly when they feel left out.

The diligent and hard-working young **4** will usually do well at school, providing they respect the integrity of their teachers. They are Self-starters when it comes to their homework, but if they can't see the value of a particular task you ask them to do, they will either fail to do it, or rush through it half-heartedly.

As they grow up, the serious and often shy **4** teen may struggle to make friends, but the friends they do have will often be theirs for life. Even as a teenager, the **4** will exhibit their Life Path's signature trait of loyalty and honesty, and once they make a friend they will stick by them no matter what.

Children born with a **4** as their Life Path Number are reliable, practical, honest and dependable. They are natural conservatives and rarely take a decision without having all the facts, but once they are set on a course of action it is almost impossible to stop them.

This natural tendency towards stubbornness must be countered by teaching them that they can't control everything that happens in their life. The best life lesson a parent can give a **4** child is to teach them to be flexible and go with the flow.

On the negative side, the young **4**'s need to fully understand the reasons they are being asked to do something can sometimes make them appear disobedient. This is not the case. You merely need to sit down and explain precisely what is expected of them.

The same headstrong quality can make **4**s rebellious at school, which can get them into trouble with authority. Again, patient and frank explanation is the solution, as well as allowing them to feel safe enough to tell you why they disagree with their teacher.

Honesty is absolutely vital when talking to **4** children. As long as parents are upfront with them at all times (which they should be with all Life Path children, not just **4**s), they won't have a problem.

Also, when a **4** child vents they must be heard, or deep resentment may fester. **4** children have a tendency to withdraw into their shells if they don't feel safe to communicate how they feel. If this continues, it may lead to loneliness and depression during their teenage years.

Playtime activities

4 children need to be encouraged to take part in playful and frivolous activities to balance out the innate seriousness of their young personalities. Sports and other pastimes that don't have a "point" can sometimes frustrate them.

Young **4**s excel at solving problems and games that are task-oriented, such as quizzes and puzzles. They also love being out in nature, so hiking and bike riding will give them joy. Anything that involves animals is perfect too, such as trips to the zoo and the aquarium. And if you can get them a pet, even better. A dog or a cat is preferable to birds and fish because **4** children are both tactile and nurturing and they like to be able to hold and cuddle their pet.

* * *

Your child's three-digit Birth Code

As we have seen in Part Two, we always work primarily with the energy of our Life Path Number right from the outset, but in our childhood years from 0 to 18 we do so in conjunction with the energy of our first Supplementary Birth Number, and in our second 18 years – until we reach full emotional maturity at 36 – we do so in conjunction with the energy of our second Supplementary Birth Number.

It's worth taking the time to read the main Life Path Number listings here in Part Three for the numbers that make up your child's two Supplementary Birth Numbers to give you a better understanding of their positive and negative qualities.

Also, as you read about your child's three-digit Birth Code, real-eyes that the difference between "feeling the force" of any Life Path and flipping to the "dark side" is determined by the amount of Self-confidence we develop in our childhood years, and then the amount of Self-love we develop in our teenage years.

That, in a nutshell (squirrel!), is your role as a parent: to instill in your child first Self-esteem, and then Self-love.

The 00/4 'Millennium' child

As we saw earlier in the Life Choices section of this listing, there are only four possible birth dates that contain this most rare of Birth Codes: January 1, 2000, January 10, 2000, October 1, 2000 and October 10, 2000.

The last child with this Birth Code was born on October 10, 1100 – more than 900 years ago – and the next one won't be born until January 2, 10,000 – an astonishing 8000 years from now. (To give you an idea of how far away that is in the future, human history began only 5500 years ago. Anything before that is called "pre-history".)

Clearly, from a numerological perspective, a child born with this Birth Code at the start of this new millennium has the potential to achieve something truly special with their life – because they are working with the double (00) amplified energy of their Life Path Number **4**. But they also have an exact and equal opposite potential to experience great disappointment.

This means the parents of a 00/4 Millennium Child must take extra care to nurture their positive humanitarian potential and guard against the negative stubborn and intractable characteristics of this rare Birth Code.

All the positive and negative qualities of the **4** detailed in this listing for the Builder still hold true, but the 00/**4** child will be working with them on a rarefied level. This means they are born with the capacity to make a real difference in the world.

But there is no pressure on them to do so. If they choose simply to use the innate practical and humanitarian qualities of the **4** to build a happy and stable home for themselves and their family and help out where they can, this is their choice and should never be questioned.

All we can ever do is what we can, and our highest potential is always to make ourselves and those around us as happy as they can be. If it's just the 00/**4**'s immediate family and their local community, that is perfect. The fact that their Birth Code is so rare should never be dumped on their shoulders as a burden. That could be ruinous to their highly sensitive nature, and must never be allowed to happen.

The 13/**4** child

The presence of 1 as the first Supplementary Birth Number means children born with this Birth Code will work with the powerful fire (forceful) energy of the Leader during the first formative 18 years of their life, and the creative air (thought) energy of 3 until full maturity at 36 to help them pursue the highest purpose of the **4** Life Path – which is to build a stable foundation for themselves and use their time, wealth and energy to fight for justice and fairness in the world.

These children will tend to be outgoing from an early age (the energy of 1) and have the capacity to be quite headstrong. Then, as they mature into young adulthood from 18 years and up, they will likely veer off into more artistic pursuits as the creative energy of 3 kicks in.

All the while they will be working diligently on their studies (the Life Path energy of **4**). And as long as they are treated always with honesty and respect, their remarkable capacity for hard work and their impressive attention to detail should give them excellent results.

Because of the absence of any water (emotion) energy in their Birth Code, these earthy Builders will be focused almost exclusively on the practicalities of life, and as children they must be encouraged to relax and enjoy the ride.

Parents would do well to re-mind their admirably goal-oriented 13/4 child that the joys to be found on the journey are just as valuable as the pleasure of arriving at their destination.

The 31/4 child

This is a mirror of the previous Birth Code, and children walking this Life Path will share many qualities with their 13/4 cousins. The key difference is that during their first formative years – when their personality is established – they will be working with the Supplementary Birth Number energy of the artistic, social and fun-loving 3 instead of the serious, driven and ambitious 1.

Yes, they will still be a 4 through and through – and will therefore be pragmatic, diligent and hard-working – but they will be much less of a loner than the driven and focused 13/4 and they will lean towards building their success at home and at school around creative pursuits.

The 31/4 will also tend to be slightly less serious and have a richer and more varied social life, due to the outgoing energy of 3 operating during their childhood and teenage years.

The forceful and determined leadership energy of 1 then kicks in during early adulthood, helping them climb the corporate ladder, or strike out in business for themselves.

Again, as we saw with the 13/4, the absence of any water (emotion) energy in their Birth Code means these earthy children will be focused almost exclusively on the practicalities of life, able to take charge of a situation (1), motivate others to join their cause (3) and see all their projects through to a successful conclusion (4). But they must still guard against being too serious, and may need to be encouraged to let their hair down and smell the roses on the way.

Life Path 4: Choices for Children

The 40/4 child

Talk about stubborn! Any parent who has a 40/4 child will know what it's like when an unstoppable force meets an immovable object.

Here we have the truly focused Builders whose capacity for material success is matched only by their heightened sense of right and wrong. As children and young adults, they will work exclusively with the diligent and pragmatic energy of **4** with no distractions, and they will do so with the extra focus and determination provided by the amplified energy of their 0 Supplementary Birth Number.

The 40/4 child can sometimes be a little too serious and may need coaxing to enjoy the carefree years of their youth.

They can easily become stubborn and inflexible, leading them to not only miss out on the juice of life but also be in danger of collapsing in a heap when things don't go their way and their routine is shattered by outside influences.

These negative pitfalls afflict all the **4** Birth Codes, but none so painfully or frequently as the 40/**4**.

The difference, as always, is how much they are able to step out of their ego (fear) and into their heart (pure love).

The 22/4 'Master Builder' child

As well as working with the practical and humanitarian energy of their Life Path Number **4**, these children will spend the first 36 years of their life focusing intently on the double energy of 2 (the Intuitive).

So while the main purpose of their life is to create a solid foundation and help others less fortunate than themselves, they will be doing so in close co-operation with the people around them, both at home and at school and later in their professional life.

The double "water" (emotional) energy of 2 gives the 22/**4** child an innate empathy and compassion. This, combined with the practical qualities of their Life Path Number, means they will often be successful at school, excelling in their academic work and making many friends.

Life Path 4: The Builder

22/4s are often the proverbial rock on whom others lean when times get tough. It is a role they are usually happy to play, even from a young age, because 4s are fiercely loyal friends and 2s are always concerned about the welfare of others, so these Master Builder children are normally happy to help anyone who might be in need.

However, the 22/4 child also has an equally heightened potential for walking the dark side of their Life Path. Their challenges will be many, particularly as they often choose to incarnate into a family where they suffer abuse of some kind so they experience the sort of injustice they will battle throughout their life.

22/4s are also prone to be the most rigid and inflexible of children for whom the slightest upset or departure from their routine can be devastating. They must learn to go with the ebb and flow of life and accept that change is an unavoidable part of every Life Path journey.

On the whole, 22/4 children, like all the Master Numbers, are far more likely to work with the positive energy of their Life Path Number. But they must take the time to nurture themselves and remember not to take themselves – or life – too seriously.

LIFE PATH 5:
The Rebel

1. **Growth cycle:** Fifth stage (the number of change)
2. **Influences:** Fire (action, masculine) and Mercury (fluidity)
3. **Positive qualities:** Quick-witted, adventurous and imaginative
4. **Negative potential:** Quick-tempered, scattered and shallow
5. **Highs and lows:** Brave freedom fighter, or timid jack of all trades
6. **Highest purpose:** Fight oppression to help others break free of fear
7. **Love matches:** 1, 3, 5 and 7 for compatibility (the rest for growth)
8. **Possible careers:** Journalism, sales, politics, arts, advertising
9. **Words to live by:** "True freedom comes from within"

1. LIFE CHOICES FOR THE REBEL

THE bright, fun-loving **5** has come into the world bristling with energy and a burning desire to make their mark. They are quick-witted and curious, pursuing both knowledge and experience with a passionate desire to find out all there is to know about life.

This is the fifth stage of a growth cycle and it marks a return to the forceful fire energy of **1**. But whereas **1**s are driven by the "leadership fire" of creation, **5**s are driven by the "rebellious fire" of change.

Having circled through the four elements, our Spiritual Growth Cycle now switches from our personal growth in the physical realm and focuses instead on our metaphysical growth in the spiritual realm.

While the first four Life Paths were primarily concerned with the "human" issues of personal power (**1**), co-operation (**2**), expression (**3**)

Life Path 5: The Rebel

and material stability (**4**), the Rebel **5** brings about a radical change by showing us how to cast off our mortal concerns as we embark on our "divine" quest to rid the world of fear and help everyone live in love.

To help them in this daunting task, **5s** are blessed with a well-developed intellect and an uncanny instinct for understanding the human condition, which lets them see exactly what is wrong with the world we live in… as well as what's right.

However, because what we are here to do is not necessarily what comes easiest to us, the **5** will also face challenges on their Life Path that are put there specifically to help them grow. And they will usually come in the form of commitment and consistency, which for the restless Rebel are both essential and extremely hard to achieve.

Those who work with the positive energy of **5** will be brave explorers, creative artists and powerful, lion-hearted revolutionaries. But those who work with the negative energy of this Life Path will tend to skim the surface of experience, bluffing their way through life… true rebels without a cause.

Most **5s** are extremely intelligent and are almost impossible to outsmart – so they can be a handful, no doubt about it. Just keeping track of where they are is hard enough, let alone trying to persuade them to do what you want them to do. Whenever they are confronted with a rule, their brain automatically starts thinking of ways to break it.

People born with a **5** as their Life Path Number are concerned with one quality above all others – freedom. These are the non-conformists of society. They hate to be tied down, and no matter what they choose to do with their life, they will always value independence, variety and the freedom to choose their own path above all else.

5s are also social butterflies. They make friends instantly with almost everyone, and then forget their name seconds later. This doesn't mean they are superficial, it just means their hyperactive minds are working so fast to take in everything about the person they are meeting on the deepest energetic level, and to them their name is an "irrelevant" politeness that is quickly forgotten as they rapidly explore the much more interesting depths of the person's mind.

Life Path 5: Life Choices

These are the courageous revolutionaries who, when working with the positive aspects of their Life Path Number, will stand up to the forces of oppression and go into battle for the downtrodden and the disadvantaged people of the world.

They will use their almost inexhaustible supply of energy to voice their anger at the "Fat Controllers" and fight for the rights of all God's creatures great and small, animal as well as human.

However, if they fail to do the necessary inner work on themselves to overcome their fear of being heard, they risk flipping to the "dark side" of this Life Path Number. If this happens, the disillusioned **5** may internalise their anger and stomp miserably through life, flitting from one dead-end job to another, one place to another and one relationship to another like a disgruntled teenager.

Rebels, as their name suggests, seldom ever fully grow up – which can manifest as either a wonderfully contagious youthful enthusiasm, or a petulant and irritating immaturity, depending on whether they are working with the positive or negative energy of this Life Path.

Similarly, all **5**s who are on a spiritual growth path will choose to incarnate into a "tribe" in which they do not fit because this is the first prerequisite of a rebellious life. When still quite young, they will look around the dinner table at their extended family and friends and real-eyes they are different and don't really fit in. This doesn't mean they don't love their family (all positive **5**s love everyone), it just means they are meant to go their own way and explore the world on their own.

* * *

Highest purpose of The Rebel

The highest purpose of this Life Path is to make the world a better place for as many people as possible by flying the flag of freedom and going into battle against the evil forces of oppression.

If this makes it sound as though **5**s have to be a combination of Princess Leia, Luke Skywalker and Han Solo… then, yes, that's exactly

Life Path 5: The Rebel

what their highest purpose is – to shine the spotlight on unfairness wherever they see it and lead the rebellion against the Fat Controllers.

But, as we saw earlier, all change comes from within, so before the rebellious **5** can hope to defeat the "evil empire", they must first slay their inner enemy. Which, for all Rebels, is Self-doubt.

Remember, the most important goal for all Life Paths is always the same: to first "wake up" to the truth that we are an extension of Source energy, and to help other people wake up as well. Then, and only then, will the path to our highest potential open up before us.

* * *

Key words are… 'confidence' and 'discipline'

To fulfill their life's highest purpose, **5**s must first learn to develop a robust inner confidence in their abilities.

Confidence is central to all the Life Paths as we embark on our common journey from pure unaware love to pure conscious love. As we saw in Part One, developing a healthy Self-esteem is the first crucial step towards Self-love that we all must take.

(If you've come straight to this Life Path listing in Part Three and are wondering what a "Self" is, please try to find the time to read Part One because it's way too complicated to explain again here.)

For the always flighty **5**, however, developing a strong sense of inner confidence is much more than just the key to their personal happiness – it will determine whether they walk the positive Life Path of the optimistic and courageous Rebel, or veer down the negative path towards cynicism, depression and eventual Self-destruction.

All **5**s are born with an innate desire to change the world for the better, and – as I'm sure you have read many times before, not least in the extraordinarily courageous life story of Nelson Mandela – changing the world around us first requires us to change our Self. (The great Madiba once said: "It is more difficult to change yourself than it is to change a country, and I know … because I have done both.")

Life Path 5: Life Choices

That is the secret to the **5**'s success: to first see the world as it is with their unique capacity for understanding the human condition, then see what needs to change... and finally to BE the change in themselves before helping to create it in the world.

This third stage is where so many **5**s come unstuck if they lack the confidence to share what they know with others. The shy Rebel may be doomed to a life of frustration, unable to command the forces they need to take on the Fat Controllers. After all, if they don't believe in themselves, how can they expect anyone else to believe in them?

That is why **5**s also need to learn the crucial qualities of discipline and determination to stay the course. Otherwise, even if they do have the confidence to step up to the fight, it will be all too easy for them to run away at the first sign of a setback.

The "dark side" of this most rebellious of all Life Paths is that ill-disciplined and unconfident **5**s will fail to achieve anything in their life that is truly worthwhile. They will rush around trying to do everything all at once but achieve very little, because they have neither the courage nor the perseverance to see their projects through to completion.

If this happens, negative **5**s – who are prone to having an addictive personality – can quickly burn themselves out, turning to drugs and alcohol to give them the buzz they so desperately need to feel alive.

None of this need happen, though, as long as the always impatient and passionate **5** learns both the value of commitment and the power of discipline to stay the course.

There's an old saying that all **5**s would do well to live by: "Success is 5 per cent inspiration, and 95 per cent perspiration."

* * *

Positive and negative potential

All Life Paths contain an equal measure of positive and negative potential. Our challenge in every lifetime, no matter our Life Path Number, is to nurture our positives and overcome our negatives.

Life Path 5: The Rebel

The reason we are given negative potential as well as positive potential is because people usually respond more effectively to the threat of pain than they do to the promise of pleasure. Also, while it is admirable to do what we are good at in life, we will only ever become the best we can be by facing our "dark side" and digging deep into our Self to overcome the obstacles that appear on our path.

As we have already seen in Part Two, it is only when the chips are down and we are up against it that we find out who we truly are and what we are truly capable of doing. For example, the liberty-loving **5** is only ever truly happy when they are free to do whatever they want, when they want and with whom they want. They crave variety and are easily bored, flitting from one sensual adventure to another in carefree abandon, living in the moment and always focused on having as much fun in the present without thinking too much about tomorrow.

The inconvenient truth for the **5** is that someone, sooner or later, is going to have to pay for their lavish party lifestyle. And that someone is them. Until they learn the value of discipline by staying in one place long enough and working hard enough to amass enough money before they take off on their next grand adventure, the **5** will often career helplessly between the positive side of their Life Path, which is an ebullient, devil-may-care love of life, and the negative side, which is an impoverished financial prison of debt and despair.

Many **5**s will also smoke cigarettes, drink alcohol, eat unhealthy food and even take recreational drugs… because, "Hey, it feels good!", without any thought to what they are doing to their long-term health.

The word "moderation" may as well be written in Swahili for all the meaning it has for the free-spirited **5**, who wants to live life to excess all the time. Ironically, though, it is by living a life of discipline and moderation that they will find the freedom – both financially and in their physical health – to experience all the world has to offer.

Scattered **5**s who don't learn how to apply themselves to a task until it is thoroughly finished can easily become disillusioned with the world. Yes, they might make the best comedians and entertainers, but they can also make the worst depressives and cynics.

Life Path 5: Life Choices

They can also become righteous and overbearing, telling anyone who will listen to them how to be happy, rather than showing them by example. The Rebel always knows the secret to happiness, but if they haven't done the necessary inner work (ie, discipline) to achieve it themselves, they may try to ram their so-called "wisdom" down the throat of others in the hope that their life hasn't been entirely wasted.

No one wants to follow a revolutionary who is drunk, overweight and disenchanted. They want Che Guevara, or Joan of Arc – fit, brave, healthy and leading from the front.

Because all **5**s are at the fifth (freedom) stage of their Spiritual Growth Cycle, they are here to implement change. The fire element that governs this Life Path burns inside the **5** like a furnace, driving them forward. And the quicksilver influence of their guiding planet Mercury ensures they never stay in one place, or do one thing, for long.

Fiery **5**s are known as the non-conformists of society, blazing their own trail and taking each day as it comes. They seldom spend too much time thinking about tomorrow, let alone the day after that. They tend to live for the experience, and the more pleasure and variety each of their experiences brings them, the better.

5s are quick to accept new ideas and to experiment with life, and anything that holds them back will be deeply resented and promptly jettisoned. Get in a **5**'s way, or try to tie them down, at your peril.

They are usually stylish, brave and well-travelled, often jetting off to exotic parts of the world just to see what it's like. They seldom need a reason to do something other than the fact that they want to do it. Taking the conservative approach is just not in their nature.

5s are free spirits and enjoy nothing more than trying something new just for the hell of it. Hungry for knowledge, they are always striving to find the answers to as many questions as they can think of. They tend to live life to the fullest and seldom worry about what tomorrow brings because they know that whatever it is, they are adaptable and quick-witted enough to be able to deal with it.

Other people tend to look on **5**s as reckless risk-takers, but that is far from the truth. The Rebel has a razor-sharp mind that is able to

Life Path 5: The Rebel

sum up a situation quicker than anyone else, which means that when they appear to rush off recklessly on a new adventure, they have in fact already thought through all the implications faster than their friends can say: "Where did they go?"

Most **5**s are also good communicators who are articulate and able to motivate other people easily and at will. They find it hard to sit still, which is why at parties you will seldom see a **5** stay in one place and talking to one person for more than the most fleeting of moments.

It can definitely be hard to keep up with a **5**. Even when you do get them to sit still for more than a few seconds, you may think you have their attention but unless what you are telling them is of global significance – and not just your personal story – their minds will be miles away, thinking of much bigger and life-changing issues.

The **5**'s passion for justice makes them deeply compassionate and considerate of how others are feeling, because their love of freedom extends to their fellow man and woman. They are revolutionaries who stand up for the "little guy" and have a healthy disregard for authority.

Many **5**s set out to change the world for the better. Everywhere they look, **5**s see oppression – because it is the one thing they themselves fear the most. And they will be quick to leap to the defence of oppressed people all over the world.

No one epitomises the freedom-loving passion of the **5** more than the 23/**5** 16th president of the United States Abraham Lincoln. He was the ultimate progressive thinker who not only set all his country's slaves free with the Emancipation Proclamation in 1863, but is to this day by far the most popular of all America's 45 presidents.

On the negative side, those **5**s who have failed to do the inner work to develop their Self-discipline and Self-confidence can easily become scattered and lose focus, leading them to become a disgruntled jack of all trades and a master of none.

The **5**'s greatest strength is also their greatest weakness because their multi-talented natures mean they often struggle to know what to do. Restless and impulsive, the **5** can flit from one job to the next, never staying in one place long enough to achieve anything of real

Life Path 5: Life Choices

significance. Their impulsive nature can make them irresponsible and thoughtless to the point where they leave a trail of damage behind them in the form of angry bosses, disillusioned friends and heart-broken lovers, all of whom feel as though they have been abandoned.

The restless Rebel would do well to slow down and plan what it is they really want to achieve by setting clear goals and sticking to them.

* * *

On a more personal level, **5**s have a tendency to skim the surface of life, seldom staying in one place long enough to reap the fruits of commitment to a task, or a partner. This is the **5**'s ultimate double-edged sword, because although it is their highest desire to have as many different experiences as possible, the best rewards in life come from focusing on one task until it is finished, just as true love comes only from committing to one partner, through thick as well as thin.

In a relationship, the unevolved **5** often has one foot out the door the entire time, which is simply not fair to their partner, or themselves. What's worse, at the first (or maybe second, if they are really in love) sign that their partner is trying to cramp their style, the other foot will follow quicker than either of you can sign the divorce papers.

As with every area of their life, the **5** must learn the value of sticking to their original commitment, whether it be to a job, a cause, or a relationship. On the whole, though, the free-spirited **5** makes a wonderful partner because life will never be boring, no matter how many years you are with them. They are sharp, quick-witted and humorous, while also being deep, passionate and devoted.

Although they are flirtatious, if you give the **5** the space they need to express their freedom-loving firefly personalities, they will worship the very ground you walk on and will never stray, nor be unfaithful to you. Quite the opposite, in fact, because nothing – and no one – will ever come between the romantic **5** and their one true love.

* * *

Life Path 5: The Rebel

Summary of the positives

Providing the freedom-loving and easily distracted **5** learns the valuable lessons of discipline and commitment – and, by doing so, is able to stay in one place long enough to reap the rewards of their efforts – they will have the potential to achieve great success.

The highest purpose of the Rebel is to show the world that true freedom comes from within, because we are all pure love and we are all Source energy. When we real-eyes that, we can break free from the Fear Matrix and nothing – not all the Fat Controllers in the world – can ever touch us, or harm us.

This is the central lesson of this fifth stage of the Spiritual Growth Cycle, when the focus switches radically from the outside world to our inner spiritual and immortal identity.

As the rebellious change-agents of this transformation, none of us needs to real-eyes this truth more than the **5**, otherwise, instead of "leading the Israelites to the Promised Land", they will collapse in a heap of despair, sucking the juice out of life in a hollow yet fruitless attempt to fulfill their purpose.

Key positive words

Fun, adventurous, free-spirited, imaginative, quick-witted, brave, humorous, insightful, energetic, vivacious, motivational, intellectual, idealistic, unconventional, sensual, spirited, imaginative, inventive, sympathetic, magnetic, inspirational, courageous and revolutionary.

* * *

Summary of the negatives

If the **5** fails to find within themselves the courage and discipline to focus on what they know needs to be done, they may slump into a pit of despair borne of their own inability to create the opportunities – both financially and courageously – to change the world.

Life Path 5: Life Choices

The negative **5** is like the thirsty man who rushes round the field, digging well after well to try to find the water he needs, but he only digs for a few seconds in one place before giving up and moving on to find another place to dig. If only he just stayed in one place, and kept digging, he would eventually hit the spring water and drink all he needed.

So, too, the negative **5** will dash about, never staying in one place long enough to reap the rewards of his, or her, labours and eventually collapse in a heap of Self-destructive despair.

The **5** yearns to change the world, but unless they can first change their own flighty nature, they won't have a hope. They must learn that true freedom comes from within. For only when they master their own destiny can they hope to help others master theirs.

Key negative words

Scattered, quick-tempered, unreliable, disillusioned, inconsistent, righteous, overbearing, restless, resentful, dishonest and depressed.

* * *

Self-love is the difference

If you have read Part One, you will already know that your ability to walk the positive side of your Life Path, as opposed to the negative side, is determined by whether you have undertaken the two key stages of personal growth. Or, to put it another way, whether you have taken the two crucial first steps on the path to your life's highest purpose.

The first step towards living your Life Path in the positive is to develop Self-esteem (and if you're wondering what a "Self" is, please take the time to read Part One because it's way too complicated to explain again here). This feeling of inner confidence is essential because it allows you to tap into your innate strengths, which you will need if you are going to have any hope of overcoming the numerous obstacles on your path. Be aware, though, that on its own this first step is never enough, because Self-confidence and Self-esteem are still the

Life Path 5: The Rebel

work of the ego. The feeling of being "good enough" carries with it an implied sense of needing to be "better than".

So to reach your full potential and achieve your life's highest purpose, you must also take the second step – which is to rise above the egoic concept of Self-esteem and climb to the much higher ground of Self-love.

Loving your Self does not mean being "full of your Self". It means the opposite. It means being humble because you understand that you are the same as everyone else, no better and no worse. Above all, it means you understand that we are all immortal spirits having a human experience, and therefore we are all, at our core, the same – pure love and pure Source energy. (The Source is also explained in Part One.)

We can see it easily in new-born babies because when we are born into physical form, and before our fear-based ego has had a chance to develop, we are all gorgeous, gurgling bundles of pure, exquisite love.

I am not suggesting you do this, but just imagine you were to place a new-born infant on the pavement of a crowded street and then stand back out of sight. Everyone – and I mean everyone – would stop and tend to it. And the reason they would do this is because, deep down, we all recognise pure love when we see it. We are drawn to it at the most basic level of our being because it is the most strikingly beautiful and compelling force on the planet.

But sadly, as we grow up and go out into the world, our ego takes over and we start to believe – usually during our teenage years – that our ego is who we are. It isn't. Love is who we are.

We are all pure love. We are all extensions of Source energy (or children of "God", whichever phrase you are more comfortable with).

If you can rise above the quasi-religious terminology, I can summarise the two steps like this: Self-esteem is about feeling "good enough", while Self-love is about feeling "God enough".

The reason why loving your Self is so important for your Life Path is because when you start to live your life from the perspective of being pure love, everything changes. Suddenly you understand that nothing "out there" in the material world can ever harm you in any way.

Life Path 5: Life Choices

Equally, you real-eyes you don't need anything "out there" in the material world to make you feel happy – not the approval of others; no amount of money, fame and power; and not even the love of a good man or woman – because you have all the love you need right there in your own heart, and you can therefore relish the exquisite joy of loving everyone unconditionally without needing anything in return.

That is why Self-love is the secret to working with the positive energy of your Life Path Number. Because when you truly love your Self, the rocky mountain path you've been climbing suddenly becomes an express elevator ride all the way up to the summit of your bliss.

* * *

No Life Path is an island

Although your Life Path Number denotes the main issues you will focus on, you will always work to some degree with the energies of the other numbers as well to become a fully rounded Self.

As a **5** your main work will be in the areas of discipline and freedom, but you will also tackle the issues of patience and Self-confidence (**1**), co-operation and balance (**2**), creative expression (**3**), stability and flexibility (**4**), acceptance (**6**), trust (**7**), abundance and power (**8**) and wisdom and integrity (**9**).

It's therefore worth your while to read through the listings for the other Life Path Numbers when your time allows.

* * *

Qualities of your three-digit Birth Code

(Note: Please read the description in Part Two of how 0 operates in your three-digit Birth Code. Also, you can consult the main Life Path listings here in Part Three for each of your Supplementary Birth Numbers (the four possible ones for the Rebel are 1, 2, 3 or 4) to give you a clearer understanding of how their qualities govern your formative years.)

Life Path 5: The Rebel

'Millennium Child' 00/5

A Millennium Child born with the remarkably powerful single-digit Birth Code of **5** has come into the world with the potential to achieve something truly spectacular with their life.

All the Millennium Children (those born at the beginning of this century without any Supplementary Birth Numbers) are endowed with extra potential because they will all work with the energy of their Life Path Number with absolute focus and an incredible amount of commitment. (The qualities of the Millennium Children are described in detail in Part Two, Chapter 2.)

The doubly amplified presence of the two 0s in place of their two Supplementary Birth Numbers means they will be working solely with the supercharged energy of **5** their entire life, right from the moment they take their first breath.

This gives them a unique capacity to bring about radical and wide-reaching change in the world, as denoted by the rebellious energy of their Life Path. And if they follow the highest purpose of the **5**, which is to help as many people as possible break free of their limiting beliefs and "wake up" to their divine nature, they will be capable of achieving a huge spiritual shift in the way we live our lives.

These rare Millennium Child Rebels have an added potential to bring about considerable change in the world because there are only a handful of dates in that add up to 00/**5**, starting with January 2, 2000 and finishing with October 10, 2010.

What makes this Birth Code even more remarkable is the fact that before the start of this millennium, the most recent child with a Life Path of 00/**5** was born on October 10, 1200, more than 800 years ago, and there won't be another one born until January 1, 3000 – almost 1000 years from now.

(If this is your child's number, they will be aged between seven and 17 as *Messages from Your Self* is published, so please flip forward to the Choices for Children section under this listing for the Rebel to find out more about their positive potential, and the negatives to avoid.)

Life Path 5: Life Choices

14/5

The presence of 1 as the first Supplementary Birth Number of this Birth Code means these Rebels will work with the forceful fire energy of the Leader (1) during the first 18 years of their life, and then with the practical earth energy of the Builder (4) during their next 18 years until they reach full emotional maturity at 36.

Their personality and life choices will still be governed by the overarching energy of their Life Path Number 5 (more fire) right from the start, but their Supplementary Birth Numbers will have a significant impact on how they do so during their crucial formative years.

The leadership energy of 1 from birth to adulthood means these young 5s may be particularly rebellious from a young age and will often have no trouble stepping outside their comfort zone to tackle injustice anywhere they find it.

In fact, they may find themselves landing in trouble more often than they (or their parents) might like, and they must be careful not to become too outspoken until they are old enough to understand all sides of the issue they are fighting against.

At school and elsewhere, the 14/5 Rebel will often stand out from the crowd. And while they might not take the lead in social activities in the same way young Leaders do, they will almost always be voices of dissent (how loud depends on their level of Self-confidence) and may eventually break away from the mainstream to establish their own "gang" or social group.

Their double energy of fire (1 and 5) endows these Rebels with a passionate desire to change and improve their world, which on its own could lead them to pick fights they might not necessarily be able to win. Fortunately, the earth energy of 4 that kicks in just as they reach 18 and get ready to strike out on their own will help ground them and teach them the value of building a strong castle – complete with moat and ramparts – before declaring war on the world.

As long as they clear their emotional blockages and work with the positive energy of these numbers, their passion and practicality should

Life Path 5: The Rebel

guide them towards achieving their life's highest purpose of fighting the forces of oppression and showing us a better way forward.

41/5

This is a mirror of the previous Birth Code, and people walking this Life Path will share many qualities with their 14/5 cousins. The key difference is that during their first formative years – when their personality is established – they will be working with the supplementary earth energy of the practical and well-grounded 4 instead of the driven and ambitious fire energy of 1.

Yes, they will still be a rebellious **5** through and through – and will therefore be quick-witted, adventurous and contrary – but they will be much less of a hothead child than the outspoken 14/**5**, and they will tend to become more balanced and mature young adults as well.

The 41/**5** will also tend to be slightly more serious and have a better understanding of the consequences of their rebellious actions, due to the practical energy of 4 operating throughout their childhood and teenage years. Their 1 leadership energy then kicks in during early adulthood from 18 years onwards, helping them gain the confidence to follow their dreams and make a real difference in the world.

As with the 14/**5**, the absence of any water (emotion) energy in their Birth Code means these Rebels will be focused almost exclusively on their career path, able to take charge of a situation (1), follow through on their projects (4) and experience much success in their primary goal of improving the way we all live our lives (**5**).

In their personal life, though, the absence of emotional energy in their numbers means both 41/**5**s and 14/**5**s must guard against being too much in their head, fighting the good fight, and not enough in their heart, nurturing their romantic relationships.

23/5

The presence of both the loving 2 (water) and creative 3 (air) Supplementary Birth Numbers gives these fiery **5**s (and their 32/**5**

Life Path 5: Life Choices

cousins) some much-needed emotional and intellectual energy, which is missing in the passionate and headstrong 14/5 and 41/5 Birth Codes.

This means these Rebels will work with the co-operative energy of 2 and the expressive energy of 3 during their early formative years, allowing them to relate to others and voice their opinions in ways that will help them fulfill their highest purpose of fighting against the forces of oppression and showing the world a better way to live.

On the flip side, however, their lack of earth energy (4 or 8) means they may sometimes find themselves living in a dream world, unable and unwilling to face up to the harsh realities of day-to-day life.

Plus, without the leadership energy of 1, they may suffer from a lack of Self-confidence in their teenage years and a lack of Self-love in their adult years, causing them to shrink back into Self-doubt. There is nothing worse for a Rebel than shyness, because if they don't have the courage to fight their fight, they will be doomed to a life of frustration.

Providing they do the necessary inner work to discover that they are pure love and pure Source energy – and therefore nothing and no one can ever harm them – the 23/**5** has the potential to be a powerful change-agent by using the intuitive energy of 2 and the communicative energy of 3 to become a compassionate and rousing revolutionary.

In their first 18 years, the supplementary qualities of 2 will ensure they develop their emotional selves before then embarking on more creative pursuits with the expressive energy of 3 until they reach full emotional maturity at the age of 36. But if they lack the confidence to work with the positive energy of these numbers, they risk becoming introverted and shy children (negative 2) and then stifling their creative urges due to Self-doubt as they enter the workforce (negative 3).

That's OK. If you are one of them, read Part One so you can "wake up" to the fact there is no need to fear anything, because you are magnificent beyond words and more wondrous than you know.

32/5

This is a mirror of the previous Birth Code, and people walking this Life Path will share many qualities with their 23/5 cousins. The

Life Path 5: The Rebel

key difference is that during their first formative years – when their personality is established – they will be working with the supplementary air energy of creative expression (the Creative 3), rather than with the emotional and co-operative water energy of the Intuitive (2).

Yes, they will still be a rebellious **5** through and through – and will therefore be quick-witted, adventurous and contrary – but they will be more creative and individual than the compassionate and conformist 23/**5**, and they will tend to be more of a loner and misfit too.

The 32/**5** will also tend to be slightly more withdrawn and spend more time on their own, pouring through books or drawing pictures as they dream up ways they can change the world.

The impact of the air energy of 3 in their childhood years imbues the 32/**5** with a thoughtful and contemplative nature. It is usually only when they reach young adulthood at 18 – when the co-operative and social energy of 2 kicks in – that they pluck up the courage to form close relationships and discuss their ideas freely with others.

And even then, it may take until they reach full emotional maturity at 36 before they truly feel able to stand on their own two feet and speak what is in their heart.

I would like to add a personal note here for my fellow 32/**5**s, if I may. This is my Birth Code, and during my early childhood years I was extremely thoughtful and creative (the energy of 3), and my loving family relished – and encouraged – my individuality. I had fire in my belly (rebellious **5**) and wild creative thoughts in my head (expressive 3) but when I was packed off to boarding school at the age of 13, I was violently bullied for expressing that exact same individuality my family loved. As a result, I shrank back into my shell and became extremely shy – and it was only when the co-operative energy of 2 kicked in at the age of 18 and I left school to go out into the world that I found the courage to speak what was in my heart as I learned how to connect with other people.

This is the classic 32/**5** Life Path, so if you are not yet feeling strong enough to fulfill your life's highest purpose as a Rebel and you haven't yet reached the age of 36, fear not. Focus on boosting the compassionate qualities of the Intuitive (2), and all will be well.

* * *

2. CAREER AND BUSINESS CHOICES

ENERGETIC, brave and quick-witted **5**s make the most adventurous explorers and courageous revolutionaries, no matter what field of employment they choose to pursue.

They love to meet new people, adore discovering new places and delight in changing the way we view the world.

In a professional sense, persuasive **5**s make excellent sales people thanks to their ability to talk the hind leg off a one-legged donkey. They are also good travel agents, tour guides, writers, journalists, promoters, public relations executives, politicians and diplomats.

The truth is, fast-learning **5**s are so adaptable they can pretty much do anything they turn their minds to – as long as the work isn't repetitive or boring.

They also do best when given a large amount of autonomy, and will often wind up going into business for themselves because they have an innate dislike of authority, orders and rules and thrive when put in charge of their own destiny.

The **5**'s natural charm, warm sense of humour and insightful wit means they also work well in a team, providing they have the freedom and flexibility to express themselves at all times.

The arts, entertainment and show business sit well with the always imaginative **5**, who – like the expressive **3** – loves to "put on a show" and take their audiences to places they have never been.

Most **5**s will try several different careers during their early working years before alighting on the one they want to pursue. In fact, it is not uncommon for a **5** to flit from job to job, lasting barely long enough in each one to pull a pay packet from their employer, as they search for their special niche in the world.

The restless **5** detests routine and should avoid jobs that involve repetitive tasks, such as finance, retail and manufacturing. Instead, they should turn their flair to professions that value their ability to adapt to change, such as sales, politics, marketing, journalism and the arts.

Many **5**s will choose careers that involve a lot of travel, because even if they do have to perform the same task over and over again, at least doing it in different places will make the repetition seem bearable.

On top of that, the **5** is frequently outgoing and charismatic – as well being versatile, adaptable and social – so any career that involves charming clients will suit them perfectly. And if a **5** does choose to work in an office, they will often be a happy mood-lifter who is popular with their colleagues.

Beneficial career paths

Sales, marketing, promotions, PR, events management, TV, acting and journalism are tailor-made for the persuasive and effervescent **5**.

Other jobs that give them the variety and human contact they crave include travel, hospitality, airline work, tour guides, advertising, chauffeuring, teaching, psychology, therapy and personal growth.

Careers that suit the **5**'s need to change the world for the better include politics, environmentalism, diplomacy, trade, film-making, photography, art, design, the law, detective work and playwright.

Best business matches

The undisciplined and mercurial **5** will often struggle to make a success of a business without a grounded and financially savvy partner, because they are usually incapable of staying still long enough to grow it from the ground up.

However, with the right partner – someone who is prepared to cost it all out and deal with the "irritating demands of customers and suppliers" – there is no reason why the ground-breaking **5** can't turn one of their gazillion bright ideas into a successful business.

Life Path 5: Relationship Choices

An ambitious **1** or a hard-working **6** would be perfect partners, because **5**s don't care if they take control of the day-to-day running of the business, as both the **1** and the **6** will probably do. Other numbers may feel threatened, but not the **5** who hates repetitive meetings and the boring chore of paperwork and will love having the freedom to go out and charm the dollars off clients or brainstorm their next Big Idea.

As for the rest of the senior roles in the business, the **5** would do best to leave that up to the **1** or the **6** – who would probably choose to employ a **2** for their human resources manager, an earthy **4** or **8** as financial controller, a **3** as creative director, a **7** as systems manager and a **9** as project manager.

* * *

3. RELATIONSHIP CHOICES

ONE of the most rewarding aspects about the Self-Awareness System™ is how equitable it is. Each Life Path offers the same opportunities for happiness and fulfillment, albeit in markedly different ways. And each of them also offers the same amount of challenges to force us to grow, although again in very different ways.

This means that no Life Path Number is any "better" or "worse" than any of the others. All of them have their blessings, and all of them have their obstacles.

In the case of **5**, the blessings centre around their charm, sense of humour, childlike enthusiasm and adaptability, which are all wonderful qualities in a partner, and their obstacles show up as inconsistency, unreliability, flirtatiousness and an inability to commit, which are sure to cause a certain amount of conflict, to say the least.

On the positive side, life with a mercurial **5** will seldom be boring. They have a seemingly inexhaustible supply of energy and curiosity, they love to try new things, meet new people and visit new places, and

Life Path 5: The Rebel

they usually possess an infectious sense of humour that can lighten up even the gloomiest of situations.

They are adventurous, charming, outgoing and always fun to be around. And they are great conversationalists too, which allows them to fit in effortlessly in any social setting.

They are also extremely versatile and adaptable, which are great qualities in a relationship, where compromises are inevitable. Where others might flip their lid if they come home to find their partner has repainted the entire house and rearranged all the furniture without consulting them, the **5** will clap their hands with glee.

Change and variety are absolutely essential for the easily bored Rebel, who craves new experiences and absolutely loathes repetition. This can certainly throw up some challenges in a relationship for their partner, who may be afraid their **5** will get bored of them too and rush off to find someone new.

They needn't worry, though, because few people are more loyal than an evolved **5**. Yes, they might come home a bit later than they said they would because they simply lost track of time, and they might even forget to call… but providing they have done the necessary inner work and cleared out their fears, they are as faithful as an old dog.

*(Note: If they haven't done the inner work, unevolved **5**s can be liars and cheaters just like all the other unevolved numbers who succumb to the "dark side".)*

Problems arise when the evolved **5** feels their partner is stifling them. Like William Wallace in the movie *Braveheart*, "Freedom" is the Rebel's battle cry. They are ever-curious risk-takers who never sit still for more than five minutes, hate spending too much time around serious people and absolutely crave constant change and stimulation.

As long as their partner gives them enough space, all will be well. After all, no partner can ever hope to stimulate a **5** all the time – that is simply too much pressure. Plus, the faithful **5** who is allowed to spread their wings will always fly straight home, bubbling over with exciting tales of their grand adventure and bearing wacky gifts.

But woe betide the partner who tries to clip the **5**'s wings and denies them the trust and freedom they need. Jealousy and mistrust are like shackles around the **5**'s wrists and ankles, and they will end the relationship as quickly as they began it.

If you are in a relationship with a **5**, never make the mistake of trying to tie them down. Not only will they be straight out the door (probably leaving all their belongings behind as well, because most **5**s regard possessions as little more than baggage), but they are also likely to move straight on to date someone else – and maybe several people at once – which can be hard for their abandoned partner to take.

While **5**s are extremely passionate, their constant curiosity and need for adventure can distract them from how their partner is feeling, causing them to miss the telltale signs that something is wrong. It is not unusual for a **5** to be suddenly faced with an outburst of anger and be genuinely surprised. "What have I done wrong now?" is the multi-tasking **5**'s usual shocked response, which only proves how clueless they are and makes the situation even worse.

Chances are when their partner needs them the most, the **5** is out riding their motorbike, or visiting friends, or any one of the hundreds of adventures they long to pursue – when they should be at home.

Ever-curious **5**s also have a tendency to change their minds as often as they change their underwear, although never without a good reason. The **5** is such a quick thinker that they are able to weigh up all sides of a decision in the blink of an eye, which can be challenging for their partner to say the least – unless, of course, they are also a **5**.

For this reason, and many others, the apparent "freedom" of being single is often more appealing to a **5**, but this is a mistake because it is only in relationship that we are able to see our faults reflected in those of our partner and have a chance to correct them and grow.

As we have already seen, the biggest challenge for the **5** is to real-eyes that true freedom comes from within – specifically by learning the essential qualities of discipline and commitment.

The unevolved **5** will rush around in pursuit of "freedom", flitting from one failed relationship to the next and frittering away what little money they have as they try (and fail miserably) to satisfy the never-ending cravings of their insatiable ego.

Life Path 5: The Rebel

Ironically, tragically even, their greatest fear will eventuate when they end up broke and alone, trapped in a prison of their own making.

If they simply stay in one place and master their emotions, as well as their finances, the **5** will discover what it feels like to be truly free. And they will enjoy the blissful connection of true love as well.

* * *

Sex drive of the 5

Rebels tend to be as adventurous in the bedroom as they are in every other area of their life, choosing to experience as many of the wilder and kinkier aspects of sex as they can. This cat-like curiosity can manifest in all manner of fetishes, although the often insecure **5** will usually wait until they feel completely safe with their partner before taking the lid off their Pandora's Box of sexual appetites.

Bondage is something that can appeal to the **5**'s obsession with freedom, just so they can experience the thrill of having it taken away from them by a dominant lover. The Golden Rule of "Never tie down a **5**" definitely doesn't apply in the bedroom. Although as soon as you do tie them down they will probably be more focused on figuring out how to break free than whatever you are doing to them because their hyperactive mind can't resist a challenge.

In fact, some **5**s can be so in their head while making love that they never fully relax into the sensuality of the experience, which can be a challenge for their partner who never feels the **5** is fully "present" in the moment. Another challenge for the **5**'s partner is that it can be impossible to keep up with their ever-changing tastes and desires. Just as they are starting to get the hang of one particular fetish or kinky game, the **5** is already bored with it and wants to move on to try something else.

Their passionate need for variety means **5**s are also almost always broadminded lovers for whom nothing is too shocking. They will be happy to try anything at least once, including imaginative role-playing and even role-swapping games. I know many **5**s who have been driven

Life Path 5: Relationship Choices

to explore both their feminine and masculine sides, including playing dress-ups in public as well as in the privacy of their boudoir.

Indeed, while the "Sex drive" section of the other eight Life Path Numbers includes separate descriptions for the feminine and masculine partners in a relationship, there is no need to do so for the **5** because they are so in touch with both sides of their personality, and their sexuality too. The masculine **5** will be happy to play a feminine role in bed, just as the feminine **5** will be happy to play a masculine one. So whether their genitals are "inies" or "outies" makes no difference.

* * *

The compatibility listings that follow will help free-spirited **5**s get the most out of their relationships, whether it's with someone they love, a friend or a business partner. You will notice the fire energy of **5** is well-matched with other **5**s and their fiery cousin **1**, as well as a **3** or a **7**, whose air energy is able to fan their flames. Water (**2** and **6**) and earth (**4** and **8**), on the other hand, can douse a fire, so these pairings will throw up more challenges. **9** usually matches well with all numbers.

However, what appears to match you best on the surface may not be what you need in your life right now. All relationships are designed to help us grow along our Life Path. Yes, of course we enjoy the companionship, close connection, sexual intimacy and deep love that relationships give us. But that is now why we have them.

The reason we choose a partner (or, to be more accurate, why our all-knowing Self chooses them for us) is because they are a mirror in which we see our shortcomings and strengths reflected back at us through their shortcomings and strengths.

That is why opposites so often attract, especially in love.

I have written an entire book on this subject called *Leap into Love* which goes into the way relationships work in our lives in great detail. But for now, please real-eyes that when your partner presses one of your buttons, they are doing so not to "piss you off" but because your Self is using them to show you the areas you need to work on.

Life Path 5: The Rebel

If you fail to understand this is the main reason why you attracted them into your life in the first place, you will fight each other and may eventually break up. And you will believe their faults were exactly that – their faults – rather than yours reflected back at you. Worst of all, you will then take the unchanged you with you to your next relationship, and – lo and behold! – exactly the same issues will come up again.

If this sounds familiar. If you have ever asked any of these questions – "Why does this always happen to me?" or "Why do all men cheat?" or "Why are all women so demanding?" or whatever it is for you – then now you know why. It's because you didn't learn from your last partner, so of course your new one will do the same thing.

And this will continue to happen, relationship after relationship, until you real-eyes it is meant to be happening to show you what areas you need to work on in your Self to change and grow.

* * *

One final quick point before we get into it: I need to stress that I disagree with almost every numerologist I know who likes to label relationships "a natural fit", "a neutral fit" or "an unnatural fit", depending on the compatibility of the numbers of the two partners.

All relationships are challenging. That is why we have them, as we have just seen. Yes, sometimes we might choose a partner who is "just like us" for the sake of harmony, but that could be regarded as a cop out if we are truly serious about our personal and spiritual growth.

If you are on a spiritual growth path in this lifetime (and there is no doubt in my mind that you are if you made it through Part One without throwing it in the bin!), then your Self will choose your relationships for you – and they will always be with a partner who will challenge you to grow in exactly the ways you need to grow.

Just because you might discover your current partner has a Life Path Number that doesn't dovetail perfectly with yours, don't fall into the trap of thinking there must be something wrong – or worse, end it with them so you can go out with someone with a "better" number.

Life Path 5: Relationship Choices

Where you are right now on your Life Path is exactly where you are meant to be, and who you are with is exactly who you are meant to be with. So please let these listings help you to look for the lessons in your relationship, rather than look for the door.

And if you are single at the moment, try to remain open-hearted about your next relationship. It doesn't matter what Life Path Number they have, so don't "cherry pick". All that matters is you follow your heart and be open to learning the lessons they can teach you. After all, that's the reason you will attract them into your life in the first place.

* * *

<u>5 & 1</u>
(Freedom and Independence)

Love

This can be a brilliant pairing full of fun, because both these fire numbers are highly motivated go-getters who are happiest when they are rushing about all over the place pursuing their latest goal, rather than sitting around at home wondering where the other went and growing resentful at the lack of attention.

Both **5** and **1** like to have a lot of personal space in a relationship and they are more than happy to give it to each other – so the **1** can seek new opportunities for the material wealth and personal success they crave, and the **5** can seek the adventure and new friendships they need more than the air they breathe.

However, herein lies a major challenge for this pairing because neither may take the time to properly nurture the relationship and they are likely to end up just drifting apart – or else they will find someone new and move on. (Both the **5** and the **1** find it very easy to meet potential mates, and they find it just as easy to let go of their old one.)

For this relationship to last longer that a few months of wild sex and thrilling adventures, both partners must make the effort to spend quality time together. Regular romantic dinners and weekends away,

Life Path 5: The Rebel

just the two of them (without the kids if they have them) are the perfect way for them to reconnect and rekindle the spark of desire.

Sexually, this is a passionate and adventurous coupling that will almost certainly result in broken bedroom furniture. Both partners like to experiment in all areas of life and will therefore happily push the boundaries of their sexual experiences in every direction.

Perhaps the biggest obstacle this pairing will face, though, is the lack of initial attraction, other than on a purely physical level. The ambitious **1** will tend to regard the mercurial and ever-changing **5** as being too unpredictable and irresponsible, while the freedom-loving **5** will see the focused and driven **1** as boring and way too serious.

It's worth sticking at it, though, because the humorous **5** is able to bring the goal-driven **1** out of their shell and teach them how to relax and smell the roses, while the disciplined **1** can teach the restless **5** that true freedom comes from focusing on one project and bringing it to fruition, rather than dashing about starting numerous projects and never finishing any of them, as Rebel **5**s tend to do.

Remember that when disagreements arise (and they will because all relationships are about growth, as we saw earlier), take the time to sit down and figure out what you are meant to be learning from your partner – then kiss them and thank them for the lesson.

Good luck, stay open and honest... and enjoy all the thrilling adventures and fun times this fiery relationship can give you.

Friendship

This is an unlikely friendship, for the reasons discussed above. Usually, the always driven and focused **1** will become frustrated with the irresponsible and ever-changing personality of the **5**. And the fun-loving **5**, who just wants to party and socialise, will quickly tire of the **1**s serious nature and career-driven monologues about their latest plan to conquer the world.

They would do well to listen to each other, though, because each holds the secret to the other's success.

The focused **1** can teach the ill-disciplined and flighty **5** to see a project through to the finish, thus creating the material wealth that the **5** needs to obtain the true freedom they crave.

Equally, the **5** can teach the **1** that achievement leads to nowhere, and the real joy of life is to be found in enjoying the moment and going with the flow, rather than missing out on all the fun of life because they are too busy planning what they are going to do next week, next month, or next year.

Business

This a good business partnership, as long as the **1** is allowed to choose the direction of the company and the **5** is not required to sit in on every meeting, which would bore them to death.

Dominant **1**s love to be in charge, but they can tend to become a bit blinkered in their single-minded pursuit of a goal. Which is why the **5**'s constant search for new and improved ways of doing things can make this a very powerful corporate combination.

The **5** will usually be happy to let **1** lead the way and shoulder the responsibility (just the word "responsibility" makes the **5** cringe), leaving the firefly **5** free to come up with brilliant new ideas that almost certainly wouldn't have occurred to the single-minded **1**.

Make sure the **1** is the boss and the **5** doesn't have to sit at a desk all day, and watch the dollars roll in.

* * *

5 & 2
(Freedom and Co-operation)

Love

This pairing is the ultimate attraction of opposites between the fun-loving and fiercely independent **5** who yearns to be free but desperately needs to learn the lesson of discipline, and the disciplined but co-dependent **2** who desperately needs to learn how to relax and enjoy life as a confident and independent free spirit.

When the rebellious **5** and the conformist **2** come together, the relationship is going to go one of two ways: it will either last five minutes during which the **5** will accuse the jealous **2** of cramping their style and the **2** will harangue the fickle **5** for being too irresponsible. Or else, if both partners are smart enough to know that the other one possesses exactly the qualities they lack and need, it will blossom into the most perfect mutual growth pairing it is possible to imagine.

Yes, there will be plenty of disagreements but change is never easy, and both partners' egos will resist the valuable spiritual and emotional lessons each has to teach the other. But providing there is a solid bedrock of love and trust, and neither partner does anything to betray that trust, the aware **5** will learn everything they need to learn about discipline, commitment and perseverance from the always patient and loving **2**, who in turn will learn everything they need to learn about optimism, tolerance and forgiveness from the always ebullient **5**.

One word of caution, though: the often jealous and insecure **2** must give their **5** partner all the trust and freedom they need and avoid being too serious, while the flighty **5** must make sure they always put their **2** lover first in everything they do and balance their need for time alone with the **2**'s need for quality time together.

Good luck, stay open and honest… and make sure you learn the life-changing lessons your partner has come into your life to teach you.

Friendship

These two are going to struggle to find much in common outside a romantic relationship, because friendship is seldom enough of a bond to force them to look past their differences and see the valuable lessons these two radically different numbers have to teach each other.

In fact, the **5** and the **2** will usually only ever come together to form a meaningful relationship if they are either lovers or best friends. Anything less, and their differences will merely irritate each other.

However, providing the impatient **5** takes the time to really listen to the always talkative **2** and hear what they have to say, and the serious **2** understands that the average **5**'s attention span is only slightly longer than that of a gnat who's busting to pee – and therefore tries to keep their monologues as short as possible – then these two can form a friendship that will stand the test of time.

Business
No. Definitely not. The lightning-fast **5** will go bonkers having to explain every little detail of what they are doing to the **2**, and the detail-oriented **2** will despise the irresponsibility and recklessness of the **5**. Pick any other number to go into business with, preferably a **1, 6** or **9**.

* * *

<u>5 & 3</u>
(Freedom and Expression)

Love
On the surface, the passionate fire energy of the **5** and the creative air energy of the **3** appear to be an excellent match in all areas, and especially in love. These two will certainly enjoy a rich and varied social life, but it may all feel a bit shallow from a lover's perspective.

They make great friends, and all the best relationships are founded on being best friends above all else. But their passion can sometimes flare too brightly and be over almost as soon as it has begun because neither number is serious enough about doing the hard work to build a solid relationship from the ground up.

The curious **5** will be off doing their own thing, delighted that the equally adventurous **3** understands their need for freedom. And the creative **3** will be off following their dreams, equally delighted that the independent **5** is happy spending large amounts of time without them.

The trouble is, the whole point of being in a relationship is to spend time together, learning from each other and helping each other to grow. So, from a personal growth perspective, there is very little point in these two numbers falling in love and committing to each other when they could achieve the same result by staying best friends.

However, if a **5** does find themselves in a romantic relationship with a **3**, they can make it work – and last – by sharing as much as they can of themselves with their partner, and by taking the time to involve themselves in the **3**'s creative projects wherever possible.

The partners will have to be very secure in themselves, however, because the **5** and the **3** are both fiercely social and incorrigible flirts. If they become jealous, they will push each other away and into the arms of another lover faster than either of them can say "Next!"

Good luck, stay open and honest… and try to make enough time for each other to keep the flames of passion burning bright.

Friendship

As we have just seen, this is one of the best and most mutually fulfilling friendship pairings in the entire Self-Awareness System™. The expressive air energy of the **3** will fan the flames of the fiery **5**'s passionate need to explore the world and make a difference in the lives of others, while the **5**'s quick-witted intelligence and love of adventure will inspire the **3** to ever higher creative achievements.

These two can be best friends forever, firing off each other and driving each other forward with not a hint of jealousy or insecurity. If they are sexually matched, though, they should probably avoid falling in love and ruining everything, unless they are prepared to learn the valuable life lessons each has to teach the other.

Business

For all the reasons that we have discussed in the Love and Friendship sections, these two numbers have so much in common creatively that they may feel tempted to combine their resources and go into business together to make their dreams come true.

They will certainly inspire and push each other, as well as give each other the space they need to do their own thing and follow their own separate creative instincts. But problems may arise when they disagree on the creative direction the business needs to take.

Also, while the well-rounded **3** is certainly better qualified to run the business, file the invoices, collate the expense accounts and handle the finances than the unreliable **5**, if they spend too much time on the mundane day-to-day tasks, the **3** may quickly grow to resent the reckless and irresponsible **5** and decide they are better off on their own.

Just as we saw with their relationships, this pairing, even if they are sexually matched, would be best advised to remain best friends – neither falling in love, nor going into business together.

* * *

5 & 4
(Freedom and Stability)

Love

OMG! Just look at the diametrically opposed qualities that define these two most incompatible of Life Path Numbers: "Freedom" and "Stability". How is that ever going to work? You'd have more luck mixing oil and water, or mating a Great Dane with a chihuahua.

The conservative **4** is a feminine earth number who wants to diligently build a stable home life focused on financial security and physical health, while the rebellious **5** is a masculine fire number who wants to charge around the world tilting at windmills and partying until dawn with a bunch of prurient, pill-popping Patagonian polyamorists.

Talk about chalk and cheese! These two have as much in common as a blackboard and a water biscuit.

If both partners are still stuck in their ego and have not yet woken up to the fact that the whole reason we attract a partner into our life is so we can learn the valuable lessons they have to teach us, then this pairing will last about 30 seconds.

However, and I speak from experience here as a mercurial **5** who dated a wonderfully loyal **4** for five years, the opportunity for these two numbers to teach each other the lessons they need to learn to grow both spiritually and emotionally are unparalleled.

The reckless and risk-taking **5** values their freedom above all else, but they will never be truly free until they learn the value of discipline and commitment that is second nature to the well-grounded **4**.

Equally, the conformist and risk-averse **4** values their stability above all else, but they may miss out on all the joys of life unless they learn to live in the moment, which is second nature to the epicurian **5**.

Good luck, stay open and honest… and make sure you try to learn the valuable life lessons that each of you can teach the other.

Friendship

As well as being fiercely loyal, which makes them a most trusting and trustworthy friend, the **4** is also passionately honest, which means they usually speak the truth without pausing to consider that perhaps the truth is not something their restless **5** friend wants to hear.

Most **5**s spend much of their time in denial of the harsh realities of life, preferring – like Don Quixote – to live in a fantasy world where they battle the forces of oppression without achieving anything other than perhaps a wounded windmill or two. They certainly don't want some super-fit and impossibly wealthy **4** telling them that their entire life is a pointless waste of time… even when it is.

This, as well as their radically different approaches to life, is why these two numbers will seldom become friends, let alone close friends. Which is a shame, because – as we saw just now in the "Love" section – they both have so much to teach each other.

Business

Aha! Now this is one area where the outgoing and charming **5** and the grounded and diligent **4** can benefit each other in ways that are not only mutually beneficial but profoundly profitable as well.

Providing each takes the time to appreciate the other for all they do – the **4** for running a tight ship and the **5** for navigating effortlessly through the storm – this can be a most beneficial business pairing.

Life Path 5: Relationship Choices

On their own, the reckless and easily bored **5** would be completely incapable of managing the business, just as the **4** would be incapable of looking up from the accounts to see the big picture and take advantage of the growth opportunities when they come along.

But together, they can fill in the gaps of each other's skill sets and enjoy considerable success – the **4** holding the purse strings and driving the business with their knack for organisation, and the **5** winning new clients and broking new deals with their tireless optimism.

* * *

5 & 5
(Freedom and Adventure)

Love

Imagine two peas in a pod. Now imagine that both peas are off-the-charts crazy party animals, desperate to have as much fun as they possibly can before someone plucks them off the grocery store shelf and throws them into a pot of boiling water to make pea soup.

If you can picture this, you will have a perfect image in your mind of what the inside of the pod looks like when the vodka begins to flow, the disco lights are turned on and the music is cranked up to the max.

It will be a riot! In fact, when the pod is cracked open in the kitchen, the soup chef will be surprised to discover both peas are not only dressed in togas but are wildly drunk and laughing like drains.

Such is life when two **5**s meet, fall in love and decide to party their lives away together in a toga-party frenzy of sensual indulgence and devil-may-care irresponsibility. Both reckless **5**s will egg each other on (no, I have no idea if egg goes well with pea soup) and delight in cooking up new adventures to pursue without giving the slightest thought to the consequences of their pants-on-fire dilettante lifestyle.

And therein lies the problem with this love match. Yes, two **5**s will probably have more fun than Joan Collins in a room full of male strippers. But having fun is only one of the two reasons we humans

Life Path 5: The Rebel

are here on this planet. The other is to learn the Big T spiritual truth that we are pure love and therefore pure Source energy, so we can return to "replenish the Source". (If that statement elicits in you a "What the...?" response, please stop and read Part One.)

On that level, two **5**s in relationship will almost never achieve their highest purpose because neither one will ever say to the other: "That's enough booze for now, let's drink some herb tea and meditate on what it means to be pure Source energy." It just isn't going to happen.

But you know what... maybe in your past lives you have paired up with serious **4**s or intellectual **7**s and have had a gutful of personal growth, in which case just go with it and order another round of caprioscas. Maybe you have earned your frivolous life this time around and should just embrace it – and each other – and have a blast.

Good luck, stay open and honest... and try to get enough sleep and eat enough vegetables so you don't end up like John Belushi.

Friendship

This will always be a fun and frivolous friendship, marked by frequent all-night parties, exciting adventures and a passionate mutual rebellion against the forces of oppression. Two **5**s who forge a close friendship will find much in common and push each other to flick two large fingers at authority. They will get into trouble for sure, but every time they do their bond will deepen and broaden exponentially.

5s are here to rebel against the institutions and effect change for the better for the huddled masses, so who better to stand by their side as they fight the good fight than another **5**?

Think of a combination of Angelina Jolie and Mick Jagger, or Dudley Moore and Marlon Brando (all wild, rebellious **5**s) and you'll know exactly why these two numbers can not only party themselves silly long into the night but achieve great change in the world together.

Business

At the risk of sounding like your parents or your school teacher, I would caution even the most responsible **5** from going into business with another **5** because neither of you will have either the emotional maturity nor the financial responsibility to prevent the company from going quickly into debt, and just as quickly into bankruptcy.

Reckless and irresponsible **5**s might be chock-a-block full of great ideas and boundless enthusiasm but, as any boring old bank manager will tell you, the secret to business success is first creating a water-tight business plan and then sticking to it. And when it comes to sticking to a plan, the impulsive **5** is about as reliable as a beer-swilling baboon with ants in its pants.

The freedom-loving **5** would do much better partnering up with an earthy **4** or **8**, who will happily work around the clock ensuring the company's finances are rock solid, or their fiery cousin **1**, who will be happy to pay attention to the finer details of the business, leaving the independent **5** free to focus on charming new clients and pursuing new value-added ventures to bring in more money.

* * *

5 & 6

(Freedom and Romance)

Love

There's an old proverb that says: "Expectation is a one-way street that leads to disappointment." (Well, it's not that old really because I just made it up, but it sounds better that way.) The point is, expectation in relationships is always going to end in tears. And when two partners are as incompatible as the committed **6** and the commitment-phobic **5**, the tears will start flowing the moment the controlling **6** tries to tell the rebellious **5** what to do, or the irresponsible **5** goes on a three-day bender without telling the **6** where they went.

These two lovers have about as much in common as Pussy Riot and Vladimir Putin. Yes, they will often be attracted to each other when they meet at a party, because the **5** will admire the **6**'s ability to stand out from the crowd, and the **6** will be drawn to the fiery **5**'s

Life Path 5: The Rebel

burning desire to change the world for the better. After all, both numbers share the common goal of raising the level of love for all of us. It's just that they will go about it in radically different ways.

The nurturing **6** wants a strong, committed relationship and a peaceful home where they can raise a family, while the adventurous **5** cares little for home life and wants to travel the globe in a never-ending series of quests to right what they see as society's wrongs.

The **6** craves commitment and consistency and will be aggressively controlling if they fail to get it, while the **5** needs constant change and stimulation from other people and will run a mile at the first sign of their partner trying to limit their freedom of choice.

It's ironic, really, because both these numbers have so much to teach each other. The serious and judgmental **6** would benefit from the courageous **5**'s love of adventure and ability to live and let live, while the ill-disciplined and freedom-loving **5** desperately needs to learn how to commit to anything for more than 30 seconds to prevent them from winding up in the poor house, a prisoner in a jail of their own making.

If these two opposites do attract each other and figure out a way to respect their differences, there is potential for spectacular mutual growth – which, after all, is why we have relationships in the first place. It won't be easy, and there will need to be almost constant compromise – such as the **5** agreeing to spend more time at home, and the **6** letting them fly when they really need to – but it will be well worth it.

Just real-eyes this relationship is unlikely to be long-lasting simply because the differences are too great. Learn all you can while you can, and try to see your partner's "negatives" as being exactly the positive areas you need to focus on to move along your growth path.

Good luck, stay open and honest… and enjoy the life-changing lessons each of you has for the other.

Friendship

The quick-witted **5** and the attractive **6** will find much to admire about each other when they first meet. The passionate **6** will be thrilled by the effervescent **5**'s lust for life, and the crusading **5** will be drawn to the **6**'s idealistic vision of a world where love triumphs over the fear-mongering forces of oppression. But that's often as far as it will go.

These two friends are unlikely to stick around beyond the point when the **6** gets fed up with the **5** changing their mind every two minutes, and the **5** gets bored of the **6**'s lack of mental stimulation.

They'll probably stay friends on Facebook, occasionally sharing visionary posts about ways to improve the world, but that's about it.

Business

This business pairing is such a bad idea that if someone published a book called *The 1000 Worst Ideas Of All Time* (including JFK saying: "Let's go for a nice long drive through Dallas" and Napoleon telling his troops: "I'm going to invade Russia, what can possibly go wrong?"), this would come in at number 27. Don't do it. Just don't.

* * *

5 & 7
(Freedom and Understanding)

Love

These two lovebirds have a lot of their core values in common, including their need for variety and their desire for plenty of time to do their own thing without feeling pressured by their partner.

Their relationship will be similar to that of a **5** and a **3** in that they will enjoy the freedom each is happy to give the other, as well as the mental stimulation of great conversation and the sharing of exciting new ideas.

The **5** will admire the **7**'s impressive intellect and will quickly come to cherish the lack of demands their new partner puts on their time, while the **7** falls in love easily and will be instantly attracted to the **5**'s rapid-fire wit and intelligence.

Both will delight in the never-ending stream of fascinating topics of conversation these two will share, and they will happily stimulate each other's minds with long discussions deep into the night about all the Big Issues facing the world.

No, the challenge for these two will never be long, awkward silences or making too many demands on each other for attention. Quite the opposite. They must watch that their relationship doesn't become too distant or else the passion could fade and die, leading one or both to look for excitement in the arms of someone else.

Another point of concern is that the often insecure **7** usually wants more affection than the **5** can give them, and they may take their Rebel partner's lack of effusive romantic displays as a sign they aren't fully committed. This is not the case, and all the **5** needs to do to reassure them is tell them and show them regularly how much they are loved.

The **5** must also curb their flirtatious nature and remember that while they are the kings and queens of a social situation, the **7** struggles with informal chit chat and is never truly comfortable among strangers.

As long as the **5** looks out for the **7** when they are out, and the **7** learns to trust that the firefly **5**'s flirtatious behaviour is absolutely no threat to their relationship (it's not, because no one is more faithful than a devoted **5**), then problems should seldom arise. And provided both are as committed as each other, this relationship can be both mutually rewarding and long-lasting.

Good luck, stay open and honest... and enjoy the blissful freedom and stimulating conversations this relationship will give you.

Friendship

For all the reasons we have just seen, these two numbers can be excellent friends, bouncing ideas off each other and talking for hours about anything and everything. The adventurous and inquisitive **5** will stimulate the **7**'s mind in all the right ways, while the deep-thinking and intuitive **7** will be the perfect sounding board for the **5**'s latest radical ideas to change the world.

Socially, they are not so well-matched, with the **7** preferring to stick with the company of close and loyal friends and the **5** craving the company of new and exciting strangers. But outside the expectations of a romantic partnership, this shouldn't cause too many upsets for these two mutually stimulating friends, who will relish the fact that neither makes too many demands on the other's time.

Business

This is where these two cerebral numbers could come unstuck because they will struggle to agree on whose intellectual vision for the business is best, while also both wanting to be in control. Also, neither likes being told what to do, and they both abhor getting bogged down in petty details – which means no one will look after the admin.

If they do decide to venture into commerce together, it will normally work best if the **5** is given free rein to bring their creative ideas to fruition and the **7** takes overall responsibility for the direction of the business. But they must employ a well-grounded manager (preferably a **4** or an **8**) to run the back-office operations for them.

* * *

5 & 8
(Freedom and Ambition)

Love

Imagine you have a large, roofless cage in your garden. And in it you put a small lion, and an owl tethered to a tall wooden post.

The lion, being a proud little lion (as all lions tend to be, even the small ones), pads around the cage trying to look as brave and strong as it possibly can – and doing a pretty good job of it too, or so it thinks.

On the inside, though, the proud little lion is trembling with fear under the unblinking and decidedly unnerving gaze of the owl's piercing black eyes.

The owl, meanwhile, shakes the rope attached to its leg and flaps its huge wings in frustration as it stares down at the lion, wondering if it is really as frightened as it looks, or if it's going to suddenly climb up the post at any moment and eat it for breakfast.

Life Path 5: The Rebel

The lion, of course, is the **8**, who wants nothing more than to be powerful enough to smash down the door of the cage and escape from this scary-looking bird, while the owl is the **5**, who wants nothing more than to be free of its chains and fly high into the sky.

This is how these two numbers will probably feel should they meet, fall in love and begin a relationship together. The freedom-loving **5** will fear being caged by their relationship and is, in fact, in grave danger of being eaten alive by the much more powerful **8**.

The normally Self-assured **8**, meanwhile, will be freaked out by the **5**'s ability to look straight through their tough façade – which fools pretty much everyone else – and see the frightened child within.

No one is more proud, and therefore more vulnerable, than the competitive and egotistical **8**. (Ego equals fear, remember.) In the normal course of their day-to-day life, the **8** is able to hide their deep-seated insecurities behind their impressive take-charge persona as they battle it out in the boardroom or on the sporting field, pursuing victory at all costs to satisfy the cravings of their ego.

But if one day they decide to open their heart to a **5**, they will real-eyes there is nowhere to hide from their ability to read them like a nursery rhyme book. This can be the most unnerving experience for the Self-conscious **8**, while also a wonderful opportunity to allow their lover to help them let go of their crippling fear.

For their part, the **5** who falls for a powerful **8** will also be unnerved by their partner's single-minded ability to set a goal and focus on achieving it, such as a lion does when stalking its prey. The **5** yearns for freedom, but the hard work and discipline required to achieve it sit about as well with them as the proverbial princess on a pea.

If the **5** could see that the **8** knows the answer to all their problems – which is to stop flitting from one job to another and one relationship to another and learn that discipline and focus will give them the success, and therefore the freedom, they crave – the owl will discover that the lion is in fact a pussycat and they can live happily ever after.

Equally, if the **8** could see that the **5** knows the answer to all their problems – which is to real-eyes there is nothing to be afraid of once

Life Path 5: Relationship Choices

they step out of their ego and into their heart, where all the power of their love resides – the lion won't need to smash down the door. It will climb up the post and chew through the owl's rope, whereupon the owl will latch onto the lion's mane with its claws, flap its massive wings several times and then fly them both to freedom.

It doesn't really matter if these two mismatched lovers choose to stay together after that. If they do, they can enjoy an exciting relationship with plenty of adventures and a good deal of financial abundance. And if they decide to go their separate ways, they will be eternally grateful to each other for the life-changing lessons they shared.

Good luck, stay open and honest… and hopefully you will both sail happily through life together in a beautiful pea-green boat.

Friendship

Continuing with the owl and the lion theme, these two will most likely be drawn to each other when they first meet, the proud **8** liking the way the quick-witted **5** makes them roar with laughter, and the intelligent **5** appreciating the **8**'s compliments about their wisdom.

The (ahem!) mane problem, though, is that the **8** may usually grow tired of the **5**'s unreliability and their penchant for flying off into the night without a moment's notice, and the **5** may find it impossible to resist poking fun at the **8**'s puffed-up sense of personal pride (which really ruffles the **5**'s feathers), thus alienating their **8** friend.

The friendship may end around the time both real-eyes they have very little in common. About as much as a lion and an owl, in fact.

Business

OK. Down to business. No more animal jokes.

The creative and adventurous **5** will often choose to partner up in business, but it will usually be with an equally creative **1**, a worldly **9**, or a compassionate **6**. I can tell you that it certainly wouldn't be with a controlling and bossy **8**. And I ain't lion.

* * *

Life Path 5: The Rebel

5 & 9
(Freedom and Passion)

Love

These two feisty and passionate lovers of life — who are always on the go and require almost constant stimulation to maintain their interest — can certainly make sparks fly when they get together. The trouble is, before the sparks have had a chance to ignite the bonfire of their love, one or both of them will probably have already moved on somewhere else and to someone new.

The **5** and the **9** have much in common, not least their tendency to be in a constant state of flux in all areas of their life. In this regard, they are perfectly matched. No one other than a **5** fully understands the **9**'s need to uproot and go travelling at the drop of a hat, and no one other than a **9** can cope as well with the mercurial **5**'s rapid changes of mind and their need for variety.

If they do meet and fall in love they will certainly never be bored or stuck for conversation because both have a wide range of interests and share a common lust for adventure. No, the challenge won't be falling in love, it will be staying in love unless both are able to find the time to nurture their relationship in their crazy-busy lives.

Committing to anything for than more than five minutes is never easy for the unpredictable **5**. And while the **9** is better at making a commitment and sticking to it, they still like to know they are free to do whatever they want, whenever they want.

For this reason, the **5** will be instantly attracted to the idea of a relationship with a **9**, who will be only too happy to give them all the freedom they need — as long as they get it back in return.

And therein lies the rub. When neither partner values the other one more than they value their freedom to be apart from them, the point of being in the relationship becomes harder and harder to justify. In some ways, they might be better off just being friends. Or, if the physical attraction is there, maybe friends with benefits.

Life Path 5: Relationship Choices

The only way this pairing is really going to work in the long-term (and work spectacularly well, I might add) is if they have both reached a point in their lives when they feel they have sown all the euphemistic oats they need to sow and climbed all the metaphorical mountains they need to climb and are ready to "settle down" with their slippers, a good book, a couple of golden retrievers and a nice cup of tea by the fire.

Until then, short, romantic flings and steamy, passionate affairs will be much more their cup of tea – or, to be more accurate, their bucket of cocktails by the pool of their five-star waterfront hotel.

Good luck, stay open and honest, make sure you have plenty of hangover cures in the medicine cabinet … and enjoy it while it lasts.

Friendship

Talk about a match made in heaven. This is a perfect match of two like-minded party people that isn't just made in heaven – it's carefully hand-crafted on Cloud Nine by a team of highly skilled angels whose lives have been dedicated to studying the fine art of having fun.

Not even "God" could have created such a boisterous friendship if he had kicked back in his banana chair on the evening of the fifth day and downed a bottle of tequila and half a pound of Bolivian blow.

These two should never go into business together, unless they want to do all their dough in the first six months. And they will struggle to stay together as lovers, unless they are old enough and wise enough to put their partying days behind them. But as friends? Oh, yes.

This is definitely going to work!

Business

For all the reasons we have just seen, the **5** would be better off partnering up in their business venture with Russell Brand or Miley Cyrus than a **9** for all the work they'll get done. Their loan from the bank will last about 10 minutes, and the company will go belly-up faster than a lapdog with an itchy tummy.

* * *

Life Path 5: The Rebel

4. HEALTH CHOICES

MOST **5**s will approach decisions regarding their physical health with the same cavalier attitude they bring to every other decision they take … which means they will ignore their health tomorrow in favour of sucking as much fun out of life today as they possibly can.

"Live for today and to hell with tomorrow" perfectly sums up the rebellious and contrary **5**'s attitude to life, and this is nowhere more prevalent than with their physical health.

Of all the Life Paths, the **5** is the least concerned with issues of physicality, and for good reason. The robust Rebel is blessed with the constitution of an ox (and a rather large, vibrant ox at that), so health is seldom a worry for them. They can drink all their friends under the table and still be up with the sun before all of them have stirred, sipping on their third mug of Earl Grey, puffing on their fifth pre-breakfast cigarette and laughing at their friends' hangovers when they do appear, while chiding them mercilessly for being such "lightweights".

It's almost as though the toxins that afflict everyone else have no effect on the **5**, who seem to function as well on a diet of booze and fags as everyone else does on a diet of salad and alfalfa sprouts.

No, the issues that affect the **5**'s health are almost never physical ones based on diet or exercise, but emotional ones based on anger and frustration. Anger is the **5**'s Achilles Heel. It is the byproduct of their failure to rise above their Self-doubt and stand in their light to show the world a better way. If unresolved, this anger – which is always directed at themselves – can lead to all manner of physical dis-eases, including high blood pressure, cardiac problems and depression.

Many **5**s suffer from nervous disorders as well, including Bell's Palsy, migraines, insomnia, skin rashes and hypertension.

Ailments to watch out for

As we have just seen, most of the **5**'s ailments are nervous and emotional rather than physical. Their body is often extremely robust,

Life Path 5: Health Choices

but their nervous system is anything but. Anger, frustration and disillusionment can play havoc with the **5**'s physical body, manifesting as stress, insomnia, heart trouble, organ problems (especially the spleen and gall bladder), nervous tension and high blood pressure.

Sleepless nights and periods of Self-doubt can also cause the Rebel to languish in depression and exhaustion. It's not uncommon for a depressed **5** to stay in bed all day, and much of the next day as well.

Skin problems (vulnerability) are also common with **5**s, especially when young, because one of their main challenges is to overcome their fear of rejection, and their skin is always their last line of defence. Many **5**s will suffer from eczema and psoriasis as shy children before they have learned that nothing "out there" can ever harm them.

Effective therapies

The best therapy for the hyperactive and nervous **5** is to engage in deep relaxation interspersed with regular physical exercise. No one needs their eight hours of sleep more than the **5**, and no one needs to burn off their superfluous energy more than them either.

Regular physical exercise is essential for the hyperactive **5**. Not only does it release their pent-up emotional energy and burn off the excess calories that their Self-indulgent lifestyle puts into their digestive system, but it also helps them release their nervous tension.

More calming activities such as mediation, yoga and Pilates are also beneficial, as are long walks in nature. All **5**s love nature, and if they come across wild animals then all the better because the Rebel derives enormous amounts of energy from the natural world.

Diet choices

All **5**s need to focus on drinking plenty of water because they can become dehydrated very easily. They also tend to veer sharply between the extremes of eating healthily and indulging in unhealthy pursuits, such as drinking and smoking. Trying to find a well-balanced middle path is crucial, because although the **5** is blessed with a robust digestive system, their complete lack of concern about the effect their diet has on their body can lead them to suffer from serious heart trouble.

The expression "The **5** is all heart" can be taken one of two ways: yes, they are one of the most compassionate of numbers, but they are also prone to heart dis-ease more than any of the other Life Paths, except perhaps the indulgent **1**.

Plenty of rest, regular physical exercise and a well-balanced diet should guarantee their physical body keeps pace with their million-miles-an-hour mind.

Eat plenty of leafy green vegetables, as well as carrots, turnips, almonds and citrus fruits. Other beneficial foods include parsnip, parsley, mushrooms, cabbage, oatmeal, potato, sweet potato, rice, cumin seeds, caraway seeds, apricots, eggs, olives and seaweed.

* * *

5. CHOICES FOR CHILDREN

YOUNG children working with the energy of **5** will usually explore the negative energies of their Life Path Number before moving on to master the positive aspects. This is true of all the nine Life Paths because children need to first understand the boundaries of what is and isn't acceptable behaviour.

However, once their boundaries are in place – and your child has understood the crucial lesson of cause and effect – young **5**s can then start tapping into their natural rebellious strengths with the assistance of a positive parental guiding hand.

Children working with the energy of **5** are usually quite a handful from the earliest age because this Life Path is concerned with freedom above all else, and for very young **5**s freedom to do whatever they want is a commodity that is in very short supply.

Life Path 5: Choices for Children

Parents must prepare for almost all their instructions and requests to be not only questioned but resisted, often with heated tantrums. The solution to a **5**'s resistance to authority is relatively easy, however. Simply use reverse psychology by asking your **5** child to do the exact opposite of what you want them to do, and nine times out of 10 they will happily do whatever it was you wanted them to do in the first place, thinking they are rebelling when they are in fact conforming.

This won't always work, of course, especially as the **5** child grows older and sees what you are doing. There will definitely be times when the rebellious **5** child needs the firm hand of discipline. They might not thank you for it at the time, but the day will come when they look back as a young adult and appreciate the boundaries you gave them.

The positive qualities of **5** children are that they are very quick to learn and they adapt easily to change. They are inherently cheerful, as long as variety is a part of their life and they do not feel restricted by too many rules and regulations.

5 children make friends easily and are usually extremely popular at school. Studying is not usually their forte, unless you can find new and varied ways for them to do it. For example, they will be more likely to finish their homework if you let them do it in their bedroom one night, on the dining room table the next night, in the living room the next night, and so on.

On the negative side, the non-conformist **5** child does not like being told what to do. At school, the need for rules can spark their rebellious streak, causing them to get into trouble with authority. If a parent tells them to do something and they do the opposite, they might get away with it – but not at school.

The trouble is, the more the school authorities try to make the **5** child conform, the more they will rebel. Ironically, if schools outlawed studying and working hard, **5** children would be top of their class.

The best way for parents to deal with the **5**'s rebellious nature is to allow them some freedom in areas that don't matter (let the boys have long hair and the girls wear their skirts short, for example). They

Life Path 5: The Rebel

have expressed their individuality and therefore will be happy to conform in more important areas such as studying and homework.

Non-conformist **5** children will usually want to do the opposite of whatever it is you are asking them to do, so clever parenting is needed.

Often the best way is to ask them what they want to do and make sure they give you several different options – then pick the one that is closest to what you want them to do.

That way they are not conforming because they are doing what they want to do, but at the same time you are getting your desired outcome without an argument.

Playtime activities

The **5** child loves adventure games, exploring, hide-and-seek and treasure hunts. Their inquisitive minds also love puzzles and quizzes. In fact, **5**s love all games as long as they are not repetitive and boring.

Because young **5**s have a lot of energy, all sports are good for them – and the fewer rules the better. If you give them a cricket bat and ball, they will probably end up playing golf or baseball with them.

At home, **5** children want to be involved in everything and hate to feel left out. If you have friends over and send them to bed, they will pretend to be asleep and then creep downstairs to listen at the living room door.

The best way to deal with this is never to send them back to bed in disgrace. Instead, invite them in, give them their social "fix" and let them interact with your friends – then take them lovingly back to bed and satisfy their insatiable curiosity by telling them that if they go to sleep now, in the morning you will take them on an adventure.

Strangely, although **5**s value freedom of choice, they love it when given specific tasks to perform. Hand them a list of everything they need to do, and they will usually dutifully tick them off one by one.

* * *

Life Path 5: Choices for Children

Your child's three-digit Birth Code

As we have seen in Part Two, we always work primarily with the energy of our Life Path Number right from the outset, but in our childhood years from 0 to 18 we do so in conjunction with the energy of our first Supplementary Birth Number, and in our second 18 years – until we reach full emotional maturity at 36 – we do so in conjunction with the energy of our second Supplementary Birth Number.

It's worth reading the main listings here in Part Three for the numbers that make up your child's two Supplementary Birth Numbers to gain a better understanding of their positive and negative qualities.

Also, as you read about your child's three-digit Birth Code, real-eyes that the difference between "feeling the force" of any Life Path and flipping to the "dark side" is determined by the amount of Self-confidence we develop in our childhood years, and then the amount of Self-love we develop in our teenage years.

That, in a nutshell (squirrel!), is your role as a parent: to instill in your child first Self-esteem, and then Self-love.

The 00/5 'Millennium' child

As we saw earlier in the Life Choices section of this listing, there are only a handful of possible birth dates at the start of the new millennium that contain this rare Birth Code, between January 2, 2000 and October 10, 2010.

Before them, the last child with this Birth Code was born on October 10, 1200 – more than 800 years ago – and the next one won't be born until January 1, 3000 – almost 1000 years from now.

Clearly, from a numerological perspective, a child born with this Birth Code at the start of this new millennium has the potential to achieve something truly special with their life because they are working with the double (00) amplified energy of their Life Path Number **5**, which endows these young Rebels with an extraordinary capacity to bring about radical change for the better in our world.

Life Path 5: The Rebel

But because the Self-Awareness System™, like everything else in the universe, is governed by the Law of Duality, this also means they have the capacity for equal amounts of disappointment.

Parents of a 00/5 Millennium Child must take extra care to nurture their positive potential and guard against the negative flighty and undisciplined characteristics of this rare Birth Code.

All the positive and negative qualities of the **5** detailed in this listing for the Rebel still hold true, but the 00/5 child will be working with them on a rarefied level. This means they are born with the capacity to make a real difference in the world by showing all of humanity how to unplug from the Fear Matrix and live their lives as pure, perfect spirits, blissfully free of fear.

But there is no pressure on them to do so. If they choose simply to use the innate freedom-fighting qualities of the **5** to help free their loved ones and close friends from the forces of oppression, this is their choice and should never be questioned.

All we can ever do is what we can, and our highest potential is always to make ourselves and those around us as happy as they can be. If it's just their immediate family and their local community, that is perfect. The fact that their Birth Code is so rare should never be dumped on their shoulders as a burden.

That unwelcome pressure could be ruinous to their highly sensitive nature, and must never be allowed to happen.

The 14/5 child

The presence of 1 as the first Supplementary Birth Number means that children born with this Birth Code will work with the powerful fire (forceful) energy of the Leader during the first formative 18 years of their life, in conjunction with their Life Path energy of **5**.

The 4 as their second Supplementary Birth Number means they will then spend their next 18 years – until full emotional maturity at age 36 – working with the practical (earth) energy of the Builder to create a strong foundation for their life.

These children will tend to be outgoing from an early age (the leadership energy of 1) and have the capacity to be quite headstrong. Then, as they mature into young adulthood from 18 years and up, they will focus on creating a solid foundation for themselves (the practical energy of 4) in terms of financial security and emotional stability.

All the while they will be questioning everything that "authority" throws at them (and by "authority I mean their parents and teachers when they are young, and the Fat Controllers as they reach adulthood) because their overarching and rebellious Life Path energy of **5** will drive them to search for a better way, free of the forces of fear.

Parents must be prepared that the rebellious nature of their Life Path Number **5**, combined with the egotistical qualities of the Leader (1) from birth to adulthood, means these young Rebels may have frequent run-ins with authority at home, at school and possibly even with the police.

They must re-mind their 14/5 child that rebellion for the sake of it is nothing more than immature petulance, and they would do better to first conform and understand the world they live in before trying to change it for the better. There is no rush. Grow up first. Understand the world you live in, and then calmly figure out – responsibly and maturely – how to change it. After all, no one can effect lasting change in the world from inside a prison cell, or a drug rehab centre.

The 14/5 child will always want to go their own way. All their parents can do is persuade them to wait until they are old enough to understand the consequences of their actions before doing so.

The 41/5 child

As we saw earlier in the Life Choices section, this is a mirror of the previous Birth Code, so children walking this Life Path will share many qualities with their 14/5 cousins. The difference is that during their first formative years – when their personality is established – they will be working with the supplementary earth energy of the practical and grounded 4, instead of forceful and ambitious fire energy of 1.

Yes, they will still be a rebellious **5** through and through – and will therefore be quick-witted, adventurous and contrary – but they will be much less of a hothead than the outspoken 14/**5**, and they will tend to become more balanced and mature young adults as well.

The 41/**5** will also tend to be slightly more serious and have a better understanding of the consequences of their rebellious actions, due to the practical energy of 4 operating throughout their childhood and teenage years. Their 1 leadership energy then kicks in during early adulthood from 18 onwards, helping them to gain enough confidence to follow their dreams and make a real difference in the world.

As with the 14/**5**, the absence of any water (emotion) energy in their Birth Code means these Rebels will be focused almost exclusively on their career path, able to take charge of a situation (1), follow through on their projects (4) and experience much success in their primary goal of improving the way we all live our lives (**5**).

In their personal life, though, the absence of any emotional energy in their numbers means both 41/**5**s and 14/**5**s must guard against being too much in their head, fighting the good fight, and not enough in their heart, nurturing their romantic relationships.

The 23/5 child

The presence of both the loving 2 (water) and creative 3 (air) Supplementary Birth Numbers gives these fiery **5**s (and their 32/**5** cousins) some much-needed emotional and intellectual energy, which is missing in the passionate and headstrong 14/**5** and 41/**5** Birth Codes.

This means these Rebels will work with the co-operative energy of 2 and the expressive energy of 3 during their early formative years, allowing them to relate to others and voice their opinions in ways that will help them fulfill their highest purpose of fighting against the forces of oppression and showing the world a better way to live.

On the flip side, however, their lack of any practical earth energy (4) means they may sometimes find themselves living in a dream world, unable and unwilling to face up to the harsh realities of day-to-day life.

Life Path 5: Choices for Children

Plus, without the leadership energy of 1, they may suffer from a lack of Self-confidence in their teenage years and a lack of Self-love in their adult years, causing them to shrink back into Self-doubt. There is nothing worse for a Rebel than shyness, because if they don't have the courage to fight their fight, they will be doomed to a life of frustration.

Providing they do the necessary inner work to discover that they are pure love and pure Source energy – and therefore nothing and no one can ever harm them – the young 23/5 has the potential to be an effective change-agent by using the love of the 2 and the creativity of the 3 to become a compassionate and rousing revolutionary.

In their first 18 years, the supplementary qualities of 2 will ensure they develop their emotional intelligence before embarking on more creative pursuits with the expressive energy of 3 until they reach full emotional maturity at the age of 36. But if they lack the confidence to work with the positive energy of these numbers, they risk becoming introverted and shy children (negative 2) and then stifling their creative urges due to Self-doubt as they enter the workforce (negative 3).

Parents of 23/5 children should make sure that they have plenty of interaction with other children from an early age, and also have the freedom to express their original creative ideas as they grow older into their 20s and 30s.

The 32/5 child

This is a mirror of the previous Birth Code, and children walking this Life Path will share many qualities with their 23/5 cousins. The key difference is that during their first formative years – when their personality is established – they will be working with the supplementary air energy of creative expression (the Creative 3), rather than with the social and co-operative water energy of the Intuitive (2).

Yes, they will still be a rebellious **5** through and through – and will therefore be quick-witted, adventurous and quite a handful – but they will be more creative than the compassionate and conformist 23/**5**, and they will tend to be more of a loner and a misfit too.

Life Path 5: The Rebel

The 32/5 child will also tend to be slightly more withdrawn and spend more time on their own, pouring through books or drawing pictures as they dream up ways they can change the world.

The impact of the air energy of 3 in their childhood years imbues the 32/5 with a thoughtful and contemplative nature. It is usually only when they reach young adulthood at 18 – when the co-operative and social energy of 2 kicks in – that they pluck up the courage to form close relationships and discuss their ideas freely with others.

And even then, it may take until they reach full emotional maturity at 36 before they truly feel able to stand on their own two feet and speak what is in their heart.

Parents of a 32/5 child would do well to coax them out of their naturally shy shell to play with other children, while keeping a close eye on their welfare. Most 32/5 children are so creative and non-conformist from the earliest age that they never truly fit in with any social group, and can therefore be subjected to bullying – simply because they are so different.

Watch out for this and always take the time to reassure your 32/5 child that the only reason the bullies pick on them is because they are indeed different and will one day grow up to change the world – while the bullies will always be bullies, stuck in the Fear Matrix, never able to escape their anger or their fear of anything they don't understand.

LIFE PATH 6:
The Visionary

1. Growth cycle: Sixth stage (the number of beauty)
2. Influences: Water (emotion, feminine) and Venus (love)
3. Positive qualities: Loving, supportive and nurturing
4. Negative potential: Meddlesome, intrusive and controlling
5. Highs and lows: Inspirational idealist, or intolerant perfectionist
6. Highest purpose: Show others their true loving potential
7. Love matches: 2, 4, 6, 8, 9 for compatibility (the rest for growth)
8. Possible careers: Social work, nursing, counselling, the arts
9. Words to live by: "Everything happens perfectly"

1. LIFE CHOICES FOR THE VISIONARY

THE caring and compassionate **6**, as the Life Path's name suggests, is the most idealistic and romantic of numbers. They are instinctive nurturers who have come into the world to be a beacon of love for all of us, and to share their vision of a Utopian "heaven on earth" where everyone lives in love, without any fear, greed or violence.

6s are the idealists of the world, holding in their hearts the best qualities of humanity as a romantic ideal that sadly is so seldom experienced today. Eternally optimistic, the positive **6** will always bounce back time and again from disappointment – determined to believe in the power of love no matter what life throws at them.

This is the sixth (feminine) stage of a growth cycle, and it follows on from the rebellious masculine energy of the **5**, who paved the way

Life Path 6: The Visionary

for radical change in the way we grow and interact with each other. The first four Life Paths are called the "human cycle", where our primary focus is on worldly issues such as career (**1**), relationships (**2**), creativity (**3**) and material stability (**4**). Then the rebellious **5** comes along and flips everything on its head, beginning the second "divine cycle" by showing us how to rise above our mortal concerns and focus instead on ridding the world of fear and helping everyone live in love.

6 marks the second stage of this "divine cycle" (**5** to **8**) where we learn that the answers to all our questions lie not "out there" in the physical world but inside us in our hearts. Specifically, the **6** is here to show us our divine beauty and teach us that love is not just something we give and receive, it is who we are.

It's no surprise that Venus is the **6**'s guiding planet, because they are here to teach us all about love. It's a lesson we must all learn as we transform ourselves from unaware carbon-based life forms having a physical experience into pure spirits having a human experience.

This is when we make the most profound shift in our lives as we real-eyes that, contrary to everything we learned in Sunday School, we are divine love and "God" is not separate from us… "God" is us.

Because **6**s are also governed by the element of water (emotion), they are deeply caring and considerate people who instinctively adopt the role of caretaker and nurturer in their family.

In fact, family is always of the highest importance for this most domestic of numbers.

The **6**'s cheerful, optimistic personality ensures they will have plenty of friends, but their life almost always revolves around their home, where they delight in supporting and encouraging their loved ones – as well as picking them up and dusting them off when they fall.

The **6** is never happier than when they feel they are being useful in a social situation, or at home with their family. Long periods of solitude are like a prison sentence for them and it is vital that they are included in all family decisions because they love to feel they are contributing to making their home a happy and harmonious place.

Life Path 6: Life Choices

But because what we are all here to do is not necessarily what comes easiest to us, the **6** will also face challenges on their Life Path that are put there specifically to help them grow. These challenges will usually involve them being let down over and over again by the people around them, who are seldom able to measure up to their idealistic view of how beautiful and loving the world should be.

Worst of all they will frequently wrestle with chronic issues of Self-worth and Self-doubt. Not only are Visionaries their own worst critic, quick to beat themselves up when their own thoughts and actions don't match their perfectionist ideals, but they are also naturally submissive and must take care to prevent other more forceful people walking all over them.

Those who work with the positive energy of **6** will learn to love and accept themselves just as they are, warts and all, which will also allow them to see the divine beauty in others. But those who work with the negative energy of this Life Path will be overly Self-critical, seeing faults in themselves and in others and getting bogged down in the petty details of perfectionism.

Negativity can bring **6**s down quite easily, especially if it's in their home or at work. If exposed to it over long periods they can become cranky, downcast and even vindictive in their behaviour. Thankfully, it is rare for the **6** to suffer these negative traits because they are naturally happy and optimistic… provided their home is harmonious and they receive tonnes of love from their nearest and dearest.

* * *

Highest purpose of The Visionary

The highest purpose of the **6** (and the Master Visionary 33/6 – more about you "33s" in a moment) is to hold the vision of a pure, perfect world where everyone lives together in peace and love. If that sounds like the cringeworthy answer to one of those Miss World questions, so be it. The cynics of the world have far too loud a voice these days and someone has to speak up for the blissful Utopian ideal of what we as a human race are capable.

That someone is the beautiful and eternally optimistic **6**.

Because the Visionary's highest purpose is to show humanity that love is the noblest quality to which we can aspire, they will face the central challenge of accepting themselves to be worthy of love as much as they preach the qualities of love to others.

The risk is that in holding the vision of divine love as the highest goal of mankind, the **6** can sometimes suffer long bouts of frustration and even depression if they spend too much time focusing on their own "human imperfections", as well as those of others. This dissatisfaction with the so-called "real world" they find themselves in can lead them to become overly critical, judgmental and intolerant.

Therefore, as well as holding the torch of love for the entire human race, the **6** also has to pursue a more personal highest purpose of achieving a healthy balance between nurturing others and helping them achieve happiness and peace, and nurturing themselves so that they can experience happiness and peace as well.

Remember, the most important goal for all Life Paths is always the same: to first "wake up" to the truth that we are an extension of Source energy, and to help other people wake up as well.

Then, and only then, will the path to our highest potential open up before us.

* * *

Key words are… 'confidence' and 'acceptance'

To fulfill their life's highest purpose, **6**s must first learn to develop a robust inner confidence in their abilities.

Confidence is central to all the Life Paths as we embark on our common journey from pure unaware love to pure conscious love. As we saw in Part One, developing a healthy Self-esteem is the first crucial step towards Self-love that we all must take.

Life Path 6: Life Choices

(If you've come straight to this Life Path listing in Part Three and are wondering what a "Self" is, please try to find the time to read Part One because it's way too complicated to explain again here.)

For the always emotional **6**, however, developing a strong sense of inner confidence is much more than just the key to their personal happiness – it will determine whether they walk the positive Life Path of the inclusive and idealistic romantic, or veer down the negative path towards intolerance, disillusion and Self-loathing.

All Visionaries are born with a deep, intuitive desire to help and nurture others, especially in their time of need. They have incredible staying power, willingly shouldering much more than their share of the burden. And talking of shoulders, theirs is almost always the one others use to cry on because they also have a remarkable capacity for patience and understanding.

However, unless the **6** develops a strong inner confidence in their own Self-worth and learns when to say "enough", they can easily be taken advantage of and become loaded up with everyone else's problems to the point of exhaustion.

As idealists who hold the highest potential of mankind close to their heart, they can also become dispirited by the far-from perfect actions of others. They are deeply affected by any signs of anger or violence and fret excessively if anyone close to them is sad or hurt.

The **6** must learn that not everything is always going to be perfect all the time, and not everyone is going to be sweetness and light 24/7. The secret to their long-term happiness lies in the famous phrase: "Grant me the serenity to accept the things I cannot change, the courage to change the things I can – and the wisdom to know the difference."

This leads to the second key word for the perfectionist Visionary to focus on, which is "acceptance". To avoid a life of continual frustration and disappointment, they must accept that the world is far from perfect and they can only do so much to raise the level of love.

Just as importantly, they must also accept that they too are far from perfect and forgive themselves fully when they fall short of their own impossibly high standards. "Guilt" is the go-to emotion for the **6**,

Life Path 6: The Visionary

and I don't need to tell you that guilt is the single most damaging emotion there is – spiritually, emotionally and physically as well.

Spiritually, it guarantees you never fully feel your Self to be pure, perfect love. Emotionally, it leads to a deep resentment of others. And physically, it is a direct path to all manner of ailments, including cancer.

By accepting that nothing and no one is perfect, including themselves, the confident **6** can avoid the "guilt trap" and maintain both their health and their humour by knowing when it is time to stop helping everyone else and look after themselves.

* * *

Positive and negative potential

All Life Paths contain an equal measure of positive and negative potential. Our challenge in every lifetime, no matter our Life Path Number, is to nurture our positives and overcome our negatives.

The reason we are given negative potential as well as positive potential is because people usually respond more effectively to the threat of pain than they do to the promise of pleasure.

Also, while it is admirable to do what we are good at in life, we will only ever become the best we can be by facing our "dark side" and digging deep into our Self to overcome the obstacles that appear on our path.

As we have already seen in Part Two, it is only when the chips are down and we are up against it that we find out who we truly are and what we are truly capable of doing.

For example, the caring and humanitarian **6** is only too happy to spread their love around and help others wherever they are needed. They are instinctively nurturing and will stop at nothing to create a loving and peaceful home for their family, as well as a supportive and safe workplace for their colleagues.

But on the flip side, they can overstep the mark quite easily and put their nose in where it isn't welcome. So instead of being seen by others as helpful, they can become intrusive and meddlesome. Equally, where the positive **6** is usually loving and supportive, the negative **6** can sometimes be overly controlling and dominating.

All **6s** must therefore learn the key lesson of this Life Path – which is to live and let live.

It's dangerously easy for the perfectionist Visionary to fall into a pattern of being critical of others, especially when they fail to live up to the **6**'s idealistic view of the world. Just as they are the most supportive of all the Life Paths, they can also be the most intolerant.

Although it appears to others that the **6** is judging them, they are usually judging their own perceived shortcomings and then projecting their dissatisfaction onto those around them. This can be hard to live with, and **6s** must learn to go easy on themselves and others when their impossibly high standards are not being met.

Another challenge that the **6** can, and usually does, encounter on their Life Path is the lesson of unconditional love. Yes, going out of their way to help others is a noble cause but unless the person they are healing or helping is another **6**, they are unlikely to find their generosity and patience reciprocated.

Much of the time the other person hasn't asked for their love or support (they never need to because the nurturing **6** instinctively knows where their help is needed the most), so the **6** would do best to give of themselves without expecting anything in return. If they don't do this, they can become hurt and resentful when other people – who usually aren't as loving and considerate as they are – fail to return it in kind.

Because all **6s** are at the sixth (divine inner beauty) stage of their Spiritual Growth Cycle, they will focus most of their optimistic energy on spreading love wherever they go. While the **1** wants to conquer the world, the **2** wants to heal the world, the **3** wants to travel the world, the **4** wants to understand the world and the **5** wants to change the world, the idealistic **6** has come here to show the world its highest potential – namely that we are all made of pure love, and love is all that matters.

Some **6s** will take this romantic crusade out into the world by taking up arms in the fight against fear and oppression. Famous

Life Path 6: The Visionary

romantic **6**s from history who have shone their beacon of love far and wide include best-selling authors Lewis Carroll, whose *Alice* books have taught countless millions the power of love, JRR Tolkien and Alexander Dumas (ditto) and Agatha Christie, whose novels contain equal parts romance and suspense. Add to this list other great romantic **6**s such as John Lennon, Michael Jackson, Stevie Wonder, Cary Grant, James Dean, Fred Astaire, Greta Garbo, James Brown and Robert De Niro – among many others – and you can start to see how much of an influence the creative Visionaries have had on our world.

Indeed, almost all **6**s have a strong and passionate creative flair in at least one of the arts, especially music and literature.

However, because this is also the most domestic of all the Life Path Numbers, many **6**s are content to shine their love light much closer to home, raising their children and helping out in their local community. Family is always of primary importance to the **6**, and even if they do go out into the world to spread their message of love, they will never stray far from home for long.

And because they are such passionate animal lovers too, the **6**'s home will almost always have at least one four-legged family member as well. (I say "family member" advisedly because the pet of a **6** will invariably be the most pampered puss or pooch in the neighbourhood, sharing beds as well as meals with the rest of the household.)

And if the family goes on holiday, chances are the pet will come too – especially if it's a dog – and probably be allowed to ride up front in the passenger's seat too.

As well as being dedicated homemakers, **6**s are often conservative in their views and are acutely aware of the value of a strict and disciplined upbringing. This, along with their instinctive need to care for and nurture others, makes them excellent mums and dads.

It's also not unusual to find **6**s volunteering at their local church, mosque, synagogue or ashram because many Visionaries belong to one of the mainstream religions. They are also happy to give freely of their time to help out at community halls, charity centres, animal rescue pounds and other worthwhile causes.

Life Path 6: Life Choices

Volunteering is in their DNA, which leads many **6**s to work with overseas aid organisations helping the poor and the displaced get back on their feet. In this line of charitable work, they will always regard their colleagues, and the victims they tend to, as their "other family".

Their cheerful personality means **6**s usually have a large group of good friends, who will not hesitate to lean on them and turn to them for advice. Again, as we have already seen, the **6** must beware of giving too much of themselves to family, friends, charities and colleagues, which can leave them exhausted both physically and emotionally. They must also be wary of becoming discouraged when others in their group do not share their passionate need for love and harmony at all times.

Sometimes the burden of caring for everyone can weigh so heavily on the **6**'s shoulders that they just give up and abdicate all their responsibilities. This rejection of their own sense of duty will make them feel deeply guilty and can cause havoc with their relationships, as well as with their physical health and emotional wellbeing.

To illustrate what I mean, it's telling that the architect of the most famous abdication in world history – Britain's King Edward VIII – was not just a **6** but a Master Number 33/**6**.

In truth, though, there are relatively few negative pitfalls for this most upbeat and generous of Life Paths. And even if they do fall in a heap, or simply become disgruntled, it's never long before the cheerful **6** picks themselves up and takes their love light back out into the world.

* * *

On a more personal level, the always loving **6** makes a wonderfully generous and loyal partner. They are eternally patient, passionately romantic, always supportive – and, if children come along, they will usually be the most doting and devoted parent it is possible to imagine.

They will go to great lengths to ensure their home is beautifully decorated, immaculately clean and always warm and welcoming for their many friends and acquaintances – who, when they come to call, will find the **6** is always the most perfectly charming host.

Life Path 6: The Visionary

Pots of piping hot tea, plates piled high with biscuits and cakes (usually homemade) and lashings of love and attention will greet them every time… along with a loving hug, a listening ear and an outpouring of helpful and uplifting words of encouragement.

The **6** is almost always attractive and immaculately well-groomed. There really is nothing they won't do for others, and they are usually deeply loved by many people as a result. In fact, it's this love that the **6** craves. It's their reward for all their hard work and tireless support.

If there is a "dark side" to this Life Path, it comes only from the best of intentions. The **6** is so keen to rid the world of all negativity that they often go too far with their desire to help, dishing out advice where it isn't wanted and sticking their face in where it isn't welcome.

This negative tendency to try to "fix" everyone can make the over-zealous **6** appear irritatingly controlling and domineering. And if the the mouth they are trying to feed then bites them, they can react with angry outbursts of righteousness. The **6** must remember not everyone wants to be helped, so it's best to offer people advice rather than force it on them. That way, if it's politely refused, a conflict can be avoided.

* * *

Summary of the positives

Providing the idealistic **6** develops the ability to accept the things they can't change in the world and the courage to change the things they can, they will fulfill their life's highest purpose of holding a vision for mankind's loving potential by shining the light of love onto others and helping as many people as possible discover their divine beauty.

This is the essential role of the Visionary, because true romance is not Romeo singing up at Juliet – it's Joan of Arc, a lowly peasant girl **6** who stood up to the forces of oppression, and Charles de Gaulle, another famous **6** who rallied his country against the Nazis.

The fact both were French is no surprise, considering France has long been regarded as a nation of passionate romantics.

Life Path 6: Life Choices

Those who work with the positive energy of **6** will make excellent healers, social workers, teachers, counsellors and homemakers. But no matter what they do, their family life will always come first, where they will be the proverbial rock everyone depends on.

The aware and evolved **6** is a tower of strength and compassion, a devoted and dedicated nurturer and an inspirational beacon of love, peace and tolerance for all of us to follow.

Key positive words

Idealistic, generous, nurturing, loving, optimistic, hospitable, kind, caring, considerate, domestic, charitable, faithful, emotional, honest, humanitarian, empathetic, graceful, warm, patient and supportive.

* * *

Summary of the negatives

As long as they clear their emotional blockages and develop a clear balance in their life between looking after everyone else and looking after themselves, there are relatively few negatives to this Life Path.

Problems for the always positive and cheerful **6** arise only when they lack the confidence to say "enough" to the crowd of needy victims beating a path to their door, including their entire family, all their friends and workmates, and everyone else who has ever heard about the amazing amount of patience and love they have to offer.

Unless they strike a balance between healing others and tending to their own needs, the negative **6** can become exhausted and resentful. They might even lash out in righteous anger, and they will also find themselves trying to control others rather than support them. No one is more meddlesome than a negative **6** who finds fault when someone or something doesn't live up to their impossibly high standards.

They must learn to live and let live, and must also develop a strong sense of Self-worth and Self-love so they avoid beating themselves up with the same "judgment stick" they use to berate others.

Key negative words

Controlling, intrusive, critical, meddlesome, righteous, superior, submissive, weak-willed, stressed, worrisome and judgmental.

* * *

Self-love is the difference

If you have read Part One, you will already know that your ability to walk the positive side of your Life Path, as opposed to the negative side, is determined by whether you have undertaken the two key stages of personal growth. Or, to put it another way, whether you have taken the two crucial first steps on the path to your life's highest purpose.

The first step towards living your Life Path in the positive is to develop Self-esteem (and if you're wondering what a "Self" is, please take the time to read Part One because it's way too complicated to explain again here). This feeling of inner confidence is essential because it allows you to tap into your innate strengths, which you will need if you are going to have any hope of overcoming the numerous obstacles on your path. Be aware, though, that on its own this first step is never enough, because Self-confidence and Self-esteem are still the work of the ego. The feeling of being "good enough" carries with it an implied sense of needing to be "better than".

So before you can reach your full potential and achieve your life's highest purpose, you must also take the second step – which is to rise above the egoic concept of Self-esteem and climb to the much higher ground of Self-love.

Loving your Self does not mean being "full of your Self". It means the opposite. It means being humble because you understand that you are the same as everyone else, no better and no worse.

Above all, it means you understand that we are all immortal spirits having a human experience, and therefore we are all, at our core, the same – pure love and pure Source energy. (The Source is also fully explained in Part One.)

Life Path 6: Life Choices

We can see it easily in new-born babies because when we are born into physical form, and before our fear-based ego has had a chance to develop, we are all gorgeous, gurgling bundles of pure, exquisite love.

I am not suggesting you do this, but just imagine you were to place a new-born infant on the pavement of a crowded street and then stand back out of sight. Everyone – and I mean everyone – would stop and tend to it. And the reason they would do this is because, deep down, we all recognise pure love when we see it. We are drawn to it at the most basic level of our being because it is the most strikingly beautiful and compelling force on the planet.

But sadly, as we grow up and go out into the world, our ego takes over and we start to believe – usually during our teenage years – that our ego is who we are. It isn't. Love is who we are.

We are all pure love. We are all extensions of Source energy (or children of "God", whichever phrase you are more comfortable with).

If you can rise above the quasi-religious terminology, I can summarise the two steps like this: Self-esteem is about feeling "good enough", while Self-love is about feeling "God enough".

The reason why loving your Self is so important for your Life Path is because when you start to live your life from the perspective of being pure love, everything changes. Suddenly you understand that nothing "out there" in the material world can ever harm you in any way.

Equally, you real-eyes you don't need anything "out there" in the material world to make you feel happy – not the approval of others; no amount of money, fame or power; and not even the love of a good man or woman – because you have all the love you need right there in your own heart, and you can therefore relish the exquisite joy of loving everyone unconditionally without needing anything in return.

That is why Self-love is the secret to working with the positive energy of your Life Path Number – because when you truly love your Self, the rocky mountain path you've been climbing suddenly becomes an express elevator ride all the way up to the summit of your bliss.

* * *

Life Path 6: The Visionary

No Life Path is an island

Although your Life Path Number denotes the main issues you will focus on throughout your life, you will always work to some degree with the energies of all the other numbers as well to become a fully rounded Self.

As a **6** your main work will be in the areas of vision and acceptance, but you will also tackle the issues of Self-confidence (**1**), co-operation and balance (**2**), creative expression (**3**), stability and flexibility (**4**), discipline (**5**), trust (**7**), abundance and power (**8**) and integrity (**9**).

It's therefore worth your while to read through the listings for the other Life Path Numbers when your time allows.

* * *

Qualities of your three-digit Birth Code

(Note: Please read the description in Part Two of how 0 operates in your three-digit Birth Code. Also, you can consult the main Life Path listings here in Part Three for each of your Supplementary Birth Numbers (the five possible ones for the Visionary are 1, 2, 3, 4 and 5) to give you a clearer understanding of how their qualities govern your formative years.)

'Millennium Child' 00/6

A Millennium Child born with the remarkably powerful single-digit Birth Code of **6** has come into the world with the potential to achieve something truly spectacular with their life.

All the Millennium Children (those born at the beginning of this century without any Supplementary Birth Numbers) are endowed with extra potential because they will all work with the energy of their Life Path Number with absolute focus and an incredible amount of commitment. (The qualities of the Millennium Children are described in detail in Part Two, Chapter 2.)

The doubly amplified presence of the two 0s in place of their two Supplementary Birth Numbers means they will be working solely with the supercharged energy of **6** their entire life, right from the moment they take their first breath.

This gives them a unique capacity to generate a massive shift in awareness for a great many people (the highest purpose of the Visionary **6**) by teaching them that love is not something we merely give and receive – it is who we are at the very core of our being.

All **6**s are first and foremost romantic idealists who are here to show us our divine inner beauty, so these Millennium Children have an opportunity to initiate a worldwide awakening at a time when their message of love is more desperately needed than perhaps at any time in our human history.

Before the start of this century, the last 00/**6** child was born on October 10, 1300, more than 700 years ago, but there are more coming soon, starting on January 1, 2020. Which is just as well, because we urgently need their help to rid our fragile little planet of the rampant fear, greed and religious warfare that threatens our very existence.

On a more personal level, 00/**6** children and adults will have the potential to create exquisitely harmonious homes, raise spectacularly loving children and enjoy a large and loyal circle of close friends.

And because the loving energy of **6** is the only number they will work with throughout their life, they may find themselves channeling their beautiful messages of hope and compassion to a wider audience through creative outlets such as music, writing and film.

As with all the Millennium Children, however, they must never feel pressured in any way to live up to the special promise of their amplified Birth Code. There is no "Life Path contract" that requires them to use their gifts for anything other than making themselves and their family happy. If all they do is shed their ego and live in love, they will achieve what we are all here to achieve… which is to real-eyes that we are pure love, and show the Source that it is pure love too.

15/6

The presence of both the fire numbers (1 and 5) as Supplementary Birth Numbers in this Birth Code means these fired-up Visionaries will

Life Path 6: The Visionary

burn their beacon of love especially brightly, both in their home life and in whatever they choose to do as a career.

For the first formative 18 years of their life, they will work with the supplementary take-charge energy of the Leader (1) to develop the confidence to spread their message of love, which is the primary goal of their Life Path Number 6. This will endow young 15/6s with both a strong personality and a single-minded determination to succeed.

Then for their next 18 years, up until they reach full emotional maturity at the age of 36, they will invoke the rebellious energy of 5, which will drive them to stand up to the forces of oppression in their quest to spread their Utopian ideal of a world free of fear and living in love (legendary Visionary Joan of Arc is the epitome of the 15/6).

All the while their main work will be influenced by the watery (emotional) energy of their Life Path 6, but their fiery Supplementary Birth Numbers mean they will not only be the head of their well-nurtured family (1) but will also seek out ways to improve the lives of others less fortunate than themselves (5).

As long as they clear their emotional blockages and work with the positive energy of their three Birth Code numbers, the 15/6 will enjoy much success both at home and in their work. Their lives will be filled with love – which is all any 6 ever really wants.

One word of caution, though: the lack of an earth number (4 or 8) in their Life Path means they must work especially hard to ground themselves and not take too many risks, and the absence of any air numbers (3 or 7) could result in disappointment if they blindly follow their emotions without failing to think things through.

Romantically, 15/6s will be enjoy deep and fulfilling relationships full of love (6), spontaneity (5) and passion (1). They will almost always seek out marriage and have children because nothing matters more to the nurturing 6 than taking care of their family.

24/6

The presence of 2 as the first Supplementary Birth Number of this Birth Code means these dyed-in-the-wool Visionaries will be deeply

Life Path 6: Life Choices

emotional beings because they will work with the water (emotion) energy of the Intuitive (2) during the first formative 18 years of their life alongside the equally watery qualities of their Life Path Number **6**.

Talk about wearing their heart on their sleeve! The highly sensitive and idealistic 24/**6** will be so in touch with their emotions during their childhood and teenage years that they will probably have to stash an entire box of tissues up their sleeve as well. They will experience life and relationships on such a deep level that seldom will a day go by without them crying both tears of sadness and tears of joy.

Mercifully, just as they reach adulthood at 18, the practical earth energy of the Builder (4) kicks in to plant their feet firmly on the ground and stop them drifting off high into the castle-filled sky of a Utopian dream world like an untethered heart-shaped helium balloon.

The 24/**6** will still always be a dreamer who holds aloft the image of a perfectly loving world for all to see, which is the main purpose of the idealistic **6**. But their focus will be fairly and squarely on building a happy and harmonious home (the energy of 4) where they can raise a family and surround themselves with the love they need.

Family will always come first for all **6**s, but for the emotional and practical 24/**6** it is their whole reason for being. Right from a young age they will crave close loving connections with friends and family members and will seldom allow their work, or anything else, to take them far from the bosom of their home.

As long as they clear their emotional blockages and work with the positive energy of these numbers, the submissive and super-sensitive 24/**6** will be able to control their swirling emotions and balance their desire to help others with their need to look after themselves. But if they fall into the "fear trap" of their ego, they run a very real risk of being trodden on and taken for granted.

Also, because of a lack of any fire (1 or 5) and air (3 or 7) numbers in their Birth Code, they need to guard against becoming too much of a homebody, devoid of direction and lacking the courage to go out and explore all this magnificent world has to offer.

Life Path 6: The Visionary

Romantically, they must also real-eyes that not everyone wants unicorns, fairytales and happy endings all the time as much as they do, so they must guard against feeling let down and reacting aggressively when their partner doesn't experience emotions as deeply as them.

42/6

This is a mirror of the previous Birth Code, and people walking this Life Path will share many qualities with their 24/6 cousins. The key difference is that during their first formative years – when their personality is established – they will be working with the supplementary earth energy of the practical and well-grounded 4, which will temper their idealistic and dreamy nature and teach them that although love is the most valuable commodity in our life, we still need to put food on our table and keep a roof over our head.

Yes, the 42/6 will still be a Visionary through and through – and will therefore focus almost all their energy on nurturing their loved ones with an almost superhuman capacity for patience and kindness – but they will be all the more effective in this role by learning early on that before we can love everyone else we first have to build a stable foundation for ourselves.

The more grounded 42/6 will also be better equipped to deal with life's little setbacks during their difficult teenage years than the 24/6, who will be more likely to succumb to their roller-coaster emotions without the benefit of any earth energy in their first 18 years.

Also, by the time their second water number 2 kicks in for the next 18 years of their life up to full emotional maturity at age 36, they will have already learned how to put down roots (4) and do what is necessary to survive in the so-called "real world".

Again, as we saw with the 24/6, the absence of any fire (1 or 5) and air (3 or 7) energy in their Birth Code means these Visionaries must guard against being too much of a homebody and remember there is a wide world out there to explore.

As long as they clear their emotional blockages and work with the positive energy of these numbers, the sensitive 42/6 will develop the inner confidence to leave the safety of their home and explore all that life has to offer. But if they fall into the "fear trap" of their ego they run a very real risk of shrinking back into the arms of their loved ones when they see that the world outside their window is not as rose-coloured as they thought.

Romantically, they make superbly loyal and supportive partners. However, like their 24/6 cousins, they must ensure they are not taken for granted or else they could shrink back into sadness and resentment.

Master Number 33/6 – 'The Master Visionary'

These Master Visionaries have the potential to manifest love and joy wherever they go. They are born optimists whose sole (soul) purpose is to raise the loving vibration of the planet for all of us.

The double energy of 3 means that in their first formative years up to the age of 18, as well as working with their Life Path Number 6 (the Visionary), the 33/6 will be deeply influenced by the artistic and expressive energy of 3 (the Creative).

This means that while the main purpose of their life is to uphold and teach the lofty romantic ideals of love to show humanity what it is capable of (the highest purpose of 6), they will also have excellent communication skills (the energy of 3) to motivate others to follow in their footsteps and become the best they can be.

The double "air" (thought) energy of 3 means they are insightful and expressive, able to communicate their ideas effectively to motivate those around them.

This, combined with the nurturing qualities of their "watery" (emotional) 6, enables them to take their message of love to a wide audience. Not only will they see the best in everyone, they will teach others how to see the best in themselves as well.

33/6 is called the number of the Master Visionary because the highest purpose of the 6 is to hold a vision of beauty and love for all mankind and to show them how the world is meant to be… and indeed can be, if only everyone were to focus on love rather than greed.

Life Path 6: The Visionary

This, combined with the double communication energy of 3, gives 33/6s the opportunity to become powerful writers and orators whose ultimate goal is to convey their message of love to a wide audience.

However, by no means all 33/6s will shoulder this burden. Many will choose instead to focus their attention on their family and friends, for whom they will go to the ends of the Earth and back again. Family life is fundamental to all 6s, and the 33/6 is no exception. After all, love – like charity – begins at home.

Famous Master Visionaries include Agatha Christie, one of the most widely-read writers in history with book sales of more than 4 billion. She infused all her detective stories – as well as the love stories she wrote under the name Mary Westmacott – with a healthy dose of charm and romanticism. Another is Francis Ford Coppola, whose *Godfather* trilogy has as its central theme – behind all the violence – the importance of family. And what about Fred Astaire and Greta Garbo? Both these 33/6s epitomised the romance of cinema in its early days.

Unlike the other three Master Numbers (11/2, 22/3 and 44/8), all of which have plenty of pitfalls to worry about, there are relatively few negatives to this Master Number Birth Code. However, as with all 6s, the 33/6 must be wary of giving too much of their energy to their loved ones – as well as to every charitable cause that comes their way – and remember to take time to nurture their own hearts as well.

If they become overwhelmed, Master Visionary 33/6s can quickly spiral into emotional distress as they fret about the problems of the world and beat themselves up for not being able to do more to help. They tend to see images of brutality, starvation and oppression on the nightly television news and feel the pain of the victims as if it were their own.

They must learn that no one person can change the whole world by themselves, and so to avoid disappointment and despair 33/6s must remember that they are not Superman or Wonder Woman. They must also remember that the key lesson for their life is to learn to love themselves first so that the love they give to others is unconditional and not tainted with the energy of "…now love me back".

Life Path 6: Career Choices

In general, though, these beautiful Selfs are like angels among us, always wanting to help in any way they can. You will usually know a 33/6 as soon as you meet one because they will have a beatific smile on their face and seem to almost glow with warmth, love and kindness.

* * *

2. CAREER AND BUSINESS CHOICES

THE **6**'s extraordinarily nurturing personality often leads them to take on roles where their primary task is to help people who are sick, lonely, vulnerable or otherwise in need. These roles may include nurses, doctors, social workers, child carers, teachers, counsellors, aid workers, lawyers, environmentalists and charity administrators.

Other roles that suit them are to be found in fire and ambulance services, police work, corrective services, human resources, hospitality, vocational guidance and anything to do with animals.

Their creative streak (especially the 33/6 Master Visionaries) also makes them suited to careers in music, acting, film, fashion, graphic design, interior design and cooking.

All **6**s are blessed with charm and charisma, which they can use to attract people to whatever worthy cause they are representing. They don't usually have the thick-skinned resilience that is necessary for commercial sales work, but are quite happy to work tirelessly to raise money and awareness for a charity or non-profit organisation.

Most **6**s will prefer to be an officer than a foot soldier, and so they should spend the time and money to gain the qualifications they need to become management material in their chosen field.

And when it comes to spreading their message of love to as many people as possible, they will gain enormous pleasure from studying one or more of the creative arts – especially filmmaking, writing and music. It's no coincidence that the list of famous **6**s in the Appendices at the back of this book is littered with extraordinarily influential actors, directors, singers and authors.

Having said all that, the Visionary's main focus will always be on creating a loving home for their family and friends to enjoy, and no matter what work they choose to do to pay the rent or the mortgage, it will usually come second to looking after their loved ones.

For this reason, many **6**s choose to shun the business world altogether and instead become homemakers who spend their time and energy raising children and supporting their partner. (Yes, this applies to the masculine partner in a loving relationship as well as to the feminine partner. Many stay-at-home "Mr Mums" are **6**s.)

No **6** should ever allow themselves to be judged for choosing to be a homemaker and devoting their life to raising their family. There is all too little value placed on full-time homemakers these days of either sex, which in my opinion is one of the main reasons why so many children are going off the rails for lack of attention, support and love.

Beneficial career paths

Teaching, nursing, medicine, counselling, charity work, social work, childcare, vet science or vet nursing, environmentalism, animal rights and welfare, church work, law, emergency services (fire and ambulance), administration, human resources, police work, corrective services, hospitality, vocational guidance, music, acting, film, fashion, graphic design, beauty, interior design, writing and cooking.

*(Note that the nurturing **6** is so concerned with helping others that much of their best work will be done on a volunteer basis, whether it be pro bono law, free financial advice for charities, or dedicating their time and energy to support a worthwhile cause.)*

Best business matches

The idealistic **6** suffers from the curse of perfectionism (and especially the Master Number 33/**6**), so they would do best to choose a business partner who is equally pragmatic and prepared to dot every

Life Path 6: Relationship Choices

i and cross every t, or else the **6** will quickly become frustrated by their lack of attention to detail.

An earthy **4** or **8** would be ideal, as long as they share the **6**'s vision for the business.

The romantic **6** is a natural optimist with lofty ideals, but they can sometimes lack confidence when it comes to hard-nosed business dealings. The always optimistic and efficient **9** is perfect for this role, but the bossy **1** should be avoided, unless they are evolved Leaders.

For their human resources manager, they would do best to choose an intuitive **2** or another nurturing **6**. For their creative team (marketing and sales) they would pick the imaginative and creative **3** or the quick-witted and persuasive **5**.

And for the more mundane but equally important back-office roles such as research and development and IT, they can do no better than the thoughtful **7** or the diligent **4**.

* * *

3. RELATIONSHIP CHOICES

ONE of the most rewarding aspects about the Self-Awareness System™ is how equitable it is. Each Life Path offers the same opportunities for happiness and fulfillment, albeit in markedly different ways. And each of them also offers the same amount of challenges to force us to grow, although again in very different ways.

This means no Life Path is any "better" or "worse" than any of the others. All of them have their blessings, and all have their obstacles.

In the case of the **6**, the blessings centre around their seemingly endless capacity to love and nurture their partner through thick and thin, which are wonderful qualities in a relationship, and their obstacles show up as righteousness, intolerance and impossibly high standards, which are sure to cause a certain amount of conflict.

Life Path 6: The Visionary

Of all the nine Life Paths, the Visionary is the most likely to enjoy a close, passionate and long-lasting relationship with their marriage partner. Nearly all 6s want a traditional marriage, no matter their gender or sexuality. This is because they value love above everything, and will always put their home life at the very top of their list of priorities.

On the positive side, the cheerful and non-judgmental 6 will be the most faithful, patient and supportive of lovers. They will happily shoulder the burden of running the family home and will be the rock on which their partner can rely. Plus, if children come along, the positive 6 is able to give them more love, patience and attention than all the other eight Life Paths put together.

They might sometimes be a little too controlling and must learn to listen to all points of view during family discussions. But as long as they receive the regular love and appreciation they need, the always energetic 6 will quite literally work around the clock to ensure every aspect of their relationship and their family home is harmonious, light and full of laughter.

As we have seen, the 6 performs at their best when surrounded by people they love and who love them back. Problems can arise if they are forced to endure long periods of solitude, or if they feel that their love and support is not reciprocated. They don't need, or expect, as much love back as they give out because they know no one else is anywhere near as compassionate as they are. But they do need some recognition, and if they don't receive anything in return for all the love they give out they can easily flip to the dark side of this Life Path by becoming needy, meddlesome, critical and resentful.

The jilted 6 is a truly fearsome creature to behold. When they feel appreciated, they radiate light and love like one of those beatific angels you see on the front of Christmas cards. But when they feel neglected or used, they can flip from Gabriel to Godzilla quicker than Superman can change his underpants.

Sadly, this happens more often than you might imagine. If the unevolved 6 fails to do the necessary inner work on themselves to learn the difference between unconditional love and the other kind, their

Life Path 6: Relationship Choices

naturally submissive personality will almost always lead them to be a doormat that everyone in the family uses to wipe the "emotional mud" off the metaphorical shoes of their life.

The **6** will put up with this for only so long before exploding. So if you are in a relationship with a wonderfully giving Visionary, please never make the mistake of taking their love and generosity for granted. You'll live to regret it – as indeed you should, because no one will ever have life as good as the partner of a devoted **6**. So don't stuff it up!

The truth is, nurturing **6**s need relatively little love in return for working tirelessly to meet all their loved ones' needs. A bunch of roses or a bottle of scotch here, and a romantic weekend away in the country or a loving note on their pillow there, will be more than enough to make them feel appreciated at the deepest level.

If you haven't read the marvellous book by Gary Chapman called *The Five Love Languages*, I recommend you find the time to do so, especially if you are in a relationship with a **6**. In the book, Gary breaks down the five different ways we all like to be loved, and it's unlikely your partner prefers the same method that you do. So, if you are like most unaware people, you will love your partner in the same way you like to be loved – and unless their method happens to be the same as yours, you will miss the mark and risk your partner failing to feel loved by you. Gary's book can show you how.

This is important for all relationships, of course. However, if your partner is a **6** – for whom loving and being loved is their No.1 value in life – then knowing how to love them properly will be the single most valuable skill you will ever learn.

As we have seen, the reason this is so important for the Visionary **6** is that they have come here with one purpose and one purpose only – and that is to teach the world about love by showing all of humanity (starting with their partner) their highest loving potential.

If they suffer the unimaginable pain of not being able to love their partner and be loved by them in return, then what chance will they have of fulfilling their life's highest purpose? So although relationships are important for all the Life Paths, they are life and death for the **6**.

Life Path 6: The Visionary

Which is why when things don't go well, the negative **6** will raise the hounds of hell before giving up on their partner. But if that still doesn't work, don't expect the **6** to stick around in an unhappy relationship. That, to them, is a life simply not worth living. They will leave, no matter how painful it may be for them, and pursue the love they crave elsewhere.

A couple of words of warning for the always nurturing **6** before we move on to the bedroom: if this is your Life Path, you have a deep and innate desire to rescue injured birds, fix up their wings and help them to fly again. This is noble, but it will never lead you to the long-term happiness you seek.

Young masculine **6**s will choose a damsel in distress to soothe and comfort, and young feminine **6**s will choose a "hurt little man-child" to nurture and repair. The trouble is, once you have healed them, they will be off, leaving you feeling abandoned and rejected.

Try to save your nurturing instincts for children and pets and pick a partner who wants your love, but doesn't need it.

* * *

Sex drive of the 6

Every Life Path number approaches sex in a unique and quite distinct way. For the **1**, sex is often about power and conquest. For the **2**, it's about connection and feeling desired. For the **3**, it's about the mental stimulation of the experience. The pragmatic **4** views sex as something they enjoy when they feel like it. And the quicksilver **5** regards it as a frivolous adventure, just like everything else they do.

With the **6**, though, our Spiritual Growth Cycle enters a whole new phase. This is the Life Path of divine love, and those who walk it are focused on manifesting a level of divine beauty in the world that matches the Utopian vision of perfection they hold in their hearts.

So when it comes to their sex drive, the Visionary **6** has absolutely no time for power play (**1**), co-dependence (**2**), mind games (**3**), mutual satisfaction (**4**) or kinky pleasures (**5**). What they want – actually, no, make that what they need – is nothing less than a spiritual experience where they dissolve with their partner and merge together in the infinite and unbounded bliss of mutual surrender to love

All **6**s, whether they are masculine or feminine, yearn to give themselves completely to their partner… and to have their partner do the same to them. To quote a phrase from my favourite sexual guru David Deida, they long to open each other's heart and "touch the face of God" together as they momentarily set their spirits free from their mortal shells and merge in the endless oneness of bliss.

Now that's not to say that the **6** – like the rest of us – doesn't like the occasional cheeky quick one on the washing machine when it's set to "spin". But fun though sex is, for the **6** it will always play second fiddle to the Stradivarius of making love like angels do.

The "feminine energy" **6** in a relationship (and this is a deeply feminine and nurturing number) will love to pamper and please her partner with her passionate sexuality in the bedroom, just as she does with her cooking in the kitchen and her graceful elegance everywhere else. Feminine **6**s are the givers who just keep on giving, and there really is nothing she won't do for the ones she loves, providing she feels both appreciated and safe enough to open up her innermost beauty. So when she does open up completely to her partner, the love-light that radiates out from her heart is truly dazzling.

The "masculine energy" **6** will have a more equal balance of masculine and feminine energy, but he too yearns to surrender fully to the bliss of divine ecstasy when he and his partner give themselves completely to each other. He doesn't care whether he is in a female body or a male body, any more than he cares what birth gender his partner is. For him, sex is never about being on top or on the bottom, it's about merging his unwaveringly masculine god essence with the infinitely receptive goddess energy of his lover. At the point of divine surrender, when both partners cease to exist as separate entities and become pure Source energy, neither will have any sense of who is who, let alone who is inside who. They will be one, for one blissful moment.

Life Path 6: The Visionary

The compatibility listings that follow will help romantic **6**s get the most out of their relationships, whether it's with someone they love, a friend or a business partner.

You will notice that the water energy of **6** is well-matched with other **6**s and their watery cousin **2**, as well as a **4** or an **8**, whose earth energy combines with water to create new life, and new love. On the other hand, fire (**1** and **5**) can boil water, and air (**3** and **7**) can evaporate it, so these pairings will normally throw up more challenges.

Also, note that unlike the emotional and sensitive watery **2**, the idealistic **6** also shares much in common with the evolved **9**.

However, what appears to match you best on the surface may not be what you need in your life right now. All relationships are designed to help us grow along our Life Path. Yes, of course we enjoy the companionship, close connection, sexual intimacy and deep love that relationships give us. But that is now why we have them.

The reason we choose a partner (or, to be more accurate, why our all-knowing Self chooses them for us) is because they are a mirror in which we see our shortcomings and strengths reflected back at us through their shortcomings and strengths.

That is why opposites so often attract, especially in love.

I have written an entire book on this subject called *Leap into Love* which goes into the way relationships work in our lives in great detail. But for now, please real-eyes that when your partner presses one of your buttons, they are doing so not to "piss you off" but because your Self is using them to show you the areas you need to work on.

If you fail to understand this is the main reason why you attracted them into your life in the first place, you will fight each other and may eventually break up. And you will believe their faults were exactly that – their faults – rather than yours reflected back at you.

Worst of all, you will then take the unchanged you with you to your next relationship, and – lo and behold! – exactly the same issues will come up again.

If this sounds familiar. If you have ever asked any of these questions – "Why does this always happen to me?" or "Why do all

Life Path 6: Relationship Choices

men cheat?" or "Why are all women so demanding?" or whatever it is for you – then now you know why. It's because you didn't learn from your last partner, so of course your new one will do the same thing.

And this will continue to happen, relationship after relationship, until you real-eyes it is meant to be happening to show you what areas you need to work on in your Self to change and grow.

* * *

One final quick point before we get into it: I need to stress that I disagree with almost every numerologist I know who likes to label relationships "a natural fit", "a neutral fit" or "an unnatural fit", depending on the compatibility of the numbers of the two partners.

All relationships are challenging. That is why we have them, as we have just seen. Yes, sometimes we might choose a partner who is "just like us" for the sake of harmony, but that could be regarded as a cop out if we are truly serious about our personal and spiritual growth.

If you are on a spiritual growth path in this lifetime (and there is no doubt in my mind that you are if you made it through Part One without throwing it in the bin!), then your Self will choose your relationships for you – and they will always be with a partner who will challenge you to grow in exactly the ways you need to grow.

Just because you might discover your current partner has a Life Path Number that doesn't dovetail perfectly with yours, don't fall into the trap of thinking there must be something wrong – or worse, end it with them so you can go out with someone with a "better" number.

Where you are right now on your Life Path is exactly where you are meant to be, and who you are with is exactly who you are meant to be with. So please let these listings help you to look for the lessons in your relationship, rather than look for the door.

And if you are single at the moment as you read this, I urge you to remain open-hearted about your next relationship. It doesn't matter what Life Path Number your next partner has, so don't "cherry pick". All that matters is you follow your heart and be open to learning the

Life Path 6: The Visionary

lessons they can teach you. After all, that's the reason you will attract them into your life in the first place.

* * *

6 & 1
(Romance and Independence)

Love

Both these numbers have sexuality coming out of their ears, so when it comes to falling in love they will find it as easy as falling entwined off the four-poster bed in their suite at the five-star tropical resort, where they will surely go on their lust-filled luxury honeymoon.

No, the challenge for the loved-up watery **6** and the dominant and fiery **1** is never falling in love – it's staying in love after the first thrilling fires of love-making have faded. One day, not too long into the relationship, the homemaker **6** will wake up and wonder where the independent **1** went. The answer is they probably left a hastily written note on the **6**'s expensive Egyptian cotton pillowcase saying: "Gone to a meeting in Caracas, back in a couple of days."

That's bad enough for the **6**, who is all about creating a loving and comfortable home full of warm family energy. But what really hurts them to their core is the lack of an "I love you" at the end of the note.

The **1** is ruled by masculine energy, so whether they are a male or a female in the traditional birth-gender sense, they will just assume their partner knows that they love them – because, after all, they are with them, aren't they? But the feminine energy of **6** needs to be told they are loved about 3.7 million times every day, give or take a few million.

Children and/or pets will often be the difference between this pairing working, or not, no matter whether the **6** is the male or female energy in this relationship. As long as the **6** is surrounded by people and animals who they can love and nurture, they will be able to cope with their partner being away from home for relatively long periods.

Life Path 6: Relationship Choices

But if they are left on their own too long or too often, one day the **1** will return home to find the **6** has left to find the loving connection they need with someone else. And they will have only themselves to blame because it's really not hard to keep a **6** happy. All you have to do is tell them you love them. A lot.

The lesson for the **1** is to make sure their devoted **6** partner feels loved and appreciated. And the lesson for the **6** is to real-eyes their desire for love and connection is so strong, it is too much to ask the task-focused **1** to provide it all the time. By looking to their family and friends as well for their regular doses of love, the **6** can avoid stifling the **1**. And in return, the **1** will shower them not only with love, but with the money to build an even bigger and more beautiful home.

Good luck, stay open and honest… and enjoy the deep feelings of trust and devotion this passionate relationship can give you.

Friendship

It is rare for the homemaker **6** and the goal-driven **1** to form deep and lasting friendships simply because they get their needs met in such radically different ways. The **1** wants to conquer the world, while the **6** is seldom happy roaming too far from their family, which always comes first for them. But **1**s are not always keen on long Sunday family lunches when they could be out riding their customised Harley with their wild and crazy friends, or playing sport… or just watching it.

However, when these two numbers reach the highest purpose of their Life Paths they can connect on a deep level as friends because the idealistic and romantic vision of the **6** – who knows that "love is all that matters" – will resonate with the impassioned **1**, who wants to use their considerable talents and energy to spread love to as many people as possible.

And the firebrand energy of the **1**, who wants to spread love through their many endeavours, will earn the lasting admiration of the evolved **6**, who knows their idealistic romantic vision for the world needs the take-charge energy of the **1** to make it happen.

Life Path 6: The Visionary

Business

This can be an auspicious commercial partnership because of what we have just spoken about. The leadership energy of **1** is ideal for starting a dynamic business, and the idealistic vision and boundless energy of **6** will ensure the business grows in ways that benefit as many people as possible – and is therefore more likely to succeed.

The **1** must take great care to always consult the **6** on all the big decisions, or else the **6** will feel unappreciated. Equally, the supportive **6** must ensure they are happy to let the **1** be the public face of the business who goes "out there" into the world to make things happen, or else the **1** will feel restricted and may become equally resentful.

* * *

<u>6 & 2</u>
(Romance and Co-operation)

Love

This pairing will never be able to complain that there isn't enough passion and emotion in their lives, because both these feminine water numbers wear their hearts on their sleeve and value their relationship and their family high above every other area of their life.

The homemaker **6** is by far the most domestic of all the Life Path Numbers, and the compassionate **2** leaves them all floundering in their wake when it comes to their capacity for love and connection.

Just the words that describe their Life Paths – Visionary and Intuitive – tell you all you need to know about how these two will be together when they first meet and fall in love. Violinists will appear out of nowhere and the rest of the world will cease to exist as they stare deeply into each other's eyes like a scene from an old black and white Cary Grant movie.

No, falling in love will never be a challenge for these two romantic idealists. Dealing with the realities of everyday life after the flames of their initial attraction have died down is another matter, though.

The forthright **6**, who likes to speak what's on their mind with a confronting directness, must be careful not to offend the sensitive and often insecure **2**, just as the **2** must guard against becoming too jealous of the more dominant energy of the busybody **6**.

The key to making this work is for both partners to give each other plenty of room to breathe and grow, while also avoiding the very real potential for jealousy by constantly acknowledging their partner and expressing clearly how much they are loved and appreciated.

Family will always be the focus of this pairing, and their home will be immaculate, warm and nurturing. They will gladly share everything they have with each other, knowing that it will be returned in kind. But communication, or rather the lack of it, could sometimes become a problem. Both the **6** and the **2** have a tendency to bottle up their true feelings, expecting the other to just know instinctively what is going on for them. Should their partner miss something, or fail to be a world-beating mind-reader every second of every day, both of them can react in anger and lash out, claiming the other "doesn't love them any more".

This can be as devastating as it is simple to avoid. Neither the **6** nor the **2** can bear any kind of negativity in their peaceful, loving home, and arguments can cut them to their core. Yet, all they needed to do to prevent it happening was to say something right at the beginning.

Communication is important in all relationships. For the **6** and the **2**, though, it is the difference between a long and happy life together or a short and angry affair. Good luck, stay open… and enjoy the passion and blissful connection this relationship can give you.

Friendship

These two have so much in common, they can't help but get along. Yes, problems can sometimes arise in a relationship where expectations are much higher. But between friends, their mutual love of people, their love of animals – and their love of love itself – can quickly bring them together to forge a strong and long-lasting emotional connection.

These two romantics will feed off each other, sharing their dreams and buying each other ever brighter pairs of rose-coloured sunglasses for each other's birthdays. They will delight in teaming up to help fight for worthy causes, and every moment they are not needed at their own homes they will probably pop round to visit each other to get their fix of mutual validation that they both crave.

As with lovers, though, the forthright **6** must guard against hurting the **2**'s feelings by voicing harsh criticisms, and the sensitive **2** must speak up when they do feel hurt to avoid deep resentment from festering.

Business

This match has the potential for success because both partners will find it easy to share a common vision for the business, which will almost always be focused on healing, teaching or helping others.

The **6** is the more grounded of these two watery numbers, so it would be best to give them control of the finances. In return, the **2** will thrive if given free rein to control the creative aspects and drive the business forward into exciting new markets.

However, the perfectionist **6** must real-eyes no one, not even the diligent **2**, is ever perfect. And the brooding **2** must always speak their mind and not be intimidated by the **6**'s tendency to be controlling.

* * *

6 & 3
(Romance and Expression)

Love

The emotional and idealistic **6** is usually happiest with another **6** or an equally watery **2**, or else with an earthy **4** or **8** with whom they can build a safe and loving home to share.

More challenges arise when they pick one of the two air numbers (**3** or **7**), because both these Life Paths are more concerned with exploring the world to feed their inquisitive minds than they are with spending intimate evenings at home, watching movies and making love in front of an open fire.

Life Path 6: Relationship Choices

Of the two air numbers, the sensitive and creative **3** is definitely better suited to the **6** than the aloof **7** (and both will be more attentive than either of the freedom-loving fire numbers **1** and **5**), but this pairing will always be more about personal growth than anything else.

The nurturing **6** wants to shower their partner with love and open up their exquisitely affectionate heart to them in a demonstrative and dazzling display of devotion – which may only make the intellectual and relatively restrained **3** feel guilty that they are nowhere as "deep".

Equally, the always curious and expressive **3** wants to talk long into the night about conceptual issues such as human rights, politics and oppression, while the idealistic **6** – although deeply concerned about these subjects – doesn't like to dwell on negativity and just wants to make love, believing (correctly) that the best way to raise the vibration of the planet is to literally "make" love.

As long as the intellectual **3** puts aside their need for mental stimulation long enough to satisfy the **6**'s craving for physical intimacy, and the faithful **6** trusts that the **3**'s need to spend time away from home with a broad spectrum of friends doesn't mean they don't value them above all others, this can be a mutually rewarding relationship.

The **6** will help the **3** get in touch with their divine inner Self, which is crucial for all creative artists. And the **3** will encourage the often shy **6** to take their much-needed message of love out into the world.

The social **3** must curb their flirtatious personality, which can wound the **6** even if there is nothing to worry about. Similarly, the domestic **6** must real-eyes the **3** needs more mental stimulation than they do and be prepared to step outside their comfort zone to prevent the **3** becoming bored and looking elsewhere for excitement.

Good luck, stay open and honest… and enjoy the mutual growth opportunities that this relationship can give you.

Friendship

On the surface, these two numbers appear to have little in common, with the nurturing **6** wanting to stay close to home and the adventurous **3** wanting to travel far and wide to explore the world.

However, without the constraints of a romantic relationship, this friendship can work extremely well because the one thing both these numbers fear the most is failing to achieve their life's ambition.

The **6** has come here to show the world its true loving potential, but they are often too timid to take their inspirational message to a worldwide audience. By supporting and inspiring their **3** friend to create art that spreads love throughout the world, they can achieve their highest purpose vicariously.

Equally, the intellectual **3** needs the loving **6** to re-mind them that while conceptual negative "dark art" may fill galleries and cinemas with arrogant, Self-important elitists, the highest purpose of art is to improve the lives of the common man and woman and raise the vibration of the planet with messages of love and compassion.

Business

Yes, this can work. But the expressive **3** must have full control of the creative side of the business, while the diligent and hard-working **6** must feel acknowledged for their tireless leadership role. Creative **3**s are well-organised, but this is not their area of greatest expertise. Far better for the **6** to run the business, allowing the **3**'s ideas to flow freely.

***

<u>6 & 4</u>
(Romance and Stability)

Love

Have you ever visited someone's house and been struck by the warm, welcoming energy of the place before you've even stepped through the architecturally designed front door into a stylish hallway straight from the pages of *Vogue Living*, as homely smells of freshly baked bread and furniture polish mix with the sound of well-behaved children playing with a puppy in the immaculately groomed garden?

Life Path 6: Relationship Choices

If you have, the chances are the people who live there are a **6** and a **4**, because these lovers are all about making their home as comfortable, welcoming and harmonious as they possibly can.

Yes, some other Life Paths love to create stylish and hospitable homes as well, especially the watery **2** and earthy **8**, but this perfectly matched pairing takes the art of domestic bliss to a whole new level.

The nurturing Visionary wants nothing more than to raise a family and shower them with love in a beautiful home, while the pragmatic Builder's attention to detail means everything in their home matches perfectly. There will not be a single vase or pot plant out of place.

Both the **6** and the **4** are dyed-in-the-wool perfectionists, a quality that can cause a great deal of friction in many relationships. But these two are so well-matched in their fastidious need for everything to be "just so" that it will seldom become a problem.

They both share the same ideals, they are both loyal and honest, and they are both willing to shoulder more than their fair share of the domestic responsibilities.

Towels left lying on the bathroom floor after a shower, or dirty clothes piled up on the bedroom floor, would send either of these nit-pickers into spasms of apoplectic rage. But it just isn't going to happen when they live together. Even their kids will be tidy – because, when they were younger, they would have been properly schooled by their parents in the old-fashioned values of manners and respect.

Neither of these partners is particularly touchy-feely, so physical intimacy could be an area of concern that these two will need to work on. Also, the **4**'s serious nature can sometimes be draining for the more upbeat **6** and they would do well to lighten up, while on the other side the controlling **6** must be careful not to step on the **4**'s toes too often and would do well to learn the relationship-saving skill of compromise.

This pairing is one of the most harmonious in the entire Self-Awareness System™ and bodes well for a long and happy life together.

Good luck, stay open and honest… and enjoy the many comforts of a peaceful and loving home that this relationship can give you.

Life Path 6: The Visionary

Friendship

The nurturing **6** and the loyal **4** will usually find they have a lot in common as friends, just as they do in a relationship. Both these numbers are open, honest and generous, which will allow them to forge a close bond based on mutual trust and admiration.

They are both naturally cautious and sensible and have similar goals in life, which will give them much to talk about. The pragmatic and well-grounded **4** may sometimes find the idealistic **6** a little flighty for their taste, just as the passionate **6** might occasionally tire of the **4**'s obsession with details. But overall, they are so alike that forming a lasting friendship will be as easy for them as stepping purposefully off a log.

Business

"Compromise" is the buzzword here. It's not a quality that comes easily to either of these fastidious numbers and, just as in a romantic relationship, the success of this pairing will depend largely on whether these two perfectionists can find a middle ground when disputes arise.

In many ways, running a business is harder than living together, so the need for compromise is even more crucial. But providing both have clearly defined roles and resist the urge to nitpick, these diligent partners can patiently build a successful business from the ground up.

* * *

<u>6 & 5</u>

(Romance and Freedom)

Love

There's an old proverb that says: "Expectation is a one-way street that leads to disappointment." (Well, it's not that old really because I just made it up, but it sounds better that way.) The point is, expectation in relationships is always going to end in tears. And when two partners are as incompatible as the committed **6** and the commitment-phobic **5**, the tears will start flowing the moment the controlling **6** tries to tell the

Life Path 6: Relationship Choices

rebellious **5** what to do, or the irresponsible **5** goes on a three-day bender without telling the **6** where they went.

These two lovers have about as much in common as Pussy Riot and Vladimir Putin. Yes, they will often be attracted to each other when they meet at a party, because the **5** will admire the **6**'s ability to stand out from the crowd, and the **6** will be drawn to the fiery **5**'s burning desire to change the world for the better. After all, both numbers share the common goal of raising the level of love for all of us – it's just that they will go about it in radically different ways.

The nurturing **6** wants a strong, committed relationship and a peaceful home where they can raise a family, while the adventurous **5** cares little for home life and wants to travel the globe in a never-ending series of quests to right what they see as society's wrongs.

The **6** craves commitment and consistency and will be aggressively controlling if they fail to get it, while the **5** needs constant change and stimulation from other people and will run a mile at the first sign of their partner trying to limit their freedom of choice.

It's ironic, really, because both these numbers have so much to teach each other.

The serious and judgmental **6** would benefit from the courageous **5**'s love of adventure and ability to live and let live, while the ill-disciplined and freedom-loving **5** desperately needs to learn how to commit to anything for more than 30 seconds to prevent them from winding up in the poor house, a prisoner in a jail of their own making.

If these two opposites do attract each other and figure out a way to respect their differences, there is potential for spectacular mutual growth – which, after all, is why we have relationships in the first place. It won't be easy, and there will need to be almost constant compromise – such as the **5** agreeing to spend more time at home, and the **6** letting them fly when they really need to – but it will be well worth it.

Just real-eyes this relationship is unlikely to be long-lasting simply because the differences are too great. Learn all you can while you can, and try to see your partner's "negatives" as being exactly the positive areas you need to focus on to move along your growth path.

Life Path 6: The Visionary

Good luck, stay open and honest… and enjoy the life-changing lessons each of you has for the other.

Friendship

The attractive **6** and the quick-witted **5** will find much to admire about each other when they first meet.

The passionate **6** will be thrilled by the effervescent **5**'s lust for life, and the crusading **5** will be drawn to the **6**'s idealistic vision of a world where love triumphs over the fear-mongering forces of oppression. But that's often as far as it will go.

These two friends are unlikely to stick around beyond the point when the **6** gets fed up with the **5** changing their mind every two minutes, and the **5** gets bored of the **6**'s lack of mental stimulation.

They'll probably stay friends on Facebook, occasionally sharing visionary posts about ways to improve the world, but that's about it.

Business

This business pairing is such a bad idea that if someone published a book called *The 1000 Worst Ideas Of All Time* (including JFK saying: "Let's go for a nice long drive through Dallas" and Napoleon telling his troops: "I'm going to invade Russia, what can possibly go wrong?"), this would come in at number 27. Don't do it. Just don't.

* * *

6 & 6

(Romance and Nurturing)

Love

It's tempting to think that falling in love with someone who has so much in common with you is the perfect way to experience the bliss of a close, loving relationship. After all, who could possibly understand your deepest dreams, desires and needs better than another passionate and nurturing Visionary?

Life Path 6: Relationship Choices

There's no doubt we all love it when we meet a new partner and discover that, "Oh happy day! They are just like me!" And these two nesting lovebirds will certainly enjoy a great number of similarities in the early stages of their relationship that will lead them to move in together almost immediately so they can create a warm and supportive home for themselves – which is the highest priority for all romantic **6**s.

But there's a reason opposites attract. Lots of reasons in fact, not least – as I have said repeatedly throughout these Life Path listings – that relationships are all about helping us grow, spiritually as well as emotionally, as both partners bring a whole range of lessons to the table for each other to learn. And this simply isn't going to happen when they are mirror images of themselves.

Add to that the **6**'s powerful desire to be the head of their family and in control of all aspects of their life, and it's easy to see how quickly the initial heady days of domestic bliss can give way to conflict and competition between two headstrong people who want to occupy the same space in their home and play the same role in their relationship.

That's not to say this pairing can't be wonderfully happy and long-lasting. It can, because each will understand the other on the deepest level and know exactly what to do or say to make them feel truly loved and appreciated (both of which are fundamental needs of the **6**).

Just be aware that you will have to decide early on who's in charge of which aspects of your life to avoid running into any damaging power struggles in your relationship.

The ability to share the responsibilities of their day-to-day life and a willingness to compromise when conflicts arise – which they will – are the twin secrets to this couple's success.

Providing these issues are dealt with from the start, the Visionaries' mutual love of family and home and their shared vision for a more loving world will give these two rose-visioned idealists every chance of dancing through life together in a tango of togetherness.

Good luck, stay open and honest… and enjoy the warmth of your close connection (not to mention the mind-bendingly good sex).

Life Path 6: The Visionary

Friendship

These two romantic idealists are likely to be instantly attracted to each other, thanks to their common values and shared vision of a world where everyone lives in peace, and violence and fear are defeated by the irresistible power of love. Rather like a Disney children's film.

In fact, if they don't ring each other up at least once a month and plan a trip to the movies together to see the latest feel-good rom-com, I'll eat my numerological hat.

This is such a feminine number that even male **6**s love a good tear-jerker. So no matter what birth gender they are, two **6**s who take the time to get to know each other can easily become BFFs, sharing their love and supporting each other through life's ups and downs.

Business

A shared vision is always a good basis for a business partnership, and these two Visionaries can create something truly special if they set their mind to it. But, just as we saw with romantic relationships, a clear delineation of responsibilities is essential if this pair of control freaks are going to avoid squabbling over who takes the lead and when.

The **6** may well find themselves better off going into business with an equally compassionate and emotional **2**, or else a practical and hard-working **4**, who will happily let the **6** be in control of the direction of the business, as long as they are always kept in the loop.

* * *

6 & 7
(Romance and Understanding)

Love

Atop the list of things that were never meant to be mixed together, there's chalk and cheese at No. 3, there's oil and water at No. 2… and then, high above them both, sitting as far apart from each other on the top of the table as they possibly can, there's a **6** and a **7**.

Life Path 6: Relationship Choices

These two have about as much in common on a social level as a snowflake and a blowtorch. In fact, it's highly unlikely they will ever even meet because the reserved **7** is way too quiet and withdrawn for the effusive **6** to notice in a crowded room, and the **6**'s immaculately groomed image will not impress the suspicious and distrusting **7**.

However, if these two polar opposites do find themselves attracted to each other they may be surprised to discover that they share more in common than either of them first thought. Both love to be in love, and they both enjoy feeling supported by their partner. But that's just about where their similarities stop.

The fiercely independent **7** will react badly at the first sign that their controlling **6** partner wants to dictate how they spend their time. And the emotionally expressive **6** will react equally badly every time the **7** refuses to engage in deep-and-meaningful share sessions and goes back into their shell – which they will do with a meddlesome **6** more often than a paranoid tortoise with chronic confidence issues.

For this relationship to work, both partners will have to do more than study and learn each other's needs. They will need to qualify with a Masters in Applied Understanding and a doctorate in Advanced Compromising Skills from the University of As You Wish.

But before they both throw in the towel, and the bedsheets too, they would do well to re-mind themselves that relationships are not all about cuddles and smooches, they are about growth.

These two are together for a very specific reason – namely to reflect each other's shortcomings and show each other the areas they most need to work on. If they can stop bickering long enough to do this, there's every chance their relationship can grow into a mutually rewarding marriage of opposites, each teaching the other and helping them to fulfill their life's highest purpose – which, to re-mind you, is not canoodling on a sofa surrounded by love-heart cushions, but learning to master your fears and stepping into your light, then helping others do the same.

Good luck, stay open and honest and enjoy the life-changing lessons your partner can teach you… if you give them a chance.

Life Path 6: The Visionary

Friendship

Maybe, possibly, but unlikely. Even if they were the last two people on Earth and found themselves marooned on a desert island, they would probably draw a big line down the middle of it and live out their lives sitting on their side with their backs to each other.

This is a shame because if these two friends were able to look past the 76,835,891 points of difference on which they vehemently disagree, they might just find that – "OMG! You like Leonard Cohen too!" – there is enough common ground on which they can sow the seeds of a highly unusual but ultimately mutually rewarding friendship.

Business

No! OK? Got that? Great. Then let's move on...

* * *

6 & 8

(Romance and Ambition)

Love

You know those Census articles in the newspaper, when they talk about the traditional "family unit" of two loved-up happy, healthy and wealthy adults who live in a nice home with four attractive children, complete with a photograph of said family all cuddled up together on their plush velour sofa and grinning like Cheshire cats?

The chances are those two loved-up happy, healthy and wealthy adults are a Visionary **6** and an Achiever **8**, because this is one of the most family oriented and materially focused romantic pairings in the entire Self-Awareness System™.

Almost always, the masculine partner in the relationship (whether they be "male" or "female" in the birth gender sense) is the breadwinner **8**, and the feminine partner (again, it doesn't matter if they are "female" or "male") is the homemaker **6**.

Life Path 6: Relationship Choices

Both the nurturing, family-focused **6** and the material and career-focused **8** are feminine numbers. They are honest and hard-working, and they are able to set – and achieve – lofty goals for themselves, both individually and together as a couple.

When they meet, the perfectly groomed and elegant **6** will stand out from the crowd and catch the refined eye of the **8**, whose confidence and strength of character will in turn appeal to the **6**. This initial attraction will deepen when they start to discuss their dreams and goals and discover they dovetail almost perfectly.

Should they take it further and fall in love, these two will want to build a comfortable and often luxurious home for themselves, where kids will usually quickly follow – depending on their age and the timing of their meeting. Just as in nature, the water of **6** will mix with the earth of **8** to create abundant life – both in the form of children, and in the accumulation of considerable wealth.

In fact, these two are so compatible, it's almost like one of those 1960s American family sitcoms where everyone smiles at everyone else for 30 minutes once a week – giving you the distinct impression that after the credits roll and the cameras are turned off, this impossibly happy make-believe family goes on smiling at each other for the other 10,020 minutes of every week as well.

Of course, in real life nothing is ever perfect. Problems for these two can arise if the hard-working **8** spends too much time in the office away from home, or the possessive **6** makes too many demands on the **8** and cramps their executive lifestyle.

But all should be well, providing the **8** tells the **6** how loved and appreciated they are every single day (yes, the **6** needs almost constant reassurance) and makes regular quality time for their family, and the **6** curbs their neediness and gives the **8** all the freedom they need to go out and conquer the world.

Good luck, stay open and honest… and enjoy annoying everyone else by living a blissful family life and smiling all week long.

Life Path 6: The Visionary

Friendship

These two can become great friends because they have so many core values and beliefs about life, money and family in common. The **6**, who sometimes has a little bit of a fondness for status (in the nicest possible way, of course) and loves many of the finer things in life, will be impressed by the **8**'s ambition and drive, while the **8** will admire the **6**'s traditional values and exemplary work ethic.

In fact, if these two are single and sexually matched, all it will usually take for their friendship to go to the next level is for either of them to make the first move – and before they can say "I do" they'll be buying a house, decorating the nursery and flicking through expensive private school brochures over a lavish breakfast of home-baked chocolate croissants, quails' eggs and fresh Columbian coffee served by their butler on the east terrace.

Business

The **6** who chooses to go into business for themselves will always have a strong vision for what they want their company to achieve. But they will be so loving towards their customers and suppliers, not to mention their competitors, they may end up wanting to make everyone else's business a success instead of theirs. Which is where the **8** comes in. The business savvy **8** will give the idealistic **6** a much better chance of making money, while at the same time satisfying their desire to create a humanitarian company that can help other people.

* * *

6 & 9
(Romance and Passion)

Love

Both the romantic **6** and the independent but equally romantic **9** are passionately spiritual numbers and will find a lot of common ground in their values and beliefs, which can form the basis for a

Life Path 6: Relationship Choices

beautiful relationship. The idealistic **6** has come here to hold aloft a vision of mankind's divine beauty, and the humanitarian and evolved **9** has come here to teach this exact same vision to the world.

The one dovetails perfectly with the other. And even though the nurturing **6** is most comfortable at home where they can look after their loved ones, while the social **9** needs to put themselves "out there" in the world, these two will usually find it easy to support each other's different needs because they share a common goal.

Plus, the hard-working **6** is only ever truly happy and content when they are showered with heaps of love and gratitude for all they do (and they do a lot). This is never a problem for the effusive **9**, who wants nothing more than to be able to love their partner with all their being and will never tire of expressing their appreciation for their **6**.

In fact, many numbers find the spiritually evolved **9** too much to handle because they know in their hearts they can never hope to match the depth of the **9**'s passion. Not so the Visionary **6**, whose very reason for living is to show the world that we are all infinite, immortal and unbounded loving beings. They will therefore delight in finally finding someone who can love them as deeply as they can love them back.

One word of caution: if the **6** should feel in any way insecure or unappreciated, they can tend to flip to the dark side of their Life Path and become both meddlesome and controlling… which is going to make the **9** run faster than a rat up Usain Bolt's drainpipe. But this will only happen if the **9** commits the cardinal sin of all relationships and takes their partner for granted. And if they're dumb enough to do that, then they really don't deserve the love of the **6**'s big, beautiful heart.

Good luck, stay open and honest… and enjoy spreading the love you have for each other out into the world to inspire others.

Friendship

For this friendship to move beyond the "Yeah, I really like them but they can be a little bit full on" stage, these two will have to pluck up the courage to fully open up their hearts to each other and risk revealing their darkest fears, as well as their deepest desires.

Life Path 6: The Visionary

Within the dreamy, loved-up context of post-sex pillow talk that a relationship provides, this is as easy as it is essential for these highly emotional numbers to feel they have fully connected with each other. But over a couple of beers and a game of pool on a Friday night, it's another matter altogether. ("It's another matter!" I hear you all shout at once. Sorry, that was a *Flying High* joke.)

Don't worry. The **6**'s heart will be perfectly safe with a **9**, and vice versa, and the rich friendship they create will likely last a lifetime.

Business

Their shared vision for a better world make the **6** and the **9** just as well-suited for business as they are for love and friendship.

Challenges will arise if their respective roles aren't clearly defined because both these numbers like to be in control. For best results, the **9** should take overall responsibility for the direction of the company and the nurturing **6** should look after staff and customer morale.

* * *

4. HEALTH CHOICES

THIS is usually one of the healthier Life Paths because the **6**'s eternal optimism and cheerful, loving personality creates an emotionally happy body, which is the best weapon we human beings have in the fight against disease (or "dis-ease", as it should be spelled).

However, problems can arise when the **6** flips to the "dark side" of their Life Path and fails to look after themselves because they are too busy looking after everyone else. In their passionate desire to heal and support those around them they can easily neglect their own needs, and if this persists real physical damage can be done.

The most common afflictions include nervous disorders (no one gets as stressed as a **6** when things don't go their way), as well as

Life Path 6: Health Choices

frequent colds, flu and high temperatures – all of which are the body's way of saying "slow down and pay attention to me for a change".

Most **6**s are such spiritual, loving beings that they sometimes need to be re-minded they are spirits having a human experience, not spirits having a spiritual experience. Yes, they are here to spread love from their hearts and teach us that we are all pure love, but they must all also take care of their Self's "vehicle" – their physical body.

In their day-to-day life, **6**s expend so much energy rushing around tending to everyone's needs, cooking for their family, cleaning their home, dashing over to visit a friend in need, and volunteering to help out wherever and whenever they can that they have little need for a gym membership or a pair of jogging shoes.

However, they can suffer from weight gain due to their deep emotional sensitivity, whereby their subconscious mind loves "having a little extra padding" to protect their hearts from being hurt by others who are less loving than themselves.

The evolved **6** who learns that nothing outside them can ever hurt them because they are pure love, and love is invulnerable, will find their weight falls off without having to endure those awfully loud aerobics classes at the gym, or those unpleasant morning runs in the rain.

Having said that, all **6**s should get outdoors as much as possible for walks in nature, because the trees, the birds and the animals will re-mind them of the divine beauty of the world we live in. And divine beauty is absolutely what the **6** is all about.

Another affliction to which the **6** is prone is diabetes, thanks to their insatiable desire for all things sweet. Their sweet tooth is simply a physical manifestation of their sweet and loving heart, which sees the world through candy-coloured glasses and wants everyone to be as happy as the children in Willy Wonka's chocolate factory.

Ailments to watch out for

On the whole, the **6** is healthier than most of the other Life Path Numbers. But as we have just seen, they can be prone to stress-related

Life Path 6: The Visionary

problems because they carry the weight of the entire world on their shoulders and are often disappointed when the world fails to live up to their idealistic standards. This can manifest as nervous disorders, migraines, fevers, joint pain, back pain, and leg and ankle problems.

In times of stress, the **6** will turn to sweets and ice cream as comfort food, neither of which sit well with their sensitive digestive system. They must be strict with the amount of sugar they consume or diabetes, constipation and other digestive issues can arise.

Infections of the throat (fear of expressing their truth) are also common, because the concerned **6** needs to be heard, and if their loving advice falls on deaf ears they may feel afraid to speak out again.

In extreme cases, the **6**'s craving for love (and therefore attention) can manifest in far more serious ailments such as chronic anxiety, hypochondria and even Munchausen Syndrome.

Effective therapies

By far the best therapy for the stress-prone and often highly strung **6** is relaxation – whether it's in the form of meditation, massage, saunas, hot baths with bubbles and scented crystals, or simply sitting in the sunshine with a good book and a lovely hot cup of tea.

Exercise is fine in moderation, but long, leisurely walks in nature are much more beneficial because they will nourish the **6** on every level of their deeply spiritual being, not just their physical body.

Almost all **6s** will have a four-legged best friend because they crave to be around animals' unconditionally loving energy. If it is a dog, they should walk him or her every day. And if it is a cat, they should spend considerable amounts of time stroking and cuddling them, which will calm their overactive nervous system.

Diet choices

Ah, food! Show me a **6** who doesn't like their food and I'll show you someone who made a mistake in adding up the numbers of their date of birth. There simply isn't a **6** in all the world who doesn't like to cook, bake, barbecue and otherwise create yummy dishes with the richest ingredients, all topped off with lashings of love.

6s are born entertainers and hosts for whom food is a fabulous way of nurturing and nourishing those they love. And often the richer, the fatter, the sweeter and the more cream topping the better.

All **6**s much watch their diet if they don't want to put on weight and increase the stress on their already over-stretched nervous system.

Healthy foods for the **6** include anything blue (figs, blueberries and cranberries), as well as tomatoes, cucumbers, apples, beans of all kinds, bananas, walnuts, watermelon, apricots, pears and fresh greens.

For energy, brown rice and wild rice are best. Avoid too many sugar-heavy carbohydrates (cakes, biscuits etc) and eat plenty of herbs and spices, including mint, parsley, fennel, cloves and cardamom.

* * *

5. CHOICES FOR CHILDREN

YOUNG children working with the energy of **6** will usually explore the negative energies of their Life Path Number before moving on to master the positive aspects. This is true of all the nine Life Paths because children need to first understand the boundaries of what is and isn't acceptable behaviour.

However, once their boundaries are in place – and your child has understood the crucial lesson of cause and effect – young **6**s can then start tapping into their natural strengths with the assistance of a positive parental guiding hand.

Children working with the energy of **6** will often surprise their parents with their "adult-like" capacity to shoulder responsibility from an early age. If neither of their parents is a **6**, they may even want to

Life Path 6: The Visionary

play the role of family peacemaker right from the moment they can talk – a quality that should be encouraged, not resisted.

These are the natural nurturers of our society. They are usually the most compassionate and domestic of individuals and their cheerful, optimistic personality ensures they will have plenty of friends. Parents of a **6** child must let them spend a lot of quality time with their friends because they are never happier than when they feel they are being useful in a social situation.

6 children develop their ability to read others' emotions from a very early age, making them appear wise beyond their years. It is not unusual for child **6**s as young as four or five to play a nurturing role for their older siblings... and even their parents.

Long periods of solitude are like a prison sentence for young **6**s. It is also important to include them in family decisions because they love to feel that they are contributing to making the family home a happy and harmonious place.

It is rare for a **6** child to show negative traits because they are naturally happy and loving individuals. However, negativity can bring them down, and if exposed to it over long periods they can become cranky, downcast and even vindictive in their behaviour. Too many arguments can cause them to become anxious, and this may manifest in outbursts of anger and a tendency to withdraw from family life.

Teenage **6**s in unhappy families will spend as little time in the home as possible and will usually rebel against their parents altogether. The reason for this is that negative energy is toxic to a young **6** and they will go in search of love and harmony elsewhere.

Ask a **6** child lovingly to do their homework, and they will perform to the highest possible standard. Tell them angrily to do it and they will probably climb out of their bedroom window and go in search of a friend to give them a dose of loving energy.

Providing their home is harmonious and they receive tonnes of love from an early age, **6** children will blossom into caring and compassionate young adults. But please be aware that if you have a **6** child as an only child, buy them a pet so they do not feel alone.

Life Path 6: Choices for Children

Playtime activities

6 children thrive in company, so play groups and school activities will give them the perfect environment where they can connect with other children and get to know them well.

Team sports are preferable to solo pursuits, and games that involve role playing – such as play-acting and drama – allow them to express their deep love without feeling the embarrassment of doing it as themselves. And all young **6**s absolutely love animals, so family pets will always be a welcome addition to the home – especially if the **6** happens to be an only child.

Because home life is so important to the **6** child, family games, outings to the park or the beach, picnics and BBQs are all great entertainment. And to cater to their nurturing instincts, teddy bears, dolls and toy animals are perfect gifts for them when they are young.

* * *

Your child's three-digit Birth Code

As we have seen in Part Two, we always work primarily with the energy of our Life Path Number right from the outset, but in our childhood years from 0 to 18 we do so in conjunction with the energy of our first Supplementary Birth Number, and in our second 18 years – until we reach full emotional maturity at 36 – we do so in conjunction with the energy of our second Supplementary Birth Number.

It's worth taking the time to read the main listings here in Part Three for the Life Path Numbers that make up your child's two Supplementary Birth Numbers to gain a better understanding of their positive and negative qualities.

Also, as you read about your child's three-digit Birth Code, real-eyes that the difference between "feeling the force" of any Life Path and flipping to the "dark side" is determined by the amount of Self-confidence we develop in our childhood years, and then the amount of Self-love we develop in our teenage years.

Life Path 6: The Visionary

That, in a nutshell (squirrel!), is your role as a parent: to instill in your child first Self-esteem, and then Self-love.

The 00/6 'Millennium' child

As we saw earlier in the Life Choices section of this listing, there are only a few possible birth dates that contain this rare Birth Code, starting with the dawn of the new millennium on January 3, 2000.

The last child with this Birth Code was born on October 10, 1300 – more than 700 years ago – which tells you how important it is that these compassionate angels have arrived here on Earth at a time when their message of divine love is needed more than ever.

From a numerological perspective, a child born with this extremely loving and idealistic Birth Code at the start of the 21st century has the potential to achieve something truly special with their life, because they are working with the double (00) amplified energy of their Life Path Number **6**. But I'm sorry to say they also have an equal potential to experience great disappointment.

This means the parents of a 00/**6** Millennium Child must take extra care to nurture the positive humanitarian potential of their child and guard against the negative characteristics of this rare Birth Code.

All the positive and negative qualities of the **6** contained in this this listing for the Visionary still hold true, but the 00/**6** child will be working with them on a rarefied level. This means they are born with the capacity to make a real difference by shining their lofty vision of mankind's loving potential for the whole world to see.

But there is no pressure on them to do so. If they choose simply to use the innate caring qualities of the **6** to build a happy and stable home for themselves and their family and help out where they can, this is their choice and should never be questioned.

All we can ever do in life is our best, and our highest potential is always to make ourselves happy and healthy – and help those around us do the same. In the case of the idealistic and romantic 00/**6**, if it's just their immediate family and friends, and members of their local

Life Path 6: Choices for Children

community, that is perfect. The fact that their Birth Code is so rare and auspicious should never be dumped on their shoulders as a burden. That could be ruinous to their highly sensitive nature, and must never be allowed to happen.

The 15/6 child

The presence of 1 as the first Supplementary Birth Number means children born with this Birth Code will work with the powerful fire (forceful) energy of the Leader during the first formative 18 years of their life, and then with the equally forceful fire energy of 5 until full maturity at 36.

This double fire energy will drive them to step outside their comfort zone in pursuing the highest purpose of the **6** Life Path, which, to re-mind you, is to shine a beacon of hope and optimism for all mankind and show us the divine love inside all of us.

These children will tend to be outgoing from an early age (the energy of 1) and will also be quite headstrong. Then, as they mature into young adulthood from 18 to 36, they will become even more headstrong as they work with the rebellious energy of the Rebel 5.

This means these children may very well be a handful for even the most tolerant parent, and it would be wise to teach them the discipline to see their projects through to completion and ensure they understand the potentially negative consequences of their impulsive actions.

From the earliest age, they will also play the role of family leader and nurturer (their Life Path energy of **6**), so don't be surprised if your young 15/**6** wants to decide not just what's for dinner, but what will be discussed at the dinner table… as well as what the family will watch on the TV after dinner!

Because of the absence of any grounded earth numbers or thoughtful air numbers in their Birth Code, these children will tend to be flighty and argumentative as well as extremely emotional. They may react badly to family fights and must be taught not to freak out or run away at the first sign of negativity.

Life Path 6: The Visionary

It's definitely a good idea to let these emotionally attuned children be involved in all the major family decisions, or else they may feel left out and become deeply wounded. And if family disagreements do arise, don't be shocked when your 15/6 child steps in gracefully to smooth things over. Even when very young, their unwaveringly loving and nurturing persona will come to the fore.

As with all **6** children, they thrive best in company and must be allowed to mix with a wide circle of friends. They also love animals, so if they are an only child make sure you have a pet they can care for.

The 24/6 child

This child is very different to the 15/6 Visionary because they lack any fire (forceful) numbers in the Birth Code and may therefore need encouragement to break out of their shell. They may tend towards shyness in their early years as they struggle to come to terms with the swirling torrent of emotions welling within them.

As well as working with the water (emotional) energy of their Life Path Number **6** (the Visionary), they will be focused in their first formative years up to 18 on their equally watery first Supplementary Birth Number of 2 (the Intuitive).

Talk about sensitive! These children will cry rivers of both sad and happy tears that could cause a flood in all but the best-drained family home. Parents must take the time to explain to them what it is they are experiencing so they don't feel alienated from their family members and friends, who never seem to react to positive and negative experiences as intensely as they do.

Teenage years may be particularly traumatic for the 24/6 child because they will experience the same terrifying challenges all teenagers face with only their emotions as a guide (the double water energy of 2 and **6**), with no Self-confident fire energy (1 or 5) and no analytical air energy (3 or 7) to help them make sense of what is happening to them.

Fortunately, just as they leave school and go out into the world by themselves as a young adult aged 18, the practical earth energy of their second Supplementary Birth Number 4 (the Builder) kicks in to help them put down roots and balance their idealistic vision of a perfect loving world with a desire to look after both their physical body and their material needs (job, money, roof over their head etc.)

As with all **6** children, they thrive best in company and must be allowed to mix with a wide circle of friends. They also love animals, so if they are an only child make sure you have a pet they can care for.

The 42/6 child

This is a mirror of the previous Birth Code, and children walking this Life Path will share many qualities with their 24/**6** cousins.

The key difference is that during their formative young years – when their personality is being established – the 42/**6** will be working with the earthy and grounded Supplementary Birth Number of 4 alongside their idealistic Life Path energy of **6**, rather than the double-helping of emotional water energy that the sensitive and intense 24/**6** has to cope with.

Yes, they will still be a romantic and nurturing **6** through and through – and will therefore be focused on being as supportive and loving in their family as they can – but they will be less sensitive to negativity than the dreamy 24/**6**, and they will lean towards finding practical solutions to their problems, rather than escaping into an unrealistic dream world at the first sign of disappointment or rejection.

The 42/**6** will also tend to be more studious at school because they value hard work and diligence, whereas the idealistic 24/**6** child will often tend to shrink from a challenge and just hope for the best.

However, as we saw with the 24/**6** child, the absence of any fire energy (action) or air energy (thoughtfulness) in the 42/**6**'s Birth Code could lead them to shrink back into their shells and be afraid to come out of their comfort zone to try something new.

Parents would do well to encourage their 42/**6** child to try new sports, study new subjects and make new friends to prevent them becoming stuck in a comfortable rut of familiarity.

Life Path 6: The Visionary

Attention must also be given to make sure the teenage 42/**6** child has indeed learned the practical lesson of their first Supplementary Birth Number of 4 – which is to create a strong foundation in the physical world before rushing off to preach their lessons of spiritual love – because when they hit 18 and strike out on their own, the watery energy of their Second Supplementary Birth Number 2 (the Intuitive) will amplify the equally idealistic loving energy of their Life Path Number of **6** to create a raging torrent of emotions and a potentially risky desire to throw caution to the wind in pursuit of their dreams.

Providing their practical childhood energy of 4 taught them that we are spirits having a human experience rather than spirits having a spiritual experience – and therefore we must take care of our material wealth and our physical body as well as coming to know ourselves as pure Source energy – then all will be well. But if they didn't learn to ground themselves as children and teenagers, emotional 42/**6**s can easily lose all track of "reality" in their adult years as they pursue a fearless Utopia that can never exist, which could lead to all kinds of dangerous addictions, including potentially life-ending drugs that they foolishly believe might give them the freedom from fear they seek.

No one is more idealistic than the 42/**6** whose early years were not grounded in building a stable foundation for their life. And no one is more likely to want to escape the disappointments of "reality" either.

I don't mean to sound alarmist, but parents of 42/**6** children must ensure they keep an eye out for them as they leave school at 18 and embark on adulthood armed only with the double emotional and sensitive energy of 2 and **6**.

The 33/6 'Master Visionary' child

Master 33/6 children have a unique ability to create love and joy wherever they go. They are born optimists whose sole (soul) purpose is to hold aloft a vision of love, peace and acceptance for all of us.

The double creative air energy of 3 means that in their formative years up to the age of 18, as well as working with their watery and

Life Path 6: Choices for Children

emotional Life Path Number of **6**, the 33/**6** child will be driven to find new and original ways to express their nurturing and idealistic ideas. They will then continue to do this right through until they reach full emotional maturity at age 36.

While the main purpose of their life is to uphold and teach the lofty romantic ideals of love to show humanity what it is capable of (the highest purpose of **6**), they will also have excellent communication skills (the energy of 3) to motivate others to follow in their footsteps and become the best they can be.

The 33/**6** will be an insightful and sensitive child and teenager, able to communicate their ideas effectively to motivate those around them, both at home and at school. This, combined with the nurturing qualities of their emotional Life Path **6**, enables them to take their message of love to a wide audience. Not only will they see the best in everyone, they will help them to see the best in themselves as well.

33/**6** is called the Master Visionary because the highest purpose of Life Path **6** is to hold a vision of beauty and love for all mankind and to show them how the world is meant to be… and indeed can be, if only everyone were to focus on love rather than greed.

This, combined with the double expressive energy of 3, gives 33/**6** children the opportunity to become the true "angels" who walk among us, showering everyone they meet with love, patience and compassion.

Parents will be delighted to discover that their 33/**6** child will be expressive, creative and inspirational (the supplementary energy of 3) from the earliest age, and their message will always be the same: "Mum, Dad, why can't we all just love each other and get along?"

Why indeed?

Therein lies the challenge for a 33/**6** child's parents, who must try to explain to them that, sadly, some angry and fearful people in the world just don't think and feel the same way they do.

The absence of fire energy (action) and earth energy (practicality) in the 33/**6** child's Birth Code could create a concern around their lack of direction and their inability to take care of the practical issues of life, such as money and health. However, as long as their parents instill in

Life Path 6: The Visionary

them enough Self-confidence to speak up for love in the face of fear and anger, and the resilience to accept that some people just aren't ready to hear it, their little "angels" will grow up into big "angels", able to pursue creative careers (the energy of 3) that will allow them to spread their message of love (the energy of **6**) to a wide audience.

As with all **6** children, they thrive best in company and must be allowed to mix with a wide circle of friends. They also love animals, so if they are an only child make sure you have a pet they can care for.

LIFE PATH 7:
The Seeker

1. **Growth cycle:** Seventh stage (the number of truth)
2. **Influences:** Air (thought, masculine) and Neptune (inspiration)
3. **Positive qualities:** Inquisitive, intelligent and clear-sighted
4. **Negative potential:** Superior, aloof and detached
5. **Highs and lows:** Insightful scholar, or arrogant "know-it-all"
6. **Highest purpose:** Seek out the truth and teach it to others
7. **Love matches:** 1, 3, 5, 7, 9 for compatibility (the rest for growth)
8. **Possible careers:** Teaching, research, therapy, science, technology
9. **Words to live by:** "The truth will set us free"

1. LIFE CHOICES FOR THE SEEKER

THE intelligent and insightful **7** is known as "The Seeker of Truth" because this is the most cerebral of all the Life Paths and is governed by the energy of air (thought). Like their airy **3** cousins, **7**s tend to be curious, studious and introspective, and they have a passionate desire to find out as many answers as they can to the "Big Questions" of life, the universe and everything.

Here we have the academics, the gurus, the soothsayers and the clairvoyants among us who are driven to solve the great mysteries of our existence and then share them with others.

This is the seventh stage of the Spiritual Growth Cycle and the third of the four Life Paths (**5** to **8**) that are focused on looking for the spiritual answers that lie within us, as opposed to Life Paths **1** to **4**

Life Path 7: The Seeker

which are more concerned with finding their answers "out there" in the material world.

The "human cycle" of the first four Life Paths was concerned with external issues of personal power (**1**), co-operation (**2**), expression (**3**) and security (**4**). Then along came the rebellious **5** to flip everything on its head and begin the second "spiritual cycle", where we rise above our mortal concerns and focus instead on ridding the world of fear.

This spiritual cycle continued with the idealistic **6**, who taught us we are all pure love and extensions of Source energy, and now moves on to the insightful **7**, who seeks to explain what "Source energy" is and show us that "God" is not separate from us… because we are ALL collectively "God", and we are all co-creators of our reality.

Just as **6** is the number of divine love, **7** is the number of divine truth. The one follows perfectly from the other because, without the **6**'s prior vision of our loving perfection, the intelligent **7** would too easily fall into the egoic trap of pursuing knowledge for knowledge's sake, rather than using their well-honed mind to first understand and then illuminate for all humanity the magnificence of our infinite being.

(Talking of illumination, it's worth noting the original Illuminati were persecuted by the Christians as "heathens" simply because they were trying to tell us the truth about our divine nature. But I digress...)

Because this Life Path is governed by the masculine element of air and its ruling planet is Neptune (inspiration), the Seeker **7** will spend much of their life soaking up vast amounts of knowledge on all manner of subjects. This is because their purpose is to understand the nature of the universe from the perspective of divine truth.

I have called this Life Path the Seeker because it most accurately describes their spiritual quest. But it could equally be called the Thinker, because **7**s will usually pursue the "Big T" Truths at all costs… and, I'm sad to say, the cost to these sensitive Selfs can sometimes be quite high.

The studious **7** is often so wrapped up in their thoughts that they have a tendency to take everything, including themselves, too seriously, causing them to miss out on the juice of life. When they work with the positive energy of this Life Path they freely and joyously share their insights about the human condition, but when they fail to develop a strong inner confidence to express themselves they can easily flip to the "dark side" of this number and withdraw into their own inner world.

Loneliness and a lack of Self-trust are the negative **7**'s constant companions, borne of their fear of never being "bright enough" or "smart enough" or "good enough" to speak what is truly in their hearts. Invariably, what they instinctively know in their heart about divine truth is worth a hundred times more than anything even their impressive intellect can grasp, if only they would step outside of their heads long enough to listen to the messages from their Self.

This is the agonising dichotomy for all **7**s. They want to understand and illuminate divine truth with their minds by spending their lives in a succession of dusty libraries, when all along they already know the truth they are seeking is in their heart, and all they need do is switch off their brains and go inside… where all their answers are waiting for them.

* * *

Highest purpose of The Seeker

The highest purpose of the **7** is to study the mysteries of life and share what they discover with others. As an air number, they are almost always in their heads, seeking out answers to every question their hyperactive and endlessly inquisitive minds can come up with.

Their role, of which they are acutely and often painfully aware, is to sort the wheat of divine truth from the chaff of human delusion – and, by doing so, light the way for all of us to rise above our mortal fears and embrace our immortal and infinite beauty.

No pressure!

The enormity of their task, and the very real potential for harming the lives of others if they get their message wrong, is a heavy burden for even the most Self-confident Seeker to bear. Which is why so many **7**s suffer from Self-doubt – especially in their teenage and early adult years – and are at risk of succumbing to the negative energy of this Life

Life Path 7: The Seeker

Path by becoming detached and aloof "know-it-alls", rather than humble, quietly spoken illuminators of the truth.

Blockbuster filmmaker James Cameron (*Avatar* and *Titanic*) is a classic example of a **7** who flips repeatedly between these two Life Path extremes, displaying in equal measure the arrogance of his extraordinary intelligence and the humility of his "God"-given gift to show us all what we are truly made of – namely, pure perfect love.

Remember, the most important goal for all Life Paths is always the same: to first "wake up" to the truth that we are an extension of Source energy, and to help other people wake up as well. Then, and only then, will the path to our highest potential open up before us.

* * *

Key words are… 'confidence' and 'trust'

To fulfill their life's highest purpose, **7**s must first learn to develop a robust inner confidence in their abilities.

Confidence is central to all the Life Paths as we embark on our common journey from pure unaware love to pure conscious love. As we saw in Part One, developing a healthy Self-esteem is the first crucial step towards Self-love that we all must take.

(If you've come straight to this Life Path listing in Part Three and are wondering what a "Self" is, please try to find the time to read Part One because it's way too complicated to explain again here.)

For the always intelligent **7**, however, developing a strong sense of inner confidence is much more than just the key to their personal happiness – it will determine whether they walk the positive Life Path of the inspirational and insightful scholar, or veer down the negative path towards arrogance, Self-doubt and distrust.

All **7**s develop their powerful, analytical minds from an early age to prepare them for a life of contemplation. They are deep thinkers, steeped in the masculine air energy of intellect, and they have excellent problem-solving skills as well as an insatiable curiosity.

Life Path 7: Life Choices

Many choose to live in their own world, where they are masters and mistresses of their intellectual domain, because they feel more at home there than they do in the emotional hurly burly of everyday life.

Like all of us, they crave connection with the ones they love, but their lack of confidence in their ability to function socially as well as they do in their private inner world of ideas can lead them to become withdrawn and afraid that they – and their beliefs – won't be accepted.

Just as for their airy **3** cousins, positive feedback is essential for boosting the **7**'s confidence when they are young. If they post their thoughts on Facebook and don't receive enough Likes, it may take them a long time to pluck up the courage to do so again. And in a family setting, their ideas – no matter how "way out" they might appear – must be treated seriously, or they may retreat into their shell.

All **7s** are attracted to the deep mystical and spiritual elements of life. After all, they instinctively know from the earliest age that is where all the answers they seek are to be found. As a result, they can suffer from shyness and awkwardness when faced with what they regard as the shallow charade of social chitchat. Indeed, it is not uncommon for young **7s** to be teased at school and at parties for being "too intense", which only causes them to become even more withdrawn.

In conjunction with developing a strong inner confidence to express the ideas swirling constantly in their head, and thus experience the blissful release of sharing their intellectual burden with others, the naturally guarded **7** must also learn the valuable lesson of trust.

This is not trust in the sense of believing others will do the right thing by them, because more often than not they won't. No Life Path is more prone to bullying, especially when young, simply because they are so socially inept and their ideas are so far from the mainstream.

Trust for the **7** means trusting that what they know in their heart to be true is indeed true (because it is). And just because their divine message of Self-love flies in the face of what everyone around them (parents, teachers, priests etc) believes doesn't make it any less so.

* * *

Life Path 7: The Seeker

Positive and negative potential

All Life Paths contain an equal measure of positive and negative potential. Our challenge in every lifetime, no matter our Life Path Number, is to nurture our positives and overcome our negatives.

The reason we are given negative potential as well as positive potential is because people usually respond more effectively to the threat of pain than they do to the promise of pleasure.

Also, while it is admirable to do what we are good at in life, we will only ever become the best we can be by facing our "dark side" and digging deep into our Self to overcome the obstacles that appear on our path.

As we have already seen in Part Two, it is only when the chips are down and we are up against it that we find out who we truly are and what we are truly capable of doing.

For example, the **7** is a tireless seeker of truth and is blessed with both a keen intellect and an instinctive spiritual wisdom that guides them in their quest to find the answers to mankind's biggest and most important questions. They are usually soft-spoken and affectionate people, and when they work with the positive energy of this most focused of Life Paths they will freely share their knowledge with others to help guide them towards a happier and more peaceful life.

But if they lack faith in their own abilities, or fail to rise above their ego's fear of being judged, they may flip to the dark side of this number and become solitary intellectuals who, at their worst, can be dismissive of everyone's beliefs but their own.

Fortunately, most **7**s are blessed with a good deal of charm and refinement, which makes them attractive, but they are not inherently social and sometimes their reserved nature is mistaken for aloofness when it is actually a cover-up for their emotional insecurity.

They like going their own way and need lots of quiet time to just sit and be with their thoughts. They are not "joiners" and prefer to stay well away from noisy crowds, choosing instead the company of like-minded, level-headed friends and colleagues.

Life Path 7: Life Choices

Because Seekers are at the seventh (truth) stage of a growth cycle they possess an intuitive and even psychic ability to know what others are thinking and feeling. This can be unnerving for young and timid 7s, especially if they belong to a family that has not yet "woken up".

It's a universal spiritual truth that everyone who is on a growth path in their lifetime will always choose to incarnate into a "tribe" in which they do not fit, otherwise the pull of peer pressure from their family and friends will prevent them ever breaking free from the tribe's collective limiting beliefs. They can always go back home after they have found their purpose – and have navigated their way through their Dark Night of the Self – to share with their tribe what they have learned. But as young, fledgling Selfs they will often look around the dinner table at home and the playground at school and wonder why they feel so different from everyone else.

This is as unavoidable as it is painful, and if you have read this far I have no doubt you know exactly what I am talking about. It's difficult for all children to feel they don't "belong", but for the introverted and sensitive 7 it can be particularly distressing – which is why the negative side of this number, more than all the others, is an ever-present threat.

The pitfalls of the 7 Life Path are only too apparent. If Seekers spend too much time on their own and in their head they can become aloof and even reclusive, distrusting everyone and afraid to express what is in their hearts.

This is the number of the introspective loner. But although 7s are happy to spend long periods of time by themselves, scouring books and the internet for the answers they seek, they will never find true fulfillment unless they are able to come out of their shell and share what they have learned with others – for that is their highest calling.

"No man is an island" is a phrase 7s would do well to remember. Yes, studying is a solitary process but it doesn't always have to be. They can join study groups and even debating societies, where they can learn the value of freely exchanging ideas with other like-minded seekers of truth. After all, the joy of knowledge lies not in solitary contemplation but in sharing our ideas with others, playfully bouncing them around like a basketball and occasionally slam-dunking an exciting distinction or breakthrough we could never have discovered on our own.

Many 7s shun frivolous social situations because they make them feel uncomfortable, preferring the company of close friends instead. And while they may not have a lot of friends (and we're talking proper flesh-and-blood friends here, not the one-dimensional social media kind), those they do have will usually be friends for life.

They sometimes find it hard to trust, but this is invariably a projection of their lack of trust in their own abilities. As soon as they develop a healthy sense of first Self-esteem and then Self-love they will find it much easier to open up and share their thoughts with others.

Also, the 7's keenly analytical mind frequently finds fault with people's behaviour, just as they do with everything else, and they would do well to remember that not everyone thinks as deeply as they do, nor do they share the 7's acute awareness of how their words and their actions affect others' feelings.

Pessimism is another negative trait common to the 7, borne of their clairvoyant ability to see into the future and their grasp of the crucial process of cause and effect. Again, the solution is for the Seeker to learn to look on the bright side and trust that all will be well – because it will be, as long as they believe it will.

All prophecies are Self-fulfilling, thanks to the Law of Attraction. This is another immutable spiritual truth that the 7 has come here to learn and then teach to others – namely, that whatever we focus on in life, we attract. So if we believe all will be well, it will be. And if we believe it won't, it won't. That's why of all the nine Life Paths, it is particularly important for the frequently cynical 7 to be as positive and optimistic as they possibly can to prevent their imagined fears from manifesting in their life.

Talking about cynicism, in their quest for knowledge the 7 will usually develop a healthy skepticism relatively early on in their life that allows them to sort the conspiracy theory garbage and pseudo new-age gobbledegook from the genuine spiritual truths they seek. They will question everything they read, and they will never take anything at face

Life Path 7: Life Choices

value. Jumping on a bandwagon just isn't in their nature, and they won't accept any kind of premise until they have examined it from every angle and considered all sides of every argument.

This is an admirable quality, especially for someone whose highest purpose is to uncover the big truths and teach them to the world. But, as ever with this Life Path, the potential pitfalls are always close at hand and the **7** must guard against becoming too critical and dismissive of other people's points of view.

It is too easy for the negative **7** to be arrogant and dismissive of anything they don't happen to agree with, and they don't want to wind up as a leather-patched academic locked away in some book-lined ivory tower looking down with disdain on the uneducated muddled masses. That is not their purpose at all, nor will it ever make them happy.

They need to walk among us, teaching us and helping us discover our truly infinite and divine loving nature. Nothing less will do.

When they work with the positive energy of their Life Path – and providing they have cleared their emotional blockages so they trust their judgment and feel confident to speak what is in their hearts – the evolved **7** is the most uplifting of Selfs, able to inspire others with their almost mystical spiritual insights about the human condition.

They will delight in sharing their knowledge freely and seeing the transformational effect their message of love and truth has on those whose lives they touch. This, in turn, will drive them to want to get their message out to a wider audience – and before long they will find themselves walking the bright side of this Life Path, spreading beauty and truth everywhere they go.

* * *

On a more personal level, **7s** can sometimes struggle in their romantic relationships because they are in their heads so much of the time. They would do best to choose an understanding partner who is happy to give them plenty of space to contemplate the mysteries of the universe, and who makes relatively few demands on their time.

Life Path 7: The Seeker

They are also not the most practical of people, so the daily chores of running a household will be a challenge. And for love to thrive in their lives, they must learn to step outside themselves and consider the needs of their partner – who will be less than impressed if the **7** bursts out of their study to lecture them on the findings of the latest Swiss experiment into cosmic dark energy or share their fascinating insights into the mating habits of pufferfish, having completely forgotten that today is their wedding anniversary.

Ironically, most **7s** crave a close and loving connection with their partner and yet fear making themselves feel vulnerable if they open up the deepest part of themselves. If they are going to be able to nourish their relationship and forge a lasting bond with their partner, they must learn yet another spiritual truth – namely, that the more honest and open we are, the less we can be hurt. There is nothing to fear but fear itself, and genuine love – when expressed without caution or concern – is the strongest and most invulnerable force on the planet.

* * *

Summary of the positives

In the positive, the confident and Self-aware **7** is a refined, elegant and charming conversationalist, brimming with interesting stories and piercing insights into issues others struggle to comprehend. What they lack in emotional warmth they more than make up for with their deep, spiritual wisdom and intuitive understanding of how others feel.

They operate best when given plenty of space and time to expand their impressive knowledge library and organise their thoughts without feeling rushed to make a decision. And when they do decide to do something, it is virtually impossible to make them change their mind, making them reliable and consistent friends, colleagues and partners.

The **7** is also valued as a wise, even psychic adviser thanks to their almost mystical ability to read people and situations accurately. The can spot frauds easily, and their hunches are almost always right.

Life Path 7: Life Choices

Yes, they can sometimes appear cold and detached, but give them time to feel safe with you and they will open up into the most trusting – and trustworthy – friend, or lover, it is possible to imagine.

Key positive words

Intelligent, insightful, spiritual, psychic, intuitive, honest, loyal, thorough, discerning, trustworthy, independent, resourceful, persistent, knowledgeable, individual, clairvoyant, inventive and determined.

* * *

Summary of the negatives

As we have seen, many of the apparent "negative" qualities of the brooding and solitary **7** are in fact defence mechanisms they employ to paper over their deep insecurity in social situations and their gnawing Self-doubt about their intellectual ability.

The only truly damaging negative traits to watch for include a tendency to feel superior and treat other, less-informed people with disdain simply because they don't know as much about whatever it is the **7** has spent countless hundreds of hours studying.

Knowledge is only of any real value if we use it for the common good and share it around freely. It is certainly nothing that we should ever feel superior about.

Another potentially harmful negative for the **7** is their lack of consideration for others, because they are so internally focused that they may be tempted to think what they are doing or saying is more important than anything anyone else wants to do, or has to say.

Awareness of their surroundings and how others are feeling is never their strong suit, which is unforgivable, really, because when they do stop being so selfish and look up from their latest edition of *New Scientist* to consider the needs of others, their heightened ability to tune into people's thoughts and feelings gives them a unique ability to help, advise and comfort wherever it is required.

Life Path 7: The Seeker

Just as the positive **7** has the capacity to be the most benevolent and generous guru, the negative **7** can be the most inconsiderate and disdainful snob for whom nothing and no one is ever good enough.

Key negative words

Judgmental, insecure, arrogant, unemotional, inconsiderate, cold, calculating, aloof, pessimistic, critical, intolerant and cruel.

* * *

Self-love is the difference

If you have read Part One, you will already know that your ability to walk the positive side of your Life Path, as opposed to the negative side, is determined by whether you have undertaken the two key stages of personal growth. Or, to put it another way, whether you have taken the two crucial first steps on the path to your life's highest purpose.

The first step towards living your Life Path in the positive is to develop Self-esteem (and if you're wondering what a "Self" is, please take the time to read Part One because it's way too complicated to explain again here). This feeling of inner confidence is essential because it allows you to tap into your innate strengths, which you will need if you are going to have any hope of overcoming the numerous obstacles on your path. Be aware, though, that on its own this first step is never enough, because Self-confidence and Self-esteem are still the work of the ego. The feeling of being "good enough" carries with it an implied sense of needing to be "better than".

So to reach your full potential and achieve your life's highest purpose, you must also take the second step – which is to rise above the egoic concept of Self-esteem and climb to the much higher ground of Self-love.

Loving your Self does not mean being "full of your Self". It means the opposite. It means being humble because you understand that you are the same as everyone else, no better and no worse.

Life Path 7: Life Choices

Above all, it means you understand that we are all immortal spirits having a human experience, and therefore we are all, at our core, the same – pure love and pure Source energy. (The Source is also fully explained in Part One.)

We can see it easily in new-born babies because when we are born into physical form, and before our fear-based ego has had a chance to develop, we are all gorgeous, gurgling bundles of pure, exquisite love.

I am not suggesting you do this, but just imagine you were to place a new-born infant on the pavement of a crowded street and then stand back out of sight. Everyone – and I mean everyone – would stop and tend to it. And the reason they would do this is because, deep down, we all recognise pure love when we see it. We are drawn to it at the most basic level of our being because it is the most strikingly beautiful and compelling force on the planet.

But sadly, as we grow up and go out into the world, our ego takes over and we start to believe – usually during our teenage years – that our ego is who we are. It isn't. Love is who we are.

We are all pure love. We are all extensions of Source energy (or children of "God", whichever phrase you are more comfortable with).

If you can rise above the quasi-religious terminology, I can summarise the two steps like this: Self-esteem is about feeling "good enough", while Self-love is about feeling "God enough".

The reason why loving your Self is so important for your Life Path is because when you start to live your life from the perspective of being pure love, everything changes. Suddenly you understand that nothing "out there" in the material world can ever harm you in any way.

Equally, you real-eyes you don't need anything "out there" in the material world to make you feel happy – not the approval of others; no amount of money, fame and power; and not even the love of a good man or woman – because you have all the love you need right there in your own heart, and you can therefore relish the exquisite joy of loving everyone unconditionally without needing anything in return.

That is why Self-love is the secret to working with the positive energy of your Life Path Number. Because when you truly love your

Life Path 7: The Seeker

Self, the rocky mountain path you've been climbing suddenly becomes an express elevator ride all the way up to the summit of your bliss.

* * *

No Life Path is an island

Although your Life Path Number denotes the main issues you will focus on, you will always work to some degree with the energies of the other numbers as well to become a fully rounded Self.

As a **7** your main work will be in the areas of trust and openness, but you will also tackle the issues of Self-confidence (**1**), co-operation and balance (**2**), creative expression (**3**), stability and flexibility (**4**), discipline (**5**), acceptance (**6**), abundance and power (**8**) and integrity (**9**).

It's therefore worth your while to read through the listings for the other Life Path Numbers when your time allows.

* * *

Qualities of your three-digit Birth Code

(Note: Please read the description in Part Two of how 0 operates in your three-digit Birth Code. Also, you can consult the main Life Path listings here in Part Three for each of your Supplementary Birth Numbers (the six possible ones for the Seeker are 1, 2, 3, 4, 5 and 6) to give you a clearer understanding of how their qualities govern your formative years.)

'Millennium Child' 00/7

A Millennium Child born with the remarkably powerful single-digit Birth Code of **7** has come into the world with the potential to achieve something truly spectacular with their life.

All the Millennium Children (those born at the beginning of this century without any Supplementary Birth Numbers) are endowed with extra potential because they will work with the energy of their Life Path

Life Path 7: Life Choices

Number with absolute focus and an incredible amount of commitment. (The Millennium Children are described in Part Two, Chapter 2.)

The doubly amplified presence of the two 0s in place of their two Supplementary Birth Numbers means they will be working solely with the supercharged energy of 7 their entire life. For obvious reasons, these 00/7 children are the "James Bonds" of the Self-Awareness System™. They are special agents of truth and are born with a licence to thrill the entire world with their ground-breaking insights.

But 7s are first and foremost soothsayers and mystics who have come here to teach us about the power of divine love, so these hyper-intelligent "James Bond Children" have a fantastic opportunity to fight the evil spectre of ignorance at a time when their help is more desperately needed than perhaps at any time in our history.

The world hasn't seen a 00/7 Millennium Child since October 10, 1400, more than 600 years ago, but there are more coming soon, starting on January 2, 2020. Which is just as well, because we urgently need their help to rid our fragile little planet of the rampant fear, greed and fundamentalist aggression that threatens our very existence.

On a more personal level, 00/7 children and adults will have the potential to enjoy great success in their chosen career thanks to their laser-like mental focus and ability to effortlessly solve a problem long before anyone else even knows there is one. And because the energy of 7 is the only number they will work with throughout their life, they also have the capacity to break new ground in their chosen field.

As with all the Millennium Children, however, they must never feel pressured in any way to live up to the special promise of their amplified Birth Code. There is no "Life Path contract" that requires them to use their gifts for anything other than making themselves and their family happy. If all they do is shed their ego and live in love, they will achieve what we are all here to achieve – which is to real-eyes that we are pure love, and show the Source that it is pure love too.

(If this is your child's number, they will be aged between five and 17 as *Messages from Your Self* is published, so please flip forward to the

Life Path 7: The Seeker

Choices for Children section under this listing for the Seeker to find out more about their positive potential, and the negatives to avoid.)

16/7

Their first Supplementary Birth Number of 1 means these Seekers will work with the forceful fire (action) energy of the Leader during the crucial early formative years of their life up until they turn 18. And they will do so in conjunction with the dominant air (thought) energy of their Life Path Number 7, which will still govern how they behave and the way their intellectual personality develops.

Then in their second 18 years, up to full emotional maturity at 36, they will flip to work with the watery (emotion) energy of their second Supplementary Birth Number 6, ensuring they balance their detached and studious nature with much-needed warmth and compassion.

This means that while the primary focus of their life will always be governed by the intellectual and solitary energy of their Life Path Number 7, they are able to have the courage (1) to express their innermost thoughts both at home and at school and then, as they reach young adulthood and head out into the world, they will develop the emotional confidence (6) to connect with other like-minded people and share their message of truth and beauty with the world.

As long as they clear their emotional blockages and work with the positive energy of their three Birth Code numbers, the 16/7 will be able to enjoy much success both at home and in their work. Their lives will be based on learning the Big Truths about the world and then teaching them to others – which is all the 7 really wants to do.

One word of caution, though: the lack of an earth number (4 or 8) in their Birth Code means the 16/7 must work especially hard to ground themselves or they may become dangerously detached from the material world of financial stability and physical health.

Romantically, 16/7s have the potential to forge close and loving relationships in their early adult years, when the supplementary energy of 6 kicks in. But until then they may struggle with social interaction, even with their family, due to the headstrong energy of 1 operating in

Life Path 7: Life Choices

their early childhood years alongside the solitary and contemplative energy of their Life Path **7**.

25/7

These Seekers are likely to be more outgoing and social than the 7's other four Birth Codes thanks to the feminine water energy of their first Supplementary Birth Number **2** (emotion) operating during their early formative years up until they reach 18.

Then during their next 18 years, until full emotional maturity at 36, they will be driven by the masculine fire energy of **5** (action) to go out into the world and use their intellectual power to make a difference in people's lives, spreading their message of divine truth far and wide.

All the while their main focus will be on pondering the mysteries of life and accumulating vast amounts of information, as governed by their Life Path Number **7**. But unlike the other more solitary Birth Codes, they will be happy to work in co-operation with others (**2**) – providing, of course, they develop the necessary inner confidence to share their ideas and beliefs without fear of rejection.

Be warned, though, that the flip side of the Intuitive (**2**) is a tendency towards being overly sensitive and shy, especially when young, and this – combined with the natural introspection of the **7** – could have the reverse effect and cause the young **25**/**7** to withdraw even deeper into their shell during their school years.

On the whole, though, these Seekers will benefit greatly from the water energy of their first Supplementary Birth Number **2** while their personality is being formed as a child, giving them a nicely balanced emotional depth to match their intellectual prowess.

Then, at age 18 as they kick-start their working life with the adventurous and courageous energy of the Rebel (**5**), they will likely develop into truly original and motivational Seekers who are capable of making a real difference in the world.

As long as they clear their emotional blockages and work with the positive energy of their three Birth Code numbers, the **25**/**7** will be able to enjoy great success in all areas of their life.

One more word of caution: the lack of an earth number (<u>4</u> or <u>8</u>) in their Birth Code means the <u>25</u>/7 must work especially hard to ground themselves and look after their money and their health. Neither the rebellious <u>5</u> nor the introspective 7 are particularly concerned with such "worldly concerns" as financial wealth or physical health, so they would do well to partner up (both in business and love) with someone who is and who can therefore help the <u>25</u>/7 focus on these issues.

Romantically and socially, <u>25</u>/7s are far better equipped than their other Seeker cousins thanks to the early presence of the Intuitive (<u>2</u>) in their Birth Code This bodes well for a happy and outgoing childhood, as well as close and loving relationships in their adult years.

<u>34</u>/7

Wow! These high-powered Seekers have so much air (thought) in their Birth Code while their razor-sharp mind is developing in their first formative years that they will likely find themselves outsmarting their schoolteachers before they even reach double figures.

The inquisitive nature of the <u>3</u> and the intellectual capacity of the **7** means these young Seekers will spend much of their childhood with their heads buried in a book or online, devouring as much knowledge as they possibly can from every available source. They will pepper their parents and teachers with questions, wanting to know how everything works and asking "why?" every time someone tells them to perform even the most menial task.

They will often be artistic from an early age as well (the energy of their first Supplementary Birth Number <u>3</u>), but the insecurity that often afflicts the solitary **7** may prevent them from expressing their creativity freely. They may choose to draw or write, rather than act or sing, and keep their work safely locked away in a drawer or a box under the bed.

At school, the outgoing energy of <u>3</u> will give the introspective **7** a better chance of interacting with teachers and classmates, although they will tend to have a few close friends rather than a wide social circle.

Then when they hit adulthood at 18, the <u>34</u>/7 will begin to work with the pragmatic earth energy of <u>4</u> (the Builder), leading them to put down roots and establish a firm foundation for both their professional life and their home life.

All the while their main work will be focused on understanding the mysteries of life and sharing the truths they learn with others, as governed by their Life Path, and their heightened intelligence all but guarantees that they will succeed in whatever they choose to do.

One word of caution, though: the lack of a water number (2 or 6) in their Birth Code means they may struggle to express and process their emotions, leading to some challenges in their relationships and, potentially, bouts of depression. And the absence of any fire (action) numbers as well (1 or 5) could cause them to become stuck in a rut of Self-doubt, unable to move forward unless they can wrest their highly developed ego from the controls of their life and conquer their fears.

43/7

This is a mirror of the previous Birth Code, and people walking this Life Path will share many qualities with their 34/7 cousins. The key difference is that during their first formative years – when their personality is established – they will be working with the supplementary earth energy of the pragmatic and responsible 4 instead of the outgoing and creative air energy of 3.

Yes, they will still be a studious **7** through and through – and will therefore focus on accumulating knowledge to help them understand how the world works – but as children and teenagers they will tend to be more serious and inwardly focused than the 34/**7**, and will be happy to spend long periods on their own pondering the meaning of life.

For their first 18 years, the 43/**7** child will probably have fewer friends than most, but those they do have will likely be theirs for life. All 4s are unwaveringly loyal and can spot a faker a mile away, leading them to be picky about who they choose to befriend, and the equally deep **7** has no time for anyone who isn't as genuine as they are.

The humanitarian aspects of the 4 means these young Seekers will be concerned with issues of fairness and justice from an early age, sparking a desire to use their powerful analytical minds (the quality of the **7**) to find ways to help improve the lives of others, especially their loved ones. Then, as the artistic and expressive energy of their second Supplementary Birth Number <u>3</u> kicks in from 18 to full emotional maturity at age 36, they will focus their impressive intellect on solving the great problems of the world in new and creative ways.

As we saw with the <u>34</u>/**7**, the absence of any water numbers (<u>2</u> or <u>6</u>) means they may suppress their emotions and struggle in romantic relationships, while the lack of a fire (action) number (<u>1</u> or <u>5</u>) may cause them to procrastinate and get bogged down in petty details.

Providing the reserved <u>43</u>/**7** develops enough Self-confidence to step outside their solitary shell and share the truths they know in new and original ways, they can enjoy great financial and creative success.

* * *

2. CAREER AND BUSINESS CHOICES

THE **7** Life Path is usually well-suited to problem-solving roles such as analysts, investigators, private detectives, police work and the law. Their acute intelligence also makes them excellent academics, teachers, scientists and researchers, and they will thrive particularly well in the protected world of colleges, universities and government think-tanks where they can enjoy a welcome level of freedom and autonomy.

Many **7**s do not feel comfortable if they have to adhere to too many rules laid down by others, and they also prefer to work alone rather than as part of a team. Their extraordinary capacity for studying and retaining information means the scholastic **7** usually excels in exams and may extend their education well past school to include all manner of advanced qualifications. (It's rare to find a mature **7** without at least a handful of letters after their name.)

Medicine is one arena that is well-suited to the **7**'s intellectual and humanitarian personality, and they will often ascend all the way to the

Life Path 7: Career Choices

top of their chosen field. Another career choice suited to their solitary style would be accounting and finance, where they may learn the ropes within a large organisation before branching out on their own.

They are also excellent diagnosticians and forensic analysts, which leads many 7s to don the white lab coat of the scientific researcher, whether it be in pharmaceuticals, medical research, computers, law enforcement or academia.

Most 7s dislike manual labour and will work best in a refined and cultured environment, where they can use their vast knowledge and nimble problem-solving skills to their best advantage. But they must guard against putting their colleagues' noses out of joint by being too insular. The 7 does not normally "play well with other kids", and because almost all careers involve at least some form of teamwork, they would do well to make a concerted effort to fit in.

No one likes an arrogant know-it-all (and the intelligent 7 certainly does know it all). But arrogance is always a sign of insecurity, and as long as the 7 has done the necessary inner work to boost their levels of Self-worth and Self-love they should be able to steer well clear of the negative side of this Life Path, which can lead to stubbornness, superiority and disdain for anyone who doesn't measure up to their high standards.

One other area that holds many rewards for the 7 is spirituality in all its forms. These are the truth-sayers and truth-seekers of the world, and they may be drawn to life of faith in one of the churches, where they can satisfy their need for plenty of solitary time for contemplation. Less-conventional spiritual paths such as psychic medium, faith healer, astrologer and (of course!) numerologist will also appeal.

Beneficial career paths

People working with the intellectual and analytical energy of 7 make excellent scientists, researchers, academics, forensic analysts, lab technicians, private detectives, accountants, bankers, lawyers, doctors, surgeons, dentists, health professionals, administrators, psychologists, therapists, counsellors, dieticians, spiritual teachers, psychics, priests,

Life Path 7: The Seeker

strategic planners, computer analysts, programmers, personal trainers, archaeologists, engineers, farmers, authors and investigators.

Best business matches

If a **7** goes into business for themselves, they will usually try to go it alone – because this is the most solitary of all the numbers. Plus, the deep-thinking **7** always believes they know best (they usually do), so any form of corporate partnership may be a challenge for them.

The fellow air energy of **3** could be a good match, injecting some much-needed creativity and flair, and the "people person" **2** would provide a good counterbalance to the rather cold rationality of the **7**'s thought processes, especially when it comes to staff morale.

Avoid the dominant **1**, the unreliable **5** and the controlling **6**. Pick a practical **4** or **8** for finance manager, a persuasive **3** for sales and marketing and a **9** or another **7** for the essential back-office roles.

* * *

3. RELATIONSHIP CHOICES

ONE of the most rewarding aspects about the Self-Awareness System™ is how equitable it is. Each Life Path offers the same opportunities for happiness and fulfillment, albeit in markedly different ways. And each of them also offers the same amount of challenges to force us to grow, although again in very different ways.

This means no Life Path is any "better" or "worse" than any of the others. All of them have their blessings, and all have their obstacles.

In the case of **7**, the blessings centre around their spiritual and intellectual intelligence and their remarkably astute analytical minds, and their obstacles are found in their social and romantic relationships, due to their reluctance to open up and share what is in their heart.

Life Path 7: Relationship Choices

Clearly, when it comes to matters of love, this lack of openness and fear of vulnerability poses a significant challenge for the 7, but it is by no means insurmountable. It just means that, more than any other Life Path, they will need to work on nurturing their relationships, as well as improving their emotional confidence.

The truth is, while most 7s prefer spending time on their own, they fall in love easily because they crave a close emotional connection with their partner and want to share the deepest part of themselves. They just often have no idea how. Plus, if it came down to a choice, as much as they want to experience the joy of a committed relationship, they would sacrifice it in a heartbeat if it meant having to give up too much of their precious "me time" to achieve it.

If your partner is a 7 you must be prepared to give them plenty of space and not violate their inner sanctuary too often, or else they will grow to resent you as an "intruder". The rewards will be worth it, though, because providing they feel free to take time out for their latest solo project, they will be the most devoted and trustworthy of lovers, unwavering in their commitment to you and loyal to the end.

Understanding their emotions is never easy for the 7, let alone expressing them freely, so it is also important to listen closely when a Seeker does open up about how they are feeling. They are extremely sensitive to rejection and will retreat back into their shell if they are mocked, dismissed or made to feel vulnerable in any way. But if they are met with love and encouragement each time they reveal an intimate part of themselves, their Self-confidence can grow quickly, allowing them to deepen their connection with their partner.

Although they are sometimes afraid of intimacy, many 7s are charming and generous in social situations, as long as the topics of conversation remain on an intellectual or spiritual level, where they feel most comfortable. Should a "deep and meaningful" heavy emotional discussion break out, they will probably make their excuses and move on. Plus, all social outings will need to be interspersed with frequent retreats to their "lair" to let them gather their thoughts.

Life Path 7: The Seeker

In the family home, there must always be a room (a study, a den, a spare bedroom or even a garage or shed in the garden) where the **7** can go and close the door behind them, knowing they will not be disturbed. This makes them best-suited to partnering up with their fellow air number **3**, another **7** or one of the two fire signs (**1** or **5**), all of whom also like time by themselves and will best understand and accept the **7**'s need for solitude.

A co-dependent **2** or a controlling **6**, both of whom need regular contact with their partners, will definitely struggle and may run the risk of pushing the **7** away if they fail to respect their inner sanctum. And the two earthy numbers (**4** and **8**), who are focused mainly on the practical day-to-day aspects of life, will be infuriated by the **7**'s need to spend so much time with their thoughts, mulling over concepts that to the **4** and **8** may appear to have no practical value whatsoever.

While the intelligent and intuitive **7** will be a devoted partner and an excellent companion who is never short of fascinating topics of conversation, they must guard against becoming too egotistical and Self-centred, especially when they perceive their partner's worries and concerns as "trivial" in the big scheme of things. Yes, they may be. But that is no excuse for dismissing them or undervaluing them, and the **7** must learn to listen to everything their partner says as though it is the most important thing in the world for them at that moment – which, of course, it is.

On the positive side, the **7**'s home will invariably be elegant and refined – just like everything else about them – and decorated in good taste with plenty of fine art and tasteful furnishings. But it may just feel a little bit too cold, and would benefit from the warmth of a more emotional and sensitive partner.

On the negative side, the **7** is so reluctant to ever reveal the full extent of their Self – even in a safe, loving relationship – that their partner can live with them for year, decades even, without ever fully feeling that they know all there is to know about them.

Also, because the trivialities of life don't interest the **7**, they can sometimes appear aloof and uncaring, which is not true at all. They just need to be taught why the challenges facing their partner are as important to them as the need to find a cure for cancer or bring about world peace. Once they real-eyes that loving their partner completely, and being loved by them completely in return, is more fulfilling to them and will bring them more joy than all the answers to all their Big Picture questions put together, the **7** will happily and eagerly become the most attentive and devoted of lovers.

* * *

Sex drive of the 7

They say the brain is the biggest and best erogenous zone of them all, and if this is true then the Seeker is the surely the Casanova, John Holmes, Jenna Jameson and Joan Collins of the bedroom all rolled into one. Sadly, though, the reality is not quite so toe-curlingly multi-orgasmic, because most **7**s are defensive to the point of shyness when it comes to the fine art of horizontal folk-dancing… at least until they feel safe enough with their partner to let their inhibitions go.

As with everything else in their life, they tend to approach love-making from an intellectual or spiritual perspective, when their partner probably just wants to get naked and "get it on", Marvin Gaye-style. Never one to feel comfortable with emotional intensity, the **7** may often regard sex as a problem to be solved or a skill to be mastered, when in reality they need to just go with the passion and be more Barry White or Cleopatra and a lot less Albert Einstein or Angela Merkel.

However, once the **7** feels safe enough to open up their triple-locked vault of "scary emotions" deep inside themselves, they can be fantastically skilled lovers – for the same reason that they can be frigid ones if they don't. The **7** will never attempt to do anything in life unless they can master it, so when they do decide to learn the libidinous ropes of languid love-making, they will not stop until they are able to give their partner the best sex they have ever had in their life. But in order to do that, they need to get in touch with their feelings and not be afraid to open themselves up to the feelings of their partner either.

Life Path 7: The Seeker

This is an overwhelmingly masculine Life Path Number, which means even feminine **7** lovers will be stuck in their heads most of the time, calculating and processing data rather than blissing out to the exquisite sensations that their body is feeling.

As we saw earlier, the central dichotomy in relationships for all **7**s is that they crave a close connection while at the same time being afraid to open up to the vulnerability such a close connection entails.

If the "masculine energy" partner in a relationship is a **7**, he will tend to want to dominate his feminine partner with the forcefulness of his superior intellect. This might be awesome when it comes to "quickies" in the wood, or in the back of the car, or in the toilet at restaurants. But when it comes to making love under the stars, or on a four-poster bed strewn with rose petals and all set about with scented candles, he needs to be able to open up his feminine partner with the force of his emotional and physical desires as well. The mind alone just isn't going to cut the mustard, sexually speaking.

Equally, if the introspective **7** is the "feminine energy" partner in a relationship, she may tend to over-analyse every aspect of her and her partner's love-making and, if she finds a "problem", will not feel comfortable until it is "solved".

Yes, of course it is good to be aware of how we can improve our sexual experience. But if she just relaxed into her feelings and opened up her innermost Self to her lover, she might find that the "problem" was merely that she had failed to switch off her mind and switch on the pleasure receptors in her body, as well as the deep feelings of love in her heart.

*　*　*

The compatibility listings that follow will help thoughtful **7**s get the most out of their relationships, whether it's with someone they love, a friend or a business partner.

You will notice the air energy of **7** is well-matched with other **7**s, their air cousin **3** and the evolved **9**, as well as a **1** and **5**, whose fire combusts with the presence of air. But air evaporates water (**2** and **6**) and erodes earth (**4** and **8**), so these pairings throw up more challenges.

However, what appears to match you best on the surface may not be what you need in your life right now. All relationships are designed to help us grow along our Life Path. Yes, of course we enjoy the companionship, close connection, sexual intimacy and deep love that relationships give us. But that is now why we have them.

The reason we choose a partner (or, to be more accurate, why our all-knowing Self chooses them for us) is because they are a mirror in which we see our shortcomings and strengths reflected back at us through their shortcomings and strengths.

That is why opposites so often attract, especially in love.

I have written an entire book on this subject called *Leap into Love* which goes into the way relationships work in our lives in great detail. But for now, please real-eyes that when your partner presses one of your buttons, they are doing so not to "piss you off" but because your Self is using them to show you the areas you need to work on.

If you fail to understand this is the main reason why you attracted them into your life in the first place, you will fight each other and may eventually break up. And you will believe their faults were exactly that – their faults – rather than yours reflected back at you.

Worst of all, you will then take the unchanged you with you to your next relationship, and – lo and behold! – exactly the same issues will come up again.

If this sounds familiar. If you have ever asked any of these questions – "Why does this always happen to me?" or "Why do all men cheat?" or "Why are all women so demanding?" or whatever it is for you – then now you know why. It's because you didn't learn from your last partner, so of course your new one will do the same thing.

And this will continue to happen, relationship after relationship, until you real-eyes it is meant to be happening to show you what areas you need to work on in your Self to change and grow.

One final quick point before we get into it: I need to stress that I disagree with almost every numerologist I know who likes to label relationships "a natural fit", "a neutral fit" or "an unnatural fit", depending on the compatibility of the numbers of the two partners.

All relationships are challenging. That is why we have them, as we have just seen. Yes, sometimes we might choose a partner who is "just like us" for the sake of harmony, but that could be regarded as a cop out if we are truly serious about our personal and spiritual growth.

If you are on a spiritual growth path in this lifetime (and there is no doubt in my mind that you are if you made it through Part One without throwing it in the bin!), then your Self will choose your relationships for you – and they will always be with a partner who will challenge you to grow in exactly the ways you need to grow.

Just because you might discover your current partner has a Life Path Number that doesn't dovetail perfectly with yours, don't fall into the trap of thinking there must be something wrong – or worse, end it with them so you can go out with someone with a "better" number.

Where you are right now on your Life Path is exactly where you are meant to be, and who you are with is exactly who you are meant to be with. So please let these listings help you to look for the lessons in your relationship, rather than look for the door.

And if you are single at the moment, try to remain open-hearted about your next relationship. It doesn't matter what Life Path Number they have, so don't "cherry pick". All that matters is you follow your heart and be open to learning the lessons they can teach you. After all, that's the reason you will attract them into your life in the first place.

* * *

7 & 1
(Understanding and Independence)

Love
This is an extremely compatible match that can often turn into a lifelong relationship, providing both partners come to each other at similar stages of their spiritual and personal development.

Life Path 7: Relationship Choices

In the beginning of the relationship there can be challenges as the guarded **7** waits to reveal their true emotions until they feel safe enough with their **1** partner to do so without fear rejection, and the always confident (if not arrogant) **1** struggles to accept that the insightful and brilliantly aware **7** is not only much smarter than they can ever hope to be, but probably has a keener insight into the **1**'s strengths and weaknesses than they have themselves.

This can sometimes lead the insecure **1** to break up with the **7**, simply because they are unnerved by their superior intelligence.

The **1** needs to learn that the **7** has absolutely no intention of stealing the **1**'s thunder. Yes, of course they are more evolved because **1**s are only at the beginning of their cycle, forging their successes in the fires of material wealth, while **7**s are well past that materialistic stage and are working with the advanced air energy of spiritual expression.

The truth is, the evolved **7** is a loving and supportive partner who is happiest when they see the love of their life succeeding in whatever they choose to do. This can sometimes make the **1** feel guilty, because they are acutely aware that their capacity for selfless support is nowhere near as strong, or as evolved, as that of their faithful and devoted **7**.

This is a huge mistake, because the **7** does not want back what they give out. They will support their independent and ambitious **1** lover through thick and thin and all they will ever need is recognition and appreciation in return. Well, that and enough solitary time to do their own thing – which the independent **1** will usually be only too happy to give them.

The often wayward **1** must always treat their devoted **7** with the utmost respect and communicate their innermost feelings with absolute honesty. The **7** can see through a lie easier than an x-ray can see through skin. And for them, honesty – no matter how painful it might be to hear – is paramount.

Remember that when disagreements arise (and they will because all relationships are about growth, as we saw earlier), take the time to sit down and figure out what you are meant to be learning from your partner – then kiss them and thank them for the lesson.

Life Path 7: The Seeker

Good luck, stay open and honest… and enjoy the wonderfully free and mutually respectful connection this relationship can give you.

Friendship

Yes, yes and yes again! These two can be Best Friends Forever, with the intellectual **7** inspiring the ambitious **1**, and the confident **1** helping the often shy **7** bring their lofty ideas to fruition.

These two friends will gleefully feed off each other energetically, with the forceful **1** encouraging the insightful **7** to put their ideas out there into the world, and the thoughtful **7** using their air energy to fan the flames of the passionate **1**.

In fact, these two numbers get along so well together that if their sexualities match and the **7** is in a relationship, they must be careful their close connection with their **1** BFF doesn't become an issue that could threaten their partner.

Business

This is a positive combination for business, for all the reasons we have already seen. The insightful **7** and the firefly **1** will usually work well together – the intelligent **7** stoking the flames of the **1**'s energetic drive with their knowledge of what people really want, and the ambitious **1** taking the **7**'s inspiring ideas and making them happen.

The air energy of **7** and the fire energy of **1** can drive this business to grow beyond their wildest dreams. But growing a business is only one side of the coin. Neither of these air and fire numbers has the first clue about the day-to-day practicalities of running a company, so the first thing they should do after signing their partnership agreement is employ an earthy manager to make sure everything runs smoothly.

And, as we have already seen, that requires a **4**. A business with a tireless **1** driving its growth, an aware **7** targeting its market, and a loyal **4** managing the back-office operations is almost guaranteed to succeed.

* * *

7 & 2
(Understanding and Co-operation)

Love

As long as a healthy balance can be achieved, whereby the **7** takes the time to listen to all the **2**'s social media gossip with genuine interest and the **2** respects the **7**'s need to spend five million hours every single day in their study wrestling with the intangible questions of conceptual metaphysical identity, then this relationship can work harmoniously without the slightest sign of a disagreement.

I'm kidding! Sorry, it's a cheap joke, I know, but it's more likely that Donald Trump will admit he's a lying bastard on the same day that someone in rural Slovakia films a flying pig and posts it on Instagram.

These two numbers have so little in common that it's a stretch to imagine them ever meeting and falling in love in the first place. Before they have even finished their starters, the emotionally closed **7** will be looking for the restaurant door to escape the fire of the **2**'s passionate and always open heart, and the free-loving **2** will be yawning into their soup as the intellectual **7** tries to explain the finer points of existential libertarianism for the 15th time.

Of all the eight other Life Path Numbers, the independent and reserved **7**, who requires long periods of time alone to contemplate the big mystical questions of life, is perhaps the most challenging match for the co-dependent and emotional **2**, who wants to curl up together on the lounge and watch movies together while the cerebral **7** wants time alone to read a treatise on quantum physics.

However, if they do experience an attraction of opposites, this has the potential to be one of the most powerful growth combinations it is possible to imagine. Think about it. What does the analytical and independent **7** need more than anything else to live a happy, healthy and fulfilling life? The answer is emotional connection, which the **2** can teach them before they've even had their first mug of Earl Grey in the morning. And what does the deep-feeling yet insecure **2** need more than anything else to live a happy, healthy and fulfilling life? The answer is loyalty and devotion from their partner, as well as a powerful lesson in how to stand on their own two feet and not sweat the small stuff – which the **7** can give them and teach them without even stopping to think about it for a single second.

If these two lovers can get out of their own way and real-eyes that each has everything the other needs, this can be a powerful growth relationship. They are unlikely to be lovers for life, but that's OK. Sometimes the best relationships flare and fade in a matter of moments, but they change the way we view the world forever.

Good luck, stay open and honest… and enjoy the challenging but ultimately life-changing growth lessons you have to teach each other.

Friendship

Unless these two are very evolved, this pairing is seldom going to work outside the "mutual growth" construct of a loving relationship that is explained above, because these two opposites will meet on a social level, freak each other out, bore each other to death and then run as fast as they can in the opposite direction. Anything other than a Facebook friendship based on the **7** liking the **2**'s photo of a pot roast they cooked the previous night for 462 of their closest, most intimate friends, or the **2** liking the obscure Renee Descartes quote they posted about mankind's quasi-spiritual struggle to discover their true identity will definitely be a stretch.

It's a shame because these two friends have so much to teach each other, if only they could see past their differences.

Business

Strangely, given their polar opposite values in life, these two could come together to form a relatively successful business partnership, because without the expectation of familiarity that is necessary for both love and friendship, they might just be able to see that each perfectly plugs the gaps in the other's skill set and is therefore able to perform the roles they themselves suck at.

Life Path 7: Relationship Choices

The intellectual and contemplative **7** needs the co-operative **2** to connect with their customers and motivate their staff, while the often scattered **2** needs the insightful and intelligent **7** to solve the day-to-day problems that will inevitably arise in any business.

There will be conflict, of course, but if there is enough mutual respect for the other's abilities, these two can definitely work well together, perfectly complementing each other's abilities.

* * *

<u>7 & 3</u>
(Understanding and Expression)

Love

No one is better able to understand the spiritual and intellectual nature of the cerebral **7** better than their fellow conceptually focused air cousin **3**, making this a good match – as long as both partners are secure enough to trust each other during long periods of separation.

The solitary **7** needs to be given plenty of time alone without being made to feel guilty that they are neglecting their partner, and no one is better able to give this gift to them than the outgoing and equally independent **3**, who needs to feel free to go out and explore the world to fuel their creative fire.

This mutual need for time apart makes this romantic match one of the most harmonious it is possible for the **7** to find, because they can support and love their expressive and creative **3** partner without feeling that they need to devote too much of their precious thinking time to stroking either their hair or their ego to make them feel loved.

As we will see in a moment, even a fellow **7** is not as understanding a lover as the carefree **3** because they may want to occupy the same space in the relationship as their **7** partner does, and they may fight them constantly to be top dog, both intellectually and spiritually.

No such competitive drive afflicts the individualistic and artistic **3**, for whom a relationship will always be of secondary importance to their need to feel free to take their message of love and hope out into the world, through whatever creative medium they choose.

The principal challenge that can arise with this pairing – and it probably will, so be forewarned and forearmed – is that both partners will be so content to let each other have all the time and space they need, they may neglect the romantic side of their relationship and simply drift apart, becoming more like friends than lovers.

As long as they take time out from their individual career goals to spend quality and passionate time together every once in a while – whether it be away on romantic weekends just the two of them, or even just out for dinner with a baby-sitter at home looking after the kids – this shouldn't become too much of a problem.

Good luck, stay open and honest… and enjoy the mutual support and understanding that this relationship can give you.

Friendship

The spiritual air energy of **7** is well-suited to the creative air energy of **3**, meaning these two analytical observers of life have the potential to forge a great friendship that will stand the test of time. Their mutual interest in understanding the world around them and finding ways to improve the lives of others will let these two friends fire off each other, sharing their Big Ideas and egging each other on to ever greater heights of creativity and professional success.

These two air (thought) numbers have so much in common they can't help but become good friends and mutual admirers almost as soon as they meet. Their conversation will soar and plunge through issues great and small, like some sort of intellectual roller-coaster, as they share their ideas with a tangible sense of relief that – at last! – they have finally found someone who "gets it".

What the **7** lacks in confidence, the **3** has in spades to help them have the courage to bring their grand designs to the world. And what the **3** lacks in depth, the intellectual **7** seamlessly provides to shore up the **3**'s paper-thin Self-esteem and give them the boost they need to express their creative ideas without fear of rejection or failure.

Business

Just as in love and friendship, this is a brilliant match for business, because both these air numbers will have an immediate and intuitive grasp of each other's creative Big Ideas, thus allowing them to share a vision for where the business needs to go, and how it can get there.

Generally, the enterprise will work best when the intuitive and thorough **7** is in charge of running the company and the creative **3** is free to pursue new directions for growth.

However, because these two air numbers have so much in common, care must be taken to avoid treading on each other's toes. A clear delineation of roles is essential to allow both partners to operate most effectively.

Neither air number will be especially good at looking after the mundane day-to-day details of running a business, so they would do well to employ an earthy **4** or **8** to look after the finances, freeing them to focus on the big creative and conceptual ideas.

* * *

7 & 4
(Understanding and Stability)

Love

The air energy of the **7** and the earth energy of the **4** seldom make for a particularly harmonious loving relationship, simply because both are just as set in their ways as the other and are equally as reluctant to compromise on their basic values, so they have limited potential to find a peaceful middle ground.

The solitary and spiritual **7** wants to have plenty of space to pursue their studies, free from the expectations of their partner. Meanwhile, the particular and fussy **4** wants to feel free to consult their partner about a million times a day on every single decision, ranging from what they are going to eat for dinner (the **7** couldn't care less) to where their lives are going (the **7** has absolutely no idea).

Life Path 7: The Seeker

In some respects, the earthy **4**'s pragmatic and well-grounded personality is the perfect foil for the airy **7**'s idealistic and spiritual focus, allowing them to ground themselves in the so-called "real world" of material stability. However, the **7** may quickly tire of what they see as the **4**'s mundane concerns. All they want to do is solve the big riddles of human existence, while the **4** wants to know if they are going to insure their home with this company or that.

Equally, the financially savvy **4** may tear their hair out trying to convince their **7** partner to come out of their study and look through the latest energy company brochures with them so they can save 30c a year on their gas bill, while the **7** is trying to come to grips with the finer points of astrophysical energetic spectro-dynamics as defined by the latest reimagining of the Keynesian economic paradigm.

These two have much to teach other about love, life and stopping to smell the roses. But they are both so serious, even Eddie Izzard might struggle to get them to lighten up over dinner and a show.

Good luck, stay open and honest… and enjoy the lessons about compromise and flexibility you can learn from each other.

Friendship

On the surface, the deep-thinking and conceptual **7** and the pragmatic and realistic **4** appear to have little in common, but look a little deeper and you will see how these two can sometimes find a great deal of common ground as friends and mutual admirers.

Both numbers have a highly evolved intuition and are acutely aware of their divine, spiritual nature. Plus, they both have finely tuned "bullshit meters" that allow them to stay well clear of cheaters and fakers, which repulse the honest **4** and appall the idealistic **7**.

Add to this their common desire to think through every problem they encounter by researching the issue in great detail and exploring all possible avenues towards finding the best solution, and it's easy to see how these two can see eye to eye on a great many topics.

The **4**'s obsession with the minutiae of life may irritate the **7**, who instinctively knows the best way forward. And the **7**'s need to spend long periods alone contemplating the big questions of life may frustrate the practical **4**, who just wants to get the job done as quickly as possible.

But on the positive side, these two friends will always respect each other's attention to detail and value the other for their generosity and humanitarian qualities.

Business

This is a beneficial partnership for business, because the practical earth energy of **4** will be happy to look after the everyday details of running and growing the company, leaving the egotistical and dominant **7** to steer the ship.

As long as the often aloof and solitary **7** takes the time to share with their **4** partner everything they are thinking (which is a lot), and the detail-focused **4** is happy to let the extraordinarily intelligent **7** take the reins and decide the direction of the business, this pairing can create an extraordinary amount of wealth and success.

* * *

7 & 5
(Understanding and Freedom)

Love

These two lovebirds have a lot of their core values in common, including their need for variety and their desire for plenty of time to do their own thing without feeling pressured by their partner.

Their relationship will be similar to that of a **7** and a **3** in that they will enjoy the freedom each is happy to give the other, as well as the mental stimulation of great conversation and the sharing of exciting new ideas.

The **7** falls in love easily and will be instantly attracted to the **5**'s rapid-fire wit and intellectual mind, while the **5** will admire the **7**'s intelligence and will quickly come to cherish the lack of demands their new partner puts on their time.

Life Path 7: The Seeker

Both will delight in the never-ending stream of fascinating topics of conversation these two will share, and they will happily stimulate each other's minds with long discussions deep into the night about all the Big Issues facing the world.

No, the challenge for these two will never be long, awkward silences or making too many demands on each other for attention. Quite the opposite. They must watch that their relationship doesn't become too distant or else the passion could fade and die, leading one or both to look for excitement in the arms of someone else.

Another point of concern is that the often insecure **7** usually wants more affection than the **5** can give them, and they may take their Rebel partner's lack of effusive romantic displays as a sign they aren't fully committed. This is not the case, and all the **5** needs to do to reassure them is tell them and show them regularly how much they are loved.

The **5** must also curb their flirtatious nature and remember that while they are the kings and queens of a social situation, the **7** struggles with informal chit chat and is never truly comfortable among strangers.

As long as the **5** looks out for the **7** when they are out, and the **7** learns to trust that the firefly **5**'s flirtatious behaviour is absolutely no threat to their relationship (it's not, because no one is more faithful than a devoted **5**), then problems should seldom arise. And provided both are as committed as each other, this relationship can be both mutually rewarding and long-lasting.

Good luck, stay open and honest… and enjoy the blissful freedom and stimulating conversations this relationship can give you.

Friendship

For all the reasons we have just seen, these two numbers can be excellent friends, bouncing ideas off each other and talking for hours about anything and everything. The adventurous and inquisitive **5** will stimulate the **7**'s mind in all the right ways, while the deep-thinking and intuitive **7** will be the perfect sounding board for the **5**'s latest radical ideas to change the world.

Socially, they are not so well-matched, with the **7** preferring to stick with the company of close and loyal friends and the **5** craving the company of new and exciting strangers. But outside the expectations of a romantic partnership, this shouldn't cause too many upsets for these two mutually stimulating friends, who will relish the fact that neither makes too many demands on the other's time.

Business

This is where these two cerebral numbers could come unstuck because they will struggle to agree on whose intellectual vision for the business is best, while also both wanting to be in control. Also, neither likes being told what to do, and they both abhor getting bogged down in petty details – which means no one will look after the admin.

If they do decide to venture into commerce together, it will normally work best if the **7** takes overall responsibility for the direction of the business and the **5** is given free rein to bring their creative ideas to fruition. But they must employ a well-grounded manager (preferably a **4** or an **8**) to run the back-office operations for them.

***

7 & 6
(Understanding and Romance)

Love

Atop the list of things that were never meant to be mixed together, there's chalk and cheese at No. 3, there's oil and water at No. 2… and then, high above them both, sitting as far apart from each other on the top of the table as they possibly can, there's the intellectual **7** and the romantic **6**.

These two have about as much in common on a social level as a snowflake and a blowtorch. In fact, it's highly unlikely they will ever even meet because the reserved **7** is way too quiet and withdrawn for the effusive **6** to notice in a crowded room, and the **6**'s immaculately groomed image will not impress the suspicious **7**.

However, if these two polar opposites do find themselves attracted to each other they may be surprised to discover that they share more in common than either of them first thought. Both love to be in love, and they both enjoy feeling supported by their partner. But that's just about where their similarities stop.

The fiercely independent **7** will react badly at the first sign that their controlling **6** partner wants to dictate how they spend their time. And the emotionally expressive **6** will react equally badly every time the **7** refuses to engage in deep-and-meaningful share sessions and goes back into their shell – which they will do with a meddlesome **6** more often than a paranoid tortoise with chronic confidence issues.

For this relationship to work, both partners will have to do more than study and learn each other's needs. They will need to qualify with a Masters in Applied Understanding and a doctorate in Advanced Compromising Skills from the University of As You Wish.

But before they both throw in the towel, and the bedsheets too, they would do well to re-mind themselves that relationships are not all about cuddles and smooches, they are about growth. These two are together for a very specific reason – namely to reflect each other's shortcomings and show each other the areas they most need to work on. If they can stop bickering long enough to do this, there's every chance their relationship can grow into a mutually rewarding marriage of opposites, each teaching the other and helping them to fulfill their life's highest purpose – which, to re-mind you, is not canoodling on a sofa surrounded by love-heart cushions, but learning to master your fears and stepping into your light, then helping others do the same.

Good luck, stay open and honest... and enjoy the life-changing lessons your partner can teach you if you give them a chance.

Friendship

Maybe, possibly, but unlikely. Even if they were the last two people on Earth and found themselves marooned on a desert island, they would probably draw a big line down the middle of it and live out their lives sitting on their side with their backs to each other.

This is a shame because if these two friends were able to look past the 76,835,891 points of difference on which they vehemently disagree, they might just find that – "OMG! You like Leonard Cohen too!" – there is enough common ground on which they can sow the seeds of a highly unusual but ultimately mutually rewarding friendship.

Business

No! OK? Got that? Great. Then let's move on…

* * *

7 & 7
(Understanding and trust)

Love

These "Twins" will operate much like Arnie and Danny DeVito, in that they will have much in common on a deep, intuitive level but on the surface – both in their personality and their tastes – they will be polar opposites, just like the two stars of that 1980s comedy classic.

The reason each will differ from the other on a superficial level is simple: if two **7**s were as alike in their tastes as they are in their deep-seated values, there would be no point in them having a relationship together in the first place. They would literally be mirror-images of each other, so they might as well stay single for all the growth lessons they would be able to share.

As we have already seen, the purpose of romantic relationships is to help each other grow, and this process can only happen when both partners are different enough to bring unique qualities to the table, while similar enough to dress the table with all the trimmings for long, romantic candle-lit dinners together.

In the case of two cerebral and spiritual **7**s, their lessons will take the form of helping each other trust in their abilities, and encouraging

Life Path 7: The Seeker

each other to express their emotions – neither of which comes easily to the socially shy and emotionally insecure Seeker.

On the positive side of this pairing, both 7s will be on the same intellectual and spiritual wavelength, able to effortlessly understand each other's needs without resorting to angry outbursts or tiresome emotional debates. They will both be happy to give each other the space they require, and they will also match up well in the limited amount of affection and attention they need on a day-to-day basis.

These twins will also enjoy spending quality time together engaged in long philosophical conversations, while other numbers might struggle to follow their train of thought or simply become bored and nod off. There will certainly never be a lack of mutually fascinating subjects for these two 7s to discuss. And when they are not deep in a heated debate about lofty conceptual notions, they will enjoy just sitting quietly reading their books – separate, but together.

There is a negative side to this pairing, however, that might rear its ugly head in the form of power struggles if neither 7 is prepared to compromise on their need to control all aspects of their life. Whereas the 7's other best-matched partner, their fellow air number 3, is usually happy to let the 7 run the household while they pursue their creative careers, another 7 will seldom want to take a back seat.

The simplest solution is to divide up the domestic responsibilities evenly, giving each partner full control of their allotted tasks. If (and it's a relatively large "IF") they can resist putting their nose in each other's business, they should be able to avoid locking horns more than about three million times a day.

All up, though, this relationship will probably get the "green light" right from the start, a pair of identical "his and hers" Maseratis to roar through life in side by side... and a long, clear road ahead with which to explore all this wonderful world has to offer.

Good luck, stay open and honest... and enjoy the journey of deep personal growth that this relationship will give you.

Life Path 7: Relationship Choices

Friendship

This meeting of like minds bodes well for an excellent friendship based on shared values and common goals. No one understands the depths of the **7**'s spiritual and intellectual personality better than another **7**, and if they are on the same psychic wavelength as well then these two twins will see eye to eye on just about everything.

Whereas in a romantic relationship two identical twins serve no valuable purpose for each other's personal growth and will therefore seldom attract each other, in a friendship there is no need for points of difference, which means these BFFs can dance through life together, bouncing ideas off each other and gleefully solving all the world's problems without either of them needing to argue about who came up with the solution first.

Business

Love? Tick. Friendship? Tick. Business? Hmmm… this is another matter entirely, because the stubborn **7**'s need for complete control of their professional life will result in neither one being able to back down even for a second. They will both want to run the business their way or the highway, and they would be better-suited choosing a fellow air number **3** or an earthy but equally humanitarian **4** to partner with.

* * *

<u>7 & 8</u>
(Understanding and Ambition)

Love

Although **8** is a materially focused Life Path, concerned above all else with working through their personal and professional issues of power and abundance, they are also spiritual beings at their core, which gives them at least some common ground with the highly spiritual **7**, who is primarily focused on solving the big mysteries of life.

That having been said, the earthy and pushy **8** and the airy and intelligent **7** have about as much in common in terms of a romantic relationship as a bulldozer and a butterfly.

In business, as we'll see in a minute, the delicate insights of the truth-seeking **7** would be of great value to temper the egotistical "crash or crash through" mentality of the win-at-all-costs **8**. But in the much more sensitive arena of love, these two may struggle to find common ground due to their diametrically opposed approach to relationships.

The **8** has a tendency to want to control their partner, just as they want to control everyone else in their life. But the fiercely independent and free-thinking **7** hates to be controlled in any way. They need to feel free to fly away to their ivory tower to contemplate the meaning of life without being disturbed, and they may resent their **8** partner's attempts to exert their authority over them.

Similarly, the impulsive and Self-confident **8** will be hair-tearingly frustrated by the **7**'s need to think for hours – days even – before they leap into making even the smallest decision. Plus, the **8** will never in a million years understand the point of the **7** spending $60,000 to study for a degree in Theosophical Sectoral Dynamics in a Post-Apocalyptic World when they could be out there earning decent money.

Putting material concerns aside, these two highly intelligent lovers should be able to connect well on a spiritual level and enjoy lively conversations about the Big Issues facing the world.

Another quality they have in common is that beneath their markedly different exteriors, they both crave to love and be loved at the deepest level of their being.

If they can agree to give each other the space they need – the **8** to work and socialise, and the **7** to study in peace – then these two can forge a very strong, loving connection. There will always be problems socially, because the networking **8** needs to mix in high-powered circles while the often withdrawn **7** is uncomfortable around strangers. And there will definitely be regular verbal disagreements.

But as long as the love and mutual respect are there, these two have much to teach each other about the core lesson of personal and

Life Path 7: Relationship Choices

spiritual growth – which is to conquer their fears and live blissfully and peacefully in love.

Good luck, stay open and honest… and enjoy the lessons about letting go of your ego that you both have to teach each other.

Friendship

There's not much common ground for these two to grow anything other than the most spindly and fragile of friendships. The deal-making and persuasive **8** loves to network and is comfortable in the company of strangers, while the introverted and solitary **7** prefers to shun the social whirl of cocktail parties in favour of the company of close, like-minded friends and colleagues.

Yes, they will both see eye to eye on many spiritual and political subjects and will enjoy conversing heatedly and at length on a wide variety of topics. But when the **8**'s material push comes to the **7**'s intellectual shove, they will more likely fight like cat and dog and go their separate ways.

Sometimes, however, a lasting friendship can be forged in the fires of their equally matched passion for making a difference, with the **7** inspiring the **8** to use their power for the greater good, and the **8** urging the **7** to have the courage to teach their truth to a wide audience. When this happens, these two friends can really rock the world.

Business

Although most **7**s will choose to go into business on their own, because they like to do everything themselves, occasionally they will real-eyes they could benefit from the input of a partner who can bring something new and valuable to the table.

In the case of the **8**, this would come in the form of their powerful and goal-oriented business acumen combined with their art of making the deal, which could help the **7** take their lofty humanitarian ideas to market and turn them into a roaring success.

When the thoughtful and spiritual masculine **7** teams up with the aggressive but socially aware feminine **8**, they have the potential to create something truly special. Think Deepak Chopra (**7**) partnered with Jane Fonda (**8**) and you'll know what I'm talking about.

* * *

<u>7 & 9</u>
(Understanding and passion)

Love

The spiritual **7** has so much in common with the equally spiritual **9** that these two will probably fall madly in love – complete with cute little Bambi-style tweety birds circling around their heads – before the barman has even brought them their second drink on their first date.

They won't be able to keep their hands off each other. And they should probably warn their friends, when inviting them for dinner, to bring a bucket, because their incessant oochy-koochy smoochy-smoochy canoodling will make everyone within 10 miles of them physically sick.

It's ironic that we all want the luvvyduvvy dream, but when we meet two people who have found it and aren't afraid to show it, we feel the urge to either throw up or punch them in the head. Ah, jealousy! The monster whose eye is the same colour as the contents of the bucket.

In all seriousness, this is one of the most rewarding partnerships for the **7** because, like them, the **9** is not afraid to declare their undying love and jump in the deep end with both feet… and fully clothed to boot. These two want nothing more than to find someone who is sufficiently evolved spiritually and emotionally to accept the depth of their love, and return it just as passionately.

Well, actually that's not strictly accurate because both the solitary **7** and the independent **9** value their time alone just as highly. And when they discover that the love of their life understands this need too… well, that's why their friends need the bucket, because if someone gave you your cake and then fed it to you naked on a silk-sheeted four-poster bed, you would be so ecstatically grateful you wouldn't be able to stop kissing and hugging them either.

Not to burst this Bambi bubble, but it's worth pointing out that this idyllic relationship – in which both partners are happy to trust the other to have plenty of space – would end about as well as the Disney film if either of them betrayed that trust. Infidelity is never good, but for these two doe-eyed dears it would be a curtain-dropper for sure.

Good luck, stay open and honest, enjoy this blissfully loving and liberating connection… and for Source's sake, don't stuff it up!

Friendship

These two open-hearted and broad-minded numbers can become fantastically close and understanding companions who support each other through thick and thin and enjoy a lifelong friendship.

Providing, of course, they are not sexually compatible.

If they are, there's a very real chance they might be tempted to turn this into something altogether more horizontal – even if they are already in love with someone else. If this is the case, they would be advised to take one of three courses of action: 1) Fall in love and live happily ever after; 2) Walk away because they can't trust themselves and they don't want to ruin the relationships they have; 3) Pack their underpants with ice every time they catch up for a coffee.

These two can definitely be BFFs thanks to their common values and beliefs. Whether they also become BFBs is another matter and a choice I leave up to them. (What? Oh, I see. Well… what if I tell you the first word is the same, and the last word is "Buddies"?)

Business

As with a friendship, this could go either way depending on their sexual compatibility. There's no doubt the **9**, who needs to be in control, would welcome the wise counsel of the intelligent **7**, and the solitary **7** would be happy to let the **9** run things and hog the limelight. So, on the surface, this is an excellent business match. But if there's also an attraction, the BFB thing could be an issue here as well.

* * *

Life Path 7: The Seeker

4. HEALTH CHOICES

THE cautious and knowledgeable **7** will usually enjoy relatively good health because they tend to be as studious and diligent about what they eat as they are in every other area of their life.

The main concerns arise when they ignore physical exercise in the gym in favour of mental workouts in their study. However, the typical **7** is usually either a lanky ectomorph or a slim mesomorph with a fast metabolism, so weight gain is not normally a problem for them.

Because the thoughtful and studious **7** is in their head almost all the time, they can sometimes suffer from stress-related illnesses if they fail to learn how to quiet their mind when they need to. Also, their innate spiritual nature means they can sometimes become too detached from the messages of their physical body and may therefore miss the early warning signs when something is wrong.

On the whole, though, this is one of the healthiest Life Path Numbers, providing the **7** pays attention to their physical body. They usually have a strong intuition about what they need to eat and what exercise suits them best, and their laser-like ability to focus on any goal they set themselves means they are able to follow a wellness routine to the letter, seldom wavering or succumbing to temptation.

Emotionally, however, it's a very different kettle of delicious and nutritious fish. The often blocked and occasionally even repressed **7** can tend to suffer from all manner of psychosomatic "dis-eases" if they fail to do the necessary inner work on themselves to process and release their negative emotions.

These will range from stress and headaches to insomnia, skin rashes allergies, poor circulation and even bouts of depression. Regular mental exercise in the form of meditation, deep breathing and relaxation are essential to ensure their negative thoughts don't manifest in a wide range of physiological dis-eases.

Similarly, their diet needs to be kept as simple as possible because their sensitive digestive system does not usually cope well with heavily processed foods and they will do best when eating their meals "clean" without too many spices, rich sauces or condiments.

The mantra for the metaphysical **7** to obtain maximum physical health needs to be: "The Source nourishes me, but the Sauce doesn't."

Ailments to watch out for

The most common afflictions for the **7** are emotional, rather than physiological, including stress, skin problems and allergies (fear) caused by emotional blockages. Skin is a particular area of concern because most **7**s feel vulnerable to attack, which may show up in their lives on their "last line of defence" as eczema, psoriasis and sores.

The **7**'s emotional blockages can also manifest as viral infections (toxic thoughts), indigestion (an unwillingness to let life and love in), arthritis (inflexibility and stubbornness) and poor blood circulation (inability to relax into the flow of life).

Nervous disorders such as hypertension, insomnia and high blood pressure are also common, for obvious reasons. It's way too easy for the all-seeing, all-knowing **7** to over-think things and take on the world's problems as if they were their own, leading to all manner of stress-related problems.

Effective therapies

Relaxation is the solution to almost all the **7**'s physical and emotional ailments. They need plenty of sleep, and will also benefit from meditation to quiet their mind and deep-breathing exercises to remove the tension from their body.

Regular physical exercise is also important to force them out of their study and into the fresh air. This can take the form of jogging or walking in nature, but they should give their minds a rest at the same time and refrain from plugging in their ear buds and listening to music or their latest audio book so they are free to drink in the relaxing beauty of their surroundings.

Life Path 7: The Seeker

Other beneficial solitary exercise options (the independent **7** usually prefers solitary sports to team ones) that will take them outdoors into the fresh air include swimming, rowing and cycling.

Indoor activities such as dancing, kick-boxing, gym classes and martial arts are also recommended for their stress-reducing benefits, as well as being excellent for getting the **7**'s blood flowing.

Regular massages will also help the cerebral and spiritual **7** get in touch with their physical body.

Diet choices

Clean and simple is the catch cry for the **7**'s optimum diet because their sensitive digestive system does not function well when loaded up with rich or processed foods. Plus, they must concentrate on eating small regular meals rather than occasional large ones.

The intellectual **7** is often so caught up in the latest book they are reading, or the latest project they are working on, that they simply forget to eat until their stomach starts to growl with hunger — whereupon they will gorge themselves on whatever they have to hand. This is the very worst way to overload their stomachs and can lead to all manner of digestive complaints.

Seafood of all kinds is good for the **7**, who are governed both emotionally and physiologically by the watery energy of their ruling planet Neptune. Plenty of fresh vegetables is essential, including cabbage, lettuce, olives, cauliflower, cucumber, broccoli, spinach, sorrel and celery. Vegetable juices are also excellent.

Fruits that agree with the **7** include lemons, apricots, watermelon, grapes, apples, pears, prunes and pawpaw, either fresh or in a juice. And make sure there is plenty of ginger, ginseng and chicory in the diet too.

As well as juices of all kids, which are easily digestible, the best beverages for the **7** include green tea, chicory and coffee. Try to stay away from alcohol and sugary drinks as much as possible.

* * *

5. CHOICES FOR CHILDREN

YOUNG children working with the energy of **7** will usually explore the negative energies of their Life Path Number before moving on to master the positive aspects. This is true of all the nine Life Paths because children need to first understand the boundaries of what is and isn't acceptable behaviour.

However, once their boundaries are in place – and your child has understood the crucial lesson of cause and effect – young **7**s can then start tapping into their natural strengths with the assistance of a patient and loving parental guiding hand.

Children working with the positive energy of **7** as their Life Path Number have powerful analytical minds. They are deep thinkers and diligent students who have excellent problem-solving skills. They also have a spiritual wisdom that manifests from a very early age, usually leading them to be wise and insightful beyond their years.

In the positive, this usually causes them to perform well at school because their thirst for knowledge and their ability to study hard and for long periods on their own means they will be able to finish all their homework and post good scores in their exams.

On the negative side, however, the **7** child sometimes spends too much time on their own, risking them becoming aloof and detached. Without enough interaction with other children they may also lack the confidence to speak what is in their hearts as they suppress their emotions and take refuge in their inner dream world.

Parents and teachers must be careful not to patronise the **7** child because they are able to understand even complex issues quickly and at a deep level. They should talk to them as they would an adult and teach them that it is safe to discuss their feelings.

Unless they nurture the young **7**'s emotional confidence by letting them express how they feel without judging them, their **7** child is likely to withdraw behind the impregnable fortress of their intellect, believing their parents and teachers – along with everyone else – are "inferior" to them and, even worse, cannot be fully trusted.

Life Path 7: The Seeker

Young **7**s must be encouraged to talk about their feelings in a safe environment. The only reason they judge others so harshly for their imperfections is because they judge their own imperfections even more harshly. Being the parent of a **7** child can certainly be a challenge. My advice is to never engage them in intellectual battle. Instead, teach them that it is OK to be imperfect and that it is actually our imperfections that make us human and lovable.

Many young **7**s will not be overly sociable, preferring to read in their room or spend time alone in nature while they contemplate the mysteries of life. They are deep thinkers and take criticism personally, so it is important for parents to make their communication with them not only considered and accurate, but gentle and compassionate.

They often find it difficult to make friends, and even if they do there may come a time when the friend does something that annoys them – in which case they may often be quickly dumped. However, the close friends they do have will usually be theirs for life

Remember, **7** is the number of spirituality and **7** children are budding little spiritual gurus. They are often more advanced in this regard even than adults living birth numbers **1** to **6**, but they haven't yet arrived in the cycle at **8**, so they may need help in coming to terms with the material world around them. And to do this they must feel safe to share their deepest inner thoughts and feelings.

Playtime activities

7 children will often prefer to engage in solo pursuits, such as reading, writing, drawing and playing computer games, rather than group activities. Parents should be prepared to give them plenty of time on their own, but not too much time.

They need to be encouraged to take an active part in family and school activities, because when a **7** child learns that they can share their thoughts and feelings with others without getting hurt, they will be more likely to succeed in finding that elusive balance between solitude and socialising later in life.

Life Path 7: Choices for Children

Most young **7**s are not naturally drawn towards physical sports, preferring mental challenges such as puzzles, crosswords and even debating societies, where they can joust intellectually with other like-minded children.

And they will often while away the hours long into the evening playing complex computer games that allow them to become the undisputed master of their own fantasy world.

Sports that will appeal most to the **7**'s inherently solitary nature include swimming, cycling, rowing, sailing and running. But don't be surprised if they shun physical exercise altogether in favour of reading anything and everything they can get their hands on – from non-fiction books to the newspaper, and even the fine print on the back of the breakfast cereal packet.

* * *

Your child's three-digit Birth Code

As we have seen in Part Two, we always work primarily with the energy of our Life Path Number right from the outset, but in our childhood years from 0 to 18 we do so in conjunction with the energy of our first Supplementary Birth Number, and in our second 18 years – until we reach full emotional maturity at 36 – we do so in conjunction with the energy of our second Supplementary Birth Number.

It's worth reading the main listings here in Part Three for the numbers that make up your child's two Supplementary Birth Numbers to gain a better understanding of their positive and negative qualities.

Also, as you read about your child's three-digit Birth Code, real-eyes that the difference between "feeling the force" of any Life Path and flipping to the "dark side" is determined by the amount of Self-confidence we develop in our childhood years, and then the amount of Self-love we develop in our teenage years.

That, in a nutshell (squirrel!), is your role as a parent: to instill in your child first Self-esteem, and then Self-love.

Life Path 7: The Seeker

The 00/7 'Millennium' child

A Millennium Child born with this remarkably powerful Birth Code has come into the world with the potential to achieve something truly spectacular with their life. The doubly amplified presence of the two 0s means they will work solely with the supercharged intellectual energy of **7** their entire life, right from when they take their first breath.

For obvious reasons, these 00/**7** children are known as the "James Bonds" of the Self-Awareness System™, although their childhood idol is more likely to be an intellectual superhero such as Dr Strange rather than MI6's suave but ultimately rather thuggishly physical super spy.

All the Millennium Children (those born at the beginning of this century with two 0s as their Supplementary Birth Numbers) are endowed with extra potential because they will work with the energy of their Life Path Number with absolute focus and an incredible amount of commitment, as supplied by the amplifying power of their two 0s. (The Millennium Children are described in detail in Part Two.)

The 00/**7** child therefore has the capacity to become a deeply intelligent and insightful Seeker, as well as an intuitive spiritual mystic able to teach us all about the divine nature of who we are at our core.

The world hasn't seen a 00/**7** Millennium Child since October 10, 1400, more than 600 years ago, but there are more coming soon, starting on January 2, 2020. Which is just as well, because we urgently need their help to rid our fragile little planet of the rampant fear, greed and fundamentalist aggression that threatens our very existence.

And because the thoughtful energy of **7** is the only number they will work with throughout their life, they also have the capacity to break new ground in whatever career they choose to pursue.

On a more personal level, 00/**7** children could more easily flip to the negative side of their Life Path because of the lack of any emotional water numbers (**2** or **6**) or practical earth numbers (**4** or **8**) in their Birth Code to help them interact with the world around them. They will be so much in their heads that they may risk shutting off from their feelings completely and losing themselves in their fantasy world.

Life Path 7: Choices for Children

Similarly, the absence of any fire energy (<u>1</u> or <u>5</u>) could cause them to procrastinate if they lack a strong inner drive to succeed. They could wind up accumulating knowledge for knowledge's sake, rather than taking what they have learned to teach others and help make a real difference in the world.

When they are young they may need a lot of gentle coaxing to come out of their shell and interact with others. And, of course, as with all the Millennium Children, the <u>00</u>/**7** child must never feel pressured to live up to the special promise of their amplified Birth Code. There is no "Life Path contract" that requires them to use their gifts for anything other than making themselves and their loved ones happy.

If all they do is shed their ego and live in love, they will achieve what we are all here to achieve – which is to real-eyes that we are pure love, and show the Source that it is pure love too.

The <u>16</u>/7 child

Of the five possible Birth Codes for the Seeker, this one is the most focused and ambitious thanks to the presence of the fire (action) energy of the Leader <u>1</u> as their first Supplementary Birth Number, which will operate in conjunction with the intellectual and spiritual qualities of their Life Path Number **7** during their first formative 18 years.

This endows the young <u>16</u>/**7** child with more confidence than other **7** children, although they will probably still be introspective and be happy to have plenty of time to themselves. Like all **7**s, they may also tend to bottle up their emotions and struggle to understand what they are feeling, which is the central challenge for all young Seekers.

Then in their late teens, up to full emotional maturity at 36, the <u>16</u>/**7** will flip to work with the watery (emotion) energy of their second Supplementary Birth Number <u>6</u>, which will give them a much-needed dose of emotional intelligence to match their heightened mental and spiritual awareness.

Their primary focus will always be governed by the studious and intellectual qualities of their Life Path Number **7**, but they will have

Life Path 7: The Seeker

more courage (1) to express their innermost thoughts, both at home and at school, when they are young. Then, as they reach young adulthood and head out into the world, they will develop the emotional confidence (6) to connect with other like-minded people and share their message of truth and beauty with others.

As long as they clear their emotional blockages and work with the positive energy of their three Birth Code numbers, the 16/7 will be able to enjoy much success both at home and in their work. Their lives will be based on learning the Big Truths about the world and then teaching them to others – which is all the **7** really wants to do.

One word of caution, though: the lack of an earth number (**4** or **8**) in their Birth Code means the 16/7 must work especially hard to ground themselves or they run the risk of becoming overbearing and bossy (negative 1), finding fault with others (negative 6) and driving themselves deeper into their private inner world (negative **7**).

16/7s have the potential to forge close and loving relationships in their adult years, when the supplementary energy of 6 kicks in. But until then they may struggle with social interaction, even with their family, due to the egotistical and headstrong energy of 1 operating in their childhood alongside the contemplative Life Path energy of **7**.

The 25/7 child

These Seekers are likely to be more socially interactive than the other four Birth Codes thanks to the feminine water (emotion) energy of their first Supplementary Birth Number 2 (the Intuitive) operating during their formative years up until they reach 18. Then during their next 18 years, until full emotional maturity at 36, they will be driven by the masculine fire (action) energy of 5 (the Rebel) to go out into the world and use their intellectual power to make a difference in people's lives, spreading their message of divine truth far and wide.

All the while their main focus will be on pondering the mysteries of life and accumulating vast amounts of information, as governed by their Life Path Number **7**, but unlike the other more solitary Birth

Life Path 7: Choices for Children

Codes they will be happier to work in co-operation with others (2) – providing, of course, they develop the necessary inner confidence to share their ideas and beliefs without the fear of being vulnerable that afflicts so many **7** children.

Be warned, though, that the flip side of the Intuitive (2) is a tendency towards being overly sensitive and shy, especially when young, and this – combined with the natural introspection of the **7** – could have the reverse effect and cause the 25/**7** to withdraw even deeper into their shell during their school years.

Parents must concentrate on encouraging young 25/**7**s to share how they are feeling, and must always respond warmly and with affection when they do. The slightest hurt can cause them to shrink back into themselves and bottle up their emotions again.

Like all **7** children, the young 25/**7** will want to be given plenty of time on their own to discover the answers they seek to their biggest spiritual questions. This is quite normal. Just be wary of allowing them to become too isolated from the rest of their family at home and their classmates at school, and teach them that true happiness comes not just from learning the Big Truths but from sharing them with others.

On the whole, though, these young Seekers will benefit greatly from the water energy of their first Supplementary Birth Number 2 while their personality is being formed as a child, giving them a nicely balanced emotional confidence to match their impressive intellectual and spiritual wisdom.

The 34/7 child

These children are likely to be extremely intelligent and creative from a very early age. They have so much air (thought) in their Birth Code while their personality is developing in their first formative years that they will likely find themselves outsmarting their parents and even their schoolteachers with relatively little effort.

The inquisitive and creative energy of their first Supplementary Birth Number 3 during their first 18 years, combined with their Life

Life Path 7: The Seeker

Path 7's tireless search for truth and meaning, will drive these young Seekers to spend much of their time at home and at school with their heads buried in a book or a computer, seeking answers to all their myriad questions and soaking up knowledge anywhere they find it.

The flip side is that they will struggle to form friendships with other children, and may even distance themselves from their family members as well. They need to be taught that it is safe to express their emotions, even if they don't understand exactly what they are feeling.

Nothing upsets a 34/**7** child more acutely than when they don't understand something. And the absence of any water numbers (2 or 6) in their Birth Code means these young Seekers may find it difficult to process, label and express their emotions, causing them to simply bottle them up inside.

They will often be artistic from an early age as well (the energy of 3), but the emotional insecurity that afflicts the solitary **7** may prevent them from expressing their creativity freely. They may choose to draw or write, rather than act or sing, and keep their work safely locked away from prying parental eyes. This privacy must be respected at all times because if it is violated, the 34/**7** child will find it hard to trust again.

Parents must give them plenty of time alone to read and write, respect their privacy at all times and never, ever criticise them on the rare occasions when they do share what they are feeling.

At school, the outgoing energy of 3 will give the introspective **7** a better chance of interacting with teachers and classmates, although they will tend to have a few close friends rather than a wide social circle. Then when they hit adulthood at 18, the 34/**7** will begin to work with the pragmatic energy of 4 (the Builder), leading them to put down roots and establish a firm foundation for their work and home life.

All the while their main focus will be on understanding the great mysteries of life and sharing the truths they learn with others, as governed by their Life Path **7**, and their heightened intelligence all but guarantees that they will succeed in whatever they choose to do.

One last word of caution: the absence of any fire (action) numbers (1 or 5) in their Birth Code could cause young 34/**7**s to become stuck in a rut of Self-doubt, unable to perform at school and in exams with the confidence of a 16/7 or a 25/7. They may have a tendency towards procrastination when it comes to revising for tests, and they may need regular but always gentle coaxing to do their homework.

The 43/7 child

This is a mirror of the previous Birth Code, and children walking this Life Path will share many qualities with their 34/7 cousins. The key difference is that during their first formative years – when their personality is established – they will be working with the supplementary earth energy of the pragmatic and responsible 4 instead of the creative and inquisitive air energy of 3.

They will still be a studious 7 through and through – and will therefore focus on their primary task of accumulating knowledge to help them understand how the world works – but as children and teenagers they will tend to be more serious and inwardly focused than the 34/7, happiest when spending long periods on their own pondering the meaning of life.

For their first 18 years, the 43/7 child will probably have fewer friends as well, but those they do have will likely be theirs for life. All 4s are unwaveringly loyal and can spot a faker a mile away, leading them to be picky about who they choose to befriend, and the equally deep 7 has no time for anyone who isn't as genuine as they are.

The humanitarian aspects of the 4 means these young Seekers will be concerned with issues of fairness and justice from an early age, sparking a desire to use their powerful analytical minds to find ways to help improve the lives of others less fortunate than themselves. Then, as the artistic and expressive energy of their second Supplementary Birth Number 3 kicks in from 18 to full emotional maturity at age 36, they will focus their impressive intellect on solving the great problems of the world in new and creative ways.

As we saw with the 34/7, the absence of any water numbers (2 or 6) means they may suppress their emotions and struggle in romantic

Life Path 7: The Seeker

relationships, while the lack of a fire (action) number (1 or 5) can cause them to procrastinate and get bogged down in petty details.

Providing the reserved 43/7 develops enough Self-confidence to step outside their solitary shell and share the truths they know in new and original ways, they can enjoy great academic success at school and later at college that will set them up perfectly for life.

LIFE PATH 8:
The Achiever

1. **Growth cycle:** Eighth stage (the number of power)
2. **Influences:** Earth (practical, feminine) and Saturn (karma)
3. **Positive qualities:** Strong-willed, resourceful and persuasive
4. **Negative potential:** Insecure, greedy and selfish
5. **Highs and lows:** Generous philanthropist, or egotistical power-tripper
6. **Highest purpose:** Create abundance for your Self and others
7. **Love matches:** 2, 4, 6 and 8 for compatibility (the rest for growth)
8. **Possible careers:** Business, finance, sport, law, management
9. **Words to live by:** "We are all on this journey together"

1. LIFE CHOICES FOR THE ACHIEVER

THE resourceful and ambitious **8** is the most materially focused of all the Life Path Numbers. These are the determined Achievers of the Self-Awareness-System™ who are here to manifest abundance of all kinds, not just financially but in terms of power and influence as well.

All **8**s are blessed with strong wills and clear goals, and they have an uncanny ability to rally others to their cause to help them succeed in whatever material outcome they seek. Their main life's focus will be working with the energy of abundance in all its forms, while at the same time clearing their deep emotional blockages to understand the difference between Self-worth, which is the work of their ego, and Self-love, which is who we are at our core – ie, pure Source energy.

Life Path 8: The Achiever

This is the eighth stage of the Spiritual Growth Cycle and the fourth stage of the second "divine cycle" that focuses on our inner spiritual work. It began with **5** (the Rebel), who turned everything inside out and taught us that all our answers lie within, and continued with **6** (the Visionary), the number of divine beauty, and **7** (the Seeker), the number of divine truth – specifically, the truth that we are pure love and we are here to show the Source that it is pure love too.

The feminine earth (practical) energy of **8** follows seamlessly on from the masculine air (thought) energy of **7** because the **8**'s central task is to show us we can have all the wealth, power and fame we want in the material world as long as we don't need it to feed our ego, and instead realise it is our divine right as pure, unbounded spirits having a human experience. All the abundance of the universe can manifest in our lives when we rise above our fears and want it for fun, rather than need it to feel better about who we are.

The **8** who pursues wealth and power for their own sake will never find they contain the happiness they seek, simply because their highly developed ego will always want more. In fact, they will often be forced to learn this spiritual lesson the hard way by suffering a calamity that causes them to lose all they have worked so hard to achieve.

This immutable spiritual truth about the number **8** escapes almost all those who see this as the "magical" number of material wealth and power, including the Chinese who will pay hundreds of thousands of dollars over the asking price for a house that has an **8** in its street number, and will put as many **8**s on their car number plate as they can. This is crass superstition and misses the point of this number entirely – which is to prove that wealth and power will never make us happy until we have learned the lessons of the first two numbers of this "spiritual cycle" by understanding that we are divine beauty at our core (the lesson of **6**), and we are also pure Source energy (the lesson of **7**).

Remember, this is the number of karma (the energy of its ruling planet Saturn) as well as the number of abundance. When the Chinese hosted the Olympics, they timed it so that the opening ceremony began at eight minutes past eight on the eighth day of the eighth month of the eighth year of the new century – for good luck, presumably. What they failed to grasp was that because they uprooted more than a million people and tore down their homes, many without compensation, just so they could build their grand Olympic stadiums for the world to marvel at (and, yes, many of the residents who complained were thrown in jail), these egotistical men (they were all men) invoked the law of payback – which, as we all know, is a karmic bitch.

They missed the divine quality of this number altogether, like so many power-trippers have before them, and still do. But that's OK. Just wait until Saturn gets a hold of them in their next life! They'll be sorry they ever heard of the number **8**, and rightly so.

The truth is, an **8** in your house number, your Birth Code or even your country's Olympic Games schedule will never give you the wealth or power you seek because, like all numbers, it resonates with divine energy rather than human energy – and it is therefore governed by the munificence of the Source, rather than the greed of the ego.

Because of the influence of Saturn on their Life Path, all **8**s will focus much of their work on understanding the karmic concept of cause and effect, which is something that clearly escaped the Chinese Communist Party apparatchiks.

The **8** must come to real-eyes that wealth and power over other people is wrong on every level, whereas wealth and power that can be shared with others less fortunate than ourselves is absolutely in tune with the divine energy of abundance that governs this most profoundly spiritual as well as materialistic number.

* * *

Highest purpose of The Achiever

The highest purpose of the **8** (and the Master Achiever 44/**8** – more about you "44s" in a moment) is to teach us that there is more than enough for everyone because we live in an abundant world where every single one of us can be "wealthy" in every sense of the word:

materially, emotionally, financially, physically and spiritually. The **8** will always teach this lesson by example, either by walking the positive side of this Life Path and sharing their wealth freely with others, or by flipping to the dark side which leads to greed, gluttony, pride and megalomania – and then suffering the consequences.

Indeed, many evolved **8**s will shun the material trappings of wealth altogether and spend their lives in the service of others. Nelson Mandela, who devoted his life to helping his country rise above the brutality of Apartheid, and Bob Marley, who gave almost all his wealth to the poor people of his homeland of Jamaica, are classic examples of astonishingly successful Achievers who clearly understood the karmic influence on this profoundly influential Life Path.

Remember, the highest goal of all Life Paths is always the same: to first "wake up" to the truth that we are an extension of Source energy, and then to help other people wake up as well. The evolved **8** is able to use their influence to teach this core spiritual message to a wide audience and show us that we are all in this together and there is more than enough to go around for everyone.

* * *

Key words are… 'confidence' and 'humility'

To fulfill their life's highest purpose, **8**s must first learn to develop a robust inner confidence in their abilities.

Confidence is central to all the Life Paths as we embark on our common journey from pure unaware love to pure conscious love. As we saw in Part One, developing a healthy Self-esteem is the first crucial step towards Self-love that we all must take.

(If you've come straight to this Life Path listing in Part Three and are wondering what a "Self" is, please try to find the time to read Part One because it's way too complicated to explain again here.)

For the always ambitious **8**, however, developing a strong sense of inner confidence is much more than just the key to their personal

Life Path 8: Life Choices

happiness – it will determine whether they walk the positive Life Path of the generous and humanitarian Achiever, or veer down the negative path towards selfishness and greed.

As they are growing up, all **8**s develop a strong ego to match their natural sense of ambition and their desire to succeed in whatever they do. They will usually be hard-working, focused on setting goals for themselves and then achieving them, no matter what obstacles stand in their way. Many young **8**s will excel in sport because it is a perfect arena for them to flex their competitive muscles. And even if they choose a more artistic or academic path, they will revel in competitions and exams where they can outdo their rivals and show off their skills.

Self-confidence is seldom a serious issue for the naturally outgoing and ambitious **8**, although some might suffer from shyness in their early years. No, the problem for them is not lacking confidence, it's having too much – an unwelcome byproduct of their highly developed ego that frequently leads to arrogance if it's not held in check by diligent parents and teachers.

Winning certainly feels good, and the young **8** must be taught that there is absolutely nothing wrong with winning. It is perfectly OK to stand proud atop the rostrum and enjoy the recognition they so richly deserve for all their hard work – just as long as they don't gloat.

"Pride comes before a fall" is sadly a lesson many **8**s have to learn the hard way at some point in their life. Which leads to the second key word governing the formative years for the Achiever... humility.

All young **8**s, and many older ones too, will find themselves faced with the complex issue of personal power at some point in their lives. They will be forced to grapple with the question of what power really means so they can learn the crucial difference between having power over people and having the power to help people.

Humility is the key. There is nothing wrong with having personal power or financial wealth. Some **8**s will amass large quantities of both in their lifetime, some will ride the roller-coaster of having them, losing them, and earning them back again – and some will simply avoid the issue of material success altogether in favour of a more spiritual calling.

All that matters is that the **8** learns to be humble in their times of victory, magnanimous in their times of defeat, and always mindful that power and wealth are the means to a much richer end of philanthropy rather than a greedy end in themselves.

* * *

Positive and negative potential

All Life Paths contain an equal measure of positive and negative potential. Our challenge in every lifetime, no matter our Life Path Number, is to nurture our positives and overcome our negatives.

The reason we are given negative potential as well as positive potential is because people usually respond more effectively to the threat of pain than they do to the promise of pleasure. Also, while it is admirable to do what we are good at in life, we will only ever become the best we can be by facing our "dark side" and digging deep into our Self to overcome the obstacles that appear on our path.

As we have already seen in Part Two, it is only when the chips are down and we are up against it that we find out who we truly are and what we are truly capable of doing.

For example, the strong-willed **8** has a heightened capacity for setting clear goals and achieving them. Hence their name "Achiever". But they also have an equally heightened potential for disappointment if they fail to do the necessary inner work to wrest their supercharged ego from the controls of their life.

As proof of this, you will find many **8**s among the lists of the rich and famous overachievers, but you will also find a disproportionately large number of them among the poor and the homeless.

As long as the **8** is mired in the egoic concept of Self-esteem (and therefore missed the lessons of divine truth taught by their predecessor Life Paths **6** and **7**) they will find they never hold onto their wealth and power for very long, because they have pursued it in the mistaken belief it will compensate for their deep-seated insecurity. Only when

Life Path 8: Life Choices

they "wake up" to their divine nature and step up to the much higher ground of Self-love will they real-eyes that all the wealth and power in the world can never make them feel truly happy. When that happens, they can have all the money and recognition they desire, because now they *want* it, but they don't *need* it to feel better about themselves.

This crucial distinction is central to all the Life Paths, but it is of particular importance for the **8** because their ego is about five million times bigger than anyone else's. (Did I mention that **8**s have a tendency to exaggerate as well?)

Because Achievers are at the eighth (abundance) stage of their Spiritual Growth Cycle, they tend to be positive, energetic and highly motivated to succeed in everything they do. They don't always find that success comes easily, but they are extremely resourceful and are willing to work hard to achieve the goals they set for themselves.

Put an obstacle in the **8**'s path and they will quickly find a way around the problem, or else they will simply take a deep breath and smash straight through it. They are also very persuasive and never take no for an answer, so if the obstacle is a human one they will argue their case with such single-minded determination that their opponent will almost always be forced to back down.

However, strong willpower can be a double-edged sword. In the positive, it drives the motivated **8** to succeed. But in the negative it can cause them to become stubborn, overbearing and even unpleasantly aggressive when they don't get their own way.

The focused **8** will usually want to go into business for themselves, where they will have a higher than average chance of success due to their remarkable drive and capacity for sustained hard work. It is also common for them to choose a sporting career, or an artistic one.

Famous Achievers who have dominated their chosen field include sporting greats Roger Federer and Valentino Rossi, musicians Buddy Holly, George Harrison and Bob Dylan, artists Michelangelo and Picasso and actors Laurence Olivier, Paul Newman and Matt Damon.

This preponderance of wildly successful **8**s is what has given rise to the mistaken belief that this is the number of good fortune. It isn't.

Life Path 8: The Achiever

Those who have found fame and made money on this Life Path have done so by setting clear goals and then focusing all their energy on achieving them, refusing to give up until they have done so no matter how many obstacles they encounter on the way.

If you think that simply putting an **8** on your car number plate or above your front door is going to bring you luck and make you rich, you have missed the point of the Self-Awareness System™ altogether and will be sorely disappointed. Stick with the numbers you have, set a clear goal for what you want to achieve – and then stop at nothing until you have achieved it. Just like the Achiever **8** does.

At the deepest level, the **8** is actually not a materialistic number at all – it is a profoundly spiritual one. This is the eighth and final "growth stage" of the cycle that started with the pioneering energy of **1**, and the bulk of the Achiever's work will therefore be focused on using all the qualities of the previous Life Paths – confidence (**1**), co-operation with others (**2**), creativity (**3**), hard work (**4**), persuasiveness (**5**), devotion (**6**) and intelligence (**7**) to create abundance in all its forms for as many people as possible.

The final Life Path **9** (the Teacher) is concerned with integrating all the wisdom of the previous Life Paths and teaching them to others. The real growth stops with the **8**'s manifestation of abundance for all. The **9** then wraps it all up before we go back to the beginning and start a new Spiritual Growth Cycle with the energy of **1** again.

Look at the unique shape of an **8** and you will see that is perfectly balanced, consisting of two equal halves that make up the whole. This is no accident and refers to the balance between the material and the spiritual that all **8**s must strive to attain. Too much of either throws the Achiever out of whack, causing them to become either too entrenched in their ego's material demands or too concerned with lofty spiritual truths at the expense of their financial and physical wellbeing.

Whereas the air energy of the **7** empowers them to spend a lot of time in their head without negative consequences, the **8** is an earth number and therefore must balance any spiritual pursuits with taking the necessary practical steps to ground themselves and create a strong and stable foundation for their life.

Newton's third law, which states that every action has an equal and opposite reaction, is particularly apposite for **8**s, who have to deal with the karmic forces of their ruling planet Saturn in everything they do, or don't do. We all reap what we sow, but for the **8** the laws of karma apply almost instantly to keep their rampant ego in check.

In the positive, the **8** balances their material, money-making focus with the pursuit of spiritual knowledge. They are practical, realistic and hard-working and they enjoy the process of manifesting abundance in their life. But they also know that money is nothing more than a tool and therefore they will tend to be extremely generous in sharing their wealth with those less fortunate than themselves. They are the living proof that the more we give, the more we have.

They are also courageous risk-takers, unlike their more cautious earthy **4** cousins, so if they do suffer a financial crisis such as bankruptcy they won't mope about it or give up and collapse in a heap. They will simply create another fortune the way they made their first one – with sustained hard work, building it from the ground up.

However, if they fail to clear their emotional blockages and rise above the fear-based limitations of their insatiable ego, the negative **8** can suffer from all manner of "instant karma" setbacks, which will depend on their level of selfishness and greed. They may lose their money, their relationship and even their physical health as they subliminally sabotage everything they have fought so hard to achieve.

A fact that is not always commonly known about karma is that it is not imposed on us by some external and judgmental "God", as many new-age dabblers in the eastern religions mistakenly believe. It is Self-imposed, a function of our divine inner Self's awareness of what we need to experience before we can know ourselves to be pure, perfect love and pure Source energy.

It's no coincidence that the eightfold path to enlightenment in Buddhism involves eight spiritual and personal disciplines, because **8**

Life Path 8: The Achiever

is the number of nirvana. And nirvana lies within us, not "out there" in some magical palace or playground in the clouds.

Vanity is another common negative trait of the **8** whose ego is still at the controls of their life.

These are the "beautiful people" who preen in front of the mirror, drive flashy cars so they can be seen, and join exclusive clubs that make them feel important. The trouble with this approach is that when the external trappings of their material success are removed, their level of Self-worth plunges into the basement.

The lesson for all **8**s is to real-eyes that obtaining wealth and influence is perfectly fine as long as they don't need their flashy toys and their VIP membership cards to feel good about themselves. If that is their motivation, they will either have their possessions taken away from them in some Self-imposed karmic crisis, or else they will live out their lives in fear of losing it all, with 26 locks on each of their doors and even more locks and chains on their lonely and distrusting heart – prisoners in a fancy jail of their own making.

That is why so many **8**s have to go through the pain of financial loss, sometimes many times, until they open their real eyes and see that all the money in the world will never make them happy. Shedding their ego and learning to love themselves is the only way to achieve that.

One final point on the overall positive and negative potential of this most powerful of Life Paths is to repeat what I said earlier, which is that many **8**s (usually those living this Life Path for the fourth or fifth time) choose to shun material trappings altogether. Instead, they become priests, missionaries, nurses, humanitarians, aid workers and charitable volunteers whose sole (soul) purpose is to be of service to others. They will still always find they have whatever they need in terms of food and shelter, but their "wealth" will be built on the amount of love they give and receive, rather than the amount of money they make and give away.

* * *

On a more personal level, many **8**s may struggle to find the right balance between their work and personal lives. Unlike the scholastic **7** who came before them and walks a lonely, contemplative path, the **8** usually has a social nature and enjoys the company of many friends, but often feels guilty that they neglect them in favour of working long into the night and on weekends.

Relationships come easily to the **8** as well, although again they must be careful not to neglect their family by working too hard. Being a lavish provider is one thing, but partners and children need more than fancy restaurants and PlayStations to feel fully loved. The **8** must make a concerted effort to turn off their mobile phones and laptops and spend quality time with their family.

It can be a challenge for the **8** to strike the elusive balance between work and play, but if they approach it like they do every other problem – by planning their course of action carefully, working hard at it and never giving up until they achieve their goal – they will succeed.

And they will be all the happier for it.

* * *

Summary of the positives

When they operate with the positive energy of this remarkably powerful Life Path Number, the evolved **8** will work hard to create a wonderfully comfortable home for themselves and their family. They will enjoy considerable status within their community, respected both for their wisdom and their generosity in helping worthwhile causes.

In their business life, they are diligent, focused, resourceful and persuasive, able to rally others to their cause and achieve great financial success. And if they encounter a setback – just like the evolved Self in Rudyard Kipling's seminal poem *If* – they will "start again at their beginnings and never breathe a word about their loss".

In their friendships and relationships, Achievers are honest, frank and loyal, although they must try regularly to take time out from their

Life Path 8: The Achiever

impossibly busy schedule to make sure their loved ones know how important they are, or they might risk them feeling neglected.

Spiritually, this Life Path marks the end of the eight-stage growth cycle that started with the number **1** and will be wrapped up and tied together with bright-coloured bows by the number **9** before we go back to the beginning to start a new cycle. This means that the **8** is here to first learn and then show others the true meaning of what it is to be a spirit having a human experience – namely, that we can enjoy all the magnificent abundance this world has to offer as soon as we rise above the fear-based needs of our ego and live as love.

Key positive words

Confident, decisive, hard-working, determined, ambitious, wise, resourceful, generous, persuasive, powerful, spiritual, humble, sharing, giving, understanding, practical, focused, goal-oriented, professional, dependable, trustworthy, disciplined and efficient.

* * *

Summary of the negatives

Because what we are here to do is seldom what comes most easily to us, the **8** will face numerous obstacles on their path to achieving their life's highest purpose that may flip them to work with the negative energy of this powerful Life Path Number.

Right from their earliest childhood years, the materialistic **8** will develop a particularly strong ego, which is the crucial first step in their quest to create abundance in their life and the lives of others. However, to use a Space Shuttle analogy, if they fail to jettison their huge "rocket booster" ego as they reach adulthood, they will never be able to leave the Earth's gravitational pull of material gratification and fly onwards and upwards to the stars... and to their spiritual goal of Self-love.

They may try to amass as much wealth, fame and influence as they can to compensate for their rampant ego's fearful sense of being

Life Path 8: Life Choices

separate, and therefore vulnerable. And in their desperation, just like Darth Vader (who I'm sure was an **8**, but I'll need to check with George Lucas and get back to you), they will turn to the "dark side" of this Life Path, which leads to greed, pride and an ugly lust for power.

Of course, this can all be avoided – just as Vader does in *The Return of the Jedi* – by real-eyesing that love is all that matters, and no amount of fancy houses, fast cars, designer clothes, wads of cash or planet-destroying Death Stars can come close to the exquisite feeling of knowing that we are pure love and pure Source energy. Which is the only spiritual goal worth having, and the highest goal all of us have.

Key negative words

Egotistical, insecure, bossy, vain, selfish, controlling, obsessive, materialistic, impractical, demanding, wasteful, ruthless and cruel.

***

Self-love is the difference

If you have read Part One, you will already know that your ability to walk the positive side of your Life Path, as opposed to the negative side, is determined by whether you have undertaken the two key stages of personal growth. Or, to put it another way, whether you have taken the two crucial first steps on the path to your life's highest purpose.

The first step towards living your Life Path in the positive is to develop Self-esteem (and if you're wondering what a "Self" is, please take the time to read Part One because it's way too complicated to explain again here). This feeling of inner confidence is essential because it allows you to tap into your innate strengths, which you will need if you are going to have any hope of overcoming the numerous obstacles on your path. Be aware, though, that on its own this first step is never enough, because Self-confidence and Self-esteem are still the work of the ego. The feeling of being "good enough" carries with it an implied sense of needing to be "better than".

Life Path 8: The Achiever

So to reach your full potential and achieve your life's highest purpose, you must also take the second step – which is to rise above the egoic concept of Self-esteem and climb to the much higher ground of Self-love.

Loving your Self does not mean being "full of your Self". It means the opposite. It means being humble because you understand that you are the same as everyone else, no better and no worse.

Above all, it means you understand that we are all immortal spirits having a human experience, and therefore we are all, at our core, the same – pure love and pure Source energy. (The Source is also fully explained in Part One.)

We can see it easily in new-born babies because when we are born into physical form, and before our fear-based ego has had a chance to develop, we are all gorgeous, gurgling bundles of pure, exquisite love.

I am not suggesting you do this, but just imagine you were to place a new-born infant on the pavement of a crowded street and then stand back out of sight. Everyone – and I mean everyone – would stop and tend to it. And the reason they would do this is because, deep down, we all recognise pure love when we see it. We are drawn to it at the most basic level of our being because it is the most strikingly beautiful and compelling force on the planet.

But sadly, as we grow up and go out into the world, our ego takes over and we start to believe – usually during our teenage years – that our ego is who we are. It isn't. Love is who we are.

We are all pure love. We are all extensions of Source energy (or children of "God", whichever phrase you are more comfortable with).

If you can rise above the quasi-religious terminology, I can summarise the two steps like this: Self-esteem is about feeling "good enough", while Self-love is about feeling "God enough".

The reason why loving your Self is so important for your Life Path is because when you start to live your life from the perspective of being pure love, everything changes. Suddenly you understand that nothing "out there" in the material world can ever harm you in any way.

Life Path 8: Life Choices

Equally, you real-eyes you don't need anything "out there" in the material world to make you feel happy – not the approval of others; no amount of money, fame and power; and not even the love of a good man or woman – because you have all the love you need right there in your own heart, and you can therefore relish the exquisite joy of loving everyone unconditionally without needing anything in return.

That is why Self-love is the secret to working with the positive energy of your Life Path Number. Because when you truly love your Self, the rocky mountain path you've been climbing suddenly becomes an express elevator ride all the way up to the summit of your bliss.

* * *

No Life Path is an island

Although your Life Path Number denotes the main issues you will focus on, you will always work to some degree with the energies of the other numbers as well to become a fully rounded Self.

As an **8** your main work will be in the areas of power and humility, but you will also tackle the key issues of Self-confidence (**1**), co-operation and balance (**2**), creative expression (**3**), stability and flexibility (**4**), freedom and discipline (**5**), acceptance (**6**), trust (**7**) and integrity (**9**).

It's therefore worth your while to read through the listings for the other Life Path Numbers when your time allows.

* * *

Qualities of your three-digit Birth Code

(Note: Please read the description in Part Two of how 0 operates in your three-digit Birth Code. Also, you can consult the main Life Path listings here in Part Three for each of your Supplementary Birth Numbers (the seven possible ones for the Achiever are 1, 2, 3, 4, 5, 6 and 7) to give you a clearer understanding of how their qualities govern your early years.)

Life Path 8: The Achiever

'Millennium Child' 00/8

A Millennium Child born with the remarkably powerful single-digit Birth Code of **8** has come into the world with the potential to achieve something truly spectacular with their life.

All the Millennium Children (those born at the beginning of this century without any Supplementary Birth Numbers) are endowed with extra potential because they will work with the energy of their Life Path Number with absolute focus and an incredible amount of commitment. (The qualities of the Millennium Children are described in Part Two.)

The doubly amplified presence of the two 0s in place of their two Supplementary Birth Numbers means these highly focused 00/**8**s will work solely with the supercharged energy of **8** for their entire life, right from when they take their first breath.

This gives them a unique capacity to amass wealth and power. And if they follow the highest purpose of the **8**, which is to share our planet's abundance with those who need it the most, they can achieve a huge shift in the way we treat our poor and our disadvantaged.

The mantra of the **8** is "We are all in this together." It is a Big T Truth that the world desperately needs to learn right now as the gap between the "have nots" and the "have way too muches" grows ever more shamefully wide.

For the 00/**8**, however, this very rare Birth Code endows these Millennium Children with an unparallelled potential to generate enormous financial wealth, which they can use to spread their much-needed spiritual message of love and togetherness around the world.

Before the start of this century, the last 00/**8** child was born on October 10, 1500, more than 500 years ago, but there are more coming soon, starting on January 3, 2020. Which is just as well, because we urgently need their help to wrest power from the greedy hands of the Fat Controllers and share the money around.

Remember, though, that every heightened chance of achievement in our Birth Code carries with it an equally heightened risk of disappointment, so these Millennium Children must never be made to feel pressured to live up to the extraordinary potential of their Life Path.

Life Path 8: Life Choices

(If this is your child's number, they will be aged between four and 17 as *Messages from Your Self* is published, so please flip forward to the Choices for Children section under this listing for the Achiever to find out more about their positive potential, and the negatives to avoid.)

17/8

The presence of a fire number (action) and an air number (thought) as their Supplementary Birth Numbers means these earthy and well-grounded Achievers have an excellent mix of courage (1), insight (7) and persistence (8) – the three qualities above all others that are needed to succeed in any venture, financial or otherwise.

For the first formative 18 years of their life, they will work with the supplementary take-charge energy of the Leader (1), which will help them develop the confidence to perform well during their school years and master the leadership skills they will need to start amassing significant personal wealth as they enter adulthood.

Then for their next 18 years, up until they reach full emotional maturity at the age of 36, they will invoke the spiritual and intellectual energy of 7, which will give them valuable insights into human nature and how the world works.

All the while their main work will be influenced by the earthy (practical) energy of 8, but in their early childhood years they will be willing to take the lead in school projects and at home in activities with their family. And they will be brimming with original and creative ideas (the energy of 1).

They will then embark on their career with a clear understanding of what they want to achieve, they will have excellent problem-solving skills and an intuitive grasp of the big spiritual truths (the energy of 7).

As long as they clear their emotional blockages and work with the positive energy of their three Birth Code numbers, the 17/8 will enjoy much success, both financially and spiritually.

One word of caution, though: the lack of a water number (2 or 6) in their Birth Code means they may struggle with understanding and expressing their emotions as children and young adults, and they may

Life Path 8: The Achiever

become so focused on material and intellectual pursuits as they grow older that they miss out on the joy of close, loving relationships.

Romantically, the 17/**8** longs to share their success with their loved ones, but because they will be in their heads so much of the time (the energy of 7) they may never learn that while providing for one's family is great, it is never the same as spending quality loving time with them.

26/8

These emotional Achievers are polar opposites of their practical and intellectual 17/**8** cousins because they have a double dose of water (emotion) in their two Supplementary Birth Numbers. This means that unlike the solitary and pioneering 17/**8**, which lacks any water numbers, the 26/**8** will spend all their first 36 formative years working with the spiritual and material qualities of their Life Path Number **8** to bring people together (2) and spread their message of love far and wide (6).

Yes, they will still be largely focused on creating abundance for themselves and others, which is the highest purpose of the **8**, but they will do so in close co-operation with others (2) during their childhood years up until the age of 18, and then as they branch out on their own from 18 to full emotional maturity at 36 they will focus on helping others see their divine inner beauty and use any power and wealth they create to raise the loving vibration of the world (6).

In fact, these Achievers might shun the material calling of their Life Path Number **8** altogether and pursue a spiritual career devoted to being of service to others. Many nurses, priests, counsellors and spiritual healers are 26/**8**s who have chosen to focus all their energy on developing the heightened spiritual wisdom of this Life Path.

If they do decide to go into business for themselves, as so many **8**s do, they will usually differ from all other Achievers by putting the needs of their family above their career. These romantic and loving 26/**8**s will value their partner and their children above all else. They will delight in being able to provide for them financially, but they will understand that no amount of money can buy lasting happiness, which comes only from sharing our successes with the ones we love.

Life Path 8: Life Choices

One word of caution, though: the lack of a fire number in their Birth Code means the 26/**8** may sometimes get bogged down by their emotions, leading them to become overwhelmed and unsure of what action to take to break out of their rut. Equally, the absence of an air number could mean that when they do decide on a course of action, it might be taken on impulse and have dire consequences because they haven't taken the time to think it through properly.

Hopefully these issues won't arise too often because the 26/**8** is a naturally resourceful and hard-working number, able to rise above any obstacles that are put in their way. And as long as they clear their emotional blockages and work with the positive energy of their three Birth Code numbers, the high-spirited 26/**8** will usually be able to enjoy great success in all areas of their life.

35/**8**

People born with this Birth Code have the potential to make a big impact on the world because they are working with their Life Path qualities of abundance and power (**8**) in conjunction with the creative and expressive energy of 3 during their first formative years, which will lead them to discover new and original ways to use their personal power (**8**) to help others on a grand scale.

Then as they reach adulthood at 18, they will invoke the rebellious and adventurous qualities of 5, which will drive them to tackle the forces of oppression head on, using their might and status to fight for the rights of the downtrodden and the disadvantaged.

There is no better example of the true power of this powerfully humanitarian Birth Code than Nelson Mandela, a 35/**8** who not only changed the fortunes of his own country but spread a message of love, forgiveness and tolerance that reached every corner of the globe.

As children, the supplementary energy of 3 (the Creative) will endow these young Achievers with an outgoing and artistic personality. They will be social and popular at school, and they will also work hard (the energy of **8**) to achieve good grades. Success may not come easily to them, but their bubbly temperament and their never-say-die attitude will stand them in great stead for when they reach adulthood and branch out on their own.

As young adults, they may lack a certain amount of discipline (the negative energy of (5), but they will fight tooth and nail for what they believe in (positive 5) and will have an insatiable curiosity to travel and experience as many adventures as they can (positive 5), while also wanting to make a real difference in the world (positive 5).

One word of caution, though: the lack of a water number (2 or 6) in their Birth Code means they may struggle with understanding and expressing their emotions as children and young adults, and they may become so focused on their professional career as they grow older that they miss out on the joy of close, loving relationships.

Nelson Mandela, for example, was a lion-hearted revolutionary but his loving relationships were fraught to say the least because he was hardly ever home.

Romantically, the 35/8 must real-eyes that to experience the love they crave they must invest just as much time and energy in their family as they do in their quest to change the world.

Master Number 44/8 – 'The Master Achiever'

If you have not already done so, please read my comments in Chapter 8 of Part Two about what numerologists like to call Master Numbers – namely, those Life Path Numbers whose Supplementary Birth Numbers are the same. There are four possible Master Numbers in numerology: 11/2, 22/4, 33/6 and 44/8.

There is no doubt that having two identical Supplementary Birth Numbers helps you focus on developing the qualities of your Life Path Number during the first 36 years of your life. However, as we have seen time and time again, having a more balanced set of elemental Birth Code numbers can sometimes be preferable to working with the energy of just one or two of the four elements.

The rare 44/8 Birth Code is unique among the Master Numbers in that all the numbers all governed by the same element – in this case the practical and materialistic element of earth. This gives them a single-minded focus on creating wealth and power, but little ability to do anything else.

That is why 44/8s are known as Alchemists, because they have an almost Midas-like power to turn anything they touch into gold. Indeed, this may be the reason why there is not one famous 44/8 in all of history, despite their phenomenal potential for success.

Perhaps the burden of such a focused Birth Code has weighed too heavily on them and they have been unable to develop the confidence (fire) they need to take action, the emotional maturity (water) they need to cope with setbacks, and the intellectual dexterity (air) they need to solve all of the problems that come their way.

The 11/2 is a watery Intuitive (2) who works with the double fire energy of the Leader (1) in their early years. The 22/4 is an earthy Builder (4) who works with the double water (emotion) energy of 2 in their early years. And the 33/6 is a watery Visionary (6) who works with the double air energy of the Creative (3) in their early years. In every case, their Supplementary Birth Numbers complement the energy of their Life Path Number by creating essential checks and balances to keep them from falling into depression when life doesn't go their way.

The all-earth 44/8 has no such balance, giving them on the one hand an extraordinary potential to manifest abundance in all areas and then use it to improve the lives of others, and on the other hand no clue how to cope with the failures and disappointments we must all experience on our path to the mountain top.

It's quite possible that some successful 44/8s don't show up on any list of famous high achievers because they have chosen to fly under the radar and donate their money and time anonymously, or else have shunned material pursuits in favour of a spiritual life in service to others.

It's more likely, though, that the majority have been driven by their rampant egos to fly too close to the Sun – and, like Icarus, they have crashed and burned in a smouldering heap of hubris, victims of drug addiction, alcoholism or emotional despair.

If this is your Birth Code, I don't mean to alarm you – merely to re-mind you that with a heightened potential for success if we walk the

Life Path 8: The Achiever

light side of our Life Path by living in love (and no one has more chance of success than the 44/8) comes an equal potential for disaster if we fail to control our ego and flip to the dark side of fear and greed.

In the positive, 44/8s will start from an early age to build a solid foundation for themselves, firmly rooted in the real world. As children they will be serious, responsible and hard-working, performing well at school and enjoying a close circle of loyal and trustworthy friends.

Then, as they hit 18 and strike out on their own, they will continue to work exclusively with the earth energy of 4 in conjunction with their equally pragmatic Life Path Number 8 to build an abundant life for themselves and their loved ones. They will also spend considerable amounts of time and energy working for charitable causes, sharing their wealth and their knowledge for the greater good.

4 marks the end of the first "human stage" of the Spiritual Growth Cycle, when we learn how to create a stable financial and emotional foundation for ourselves, and 8 marks the end of the second "divine stage" of the cycle, when we take all we have learned and then teach others how to create abundance in their own lives.

Taken together, this helps explain why 44/8s are often evolved Selfs who have a clear understanding of the law of karma, due to the lessons and achievements of their many past lives.

44/8s who do the required inner work (ie, learn that they are pure love and part of the Source) have the capacity to amass great wealth and use it in positive ways to help others. They also have the potential to become powerful and generous philanthropists who are able to improve the lives of the poor and downtrodden on a wide scale.

As well as being wise old Selfs, Alchemists are also loyal and dependable friends (the energy of 4). Not only can they metaphorically turn lead into gold, their friendships will be "solid gold" as well.

Where they may struggle, though, is in their romantic relationships, due to the lack of any water (emotion) energy in their all-earth Birth Code. I know several 44/8s who are extremely successful and widely popular (interestingly, all of them are creative artists), but they have stumbled painfully from one failed relationship to another.

Life Path 8: Career Choices

All of them have failed to wrest their powerful egos (the curse of all **8**s, and especially the **44**/**8**) from the controls of their life, which means they are stuck in the dingy basement of Self-esteem and lack the bright top-floor penthouse energy of Self-love that is essential for any romantic relationship to work at the deepest level.

One of the "Big T" Truths of the Self-Awareness System™ states that it is not possible to love someone more than they love themselves. If you try to give them more love than they subconsciously feel they deserve, they will reject it – and, in the process, they will reject you too.

That is why **44**/**8**s who fail to kill their ego and learn they are pure love and pure Source energy will not only push true love away, they may flip to the dark side of this most powerful of all Birth Codes and use their power to try to control and exploit other people, rather than help them and lift them up. This is called the "Scrooge" path, and sadly some **44**/**8**s who can't master their inner fears are tempted to take it.

If you are a **44**/**8** you need to know that nothing is expected of you. Your life is yours to live how you choose, and for most people fame and fortune are simply not worth the price we have to pay to achieve them. All that matters is you conquer your fears (ego) and learn to love your Self.

The mantra of the Achiever is: "We are all in this together". But the mantra of the Master Achiever is: "We create the most abundance when we love our Self, and allow our Self to love others too."

* * *

2. CAREER AND BUSINESS CHOICES

MANY **8**s will wind up going into business for themselves, or else they will join the corporate ladder and quickly climb their way to the biggest office with the biggest desk on the very top floor. These are the natural chief executives and entrepreneurs of the world. They are usually

Life Path 8: The Achiever

money-focused, which means they will also excel in sales, finance and any other profession that offers fat bonuses. And the cut-and-thrust world of politics will often appeal as well, not just because they love a good fight but because of the power and status it can afford them.

Most **8**s thrive in the corporate environment because they are well-organised, ambitious and willing to put in the long hours that are needed to steal a march on their rivals. They welcome responsibility and effortlessly shoulder the burden of leadership. Plus, their magnetic appeal brings out the best in the people who work for them – which also reflects favourably on them.

Sometimes the **8** can be so sure of their own abilities and so critical of anyone else's that they take on too much, causing them to become overwhelmed. They work best when focused on the Big Picture vision of their enterprise, and would therefore do well to learn the fine art of delegation by putting in place a team of trusted confidantes around them. Ideally, this would include an equally hard-working and diligent Builder **4** to keep an eye on the essential details, and a trustworthy and worldly Teacher **9** to make sure that they don't lose touch with the humanitarian goals of the business.

Outside the corporate world, many **8**s also thrive in the highly competitive cauldron of professional sport, where their natural drive to be the best can take them to the top of the tree – and, in the process, satisfy their desire for fame and fortune as well.

The same is true for many of the arts, including acting, music and painting. The creative professions are littered with successful and high-profile **8**s, as the list of Famous Life Paths in the Appendices at the back of this book will attest.

It's not unusual for an **8** to build a successful business and then lose it all. But with remarkable resilience and sheer guts and hard work, they will simply start again at the beginning and build another one.

Whatever career path the **8** chooses to pursue, their competitive spirit and their never-say-die attitude give them a much better than average chance of success. They are also excellent negotiators, able to bend other people to their will with relative ease, which makes them ideally suited for trade and diplomatic roles, as well as the deal-making world of corporate finance.

Finally, it's worth noting again that some **8**s eschew the pursuit of material trappings altogether in favour of a simple life spent in the service of others. This Life Path is the pinnacle of the Spiritual Growth Cycle, and many of those who walk it will choose to rise above the demands of their ego and use their unique understanding of the human condition to help others in a hands-on capacity. They will become priests or healers or aid workers or nurses, giving freely of their time to minister to those in need. But even if they don the humble robes of the missionary, they will still be an **8** through and through and will be extremely effective at raising funds for their worthy cause.

Beneficial career paths

People who are working with the resourceful and goal-oriented energy of **8** make excellent entrepreneurs, executives, bankers, lawyers, small business owners, sales people, sports professionals, musicians, actors, filmmakers, artists, priests, nurses, missionaries, aid workers, politicians, diplomats, counsellors, financial advisers, real estate gurus, philanthropists, fundraisers, architects, stockbrokers, archaeologists, historians, publishers, journalists, TV presenters and art gallery owners.

Best business matches

The ambitious and highly organised **8**, just like the focused and passionate **1**, doesn't need a business partner when they decide to strike out on their own. In fact, they would normally do better to go it alone and shoulder the responsibility for the business themselves.

The always focused **8** is resourceful, hard-working and determined to succeed in whatever they do. A partner would just get in the way and annoy them because they can never hope to stay as focused on the task at hand as the **8**. One exception is the **1**, but the **8** may struggle to tolerate the **1**'s need to be in control.

The single-minded and ambitious **8** would be wise to employ a great team and pay them well (money usually comes easily to the **8**) so they are prepared to work the long hours the **8** expects of them. An earthy **4** or a watery **2** would be ideal for the role of general manager. They could pick a creative **3** for marketing, a **6** for human resources, a **5** for sales, a **7** for back-office roles, and a **9** as project manager.

* * *

3. RELATIONSHIP CHOICES

ONE of the most rewarding aspects about the Self-Awareness System™ is how equitable it is. Each Life Path offers the same opportunities for happiness and fulfillment, albeit in markedly different ways. And each of them also offers the same amount of challenges to force us to grow, although again in very different ways.

This means no Life Path is any "better" or "worse" than any of the others. All of them have their blessings, and all have their obstacles.

In the case of **8**, the blessings centre around their capacity for hard work and their clear, single-minded focus that allows them to achieve virtually any goal they set for themselves, and their obstacles usually appear in their romantic relationships, where they can struggle to create close, loving connections and peaceful, harmonious homes.

Usually, this is a result of them focusing too much of their time and energy on their work to the detriment of their family life. But it often goes much deeper than that, because many materialistic **8**s suffer from a chronic lack of Self-love, of which they are often painfully unaware. They believe in their heart that they love themselves, and they point to the trappings of their success as proof, saying to themselves: "Look what I've created!" But they fail to real-eyes the crucial distinction between Self-love and Self-esteem.

Yes, their Self-esteem is probably through the roof because the unevolved **8**'s ego is usually bigger than one of Thor's biceps. But, as we saw earlier, Self-esteem is a fool's game because it's all about trying to feel "good enough", which is the ego talking – and the ego will never be satisfied. It will always want more, so it will never be able to feel "good enough". Worse, it will keep us separate from – and therefore in competition with – everyone else around us, as it battles to be "better than" its rivals, whether they are rivals at work or rivals for their partner's affections, or even their partner themselves.

This is why so many **8**s struggle in love and get bogged down in petty power struggles, because they sometimes view their relationship as a battleground where, by definition, there must always be a winner and a loser – just the same as they view every other aspect of their life.

Sadly, the **8** may suffer from this conflict just as much as, if not more than, their partner. They want to love and be loved at the deepest part of their being, and they simply cannot understand why the tactics they employ to win in business or sport don't work at home.

The answer is as simple as it is elusive for the egotistical Achiever, who must learn the crucial difference between Self-esteem (the ego) and Self-love (the Source). It is only when the competitive **8** stops seeing themselves as separate and understands that we are all the same – because we are all pure love, and therefore pure Source energy – that they can rise above the lonely "hell" of living as their fear-based ego and experience the "heaven" of feeling connected on the deepest, most loving level to everyone and everything.

This is the key lesson we must all learn on our journey towards achieving our life's highest purpose. It's not easy for any of the Life Paths, but for the achievement-oriented **8** it is particularly challenging.

Indeed, it is so difficult for the **8** to surrender their precious ego – which, after all, is the key to all the wealth, fame, power and status they have worked so hard to achieve – that after a number of failed relationships (and probably very expensive divorces) they may simply give up on trying to have a close, loving connection altogether and settle for a luxurious, but cold, marriage of convenience instead.

This is their choice, and it should not be judged. But it is always sad to see someone trying to disguise their lack of happiness by buying ever larger mansions, complete with "his" and "hers" sports cars in the garage, expensive art on the walls and walk-in wardrobes the size of Texas stacked with all the latest designer clothes – only to sleep alone in separate bedrooms.

Of course, by no means all **8**s are destined to suffer this hollow fate. At their core, they are all deeply loving and romantic individuals with voracious sexual appetites who yearn to open up their heart completely to their partner. As long as they feel safe (and this is crucial for the **8**), they can be the most passionate and adventurous of lovers, showering their partner with gifts, whisking them away for romantic weekends and dropping in unexpectedly at their workplace with flowers "just because I felt like telling you how much I love you".

Sure, there will still be plenty of fights because even spiritually evolved **8**s find it almost impossible to back down when they believe they are right. But the make-up sex will be spectacular.

The **8** can also sometimes appear insensitive, but this is just a front. They feel deeply about what is going on in their lives, they just have no idea how to express what it is they are feeling. Also, their forthright nature can make them speak harshly simply because they haven't taken the time to phrase what they want to say in a more conciliatory way.

If you are in a relationship with an **8**, all of this will sound all too familiar. They can be infuriatingly stubborn, and they will always refuse point blank to take your advice, no matter how good it is. Whenever they make a choice they have to feel it is their decision, not someone else's. The solution is never to try to fight them or bend them to your will, because it just won't work. Instead, you need to be like the bride's mother in that wonderful movie *My Big Fat Greek Wedding*, who expertly manipulates her dominant husband by making him think he is making all the decisions, when in fact it is she who plants the ideas in his mind. As she says: "He might be the head of the household, but I am the neck and I can turn him in any direction I choose."

(Again, this is not sexist. This conflict-avoidance trick works just as well if the **8** is the "feminine energy" partner in a relationship.)

* * *

Life Path 8: Relationship Choices

Sex drive of the 8

Power is at the heart of everything the Achiever does, and their sex life is no different. At work, they revel in the power of being in charge. When they buy a car, they want to know exactly how much horsepower they've got under their accelerator pedal. And when they go for a walk, it is always a power walk, never a casual stroll.

The same is true in the bedroom, where the biggest aphrodisiac for the **8** is a partner who exudes power, no matter which birth gender they are. The masculine **8** is turned on by a partner who can flip them on their back and take control, while the feminine **8** will only truly open up to a partner who has the power to ravish them and feast on their femininity like a starving carnal carnivore.

(Phew, I don't know about you, but that image has got me thinking I need to take a cold shower – and I'm not even an **8**!)

Most **8**s are either voracious and insatiable animals between the sheets, or else cold as ice, depending on whether they are working with the positive or negative energy of this Life Path.

If your partner is an **8**, you need to make them feel safe because they will never open up to you unless you open up to them first. Make your Self vulnerable and they will feed you their deepest fruits. Hold back, and they'll make you feel they're not even there in bed with you.

The secret is trust. Give your Self completely to your **8** lover and they will reciprocate with a depth of passion unlike anything you have experienced. But be warned... never show fear to an **8**, or they'll eat you alive. Instead show them vulnerability and strength (they are the same thing) and they will be yours forever.

Despite the **8**'s focus on abundance and power, this is a feminine number, which means those working with the positive energy of this Life Path are open, passionate and nurturing towards their lover, just as they are with their friends and workmates. But when they feel afraid or insecure, their ego will rear its ugly head and push away anyone it deems a threat – especially their partner – based on its belief that the best form of defence is attack.

Life Path 8: The Achiever

For the "feminine energy" partner in a relationship, this manifests in the bedroom as the silent treatment. She will probably sleep in the spare room, but if she really wants to make her masculine partner suffer, she will lie in bed like a block of ice with her back turned while she texts every single one of her masculine friends – or even calls them and laughs provocatively to really rub her lover's nose in it.

This is a test, and nothing more. She wants to know whether her masculine partner is truly "man enough" to deserve her affections. If he comes grovelling to her, he will fail miserably. But if he grabs the phone, flings it across the room and makes forceful and passionate love to her, she will know he is strong enough for her to step into her own sexual power without scaring him off or hurting him.

This dynamic works in much the same way if the **8** in a relationship is the "masculine energy" partner. Everything to him is a competition that he wants – no, make that needs – to win. And sex is no different. The last thing he wants in a lover is a doormat, because where's the fun in that. He wants to know that his partner is "woman enough" to stand up to him and make him fight for – and win – her affections, not just once but over and over again. This gives him the thrill of the chase that he craves, and if she's smart she'll let him have his little victories while never allowing him to think he has won her over completely. She will always hold something back to keep him wanting more.

* * *

The compatibility listings that follow will help ambitious **8**s get the most out of their relationships, whether it's with someone they love, a friend or a business partner. You will notice the earth energy of **8** is well-matched with other **8**s and their earthy cousin **4**, as well as a **2** or a **6**, whose water gives the earth the nutrients it needs to nurture love. Fire (**1** and **5**) can scald the fragile earth, and air (**3** and **7**) can erode it, so these pairings are likely to throw up more challenges. And even the well-rounded and worldly **9** may struggle to cope with the **8**'s single-minded career focus and over-developed ego.

Life Path 8: Relationship Choices

However, what appears to match you best on the surface may not be what you need in your life right now. All relationships are designed to help us grow along our Life Path. Yes, of course we enjoy the companionship, close connection, sexual intimacy and deep love that relationships give us. But that is now why we have them.

The reason we choose a partner (or, to be more accurate, why our all-knowing Self chooses them for us) is because they are a mirror in which we see our shortcomings and strengths reflected back at us through their shortcomings and strengths.

That is why opposites so often attract, especially in love.

I have written an entire book on this subject called *Leap into Love* which goes into the way relationships work in our lives in great detail. But for now, please real-eyes that when your partner presses one of your buttons, they are doing so not to "piss you off" but because your Self is using them to show you the areas you need to work on.

If you fail to understand this is the main reason why you attracted them into your life in the first place, you will fight each other and may eventually break up. And you will believe their faults were exactly that – their faults – rather than yours reflected back at you. Worst of all, you will then take the unchanged you with you to your next relationship, and – lo and behold! – exactly the same issues will come up again.

If this sounds familiar. If you have ever asked any of these questions – "Why does this always happen to me?" or "Why do all men cheat?" or "Why are all women so demanding?" or whatever it is for you – then now you know why. It's because you didn't learn from your last partner, so of course your new one will do the same thing.

And this will continue to happen, relationship after relationship, until you real-eyes it is meant to be happening to show you what areas you need to work on in your Self to change and grow.

* * *

One final quick point before we get into it: I need to stress that I disagree with almost every numerologist I know who likes to label

Life Path 8: The Achiever

relationships "a natural fit", "a neutral fit" or "an unnatural fit", depending on the compatibility of the numbers of the two partners.

All relationships are challenging. That is why we have them, as we have just seen. Yes, sometimes we might choose a partner who is "just like us" for the sake of harmony, but that could be regarded as a cop out if we are truly serious about our personal and spiritual growth.

If you are on a spiritual growth path in this lifetime (and there is no doubt in my mind that you are if you made it through Part One without throwing it in the bin!), then your Self will choose your relationships for you – and they will always be with a partner who will challenge you to grow in exactly the ways you need to grow.

Just because you might discover your current partner has a Life Path Number that doesn't dovetail perfectly with yours, don't fall into the trap of thinking there must be something wrong – or worse, end it with them so you can go out with someone with a "better" number.

Where you are right now on your Life Path is exactly where you are meant to be, and who you are with is exactly who you are meant to be with. So please let these listings help you to look for the lessons in your relationship, rather than look for the door.

And if you are single at the moment, try to remain open-hearted about your next relationship. It doesn't matter what Life Path Number they have, so don't "cherry pick". All that matters is you follow your heart and be open to learning the lessons they can teach you. After all, that's the reason you will attract them into your life in the first place.

* * *

<u>8 & 1</u>
(Ambition and Independence)

Love

These numbers are like two peas in a pod and will usually find it easy to form a close business relationship, but loving relationships are another matter because neither has much regard for romance. They are

Life Path 8: Relationship Choices

too busy making their mark in the world and pursuing their careers to spend much in the way of quality time with their partner.

The upside is that while other numbers may struggle with the **1**'s constant need to focus on their career, it's no problem for the equally driven **8**, who will please the **1** by allowing them the space they need.

The downside is that this can tend to feel more like a marriage of convenience than a marriage of true hearts, and both must take the time to nurture the relationship or it may quickly wither and die.

Also, for all their material focus, both the strong-willed **8** and the headstrong **1** crave the approval and support of their partner. And if it isn't there, they will look for it somewhere else. Extra-marital affairs are common, though usually short-lived, because after the disgruntled **8** or **1** has got their "fix" of approval from someone else, they will usually feel cramped by their new illicit relationship and yearn for the freedom they had before with their undemanding partner.

Another area to watch for is that both the **8** and the **1** are assertive partners who like to be on top – which can make for a great time in the bedroom, but a series of blazing rows everywhere else. The solution is to draw firm boundaries within the relationship and decide the arenas where each can be in charge.

Taking turns also works – whether it's deciding whose turn it is to pick the Sunday night movie, or choose the restaurant, or even the holiday destination each year.

As long as there is open communication and both partners feel free to speak up when their needs are not being met – which will be frequently – this relationship can be mutually rewarding. But if the high expectations of both these numbers lead either one to become too demanding or needy towards the other, it will push them away faster than they can say "divorce".

Well, that's not quite accurate. They will have to say "expensive divorce" because both the **8** and the **1** are very money-oriented and will probably want to squeeze every last penny from the other.

It need never come to this, though, as long as the busy **1** and the ambitious **8** take the time to inject even just a little bit of romance into their daily lives. Notes on the pillow, flowers or gifts for no reason, surprise dinner dates and such will work just fine.

Good luck, stay open and honest… and enjoy the material success and sizzling hot sex this exciting relationship can give you.

Friendship

The materialistic **8** and the ambitious **1** have the potential to be both best mates and sworn enemies – usually in quick succession.

Many **8/1** friendships will start off with excitement and enthusiasm, as both fire their "Big World-Changing Ideas" off each other. They will usually bond over their mutual desire for success and advancement, and may even choose to partner up (see the Business notes below), thinking – quite rightly – that by combining their ferocious appetites and energies they will form a dynamic team.

They will, there is no doubt about it. But it may last only as long as it takes one to outstrip the other. If the fragile ego of the **1** feels slighted by their sometimes ruthless **8** partner, competition will replace co-operation and the friendship could be sacrificed on the altar of ambition. The solution is to real-eyes there is more than enough to go around, and if each can rise above their ego and celebrate the successes of the other rather than resent them for their triumphs, then this can be a very rewarding friendship in every sense.

Business

Of all the possible Life Path Number combinations, this is easily the most auspicious pairing for creating lasting wealth and abundance.

The ambitious **1** can sometimes fall into the egoic trap of pursuing goals that are more about making themselves feel worthy than creating genuine abundance for all concerned.

This is the curse of the energy of fire, which sometimes can burn brightly just for the sake of it – and yet at the end of their spectacular display of energetic fireworks, when all the embers have died down, there may be little to show for their efforts other than the smouldering ashes of their failed dreams.

Life Path 8: Relationship Choices

Enter the **8**, who is equally ambitious but is governed by the stable and process-driven energy of earth, and can therefore ground the fiery **1** and keep them focused on the end result.

The materialistic **8** is balanced by their more advanced spiritual understanding that the purpose of creating wealth is not to keep it, but to share it with others less fortunate than themselves.

This is a lesson the **1** would do well to learn.

As long as the powerful personalities of the **1** and the **8** can set boundaries so they do not tread on each other's toes, this is the perfect business partnership, where both will drive each other to new heights of achievement. The secret to success here is trust. If the **1** trusts the **8** to manage the business while they rush about making deals and bringing in the money, and the **8** trusts the **1**'s vision enough to let them take the lead and drive the business forward into new markets, there is nothing this most dynamic of duos can't achieve.

* * *

8 & 2

(Ambition and Co-operation)

Love

This is one of the most compatible love matches for the **8**, both romantically and in business. In fact, these two lovebirds may well decide to partner up for both so they can live, play and work together.

While in a business setting it makes no difference which number is the feminine energy and which is the masculine, at home this pairing usually works best in the traditional roles of an **8** breadwinner and a **2** homemaker. The materialistic earthy Achiever needs to be out there kicking goals and making tonnes of money, while the emotional and watery Intuitive is happiest when they are creating a stylish, warm and harmonious home for their family.

There is nothing sexist about this. In fact, because these numbers are both feminine, it's common for the ambitious "female" **8** to be the

Life Path 8: The Achiever

breadwinner while her "male" **2** partner runs the rest of their life. The goal-oriented **8** will be delighted that their trusted **2** partner controls the family purse strings, freeing them up to go after their Next Big Deal. They will also relish the unwavering support they feel from their supporting and compassionate Intuitive **2**, who will be only too happy to stroke their ego and offer words of encouragement when the **8** suffers one of their rare setbacks.

On their side, the homemaker **2** will be thrilled they don't have to go to a boring office every day and endure interminable, dick-swinging meetings during which everyone tries to out-ego each other. They will love having the freedom to do whatever they want, whenever they want, and focus all their loving energy on raising a family – or, if they don't have children, on running their own business from home.

Yes, the **2** is governed by the emotional element of water, but money is also important to them because all Intuitives want a comfortable home and an active social life, and they also love to travel – all of which require a good income – so they will be happy to let their **8** partner focus their energy on the business of making wads of cash.

But (there's always a but in relationships, sorry) the **8** must never take their **2** partner's support for granted. If they don't feel appreciated for the part they play, and if they don't receive enough attention, the **2** can flip from "Hello darling, how was your day?" to "I've run away to Acapulco with my personal trainer, your dinner's in the dog".

Despite their busy business schedule, the **8** must always make enough time for their **2** lover. Coming home late with expensive gifts is nice, but what they really want is for them to come home early with a babysitter secretly organised and whisk them away to their favourite restaurant for a romantic candlelit dinner, followed by long, languid lovemaking in a luxury hotel suite complete with bubble bath.

And woe betide the **8** who cheats on their **2** partner. They will come home to find their precious designer dresses – or Tom Ford suits, depending on their sex – cut up into a thousand pieces and lying under the sprinkler on the front lawn.

Life Path 8: Relationship Choices

For their part, the **2** must at all costs avoid becoming too needy and making unwarranted demands on the **8**'s precious time. Nothing turns an Achiever off more than a nagging husband or wife.

Providing both partners do the necessary inner work to boost their level of Self-love, none of these issues should arise and they will enjoy a long-lasting, passionate and exciting relationship together.

Good luck, stay open and honest… and enjoy the close, loving connection and mutual financial rewards this relationship can give you.

Friendship

Although the **8** and the **2** can find much joy in a traditional loving relationship and experience mutual success in a business partnership, this pairing is not so compatible when it comes to a friendship. The ambitious **8** may look down on the simple, homely values of the **2**, and the emotional **2** may distrust the blatantly materialistic priorities of the money-oriented **8**.

Providing they can find a middle ground of mutual interests, there is the potential to forge a rewarding friendship, whereby the **8** helps the **2** set up a lucrative business and the **2** teaches the **8** to loosen up and smell the roses.

Interestingly, if their connection deepens along these lines, these two friends, if available and sexually matched, will probably wind up in bed – or in business – together.

And probably both.

Business

As we've already seen, this is a fantastic business combination because the ambitious and take-charge **8** needs a partner they can fully trust, and few are more trustworthy than the honest, open-hearted **2**. Equally, while the **2** usually has a solid head for business, they may lack the **8**'s drive and ambition to make it to the very top, not to mention the ruthless killer streak necessary to see off their rivals.

Just as in love, the **8** must make sure the **2** feels fully appreciated for all their hard work, and the **2** must trust the **8** and support them in all they do, rather than nag them and undermine their confidence.

Normally, the **8** might be tempted to feel that they perform best on their own without a business partner, and that is often true. But not in this case. A dedicated and supportive **2** in their corner will empower them to work harder, reach higher and go a lot further than they could ever hope to do on their own.

* * *

8 & 3
(Ambition and Expression)

Love

This is always going to be more of a mutual growth opportunity than a "tra-la-la-la" tiptoe-through-the-tulips-hand-in-hand-without-a-care-in-the-world-because-we're-so-in-love relationship. But that's OK. After all, some of our most valuable relationships are the ones just like this, when opposites attract – no matter how briefly – to teach each other some valuable life lessons.

The lesson the **3** has for the **8** in this marriage of opposites is to lighten up and not take life so seriously, but their time with the **3** will be far from easy and unless they have read a book like this one they will probably give up and pull the plug before they have learned it.

Try as they might to be attentive to their partner, the goal-oriented **8** will almost always be too focused on themselves and their own material interests for the attention-seeking **3**, just as the socially interactive **3** will almost always be too demanding of their partner's time for the busy **8** to cope with.

The earthy **8** needs a partner who gives them plenty of time and space to do their own thing, but the social **3** thrives on excitement and needs almost constant stimulation from their lover, otherwise they might just as well have stayed single and fancy free.

Life Path 8: Relationship Choices

For a **3** to commit happily to a relationship with an **8** they must be prepared to make their own entertainment separate from their partner, otherwise they will quickly grow to resent the Achiever for never being there for them. Equally, the **8** must let their **3** lover go out and find the entertainment they crave without them, trusting that they won't stray.

Which they probably will, one day, when they meet someone who is creative and quirky and cool and… well… more like them.

One of the biggest problems with this pairing is that the **8** will find little to admire about the **3**'s social butterfly nature, and the **3** will not value the **8**'s monetary work ethic because they are perfectly capable of making their own money.

In fact, their values are so different that it's highly unlikely these two will ever meet and fall in love in the first place. So please real-eyes that if you find your Self in one of these **8/3** relationships as you read this, you are there for a very specific and important reason.

There is something you need to change about your Self, and you have attracted your **3** partner into your life so they can teach you what it is and how to do it. You'll know what it is if you look hard enough. And, who knows, by making the change you just might find that this relationship is "the one" after all, and you will both go on to live a long and blissfully happy life together.

Good luck, stay open and honest… and try to find the crucial life-changing lessons that each of you is able to teach the other.

Friendship

The ambitious **8** will meet the free-loving **3** at a party and hit it off immediately, partying long into the night together.

Said no one. Ever.

Yes, they can be friends – even great friends, if they work at it. But on first meeting, these two will usually have very little in common.

Business

Equally, no one ever said that these two should even think about perhaps contemplating the thought of considering the possibility of

Life Path 8: The Achiever

maybe mulling over the concept of discussing the idea of talking about going into business together. Ever.

* * *

8 & 4
(Ambition and Stability)

Love

"Earth to Number **8**. Earth to Number **8**. Come in, Number **8**. Your perfect life partner is waiting for you!"

Here at the Self-Awareness System™ Ground Control Situation Room we have teams of NASA-qualified relationship counsellors working round the clock monitoring banks of computer data to find everyone in the entire universe an ideal mate.

For some lovelorn lonely hearts, this task can be more challenging than putting a man on the Moon. But for these universally compatible earth numbers, finding a love that lasts with each other is easier than putting a man on a bicycle.

The earthy **8** and the equally earthy **4** are as alike as root canal therapy and a Justin Bieber concert. (Sorry to all you young Bieber fans, but you will grow out of it one day soon, I promise you.)

In fact, they are so alike that in some ways this relationship just doesn't need to happen, unless both partners have already learned all their personal growth lessons in their 249 previous incarnations and have come here this time simply to fall in love, earn wads of cash together, drink absurdly expensive cocktails by their infinity pool overlooking Monte Carlo Harbour, and shag each other senseless while listening to any music other than Justin Bieber.

These two lovers' mutual practical and pragmatic earthiness is the key to their success.

The goal-oriented and competitive **8** will love that their equally pragmatic **4** partner understands and supports their need to go out into the world and win. And the more homely but equally professional and focused **4** will delight in their **8** lover's desire to create a strong and stable home for their family.

It doesn't matter if the masculine partner in their relationship is the **4** and the feminine partner is the **8**, or whether it's the other way around, these two well-grounded lovers will usually gladly give each other more than enough space to do their own thing without complaining that they don't spend enough quality time together.

The only real banana skin in this relationship could occur if one partner betrays the other's trust. Both numbers tend to be fiercely honest, and they demand the same in return. Plus, they both have excellent lie-detector minds, so if one decides to cheat on the other, they will be caught out and the fairytale will be over.

As long as they stay true, though, there is no reason why these two earthy lovers can't fly to the stars and back together. Good luck, stay honest… and relish the exquisite bliss of finding your "soulmate".

Friendship

For all the reasons above, these two friends will see eye-to-eye on almost every topic, leading them to forge a close and intimate connection. In fact, if they are not single but are sexually matched, they must be careful not to spend too much time together or else their friendship may threaten one or both of their relationships.

Providing clear barriers are drawn, these two BFFs can push each other to ever greater success. There's even a chance that they might decide to pool their resources, if their respective relationships are strong enough, and go into business together.

As we're about to see…

Business

When it comes to stamina and a capacity for sustained hard work, no one comes closer to the detail-focused and diligent **4** than the equally pragmatic **8**, which makes them perfect business partners.

Neither will feel the other is failing to pull their weight, and while the **8** wants to go out in pursuit of the Next Big Deal, the **4** has no

Life Path 8: The Achiever

such lofty needs and will happily run the business like clockwork while the **8** flexes their deal-making muscles.

As long as each acknowledges the other's efforts, and the spoils are shared evenly, this pairing has the potential to achieve great wealth in whatever enterprise they embark on together.

* * *

8 & 5
(Ambition and Freedom)

Love

Imagine you have a large, roofless cage in your garden. And in it you put a small lion, and an owl tethered to a tall wooden post.

The lion, being a proud little lion (as all lions tend to be, even the small ones), pads around the cage trying to look as brave and strong as it possibly can – and doing a pretty good job of it too, or so it thinks.

On the inside, though, the proud little lion is trembling with fear under the unblinking and decidedly unnerving gaze of the owl's piercing black eyes.

The owl, meanwhile, shakes the rope attached to its leg and flaps its huge wings in frustration as it stares down at the lion, wondering if it is really as frightened as it looks, or if it's going to suddenly climb up the post at any moment and eat it for breakfast.

The lion, of course, is the **8**, who wants nothing more than to be powerful enough to smash down the door of the cage and escape from this scary-looking bird, while the owl is the **5**, who wants nothing more than to be free of its chains and fly high into the sky, far from the jaws of the lion.

This is how these two numbers will probably feel should they meet, fall in love and begin a relationship together.

The freedom-loving **5** will definitely fear being caged by their new relationship... and they are, in fact in grave danger of being eaten alive by the much more powerful **8**.

Life Path 8: Relationship Choices

The normally Self-assured **8**, meanwhile, will be freaked out by the **5**'s ability to look straight through their tough façade – which fools pretty much everyone else – and see the frightened child within.

No one is more proud, and therefore more vulnerable, than the competitive and egotistical **8**. (Ego equals fear, remember.) In the normal course of their day-to-day life, the **8** is able to hide their deep-seated insecurities behind their impressive take-charge persona as they battle it out in the boardroom or on the sporting field, pursuing victory at all costs to satisfy the cravings of their ego.

But if one day they decide to open their heart to a flighty yet insightful **5**, they will real-eyes there is nowhere to hide from their partner's uncanny ability to read them like a nursery rhyme book. This can be the most unnerving experience for the Self-conscious **8**, while also the most wonderful opportunity to allow their lover to help them let go of their ego and step up to the higher ground of Self-love.

For their part, the **5** who falls for a powerful **8** will also be unnerved by their partner's single-minded ability to set a goal and focus on achieving it, such as a lion does when stalking its prey. The **5** yearns for freedom, but the hard work and discipline required to achieve it sit about as well with them as the proverbial princess on a pea.

If the **5** could see that the **8** knows the answer to all their problems – which is to stop flitting from one job to another and one relationship to another and learn that discipline and focus will give them the success, and therefore the freedom, they crave – the owl will discover that the lion is in fact a pussycat and they can live happily ever after.

Equally, if the **8** could see that the **5** knows the answer to all their problems – which is to real-eyes there is nothing to be afraid of once they step out of their ego and into their heart, where all the power of their love resides – the lion won't need to smash down the door. It will climb up the post and chew through the owl's rope, whereupon the owl will latch onto the lion's mane with its claws, flap its massive wings several times and then fly them both to freedom.

It doesn't really matter if these two mismatched lovers choose to stay together after that. If they do, they can enjoy an exciting relationship with plenty of adventures and a good deal of financial abundance. And if they decide to go their separate ways, they will be eternally grateful to each other for the life-changing lessons they shared.

Good luck, stay open and honest… and hopefully you will both sail happily through life together in a beautiful pea-green boat.

Friendship

Continuing with the owl and the lion theme, these two will most likely be drawn to each other when they first meet, the proud **8** liking the way the quick-witted **5** makes them roar with laughter, and the intelligent **5** appreciating the **8**'s compliments about their wisdom.

The (ahem!) mane problem, though, is that the **8** may tire of the **5**'s unreliability and its penchant for flying off into the night without a moment's notice, and the **5** may find it impossible to resist poking fun at the **8**'s puffed-up sense of pride, which really ruffles the **5**'s feathers.

The friendship may end around the time both real-eyes they have very little in common. About as much as a lion and an owl, in fact.

Business

OK. Down to business. No more animal jokes.

The resourceful **8** doesn't really need anyone to partner with. If they were to team up, it would be with an earthy **4**, or perhaps a "people person" **2** or **6**. I can tell you that it certainly wouldn't be with an unreliable and flighty **5**. And I ain't lion.

* * *

8 & 6
(Ambition and Romance)

Love

You know those Census articles in the newspaper, when they talk about the traditional "family unit" of two loved-up happy, healthy and wealthy adults who live in a nice home with four attractive children, complete with a photograph of said family all cuddled together on their plush velour sofa and grinning like Cheshire cats? Chances are those two loved-up adults are an Achiever **8** and a Visionary **6**, because this is one of the most family oriented and materially focused pairings.

Almost always, the masculine partner in the relationship (whether they be "male" or "female" in the birth gender sense) is the breadwinner **8**, and the feminine partner (again, it doesn't matter if they are "female" or "male") is the homemaker **6**. Both the material and career-focused **8** and the nurturing, family-focused **6** are feminine numbers. They are honest and hard-working, and they are able to set – and achieve – lofty goals for themselves, both individually and together as a couple.

When they meet, the perfectly groomed and elegant **6** will stand out from the crowd and catch the refined eye of the **8**, whose confidence and strength of character will in turn appeal to the **6**. This initial attraction will deepen when they start to discuss their dreams and goals and discover they dovetail almost perfectly.

Should they take it further and fall in love, these two will want to build a comfortable and often luxurious home for themselves, where kids will usually quickly follow – depending on their age and the timing of their meeting. Just as in nature, the earth of **8** will mix with the water of **6** to create abundant life – both in the form of children, and in the accumulation of considerable wealth.

In fact, these two are so compatible, it's almost like one of those 1960s American family sitcoms where everyone smiles at everyone else for 30 minutes once a week – giving you the distinct impression that after the credits roll and the cameras are turned off, this impossibly happy make-believe family goes on smiling at each other for the other 10,020 minutes of every week as well.

Of course, in real life nothing is ever perfect. Problems for these two can arise if the hard-working **8** spends too much time in the office away from home, or the possessive **6** makes too many demands on the **8** and cramps their executive lifestyle. But all should be well, providing the **8** tells the **6** how loved and appreciated they are every day (yes, the **6** needs almost constant reassurance) and makes regular quality time for their family, and the **6** curbs their neediness and gives the **8** all the freedom they need to go out and conquer the world.

Good luck, stay open and honest... and enjoy annoying everyone else by living a blissful family life and smiling all week long.

Friendship

These two can become great friends because they have so many core values and beliefs about life, money and family in common. In fact, if these two are single and are sexually matched, all it will take for their friendship to go to the next level is for either of them to make the first move – and before they can say "I do" they'll be buying a house, decorating the nursery and flicking through private school brochures over a breakfast of home-baked croissants, quails' eggs and fresh Columbian coffee served by their butler on the east terrace.

Business

The **8** seldom needs a business partner because they like to be in charge of every aspect of everything they do. However, if they were to partner up with a **6** they would benefit from the Visionary's equal capacity for hard work, as well as their almost superhuman ability to make everyone they work with feel validated, supported and properly motivated. Staff and customer relations are not the **8**'s strong suit, so the **6**'s nurturing and optimistic energy would be invaluable in keeping their buyers – and their workers – as happy as pigs in poop.

* * *

8 & 7
(Ambition and Understanding)

Love

Although **8** is a materially focused Life Path, concerned above all else with working through their personal and professional issues of power and abundance, they are also spiritual beings at their core, which gives them at least some common ground with the highly spiritual **7**, who is primarily focused on solving the big mysteries of life.

That having been said, the earthy and pushy **8** and the airy and intelligent **7** have about as much in common in terms of a romantic relationship as a bulldozer and a butterfly.

In business, as we'll see in a minute, the delicate insights of the truth-seeking **7** would be of great value to temper the egotistical "crash or crash through" mentality of the win-at-all-costs **8**. But in the much more sensitive arena of love, these two may struggle to find common ground due to their diametrically opposed approach to relationships.

The **8** has a tendency to want to control their partner, just as they want to control everyone else in their life. But the fiercely independent and free-thinking **7** hates to be controlled in any way. They need to feel free to fly away to their ivory tower to contemplate the meaning of life without being disturbed, and they may resent their **8** partner's attempts to exert their authority over them.

Similarly, the impulsive and Self-confident **8** will be hair-tearingly frustrated by the **7**'s need to think for hours – days even – before they leap into making even the smallest decision. Plus, the **8** will never in a million years understand the point of the **7** spending $60,000 to study for a degree in Theosophical Sectoral Dynamics in a Post-Apocalyptic World when they could be out there earning decent money.

Putting material concerns aside, these two intelligent lovers should be able to connect well on a spiritual level and enjoy lively (although probably heated) conversations about the big issues facing the world. Another quality they have in common is that beneath their markedly different exteriors, they both crave to love and be loved at the deepest level of their being.

If they can agree to give each other the space they need – the **8** to work and socialise, and the **7** to study in peace – then these two can forge a very strong, loving connection. There will always be problems socially, because the networking **8** needs to mix in high-powered circles while the **7** is usually uncomfortable around strangers. And there will definitely be regular verbal disagreements. But as long as the love and

Life Path 8: The Achiever

mutual respect is there, these two have much to teach each other about the core lesson of personal and spiritual growth – which is to conquer their fears and live blissfully and peacefully in love.

Good luck, stay open and honest... and enjoy the lessons about letting go of your ego that you both have to teach each other.

Friendship

There's not much common ground for these two to grow anything other than the most spindly and fragile of friendships. The deal-making and persuasive **8** loves to network and is comfortable in the company of strangers, while the introverted and solitary **7** prefers to shun the social whirl of cocktail parties in favour of the company of close, like-minded friends and colleagues.

Yes, they will both see eye to eye on many spiritual and political subjects and will enjoy conversing heatedly and at length on a wide variety of topics. But when the **8**'s material push comes to the **7**'s intellectual shove, they will more likely fight like cat and dog and go their separate ways. Sometimes, however, a lasting friendship can be forged in the fires of their passion for making a difference, with the **7** inspiring the **8** to use their power for the greater good, and the **8** urging the **7** to have the courage to teach their truth to a wide audience.

Business

Although most **8**s will choose to go into business for themselves so they can control every aspect of their enterprise (did I mention that all **8**s are chronic control freaks? Yes? Good), occasionally they will step down from their high money-making horse and real-eyes they could benefit from the input of a partner who can bring something new and valuable to the table.

In the case of the **7**, this would come in the form of insightful and considered spiritual wisdom to steer the egotistical but also spiritual **8** towards using their business acumen to create ethical enterprises that do more than just make money – they help to improve the lives of the disadvantaged and the downtrodden.

Life Path 8: Relationship Choices

When the goal-oriented but socially aware feminine **8** and the thoughtful and humanitarian masculine **7** come together, they have the potential to do something truly special. Think of Grace Kelly (**8**) teamed with Deepak Chopra (**7**), or Liza Minnelli (**8**) teamed with Winston Churchill (**7**), and you'll know what I'm talking about.

* * *

8 & 8
(Ambition and Strength)

Love

Twins are well-known to intuitively understand what the other is thinking and feeling at every moment of every day. In the case of two **8**s, these twins are probably thinking "How can I make money out of this?" and feeling "God, I hope no one can see through my facade and real-eyes I'm nowhere near as confident as I pretend to be."

This mutual material ambition, combined with an equally balanced deep-seated emotional insecurity, creates the possibility of a fantastically rewarding loving relationship – if only either of the two **8**s is prepared to go out on a limb and declare their undying love for the other.

All **8**s tend to be guarded with their emotions until their partner commits to them and makes them feel safe, whereupon they will open up and jump in with both feet. But if both wannabe lovers are as reticent as these two twins often are, there is a very real risk that neither of them will have the courage to make the first move, and what could have been a wonderful relationship may slip through their fingers.

At some point, one of these two externally proud but internally insecure lovers is going to have to put their cards on the table, push all their chips into the middle and gamble their heart on the belief that their partner feels the same way they do.

This will always be the hardest part of their relationship, because once two **8**s declare their love for each other, there is nothing stopping them from dancing through life together, creating fortunes, notching up career victories and building ever larger palaces in which they can live, love, laugh and raise a happy family together.

Forget Batman and Robin, these two powerful go-getters are the ultimate Dynamic Duo who can take on the world together and win, with each looking out for the other's back. Right from the start, they will be attracted to one another's confidence and personal power, while at the same time having a unique understanding about their partner's fear of being "good enough" that lurks beneath their confident facade – because they have the same fear themselves.

This couple must avoid falling into the egoic trap of competing with each other, which can quickly lead to fights and even divorce in their quest to be top dog. But as long as they recognise they are a team, and therefore each other's victories are the same as their own, there really is nothing these two goal-oriented lovers can't achieve together.

This will definitely be a passionate relationship, because both of these feminine energy numbers feel and express their emotions at the deepest level. But it is unlikely to be a particularly romantic one, for the simple reason that both **8**s are more concerned with feeding their highly developed egos with the material trappings of wealth and power, than with spending long, touchy-feely nights in front of the fire.

Good luck, stay open and honest… and enjoy the material success and mutual support this relationship can give you.

Friendship

Eight rhymes with ate, and these two friends will almost certainly share a passionate love of good food and fine wine. In fact, anything that makes these fiercely competitive Achievers feel like winners will appeal to their highly developed egos, including box seats at the theatre, a table by the window in the best restaurant in town, and upgrades to Fist Class when they fly to Greece to spend their summers in Santorini.

These two friends are so compatible in their mutual desire to experience the best life has to offer that they will delight in outdoing each other with their Instagram posts – one uploading a photo of themselves sipping orange mocha frappuccinos with Ben Stiller in LA,

Life Path 8: Relationship Choices

and the other sharing a selfie with Angelina Jolie by the pool at the Kandolhu Island Resort in the Maldives.

Business

This is not the best idea. In fact, as ideas go, the prospect of these two wannabe top dogs trying to suppress their Godzilla-size egos to partner up in an equal financial enterprise is more likely to end in tears and an expensive lawsuit than a John Grisham novel.

It's always advisable for the resourceful **8** to be in full control of their financial affairs, and therefore they should go into business by themselves. However, if they do insist on partnering up, they would do best to choose a pioneering **1**, a co-operative **2**, a creative **3**, a diligent **4** or a compassionate **6**.

But another ambitious, bossy and take-charge **8**? They'd be better off putting an angry lobster in their bathing costume and then trying to swim the English Channel with one arm tied behind their back.

* * *

8 & 9

(Ambition and Passion)

Love

The humanitarian **9** has lived all the Life Paths at least once and has come here this time to teach the world by example their evolved spiritual messages of peace and love. The materialistic **8**, on the other hand, has come here to work through their deep-seated issues of personal power – both in the positive as a generous benefactor, and in the negative as an insecure miser – and is focused on creating as much abundance as they can.

Viewed this way, it's hard to imagine two more divergent Life Paths, which is going to throw up all manner of challenges for this pairing in a romantic relationship, simply because their goals are so diametrically opposed to each other.

Life Path 8: The Achiever

The creative and artistic **9** wants a close, loving relationship almost as much as they want to travel the world teaching others about love as a free-spirited role model. The fact that the **8** will spend almost all their time working and prefers a partner who spends a lot of time at home looking after the domestic affairs won't sit well with them. And unless they are lucky enough to find one of the few creative **8**s out there, they will probably feel as misunderstood as they feel neglected.

For their part, the ambitious **8** wants a partner who is happy to give them all the room they need to pursue their career goals because they appreciate the luxuries of life and are happy to share in the spoils. But the **9** doesn't give a fig about money. And they certainly don't want to sit at home while their partner goes out and conquers the world. They need to be out there too, not conquering but teaching. So if the **8** is even the slightest bit insecure romantically, as most of them are, this could cause them to become not just jealous, but aggressively so.

Yes, these two advanced numbers have a few things in common, including their interest in metaphysics. But they are working with their spiritual energy in such different ways that the chances of them even falling in love in the first place are slimmer than Ariana Grande's waist. And even if they do, the odds of it lasting are even smaller.

Many times an attraction of opposites such as this contains a number of valuable lessons for each to learn from the other. But, unusually, these two highly evolved numbers really don't have all that much to teach each other in the romantic setting of a relationship.

The worldly **9** has probably already worked through their power issues before, and the **8** usually needs to learn their Life Path lessons the hard way for themselves.

For all these reasons, the **8** and the **9** would usually do best to remain friends. But if they do decide to give love a go, they must commit to each other with every fibre of their being, trust each other with their lives – and never, ever do anything to betray that trust.

If they can do this (and if you happen to be in this relationship as you read this, please take heart) then these two spiritual superheroes can not only rock each other's world, they can rock the whole world.

Life Path 8: Health Choices

Good luck, stay open and honest… and love each other with all your heart. Because if you can do this, the sky's the limit.

Friendship

Although these two may struggle in love, they can easily become the very best of friends. Free of the expectations of a relationship, the **9** can advise the materialistic **8** on the best ways to use their wealth and status for the greater good, and the **8** can guide, and maybe even fund, the **9**'s humanitarian efforts so they have the maximum impact.

Business

Although in a friendship these two can help each other perfectly, when it comes to money – and at the end of the day, businesses are all about the money – the **8** and the **9** will bump into all the same "issues" (a nice way of saying "blazing rows") that they would in a romantic relationship. Their core values and beliefs are just way too different to make this a harmonious business partnership.

* * *

4. HEALTH CHOICES

THE energetic and goal-oriented **8** will usually approach the challenge of physical health with the same single-minded determination to succeed that they bring to every other area of their life. Their capacity for hard work will pay dividends in the gym, although their love of the best things in life may well undo much of their good work when they gorge themselves on rich foods and fine wines at dinner time.

Most **8**s are blessed with strong physiques and robust digestive systems, which reflect both the strength of their resolve and their resilience to setbacks in their professional life. Plus, their competitive personality normally leads them to play at least one sport, and usually

Life Path 8: The Achiever

several, because they love the sensation of winning – whether it's on the football field or the tennis court, or in the boardroom.

When it comes to physical exercise, the competitive **8** does not do well on their own. Jogging and other solitary pursuits are never going to give them as much satisfaction as team sports, or working out with a close friend at the gym where they can push each other.

Many adult **8**s may struggle with their weight, simply because they are usually in a position to afford the finer things in life (and when I say "finer" I really mean "fattening"). And if they are in the corporate world, they must pay particular attention to their diet. All those long business lunches and evening cocktail parties can play havoc with their waistline, not to mention their blood pressure.

Ironically for the fine-dining **8**, they are best-suited to a vegetarian diet that puts as little strain on their digestive system as possible. This is because they expend so much energy in their day-to-day life as they fight to conquer the world that the food they eat needs to be as "clean" and healthy as possible.

If they are not working, the **8** needs regular strenuous exercise to burn off their excess energy. But if, like most **8**s, they are toiling round the clock to further their career, they must make sure they take plenty of time for relaxation. Massages, hot baths and plenty of uninterrupted sleep are truly the best medicine for the hyperactive Achiever.

Ailments to watch out for

Many **8**s are prone to experience quite serious joint problems later in life in the form of arthritis, rheumatism, gout and bursitis, which are physiological manifestations of their deep-seated lack of emotional flexibility. The more they can learn to relax and go with the flow, the less these ailments will bother them.

Other common afflictions include frequent headaches (stress), problems with their teeth (indecisiveness) and ears (refusal to listen to dissenting views), liver disorders (anger and frustration), high blood pressure (stress again) and even paralysis (fear).

Life Path 8: Health Choices

8s are so driven that any obstacle can manifest as a dis-ease, which is why it's vital they clear their emotional blockages to prevent illness.

Effective therapies

A balanced combination of strenuous physical exercise to burn off any excess energy and regular relaxation therapies such as massage and meditation will work best to keep the doctor from the **8**'s door.

Painting and music are excellent foils for their materialistic focus. Walking or jogging in nature (preferably in the morning) and interacting with animals will re-mind them of the value of beauty and tranquility. And they also need to experience the fulfilment that comes from giving and sharing, so volunteering at an animal shelter or at a children's charity can be beneficial for their overall sense of wellbeing.

Sometimes the **8** can become way too serious in their pursuit of success, so fun activities such as dancing, ice skating or even just watching a good comedy movie can work wonders in helping them to lighten up. Bascially, anything frivolous such as family charades, hide and seek with the kids or a visit to the funfair will help the goal-oriented **8** remember that we are here first and foremost to have fun and be happy, not to make more money than Rockefeller.

Diet choices

The goal here is to keep it simple and avoid fast foods. The always on-the-go **8** is known to treat food as fuel during their busy day, and they may simply grab the nearest and quickest thing to eat in a hurry so they can keep working. But sadly, the nearest and quickest thing is normally the least healthy.

A simple vegetarian diet is optimal for the **8**, but this is seldom practical because they will attend so many functions as part of their working day that they will find it impossible to resist the temptation of rich, fattening treats. As long as they keep them to a minimum, though, and watch their alcohol intake too, they should be fine.

The most beneficial foods for the **8** include plenty of fresh fruit and vegetables, grains, legumes, honey instead of sugar, herb teas (especially chamomile) and lots and lots of fresh, clean water.

* * *

5. CHOICES FOR CHILDREN

YOUNG children working with the energy of **8** will usually explore the negative energies of their Life Path Number before moving on to master the positive aspects. This is true of all the nine Life Paths because children need to first understand the boundaries of what is and isn't acceptable behaviour.

However, once their boundaries are in place – and your child has understood the crucial lesson of cause and effect – young **8**s can then start tapping into their natural strengths with the assistance of a positive parental guiding hand.

Children who work with the positive energy of **8** as their Life Path Number will usually be responsible, dedicated and resourceful from an early age. Their successes will seldom come easily to them, especially at school. But their willingness to work hard and put in the study time, combined with their ability to set clear goals for themselves and follow through on them, will normally be more than enough to ensure they do well in their exams and graduate with good grades.

At home, the young **8** will always want to have a say in the family's affairs and may even become a little bit bossy if they don't get their way. Parents would do well to remember that these are the future presidents, CEOs and entrepreneurs of the world and all they are doing is flexing their budding leadership muscles. They must teach their naturally dominant **8** child the value of teamwork and consultation, as well as the importance of humility, while at the same time making sure they don't stifle their natural flair for taking control of a situation.

Life Path 8: Choices for Children

Another positive quality that must be nurtured, while also making sure it doesn't get out of hand, is the persuasive **8** child's innate charisma and personal charm, which they can use to draw others to them. They will often have a wide circle of friends from a relatively early age, and it's not unusual for them to be the leader of their gang of friends, as well as captain of their school sports team.

The positive **8** will also happily involve themselves in money-making activities, such as Saturday jobs and newspaper rounds, and entrepreneurial activities should be encouraged. It pays to teach them the value of money early – and by that I mean the fact that money is only of value when we control it and share it, rather than hoard it and allow it to control us.

However, young **8**s need to learn from an early age that there is more to life than material success. Teach them the importance of sharing, loyalty, friendship and generosity. And explain that the beauty of having money – and the power that goes with it – is that it allows us to help those we care about and to create ethical businesses that give other people fulfilling jobs.

There are few negative qualities to trip up your **8** child because they are so naturally positive, popular and energetic. However, strong willpower can be a double-edged sword when it comes to children. In the positive, it drives them to succeed. But in the negative, it can make them rebellious and aggressive when they don't get their own way.

Providing the **8** child is taught the importance of thinking of the needs of others and not just about themselves, parents shouldn't have too much difficulty guiding them in the right direction. This is best done through plenty of interaction with other children as well as adults, so they learn early how to create a healthy balance in their lives between working hard and having fun.

Creative pursuits such as painting and music are excellent foils for the **8** child's practical personality. And make sure they understand the fulfillment that comes from giving and sharing with others. A visit to a children's hospital can be confronting for a young **8**, but it may be just the experience they need to make sure they walk the positive side

Life Path 8: The Achiever

of this Life Path as a philanthropist out to help others rather than an egotist out to help themselves.

Playtime activities

Socialising usually comes easily for young Achievers because they exude charisma and willpower and will delight in interacting with other like-minded children.

Sport is one excellent arena for them to flex their competitive muscles, and it will also allow them to learn the basics of leadership and teamwork. Many young **8**s are also extremely creative and will benefit from music lessons, drama and art classes, and writing exercises to help them express their inner feelings.

Most **8**s love the limelight and adore being the centre of attention, so they will relish any opportunity to perform on stage in school plays, local drama clubs and music recitals.

Rewards and recognition are also important for the **8**, so make sure they receive plenty of encouragement from an early age. They will delight in receiving pennants, cups and other trophies and they will usually display them prominently – and with great pride – in their bedroom.

* * *

Your child's three-digit Birth Code

As we have seen in Part Two, we always work primarily with the energy of our Life Path Number right from the outset, but in our childhood years from 0 to 18 we do so in conjunction with the energy of our first Supplementary Birth Number, and in our second 18 years – until we reach full emotional maturity at 36 – we do so in conjunction with the energy of our second Supplementary Birth Number.

It's worth reading the main listings here in Part Three for the numbers that make up your child's two Supplementary Birth Numbers to gain a better understanding of their positive and negative qualities.

Life Path 8: Choices for Children

Also, as you read about your child's Birth Code, real-eyes that the difference between "feeling the force" of any Life Path and flipping to the "dark side" is determined by the amount of Self-confidence we develop in our childhood years, and then the amount of Self-love we develop in our teenage years. That, in a nutshell (squirrel!), is your role as a parent: to instill in your child first Self-esteem, and then Self-love.

The 00/8 'Millennium' child

A Millennium Child born with this remarkably powerful Birth Code has come into the world with the potential to achieve something truly spectacular with their life. The doubly amplified presence of the two 0s means they will work solely with the supercharged abundant energy of **8** their entire life, right from when they take their first breath.

This gives them a unique capacity to amass significant wealth and power during their adult life. And if they follow the highest purpose of the **8** – which is to share our planet's abundance with those who need it the most – they have the potential to achieve a huge shift in the way we treat the less-fortunate members of society.

All the Millennium Children (those born at the beginning of this century with two 0s as their Supplementary Birth Numbers) are endowed with extra potential because they will all work with the energy of their Life Path Number with absolute focus and an incredible amount of commitment, as supplied by the amplifying power of their two 0s. (The Millennium Children are described in detail in Part Two.)

For the 00/**8**, however, their extremely rare Birth Code endows these Millennium Children with an unparalleled potential to generate enormous financial wealth, which they can use to spread their much-needed spiritual message of love and togetherness far and wide.

Before the start of this century, the last 00/**8** child was born on October 10, 1500, more than 500 years ago, but there are more coming soon, starting on January 3, 2020. Which is just as well, because we urgently need their help to wrest power from the greedy hands of the Fat Controllers and share the money around.

Life Path 8: The Achiever

Remember that every heightened chance of achievement in our Birth Code carries with it an equally heightened risk of disappointment, so these Millennium Children must never be made to feel pressured to live up to the extraordinary potential of their Life Path.

It's crucial that parents of a 00/**8** child do not allow them to feel even the slightest sense of responsibility or obligation. If all their Millennium Child does is learn to love themselves, and share their love with those they care about, they will achieve the highest purpose of all – which is to raise the loving vibration of the planet.

It is extremely likely that they will achieve much more than this, both materially and spiritually. But they must be free to choose their own life path, just like the rest of us.

The 17/8 child

The presence of a fire number (action) and an air number (thought) as their Supplementary Birth Numbers means these earthy and well-grounded children will have an excellent mix of courage (1), insight (7) and persistence (**8**) – the three qualities above all others that are needed to succeed in any venture they set their mind to.

For the first formative 18 years of their life, they will work with the supplementary take-charge energy of the Leader (1), which will help them develop the confidence to perform well during their school years and master the leadership skills they will need when they start to pursue their lofty career goals as they enter adulthood.

Then for their next 18 years, up until they reach full emotional maturity at the age of 36, they will invoke the spiritual and intellectual energy of 7, which will give them valuable insights into human nature and how the world works.

All the while their main work will be influenced by the earthy (practical) energy of **8**, but in their early childhood years they will be willing to take the lead in school projects and at home with their family and will be brimming with original and creative ideas (the energy of 1). They will then embark on their career with a clear understanding of what they want to achieve and they will have excellent problem-solving skills and an intuitive grasp of the big spiritual truths (the energy of 7).

As long as they clear their emotional blockages and work with the positive energy of their three Birth Code numbers, the 17/8 will enjoy much success, both financially and spiritually.

One word of caution, though: the lack of a water number (2 or 6) in their Birth Code means they may struggle with understanding and expressing their emotions as children and young adults, and they may become so focused on material and intellectual pursuits as they grow older that they could miss out on the joy of close, loving relationships.

Parents of these children must make sure they teach them that all the money in the world is no match for the exquisite pleasure to be found in loving someone completely and unconditionally with all their heart, and being loved completely and unconditionally in return.

The 26/8 child

These emotional young Achievers are polar opposites of their practical and intellectual 17/8 cousins because they have a double dose of water (emotion) in their two Supplementary Birth Numbers. This means that unlike the solitary and pioneering 17/8, which lacks any water numbers, the 26/8 will spend all their first 36 formative years working with the spiritual and material qualities of their Life Path Number **8** to bring people together (2) and spread their message of love far and wide (6).

Yes, they will still be largely focused on creating abundance and sharing it around, which is the highest purpose of the **8**, but they will do so in close co-operation with others (2) during their childhood years up until the age of 18, and then as they branch out on their own from 18 to full emotional maturity at 36 they will focus on helping others see their divine inner beauty and use any power and wealth they create to raise the loving vibration of the world.

In fact, these Achievers might shun the material calling of their Life Path Number **8** altogether and pursue a spiritual career devoted

Life Path 8: The Achiever

to being of service to others. Many nurses, priests, counsellors and spiritual healers are 26/**8** who have chosen to focus all their energy on developing the heightened spiritual wisdom of this Life Path.

As children, the co-operative energy of their first Supplementary Birth Number 2 will also drive them to forge close friendships at school and take an active part in family life at home.

One word of caution, though: the lack of a fire number (1 or 5) in their Birth Code means these children may sometimes get bogged down by their emotions, leading them to become overwhelmed and unsure of what action to take. Equally, the absence of an air number (3 or 7) could mean that when they do decide on a course of action, it might be taken on impulse and have dire consequences because they haven't taken the time to think it through properly.

Hopefully these issues won't arise too often because the **8** is a naturally resourceful and hard-working child, able to rise above any obstacles that are put in their way. And as long as they clear their emotional blockages and work with the positive energy of their three Birth Code numbers, the high-spirited 26/**8** will usually be able to enjoy great success at school and in all areas of their life.

The 35/8 child

Children born with this Birth Code have the potential to make a big impact on the world because they are working with their Life Path qualities of abundance and power (**8**) in conjunction with the creative and expressive energy of 3 during their first formative years, which will lead them to discover new and original ways to use their personal power (**8**) to help others on a grand scale.

Then as they reach adulthood at 18, they will invoke the rebellious and adventurous qualities of 5, which will drive them to tackle the forces of oppression head on, using their wealth and power to fight for the rights of those less fortunate than themselves.

As children, the supplementary energy of 3 (the Creative) will endow these young Achievers with an outgoing and artistic personality.

They will be popular, and they will also work hard (the energy of **8**) to achieve good grades. Success won't come easily, but their bubbly temperament and their never-say-die attitude will stand them in great stead for when they reach adulthood and branch out on their own.

As young adults, they may lack a certain amount of discipline (the negative energy of (5), but they will fight tooth and nail for what they believe in (positive 5) and will have an insatiable curiosity to travel the world and experience as many adventures as they can (positive 5).

One word of caution, though: the lack of a water number (2 or 6) in their Birth Code means they may struggle with understanding and expressing their emotions as children and young adults, and they may become so focused on material and creative pursuits as they grow older that they could miss out on the joy of close, loving relationships.

Parents must focus on teaching their 35/8 child the value of love and the need to invest just as much time and energy in their family as they do in their quest to change the world.

The 44/8 'Master Achiever' child

If you have not already done so, please read my comments in Chapter 8 of Part Two about what numerologists like to call Master Numbers – namely, those Life Path Numbers whose Supplementary Birth Numbers are the same. There are four possible Master Numbers in numerology: 11/2, 22/4, 33/6 and 44/8.

There is no doubt that having two identical Supplementary Birth Numbers helps children and young adults focus on developing the qualities of their Life Path Number during the first 36 years of their life. However, as we have seen time and time again, having a more balanced set of elemental Birth Code numbers can sometimes be preferable to working with the energy of just one or two elements.

The 44/8 child is unique among the Master Numbers in that all their numbers are governed by the practical and materialistic element of earth. This gives them a single-minded focus on creating wealth and power, but very little ability to do anything else. Of particular concern is the absence of any water numbers (2 or 6) in their Birth Code, which could lead them to bottle up their emotions.

In the positive, 44/8s will start from an early age to build a solid foundation for themselves, firmly rooted in the real world. As children they will be responsible and hard-working, usually performing well at school and enjoying a close circle of loyal friends. Then, as they hit 18 and strike out on their own, they will continue to work with the energy of 4 in conjunction with their equally pragmatic Life Path Number 8 to create an abundant life for themselves and their loved ones.

That is why 44/8s are known as Alchemists, because they have an almost Midas-like power to turn anything they touch into gold.

44/8s who do the required inner work have the capacity to amass great wealth and use it in positive ways. In fact, they have the potential to become powerful and generous philanthropists who are able to improve the lives of the poor and downtrodden on a wide scale.

As well as being wise old Selfs, young Alchemists are also loyal and dependable friends (the energy of 4). Not only can they metaphorically turn lead into gold, their friendships will be "solid gold" as well.

Where they may struggle, though, is in their ability to love, and to let love in, due to the lack of any water (emotion) energy in their all-earth Birth Code. So if your child is a supercharged 44/8 they must be taught two things: they must be taught that nothing is expected of them and there is absolutely no pressure to do something extraordinary with their life; and they must be taught that love is far more powerful – and much more rewarding – than all the money in all the world.

All that matters as they grow up is that they conquer their fears (ego) and learn to love themselves, which will empower them to love others. The mantra of the materially focused and spiritually attuned 8 is: "We are all in this together". But the mantra of the Alchemist is: "We create the most abundance in our life, and in the lives of others, when we truly love our Self… and allow our Self to love others too."

LIFE PATH 9:
The Teacher

1. Growth cycle: Final stage (the number of wisdom)
2. Influences: All four elements (balanced) and Mars (passion)
3. Positive qualities: Wise, understanding and aware
4. Negative potential: Insensitive, impatient and pushy
5. Highs and lows: Enlightened role model, or over-zealous fanatic
6. Highest purpose: Teacher of truth who spreads peace and love
7. Love matches: 1, 3, 6, 7, 9 for compatibility (the rest for growth)
8. Possible careers: Charitable work, the arts, media, health, law
9. Words to live by: "Love is all there is"

1. LIFE CHOICES FOR THE TEACHER

THE worldly and humanitarian **9** is the most evolved and insightful of all the numbers. These are the wise teachers at the end of a Spiritual Growth Cycle who take the experiences accumulated by all the previous eight Life Paths and integrate them into a clear message of divine truth and beauty, before we return to **1** again to start a brand new cycle.

This is not just the number of integration, it is also the number of integrity. Those working with the positive energy of **9** are not just here to teach the lessons of all the Life Paths, they are here to embody them as well – teaching not from behind a desk, but by example.

Because this Life Path is governed evenly by all four elements at once, those walking it tend to be well-rounded individuals who are able

Life Path 9: The Teacher

to strike a healthy balance of forceful action (fire), emotional maturity (water), material practicality (earth) and creative expression (air).

It's no surprise that Mars is the **9**'s guiding planet, because these Teachers are driven by a passionate urge to succeed in whatever they do and they will always fight for what they believe to be right. Although Mars was the god of war in traditional Roman mythology, the Romans viewed him not as a destroyer but as a creator of peace and order.

This is a masculine number. But as with the elements, the **9** has a healthy balance of masculine and feminine energy, which empowers them to make their mark in the world in a wide range of career paths.

Successful **9**s are found in all walks of life, from music (Elvis, Jimi Hendrix, Adele, Cher) to film (Harrison Ford, Morgan Freeman, Spike Lee), psychology (Carl Jung, Louise Hay), sport (Jack Nicklaus), aviation (Charles Lindbergh) and philanthropy (John D. Rockefeller) – to pick just a handful of outstanding examples.

Although this Life Path is called the Teacher, their highest calling has nothing to do with classrooms and rigid educational curriculums. We're talking about life lessons here, not the three Rs.

If you wanted a school teacher you would employ a **3**, a **6** or a **7**. The **9** is not here to teach us facts, but truths. Specifically, the emotional and spiritual truths they have learned in their many previous lifetimes. And they don't teach from textbooks, they teach by example – going out into the world to give freely of their time and wisdom.

To picture how an evolved humanitarian **9**'s Life Path might turn out, you need look no further than Mahatma Gandhi or Mother Teresa. Both are the epitome of the peaceful, calm and courageous **9**.

This is the Life Path where we tie up all the lessons of the eight-stage Spiritual Growth Cycle. It is the pinnacle of experience that can be reached only by learning the lessons of all the other eight numbers. It's also the number of nirvana – of arrival – because it manifests all the qualities of the numbers that have gone before it.

As we saw in Part Two, there is a unique power and purity about the number **9** that sets it apart from all the other eight numbers. If you

Life Path 9: Life Choices

divide any of the other single-digit numbers by 9 you get an unending string of that number:
– 1 divided by **9** equals 0.11111111111111111111111111 etc.
– 4 divided by **9** equals 0.44444444444444444444444444 etc.

Even more remarkably, when you multiply any number by 9, no matter how big it is, the number you get always adds up to 9. It is the only number that behaves in this way:
– 2 x **9** = 18 (1 + 8 = **9**)
– 14 x **9** = 126 (1 + 2 + 6 = **9**)

Now, try adding any single-digit number to **9**. The result you get reduces back to the original number. Again, no other number does this:
– 5 + **9** = 14 (1 + 4 = **5**)
– 8 + **9** = 17 (1 + 7 = **8**)

Spiritually, then, what **9** represents is heaven on earth. It is the number of bliss, paradise and never-ending perfection. In the Christian tradition, it is the number of the "final judgment", and the Hebrew Bible refers to **9** as the number of "Immutable Truth".

On a personal level, and from the point of view of the Self-Awareness System™, the number **9** represents the attainment of your goal, whatever your goal happens to be. It's the number of completion, and it is therefore also the number of death and rebirth.

There is only one place you can go after **9**, and that is back to the beginning – to **1** – to start the whole process again.

* * *

Highest purpose of The Teacher

The highest purpose of this most humanitarian of Life Paths is to be a role model for peace, love and truth and to fight for freedom and justice wherever they find oppression or discrimination.

No pressure!

Fortunately, everyone walking this Life Path is well-equipped to tackle this daunting task because they have already walked all the other

Life Path 9: The Teacher

eight Life Paths at least once. It's simply not possible for a young Self to incarnate as a fully integrated **9** and succeed in achieving this number's highest purpose unless they have already learned at least some of the lessons of leadership (**1**), co-operation (**2**), expression (**3**), stability (**4**), discipline (**5**), acceptance (**6**), trust (**7**) and karma (**8**).

That's why so many **9**s who work with the positive energy of their number – including relatively young **9**s – appear to be "old Selfs" who know far more about the ways of the world than their limited experience in this lifetime could possibly have taught them.

The key to the resourceful and wise **9**'s happiness lies in willingly embracing their exalted position and dedicating their life to improving the lives of others.

In doing so, they will also find their own fulfillment – as well as significant material success – thanks to their commanding yet compassionate nature that draws others to follow them.

Remember, the most important goal for all Life Paths is always the same: to first "wake up" to the truth that we are an extension of Source energy, and to help other people wake up as well. Then, and only then, will the path to our highest potential open up before us.

* * *

Key words are… 'confidence' and 'integrity'

To fulfill their life's highest purpose, **9**s must first learn to develop a robust inner confidence in their abilities.

Confidence is central to all the Life Paths as we embark on our journey from pure unaware love to pure conscious love. As we saw in Part One, developing a healthy Self-esteem is the first step towards Self-love we all must take. (If you've come straight to this Life Path listing and are wondering what a "Self" is, please try to find the time to read Part One because it's too complicated to explain again here.)

For the **9**, however, developing a strong sense of Self-confidence will determine whether they walk the positive Life Path of the inspiring

Life Path 9: Life Choices

role model who leads from the front, or veer down the negative path towards intolerance, arrogance and fanaticism.

All **9**s are here to teach by example, integrating what they know intuitively from their previous incarnations with what they learn in this lifetime. And when they work with the highest positive energy of this Life Path, they don't just speak their wisdom, they live it and embody it in everything they do.

Their central challenge, therefore, will always be developing enough confidence in their message and in themselves to step into the spotlight and shout out loud to the world: "Listen up, people, I have something to say!" If they fail to grow into their power and instead shrink back into their fear, the **9** can easily flip to the "dark side" of this number and become overly domineering and aggressive as they try to push their lessons onto other people instead of gently and lovingly teaching them by example.

In this they are their own worst enemy because their anger is never with the outside world, it is with themselves when they lack the courage and integrity to live their own truth and learn their own lessons.

This brings us to the second key word for the **9**… integrity. As one of the most inspirational and courageous **9**s who has ever lived, Mahatma Gandhi, is reported to have said (although there is some doubt as to whether these were his exact words): "Be the change you want to see in the world."

Gandhi was a **9** who certainly lived up to this core piece of advice that all Teachers would do well to follow, as illustrated by the famous story of the Mahatma and the little boy who ate too much sugar. (Again, there is some doubt as to whether this story is true, but it doesn't really matter because the crucial lesson for the **9** that it contains certainly is.)

Apparently, the mother of a young boy living in India in the 1930s was worried about how much sugar his son was eating. Despite her best efforts, she was unable to stop him so she decided to take him to see Gandhi, who was her son's idol, at the great man's ashram.

"Bapu (father), my son eats too much sugar and it's is not good for him," she said. "Would you please advise him to stop eating it?"

Gandhi thought for a moment and then told the woman to go away and come back in two weeks, when he would talk to her son. The woman was surprised, but did as she was asked.

Two weeks later, she reappeared with the boy at Gandhi's ashram. The great man bent down and said to her son: "Boy, you should stop eating sugar. It's not good for your health." The star-struck boy nodded and promised Gandhi that he would stop.

The mother was puzzled, though, and said: "Bapu, forgive me for asking, but why couldn't you have told him that two weeks ago?"

Gandhi replied: "Because two weeks ago I was eating sugar."

That's integrity.

***

Positive and negative potential

All Life Paths contain an equal measure of positive and negative potential. Our challenge in every lifetime, no matter our Life Path Number, is to nurture our positives and overcome our negatives.

The reason we are given negative potential as well as positive potential is because people usually respond more effectively to the threat of pain than they do to the promise of pleasure. Also, while it is admirable to do what we are good at in life, we will only ever become the best we can be by facing our "dark side" and digging deep into our Self to overcome the obstacles that appear on our path.

As we have already seen in Part Two, it is only when the chips are down and we are up against it that we find out who we truly are and what we are truly capable of doing.

For example, the wise and evolved **9** has a heightened capacity for teaching and healing, but they have an equally heightened potential for disappointment if they fail to do the necessary inner work to clear their fears and wrest their ego from the controls of their life.

Those who work with the positive humanitarian energy of **9** will live in accordance with spiritual law and dedicate their life to helping

Life Path 9: Life Choices

others. But those who work with the negative energy of this Life Path may become stuck in their ego and think they always know best. They may then try to impose their will on others, even when it's not welcome.

All **9**s have an unquenchable thirst for knowledge and experience. They like to be well-informed and they get along with almost everyone because of their innate ability to understand how people feel, which makes them adaptable, considerate and empathetic.

They are also endowed with the energy of all four of the elements, instead of just one, which gives them a unique ability to draw on the forces of fire (action), water (emotion), air (thoughtfulness) and earth (practicality) whenever they confront an obstacle in their path.

There is therefore nothing the well-rounded **9** cannot accomplish if they set their mind to it. They are usually early developers (fire) and remarkably in tune with the emotions of those around them (water). They are also level-headed and pragmatic (earth) and are blessed with a strong creative streak (air), which is why so many famous **9**s have made their mark in the arts, whether it be music, film or literature.

Having cycled through the other Life Paths at least once, the **9** has the potential to be a pioneering leader (the energy of **1**), an intuitive and open-hearted lover (**2**), an expressive and inspirational motivator (**3**), a reliable builder of friendships and financial stability (**4**), a brave and rebellious freedom fighter (**5**), a compassionate and idealistic romantic who holds aloft a radiant beacon of divine beauty for all mankind to follow (**6**), a thoughtful and diligent seeker of truth (**7**) and a powerful achiever who is able to manifest abundance, not just for themselves but for others as well (**8**).

This broad knowledge base gives the **9** a natural ability to take the lead in whatever they choose to do with their life. In fact, even shy **9**s may find themselves thrust into positions of leadership because of their open, honest and amiable personality that others want to emulate.

Now, if you're not a **9** and you happen to be reading this, I imagine that right about know you might be thinking "Hey, this isn't fair! How come **9**s get so much more positive potential than the rest of us?"

Life Path 9: The Teacher

The answer goes to the very heart of the always equitable Self-Awareness System™, which never favours one Life Path over another, because for every positive potential for health, wealth and happiness there is an equal negative potential for pain and disappointment.

In other words, no Life Path is ever better or worse than another. Some, like the influential **9** or the money-making **8**, might appear at first glance to have more chance of achieving material and spiritual success than, say, the loving but sensitive **2**, or the loyal but unambitious **4**. But who's to say that finding your one true love and sharing your hearts in a blissfully happy relationship (positive **2**), or creating a safe and harmonious home surrounded by close friends and enjoying radiant good health (positive **4**), isn't better than living in a huge mansion but being miserable, sick and lonely (negative **8**) or festering in a Self-pitying pool of tearful and angry resentment (negative **9**)?

Sadly, for as many wonderfully inspiring and successful **9**s who have been able to make a real difference in the world, there are just as many deflated and defeated Teachers who have crumbled under the crippling weight of expectation of this most challenging of Life Paths.

The biggest enemy of the **9** is a lack of Self-confidence. As we have already seen, if they fail to wrest their ego from the controls of their life and rise above their fear of "not being good enough" by going through their Dark Night of the Self (please read Part One, Chapter 6 if you don't know what this is), the **9** may try to impose their will on others aggressively, rather than teach them gently, and may therefore doom themselves to a life of Self-loathing and loneliness.

Other less-dramatic but still painful pitfalls for the **9** that lurk along their Life Path include the propensity for them to be badly hurt when people they are trying to help simply aren't ready to hear their message of love, and – in their fear and anger – lash out at them.

They can also suffer from what we here in Australia call "The Tall Poppy Syndrome", whereby cruel and jealous people go out of their way to cut successful people down at the knees simply because their own lives are so miserable. Social media trolls are the worst offenders,

Life Path 9: Life Choices

and the internet – for all its marvellous innovations – is singularly to blame for giving these cowards a voice.

The young **9** whose talents have propelled them into the limelight before their Self-confidence has had a chance to evolve sufficiently can be destroyed by this kind of disgraceful attack.

In truth, though, the **9** is such a positive Life Path that few will have to experience the pain of the dark side of this number. And even if they do, the answers are there in Part One to help them turn their life around. Plus, positive **9**s are supremely intelligent and adaptable, and their ability to understand and read people makes it relatively easy for them to avoid anger and aggression – and to quickly rise above them if they should come their way.

Most **9**s are so Self-assured, in fact, that when people see them in a shop, a restaurant or an airport, let's say, they think they work there!

* * *

On a personal level, **9**s tend to operate best when they have the close, loving support of an understanding partner who is happy to give them all the space they need to go out into the world and teach what they came here to teach, while always being there to pick them up and dust them off when they come home wounded and disillusioned.

Many **9**s will struggle to cope with the yawning gap between their rose-coloured, idealistic view of the world – and the people who live in it – and the painful reality that most of them are just not ready to hear the **9**'s uplifting messages of truth and beauty, and will react angrily if pushed. That's why having a safe and nurturing home, as well as a patient and understanding partner, is so important to help heal their wounds when they get hurt and rejected.

On the whole, though, the intuitive **9** gets on well with most people due to their ability to know what others are thinking and feeling. They are also knowledgeable and unusually well-informed, which allows them to converse easily with anyone on virtually any subject.

Life Path 9: The Teacher

Above all, **9**s exude an air of trustworthiness that will serve them well and pave the way for great spiritual, professional and material success in whatever field they choose. They also feel very strongly for those who are less fortunate than themselves and are driven by a deep inner desire to make things better.

In short, there is usually nothing a **9** cannot accomplish if they set clear goals and focus all their energy on achieving them.

* * *

Summary of the positives

This is arguably the most positive of all the Life Paths because those who walk it are at the end of a growth cycle and are therefore endowed with the wisdom and the experience of the other eight Life Paths that have come before.

They are also working with the energy of all four elements, rather than just one, giving them a well-rounded personality and a unique capacity to get the ball rolling (fire/action), work harmoniously with others to keep the ball rolling in the right direction (water/emotion), dream up new ways to decorate the ball to make it more appealing (air/creativity), and then wisely invest the money they make from selling the ball to some billionaire Russian oil tycoon so they can enjoy the fruits of their labours (earth/materialism).

The **9** is also charged with teaching the lessons of the previous eight Life Paths, and so they have a unique insight into the way the world works. This gives them the power to make a real difference in the lives of others and inspire them to be the best they can be.

Often this is achieved through one of the creative arts such as film, literature or music, which the creative and confident **9** will use to get their message of love out there to as wide an audience as possible. But sometimes the **9** will choose to make themselves the lesson, as in the case of those two splendidly congruent 20th century Teacher **9**s Mahatma Gandhi and Mother Teresa.

Life Path 9: Life Choices

Key positive words

Generous, considerate, wise, thoughtful, brave, insightful, well-rounded, observant, intuitive, humanitarian, creative, artistic, soulful, peaceful, inspirational, trustworthy, popular, knowledgeable, loving, congruent, evolved, powerful, influential, compassionate, empathetic, philanthropic, idealistic, resourceful, benevolent and altruistic.

* * *

Summary of the negatives

Because of the infallible equitability of the Self-Awareness System™, the **9** has a heightened potential for disappointment to match their heightened potential for success, making this at once the most positive of all the Life Paths and also the most vulnerable to pain should those walking it fail to shed their ego and operate from a place of love.

Whereas the Self-loving **9** is the most inspirational of teachers, the **9** who is fearful and egotistical (they are the same, remember) can be the most intolerant and arrogant of zealots, forcing their will on others rather than teaching by example.

Negative **9**s are not normally deliberately evil in the way a negative **5**, for example, can be (Hitler and Pol Pot were both negative **5**s). They mean well, but they have failed to learn the crucial difference between leading a horse gently to water, and forcing it to drink against its will.

Generally, when a **9** turns to the "dark side" of this Life Path, they suffer the consequences by feeling the pain of repeated failure and rejection from those they were trying to help.

Key negative words

Fanatical, intrusive, over-zealous, insensitive, bossy, indecisive, arrogant, overbearing, pushy, meddlesome, angry and frustrated.

* * *

Self-love is the difference

If you have read Part One, you will already know that your ability to walk the positive side of your Life Path, as opposed to the negative side, is determined by whether you have undertaken the two key stages of personal growth. Or, to put it another way, whether you have taken the two crucial first steps on the path to your life's highest purpose.

The first step towards living your Life Path in the positive is to develop Self-esteem (and if you're wondering what a "Self" is, please take the time to read Part One because it's way too complicated to explain again here). This feeling of inner confidence is essential because it allows you to tap into your innate strengths, which you will need if you are going to have any hope of overcoming the numerous obstacles on your path. Be aware, though, that on its own this first step is never enough, because Self-confidence and Self-esteem are still the work of the ego. The feeling of being "good enough" carries with it an implied sense of needing to be "better than".

So to reach your full potential and achieve your life's highest purpose, you must also take the second step – which is to rise above the egoic concept of Self-esteem and climb to the much higher ground of Self-love.

Loving your Self does not mean being "full of your Self". It means the opposite. It means being humble because you understand that you are the same as everyone else, no better and no worse.

Above all, it means you understand that we are all immortal spirits having a human experience, and therefore we are all, at our core, the same – pure love and pure Source energy. (The Source is also fully explained in Part One.)

We can see it easily in new-born babies because when we are born into physical form, and before our fear-based ego has had a chance to develop, we are all gorgeous, gurgling bundles of pure, exquisite love.

I am not suggesting you do this, but just imagine you were to place a new-born infant on the pavement of a crowded street and then stand back out of sight. Everyone – and I mean everyone – would stop and tend to it. And the reason they would do this is because, deep down, we all recognise pure love when we see it. We are drawn to it at the most basic level of our being because it is the most strikingly beautiful and compelling force on the planet.

But sadly, as we grow up and go out into the world, our ego takes over and we start to believe – usually during our teenage years – that our ego is who we are. It isn't. Love is who we are.

We are all pure love. We are all extensions of Source energy (or children of "God", whichever phrase you are more comfortable with).

If you can rise above the quasi-religious terminology, I can summarise the two steps like this: Self-esteem is about feeling "good enough", while Self-love is about feeling "God enough".

The reason why loving your Self is so important for your Life Path is because when you start to live your life from the perspective of being pure love, everything changes. Suddenly you understand that nothing "out there" in the material world can ever harm you in any way.

Equally, you real-eyes you don't need anything "out there" in the material world to make you feel happy – not the approval of others; no amount of money, fame and power; and not even the love of a good man or woman – because you have all the love you need right there in your own heart, and you can therefore relish the exquisite joy of loving everyone unconditionally without needing anything in return.

That is why Self-love is the secret to working with the positive energy of your Life Path Number. Because when you truly love your Self, the rocky mountain path you've been climbing suddenly becomes an express elevator ride all the way up to the summit of your bliss.

* * *

No Life Path is an island

Although your Life Path Number denotes the main issues you will focus on, you will always work to some degree with the energies of the other numbers as well to become a fully rounded Self.

Life Path 9: The Teacher

As a **9** your main work will be in the areas of wisdom and integrity, but you will also tackle the issues of Self-confidence (**1**), co-operation and balance (**2**), creative expression (**3**), stability and flexibility (**4**), freedom (**5**), acceptance (**6**), trust (**7**) and abundance and power (**8**).

It's therefore worth your while to read through the listings for the other Life Path Numbers when your time allows.

* * *

Qualities of your three-digit Birth Code

(Note: Please read the description in Part Two of how 0 operates in your three-digit Birth Code. Also, you can consult the main Life Path listings here in Part Three for each of your Supplementary Birth Numbers (the eight possible ones for the Teacher are 1, 2, 3, 4, 5, 6, 7 and 8) to give you a clearer understanding of how their qualities govern your early years.)

'Millennium Child' 00/9

A Millennium Child born with the remarkably powerful single-digit Birth Code of **9** has come into the world with the potential to achieve something truly spectacular with their life.

All the Millennium Children (those born at the beginning of this century without any Supplementary Birth Numbers) are endowed with extra potential because they will work with the energy of their Life Path Number with absolute focus and an incredible amount of commitment. (The qualities of the Millennium Children are described in Part Two.)

The doubly amplified presence of the two 0s in place of their two Supplementary Birth Numbers means they will work solely with the supercharged energy of **9** their entire life. This gives them a unique capacity to accumulate vast amounts of knowledge. And if they follow the highest purpose of the **9** – which is to raise the overall vibration of the planet by being a role model for love and peace – they have the potential to achieve a mass awakening among the billions of frightened Selfs who are still plugged into the Fear Matrix.

Life Path 9: Life Choices

The mantra of the **9**'s Life Path is "Love is all there is." This is the biggest "Big T" Truth of them all. As we saw in Part One, the entire universe and everything in it is made out of love energy. It came into being when the Source split in two, becoming in one glorious moment pure love ("God") and pure love energy (the universe).

Our mission as human beings, should we choose to accept it, is to learn that "God" is not separate from us… it IS us, and we are it, because we are all the same, and we are all love.

For the uniquely wise and aware 00/**9**, however, this rare Birth Code endows these Millennium Children with an unparallelled potential to create a wealth of knowledge and material success in their life, as well as in the lives of others.

The highest calling for the **9** is to first learn this lesson themselves by "waking up" to their divine nature, and then teach it to the world. It's not an easy mission, to be sure. But it's certainly not impossible, especially for these doubly focused Millennium Children.

Before the start of this century, the last 00/**9** child was born on October 10, 1600, more than 400 years ago, but there are more coming soon, starting on January 4, 2020. Which is just as well, because we urgently need their spiritual messages of love and peace as the dark forces of religious dogma blanket our world with fear.

Remember, though, that every heightened chance of achievement in our Birth Code carries with it an equally heightened risk of disappointment, so these Millennium Children must never be made to feel pressured to live up to the extraordinary potential of their Life Path.

(If this is your child's number, they will be aged between three and 17 as *Messages from Your Self* is published, so please flip forward to the Choices for Children section under this listing for the Achiever to find out more about their positive potential, and the negatives to avoid.)

18/9

All **9**s carry with them the residual awareness of having lived all the other Life Paths at least once. That's why this number is the only one governed by all four elements at the same time, so when they work

Life Path 9: The Teacher

with the elemental energy of their two Supplementary Birth Numbers – the first one for their early formative years up to 18, and the second one from 18 to full emotional maturity at 36 – they may experience the lessons they learn as more of a "remembering" than a "discovering".

In the case of the 18/**9**, the forceful fire energy of the Leader (1) during their childhood years will help them develop the confidence to perform well at school, as well as master the leadership skills they will need to stand out from the crowd and teach their lessons of love.

Then in their young adult years they will switch to working with the supplementary earth energy of the Achiever (8) to develop their personal power even further and create abundance in all areas of their life – emotionally and spiritually, as well as financially.

All the while, their primary focus will still be on amassing copious amounts of knowledge and sharing it with others, as determined by their Life Path energy of **9**. But they will do so with the benefit of added Self-confidence (1) and personal power (8), enabling them to take the lead in whatever they choose to do.

It's easy to see how the combination of the three most forcefully ambitious numbers in the Self-Awareness System™ – 1, 8 and **9** – empowers these Teachers with a remarkable potential to achieve great success. However, with great potential comes great responsibility, and by no means all 18/**9**s will find it easy to live up to the almost impossibly high expectations of this auspicious Birth Code.

Some may also have to learn their life lessons the hard way if they flip to the equally powerful negative potential of this Birth Code and become seduced by the "dark side of the Force" – ie, their fear and their ego (they are the same, remember). Their ego will grow fast and strong with the leadership energy of 1 during their childhood years and the equally powerful energy of 8 as a young adult, making it all the more challenging for them to "wake up" and discard it.

Also, the lack of any water numbers (2 or 6) means they could struggle with their romantic relationships because they will be relying solely on their Self's residual memory of the lessons they learned in their previous lives as an Intuitive **2** and a Visionary **6**.

Life Path 9: Life Choices

However, as long as they do the necessary inner work to rid themselves of their fears and work with the positive energy of their three Birth Code numbers, the 18/9 will achieve great success and enjoy the company of good friends and the respect of their peers.

27/9

As with the previous Birth Code, these Teachers will carry with them the residual awareness of having lived all the other Life Paths at least once. That's why this number is the only one governed by all four elements at the same time, so when they work with the elemental energy of their two Supplementary Birth Numbers – the first one for their early formative years up to 18, and the second one from 18 to full emotional maturity at 36 – they may experience the lessons they learn as more of a "remembering" than a "discovering".

In the case of the 27/9, the emotional water energy of the Intuitive (2) during their childhood years will help them express, process and understand their feelings and connect with others on a deep and empathetic level – both of which are invaluable qualities for a well-rounded role model whose highest purpose is to inspire others.

Then in their young adult years they will switch to working with the supplementary air energy of the Seeker (7), which will help them seek out and assimilate the Big T spiritual Truths about the world that they have come here to teach by example.

All the while, their primary focus will still be on amassing copious amounts of knowledge and sharing it with others, as determined by their Life Path energy of **9**. But they will do so with the benefit of a healthy emotional intelligence (2) as well as an insightful intellect (7), enabling them to teach their divine truths with a passion and clarity that really engages their audiences and commands a loyal following.

This healthy balance of emotion and intellect means there are fewer negative pitfalls to worry about than for the more dominant and forceful 18/**9**. But the absence of any practical earth numbers (4 or 8) could mean they will need to work especially hard to look after their finances because they will be relying solely on their Self's residual

Life Path 9: The Teacher

memory of the pragmatic lessons they learned in their previous lives as a Builder **4** and an Achiever **8**.

In fact, as they grow older and wiser, many 27/**9**s may shun the egoic trappings of the material world altogether in favour of a more spiritually focused life dedicated to helping others "wake up" to their divine loving perfection. Mother Teresa and Gandhi were both 27/**9**s who chose this Life Path, and many other 27/**9**s will do the same.

36/9

As with the previous Birth Codes, these Teachers will carry with them the residual awareness of having lived all the other Life Paths at least once. That's why this number is the only one governed by all four elements at the same time, so when they work with the elemental energy of their two Supplementary Birth Numbers – the first one for their early formative years up to 18, and the second one from 18 to full emotional maturity at 36 – they may experience the lessons they learn as more of a "remembering" than a "discovering".

In the case of the 36/**9**, the creative air energy of the (3) during their childhood years will help them express the feelings in their heart and develop their artistic talents in conjunction with the voracious knowledge-gathering appetite of their Life Path Number **9**.

Then in their young adult years, they will switch to working with the supplementary water energy of the (6), which will lead them to focus on holding a Utopian vision of a peaceful and loving world for the rest of us to follow, while also using their creativity to show others their divine inner beauty.

All the while, their primary focus will still be on amassing copious amounts of information and sharing it with others, as determined by their Life Path energy of **9**. But they will do so with the benefit of an artistic and expressive creativity (3) as well as an optimistic belief in the power of love (6), enabling them to teach their beautiful truths in original and inspirational ways to a wide audience.

Three stunningly beautiful and talented 36/**9**s who perfectly embody the creative and romantic qualities of this artistic Birth Code

Life Path 9: Life Choices

are Adele, Ariana Grande and Brigitte Bardot, all of whom have used their striking good looks and Source-given talent to inspire women all over the world to step into their feminine power.

As with their equally artistic 27/**9** cousins (Cher, Ray Charles, Morgan Freeman and Elvis Presley, to name just a few), the absence of any practical earth numbers (4 or 8) in this Birth Code could mean they will need to work especially hard to look after their finances and keep themselves well-grounded because they will be relying solely on their Self's residual memory of the pragmatic lessons they learned in their previous lives as a Builder **4** and an Achiever **8**.

However, as long as they do the necessary inner work to rid themselves of their fears and work with the positive energy of their three Birth Code numbers, the 36/**9** will enjoy great success in both their professional life and with their romantic relationships.

45/9

This is the highest three-digit Birth Code in the Self-Awareness System™. Although there are a few people who were born on dates that add up to 46, 47 and 48 (48 being the largest number and unique to those born on September 29, 1999), their numbers are added together to arrive at Supplementary Birth Numbers of 10, 11 and 12 respectively.

This means 45/**9** is also one of the rarest Birth Codes, along with the Millennium Children born at the start of the new century. None of the famous **9**s listed in the Appendices at the back of this book has this unusual set of numbers, and I have been unable to find anyone notable throughout history who does.

However, anyone born with this lofty Birth Code has a unique opportunity to right the wrongs of the world by working with the practical and disciplined earth energy of the Builder (4) in conjunction with the courageous and adventurous energy of the Rebel (5).

No one other than a 45/**9** has the benefit of this perfectly well-balanced and complementary set of Supplementary Birth Numbers, for without the courage and rebellious energy of 5, the cautious 4 would never have gumption to take on the Fat Controllers and battle the forces of oppression, just as without the discipline and commitment of 4, the impulsive 5 would rush around lunging at any Fat Controller who comes in sight – but giving up at the first sign of a setback because they lack the stamina for a sustained fight.

All the while, the 45/9's main focus will be on developing their Self-confidence and accumulating knowledge, as determined by the highest purpose of their **9** Life Path. But for the first formative 18 years they will also work with the energy of 4, which is concerned with issues of loyalty, honesty and stability and will likely drive them to study hard and succeed at school. Then from 18 to full emotional maturity at 36 they will start to tap in to the adventurous and rebellious "change energy" of 5, which will propel them to use their talents to make a real difference in the world.

The absence of any water numbers in a Birth Code is normally a cause for mild concern when it comes to romance, but in the case of the 45/**9**, the honesty and loyalty of their 4 and the fun-loving energy of their 5, combined with the intuitive emotional maturity of their Life Path **9**, gives them all the qualities they need to enjoy close, loving relationships that are based on a solid foundation of trust (4) and are also wildly adventurous and exciting (5).

As long as they do the necessary inner work to rid themselves of their fears and work with the positive energy of their three Birth Code numbers, there really is nothing the awake and aware 45/**9** can't achieve if they set their spectacularly resourceful mind to it.

* * *

2. CAREER AND BUSINESS CHOICES

OF all the Life Paths, the worldly and resourceful **9** can turn their hand to just about any career they choose and enjoy a great deal of success, making this more a matter of personal preference than anything else.

Life Path 9: Career Choices

As long as they are able to use their profession to raise the level of love in the world – which is the highest purpose of the Teacher – it really doesn't matter what they choose to do.

Most evolved **9**s are creative and confident performers – whether it be in the fields of music, dance or drama – and therefore will be drawn to the arts as being the perfect medium for them to teach their message of love and peace to a wide audience. Acting is second-nature to the **9**, who has lived all the Life Paths at least once before and so finds it easy to express the emotions of the characters they portray.

Their heightened sense of aesthetics also makes the **9** well-suited to careers in graphic design, interior decorating and architecture.

There is usually nothing a **9** can't do if they set their mind to it, and their generous, humanitarian nature means they will often take whatever money they make and give it away to help others who are less fortunate than themselves. One of the richest men who has ever lived, John D. Rockefeller, was also the most generous philanthropist who has ever lived. And he was a **9**.

Whatever career path they choose, the fiercely independent **9** will always demand a good deal of autonomy to do things their own way, so they will tend to stay away from anything that has too many rules and regulations. The stark, competitive world of commerce will not appeal to most professional **9**s, who will prefer the morally and intellectually challenging worlds of politics or the law for the cerebral stimulation they give them, as well as the opportunity to have a direct impact on the lives of the downtrodden and the disadvantaged.

This is also primarily a spiritual and compassionate Life Path, which will lead many **9**s to become healers, counsellors, doctors, surgeons and even priests and gurus, who will shun the materialistic concerns of the world altogether in order to teach their lessons of love and truth by example, which is the **9**'s highest calling.

Interestingly, for a Life Path that is called the Teacher, few **9**s will become teachers because our education systems are too restrictive for the humanitarian lessons they are here to share. Some will, though, and if they do they will always be the most popular teacher in their school.

Life Path 9: The Teacher

Beneficial career paths

People who are working with the humanitarian and role model energy of **9** make excellent actors, producers, directors, musicians, dancers, painters, writers, designers, journalists, broadcasters, politicians, lawyers, judges, architects, counsellors, nurses, doctors, surgeons, spiritual teachers, diplomats, sociologists, numerologists, astrologists, teachers, lecturers, professors, researchers, child protection agents, pharmacists, gardeners, horticulturalists, landscape designers, interior decorators and philanthropists.

Best business matches

Most **9**s would benefit from going into business by themselves because they are natural-born leaders who absolutely insist on being in full control of their own destiny.

They do work best when part of a team, though, and they should therefore try to assemble a coterie of close and trusted advisers who can look after the day-to-day running of the business and leave them free to focus on the big picture decisions.

They would be wise to employ a fiery and pioneering **1**, a co-operative and aware **2** or a loyal and diligent **4** as general manager to run the day-to-day operations of the business, because they will share the **9**'s humanitarian vision for the company while also being able to balance the books and put in the long hours that will be required to keep everything ticking over smoothly.

An equally courageous and inventive **5** would be perfect for the sales and marketing role, another **2** would be ideal for human resources and staff morale, a **7** or another **9** could handle the special projects, providing they are given enough autonomy, and a creative **3** would be ideal as their assistant-cum-special adviser.

The materialistic and power-hungry **8** should probably be avoided, unless they are evolved, to prevent conflicts from arising, as should the controlling and meddlesome **6**, for the same reason.

* * *

3. RELATIONSHIP CHOICES

ONE of the most rewarding aspects about the Self-Awareness System™ is how equitable it is. Each Life Path offers the same opportunities for happiness and fulfillment, albeit in markedly different ways. And each of them also offers the same amount of challenges to force us to grow, although again in very different ways.

This means no Life Path is any "better" or "worse" than any of the others. All of them have their blessings, and all have their obstacles.

In the case of **9**, the blessings centre around their adaptability and emotional wisdom, which stand them in good stead when it comes to romantic relationships, and their obstacles show up as insecurity and Self-doubt, which can cause them to lash out at those closest to them when they feel vulnerable or exposed.

Most deeply romantic **9**s are so desperate to feel the bliss of a close and mutually supportive loving connection that they often jump into a relationship too quickly before they have really had a chance to think it through… only to discover that their partner isn't who they thought they were. It will pay them to resist declaring their undying love at their first dinner date before the waiter has even taken their order, and instead wait to get to know the beautiful or handsome object of their affections before leaping in with both feet.

I say "beautiful" and "handsome" because the **9** sees the best in people right from the start. Everyone to them is exquisite and perfect, right up to the point when they prove them wrong, which is always a painful letdown for the eternally optimistic **9**.

Just as caution is the better part of valour, the enthusiastic **9** needs to learn that patience is by far the better part of falling in love. Plus, of course, everyone is always going to put their best foot forward on the first and second date, so we can never hope to glimpse a person's true character until we have taken the time to get to know them well.

Once in a relationship, the **9** makes the most understanding of lovers because they have already experienced all the other Life Paths at least once, which gives them a unique insight into how their partner

Life Path 9: The Teacher

is feeling. They also tend to be extremely generous with their time and their affections. And providing they have done the inner work to release their fears, they are usually willing and able to share the deepest part of themselves – which is absolutely as deep as it gets.

But if they have failed to clear their emotional blockages, or if their partner gives them even the slightest reason to doubt they are safe, they can shut down quicker than one of those anti-bandit screens in a bank. And once you lose a **9**'s trust, it is difficult, if not impossible, to ever get it back again. They will simply move on, eternally optimistic that their "one true love" is out there somewhere waiting for them.

This is a mistake, however, and the **9** must learn there is no such thing as "the one". Relationships are not about finding our so-called soulmate and living out our lives together in rose-tinted bliss, walking along the beach during a never-ending sunset and holding hands while pretty young Italian violinists play Pachelbel's Canon in D major under fuchsia-coloured silk awnings shaped like peacock feathers.

This is the stuff of Hollywood fantasy, and **9**s need to get real and understand that relationships are all about growth and showing each other the areas we need to work on in ourselves, so running away only means they will have to face the exact same issue with their next lover.

When they do settle down, **9**s make excellent partners and parents for their children. They delight in intimacy and will share all their dreams and desires with their partner, just as they will revel in the chance to teach all they know to their little bundles of joy as they grow up. And, as with every other area of their life, they will teach them not with textbooks and periodic tables, but by setting a shining example of what it means to live as pure love… pure Source energy.

* * *

Sex drive of the 9

In the bedroom, the passionate **9** usually flits between being open and adventurous and closed and cautious, depending on how safe and supported they feel with their partner.

Life Path 9: Relationship Choices

This is the most aware and emotionally attuned of the nine Life Paths because the **9** is working with the energy of all four elements, having experienced the other numbers at least once. But their intuitive awareness of how their partner is feeling can be a double-edged sword.

On the one hand, it endows them with a unique ability to know what their lover wants and needs, while on the other hand they also know the moment their partner is not feeling exactly how the **9** might want them to feel. And that can cause them to shut down out of some misplaced sense of insecurity or inadequacy, making them appear cold.

The **9** needs to open up to receiving the same pleasure from their lover that they like to give to them, so it's not a one-way street. Yes, it might be better to give than receive... but by not receiving, they are denying their lover the same joy of giving that they cherish so much.

For the "feminine energy" **9** in a relationship, whether she happens to be the female or male partner in the traditional birth gender sense, this inability to receive can make her lover doubt whether he is able to make her truly happy and satisfied sexually, which can lead to all sorts of insecurities and even aggressive behaviour on the part of the masculine partner if it is not resolved quickly.

And for the "masculine energy" **9** in a relationship, whether he happens to be male or female in the traditional birth gender sense, his inability to allow his feminine partner to seduce him and reciprocate his generous gifts can lead her to doubt whether he truly loves her.

In either situation, this can lead to serious problems in the relationship – which would be such a shame, because all the **9** has to do is let their partner love them as much as they love their partner.

I know this sounds simple, but for the **9** it can be a big step. It's a step they must take, however, if they are going to enjoy a fulfilling sex life and a long and happy relationship together.

* * *

The compatibility listings that follow will help humanitarian **9**s get the most out of their relationships, whether it's with someone they

Life Path 9: The Teacher

love, a friend or a business partner. You will notice that the thoughtful and idealistic **9**, which is governed by the energy of all four elements, is able to find much in common with all the Life Path Numbers, but is especially well-suited to the air (thought) energy of **3** and **7**, as well as the nurturing energy of **6**, and other well-balanced **9**s. The fire energy of **1** is a match, but the brash **5** can sometimes be too extreme for the **9**'s refined sensibilities. The earthy **4** and **8** can tend to be too set in their ways, and the neediness of the watery **2** may cramp their style.

However, what appears to match you best on the surface may not be what you need in your life right now. All relationships are designed to help us grow along our Life Path. Yes, of course we enjoy the companionship, close connection, sexual intimacy and deep love that relationships give us. But that is now why we have them.

The reason we choose a partner is because they are a mirror in which we see our shortcomings and strengths reflected back at us through their shortcomings and strengths.

That is why opposites so often attract, especially in love.

I have written an entire book on this subject called *Leap into Love* which goes into the way relationships work in our lives in great detail. But for now, please real-eyes that when your partner presses one of your buttons, they are doing so not to "piss you off" but because your Self is using them to show you the areas you need to work on.

If you fail to understand this is the main reason why you attracted them into your life in the first place, you will fight each other and may eventually break up. And you will believe their faults were exactly that – their faults – rather than yours reflected back at you.

Worst of all, you will then take the unchanged you with you to your next relationship, and – lo and behold! – exactly the same issues will come up again.

If this sounds familiar. If you have ever asked any of these questions – "Why does this always happen to me?" or "Why do all men cheat?" or "Why are all women so demanding?" or whatever it is for you – then now you know why. It's because you didn't learn from your last partner, so of course your new one will do the same thing.

Life Path 9: Relationship Choices

And this will continue to happen, relationship after relationship, until you real-eyes it is meant to be happening to show you what areas you need to work on in your Self to change and grow.

* * *

One final quick point before we get into it: I need to stress that I disagree with almost every numerologist I know who likes to label relationships "a natural fit", "a neutral fit" or "an unnatural fit", depending on the compatibility of the numbers of the two partners.

All relationships are challenging. That is why we have them, as we have just seen. Yes, sometimes we might choose a partner who is "just like us" for the sake of harmony, but that could be regarded as a cop out if we are truly serious about our personal and spiritual growth.

If you are on a spiritual growth path in this lifetime (and there is no doubt in my mind that you are if you made it through Part One without throwing it in the bin!), then your Self will choose your relationships for you – and they will always be with a partner who will challenge you to grow in exactly the ways you need to grow.

Just because you might discover your current partner has a Life Path Number that doesn't dovetail perfectly with yours, don't fall into the trap of thinking there must be something wrong – or worse, end it with them so you can go out with someone with a "better" number.

Where you are right now on your Life Path is exactly where you are meant to be, and who you are with is exactly who you are meant to be with. So please let these listings help you to look for the lessons in your relationship, rather than look for the door.

And if you are single at the moment, try to remain open-hearted about your next relationship. It doesn't matter what Life Path Number they have, so don't "cherry pick". All that matters is you follow your heart and be open to learning the lessons they can teach you. After all, that's the reason you will attract them into your life in the first place.

* * *

Life Path 9: The Teacher

9 & 1
(Passion and Independence)

Love

This pairing has great potential to forge a close, loving and lasting relationship, full of adventure, laughter and happiness.

No other number can captivate the normally career-focused **1**'s heart as easily as the vivacious, generous and optimistic **9**. Their love of life and sunny personality will feed the **1**'s need for a partner who is as independent as they are.

At the same time, the **9**'s inner strength and emotional maturity will help them cope with long periods apart while the **1** pursues their career-focused goals – and all they will need in return is a regular phone call or text telling them how much they mean to their Leader lover.

During the times they are together, and providing both partners have done the necessary inner work to quiet their egos, these two lovebirds will laugh and make love like teenagers. Sex is almost always passionate, intimate and adventurous.

And during their times apart – there will be many as the humanitarian **9** shares themselves freely with friends and family in need, and the **1** pursues their business interests – they will delight in planning their next fun time together.

One word of warning: the **9** is so passionate and generous that they will freely give the **1** all the time and space they need – but only on the unspoken condition that they never lose the deep, intimate connection with their lover. Intimacy is paramount to the **9**, and as long as they always know they are the most important person in the **1**'s life, all will be well. But if they feel they are being taken advantage of, they will shut down and withdraw into their shell.

1s must ensure their adoring **9** always knows they are the most important thing in their life. This usually requires nothing more than a loving phone call or a small token of appreciation now and then in the form of a gift. And on the very rare occasion when the **9** does ask for attention, the **1** absolutely must stop whatever they are doing (and fly home if necessary) to give them the intimacy they need.

It's a very small price to pay for the years and years of selfless support, love and freedom the **9** is only too happy to give their **1** partner... with this one very small proviso.

Remember that when disagreements arise (and they will because all relationships are about growth, as we saw earlier), take the time to sit down and figure out what you are meant to be learning from your partner – then kiss them and thank them for the lesson.

Good luck, stay open and honest... and enjoy the adventures and laughter this exciting relationship can give you.

Friendship

Usually, a **9** and a **1** who forge a close, trusting friendship will stay friends for life. As we saw just now in the context of a romantic relationship, both come to the table with only one expectation each: for the **1** it's the desire for a friend who is not needy, and for the **9** it is for a friend who never takes advantage of their limitless generosity.

Providing both these needs are met – and the **1** remembers to always acknowledge the **9**'s generosity and never take advantage of their giving nature, while the **9** always remembers not to cramp the **1** or make them feel guilty about their ambitious nature – these two naturally optimistic lovers of life can become great friends.

I would even go so far as to suggest they consider teaming up and starting a business. And if their sexualities match, they might even hop into bed and get married because there is little these two numbers can't achieve better together than they can on their own.

Business

As we have just seen in friendship, the **9** and the **1** can also work extremely well together in a business context. The usual provisos apply, namely that the **1** will need to feel they are in charge and the **9** will need to give the **1** all the space they require to pursue new opportunities where they find them.

In return, the **9** will need to feel appreciated and always kept in the loop. They will also need the freedom to pursue their own (usually charitable) projects that will form part of the business but will be their own responsibility for them to run as they see fit.

Where the charitable **9** can sometimes be too generous, the more ambitious **1** will keep the business coffers filling up. And where the blunt **1** can sometimes put customers' and suppliers' noses out of joint, the always diplomatic **9** can step in to smooth things over.

* * *

9 & 2
(Passion and Co-operation)

Love

Because the evolved **9** has walked all the Life Paths before and is therefore working with the energy of all four elements at once, they are usually able to enjoy long, romantic and fulfilling relationships with every number. If there is one that's going to throw up more than its fair share of challenges, however, it's the **2**.

The always compassionate Intuitive is a co-operative and deeply caring Self who works best in close, intimate relationships, which is fine up to a point because the **9** loves intimacy too. But while the **2** wants to share all their love with their partner, the humanitarian **9** wants to share their love with the whole world. Yes, they will love the **2** – but not to the exclusion of everyone else.

This can cause problems if the **2**, who dislikes being alone, hasn't done the necessary inner work to avoid being needy and co-dependent should they feel their **9** partner isn't showing them enough attention. The **9** has come here for a specific reason – and that is to share their gifts with the world. If they feel their partner is stifling them or holding them back, they will quickly grow resentful and cold towards them.

One of two things will then happen. The disconsolate **9** will either shrink back into their shell and behave so badly that the **2** will

Life Path 9: Relationship Choices

eventually break up with them, thus setting them free. Or, if they are more courageous, they will simply walk out the door themselves.

This can easily be avoided by the **2** giving the **9** the space they need to fulfill their life's highest purpose of teaching and loving as many people as they can. The **2** will then be delighted to find the **9** showers them with all the love – if not the time together – that they crave.

Equally, the **9** must make a concerted effort to make time for their **2** partner and never stop telling them how much they are loved. Regular romantic weekends away together and surprise gifts work wonders to let the **2** know they are the most important person in the **9**'s life.

Good luck, stay open and honest... and enjoy the beautiful intimacy this deeply emotional relationship can give you both.

Friendship

The ebullient **9** can pretty much make friends with anyone and everyone they meet. They are working with all the four elements, which allows them to connect with a wide variety of people – from fiery and passionate **1**s to earthy and materialistic **8**s. The one element they can sometimes struggle with, though, is water because while the **9** is a deeply emotional number, they are not overly gushy or romantic.

These friends will usually have very different views of the world because the **9** is focused on spreading themselves far and wide, while the **2** likes to stay close to their home and their family. Yes, they will have much in common to talk about, but they are unlikely to be best friends simply because their lifestyles and core values don't match.

Business

While their differences may pose a serious challenge in love and friendship, in business the **9** and the **2** can work well together. The co-operative **2** will be happy for the **9** to take the lead, as long as they are appreciated for all they do, and the **9** will love the **2**'s upbeat energy and the fact they share the **9**'s lofty vision for a better world.

* * *

Life Path 9: The Teacher

9 & 3
(Passion and Expression)

Love

Throughout this book, and indeed throughout all my books, I talk about the important role romantic relationships play in our personal and spiritual growth. That is why even the so-called "incompatible" relationships in the Self-Awareness System™ are so valuable – because we will always attract at least one partner into our life to teach us the valuable life lessons we need to learn to grow along our Life Path.

Occasionally, though, a relationship comes along with someone who is so like us and so well-matched in all the crucial areas that we immediately shut down all our internet match-making profiles, pluck out our roving eye, put a huge sign on our front door saying "SOLD! OFF THE MARKET!" and dance our lives away together in a soulmate samba of such twinkle-toed delight that, by comparison, even Fred Astaire and Ginger Rogers at their very best would look like two flat-footed walruses fighting over a fish.

This is one of those. Right from the start, when these two first meet, there will be an instant attraction as the socially charming **9** and the effervescent **3** strike up a scintillating conversation about their latest creative project. Both are naturally artistic and outgoing, both share a common love of the limelight, and both want a partner who they know won't cramp their style in any way.

Once these two lovers commit, they can enjoy a wonderfully passionate roller-coaster ride through life as they explore the world together, party together, entertain together, create fantastic art together and grow old together – while all the while giving each other all the space they need to do their own thing.

Problems can really only arise if they fail to share the limelight, because both these numbers love to perform and absolutely adore being the centre of attention. They must make sure they allow each other to shine so this doesn't become an area of conflict and jealousy.

That having been said, there is normally nothing that will prevent these two lovers of life from acting out all their romantic fantasies and growing old and happy together. They will both almost certainly have worked through their growth lessons in previous relationships, which is what has freed them to find this blissfully compatible connection.

Good luck, stay open and honest, remember to share the limelight… and enjoy every single moment of your glorious time together.

Friendship

These two perfectly matched numbers won't be just BFFs, they'll be BBFITWBWs – Best Bloody Friends In The Whole Bloody World. They will have so much in common, in fact, that they must be wary of upsetting their respective partners by rabbiting on too much about how wonderfully inventive X is, or how creative and original Y is.

As with relationships, problems can arise for these friends if they become jealous of each other's success and try to hog the limelight. The **9** must celebrate the **3**'s triumphs, even when their own lives aren't going so well, and support their friend rather than compete with them.

Business

The **9** and the **3** will likely work just as well in business together as they do in love and friendship. This is a case of the whole being more than the sum of its two parts, with both pushing the other to achieve far more success than they could on their own. Again, make sure you share the limelight and the praise… and watch the money roll in

* * *

<u>9 & 4</u>
(Passion and Stability)

Love

One numerologist I know has this to say about a **9** and a **4**: "These two have next to nothing in common. Not recommended for any kind

Life Path 9: The Teacher

of interaction, let alone a relationship." While this is definitely a bit harsh, and misses the crucial point that even the most incompatible of relationships is always worthwhile for the lessons we can learn from them, it does a pretty good job of warning that this pairing will always be more about growth than anything else.

Providing that both partners real-eyes their love for each other is based on helping each other to change and grow, rather than validating each other's faults and failings, then this can be one of the most important relationships in their lives. Sure, their time together won't be all beer and skittles, let alone champagne and lawn tennis, but it will be ultimately rewarding and well worth the effort.

Let's list the differences between these two numbers, and then look for the lessons contained in them.

Above all, the **9** is a social number who wants to mix with as wide a circle of friends and strangers as they can. They have come here to teach their messages of love and truth by example, not from behind a desk, so they need to go out into the world and give freely of their time and energy. The **4**, on the other hand, despises the superficiality of the social whirl and chooses instead to spend their time at home, or in the company of close, like-minded friends.

The **9** wants passion and fireworks and expresses their emotions freely, while the often reticent **4** wants stability and companionship.

The **9** hates to be told what to do, while the **4** can be as controlling of their partner as they are of everything else in their life.

The **9** is impatient and wants to have it all now, while the **4** wants to build their home and their relationship from the ground up.

The list goes on and on, but you get the idea. The point is that in every difference lurks a valuable lesson for both partners.

The social **9** is often hurt by superficial people taking advantage of them and would be wise to adopt some of the **4**'s skepticism, while the conservative **4** needs to get out more and learn to have fun.

The emotional **9** frequently gets burned by wearing their heart on their sleeve and would benefit from some of the **4**'s caution, while the reserved **4** could do with being more passionate and adventurous.

Life Path 9: Relationship Choices

The headstrong **9** doesn't take advice well, often to their detriment, while the often controlling **4** needs to learn to live and let live.

The impatient **9** can suffer from financial hardship and emotional rejection when they try to overreach themselves and would do well to take their time and plan properly, while the conservative **4** sometimes takes far too long to make up their mind and misses out on all manner of business and romantic opportunities.

So, yes, on the surface my numerologist friend is right – these two do have virtually nothing in common. But that is precisely why this could be the most valuable relationship of both their lives if they are open to learning from each other.

Good luck, stay open and honest… and if fights break out (they probably will) try to look past your differences and see the lessons.

Friendship

As with a loving relationship, this is definitely a case of opposites attracting. Outside their shared humanitarian views, the confident **9** and the cautious **4** have such different tastes, values and personalities that it's hard to imagine them taking the time to get to know each other unless they find themselves stuck in a lift together for at least 10 hours.

Which is a shame, because these two have so much to teach each other… IF they could see beyond the 731 things that annoy them.

That's one big-assed "if", though.

Business

There are only so many ways to say this, but I'm going to try to come up with as many as I can to make sure the message is crystal clear: No, definitely not, never in a million years, no way Jose, uh-uh, are you serious? are you kidding? are you nuts? what part of "no" don't you understand? I could say "yes" but I'd be lying, nope, nein, negative, negatory, not on your nelly, not on your life – and my favourite (thank you, Austin Powers): "How about NO, you crazy Dutch bastard!"

* * *

9 & 5
(Passion and Freedom)

Love

These two feisty and passionate lovers of life – who are always on the go and require almost constant stimulation to maintain their interest – can certainly make sparks fly when they get together. The trouble is, before the sparks have had a chance to ignite the bonfire of their love, one or both of them will probably have already moved on somewhere else and to someone new.

The **9** and the **5** have much in common, not least their tendency to be in a constant state of flux in all areas of their life. In this regard, they are perfectly matched. No one other than a **5** fully understands the **9**'s need to uproot and go travelling at the drop of a hat, and no one other than a **9** can cope as well with the mercurial **5**'s rapid changes of mind and their need for variety.

If they do meet and fall in love they will certainly never be bored or stuck for conversation because both have a wide range of interests and share a common lust for adventure. No, the challenge won't be falling in love, it will be staying in love unless both are able to find the time to nurture their relationship in their crazy-busy lives.

Committing to anything for than more than five minutes is never easy for the unpredictable **5**. And while the **9** is better at making a commitment and sticking to it, they still like to know they are free to do whatever they want, whenever they want.

For this reason, the **9** will be instantly attracted to the idea of a relationship with a **5**, who will be only too happy to give them all the freedom they need – as long as they get it back in return.

And therein lies the rub. When neither partner values the other one more than they value their freedom to be apart from them, the point of being in the relationship becomes harder and harder to justify. In some ways, they might be better off just being friends. Or, if the physical attraction is there, maybe friends with benefits.

Life Path 9: Relationship Choices

The only way this pairing is really going to work in the long-term (and work spectacularly well, I might add) is if they have both reached a point in their lives when they feel they have sown all the euphemistic oats they need to sow and climbed all the metaphorical mountains they need to climb and are ready to "settle down" with their slippers, a good book, a couple of golden retrievers and a nice cup of tea by the fire.

Until then, short, romantic flings and steamy, passionate affairs will be much more their cup of tea – or, to be more accurate, their bucket of cocktails by the pool of their five-star waterfront hotel.

Good luck, stay open and honest, make sure you have plenty of hangover cures in the medicine cabinet ... and enjoy it while it lasts.

Friendship

Talk about a match made in heaven. This is a perfect match of two like-minded party people that isn't just made in heaven – it's carefully hand-crafted on Cloud Nine by a team of highly skilled angels whose lives have been dedicated to studying the fine art of having fun.

Not even "God" could have created such a boisterous friendship if he had kicked back in his banana chair on the evening of the fifth day and downed a bottle of tequila and half a pound of Bolivian blow.

These two should never go into business together, unless they want to do all their dough in the first six months. And they will struggle to stay together as lovers, unless they are old enough and wise enough to put their partying days behind them. But as friends? Oh, yes.

This is definitely going to work!

Business

For all the reasons we have just seen, the **9** would be better off partnering up in their business venture with Russell Brand (a typical 32/**5**) for all the work they'll get done. Their loan from the bank will last about 10 minutes, and the company will go belly-up faster than a lapdog with an itchy tummy.

* * *

Life Path 9: The Teacher

9 & 6
(Passion and Romance)

Love

Interestingly, although a relationship with a watery **2** poses some considerable challenges for the globe-trotting **9** due to the **2**'s need for quality time together almost every single day, the equally watery **6** can be a good match for the social and ambitious **9** because they are more than happy to be left alone to their own devices.

Whereas the **2** dislikes being alone and will struggle to cope with the **9**'s need to spend long periods away from home, the independent **6** has so much going on in their own life that they won't mind the time apart – as long as they get regular phone calls and texts from their **9** partner assuring them how loved and appreciated they are.

Both the **9** and the **6** are passionately spiritual and will find a lot of common ground in their values and beliefs. The **9** has come here to teach their message of love by example, while the highest purpose of the **6** is to hold aloft a vision of mankind's divine beauty.

They dovetail perfectly. And even though the **6** is happiest at home where they can look after their loved ones, while the social **9** needs to go out into the world, these two will find it easy to support each other's different needs because they share a common goal.

Plus, the hard-working **6** is only ever truly happy and content when they are showered with heaps of love and gratitude for all they do (and they do a lot). This is never a problem for the effusive **9**, who wants nothing more than to be able to love their partner with all their being and will never tire of expressing their appreciation for their **6**.

In fact, many numbers find the spiritually evolved **9** too much to handle because they know in their hearts they can never hope to match the depth of the **9**'s passion. Not so the Visionary **6**, whose very reason for living is to show the world that we are all infinite, immortal and unbounded loving beings. They will therefore delight in finally finding someone who can love them as deeply as they can love them back.

Life Path 9: Relationship Choices

One word of caution: if the **6** should feel in any way insecure or unappreciated, they can tend to flip to the dark side of their Life Path and become both meddlesome and controlling – which is going to make the **9** run faster than a rat up Usain Bolt's drainpipe. But this will only happen if the **9** commits the cardinal sin of all relationships and takes their partner for granted. And if they're dumb enough to do that, then they really don't deserve the love of the **6**'s big, beautiful heart.

Good luck, stay open and honest… and enjoy the deep, romantic and passionate connection this relationship can give you.

Friendship

For this friendship to move beyond the "Yeah, I really like them but they can be a little bit full on" stage, these two will have to pluck up the courage to fully open up their hearts to each other and risk revealing their darkest fears, as well as their deepest desires.

Within the dreamy, loved-up context of post-sex pillow talk that a relationship provides, this is as easy as it is essential for these highly emotional numbers to feel they have fully connected with each other. But over a couple of beers and a game of pool on a Friday night, it's another matter altogether. ("It's another matter!" I hear you all shout at once. Sorry, that was a *Flying High* joke.)

Don't worry. The **9**'s heart will be perfectly safe with a loyal and compassionate **6**, and vice versa, and the rich friendship they create will likely last a lifetime.

Business

Their shared vision for a better world make the **9** and the **6** just as well-suited for business as they are for love and friendship.

Challenges will arise if their respective roles aren't clearly defined because both these numbers like to be in control. For best results, the **9** should take overall responsibility for the direction of the company and the nurturing **6** should look after staff and customer morale.

* * *

9 & 7
(Passion and Understanding)

Love

Just as with the **3**, the other air number in the Self-Awareness System™, the spiritually focused **7** has so much in common with the equally spiritual **9** that these two dreamers will probably fall head over heels in love – complete with cute little Bambi-style tweety birds circling around their heads – before the barman has even brought them their second drink on their first date.

They won't be able to keep their hands – or their lips – off each other. And they should probably warn their friends, when inviting them over for dinner, to bring a bucket, because their incessant oochy-koochy smoochy-smoochy canoodling will make everyone within 10 miles of them physically sick.

It's ironic, isn't it, that we all want the luvvyduvvy dream, but when we come across two people who have actually found it and aren't afraid to show it, we feel the urge to either throw up or punch them in the head. Ah, jealousy! The monster whose eye is the same colour as the contents of the bucket.

In all seriousness, this is one of the most rewarding partnerships for the **9** because, like them, the **7** is not afraid to declare their undying love and jump in the deep end with both feet... and fully clothed to boot. These two want nothing more than to find someone who is sufficiently evolved spiritually and emotionally to accept the depth of their love, and return it just as passionately.

Well, actually that's not strictly accurate because both the independent **9** and the solitary **7** value their time alone just as highly. And when they discover that the love of their life understands this need too... well, that's why their friends need the bucket, because if someone gave you your cake and then fed it to you naked on a silk-sheeted four-poster bed, you would be so ecstatically grateful you wouldn't be able to stop kissing and hugging them either.

Life Path 9: Relationship Choices

Not to burst this Bambi bubble, but it's worth pointing out that this idyllic relationship – in which both partners are happy to trust the other to have plenty of space – would end about as well as the Disney film if either of them betrayed that trust. Infidelity is never good, but for these two doe-eyed dears it would be a curtain-dropper for sure.

Good luck, stay open and honest, enjoy this blissfully loving and liberating connection… and for Source's sake, don't stuff it up!

Friendship

These two open-hearted and broad-minded numbers can become fantastically close and understanding companions who support each other through thick and thin and enjoy a lifelong friendship.

Providing, of course, they are not sexually compatible.

If they are, there's a very real chance they might be tempted to turn this into something altogether more horizontal – even if they are already in love with someone else. If this is the case, they would be advised to take one of three courses of action: 1) Fall in love and live happily ever after; 2) Walk away because they can't trust themselves and they don't want to ruin the relationships they have; 3) Pack their underpants with ice every time they catch up for a coffee.

These two can definitely be BFFs thanks to their common values and beliefs. Whether they also become BFBs is another matter and a choice I leave up to them. (What? Oh, I see. Well… what if I tell you the first word is the same, and the last word is "Buddies"?)

Business

As with a friendship, this could go either way depending on their sexual compatibility. There's no doubt the **9**, who needs to be in control, would welcome the wise counsel of the intelligent **7**, and the solitary **7** would be happy to let the **9** run things and hog the limelight. So, on the surface, this is an excellent business match. But if there's also an attraction, the BFB thing could be an issue here as well.

* * *

9 & 8
(Passion and Ambition)

Love

The humanitarian **9** has lived all the Life Paths at least once and has come here this time to teach the world by example their evolved spiritual messages of peace and love.

The materialistic **8**, on the other hand, has come here to work through their deep-seated issues of personal power – both in the positive as a generous benefactor, and in the negative as an insecure miser – and is focused on creating as much abundance as they can.

Viewed this way, it's hard to imagine two more divergent Life Paths, which is going to throw up all manner of challenges for this pairing in a romantic relationship, simply because their goals are so diametrically opposed to each other.

The creative and artistic **9** wants a close, loving relationship almost as much as they want to travel the world teaching others about love as a free-spirited role model. The fact that the **8** will spend almost all their time working and prefers a partner who spends a lot of time at home looking after the domestic affairs won't sit well with them. And unless they are lucky enough to find one of the few creative **8**s out there, they will probably feel as misunderstood as they feel neglected.

For their part, the ambitious **8** wants a partner who is happy to give them all the room they need to pursue their career goals because they appreciate the luxuries of life and are happy to share in the spoils. But the **9** doesn't give a fig about money. And they certainly don't want to sit at home while their partner goes out and conquers the world. They need to be out there too, not conquering but teaching. So if the **8** is even the slightest bit insecure romantically, as most of them are, this could cause them to become not just jealous, but aggressively so.

Yes, these two advanced numbers have a few things in common, including their interest in metaphysics. But they are working with their spiritual energy in such different ways that the chances of them even falling in love in the first place are slimmer than Gisele Bundchen's waist. And even if they do, the odds of it lasting are even smaller.

Many times an attraction of opposites such as this contains a number of valuable lessons for each to learn from the other. But, unusually, these two highly evolved numbers really don't have all that much to teach each other in the romantic setting of a relationship. The **9** has already worked through their power issues before, and the **8** needs to learn their Life Path lessons the hard way for themselves.

For all these reasons, the **9** and the **8** would usually do best to remain friends. But if they do decide to give love a go, they must commit to each other with every fibre of their being, trust each other with their lives – and never, ever do anything to betray that trust.

If they can do this (and if you happen to be in this relationship as you read this, please take heart) then these two spiritual superheroes can not only rock each other's world, they can rock the whole world.

Good luck, stay open and honest... and love each other with all your heart. Because if you can do this, the sky's the limit.

Friendship

Although these two may struggle in love, they can easily become the very best of friends. Free of the expectations of a relationship, the **9** can advise the materialistic **8** on the best ways to use their wealth and status for the greater good, and the **8** can guide, and maybe even fund, the **9**'s humanitarian efforts so they have the maximum impact.

Business

Although in a friendship these two can help each other perfectly, when it comes to money – and at the end of the day, businesses are all about the money – the **9** and the **8** will bump into all the same "issues" (a nice way of saying "blazing rows") that they would in a romantic relationship. Their core values and beliefs are just way too different for this to be a harmonious business partnership.

* * *

Life Path 9: The Teacher

<u>9 & 9</u>
(Passion and More Passion)

Love

As we have already seen, the evolved **9** is such a well-balanced old Self – because they have lived all the other Life Paths at least once and are working with the energy of all four of the elements – that they can enjoy close, loving relationships with almost all the other numbers, with just one challenging exception.

Their heightened spiritual intelligence and artistic creativity makes them a wonderful match for both the air Life Paths – the expressive **3** and the insightful **7**. And all the rest, with the notable exception of **8**, can teach them essential personal growth lessons that are invaluable in helping them achieve their life's highest purpose.

But if the passionate **9** really want to knock their socks off (and as long as they don't mind the occasional fiery argument) they will look no further than another equally evolved and splendidly humanitarian **9** to fall in love with.

These two creative and aware Teachers share the common goal of becoming spiritual role models who can help as many people as possible unplug from the Matrix and live in love, rather than fear.

They will support each other's burning desire to make a difference in the world. They will match each other artistically. And, above all, they will love each other with a depth of passion that only a **9** is capable of giving, and only another **9** is capable of receiving.

In fact, their connection has the potential to become so strong that they may seldom be satisfied with just being lovers and will want to be best friends and business partners too.

On the downside (there's always a downside, sorry), they are so alike that they may find themselves treading on each other's toes and fighting over petty issues as a result. But if they learn even the most rudimentary conflict avoidance and resolution skills available in any NLP book, their fights can be kept to a minimum. And when fights do happen, they will always turn into spectacular and furniture-breaking make-up sex faster than one of them can say "F... you!" and the other one can reply "F... me!"

Good luck, stay open and honest… and make sure you save enough money to buy new bedroom furniture because you're going to need it!

Friendship

Just as in love, these two Teachers have so much in common that if they meet in a social setting (and they absolutely love social settings), they will likely forge an instant friendship, borne of their mutual desire to help other people and their well-matched artistic tastes.

As with some other numbers who are so alike, two **9** twins who are sexually compatible but already in committed relationships with other people must be careful to draw very clear boundaries around their friendship to avoid upsetting their respective partners.

As we saw in the Love listing above, all **9**s who fall for each other will invariably be one another's best friend, and will often start up a business together too.

I'm not saying it's not possible to remain just friends, especially if there is no physical attraction, in which case it's not an issue. I'm just pointing out this is such a perfect match that if two **9**s are compatible in a sexual sense, they would be wise to "have the conversation" and then proceed with caution.

Business

At first glance, two **9**s who share a common vision for a business could be tempted to pool their talents and resources. But this might be a mistake. They will be so alike in their goals and abilities that conflicts could quickly arise, even if their respective roles are clearly defined.

I would say this: if you're in a loving relationship and want to work together too, go for it because you will be able to resolve your conflicts. But if you're not, don't. You may end up falling out, which will be costly.

* * *

Life Path 9: The Teacher

4. HEALTH CHOICES

THE compassionate and Self-sacrificing **9** is usually so concerned with looking after everyone else in their life that they can easily forget to look after themselves as well, leading to all manner of physical and emotional health challenges.

In between picking up the pieces of other people's lives and disseminating good advice to all and sundry, the always considerate **9** must take the time to look after themselves – especially as they tend to project such a powerful energy of strength and Self-sufficiency that others seldom think twice about turning to them for help in a crisis, and in the process draining them of their valuable energy.

Add to this the **9**'s deep-seated dislike of ever asking for help, even when they need it desperately, and you can see why the doctors' surgery waiting rooms are often littered with broken and battered **9**s suffering from exhaustion, stress and overwhelm.

Cardiovascular exercise is essential to maintain their overall physical health and avoid weight gain, which can sometimes be an issue for the gourmand **9**, who loves good food and fine wines. In fact, alcohol is one of the worst poisons they can put in their body. It's not great for anyone, but for the **9** it can be catastrophic.

Many **9**s who fail to clear their emotional blockages and let go of their fears can show signs of an addictive personality, leading them to seek release in alcohol and drugs as they try desperately to numb their highly advanced and sensitive feelings. You've only got to look at the list of famous artistic **9**s in the Appendices at the back of this book to see the tragic result of this inability to manage their state of mind.

Jimi Hendrix, perhaps the greatest guitarist who ever lived, died of drugs at the age of just 27.

Ray Charles battled heroin addiction for many years, and his friends said it had a worse impact on his life than losing his sight.

Kurt Cobain, one of the most influential rock musicians of his generation, was also a heroin addict who allegedly killed himself (his Self) with a shotgun, although mystery still surrounds his death.

And Elvis Presley, universally regarded as the king of popular music, battled obesity, drugs and alcohol up until his untimely death.

All these **9**s had one thing in common: they were unable to handle their fame, release their ego and conquer their fears. Which is why it's so important for all **9**s to wake up to their divine spiritual nature and rise above the deadly trap of their ego's need to be separate and afraid.

As would-be role models for divine truth, which is the highest purpose of the **9** Life Path, this is not just the key to their happiness, it is also the key to their physical health – and their very survival too.

Ailments to watch out for

Many **9**s are prone to experience problems with their immune system (failure to set clear boundaries), borne of their propensity to do too much for other people without looking after themselves. They can also suffer from all kinds of fevers (anger) if they fail to clear their emotional blockages and become resentful that they are always doing more for others than others do for them.

It's not uncommon for **9**s to experience a lot of loss in their life, whether it's the death of loved ones and pets, or the end of friendships and relationships. This is an unavoidable result of their Life Path as a role-model teacher of truth, because they would not be as effective in helping others with their pain if they hadn't experienced it themselves.

But the effects on their physical body can be traumatic, including respiratory issues (inability to let life in), throat ailments (suppressed emotions and stifled creativity), liver problems (anger at their lot in life) and trouble with their neck and their shoulders (the oppressive burden of responsibility).

Effective therapies

Lots of morning walks in nature will do wonders for the **9**'s peace of mind, as well as re-minding them what's important in life – which is to live in harmony with the world we find our Self in.

Regular strenuous (sweat-breaking) exercise to strengthen their heart for the challenges of their Life Path is also essential, as is plenty of relaxation and deep, uninterrupted sleep.

Hyperactive **9**s will benefit from massage, Reiki and other gentle "physical touch" therapies that will take them out of their head and put them back in touch with their physical body. Even a quick visit to one of those 10-minute neck and shoulder massage places you see in shopping malls will help to relieve the tension that many **9**s experience because they feel they are carrying the weight of the whole world.

Diet choices

All **9**s must guard against eating too many rich or greasy foods and drinking too much alcohol, which are dangerously toxic to their already over-burdened immune system. They should also try to stay away from hot, spicy dishes that can overheat their metabolism, causing reflux, indigestion and other stomach disorders.

Garlic is excellent for boosting their weak immune system and preventing colds and fevers, particularly in the winter months. Nettle is also good for strengthening the **9**'s immune system, either as a side vegetable with a meal or in a broth.

And because **9**s are governed by the red planet of Mars, all foods that are red in colour should be consumed freely, including red peppers, strawberries, raspberries, cranberries, red apples, red grapes, rhubarb and red cabbage.

* * *

5. CHOICES FOR CHILDREN

YOUNG children working with the energy of **9** will usually explore the negative energies of their Life Path Number before moving on to

Life Path 9: Choices for Children

master the positive aspects. This is true of all the nine Life Paths because children need to first understand the boundaries of what is and isn't acceptable behaviour.

However, once their boundaries are in place – and your child has understood the crucial lesson of cause and effect – young **9**s can then start tapping into their natural strengths with the assistance of a positive parental guiding hand.

Children working with the positive energy of **9** have a thirst for knowledge and absorb information like a sponge. They are usually quirky and quite different to children with other Life Paths, but they get on well with most of them due to their intuitive ability to know what others are feeling, which makes them adaptable, considerate and empathetic. They are often regarded as "old Selfs" because their innate spiritual and emotional wisdom belies their lack of experience.

From a very early age, **9** children tend to be social and make friends easily. Their magnetism draws people to them, and even shy **9**s may find themselves thrust into positions of leadership because of their open and amiable personality.

Young **9** children can be early developers. If they are academically minded, they will often shoot straight to the top of their class. And if they are more interested in sport, they will probably captain every team they play in, even if they are not the best player.

Because of their inquisitive young minds, the **9**'s parents would do well to enroll them in a wide variety of classes and activities and give them plenty of space to study and learn from books, computers and the TV. They are also creative and possess a strong inclination for the arts. School plays, amateur dramatics, music recitals and the like are perfect outlets that allow them to perform on a stage.

Most young **9**s love to be the centre of attention. But if they are a little shy, they need all the help they can get to develop the confidence required to stand up in front of a crowd, which is essential to achieve their life's highest purpose of teaching others by example.

Parents need to watch out for the potential negative qualities of this Life Path, including a tendency for young **9**s to get a little bit of a big head if they find themselves easily outperforming other children at school. Also, the **9** child is often so concerned with helping others with no thought of their own needs that they can get badly hurt when another child takes advantage of their generous nature.

9 children can also tend to be quite rebellious at school, and at home. They are intelligent, quick-witted and adaptable, and their ability to understand and read people – including their parents and teachers – makes it easy for them to get away with all sorts of mischief.

Also, many **9** children are determined and strong-willed, which can quickly flip into stubbornness and disobedience if it's not handled properly. And they tend to find it difficult to let go of things, such as the loss of a pet or a friendship, so they may need help in this area too.

Playtime activities

9 children do well in group activities and will usually prefer team sports to solo ones. They also make excellent debaters, often able to argue rings round much older children. Above all they love games and pastimes where they are able to help others do well. These outlets for their energy are crucial for a young **9**'s development so they learn early on that when they help others to win, they win too.

Creative pursuits such as painting, music and dance are another area where **9** children usually perform well because most of them are naturally artistic and in tune with the beauty of the world around them.

Acting usually comes easily to the **9** child from an early age, thanks to their love of the limelight and their innate understanding of the emotions of the characters they are portraying.

* * *

Your child's three-digit Birth Code

As we have seen in Part Two, we always work primarily with the energy of our Life Path Number right from the outset, but in our childhood years from 0 to 18 we do so in conjunction with the energy

Life Path 9: Choices for Children

of our first Supplementary Birth Number, and in our second 18 years – until we reach full emotional maturity at 36 – we do so in conjunction with the energy of our second Supplementary Birth Number.

It's worth taking the time to read the main listings here in Part Three for the numbers that make up your child's two Supplementary Birth Numbers, so you can gain a better understanding of their positive and negative qualities.

Also, as you read about your child's three-digit Birth Code, real-eyes that the difference between "feeling the force" of any Life Path and flipping to the "dark side" is determined by the amount of Self-confidence we develop in our childhood years, and then the amount of Self-love we develop in our teenage years.

That, in a nutshell (squirrel!), is your role as a parent: to instill in your child first Self-esteem, and then Self-love.

The 00/9 'Millennium' Child

As we saw earlier in the Life Choices section of this listing, a Millennium Child born with this remarkably powerful Birth Code has come into the world with the potential to achieve something truly spectacular with their life. The doubly amplified presence of their two 0s means they will be working solely with the supercharged energy of **9** their entire life, right from when they take their first breath.

This gives them a unique capacity to accumulate vast amounts of knowledge from an early age, making them not only more likely to be successful in their school work but also able to understand and process the deep emotions they are feeling with a surprising maturity as they enter their challenging teenage years.

All the Millennium Children (those born at the beginning of this century with two 0s as their Supplementary Birth Numbers) are endowed with extra potential because they will all work with the energy of their Life Path Number with absolute focus and an incredible amount of commitment, as supplied by the amplifying power of their two 0s. (The Millennium Children are described in detail in Part Two.)

Life Path 9: The Teacher

For the <u>00</u>/**9**, however, their rare Birth Code endows these Millennium Children with an unparallelled potential to take on a leadership role both at school and among their friends, and to develop the confidence in themselves and their abilities that is so essential for their Life Path as a role model and teacher of truth.

Before the start of this century, the last <u>00</u>/**9** child was born on October 10, 1600, more than 400 years ago, but there are more coming soon, starting on January 4, 2020. Which is just as well, because we urgently need their spiritual messages of love and peace.

Parents of these children must guard against them becoming arrogant and superior when they discover how much more evolved they are than the other children they study and play with. They need to be taught from an early age that even though the qualities of their Life Path Number give them a clearer understanding of many issues, both spiritually and intellectually, this does not mean they are "better" than other children… merely different.

Parents must also remember that every heightened chance of achievement in a child's Birth Code carries with it an equally heightened risk of disappointment, so these Millennium Children must never be made to feel pressured to live up to the extraordinary potential of their Life Path. Yes, they truly do have a gift, but this can easily be made to feel like a burden – especially is they feel they never really fit in with other children, as often happens with young **9**s.

The <u>18</u>/9 child

All **9** children carry with them the residual awareness of having lived all the other Life Paths at least once. That's what makes them stand out from the crowd, and why their birth number is the only one governed by all four elements at the same time. Parents can choose either to explain this difficult concept to them at an early age, or else wait for them to discover the concept of reincarnation for themselves when they get older. Either way, when they work with the elemental energy of their two Supplementary Birth Numbers – the first one for their early formative years up to 18, and the second one from 18 to full emotional maturity at 36 – they may experience the lessons they learn as more of a "remembering" than a "discovering".

In the case of the 18/**9**, the forceful fire energy of the Leader (1) during their childhood years will help them develop the confidence to perform well at school, as well as master the leadership skills they will need to teach their lessons of love as they grow out into the world.

Then, in their young adult years, they will switch to working with the supplementary earth energy of the Achiever (8) to develop their personal power even further and create abundance in all areas of their life – emotionally and spiritually, as well as financially.

All the while, their primary focus will still be on amassing copious amounts of knowledge and sharing it with others, as determined by their Life Path energy of **9**. But they will do so with the benefit of added Self-confidence (1) and hard work (8), enabling them to take the lead in whatever they choose to do.

The leadership energy of 1 may make these children a bit of a handful when they are young, and they must be taught the difference between confidence and arrogance. However, as long as they do the necessary inner work to rid themselves of their fears and release the positive energy of their three Birth Code numbers, the 18/**9** child will achieve great success and enjoy the company of good friends and the respect of their peers.

The 27/**9** child

As with the previous Birth Code, these young Teachers will carry with them the residual awareness of having lived all the other Life Paths at least once. That's why this number is the only one governed by all four elements at the same time, so when they work with the elemental energy of their two Supplementary Birth Numbers – the first one for their early formative years up to 18, and the second one from 18 to full emotional maturity at 36 – they may experience the lessons they learn as more of a "remembering" than a "discovering".

In the case of the 27/**9**, the emotional water energy of the Intuitive (**2**) during their childhood years will help them to express, process and understand their feelings and also to connect with others on a deep, empathetic level – all of which are invaluable qualities for a budding role model whose highest purpose is to inspire others.

Then in their young adult years they will switch to working with the supplementary air energy of the Seeker (**7**), which will help them seek out and assimilate the Big T spiritual Truths about the world, which they have come here to teach by example.

All the while, their primary focus will still be on amassing copious amounts of knowledge and sharing it with others, as determined by their Life Path energy of **9**. But they will do so with the benefit of a healthy emotional intelligence (**2**) as well as an insightful intellect (**7**), enabling them to teach their divine truths with a passion and a clarity that really engages their audience and commands a loyal following.

This is a particularly creative Birth Code and parents would do well to encourage their 27/**9** child to engage in artistic pursuits both at school and in their own time to develop their talent. A glance at the list of famous **9**s in the Appendices at the back of this book will reveal just how many successful singers and actors were born with this set of expressive numbers, including Cher, Jimi Hendrix, Ray Charles, Kurt Cobain, Elvis Presley, Tom Jones, Morgan Freeman, Harrison Ford and Shirley MacLaine.

It's telling that the qualities required to be a great role model and teacher of wisdom are almost exactly the same as those needed to be a pioneering and ground-breaking artist.

The 36/9 child

As with the previous Birth Codes, these young Teachers will carry with them the residual awareness of having lived all the other Life Paths at least once. That's why this number is the only one governed by all four elements at the same time, so when they work with the elemental energy of their two Supplementary Birth Numbers – the first

Life Path 9: Choices for Children

one for their early formative years up to 18, and the second one from 18 to full emotional maturity at 36 – they may experience the lessons they learn as more of a "remembering" than a "discovering".

In the case of the 36/**9**, the air energy of the Creative (3) during their childhood years will help them express the feelings in their heart and develop their artistic talents in conjunction with the voracious knowledge-gathering appetite of their Life Path Number **9**.

Then, in their young adult years, they will switch to working with the supplementary water energy of the Visionary (6), which will lead them to focus on holding a Utopian vision of a peaceful and loving world for the rest of us to follow, while also using their creativity to show us our divine inner beauty.

All the while, their primary focus will still be on amassing copious amounts of information and sharing it with others, as determined by their Life Path energy of **9**. But they will do so with the benefit of an artistic and expressive creativity (3) as well as an optimistic belief in the power of love (6), enabling them to teach their beautiful truths in original and inspirational ways to a wide audience.

Young 36/**9**s will often be extremely attractive children and will develop into beautiful or handsome teenagers and young adults who will enjoy the attention of many suitors. This is because they are working with the aesthetic and artistic energy of 3 in their early years, and then when they get older they will be endowed with the divinely loving and beautiful energy of 6.

As with all **9** children, parents would do well to foster their 36/**9** child's artistic talents, which will usually come to the fore from a young age. Music, dance, literature and drama are all excellent outlets, as are debating and public speaking.

Many 36/**9** children will tend to be quite unconventional in the way they behave, right from the earliest age, which is nothing for their parents to worry about. In fact, the 36/**9** will thrive best when allowed to freely express their individuality, and mums and dads should avoid trying to force them to conform wherever it's not necessary.

Life Path 9: The Teacher

The 45/9 child

This is the highest three-digit Birth Code in the Self-Awareness System™. Although there are a few people who were born on dates that add up to 46, 47 and 48 (48 being the largest number and unique to those born on September 29, 1999), their numbers are added together to arrive at Supplementary Birth Numbers of 10, 11 and 12 respectively.

This means 45/9 is also one of the rarest Birth Codes, along with the Millennium Children born at the start of the new century. None of the famous **9**s listed in the Appendices at the back of this book has this unusual set of numbers, and I have been unable to find anyone notable throughout history who does.

A child born with this "hen's teeth" Birth Code will possess a strong sense of loyalty to family and friends from the earliest age, due to them working with the supplementary earth energy of 4 during their first formative 18 years. They will tend to be hard-working, honest and diligent, and they will probably display a passionate dislike of any form of perceived injustice, leading them to become quite outspoken should they feel that they, or anyone else, is being treated unfairly.

Then, from 18 to full emotional maturity at 36, they will tap into the adventurous and rebellious "change" energy of 5, which will propel them to use their innate desire for fairness and justice to make a real difference in the world by helping those less fortunate than themselves.

To avoid conflict, parents must be aware of their 45/9 child's need to be heard and to have their opinions respected. The combination of their "old Self" Life Path Number **9**, which endows them with a wisdom far beyond their years, and the righteousness of their first supplementary number 4 means these budding young teachers of truth will have a clear grasp of right and wrong from an early age.

And then, when their rebellious energy of 5 kicks in at 18, they will almost certainly be driven to go out into the world to right as many of these perceived wrongs as they possibly can.

APPENDICES:

BONUS MATERIAL

*Strive not to be a success,
but to be of value.*

— Albert Einstein

Appendix A:
Some famous Life Paths

1. THE LEADER
(Inventive, pioneering and original)

Drew Barrymore: Leading child actor, producer and charity worker.
Chuck Berry: A leading figure of rock and roll in the 1950s.
Charlie Chaplin: A true leader and pioneer in the world of cinema.
Arthur C. Clarke: One of the world's leading science fiction writers.
Sean Connery: Hollywood's ultimate leading man.
Tom Cruise: Or maybe this is Hollywood's ultimate leading man, despite being short and a little over the top in the Scientology caper.
Rene Descartes: The leading light of The Age of Reason (1600s).
Walt Disney: Regarded worldwide as the ultimate leader when it comes to popular entertainment and having a fun time.
Placido Domingo: Led the way in bringing opera to the masses.
Eminem: Sounds like a chocolate sweet, but has undoubtedly led the way for pretty fly white guys in the black-dominated world of rap.
Henry Ford: Entrepreneur who led the way with mass production.
Lady Gaga: "Out there" singer. A leading advocate for meat apparel.
Marvin Gaye: Led the Motown movement and became *Rolling Stone*'s sixth greatest singer of all time. Tragically killed by his own father.
Mikhail Gorbachev: Global leader of peace and detente.
Hugh Jackman: Aussie nice guy and leading children's rights activist.

Appendix A

Steve Jobs: A leader among leaders in the world of technology.
Sophia Loren: You want a leading lady? Look no further.
George Lucas: A leader among filmmakers. Transformed modern cinema with just one film way back in 1977.
Martin Luther: German theologian and leading light for protestants.
Martin Luther King: Inspirational human rights activist and social revolutionary who led the black rights movement in the US.
Karl Marx: A grumpy socialist with a world-leading beard.
Rupert Murdoch: Leads a hugely influential media conglomerate.
Jack Nicholson: Another legendary leading man and party boy.
Florence Nightingale: Led the world with her bedside manner.
Dr Seuss: The undisputed leader among whacky children's authors.
Tiger Woods: Led the way in the clubhouse, and in the bedroom.

* * *

2. THE INTUITIVE
(Loving, compassionate and inclusive)

John Adams: Much-loved American statesman and libertarian.
Hans Christian Andersen: Lovely writer. A children's favourite.
Julie Andrews: Respected and universally loved English actress.
Pat Benatar: Her four Grammys look lovely in her cabinet at home.
Richard Burton: Actor who loved a drink (ie, pissed most of the time).
Maria Callas: One of the most loved singers of the 20th century.
John Candy: Lovely man. Funny, warm… and sorely missed.
Oleg Cassini: Made lovely frocks for Jackie Kennedy and Grace Kelly.
Phil Collins: Intuitively knows how to drum and sing at the same time.
Wayne Dyer: Intuitive and much-loved spiritual author and teacher.
Edouard Manet: Made a lovely impression on the art world.
Claude Monet: Ditto. Had a truly lovely beard as well.
Ronald Reagan: Love him or hate him, he did pretty well for a lousy B-movie cowboy who couldn't act his way out of a paper bag.

Some Famous Life Paths

Omar Sharif: Lover, lothario, bridge player and legendary ladies' man.
Dr Benjamin Spock: Loved long and prospered (oh, wrong Spock).
Robert Louis Stevenson: One of the most widely loved writers ever.
Gloria Vanderbilt: Fashion designer who loved a good pair of jeans.
Frank Zappa: Ground-breaking singer. Looked scary but was lovely.
Franco Zeffirelli: Filmmaker activist who spoke up for same-sex love.

11/2. THE MASTER INTUITIVE

Jennifer Aniston: Lovely! Brad Pitt was a goose to ever leave her.
JM Barrie: Wrote *Peter Pan*, the most-loved children's story ever.
David Beckham: Like Reagan, love him or not, he's done very well.
Lord Byron: Romantic poet, who was also apparently a great lover.
Charles, Prince of Wales: Loves the environment. A bit odd though.
Bill Clinton: President, orator, mad rooter and lover of fine cigars.
Davy Crockett: American frontiersman and widely loved folk hero
Paris Hilton: Loves spending money. But then, who doesn't.
Cecil B DeMille: Knew intuitively what audiences wanted to watch.
Ella Fitzgerald: What's not to love about this extraordinary singer.
Cathy Freeman: Aboriginal athlete, united the whole of Australia at the 2000 Olympic Games. What a lovely fairytale when she won gold.
John Paul Getty: Billionaire philanthropist. Loved helping the poor.
Goethe: Loved having just one name long before Cher and Prince.
Bob Hope: British-born comedian. Audiences simply loved him.
Harry Houdini: Loved being on stage, but hated being tied up.
Michael Jordan: Who doesn't love this guy? Sporting royalty.
Jackie Kennedy: Lover of frocks, presidents and rich Greek blokes.
Henry Kissinger: Master diplomat. Loved a good, long negotiation.
Jennifer Lopez: More loved for her bum than her talent. Go figure.
Madonna: Managed to love both Sean Penn and Guy Ritchie. Respect.
Wolfgang Amadeus Mozart: Child genius and one of the greatest composers ever. Total pain in the ass, but his music is simply lovely.
Barack Obama: President and Nobel Prize-winning peacemaker who embodies the co-operative qualities of the Master Intuitive.
Keith Richards: Love him! No idea how he's still alive though.

Appendix A

Anthony Robbins: Success coach who's loved by all his followers.
Diana Ross: Lovely voice… and a truly lovely lady as well.
Prince William: Has made Brits love their royal family again.

* * *

3. THE CREATIVE
(Motivational, sensitive and expressive)

Alan Alda: Creative actor who made *MASH* the biggest show ever.
Richard Bach: Author who motivated us all to love seagulls.
David Bowie: Hugely creative musician who was clearly motivated by little green spacemen with orange spiky hair. So, so missed.
Frank Capra: Created the motivational classic *It's a Wonderful Life*.
Fidel Castro: Good motivator, but not a particularly nice guy.
Kevin Costner: Created the motivational movies *Dances With Wolves* and *Field of Dreams*, but has made some truly awful ones as well.
Salvador Dali: Surreal artist, probably motivated by magic mushrooms.
Charles Dickens: Created the best characters of any writer, ever.
Judy Garland: A creative Hollywood star for 45 of her 47 years.
Ricky Gervais: Motivated to take the piss out of celebrities. Legend!
Melanie Griffith: Motivated Antonio Banderas to marry her, and in the process created worldwide jealousy among every other woman.
Audrey Hepburn: Hugely popular and motivational style icon.
Alfred Hitchcock: Creative filmmaker who set the bar in the suspense genre. Motivated millions to get rid of their shower curtains.
kd lang: Appears to be motivated by a dislike of capital letters.
TE Lawrence: Legendary army officer who was motivated by his love of Arabia, as well as his fondness for capital letters.
Og Mandino: Motivational author. What's with his first name, though?
Swami Muktananda: Indian guru, mystic and motivational teacher.
Olivia Newton-John: Created a huge market for shiny, spray-on black pants with her unforgettable role in the best musical ever… *Grease*.

Katy Perry: Creative and talented singer, but what on Earth motivated her to marry Russell Brand? (Just kidding, Russell).
River Phoenix: Tragically motivated a lot of kids to say no to drugs.
Paul Robeson: US activist and motivational black rights campaigner.
Carlos Santana: Can create truly angelic music on his guitar.
William Shatner: Boldly motivated where no one has motivated before.
John Travolta: A creative and motivational entertainer in every sense.

* * *

4. THE BUILDER
(Loyal, dedicated and humanitarian)

Pamela Anderson: The ultimate builder, really, because she built her career purely on being "built". Now a passionate animal rights activist.
Richard Branson: Builder of companies worth squillions of dollars.
Bill Gates: Built an enormous fortune and is generously giving it away.
Hugh Hefner: Built a mansion and had lots and LOTS of fun in it.
Paul Hogan: A bridge painter who built a successful acting career.
Julio Ingelsias: Seductive singer who built an army of female fans.
Sarah Jessica Parker: Built her career on just one television character.
Elton John: Enduring music star who has built an absolute fortune.
Paul McCartney: Ditto.
Michael Parkinson: Chat show host. The master of building rapport.
Brad Pitt: Well-built hunk with a heart. Has even more fans than Julio.
Arnold Schwarzenegger: Body builder, action hero and Governator.
Donald Trump: A builder of tacky hotels and imaginary walls.
Oprah Winfrey: Tireless humanitarian who built a fortune from poor beginnings to become one of the most respected women in the world.

22/4. THE MASTER BUILDER
Woody Allen: Built a career out of being a scrawny nerd. Respect.
PT Barnum: Showbiz tycoon who built the best circus of all time.

Appendix A

Bono: Irish rock god and builder of one of the greatest bands ever.
Sarah Bernhardt: One of the first women to build an acting career.
Nadia Comaneci: Had to build a cabinet for all her Olympic medals.
Joan Crawford: Screen sex goddess who built a huge male fan base.
Neil Diamond: Built his fortune on one steamy night in August.
Clint Eastwood: Loves building things, but prefers shooting them.
Thor Heyerdahl: Built a raft called Kon-Tiki and sailed into history.
Kim Kardashian: Has built a successful career with nothing but a big bum and an even bigger wardrobe. Talk about a Master Builder.
Marcel Marceau: Built a fortune without saying a word. Genius.
Steve McQueen: Tough-guy actor who built a cult following.
Leslie Nielsen: Didn't build anything, but he was seriously funny
JD Salinger: Author who built a cult following with just one book.
Frank Sinatra: Showbiz giant who, it must be said, had some dodgy Italian friends in the building trade.
Leonardo da Vinci: Artist and inventor. A true Master Builder.

* * *

5. THE REBEL
(Adventurous, rebellious and dynamic)

Ursula Andress: Bond girl who rebelled against one-piece swimsuits.
Louis Armstrong: Pioneering jazz musician with a rebellious streak.
Mikhail Baryshnikov: Ballet dancer who defected from the former Soviet Union to make it big in the West. Rebellious, or what.
William Blake: Rebellious poet, painter and literary revolutionary.
Russell Brand: A typical 5… loud and rebellious (and quite funny).
Marlon Brando: Rebellious actor, filmmaker and heavy drinker.
John Cleese: Pioneering comedian and famed grumpy hotelier. One of the decidedly rebellious Monty Python comedy team.
Charles Darwin: Revolutionary evolutionist (try saying that three times fast with a mouthful of meringue) who rebelled against the creationists.

Some Famous Life Paths

Marlene Dietrich: Decidedly rebellious Hollywood femme fatale.
Benjamin Franklin: The epitome of the rebellious, free-thinking **5**.
Vincent van Gogh: Cut his own ear off. How rebellious is that?
Adolf Hitler: Psychotic mass-murdering megalomaniac bastard. The perfect example of a rebellious **5** who went to the dark side.
Ron Howard: Rebelled against his clean-cut childhood TV star image to become one of Hollywood's most respected film directors.
Mick Jagger: One of the most influential figures in the history of rock and roll music. A true rebel in every sense of the word.
Angelina Jolie: Deliciously rebellious actress and philanthropist.
James Joyce: Ground-breaking and rebellious Irish novelist.
Beyonce Knowles: Singer who for some reason rebelled against the idea of putting an acute accent on the last letter of her first name.
Abraham Lincoln: Rebelled against slavery. The best president ever.
George Michael: Seriously talented musician and all-round nice guy who rebelled against LA police entrapment laws. We miss you, George!
Dudley Moore: Mould-breaking and delightfully rebellious comedian.
Isaac Newton: Rebellious scientist and famed fruitologist. Discovered gravity… but the bump on his head never really went away.
Pol Pot: Like Hitler, another mass-murdering bastard who turned to the dark side of this number and rebelled against his own people.
JK Rowling: Harry's rebellious streak made her richer than the Queen.
Steven Spielberg: Maybe not rebellious, but definitely revolutionary.
Malcolm X: Influential and rebellious American black rights activist.

* * *

6. THE VISIONARY
(Romantic, empathetic and idealistic)

Joan of Arc: If you want the ultimate romantic heroine, look no further.
Isaac Asimov: A truly visionary and romantic science fiction writer.
Ray Bradbury: Ditto.

Appendix A

James Brown: Singer who romanced his fans with prodigious talent.
Michael Caine: Brilliant actor who saw a vision of an "angel" in an advert on TV, tracked her down and married her. Romantic, or what?
Lewis Carroll: Visionary and romantic author of *Alice in Wonderland*.
James Dean: Unparalleled as a romantic global youth icon.
Alexander Dumas: Rousingly romantic author of *The Three Musketeers*.
Thomas Edison: Don't know how romantic he was, but he was certainly a visionary who invented just about everything.
TS Eliot: Visionary poet who liked cats. Lots and lots and lots of cats.
Ralph Waldo Emerson: Individualist, transcendentalist… and other long words as well. His wife wished he was more romantic, though.
Federico Fellini: A visionary filmmaker, although a little bit weird.
Charles de Gaulle: Leader of the Free French. Now that's romantic.
Cary Grant: Leading men don't get any more romantic than this.
Michael Jackson: Romantic? Hmmm. Talented? Yes. Nuts, definitely.
John Lennon: Dyed in the wool visionary who wanted world peace.
Charles Shultz: His central character Charlie Brown is a hopeless romantic who made him a fortune. Earned a lot more than peanuts.
JRR Tolkien: Visionary fantasy romantic novelist. Defined the genre.
Stevie Wonder: Courageous blind musician and renowned romantic.

33/6. THE MASTER VISIONARY

Fred Astaire: Romance was this twinkle-toed star's middle name.
Pearl Bailey: The first "Ambassador of Love" to the United Nations.
Bjorn Borg: Swedish tennis god who every woman wanted to romance.
Agatha Christie: The most visionary crime and romance author ever.
Francis Ford Coppola: Visionary and ground-breaking filmmaker.
Buckminster Fuller: Another visionary, this time in architecture.
Robert De Niro: Mrs De Niro says he's romantic, but I'm not sure.
Albert Einstein: Definitely a visionary, but his hair was a worry.
Greta Garbo: Another Swedish sex symbol (they're a romantic lot).
BB King: Blues guitarist who knew how to romance his audience.
Stephen King: Horror author who has written great romances too.
Gladys Knight: *Midnight Train to Georgia*. Most romantic song ever!

Jennifer Lawrence: Can play romantic leads, as well as kooky ones.
Roman Polanski: Visionary, if somewhat controversial, filmmaker.
Sylvester Stallone: His is a truly romantic rags-to-riches story.
HG Wells: A visionary writer who was way ahead of his time.
Bruce Willis: Who knew being short and bald could be so romantic?
Wilbur Wright: This aviator was both a visionary and a romantic.

* * *

7. THE SEEKER
(Thoughtful, intelligent and curious)

Sai Baba: Controversial seeker of truth who inspired millions.
Leonard Bernstein: The thinking musical fan's favourite composer.
James Cameron: Seeks new ways to push the movie envelope.
Johnny Cash: The thinking person's country music superstar.
Deepak Chopra: A sought-after expert on the power of the mind.
Winston Churchill: Thought Hitler was a bastard and kicked his ass.
Eric Clapton: The thinking rock fan's favourite guitarist.
Christopher Columbus: Sought the New World… and found it.
Johnny Depp: The thinking woman's Hollywood sex symbol.
Michael Douglas: Anyone else think he was lucky to get Catherine?
Queen Elizabeth: Thinks the whole world smells of fresh paint.
Stephen Hawking: The ultimate thinker and seeker of truth.
Bob Hoskins: British actor. The thinking man's cockney gangster.
John Fitzgerald Kennedy: Did most of his thinking in his trousers.
Peter O'Toole: The drinking woman's Hollywood sex symbol.
Al Pacino: Most people think he's the best film actor ever.
Pink: A pop poppet with a brain. Who'd have thought it.
Emmeline Pankhurst: Quite rightly thought women should vote.
Susan Sarandon: Smart and sexy. The thinking man's movie goddess.

* * *

Appendix A

8. THE ACHIEVER
(Ambitious, driven and persistent)

Alexander Graham Bell: Inventor, genius and all-round overachiever.
Michelangelo: Painted a ceiling and achieved everlasting fame.
Matt Damon: An overachiever. Sexy, nice, talented, rich. Bastard.
Bob Dylan: Achieved huge fame, but sounds like he's gargling gravel.
Roger Federer: Achieved unparallelled greatness with a tennis racquet.
Colin Firth: A massive Hollywood star who's also a thoroughly nice guy, which is quite an achievement.
Jane Fonda: Achieved more as a fitness guru than she did by acting.
Richard Gere: Achieved success despite his middle name "Tiffany".
George Harrison: Achieved the most votes for "Sexiest Beatle".
Buddy Holly: His finest achievement was making nerdy glasses cool.
Grace Kelly: Achieved every girl's dream of becoming a princess.
Nelson Mandela: No words can describe his achievements.
Bob Marley: Achieved true greatness despite being stoned 24/7.
Dan Millman: Former world champion gymnast and my favourite metaphysical author. Respect, my friend, for what you have achieved.
Liza Minnelli: Achieved superstardom both as an actress and a singer.
Paul Newman: Actor and salad king. Now that's overachieving!
Laurence Olivier: No one has achieved more respect as an actor.
Pablo Picasso: Achieved fame as a painter, but needed a big business card because his full name was "Pablo Diego Jose Francisco de Paula Juan Nepomuceno Maria de los Remedios Cipriano de la Santisima Trinidad Ruiz y Picasso". What the hell were his parents smoking?
Valentino Rossi: Has achieved the status of best bike racer ever.
Martin Scorsese: Finally achieved an Oscar after 38 years of trying.
George Bernard Shaw: Achieved fame as a playwright and drinker.
Oscar Wilde: Achieved even more fame as a playwright and drinker.

44/8. THE ALCHEMIST

I have not found any famous Alchemists in all of history. And Source knows, I have tried. If you know of any, please let me know.

Some Famous Life Paths

9. THE TEACHER
(Role model, wise and insightful)

Adele: Has taught us that you can be a star and still swear like a trooper.
Ariana Grande: Bravely taught her fans to flick two fingers at terror.
Brigitte Bardot: She taught the world about animal cruelty in the 60s.
Justin Bieber: The girls love him, but the boys want to punch him in the head. So what does that teach us about human nature?
Beau Brummell: Taught men how to dress long before David Beckham.
Jack Canfield: Author, spiritual teacher and chicken soup aficionado.
Ray Charles: Taught the world that blindness is no barrier to success.
Cher: Taught today's pop poppets all there is to know about sex appeal.
Kurt Cobain: Taught kids everywhere that looking scruffy was cool.
Harrison Ford: Not so much a teacher as a true role model for actors.
Morgan Freeman: Talk about a role model! Wonderful in every way.
Mahatma Gandhi: The ultimate teacher of, and role model for, peace.
Louise Hay: Tireless humanitarian and a powerful teacher of truth.
Jimi Hendrix: Taught us how to be cool when your guitar is on fire.
Eddie Izzard: Hilarious and inspirational, a role model for comedians.
Tom Jones: A role model for crooners and lingerie collectors.
Carl Jung: Famed teacher of spiritual truths. Paved the way for others.
Spike Lee: Used film to teach the world about racial inequality.
Charles Lindbergh: Taught us how to fly. Role model for adventurers.
John Keats: Beautiful poet. Taught us truth is beauty, and beauty truth.
Shirley MacLaine: Actor, spiritualist and a teacher of reincarnation.
Jack Nicklaus: Best golfer of all time and a role model for fair play.
Elvis Presley: Taught us how to swing our hips and shoot TVs.
John D. Rockefeller: Not a teacher, but a philanthropic role model.
Telly Savalas: Taught us that bald is sexy long before Bruce Willis.
Mother Teresa: The epitome of a **9**. A wise, humanitarian angel who walked the face of the earth teaching her message of love and healing.

Appendix B:
Easy numerology readings

The Pythagorean Square

Separate to the Self-Awareness System™ in Parts Two and Three, traditional numerology employs a 3 x 3 grid called "the Pythagorean Square" to map the numbers of your date of birth and use them to extract valuable insights into your innate strengths and weaknesses.

I do not believe it is anywhere near as powerful as interpreting your Birth Code using the Self-Awareness System™, but I have included it here in the Appendices as an add-on because it does give you a simple (and therefore, by definition, rather simplistic) method for conducting a quick numerology reading for your family and friends.

It also makes for a fun and illuminating party game.

The square contains nine cells, numbered **1** to **9**, into which you place a person's birth date numbers.

The cells that contain one or more numbers represent the person's strengths (the more numbers in the cell, the greater their strength in that particular arena of their life). And the cells that have no numbers represent the areas of their life where they will need to focus their attention because they lack an innate ability.

* * *

Easy Numerology Readings

This is what the Pythagorean Square looks like:

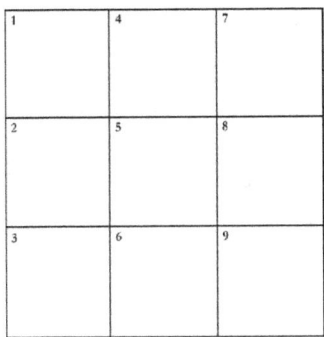

To fill out the square, write down the numbers that make up your date of birth in its relevant numbered square… or the date of birth of your family member or friend if you are doing a reading for them.

Example

Let's say you are doing a reading for someone who was born on March 24, 1993. Their numbers would look like this:

3 (for the month of March), **24** (for the day) and **1993** for the year they were born. So their numbers would be:

3 – 2 – 4 – 1 – 9 – 9 – 3

And so their square would look like this:

1	4	7
1		
2	5	8
	5 5	
3	6	9
3 3		**9 9**

Appendix B

This person has a double dose of the energy of numbers **3** and **9**, and a single dose of the energy of numbers **1**, **2** and **4**.

If you were doing a career or business reading for them, let's say, using the information that is contained under their relevant Life Path Number in Part Three, you would be able to tell them that they have the innate and latent potential to be extremely creative and expressive (**3** the Creative), and can also become wise and capable teachers and role models (**9** the Teacher).

So if they tap into their highest potential they will be able to use their creative and expressive skills (**3**) to motivate and teach others to be the best they can be (**9**).

They can perhaps do this by starting their own business using the entrepreneurial energy of **1** (the Leader). They will work well with others using the energy of **2** (the Intuitive). And they can create a stable business using the practical and nurturing energy of **4** (the Builder).

However, they must be warned that without any innate strengths in **5** (the Rebel), **6** (the Visionary), **7** (the Seeker) and **8** (the Achiever), their business could easily stagnate because they lack the capacity to adapt to change (**5**) or hold a lofty vision of their highest potential (**6**). They might also fail to see the "big picture" because they lack the insightful qualities of **7**, leading them to potentially miss out on the material achievements governed by **8**.

By becoming aware of their shortcomings, as well as their strengths, they would be able to deliberately seek out people to work with them who have plenty of **5**s, **6**s, **7**s or **8**s in their birth charts.

* * *

Let's look at another example to make sure you really get how the Pythagorean Square works. A person with a birth date of May 30, 1959 would have these numbers:

3 – 0 – 5 – 1 – 9 – 5 – 9

And so their square would look like this:

1 **1**	4	7
2	5 **5 5**	8
3 **3 (3)**	6	9 **9 9**

Note that when there is a **0** in the birth date (as in this example with a 30), the **0** is listed in the grid as an amplifier alongside the number that precedes it, giving them a double dose of that number. This is because the number **0** always amplifies the number that precedes it, so **10** is endowed with more positive and negative potential than **1**, just as **20** is endowed with more positive and negative potential than **2**, and so on.

This person has a double dose of the energy of numbers **3, 5** and **9** in their grid and a single dose of the energy of **1**, which means on the positive side they are extremely focused in certain arenas of their life (**3** the Creative, **5** the Rebel and **9** the Teacher). But they also have a lot of gaps in their square – namely **2** (the Intuitive), **4** (the Builder), **6** (the Visionary), **7** (the Seeker) and **8** (the Achiever).

If this were your friend, you would be able to tell them that they are extremely creative (double **3**) and excellent at putting their ideas across in ways others can easily grasp (double **9**), and they will do so to bring about radical change in the world (double **5**).

Their ideas will also be original, thanks to the energy of **1** (the Leader), perhaps propelling them to start their own business, or write books, to teach their pioneering concepts to the world.

However, their lack of any watery numbers in **2** (the Intuitive) and **6** (the Visionary) – which govern our ability to co-operate with others – means they may try to do everything themselves, when they might do better to work together as part of a harmonious team.

Appendix B

Also, their lack of earth energy in **4** (the Builder) and **8** (the Achiever) – both practical and material numbers – means they may fail to ground themselves and plan properly, leading them to rush around starting new projects without ever seeing them through to fruition.

Equally, their lack of any numbers in **7** (the Seeker) means they may never fully think their ideas through, leaving them unprepared and unable to cope with problems should they arise.

By making them aware of their shortcomings (as represented by the gaps in their grid) as well as their strengths, you could steer your friend to avoid frustration and disappointment by teaming up with a **4** or an **8** to manage their business affairs, as well as a marketing expert (**2** or **6**) to help them connect with their audience.

And a Seeker in their team would give them added insight (**7**) to refine their creative ideas (**3**) and their wild ideas (**5**) to teach (**9**) what they have learned in a way that inspires other people, rather than just lecturing them (negative **9**) to change for the sake of it (negative **5**).

* * *

Let's look at one more example. Someone born on October 16, 1985 would have these numbers: **1 – 0 – 1 – 6 – 1 – 9 – 8 – 5**.

So their square would look like this:

1 **1 (1) 1 1**	4	7
2	5 **5**	8 **8**
3	6 **6**	9 **9**

Someone with this birth grid has a quadruple dose of the entrepreneurial energy of **1** (the Leader), due to the three **1**s in their birth date and the amplifying energy of their **10** – which presents as another **1**. This means they have the capacity to become extremely influential leaders and courageous entrepreneurs, who will almost certainly strike out on their own to set up their own business.

They will do so with the brave and outgoing energy of **5** (the Rebel), which will lead them to branch out into new arenas, and the compassionate energy of **6** (the Visionary), which will inspire them to make the world a better place for all.

The **9** (the Teacher) in their grid means they will have an innate ability to convince people that what they do is for the benefit of all, and their **8** (the Achiever) means they are likely to take the necessary practical steps to ensure their project will succeed.

On the negative side, the blanks in **2** (the Intuitive) and **3** (the Creative) means they may struggle to create a harmonious workplace and may even flip to the "dark side" and become a tyrant who resorts to bullying those around them to buy into their view of the world.

Equally, the lack of numbers in **4** (the Builder) means they could build their empire on quicksand, failing to pay attention to the details necessary for long-term stability, meaning their successes could be short-lived. And the absence of any energy in **7** (the Seeker) means they might force their ideas on others without taking the time to think about the potential pitfalls they might encounter along the way.

* * *

Mind the gap!

Please make sure that when you perform a reading for someone you pay as much attention to the gaps in their grid – in other words the challenges they will face – as you do to their innate strengths where they have one or more numbers in a square.

Appendix B

Pythagoras, who invented this divination system, spent as much time educating his students to take steps to guard against any potential pitfalls (ie, gaps in their grid), because "knowing our limitations" guards us against the pain and disappointment that so often prevents us from fulfilling our highest potential.

As a natural optimist, I used to believe that we humans will do more to achieve pleasure in life than we will do to avoid pain. I was naive. I now real-eyes that avoiding pain is a more potent motivator for most people than the desire to gain pleasure.

So please pay as much attention to the blank spaces on someone's grid as you do to those where their birth numbers fall. That way you will be able to steer them down the stream that takes them to their success, while also making sure they don't founder on the rocks of ignorance and disillusionment.

* * *

A final thought…

During the past thousand years, before this new millennium, everyone was born with a **1** in their birth date (1000 to 1999), which gives them at least one **1** in their grid. This means most people alive today possess at least some of the qualities of the Leader, which empowers them to go out into the world to express their original ideas.

However, everyone born since 2000 will have at least one **2** in their grid, which means they will be working – at least to some degree – with the co-operative and supportive energy of the Intuitive **2**.

There will therefore be more and more people born with the desire to create closer connections and a deeper understanding of how we as a human race can benefit from working together in co-operation with each other. Which means this third millennium has the potential to create more love, and less fear. Which we so desperately need.

Appendix C:
Leap into love

There will be times, long after you put this book away on a shelf, when, despite all your best efforts to remain unafraid and living as the love in your heart rather than the ego in your head, something happens in your life that sends you spiralling back into anxiety, pain and Self-doubt. It might be as serious as an illness, the death of a loved one or the break-up of a relationship, or as simple as a goal that you set for your Self failing to turn out exactly as you wanted.

These painful experiences can be truly devastating, but they are also unavoidable because they are all a part of life, and they are also an integral part of growth. What matters is how we deal with them and whether we let them destroy us, or make us stronger.

Because I know you won't want to go trawling through all 800-plus pages of this book to find exactly the right passage that might help you in your times of dire need, I have included here for easy reference two short extracts from my book *Leap Into Love* that I hope will give you both the comfort and the strength you seek.

Nothing that I, nor anyone else, can say will take away your pain. And nor should it, because it is for you to process in your own way. You need to grieve before you can grow. That is essential. How long you grieve for, though, is up to you. The purpose of these extracts is to re-mind you who you are and why you are here, so that you can move through your pain as quickly as possible. And return to love.

Appendix C

Extract 1: The Six Laws of Spiritual Growth

In your times of trouble, and especially if you are going through the often painful and distressing Dark Night of Your Self, these six simple spiritual truths will comfort you.

1. Although you will experience pain in order to grow, your Self will never give you more pain than you can handle.

2. Once you have learned a lesson you will never have to learn it again, so you will never have to feel the same pain twice.

3. Everything you have to give up on your growth path is always replaced by something of greater value. Every time. No exceptions.

4. Every challenge you face is an opportunity for you to grow. Your choice at any given moment is always a choice between love and fear. Do I expand and grow (love)? Or do I shrink back (fear)?

5. Growth is exponential. When you conquer one fear of a certain size, every other fear of the same size or smaller is now within your comfort zone, so you won't need to face them. Ever.

6. You don't have to "do" anything to become pure love, because you already are pure love, and you always have been. Just like the Source, all you have to "do"… is be.

* * *

Extract 2: The Circle of Life

Whatever you are feeling, and whatever you are fearing, remember that you are not just the flesh and blood you see in the mirror. You are so much more than that, and more wondrous than you can imagine.

You are a spirit, a divine being, a perfect embodiment of pure Source energy playing at the game of human life. You are a living, breathing miracle of life and love. No harm can ever come to you, not even in death – because death is just another way of spelling "home".

Sometimes in the face of loss, sadness or rejection you may forget to focus on who you are, and why you are here. So let me re-mind you. You are here for one reason, and one reason only – which is to find your way back to where you started all those years ago as a perfect little bundle of newborn baby love. Only this time, instead of being pure unconscious love, like a baby, you will be conscious that you are pure love and you will be fully aware of your own divine perfection.

Life is a circle. We are all born as perfect love, and the journey of our life is to find our way back there again. Back home. Back to love.

The experiences you will have in your lifetime – all of them, whether you decide to label them "good" or "bad" – are designed solely for this one purpose… to help you find your way back to love.

Remember, you don't have to do anything, other than let go. Let go of your fears. Let go of your past hurts, because they were perfectly designed – by your Self – to help you grow. And above all, let go of all your future concerns because everything always happens perfectly.

Always. Every time.

It may not feel like it, but I can assure you that your life is perfect just as it is. And the whole complex, painful process of learning to love your Self – which is your goal in every lifetime – is perfectly designed to bring you to this one final, inescapable and blissful conclusion:

Love is not something you give, or something you get.
Love is who you ARE.

* * *

If you should ever lose sight of your purpose of finding your way back to love, don't worry – there are guides all around you to show you the path. These guides are placed deliberately in front of us to re-mind us that love is the only thing in this world that is real.

Who are these guides? They are the animals that surround us. And they are the purest spirits on the planet.

Appendix C

Have you ever wondered why animals exist? No, they are not here for us to eat. Far from it. They are here to re-mind us how to be still, how to feel no Self-pity, and how to love unconditionally.

The brilliant 19th century French author Victor Hugo once wrote: "Animals are the reflections of our souls. They appear before us as silent teachers to show us the way back to love."

So the next time you encounter an animal of any kind, please take the time to send them a silent "thank you". Or you can say it out loud, if you like. They will feel it.

And if you are not already a passionate lover of animals, I urge you to become one now because they have so much to teach you, especially in your times of greatest need.

Let the animals re-mind you that the only two qualities you ever need concern your Self with are love and courage... as they do.

Let them re-mind you to live in the moment... as they do.

Let them re-mind you to jump for joy and greet your loved ones with passion... as they do.

Let them re-mind you how to give unconditional love, not just to others but also to your Self... as they do.

Let them re-mind you that you are unique and perfect just as you are... just as they are.

Above all, let them re-mind you that the search for love outside your Self is futile. You will never find love "out there" because it isn't "out there". It is within you. It is all within you.

So even if you remember nothing else from this entire book, please remember these six, simple words that will guide you home and back to love when you have lost your way:

Don't look for love... BE IT.

If you live your life like that you can never go wrong. You can never be hurt. And you can never get lost on your spiritual journey back to where you started. Back to love.

Appendix D:
Further reading suggestions

A Return to Love (Marianne Williamson)
Anatomy of the Spirit (Caroline Myss)
Conversations with God (Neale Donald Walsch)
Dear Lover (David Deida)
God's Gladiators (Stuart Wilde)
Living in the Light (Shakti Gawain)
Many Lives, Many Masters (Brian Weiss)
Nature, Man, and Woman (Alan Watts)
No Ordinary Moments (Dan Millman)
Past Lives, Present Miracles (Denise Linn)
Radical Forgiveness (Colin Tipping)
Soul Coaching (Denise Linn)
The Alchemist (Paolo Coelho)
The Celestine Prophecy (James Redfield)
The Five Love Languages (Gary Chapman)
The Life You Were Born to Live (Dan Millman)
The Power of Now (Eckhart Tolle)
Way of the Peaceful Warrior (Dan Millman)
You Can Heal Your Life (Louise Hay)

(And please don't forget to watch **The Matrix**)

Acknowledgements

Writing a book such as this inevitably involves a large team of people, and I am blessed to have such a magnificent support network of truly inspirational friends, family and business colleagues.

To my two boys Tyson and Gigi, you are my greatest ever gifts from Spirit and I will always love you more than words can say.

To my family Sally, Mark and Ian, and all your beautiful children and grandchildren, I love you so much and am so blessed by you all.

To my mother and father who guided me in spirit, thank you for giving me my life and your love. I felt you both daily as I wrote this.

To Dana and David, thank you for your unwavering love and for believing in me and this book. You are my Aussie family. And thank you, too, to my support group of friends too numerous to mention.

To my two exquisite teachers and "spiritual gladiators" Michele and Christine, thank you for the fairy dust, love and inspiration.

And to my warrior priestess Janene ("Nene"), thank you for your love and support (and your supreme editing skills!). This book is for you. I will hold you in my heart forever, no matter where we end up.

Finally, I want to acknowledge the wisdom and insight of one of my most enlightened mentors, Dan Millman. His marvellous book on numerology, *The Life You Were Born to Live* (HJ Kramer 1993), was one of the triggers that started me on my journey to find out why something as simple as our date of birth could contain so many spiritual truths.

In researching the answer to this question, I discovered the answer to all my other questions as well.

Thank you, my most generous teacher. I owe you a debt I know I can never repay, although I hope this book goes some way towards doing so by raising the vibration of the planet on your behalf.

About the author

Simon H Firth is a professional writer, author, numerologist, teacher, presenter, journalist and Self-empowerment coach who specialises in teaching advanced communication and conflict-resolution skills in the context of intimate relationships, parenting, business, and personal and spiritual growth.

He is the author of six books about finding your true happiness with your partner, your friends, your colleagues, your children… and, above all, with your Self.

Simon has spent almost 40 years travelling the world and studying all the major religions, as well as some of the more esoteric spiritual and philosophical belief systems, in his quest for truth and beauty.

He is also a dedicated advocate for animal welfare and proudly donates 10 per cent of all his earnings to the Worldwide Fund for Nature (formerly World Wildlife Fund), because he believes passionately that if humanity can't look after the most vulnerable inhabitants of our planet, then we really don't deserve to be here at all.

Simon spends most of his time travelling and teaching, and he is based in Sydney, Australia.

www.ingramcontent.com/pod-product-compliance
Lightning Source LLC
Chambersburg PA
CBHW050642240426
43663CB00049B/2377